ADO Programming
in Visual Basic 6

ISBN 0-13-085857-9

90000

9 780130 858573

PRENTICE HALL PTR MICROSOFT® TECHNOLOGIES SERIES

PRENTICE HALL PTR MICROSOFT® TECHNOLOGIES SERIES

Steven Holzner

ADO Programming in Visual Basic 6

 Prentice Hall PTR, Upper Saddle River, NJ 07458
www.phptr.com

Library of Congress Cataloging-in-Publication Data

Holzner, Steven
  ADO Programming in Visual Basic 6/ Steven Holzner
          p.   cm. -- (Microsoft Technologies Seires)
      ISBN 0-13-085857-9 (alk. paper)
        1. Microsoft Visual BASIC.   2. BASIC (Computer program language)   3. ActiveX   4.
  Object-oriented programming (Computer science)   I. Title.   II. Series
  QA76.73.B3 H73 1999
      005.1'17--dc21   99-049907
                                                                             CIP

Editorial/Production Supervision: *Wil Mara*
Acquisitions Editor: *Jill Pisoni*
Marketing Manager: *Lisa Konzelmann*
Manufacturing Manager: *Maura Goldstaub*
Editorial Assistant: *Linda Ramagnano*
Cover Design Director: *Jerry Votta*
Cover Designer: *Talar Agasyan*
Art Director: *Gail Cocker-Bogusz*

© 2000 Prentice Hall PTR
Prentice-Hall, Inc.
Upper Saddle River, New Jersey 07458

Prentice Hall books are widely used by corporations and government agencies for training, marketing, and resale. The publisher offers discounts on this book when ordered in bulk quantities.
For more information, contact: Corporate Sales Department, Phone: 800-382-3419;
FAX: 201-236-7141; email: corpsales@prenhall.com

Or write: Corp. Sales Dept., Prentice Hall PTR, 1 Lake Street, Upper Saddle River, NJ   07458

Printed in the United States of America
10   9   8   7   6   5   4   3   2

ISBN 0-13-085857-9

Prentice-Hall International (UK) Limited, *London*
Prentice-Hall of Australia Pty. Limited, *Sydney*
Prentice-Hall Canada Inc., *Toronto*
Prentice-Hall Hispanoamericana, S.A., *Mexico*
Prentice-Hall of India Private Limited, *New Delhi*
Prentice-Hall of Japan, Inc., *Tokyo*
Pearson Education Asia P.T.E., Ltd., *Singapore*
Editora Prentice-Hall do Brasil, Ltda., *Rio de Janeiro*

Dedicated to Nancy, of course!

CONTENTS

THREE   Using the ADO Data Control   111

FIVE   Connecting to Databases   208

EIGHT   Using Recordsets in Code   362

THIRTEEN   Data Shaping and ADOX   599

INTRODUCTION

Welcome to our book on ADO database programming with Visual Basic. ActiveX Data Object (ADO) programming has a special connection with Visual Basic, and we'll see both packages at their best and most powerful in this book.

These two packages—ADO and Visual Basic—are specifically designed to work together. Visual Basic bends over backwards to make using ADO easy, and I'll cover the Visual Basic database tools like data views, data environments, the query builder, and more in depth. For example, Visual Basic data environments—often not even covered in general database programming books—are especially powerful in ADO, and we'll see that many techniques that are difficult in code, such as creating involved hierarchical recordsets, are simple using Visual Basic data environments.

In fact, the natural environment for ADO programming is Visual Basic—and I think you'll agree as you read this book.

What's in This Book

This book covers ADO programming using Visual Basic, which means there's a great deal of material to work with, from the basics of the ADO object model to the Remote Data Service (RDS), from using the ADO data control to working with shaped data, from creating disconnected recordsets to sorting and searching data, from the ADO object set to the ADO extension (ADOX) object set. ADO is intended to be the future of data access as far as Microsoft is concerned, and we'll see it all here.

Here's a list of some of the topics you'll see in this book:

The ADO object model	Data Views
The Visual Basic database tools	Creating database tables
The Visual Data Manager	Editing databases
Data Environments	Updating databases

Adding and deleting records
The Query Builder
The Data Form Wizard
Database diagrams
The Data Report Designer
The Query Builder
Data projects
Multi-tiered database architecture
Database transactions
The Microsoft Transaction Manager
The Microsoft Visual Modeler
Data validation
The ADO data control
Binding controls
The DataBindings collection
Using DataList, DataCombo, and DataGrid controls
Using the Hierarchical FlexGrid control
The Connection object
Connecting to databases
The Command and Parameter objects
The Recordset object
Creating and using recordsets
Executing commands
Sorting recordsets
Filtering recordsets
Searching recordsets
Creating and using disconnected recordsets
ADO Field objects
ADO Error objects

ADO Property objects
ADO dynamic properties
ADO collections
Creating data objects
Creating data source ActiveX controls
Creating data consumer ActiveX controls
Using commands with parameters
Handling recordsets, connections, and commands asynchronously
Navigating in recordsets
Using bookmarks
Batch updating
Using the ADO library in code
The properties, methods, and events of all ADO objects
Handling ADO events
Creating and using indexes
Synchronizing with the server
Persisting Recordsets
Creating recordsets on the fly
Exporting recordsets
Using Data Source Objects (DSOs) in Web pages
ADO and Active Server Pages (ASP)
The Remote Data Service (RDS)
Data shaping
Hierarchical recordsets
Child recordsets
Multiple child recordsets
Grandchild recordsets
ADOX-ADO extensions

ADO is a library of data objects—ActiveX and COM objects—that provides an interface to the underlying Microsoft OLE DB database access standard (the successor to ODBC), as we'll see in Chapter 1. ADO provides access to all kinds of heterogenus data using standard database techniques. It's not yet as a complete set of database access objects as other database objects sets you can use in Visual Basic, such as the Data Access Object (DAO) set, but it's growing every day. We'll see what ADO is capable of in this book, from the basics through ADO data shaping and handling child and grandchild recordsets. Chapter 1 will show where ADO fits in to Microsoft's data access scheme.

Besides showing ADO at work, this book also functions as an ADO reference. I'll cover each ADO object in detail, as well as all the ADO properties, the ADO methods and what arguments you pass to those methods, as well as the ADO events and what arguments are passed to the handler procedures for those events. The idea is that you'll be able to easily find the information you need, in depth and ready to use.

There's one convention you should know about in this book. While developing examples and introducing new code to existing code, I'll highlight the new code like this:

```
Private Sub Adodc1_MoveComplete(ByVal adReason As _
ADODB.EventReasonEnum, ByVal pError As _
ADODB.Error, adStatus As ADODB.EventStatusEnum, _
ByVal pRecordset As ADODB.Recordset)


    Set adoRecordset2 = _
    Adodc1.Recordset("ChapterOrders").Value
        .
        .
        .
```

Note also the three dots at the end of this code, indicating that there's more code to come. So, what will you need to use this book? I'll take a look at that next.

What You'll Need

To use this book profitably, you'll need a knowledge of Visual Basic programming. You don't have to be an expert, but you will need the basic skills of a Visual Basic programmer, since this book is not about teaching Visual Basic. However, when it comes to more advanced techniques like constructing ActiveX controls from scratch, I'll work through the Visual Basic code in depth. If you find things becoming obscure, you might want to take a look at a general Visual Basic text before continuing.

I'll use Visual Basic 6.0 in this book, because previous versions don't support the tools and interfaces needed. For that reason, you'll need a working installation of Visual Basic 6.0 or later, ideally, the Microsoft Visual Basic 6.0 Enterprise Edition. In addition, the database tools, libraries, and controls we'll use in this book can be very memory intensive, so I recommend that you use a machine with at least 64MB of RAM, although you can get away with less than that for much of the book.

Some of the examples in this book use the Microsoft SQL Server, because the native Microsoft Jet database engine that comes with Visual Basic isn't powerful enough to support many aspects of ADO programming. I'll use SQL Server 7 in this book, but you can also use SQL Server 6.5. You don't need SQL Server to use this book, but some examples and some projects on the CD will use it. If you have access to SQL Server, such as over a network, that's fine; if not, you can read through the examples as presented in the book.

In addition, I'll take a look at the Data Source Objects (DSOs) that come with the Microsoft Internet Explorer version 4.0 and later which let you use ADO with Web pages. To work through the examples in Chapters 11 and 12, you'll need that browser or later; note that Microsoft Internet Explorer 4.01 comes with Visual Basic 6.0.

I'll take a look at working with ADO and Active Server Pages (ASP) in this book, and if you want to take full advantage of that, you must have access to an Internet or intranet server that supports ASP. Usually, that means you use the Microsoft Internet Information Server (IIS), but you may be able to use the Microsoft Personal Web Server (PWS), which is freely available, on your own machine—see Chapter 12 for the details. I'll also take a look at using the Remote Data Service (RDS), which is now considered part of ADO, in Chapter 12. To use RDS, you'll need an Internet or intranet server that supports it, like the Microsoft IIS or PWS.

The most important resource in this book is Visual Basic itself. In the first chapter, I'll start with an overview of database programming in Visual Basic. As you'll see, there's a huge amount of material coming up, so the sooner we start, the better. It's time to turn to Chapter 1 now.

Visual Basic Database Programming

Welcome to our book on Microsoft Visual Basic and ActiveX Data Objects (ADO) programming. In this book, we're going to see a tremendous amount of database programming using ADO—from simply moving through a database by clicking buttons in a form all the way to using the Remote Data Services (RDS) on Web servers, learning about data shaping, using hierarchical recordsets, and creating ActiveX controls that act as data sources. There's an immense arsenal of ADO programming power in Visual Basic, and this is the book where we'll put it to work.

ADO is Microsoft's newest database protocol, which was built to provide an easy interface to the large Microsoft database-handling package, OLE DB. ADO is a flexible standard that is intended to supersede the two earlier standards: Data Access Objects (DAO) and Remote Data Objects (RDO). In this chapter, I'm going to start examining ADO database programming by giving an overview of Visual Basic database programming in general, then taking a brief look at both DAO and RDO before turning to ADO. I'll put all three of these protocols into historical perspective to give you an idea why ADO is so powerful and where it fits into the scheme of things.

You may wonder why there are three different sets of database protocols available in Visual Basic. As it turns out, the reason is historical.

1

At first, Visual Basic only supported DAO, which connected to the Microsoft Jet database engine (the database engine in Microsoft Access). Then, recognizing that there are other database types available, Microsoft created the Open Database Connectivity (ODBC) standard, and supported ODBC with RDO in Visual Basic. Finally, Microsoft saw that the Web and other forms of data—from email to Web content—were available too, and created ADO, which is a flexible standard that allows connections on the same computer, over networks, and the Web—and is intended to supersede ODBC.

In this chapter, we'll take a look at what databases are all about, and how to create and edit them in simple ways. I'll take a look at DAO, RDO, and ADO programming in Visual Basic in overview to create the foundation we'll use in the rest of the book, and specifically to get an idea of what ADO programming is all about, including an overview of the ADO object model, which is what we'll be exploring throughout most of the book. I'll end the chapter with an overview of another important aspect of database programming in Visual Basic—Structured Query Language (SQL). SQL is integral to a lot of database programming, and some knowledge of it is essential to database programming beyond the most basic.

So the question now is—just what *are* databases?

What Are Databases?

Like many other programming concepts, databases have become more complex over the years, but the fundamental concept is still a simple one—databases organize data for access and manipulation under programmatic or application control.

The most popular database construct is the *table*, and that provides our conceptual starting point. To see how a database table works, say, for example, that you are in charge of teaching a class and are supposed to store a grade for each student. You might make up a table much like this one to record the grade for each student:

```
Column/  Column/
Field 1  Field 2
 Name    Grade
 --------------
| Ann   |   C   |   <-- Row/Record 1
|-------|-------|
| Mark  |   B   |   <-- Row/Record 2
```

```
|-------|-------|                .
| Ed    |   A   |                .
|-------|-------|                .
| Frank |   A   |
|-------|-------|
| Ted   |   A   |
|-------|-------|
| Mabel |   B   |
|-------|-------|
| Ralph |   B   |
|-------|-------|
| Tom   |   B   |
 ----------------
```

In fact, you've already created a database—or more specifically, a database table. The transition from a table on paper to one in a computer is natural: With a computer, you can sort, index, update, and organize large tables of data in an easy way (and without a great waste of paper). You can even connect tables together, creating *relational* databases.

Each individual data entry in a table, such as a student's name, goes into a *field* in the table. A collection of fields together, such as the Name and Grade fields in our table, make up a *record*.

Each record gets its own row in a table, and each column in a row represents a different field. A collection of records—that is, rows of records where each column is a field—becomes a *table*.

What, then, is a database? In its most conventional form, a database is just a collection of one or more tables. In fact, you can go further than that in Visual Basic—you can have collections of databases. You can also have *indexes* in tables, and those are pointers to specific fields, either in the current database or another one. There are other ways of setting up databases as well—for example, you can use data *cubes* with some database protocols, and other database constructs are available too, as we'll see in this book. Even so, the table is the crucial concept to get down first, because even though ADO is intended to let you handle the data kept in *data stores* in many different formats—from email to Web content, from standard databases to spreadsheets—it all comes down to working with data with techniques adapted from handling tables.

Flat and Relational Databases

So far, we've defined a certain type of database: a flat, or flat-file database. There is a second type of database as well: a relational database. Relational databases are called relational because they are set up to relate the data in multiple tables together. To make a table relational, you choose certain fields to be *primary* and *foreign* keys.

The primary key in a table is usually the most important one—the one you might use to sort, for instance. The foreign key usually represents the primary key in another table, giving you access to that table in an organized way. For example, I might add a field for student IDs to the student grade table. That same field, the student ID, may be the primary key in the school registrar's database table, which lists all students. In this table, then, the student ID field is a foreign key, allowing us to specify individual records in the registrar's table. In a flat-file system, a file corresponds to a table and it has records and fields, whereas in a relational system, a database is made up of many tables, which each have columns and rows.

We'll elaborate on this simple concept of how databases work throughout the book, but we already have a good idea of what's going on. We've seen how a basic database of tables works, and how each table—made up of records and fields—works. Next, I'll take a look at the question of database access, which is all about client/server architecture.

Multi-Tiered Database Architecture

Your database and the software you use to work with it can all be on the same machine, and very commonly are. Today, however, *multi-tiered* database installations are becoming increasingly common, breaking things up into *client/server* relationships.

Multi-tiered installations are broken into modular layers. Probably the most common multi-tiered application today is the two-tier, server-side database. There, the data is stored in a server and the user interface is present in client applications that accept input and commands from the user. In this way, the client application can request data from the server, modify that data, and send it back.

The actual work of handling and manipulating the data in a two-tier model is done on the server, which is usually a more powerful machine than the client machines. The results are that network traffic is minimized, the data the server works on is internal to the server for very fast access, and when you want to update the data or the way that data is handled, you only need to replace the server-side component of the whole application.

The two-tier model has been expanded now to become a three-tier model in many environments. The third tier is often called the *business logic,* or *business services* layer, and it is placed between the client and server. This layer exists to check the data sent on to the actual server, making sure that the data is in the proper format, that it maintains data integrity, and that it adheres to requirements called *business rules*.

An example of a business rule might be to check to make sure that the number of items on an order form is one or greater, or to make sure that items marked for shipment are actually in stock. We'll see how to implement business rules in this book.

Here, then, is the usual division of services in a three-tiered architecture:

- Client user services—Provide the user interface, preliminary processing.
- Business services—Implement business rules for checking data.
- Data services—Handle the data crunching.

Originally, the middle layer was usually implemented with a transaction processing monitor, much like the Microsoft Transaction Server. However, the middle tier today can also be a *message server*, which is much like an asynchronous, distributed version of a transaction server, or even made up of fully distributed components. Such distributed components can be based, for example, on the Microsoft COM or DCOM model, and together, those components form an application.

The third tier is often implemented on a third machine, but that need not be the case because client machines are becoming more and more powerful. In fact, putting the third tier on a client machine can speed up processing considerably, which means you can get a lot done in this layer. As a result, client applications often do little more than present the data to the user, allowing the user to edit and modify that data, but doing little real processing; such client applications are called *thin clients*.

What type of database architecture you should choose depends, of course, on your needs and resources. For example, if you've got a lot of users that will be interacting with your data stores, the idea of using thin clients where you don't have to support many powerful computers and software installations—becomes very attractive.

There's one more concept to mention before digging into database programming: Universal Data Access. Universal Data Access (UDA) is the name for Microsoft's overall data access strategy, and it's a term you might come across when working with database programming. UDA is made up of the union of these technologies:

- **ADO**—ActiveX Data Objects, an interface for OLE DB.
- **ODBC**—Open Database Connectivity, used for SQL relational databases.
- **OLE DB**—The OLE database protocol, the specification for object-oriented database access and the basis for ADO.
- **RDS**—Remote Data Services.

Now it's time to start translating these concepts into practice by writing some working code, and to do that, I'll take a look at the three ways of handling databases in Visual Basic now: DAO, RDO, and ADO.

Using Databases in Visual Basic

How do you use a database file in a Visual Basic program? You use a database protocol: DAO, RDO, or ADO. Using one of these protocols makes the data in a database available to you in code. That is to say, DAO, RDO, and ADO are the available database *interfaces* you can use in Visual Basic.

From a programming point of view, there are two ways to work with all these protocols in Visual Basic: with the Visual Basic controls that specifically support these protocols, or with a library of programming objects that lets you handle these protocols in code (ADO also lets you use Data Environments, as we'll see throughout this book).

Using Data Controls

The Visual Basic control set includes three *data controls*: the DAO data control (which supports DAO), the RDO remote data control (which supports ODBC), and the ADO data control (which supports ADO). You use these controls to connect to and move through databases, but they don't actually display data—you bind them to other Visual Basic controls, called *data-bound controls*, and those bound controls handle the data display.

Using data controls and data-bound controls is the easiest way to work with data in databases in Visual Basic, because the programming is mostly handled for you. The process goes like this: You simply add the data control you want to a Visual Basic form, then connect that data control to a database. The data control acts as a *data source* for the rest of the project, and you can bind controls to the data control. To bind a control to a data source, you use the control's properties like `DataSource` to specify the data control, and then use properties like `DataField` and `BoundColumn` to specify what field to display in the bound control.

The data control itself presents a set of buttons with arrows to let the user move through a database, record by record, and the record pointed to at any time by a data control is that control's *current record*. The data in the field or fields of the current record is automatically displayed in controls bound to the data control, and if the user changes that data, the new data is automatically written to the database when the user moves on to another record.

Here are the Visual Basic controls that can function as bound controls:

- Picture boxes.
- Labels.
- Text boxes.

- Check boxes.
- Image controls.
- OLE controls.
- List boxes.
- Masked edit controls.
- Rich text boxes.
- Combo boxes.

In addition, there are the following special controls that are designed to be used as bound controls:

- DBList.
- DBCombo.
- FlexGrid.
- MSHFlexGrid.

Finally, there are a number of bound controls that are specially built to be used with the ADO data control only. These controls are:

- DataList.
- DataCombo.
- DataGrid.

We'll take a good look at working with data-bound controls in Chapter 4.

Besides using data controls, there's another connection technique designed specifically for ADO: Data Environments. A Data Environment can act as a data source for data-bound controls just as a data control can. Data Environments are the successors to the UserConnection objects one used to use to form connections with ODBC sources; UserConnections are mostly considered obsolete today, and now you use Data Environments to provide an ADO-based connection to your data at both design-time and run-time (not just at run-time, as with data controls and code). We'll see a great deal about using Data Environments in this book.

Note that while using data controls and data-bound controls provides a simple way to work with a database, it's also simplistic, because you typically let Visual Basic handle all the programming details—which means the most the user can do is view individual records and edit a field or two (although you can gain access to the data in the database directly as stored in a data control, as we'll see in Chapter 3). For real database programming, you usually use the database object libraries.

Using Database Object Libraries

Data controls—the DAO, RDO, and ADO controls—are useful when you want a quick solution to move through the records in a database, but as database programming became more serious, programmers turned more and more to working with databases in code, using the database object libraries. There's an object library for the DAO, RDO, and ADO protocols; in fact, there are two for the ADO protocol.

You can work with the three database object sets directly in code, without controls like the DAO data control or ADO data control. To do that, you add a reference to a database protocol library, such as the Microsoft ActiveX Data Objects Library in Visual Basic, using the `Project` menu's `References` option. When you've referenced a database object library in your code, you can connect to a database using that object library's methods.

When you connect to a database using the DAO, RDO, or ADO object libraries, you typically create a `Recordset` object (called a `Resultset` object in RDO) based on the connection protocol you used. A recordset holds the records that match the criteria you've set. A recordset can hold an entire table of data from a database, a subset of data from a table, or data from a number of tables. You can then use the methods of a recordset to move through records and manipulate them. We'll see a great deal about creating recordsets in this book.

Besides using the built-in methods of DAO, RDO, or ADO objects to manipulate and edit records, you can also execute Structured Query Language (SQL) commands directly on the records in a recordset. We'll see how that works in this book too.

Those are the two techniques for handling database protocols in Visual Basic: using data controls and data-bound controls, and using database object libraries in code. I'll start the overview of available database protocols now, beginning with the venerable workhorse of database programming in Visual Basic—DAO.

DAO

In the days when Visual Basic first started handling databases, it used the Microsoft Jet database engine, which is what Microsoft Access is built on. Using the Jet engine represented quite an advance for Visual Basic because it let you work with all kinds of data formats in the fields of a database: text, numbers, integers, longs, singles, doubles, dates, binary values, OLE objects, currency values, Boolean values, and even memo objects (up to 1.2GB of text). The Jet engine also supported SQL, in which database programmers found another significant advance. Database programming in Visual Basic took off when DAO appeared.

To support the Jet database engine, Microsoft added the DAO data control to Visual Basic, and you can use that control to open Jet database files (which have the extension `.mdb`).

To support the connection to Jet, Microsoft added the following set of data access objects to Visual Basic. You can work with these objects in code when you've added a reference to the DAO object library in your project.

- DBEngine—The Jet database engine.
- Workspace—An area that can hold one or more databases.
- Database—A collection of tables.
- TableDef—The definition of a table.
- QueryDef—The definition of a query.
- RecordSet—The set of records that make up the result of a query.
- Field—A column in a table.
- Index—An ordered list of records.
- Relation—Stored information about the specific relationship between tables.

You can also use the DAO data control, also called just the data control, to connect to databases without using any of the above objects in code.

The DAO Data Control

With the DAO data control, you can move around in a database from record to record. This control lets you bind and display data in bound controls, and displays a set of arrow buttons the user can manipulate to move through the database.

You can see a data control operating with bound controls in Figure 1.1, where I've opened the students table discussed earlier with a data control. You can see the Name and Grade fields for the first record in that figure.

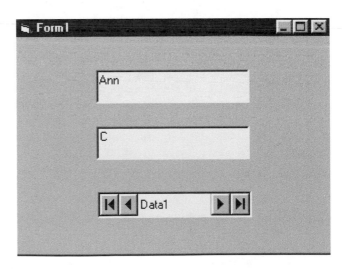

FIGURE 1.1 A DAO data control at work.

The attraction of using the DAO data control is that you can perform many data access operations without writing code. Data-bound controls automatically display data from one or more fields for the current record, and the data control performs all operations on the current record.

If the DAO data control is made to move to a different record, all bound controls automatically pass any changes to the data control to be saved in the database. The DAO data control moves to the requested record and passes back data from the current record to the bound controls, and the bound controls display that data.

Visual Basic uses a control's properties as you've set them to open a selected database, create a DAO `Database` object, and create a `Recordset` object. The data control's `Database` and `Recordset` properties refer to `Database` and `Recordset` objects, and you can manipulate the data using those properties. If you have an SQL statement to execute, you place that statement in the data control's `RecordSource` property, and the result appears in the `RecordSet` property.

RDO

You use Remote Data Objects (RDO) to connect to databases using the Open Database Connectivity (ODBC) specification, which Microsoft anticipates will be superseded by ADO. Originally, Microsoft introduced this specification to allow developers to work with databases besides those based on the Jet engine, such as Oracle databases.

Setting up a connection to an ODBC source can be a little involved. You set up ODBC connections to databases using the `ODBC Data Sources` item in the Windows `Control Panel`, and when you do, those connections are registered and available to all applications by name.

Say that you put the `students` table in a Microsoft Access database file named `db.mdb`. How would you set that database up as an ODBC data source? To set up a data source, you open the `ODBC Data Sources` item, opening the `ODBC Data Source Administrator` dialog, click the `System DSN` tab (DSN stands for Data Source Name), and click the `Add` button to open the `Create New Data Source` dialog.

You can see the ODBC drivers installed on your system in this dialog. Select the one you want to use (the `Microsoft Access` driver) and click `Finish` to install the `db.mdb` file. Doing so opens the `ODBC Microsoft Access` dialog, and you use the `Select` button to select the database file, `db.mdb`, and give a name to that new data source, such as `db`, making `db` the name this data source may be accessed with from your Visual Basic programs. Then you click the `OK` button in the `ODBC Microsoft Access` dialog.

This creates a new ODBC connection for your file, and that connection appears in the `ODBC Data Source Administrator`. Click the `OK` button to close the `ODBC Data Source Administrator`. Now you've added a new

ODBC source, db, to your computer's Data Environment. You can use that data source in your programs, such as to set an RDO control's DataSource-Name property to that data source, which makes the data in the data source available to controls bound to the RDO control.

You can also create direct connections to ODBC data sources with the objects in the RDO library. The remote data objects are (mostly) designed in parallel with data access objects; for example, the database engine is rdoEngine instead of DBEngine, Recordsets are rdoResultsets, Workspaces are rdoEnvironments, Field objects are rdoColumn objects, and so on. And although the names have changed, the command set is very similar to DAO.

The RDO Data Control

Much like the DAO data control, the RDO control gives you access to a database and displays data in bound controls. Unlike the DAO data control, however, you use the remote data control to access ODBC data sources through ODBC connections, which at this time includes databases built with nearly all the popular database programs.

You can see the RDO control at work in Figure 1.2, where I've connected that control to the db ODBC data source that holds the students table. As with the DAO data control, you can use the arrow buttons in the RDO control to move to other records, and all the controls bound to the RDO control will be updated automatically.

After creating DAO and RDO, Microsoft saw that data access needs were still multiplying, so they finally created ADO.

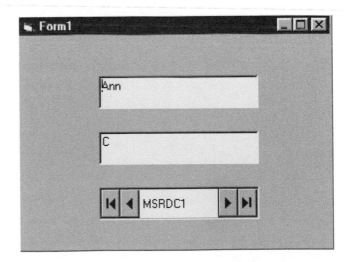

FIGURE 1.2　An RDO data control at work.

················

ADO

Both DAO and RDO are limited in many respects. DAO uses only the Jet engine, and while RDO supports many databases, it restricts you to certain formats and connection methods, and because it supports so many formats, you get a sort of least-common-denominator performance, which has left room for improvement.

Microsoft's most recent data access implementation is based on ActiveX Data Objects (ADO), which are based on OLE DB, the successor to ODBC. ADO lets you access data in a database server through any OLE DB provider. ADO is designed to provide you with a consistent interface for working with a variety of data sources, from text files to ODBC relational databases, from email to groups of databases.

ADO is based on OLE DB; in fact, ADO is only an application-level interface that exposes the objects of OLE DB. Microsoft introduced OLE DB, ADO, and the advanced data connector in 1996. The advanced data connector has since been replaced with Remote Data Services (RDS). RDS, along with the remote provider for ADO (which some people call ADO/R), give you the ability to work with remote data in distributed environments. Together with ODBC, these elements make up the core of the Microsoft Data Access Components (MDAC) package. MDAC is now in version 2, as of July 1998. The components in this package are OLE DB 2, ADO 2, a new RDS, and ODBC 3.5.

OLE DB itself is the foundation of ADO and, in turn, it is based on the COM specification. OLE DB supports a standard set of data access methods for data sources, and each such data source is called an *OLE DB provider*. ADO enables you to write an application to access and manipulate data in a database server through such OLE DB providers, and for every supported data storage platform, there is an OLE provider type.

As of this writing, here are the available OLE providers in Visual Basic:

- Microsoft Jet 3.51 OLE DB Provider.
- Microsoft Jet 4.0 OLE DB Provider.
- Microsoft OLE DB Provider for DTS Packages.
- Microsoft OLE DB Provider for Microsoft Active Directory Services.
- Microsoft OLE DB Provider for ODBC Drivers.
- Microsoft OLE DB Provider for OLAP Services.
- Microsoft OLE DB Provider for Oracle.
- Microsoft OLE DB Provider for SQL Server.
- Microsoft OLE DB Simple Provider.
- MS Remote.
- MSDataShape.

- MSPersist.
- SQL Server DTS Flat File OLE DB Provider.

As we'll see, these are the software packages that you use to connect to specific data providers using ADO. For example, to connect to a Microsoft Access database, which is based on the Microsoft Jet engine, you would use a Jet OLE DB provider.

ADO's main benefits are ease of use, high speed, low memory overhead, and a relatively small amount of disk usage. ADO supports a great many features for building client/server and Web-based applications.

ADO also features the Remote Data Services (RDS), by which you can move data from a remote server to a client application or Web page, manipulate the data on a client, and return updates to the server in a single round trip. We'll see all that in this book. For example, you may want to access data sources through non-standard data sources such as the Microsoft Internet Information Server (IIS) in a three-tier system. RDS defines a programming model to enable access to data through intermediaries such as IIS. Using RDS, you can also cache data on the client or middle tier of a three-tier application. Previously released as Microsoft Remote Data Services 1.5, RDS has been combined with the ADO programming model to simplify client-side data remoting.

ADO is actually a library of objects that you use to connect to databases. It doesn't support all the methods that DAO does now, but it will in the future. In ODBC, you used to connect to databases directly using SQL strings; now the interface has been made more modular in ADO, which is based on objects, not on passing SQL strings directly using procedures. Programming with objects is intended to make it easier to break your application up across tiers.

Here are the objects in the ADO library:

- **Connection**—Access from your application to a data source is through a connection, the environment necessary for exchanging data. The Connection object is used to specify a particular data provider and any parameters.
- **Command**—A command issued across an established connection manipulates the data source in some way. The Command object lets ADO make it easy to issue commands.
- **Parameter**—Commands can require *parameters*, which can be set before you issue a command. For example, if you require a debit from a charge account, you would specify the amount of money to be debited as a parameter in a Parameter object.
- **Recordset**—If your command is a query that returns data as rows of information in a table, then those rows are placed in local storage in a Recordset object.

- **Field**—A row of a recordset consists of one or more fields, which are stored in `Field` objects.

- **Error**—Errors can occur when your program is not able to establish a connection, execute a command, or perform an operation. ADO supports an `Error` object to hold the resulting error.

- **Collection**—ADO provides *collections*, objects that contain other objects of a particular type. ADO provides four types of collections: the `Connection` object has the `Errors` collection; the `Command` object has the `Parameters` collection; the `Recordset` object has the `Fields` collection; and the `Connection`, `Command`, `Recordset`, and `Field` objects all have a `Properties` collection, which contains all the `Property` objects that apply to them.

- **Events**—ADO uses the concept of events, just like other interface objects in Visual Basic. You use event-handling procedures with events. There are two types of events: `ConnectionEvents` (issued when transactions occur, when commands are executed, and when `connections` start or end) and `RecordsetEvents` (events used to report the progress of data changes).

Here's a quick overview showing how to use the ADO objects:

- You make a connection to a data source using the `Connection` object.
- If you want to use SQL with the data source, you can create an object to represent an SQL command using the `Command` object.
- If you're creating an SQL command, you can specify columns, tables, and values in the command as variable parameters with the `Parameter` object.
- You execute the command using the `Command`, `Connection`, or `Recordset` objects.
- If the command returns rows of data, you store them in a cache using the `Recordset` object.
- You can create a view of the cache so you can sort, filter, and navigate the data using the `Recordset` object.
- You can also edit the data by adding, deleting, or changing rows and columns with the `Recordset` object.
- When you're done making changes, you update the data source with changes from the cache using the `Recordset` object.
- You end the connection, using the `Connection` object.

Much of this book will be an exploration of the ADO object library, so it's a good idea to get an overview of the objects in the library here. I'll start with the `Connection` object.

Connection Objects

A Connection object represents a unique session with a data source. In the case of a client/server database system, it may be equivalent to an actual network connection to the server. Access from your application to the data source is through this connection, which provides the environment necessary for exchanging data. The Connection object is used to specify a particular data provider and any parameters.

You specify a connection string to connect to a data source, and that string specifies not only the database to use, but also the OLE DB provider, passwords, if any, and other options, such as what security protocol you want to use with the SQL Server. You can use the Connection object's Open method to open a connection.

When you're connected, you can execute SQL queries on the data source with the Connection object's Execute method, which can return a recordset. Or you can use a Recordset object's Open method, passing it a Connection object, to open a database.

You can also manage database *transactions* using the Connection object. Using transactions, you can group what may be many different individual actions into one coherent whole, so if one action fails, they all do. In this way, you don't end up with only partial updates to your database if there's a problem during update operations.

The Connection object supports methods to work with transactions like BeginTrans (begin a transaction), CommitTrans (update a database), and RollbackTrans (restore the state before the transaction began). Once you call the BeginTrans method, the provider will not commit changes to the database until you call CommitTrans or RollbackTrans and end the transaction. We'll use these methods in Chapter 5.

note Note that not all data providers support transactions. You can check if your provider does by seeing if the provider-defined property **Transaction DDL** appears in the **Connection** object's **Properties** collection. The Microsoft Transaction Server (MTS) is a middle-tier application that lets you support transactions, and we'll see more of it later.

Since the Connection object manages your connection with the database, it includes a ConnectionString property, which holds the connection string, and a CommandTimeout property, which sets the timeout length for commands. A command is typically an SQL query that returns a recordset or performs some other action, such as deleting a record. That's one way of sending instructions to the Connection object—using Command objects.

Command Objects

Command objects represent instructions issued across a connection to manipulate a data source, typically through SQL.

note Note that some OLE DB providers do not support `Command` objects, so you'll have to use the `Connection` `Open` or `Execute` methods with them.

You use a `Command` object to query a database and return records in a `Recordset` object, or to manipulate the structure of a database. Here's how you use `Command` objects, step by step:

1. Connect the `Command` object to an active connection by setting the `Command` object's `ActiveConnection` property.

2. Store the actual text of the command (for example, an SQL statement) in the `CommandText` property.

3. Configure parameterized queries or stored procedure arguments with `Parameter` objects and the `Parameters` collection.

4. If you wish, specify the type of command with the `CommandType` property before execution to optimize performance.

5. Execute a command and return a `Recordset` object—if appropriate—with the `Command` object's `Execute` method.

`Commands` are important objects in ADO. They can manipulate records by deleting or updating them, they can return recordsets, and you can use them to define multiple commands for each connection.

There are three important `Connection` methods that you should know about when dealing with commands: `Execute`, which executes a command; `WillExecute`, which is called just before a command executes and gives you an opportunity to modify command parameters; and `ExecuteComplete`, which is called just after a command has finished executing.

`WillExecute` causes a `WillExecute` event, which may occur because of calls to the `Connection.Execute`, `Command.Execute`, or `Recordset.Open` methods. `ExecuteComplete` causes an `ExecuteComplete` event, which may occur because of calls to the `Connection.Execute`, `Command.Execute`, `Recordset.Open`, or `Recordset.NextRecordset` methods.

The parameters you might use in a `Command` object are stored in its `Parameters` collection, and each item in that collection is a `Parameter` object. For example, to shift money between accounts, you could specify the amount as a parameter in a `Parameter` object.

Parameter Objects

`Parameter` objects hold all that you need to specify a command parameter. Here's how you use `Parameter` objects:

1. Use the `Command` object's `CreateParameter` method to create a `Parameter` object with the appropriate property settings.

2. Set the name of a parameter with the Name property.

3. Set the value of a parameter with the Value property.

4. Set parameter characteristics with attributes and the Direction, Precision, NumericScale, Size, and Type properties.

5. Pass long binary or character data (more than 255 bytes) to the parameter with the AppendChunk method.

6. Use the Command object's Append method to the Parameter object to add to the Command object's Parameters collection.

After you've created a parameter and given it a name and a value, you can refer to it by name in an SQL string, where it replaces a ? character with the value of the parameter. For example, if you created a parameter object called Name, you could use it in SQL like this:

```
cmd.CommandText = "SELECT * from students WHERE
Name = ?"
```

We'll see more about this in detail when we work with parameterized ADO commands later. When you execute a command, with or without parameters, you may generate a recordset, depending on the command you've executed (some commands, such as the SQL Delete command, don't create new recordsets). That recordset is held in an ADO Recordset object.

Recordset Objects

Recordsets are what you use to manipulate data from a data provider. When you use ADO, you manipulate data almost entirely using Recordset objects. All Recordset objects are constructed using records (that is, rows) and fields (that is, columns). We'll see more about Recordset objects throughout the book, of course, but I'll cover them here in overview.

Recordset objects include methods like MoveFirst, MoveNext, and so on that let you navigate through a recordset.

When you open a recordset, you use the recordset's Open method. Here's how you use the Open method to create a recordset:

```
recordset.Open Source, ActiveConnection, _
CursorType, LockType, Options
```

The first argument is a valid Command object variable name, SQL statement, table name, stored procedure call, or the file name of a recordset. The ActiveConnection argument is the connection you want to create the recordset from.

You can also specify the type of cursor you want in the `CursorType` argument. So what is a *cursor*? A cursor manages a recordset in ADO, and specifies how you can move through the recordset. Say, for example, that you have a database with 40,000 records and you execute a command on that database that retrieves 4 records—records 1,233, 21,607, 37,999, and 39,003. The cursor in your program is responsible for making those records appear as records 1, 2, 3, and 4 to your code as the user scrolls through them. In this way, an ADO cursor mimics a cursor you'd use on the screen to scroll through lines of text.

There are four different cursor types defined in ADO, and it's important to know the differences between them; here are the four possible options you can pass to a recordset's `Open` method:

- **adOpenDynamic**—*Dynamic cursor.* This cursor type lets you view additions, changes, and deletions by other users, and allows all types of movement through the recordset.

- **adOpenKeyset**—*Keyset cursor.* This cursor behaves like a dynamic cursor, except that it prevents you from seeing records that other users add, and prevents access to records that other users delete. Data changes by other users will still be visible.

- **adOpenStatic**—*Static cursor.* This cursor provides a static copy of a set of records for you to use to find data or generate reports. Note that additions, changes, and deletions by other users will not be visible.

- **adOpenForwardOnly**—*Forward-only cursor.* This cursor behaves the same as a dynamic cursor, except that it allows you to only scroll forward through records. This can improve performance when you only need to make a single pass through the data in a recordset.

You can set the `CursorType` property before opening a `Recordset` object to choose the cursor type, or you can pass a `CursorType` argument with the `Open` method. If you don't specify a cursor type, ADO opens a forward-only cursor by default. We'll see more about cursors when we work with `Recordset` objects in Chapter 8.

 note Although not supported in the `Open` method, you can use the `Recordset` object's `CursorLocation` property to indicate if you want the cursor to be on the client or the server (not all servers will support cursors).

When you open a `Recordset` object, you can specify the lock type using the `LockType` argument. This argument specifies how you lock records that are being updated. To update a record, you edit the data in a record's fields (by changing a `Field` object's `Value` property, or by editing the data in a bound control), which puts the recordset in Edit mode (as indicated in the `EditMode` property, which is set to `adEditInProgress`), then call the `Update` method. Various types of locking can occur when you edit or update records. Here are the possibilities; note in particular the difference between optimistic and pessimistic locking:

- **`adLockReadOnly`**—(default) read-only. You cannot alter the data.
- **`adLockPessimistic`**—Pessimistic locking, record by record. The data provider does what is necessary to ensure successful editing of the records, usually by locking records at the data source immediately when you start editing the data in the recordset's fields.
- **`adLockOptimistic`**—Optimistic locking, record by record. The provider uses optimistic locking, locking records only when you call the `Update` method.
- **`adLockBatchOptimistic`**—Optimistic batch updates; required for batch update mode as opposed to immediate update mode.

note With some providers (such as the Microsoft ODBC Provider for OLE DB and the Microsoft SQL Server), you can create `Recordset` objects without a previously defined `Connection` object by passing a connection string to the `Open` method. Behind the scenes, ADO still creates a `Connection` object, but it doesn't give that object an object variable in your code.

When you open a recordset, the current record is positioned to the first record (if any) and the `BOF` (Beginning of File) and `EOF` (End of File) properties are set to False. If there are no records, the `BOF` and `EOF` property settings are True.

You can use the `Recordset` object's `MoveFirst`, `MoveLast`, `MoveNext`, and `MovePrevious` methods, as well as the `Move` method, and the `AbsolutePosition`, `AbsolutePage`, and `Filter` properties to reposition the current record, assuming the provider supports these methods and properties. As you might expect, forward-only `Recordset` objects support only the `MoveNext` method.

When you use the `Move` methods to traverse each record, you can use the `BOF` and `EOF` properties to see if you've moved beyond the beginning or end of the recordset.

It's also useful to know that `Recordset` objects can support two types of updating: immediate and batched. In immediate updating, all changes to data are written immediately to the data source when you call the `Update` method.

If a data provider supports batch updating, you can have the data provider cache changes to more than one record and then send them in a single call to the database with the `UpdateBatch` method. Batch operations apply to changes made with the `AddNew`, `Update`, and `Delete` methods. After you call the `UpdateBatch` method, you can use the `Status` property to check for any problems.

ADO `Recordset` objects are so important that Microsoft has a whole library just for them. There are two main ADO libraries: ADOR and ADODB. The ADOR library is installed with Microsoft Internet Explorer and supports only `Recordset` objects and static cursors. The ADODB library is the full ADO library, including ADO `Recordset` objects, and it's the one we'll use except when working with the Microsoft Internet Explorer.

That's it for the `Recordset` object. How do you address the fields in an ADO recordset? With `Field` objects from the recordset's `Fields` collection.

Field Objects

A `Field` object represents a field in a database; that is, a column of data. You use the `Value` property of `Field` objects to set or return data for the current record. The `Value` property is the default property of `Field` objects, so you can refer to the data in a field called `Name` in any of these ways:

- `adoRecordset.Fields(1).Value`
- `adoRecordset("Name")`
- `adoRecordset.Fields(1)`
- `adoRecordset.Fields("Name")`
- `adoRecordset!Name`

Besides the `Value` property, `Field` objects also have properties like `Name`, `Type`, `Size`, and `Precision`. You can use their `AppendChunk` method to add longer data items to a field.

Error Objects

Errors can happen when your application can't establish a connection or execute a command. ADO supports the `Error` object to hold the resulting error. The `Connection` object contains an `Errors` collection, which contains `Error` objects. The `Error` object contains details about data access errors pertaining to a single operation involving the provider.

 Each **Error** object holds a provider error, not an ADO error. You handle ADO errors with the **On Error GoTo** statement, and they are stored in the **Err** object.

Property Objects

A `Property` object represents a characteristic of an ADO object defined by the provider. ADO objects have two types of properties: built-in and dynamic.

Built-in properties are those properties implemented in ADO and immediately available to any new object using the `Object.Property` syntax. They do not appear as `Property` objects in an object's `Properties` collection, so although you can change their values, you cannot modify their characteristics.

Dynamic properties are defined by the data provider and appear in the ADO `Properties` collection. For example, such a property may specify if a `Recordset` object supports transactions. These properties will appear as `Property` objects in that `Recordset` object's `Properties` collection. Dynamic properties can be referred to only with the `Properties` collection, like this: `adoObject.Properties(0)` or `adoObject.Properties("Name")`.

That completes our discussion of ADO. As with the other data connection protocols, ADO also has a data source control: the ADO data control.

The ADO Data Control

You can see an ADO data control at work in Figure 1.3. The ADO data control is similar to the DAO data control and the remote data control, except that it uses the ADO connection protocol. At design-time, you create a connection by setting the `ConnectionString` property to a valid connection string, then you set the `RecordSource` property to a statement appropriate to the database provider.

You can also set the `ConnectionString` property to the name of a file that defines a connection. You then connect the ADO data control to a databound control, such as a data grid, data combo, or data list, by setting its `DataSource` property to the ADO data control. At run-time, you can set the `Provider`, `ConnectionString`, and `RecordSource` properties to change the database.

The ADO data control is an important one in Visual Basic ADO programming, and it's worth getting a closer look at it here. We'll see more

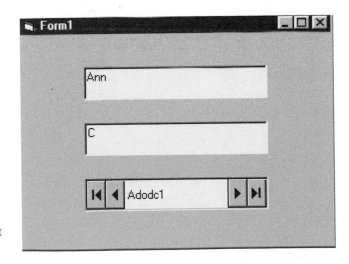

FIGURE 1.3   An ADO data control at work.

about the ADO data control in Chapter 3, but it's a good idea to start with some actual ADO programming to make it easier to put the material we'll cover between now and then into perspective.

Getting Started with the ADO Data Control

Probably the easiest way to connect an application to a data source using the ADO protocol is with the ADO data control. Because it's an easy process, I'll go through an example here, connecting an ADO data control to the `Nwind.mdb` database that comes with Visual Basic, getting us into ADO programming immediately (the `Nwind` database holds customer and sales records for a fictitious company named Northwind).

Start Visual Basic now and create a new standard EXE project by clicking the `New` tab in the dialog box that appears when Visual Basic opens, selecting the `Standard EXE` icon, and clicking the `Open` button. The new standard EXE project appears in Visual Basic as in Figure 1.4, where I've opened the code window by clicking the `View Code` button in the Project Explorer (the button at the top left in the Project Explorer). I've also labeled the parts of the Visual Basic Integrated Development Environment (IDE) in that figure because I'll be referring to those parts of the IDE throughout the book.

Select the new Visual Basic form, `Form1`, in the Visual Basic IDE now (this form is automatically selected when you create a new standard EXE

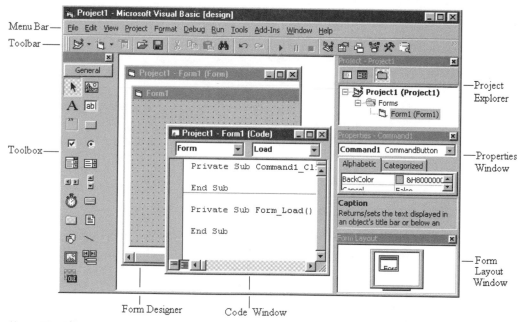

FIGURE 1.4 A new standard EXE project in Visual Basic.

project). In this example, I'll add a label, an ADO data control, and a bound control to this form. Using the ADO data control, the user will then be able to move through the Nwind database, seeing data displayed in the text box.

The label in this program will just display the caption ADO Data Control Example, so find the label tool in the toolbox, double-click it to add a new label to Form1, and use the mouse to position the new label as shown in Figure 1.5.

Add the appropriate caption to the label, ADO Data Control Example, using the label's Caption property in the Properties window. In addition, center the text by setting the label's Alignment property to Center using the drop-down list box for that property in the Properties window. Finally, set the font size to 24 points by clicking the Font data item in the Properties window, clicking the ellipsis (...) button that appears, selecting 24 in the Size list of the Font dialog box, and clicking OK to close the Font dialog. The result appears in Figure 1.6.

The next step is to add an ADO data control, and I'll take a look at that now.

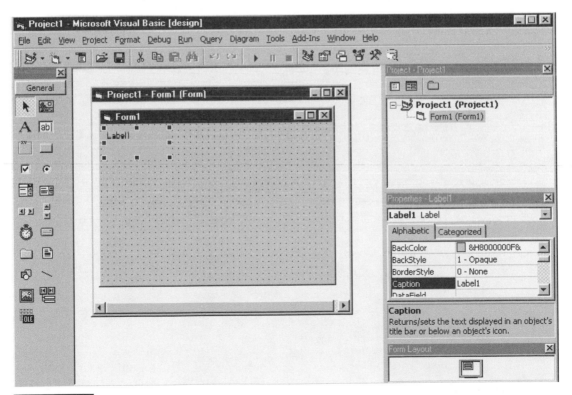

FIGURE 1.5   Adding a label to a form in Visual Basic.

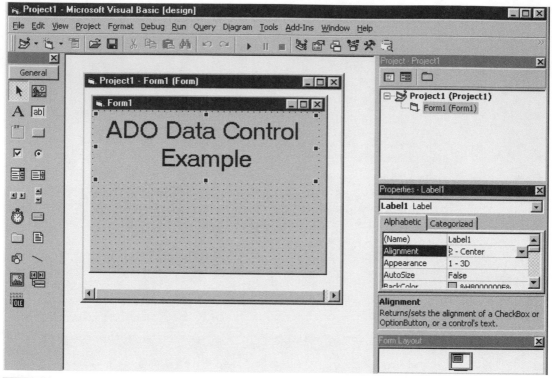

FIGURE 1.6   A label with the caption ADO Data Control Example.

Adding an ADO Data Control to a Form

Here's how you add an ADO data control to a form in Visual Basic:

1. Select the `Components` item in the `Project` menu.
2. Click the `Controls` tab in the `Components` dialog.
3. Select the `Microsoft ADO Data Control` entry in the `Controls` list box.
4. Click `OK` to close the `Components` dialog box.
5. Add an ADO data control to your form.
6. Connect the ADO data control's `Connection` object to a data source with the `ConnectionString` property, separating items in that string with semicolons.

The `Components` dialog appears in Figure 1.7, and you can see the `Microsoft ADO Data Control` entry selected in that figure. Select that entry now and click `OK` to add the ADO data control to the Visual Basic toolbox; the new ADO data control tool appears in the toolbox in Figure 1.8.

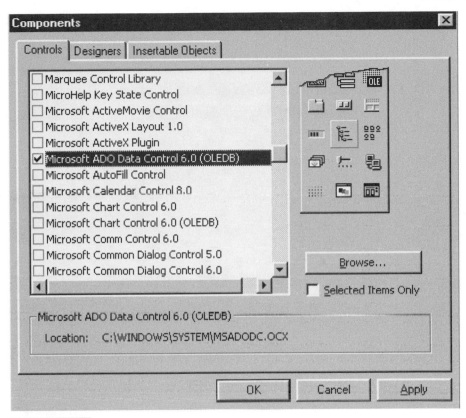

FIGURE 1.7   The Visual Basic Components dialog box.

Double-click the ADO data control tool now to add a new ADO data control, Adodc1, to Form1. Position the control with the mouse and use the sizing handles to size the control as shown in Figure 1.8.

Now that we've created this new control, the next step is to connect it to the Nwind.mdb database. In this case, that means creating a connection string for the control.

Creating a Connection String

Creating a connection string is the standard first step in connecting an ADO data control to a database. You place the connection string in the ADO Connection-String property. The ADO control supports four arguments for the ConnectionString property, as well as other arguments you pass directly to the data provider. Here are the arguments for the ConnectionString property:

- **Provider**—Name of a data provider to use for the connection.
- **File Name**—Name of a provider-specific file containing preset connection information.

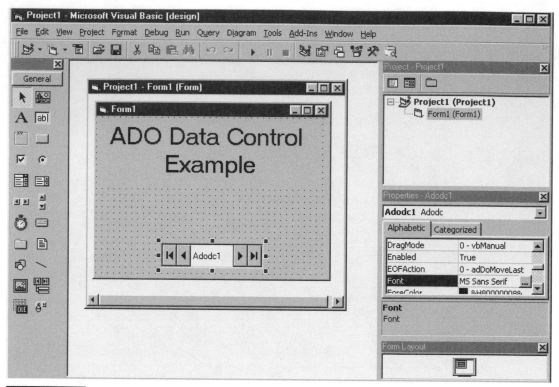

FIGURE 1.8 Adding a new ADO data control to a form.

- **Remote Provider**—Name of a provider to use when opening a client-side connection. (This applies to the RDS only.)
- **Remote Server**—Pathname of the server to use when opening a client-side connection. (This applies to the RDS only.)

In fact, you'll frequently have to add server-specific information, such as commands and so forth, directly to the server in the connection string. So where does that leave us now that we want to connect to the Nwind.mdb file? How do you create a connection string?

Fortunately, Visual Basic automates the process for every type of OLE DB data provider for which there are drivers. To see how this works, just click the ellipsis button in the ConnectionString property's entry in the Visual Basic Properties window to open the ADO control's Property Pages, as shown in Figure 1.9.

As you can see in that figure, you can specify a connection using a data link file (data link files have the extension .udl), an ODBC DSN, or a connection string. To automate the building of a connection string, click the Build button after making sure the Use Connection String option button is selected.

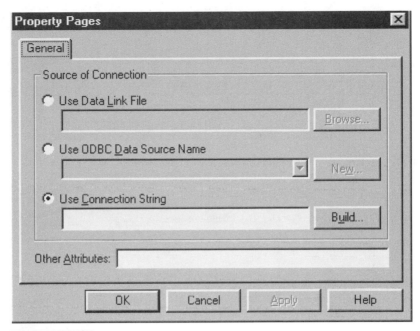

FIGURE 1.9   The ADO control's Property Pages.

Clicking the Build button opens the Data Link Properties dialog you see in Figure 1.10, and we'll see more about this dialog throughout the book. This dialog lets you select an OLE provider to use to access your data through ADO. In this case, I'll select a Jet OLE provider, the Microsoft Jet 4.0 OLE DB Provider.

Now click the Next button to move to the Connection page, as you see in Figure 1.11. In this page, you give the name of the database you want to connect to. In this case, click the ellipsis button next to the text box labeled Select or enter a database name, browse to the Nwind.mdb database, select it, and click the Open button. If applicable for a database, you can also specify the user name and password you want to use with the database at this point.

To test the connection, click the Test Connection button; you will get a message box saying Test connection succeeded or an error box indicating what the problem was (usually the database file was not where Visual Basic expected it to be).

After testing the connection, click OK to dismiss the Data Link Properties dialog. The new connection string appears in the ADO control's Property Pages, as you see in Figure 1.12.

Here's the new connection string for the Nwind.mdb database:

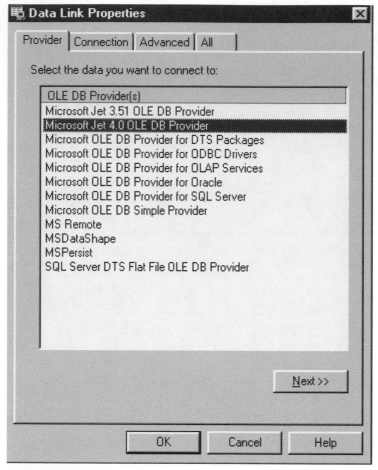

FIGURE 1.10   The `Data Link Properties` dialog, `Provider` page.

```
Provider=Microsoft.Jet.OLEDB.4.0;Persist Security
Info=False;Data Source=C:\ADO\Nwind.mdb
```

Here's how the connection string might have looked if I used another OLE DB provider—the Microsoft SQL Server:

```
Provider=SQLOLEDB.1;Persist Security Info=False;User
ID=sa;Initial Catalog=Northwind
```

At this point, we've selected a database to connect to and created a connection string, but we haven't specified what data we want to use in the database.

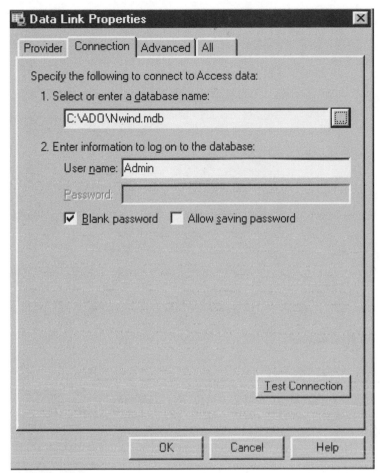

FIGURE 1.11   The `Data Link Properties` dialog, `Connection` page.

Getting Records from a Database

After indicating what database to connect to, you must still set the ADO control's `RecordSource` property to indicate where you want to get the actual records from in the database.

In this case, I'll enter the `Customers` table in the ADO control's `RecordSource` property. To do that, click the ellipsis button in the `Record-Source` property's entry in the `Properties` window, opening the `Property Pages` dialog to the `RecordSource` property, as shown in Figure 1.13.

Here, you select the `CommandType` property from the drop-down list. This property holds the command we'll execute on the data source to create the records the ADO data control will work with. The possibilities are `ad-CmdUnknown`, `adCmdText` (lets you specify an SQL statement), `adCmdTable`

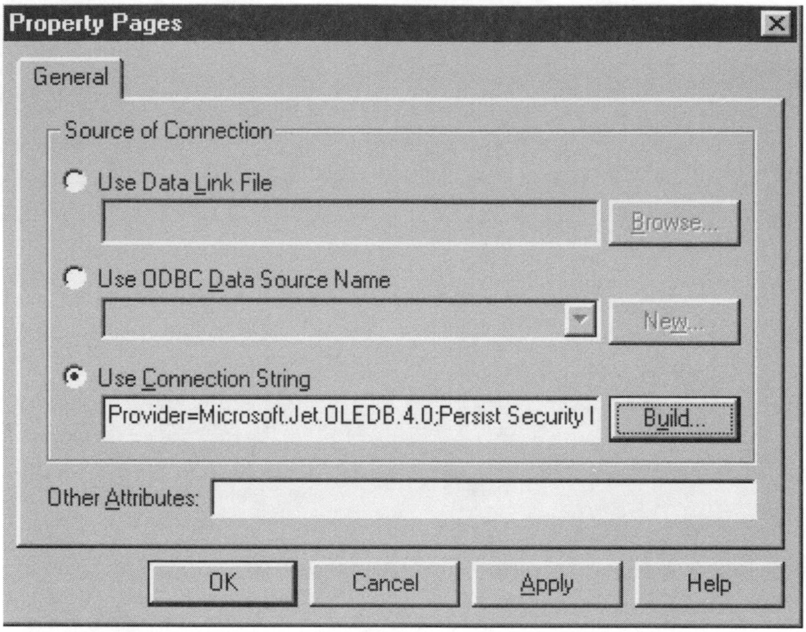

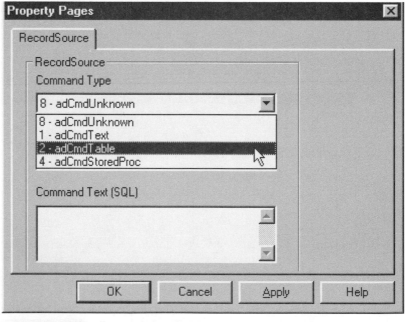

FIGURE 1.12 A new connection string in the Property Pages.

FIGURE 1.13 The Property Pages, RecordSource tab.

(lets you specify a table), and `adCmdStoredProc` (lets you specify a stored procedure), as you see in Figure 1.13. These possibilities indicate the ways of getting records from the Microsoft Jet 4.0 OLE DB provider.

In this case, I'll select `adCmdTable` to make this a table-type command, which will fetch an entire table from `Nwind.mdb`. The next step is to specify what table to fetch; in this case, I'll use the `Customers` table in the `Nwind` database. That table appears in Figure 1.14 in the Visual Data Manager, one of the Visual Basic database tools we'll take a look at in Chapter 2.

To load the `Customers` table into the ADO data control, you can use the `Table` or `Stored Procedure Name` drop-down list in the `Property Pages`, as shown in Figure 1.15. Visual Basic helps out here by examining the database immediately and filling that drop-down list with the available tables, as shown in Figure 1.15. Select the `Customers` table from the drop-down list now.

	CustomerID	CompanyName	ContactName	ContactTitle	Address	City
▶		Alfreds Futterkiste	Maria Anders	Sales Representative	Obere Str. 57	Berlin
	ANATR	Ana Trujillo Emparedado	Ana Trujillo	Owner	Avda. de la Constitución	México
	ANTON	Antonio Moreno Taquer	Antonio Moreno	Owner	Mataderos 2312	México
	AROUT	Around the Horn	Thomas Hardy	Sales Representative	120 Hanover Sq.	London
	BERGS	Berglunds snabbköp	Christina Berglund	Order Administrator	Berguvsvägen 8	Luleå
	BLAUS	Blauer See Delikatesser	Hanna Moos	Sales Representative	Forsterstr. 57	Mannhe
	BLONP	Blondel père et fils	Frédérique Citeaux	Marketing Manager	24, place Kléber	Strashn
	BOLID	Bólido Comidas prepara	Martín Sommer	Owner	C/ Araquil, 67	Madrid
	BONAP	Bon app'	Laurence Lebihan	Owner	12, rue des Bouchers	Marseille
	BOTTM	Bottom-Dollar Markets	Elizabeth Lincoln	Accounting Manager	23 Tsawassen Blvd.	Tsawas
	BSBEV	B's Beverages	Victoria Ashworth	Sales Representative	Fauntleroy Circus	London
	CACTU	Cactus Comidas para lle	Patricio Simpson	Sales Agent	Cerrito 333	Buenos
	CENTC	Centro comercial Mocte	Francisco Chang	Marketing Manager	Sierras de Granada 999	México
	CHOPS	Chop-suey Chinese	Yang Wang	Owner	Hauptstr. 29	Bern
	COMMI	Comércio Mineiro	Pedro Afonso	Sales Associate	Av. dos Lusíadas, 23	São Pau
	CONSH	Consolidated Holdings	Elizabeth Brown	Sales Representative	Berkeley Gardens 12 E	London
	DRACD	Drachenblut Delikatesse	Sven Ottlieb	Order Administrator	Walserweg 21	Aachen
	DUMON	Du monde entier	Janine Labrune	Owner	67, rue des Cinquante C	Nantes
	EASTC	Eastern Connection	Ann Devon	Sales Agent	35 King George	London
	ERNSH	Ernst Handel	Roland Mendel	Sales Manager	Kirchgasse 6	Graz

FIGURE 1.14 The `Customers` table in the `Nwind` database.

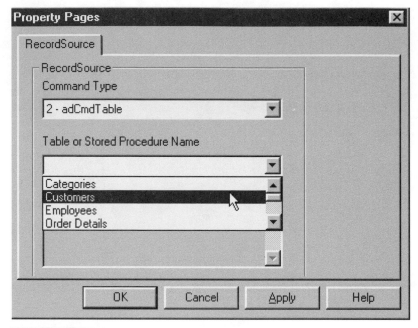

FIGURE 1.15 The `Property Pages`, `RecordSource` tab.

Finally, click OK to close the `Property Pages` dialog; doing so sets the `RecordSource` property of the ADO data control, `adodc1`, to `Customers`. And that's it—now the ADO data control is connected to a table in a database; we've specified an OLE DB provider type to use, the command to execute on the database to fetch a specific table of data, and the table we want. Note that we'll see a lot more about the ADO data control in Chapter 3, but what we've done so far already provides a useful overview.

Now that the ADO control is connected to a database, it's time to connect other controls to the ADO control itself and to see the data in the `Customers` table.

Binding Controls to the ADO Data Control

Note that a control like a text box can only display a single string of text, which means that you can use it only to display a single field of data from the current record in the ADO data control. In this case, I'll bind a text box to the `ContactName` field of the `Customers` table in the ADO control's `Recordset` object (you can see the `ContactName` field's column of data in the `Customers` table in Figure 1.14). You bind controls like text boxes by setting their `DataSource` and `DataField` properties. The `DataSource` property will hold the name of the ADO data control in the form, `adodc1`, and the

`DataField` property will hold the name of the field in the records supplied by the ADO data control that I want to display in the text box.

To add a text box to `Form1`, double-click the text box tool in the tool-box and position the new text box as shown in Figure 1.16. The new text box is named `Text1`.

Clear the text box by erasing the text in its `Text` property in the `Proper-ties` window. Now I'll bind the text box to the ADO data control. To do that, I'll start by setting its `DataSource` property to the ADO control, `Adodc1`.

Visual Basic helps here again; just click the drop-down list box in the text box's `DataSource` entry in the `Property Pages` and you'll see a list of the possible data sources, as shown in Figure 1.17; in this case, there's only one possibility—the ADO data control I've added to the form, `adodc1`. Select `adodc1` in the text box's `DataSource` property now.

The final step is to set `Text1`'s `DataField` property to the `Contact-Name` field in the `Customers` database. Visual Basic helps here once again by checking the database to see what fields are available in the table we're going to use and displaying those fields in the drop-down list box that ap-

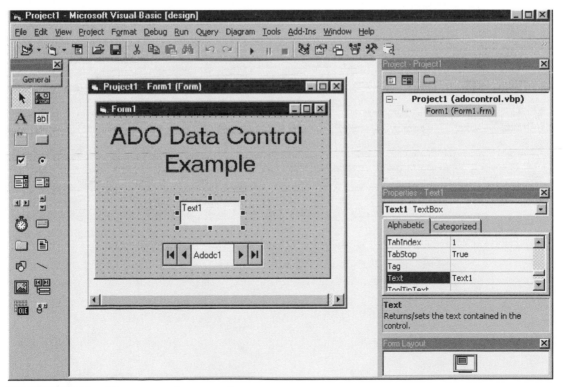

FIGURE 1.16   Adding a text box to a form.

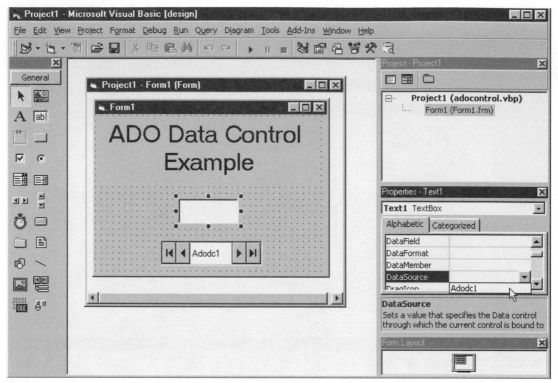

FIGURE 1.17 Setting a text box's `DataSource` property.

pears when you click the `DataField` property's entry in the `Properties` window, as shown in Figure 1.18.

That's all it takes. Now run the application by selecting the `Start` item in the Visual Basic `Run` menu. The program runs, as you see in Figure 1.19—and as you can see in that figure, the first `ContactName` entry in the `Nwind` `Customers` table appears in the text box. The ADO data control at the bottom of the form displays buttons that you can use to navigate through the records in the `Customers` table; in order, from left to right, the buttons move to the first record in the table, the previous record, the next record, and the last record.

Congratulations—you've just completed your first ADO program! As you can see, it's not too difficult to get a working program going using ADO.

So far, we've gotten an overview of the ADO object model and completed a working ADO program. I'll continue the ADO overview now by taking a look at what's new in recent versions of ADO.

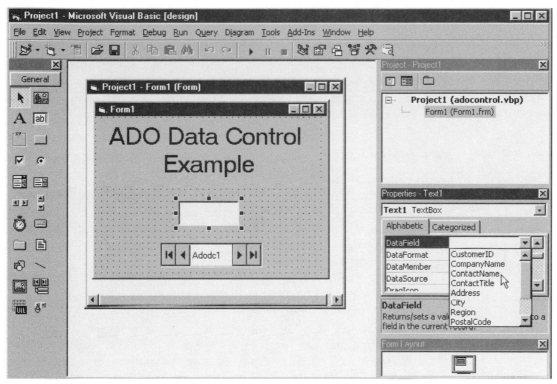

FIGURE 1.18 Setting a text box's `DataField` property.

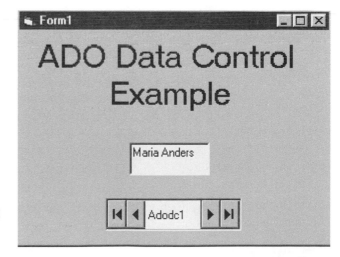

FIGURE 1.19 Using an ADO data control.

What's New in Recent Versions of ADO?

As of this writing, the current versions of ADO you can use in Visual Basic are ADO 2.0 and 2.1. I'll take a look here at what's new in these two versions. Much of this material is advanced and won't have much meaning unless you're already familiar with ADO programming, but you can refer back to this information later when we've covered the topics mentioned here.

New in ADO 2.0

Here's some of what's new in ADO version 2.0:

- There's a new shorthand method to create a recordset by appending new `Field` objects to the `Fields` collection of a recordset. After creating the recordset, you can open it and insert data from any source. You can also manufacture the data under programmatic control. The new `Recordset` object can use all the data methods available to any recordset. You can use the recordset to supply information to a visual control, or even to update an actual data source.

- Now, with recordset persistence, you can save recordset data in a file. After saving the data, you can use the data in the file, called *persisted* data, to create a `Recordset` object. As you might expect with ADO, the persisted file may exist on a local drive, network server, or as a URL on a Web site.

- The `MSPersist` provider is new and supports storing a `Recordset` object in a file with the `Save` method. The persisted file can be restored with the `Recordset` object's `Open` or the `Connection` object's `Execute` methods. To store the `Recordset` object, it's converted into a string in the file. Right now, the only supported format is the Microsoft Advanced Data TableGram (ADTG) format. The `MSPersist` provider also adds a property—`PersistFormat`—to the `Recordset` object's `Properties` collection, so you can determine or set the string format used.

- The new `GetString` method formats a `Recordset` object so that the columns and rows are delimited with characters you choose.

- The new `Sort` property determines the order in which rows of a recordset are presented.

- The new `Filter` property determines which rows are accessible when moving among rows.

- The `Find` method locates a value within an indexed column of a recordset.

- You can now create an internal index for a `Field` object by setting its dynamic `Optimize` property (this dynamic property is added to the `Field` object's `Properties` collection when you set the `CursorLoca`-

tion property to `adUseClient`). Note, however, that this index is internal to ADO—you can't gain access to it in your code.

We'll cover these concepts in more detail later.

New in ADO 2.1

Here's some of what's new in ADO 2.1:

- The new `Seek` method and `Index` property let you locate rows in a recordset quickly.
- ADO now supports row updates and synchronization.
- You can have custom control of row updates and synchronization for `Recordset` objects created by an SQL `JOIN` operation. In fact, seven new dynamic properties control the behavior of the five existing methods.
- Recordsets can now be saved in Extensible Markup Language (XML) format.
- The Microsoft Data Shaping Service for OLE DB, which supports data shaping, can now reshape previously shaped recordsets. (To support this new feature, `Recordset` objects now have a `Name` property that is available for the duration of the connection.)
- You can perform aggregate calculations on a column at any level of a shaped recordset, not just the immediate child of the parent. (This feature uses fully qualified chapter names to form a path to the desired level and column.)
- Parameterized `COMPUTE` commands can now have an arbitrary number of intermediate `COMPUTE` clauses between the `PARAMETER` clause and parameter argument.
- The Microsoft OLE DB Remoting Provider service provider became a standard service provider in ADO 2.1. This service was given new dynamic properties for better performance and compatibility with ADO 2.0 in ADO 2.1.
- The new Microsoft Cursor Service for the OLE DB service component augments the cursor support in other data providers.

Again, much of this information probably makes little sense now, but we'll cover it in more detail later.

That finishes our overview of ADO in this chapter—but there's still more to consider. This chapter is on Visual Basic database programming, and Visual Basic version 6 adds a specific capability that all database programmers should be aware of—data validation. I'll take a look at that now.

• • • • • • • • • • • • • •

Writing Bulletproof Database Programs by Validating User Data

One of the most important aspects of database programming is validating user input. Your application is responsible for ensuring that the data a user enters is in an appropriate form for your program to use and store, and checking that data is especially important when you're using databases.

In real-world database programming, this is one of the most important parts of programming; when you release a database application to users, it has to be *bulletproof*. In fact, it's not unusual to spend more time developing a program's user interface than writing the actual core code that works with a database. It's crucial that your program doesn't break if someone enters text when they should have entered a number or makes some other kind of mistake, such as asking your program to sort an empty table.

Ideally, every possible misuse of your program should be considered, planned for, handled, and tested. (After a few too many calls from mystified users, this is one of the things you learn quickly in a commercial database programming environment.)

It's hard to emphasize this part of database programming enough, which is why I'm covering it at the very beginning of this book in this chapter on general Visual Basic database programming. The feel of a program is of paramount importance to users, and if your program feels fragile to them—crashing frequently or getting stuck—they'll stop using it.

Visual Basic 6 includes a great deal of support that lets you check, that is, validate, data entered by users before you pass it on to the database part of your code. This support is an invaluable part of Visual Basic database programming, and I'll take a look at it here. Much of this support is designed to let you check the data the user entered when the user moves the *focus* to another control. The focus, more properly called the *input focus*, is a Windows concept. When you give a control the focus, usually by clicking it, that control will be able to read keystrokes. Only one control can have the focus at any one time (i.e., there's only one keyboard to enter data from).

Here are some of the properties, events, and methods that you can use in the data validation process in Visual Basic—new in Visual Basic 6 are the important `CausesValidation` property and `Validate` event:

- `Enabled` property—Enables or disables controls.
- `Locked` property—Denies user access to the data in a control if True.
- `MaxLength` property—Sets the maximum length of the text in text box controls.
- `DataFormat` property—Specifies the data format in bound controls.
- `CausesValidation` property—If True, means this control causes a `Validate` event.

- `Validate` event—Occurs if the user tries to move the focus away from the control and the `CausesValidation` property of the target control is True.
- `Change` event—Occurs if the user changes the data in a control.
- `KeyPress` event—Occurs when the user presses a key that generates an ANSI code.
- `LostFocus` event—Occurs when a control loses the focus.
- `ValidateControls` method—A form method that lets you fire the `Validate` event for the last-used control on a form, when the user is about to leave the form.

Which control event you want to use for data validation depends on how you want to validate that data. Four events that you can use are the `Change`, `KeyPress`, `LostFocus`, and `Validate` events:

- `Change` event—You can use this event to validate data if you want to catch errors as the user enters data character by character.
- `KeyPress` event—You can use this event if you want to catch errors as the user presses keys that generate ANSI codes.
- `LostFocus` event—You can use this event to validate data when the user moves the focus away from the control, although the `Validate` event is now a better event to use; in other words, when the user is done entering data.
- `Validate` event—You can use this event to validate data when the user moves the focus away from the control; in other words, when the user is done entering data.

I'll take a look at a data validation example now using the new `CausesValidation` property and `Validate` event.

Data Validation Using the CausesValidation Property and Validate Event

In this data validation example, I'll use two text boxes, `Text1` and `Text2`, written so the user must enter numeric data in each. If the user places non-numeric data in a text box and then moves away from that text box (as by clicking another control), the program will display a message box asking the user to enter numeric data in the text box and return the focus to that text box.

To start this example, I will create a new standard EXE project and add two text boxes—which Visual Basic names `Text1` and `Text2`—to the default form, `Form1`, as shown in Figure 1.20. I will also clear the text in those text boxes, as also shown in Figure 1.20.

When the user enters data into one of these text boxes and moves to another control whose `CausesValidation` property is set to True, the `Validate` event of the text box is fired. You can place code in the `Validate` event handler to check the new data in the text box and display a message

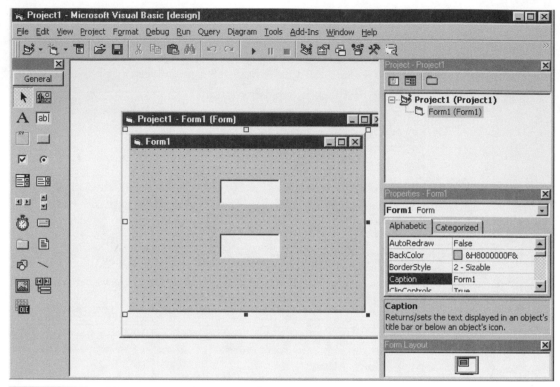

FIGURE 1.20 Adding two text boxes to a form.

box if needed. By default, the CausesValidation property of controls like text boxes is True, so I don't need to set that property.

To add code to the Validate event of each text box, you use the Visual Basic code window, which you can open by clicking the View Code window in the Project Explorer, or by double-clicking a form or control.

In the code window, select the first text box, Text1, in the upper left drop-down list box and select the text box's Validate event in the upper right drop-down list box, as shown in Figure 1.21.

Selecting the Validate event in the drop-down list box adds this code to the code window:

```
Private Sub Text1_Validate(Cancel As Boolean)
End Sub
```

This is the Sub procedure that will be called when Text1's Validate event fires. In this event handler, you can check the data in the text box. If you set the Cancel parameter to True, Visual Basic prevents the user from moving away from the text box by returning the focus to the text box.

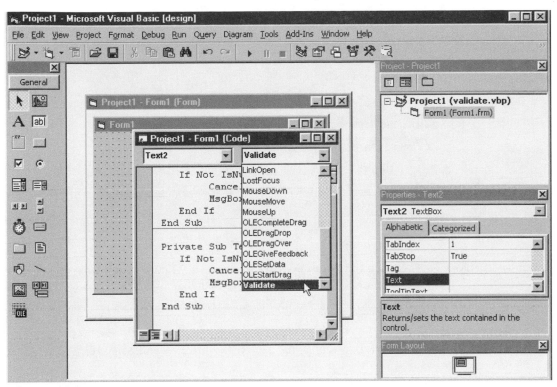

FIGURE 1.21 Selecting the Validate event.

In this case, I'll just make sure that the user entered numeric data into the text box by using the Visual Basic IsNumeric function. Here's the code to add to the Validate event handlers for Text1—note that if the data in the current text box is not in numeric form when the user tries to move the focus to a new control whose CausesValidation property is True, the code sets the Cancel parameter to True, preventing the user from moving the focus away from the text box, and displays a message:

```
Private Sub Text1_Validate(Cancel As Boolean)
    If Not IsNumeric(Text1.Text) Then
        Cancel = True
        MsgBox "Please enter a number in Text1"
    End If
End Sub
```

Next, add a Validate event handler for the other text box, Text2:

```
Private Sub Text2_Validate(Cancel As Boolean)
End Sub
```

As before, add this code—customized for `Text2`—to check the value the user entered to make sure it's numeric:

```
Private Sub Text2_Validate(Cancel As Boolean)
    If Not IsNumeric(Text2.Text) Then
        Cancel = True
        MsgBox "Please enter a number in Text2"
    End If
End Sub
```

That's it—the result appears in Figure 1.22. When the user enters data that does not represent a number in a text box and then tries to move the focus, the application displays the error message you see in that figure and returns the focus to the text box.

As you can see, the new `CausesValidation` property and `Validate` event are useful for checking user data—an essential step in database programs that you release generally.

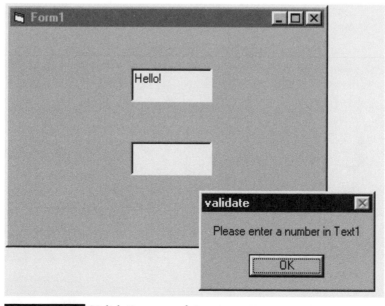

FIGURE 1.22   Validating user data.

Besides the `CausesValidation` property and `Validate` event, you can watch what the user is typing keystroke by keystroke if you want to, using the `Change` or `KeyPress` events. For example, this code checks the data the user enters into `Text1` as they're entering it:

```
Private Sub Text1_Change()
    If Not IsNumeric(Text1.Text) Then
        MsgBox "Please enter only numbers in Text1"
    End If
End Sub
```

Disabling and Hiding Controls

Another technique good user interfaces use is disabling a control when that control doesn't apply—such as disabling text boxes labeled `First Name` and `Last Name` when the user is entering data about inventory products, not people. When a control is disabled, it's grayed out and won't accept the focus, so the user can't enter data in it. Disabling controls means that the user won't enter data in them inadvertently. In Visual Basic, you can disable controls, even menu items, by setting their `Enabled` property to False.

On the other hand, if you disable too many controls, your program will seem impenetrable to the user. It's better to make controls invisible than to present too many disabled controls at any one time. You can make controls invisible by setting their `Visible` property to False.

Form-Level Data Validation

Usually you perform data validation at the control level, but you can also validate data at the form level. To do that, you use the `KeyPreview` property and the following key events: `KeyDown`, `KeyPress`, and `KeyUp`, which fire when the user types data.

By default, forms do not fire key events. However, you can change that by setting their `KeyPreview` property to True. When you do, you can use the `KeyDown`, `KeyPress`, and `KeyUp` events to preview keystrokes *before* they are sent to controls, which lets your code check that data.

The `KeyDown` event occurs when the user presses a key:

```
Private Sub Form_KeyDown(KeyCode As Integer, Shift As
Integer)
    MsgBox "You pressed a key."
End Sub
```

The `KeyUp` event occurs when the user releases a key:

```
Private Sub Form_KeyUp(KeyCode As Integer, Shift As
Integer)

    MsgBox "You released a key."

End Sub
```

Both the KeyDown and KeyUp event handlers get the same two parameters:

- **keycode**—A key code as defined by Visual Basic, such as vbKeyF1 (the F1 key) or vbKeyHome (the HOME key).
- **shift**—An integer that corresponds to the state of the SHIFT, CTRL, and ALT keys at the time of the event. The shift argument is a bit field with the least-significant bits corresponding to the SHIFT key (bit 0), the CTRL key (bit 1), and the ALT key (bit 2). These bits correspond to the values 1, 2, and 4, respectively.

If you want to determine what key was pressed in these two events, you must decipher the key code and then determine if the SHIFT or another key was pressed. On the other hand, the KeyPress event handler is passed the actual value of the struck key, KeyAscii, and you can convert that value into a character by passing it to the Visual Basic Chr function:

```
Private Sub Form_KeyPress(KeyAscii As Integer)

    MsgBox "You pressed:" & Chr(KeyAscii)

End Sub
```

The KeyPress event does not happen when the user presses a key that does not have an ANSI equivalent, such as arrow keys or function keys.

Using key previewing, you can check the value of keys the user types before they are sent to the control they were targeted to, and this provides a powerful way of validating data. For example, if you don't want the user to be able to type the character "a" in the controls in a form, you can set the KeyAscii argument to 0 in the form-level KeyPress:

```
Private Sub Form_KeyPress(KeyAscii As Integer)

    If Chr(KeyAscii) = "a" Then

        KeyAscii = 0

    End If

End Sub
```

As you can see, Visual Basic provides a lot of help when it comes to data validation, and I strongly recommend that you incorporate data validation into your database programs—doing so almost always saves you a lot of grief in real-world applications.

There's one more useful topic to complete our database programming overview in this chapter—SQL programming. SQL is the *lingua franca* of database programming, and it's hard to get by without at least a little SQL in Visual Basic database programming. You don't have to be an SQL expert, but a little can go a long way, so I'll present an overview of SQL here at the beginning of the book—we'll be using it to some extent throughout the book and won't want to stop to learn it when there are more pressing topics to be covered.

note Note that you will *not* need a profound knowledge of SQL to work with ADO in this book.

Some Basic SQL

To get an overview of basic SQL at work, I'll use the Customers table in the Nwind.mdb database that comes with Visual Basic and create SQL queries that work with that table. You can see this table displayed in Figure 1.14. Here, I'll just work through some basic SQL to get us started. The foundation of SQL is the SELECT statement, and I'll start with that.

The SELECT Statement

You use the SELECT statement to retrieve fields from a table; here's an example in which I'm retrieving all the records in the Customers table using the wildcard character, *:

```
SELECT * FROM Customers
```

This returns a recordset that holds all the records in the Customers table. This is a basic SQL statement that we'll see frequently in this book.

Selecting Specific Fields

You can also select specific fields from a table like this instance, in which I'm selecting the CustomerID, Address, and City fields from the Customers table:

```
SELECT CustomerID, Address, City FROM Customers
```

The result of this query appears in Figure 1.23 in the Visual Data Manager.

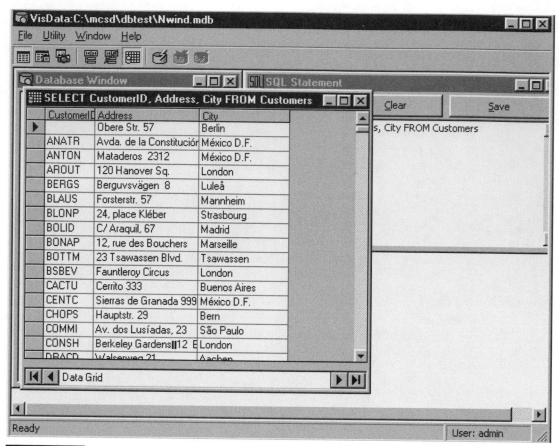

FIGURE 1.23　Selecting specific fields from a database.

The WHERE Clause

Using the WHERE clause, you can set up selection criteria that must be met by the records in the recordset generated by the query. For example, to select all the records in the Customers table where the City field equals Berlin, you can execute this statement:

```
SELECT * FROM Customers WHERE City = "Berlin"
```

　　You don't have to use an equals sign here; you can also test fields using these operators:

- < (less than).
- <= (less than or equal to).
- > (greater than).
- >= (greater than or equal to).
- BETWEEN.

- LIKE.
- IN.

The logical comparisons like < and > are familiar, but what about BE-TWEEN, LIKE, and IN? I'll take a look at them next.

The BETWEEN Clause

You use the BETWEEN clause to specify a range for acceptable values. For example, here's how to select all the records from the Customers table where the CustomerID record starts with A (the CustomerID field is alphabetic, not numeric, in this table):

```
SELECT * FROM Customers WHERE CustomerID BETWEEN
"A*" And "B*"
```

Note the use of wildcard characters: "A*" and "B*". Using these parameters indicates that you want all the CustomerID values that start with A. The results appear in the Visual Data Manager in Figure 1.24.

The LIKE Clause

The LIKE clause is specially designed to let you use partial string matching, which you can specify with wildcards like this, where I select all the records from the Customers table where the City matches the wildcard string "Be*":

```
SELECT * FROM Customers WHERE City LIKE "Be*"
```

This yields a recordset with records whose City fields match names like Berlin and Belgrade.

The IN Clause

You can use the IN clause to specify a set of values that fields can match. For example, here's how I retrieve records that have values in the City field that match "Berlin" or "London":

```
SELECT * FROM Customers WHERE City IN ("Berlin",
"London")
```

Logical Operations

You can also use logical operations on the clauses in your SQL statements. Here's an example in which I'm specifying two criteria: The City field must hold either "Berlin" or "London", and there must be some value in the Fax field (note that you use the Null keyword to test if there's anything in a field):

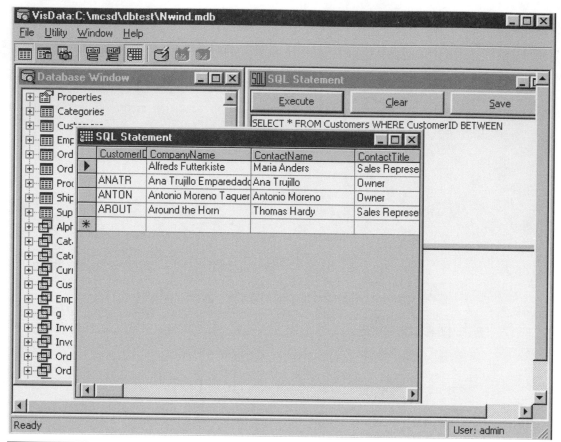

FIGURE 1.24 Selecting a range of data from a database.

```
SELECT * FROM Customers WHERE City NOT IN ("Berlin",
"London") AND Fax IS NOT NULL
```

You can use these logical operators to connect clauses: AND, OR, and NOT. Using AND means that both clauses must be True, using OR means either one can be True, and using NOT flips the value of a clause from True to False *or* False to True. The results of this query appear in Figure 1.25 in the Visual Data Manager.

The DISTINCT Clause

Sometimes, a database may hold duplicate values in the fields of the records of a table; for example, several customers come from the same city, so they'd all have the same value in the City field. You might want to take a look at

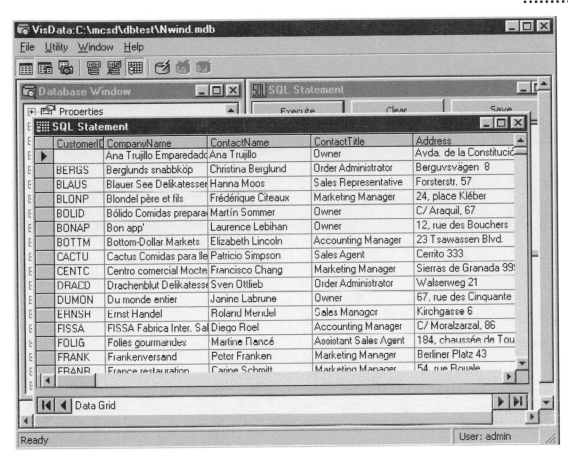

FIGURE 1.25   Using logical operations to get data from a database.

all the cities represented, without duplicates, and you can use the `DISTINCT` clause for that, like this:

```
SELECT DISTINCT City FROM Customers
```

The Order BY Clause

As you might expect, you can also order the records in a recordset produced by an SQL statement. Here's an example in which I order the records in the `Customers` table by `CustomerID`:

```
SELECT * FROM Customers Order BY CustomerID
```

You can also sort in descending order with the `Desc` keyword:

```
SELECT * FROM Customers Order BY CustomerID Desc
```

The AS Clause

Note that names of the fields returned in a recordset retain the original names they had in the table. You might want to change those names; for example, labeling a field "Name" might be more descriptive to the user than "Usr-ObjectDescriptor". You can *alias* a field's name with the AS clause like this, where I'm changing ContactName to just Name for the purposes of the returned recordset:

```
SELECT ContactName AS Name FROM Customers
```

Now in the recordset, the ContactName field will be called Name.

COUNT, SUM, MIN, MAX, and AVG

SQL comes with built-in functions like COUNT, SUM, MIN, MAX, and AVG that let you work with the records in a recordset. Here are what those functions do:

- **COUNT**—Returns a count of records.
- **SUM**—Adds values over records.
- **MIN**—Finds the minimum value.
- **MAX**—Finds the maximum value.
- **AVG**—Finds the average value.

Here are some examples in which I put those functions to work:

```
SELECT COUNT(EmployeeID) AS NumberEmployees,
AVG(BirthDate) AS AverageBirthDate, SUM(BirthDate)
AS TotalYears, MIN(BirthDate) AS MinBirthDate,
MAX(BirthDate) AS MaxBirthDate FROM Employees
```

The GROUP BY Clause

You can group the way records are returned with the GROUP BY clause like this, where I'm grouping records by city:

```
SELECT City, Count (City) AS NumberCities FROM
Customers GROUP BY City
```

The HAVING Clause

You can use the SQL HAVING clause with GROUP BY; this clause is like the WHERE clause, but is used only with GROUP BY. This clause lets you specify additional criteria that records must meet, like this, where I'm specifying only records with cities that begin with "B":

```
SELECT City, Count (City) AS NumberCities FROM
Customers GROUP BY City HAVING City LIKE "B*"
```

The DELETE Statement

Not all SQL statements are designed to return recordsets. For example, you can use the DELETE statement to delete records like this, where I'm removing all records from the Customers table that have City values that are not "Berlin" or "London":

```
DELETE * FROM Customers WHERE City NOT IN ("Berlin",
"London")
```

The UPDATE Statement

You use the UPDATE statement to update a database when you want to make changes. For example, here's how to change the value of the City in all records where it's currently "London" to "Berlin":

```
UPDATE Customers SET City = "Berlin" WHERE City =
"London"
```

Joining Tables

Relational databases are powerful databases that connect tables with specific keys and, using relational concepts, you can perform many SQL operations. For example, say you wanted to create a new recordset with customer contact names from the Customers table and the IDs of the items they've ordered from the Orders table. The key that relates these two tables is CustomerID, so you can set up the SQL query like this, making sure that the CustomerID field matches in each record you're joining:

```
SELECT Customers.ContactName, Orders.OrderID FROM
Customers, Orders WHERE Customers.CustomerID =
Orders.CustomerID
```

The results appear in the Visual Data Manager in Figure 1.26.

You can also do inner joins, where records must be in both tables, or outer joins, where records can be in either table and, of course, a lot more with SQL.

You can see how useful the Visual Basic Visual Data Manager is when you want to take a look at a database. In fact, Visual Basic includes a flood of

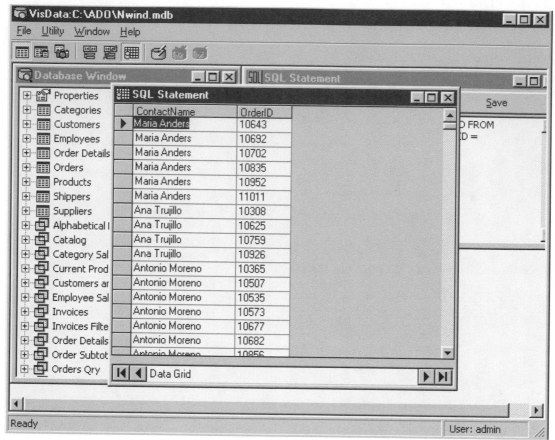

Joining tables using SQL.

database tools, and we'll be using those tools throughout this book. There are so many database tools that it can be a significant problem trying to understand what each one does—the Visual Basic database tools include the Visual Data Manager, the Data Form Wizard, the Data Object Wizard, the Data Project Wizard, the Data Report Designer, Data Environments, Data Views, Database Designers, Query Designers, and a great many others.

Some Visual Basic programmers may feel inundated by the vast tool set, especially when each tool can be very complex. However, knowing what these tools do is essential for database programming in Visual Basic, so we'll take a look at these tools and how to use them in the next chapter. And, after we're comfortable handling databases in Visual Basic, we'll start using the ADO data control in-depth in Chapter 3.

Visual Basic
Database Tools

One of the most popular topics in Visual Basic database programming is its arsenal of database *tools*. These tools provide you with ways of handling databases in Visual Basic, but unless you know your way around, the choices can be bewildering. In this chapter, I'll take a look at the Visual Basic database tools that we'll be using throughout the book.

The number of database tools has skyrocketed lately, and now there are even tools to keep track of other tools. I'll set things straight in this chapter. Once you get familiar with what database tools there are, they can be invaluable; but, threshing your way through the thicket can be a challenge. New in Visual Basic 6 are Data Views and Data Environments, for example, and it's essential that you know what they do.

The Visual Basic database tools include the Visual Data Manager, the Data Form Wizard, the Data Object Wizard, the Data Project Wizard, the Data Report Designer, Data Environments, Data Views, Database Designers, and Query Designers, not to mention various sub-tools like the Query Builder and other Microsoft applications like the SQL Server and Transaction Server. All these tools are part of handling databases in Visual Basic, and as you can see, there's quite an array here. I'll start this chapter with a popular database tool that is easy to use and has been available for quite a while—the Visual Data Manager.

The Visual Data Manager

The Visual Data Manager is the first of the Visual Basic database tools I'll cover. This venerable tool has been around for a while, and although a lot of its functionality has been taken over by the Data View window, it's still a powerful utility.

You open the Visual Data Manager from the Visual Basic Add-Ins menu. You can use this tool to create and modify databases, as well as execute SQL statements on them and see the results.

You create a new database with the File menu's New item, and open an existing database with the Open item. As an example, I'll take a look at creating a new database here. In this case, I'll create a new Microsoft Access-type database, db.mdb, based on the students table we discussed in the previous chapter. That table, which has two fields, Name and Grade, to keep track of students, looks like this:

```
   Name      Grade

   ---------------
 | Ann    |   C   |
 |--------|-------|
 | Mark   |   B   |
 |--------|-------|
 | Ed     |   A   |
 |--------|-------|
 | Frank  |   A   |
 |--------|-------|
 | Ted    |   A   |
 |--------|-------|
 | Mabel  |   B   |
 |--------|-------|
 | Ralph  |   B   |
 |--------|-------|
 | Tom    |   B   |
   ---------------
```

Creating a New Database

To create a new database, you start by opening the Visual Data Manager from the Visual Basic Add-Ins menu. To actually create the database, you select the New item in the Visual Data Manager's File menu. The Visual Data Manager lets you design databases in several different formats:

- Microsoft Access.
- Dbase.
- FoxPro.
- Paradox.
- ODBC.
- Text files.

When you select the New menu item, a submenu opens with these choices; in this example, I'll choose Microsoft Access. Selecting that item opens a new submenu, giving you the choices of Access version—version 2.0 or version 7.0. I'll choose version 7.0 here.

The Visual Data Manager then asks for a name and path for this new database with a dialog box; I'll call this new database db.mdb and click the OK button. After creating this new, empty database, the Visual Data Manager opens it as you see in Figure 2.1.

You can see in Figure 2.1 that the Visual Data Manager has given the new database a set of properties already. The first step in creating our new database is to add a table, the students table, to it.

Creating a New Table

To add a table named students to db.mdb, right-click the Properties item in the Visual Data Manager's Database Window and select the New Table item, opening the Table Structure dialog you see in Figure 2.2.

I give this new table the name students by typing that into the Table Name box, as shown in Figure 2.2. That's all it takes—at this point, the Visual Data Manager has created a new table, and I'll add two new fields in this table: Name and Grade.

Creating Fields in a Table

To add fields to the database table, click the Add Field button in the Visual Data Manager's Table Structure dialog, opening the Add Field dialog box you see in Figure 2.3.

You name a new field by entering its name in the Name box, and you can select the data type of the new field in the Type box. Here are the data types you can give the new field in the Visual Data Manager:

- Boolean.
- Byte.
- Integer.
- Long.

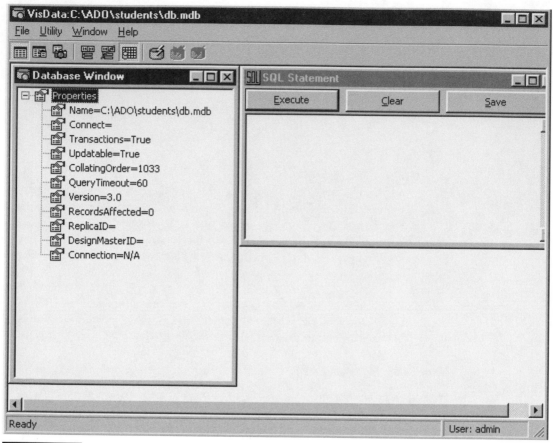

FIGURE 2.1 Creating a new database in the Visual Data Manager.

- Currency.
- Single.
- Double.
- Date/Time.
- Text.
- Binary.
- Memo.

Exactly what all these data types mean can become an important question in Visual Basic database programming, and the actual data storage format used can vary by database type. For the sake of reference, the way Visual Basic defines the common data formats—and the possible range of values they can hold—appears in Table 2.1.

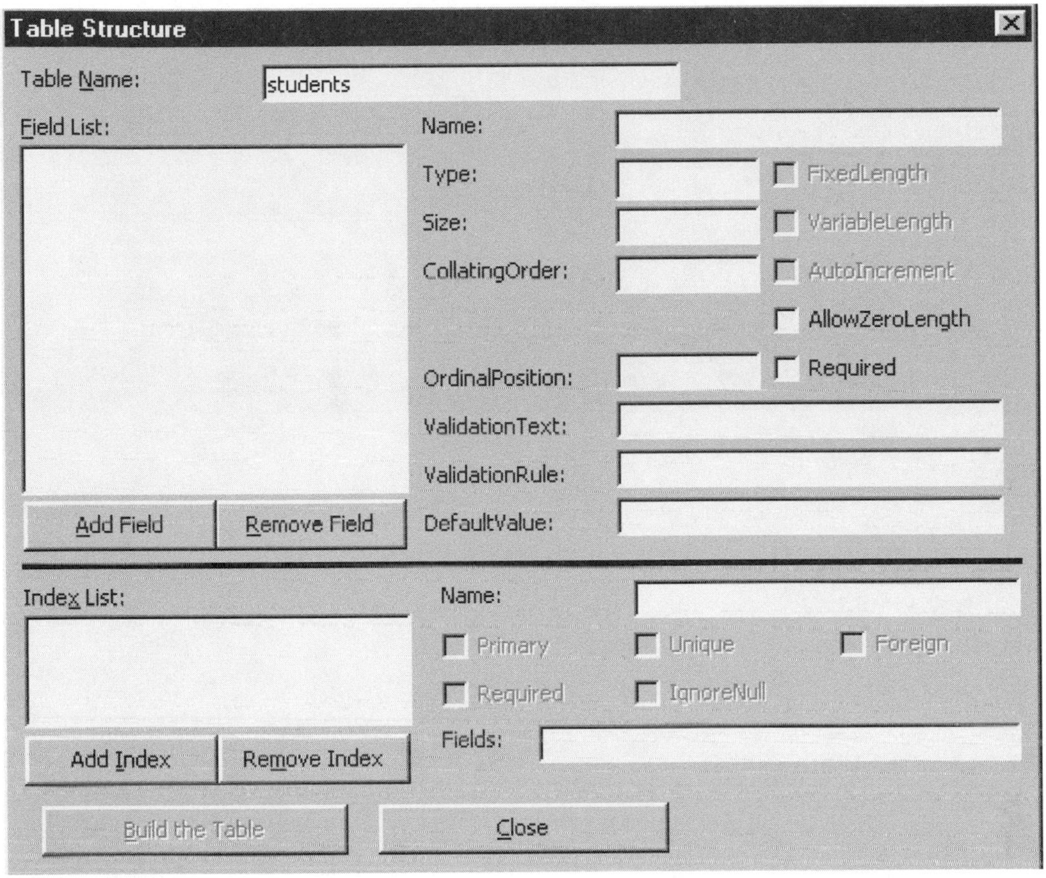

Table Structure

Table Name: students

Field List:

Name:

Type: ☐ FixedLength

Size: ☐ VariableLength

CollatingOrder: ☐ AutoIncrement

☐ AllowZeroLength

OrdinalPosition: ☐ Required

ValidationText:

ValidationRule:

[Add Field] [Remove Field]   DefaultValue:

Index List:

Name:

☐ Primary   ☐ Unique   ☐ Foreign

☐ Required   ☐ IgnoreNull

[Add Index] [Remove Index]   Fields:

[Build the Table] [Close]

FIGURE 2.2   Creating a new table.

In this case, I'll leave the new field with the default data type—Text. This type is analogous to the intrinsic Visual Basic String type, except that it's usually set to a fixed length, which you indicate in the Size box in Figure 2.3. I'll leave the length of the Name field at the default, 50 characters. (Note that you can make text fields variable length by clicking the VariableField option button you see in Figure 2.3.)

Note in Figure 2.3 that you can specify the position of this field's column in the records of the database by specifying a number in the Ordinal-Position box. You can also give the field a default value by placing a value in the DefaultValue box, as well as support data validation by entering values in the ValidationText and ValidationRule boxes.

What are the ValidationText and ValidationRule values all about? You can perform data validation with these items; for example, if you want a field named ShipDate to be in the future, you can use the Validation-

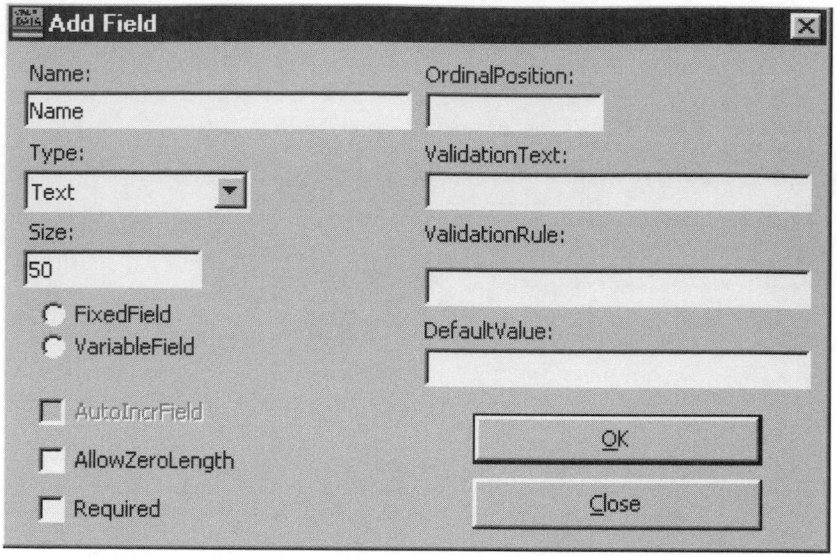

FIGURE 2.3 Creating a new field.

TABLE 2.1 Visual Basic Data Types

Variable Type	Bytes	Suffix	Range
Boolean	2	N/A	True, False
Byte	1	N/A	0 to 255
Currency	8	@	-922,337,203,685,477.5808 to 922,337,203,685,477.5807
Date	8	#...#	1 January 100 to 31 December 9999, and times from 0:00:00 to 23:59:59
Decimal	12	N/A	-79,228,162,514,264,337,593,543,950,335 to 79,228,162,514,264,337,593,543,950,335
Double	8	#	-1.79769313486232E308 to -4.94065645841247E-324 for negative values and from 4.94065645841247E-324 to 1.79769313486232E308 for positive values.
Integer	2	%	-32,768 to 32,767
Long	4	&	-2,147,483,648 to 2,147,483,647
Memo	N/A	N/A	Up to 1.2GB of text
Object	4	N/A	N/A
Single	4	!	-3.402823E38 to -1.401298E-45 for negative values and from 1.401298E-45 to 3.402823E38 for positive values.
String	N/A	$	A variable-length string can contain up to approximately 2 billion characters; a fixed-length string can contain 1 to approximately 64K characters
User-defined data type	N/A	N/A	N/A
Variant	N/A	N/A	N/A

Rule >Date() and put the text "Ship date must be after today". in the ValidationText box; that text is displayed if the validation rule is violated.

Finally, note the three check boxes at the bottom left in Figure 2.3: AutoIncrField, AllowZeroLength, and Required. Here's what they do:

- **AutoIncrField**—Automatically increments the value in the field as the number of records increases. This is good if you want to create a numerical index of records that automatically increments as you add new records.
- **AllowZeroLength**—Indicates that the field can have zero length. Sometimes when you're creating a database, you don't want to allow certain fields to have a null value, and you can use this setting to reflect that.
- **Required**—Indicates that this field is required and must hold data.

To add the new Name field to the students table, I just click the OK button. This adds the new field to the students table. Note that the Add Field dialog box stays open (although the settings you specified for the Name field are cleared) so you can add more fields.

The next step is to add another field named Grade, which will be the same type as the Name field—a text field fixed at 50 characters, which is the default. I enter that field's name and click OK to add the field, then click Close to close the Add Field dialog box. This adds the Name and Grade fields to the Field List box in the Table Structure dialog, as you can see in Figure 2.4.

You can see the properties of each field displayed in the Table Structure dialog in Figure 2.4; for example, you can see that the Name field is a text field of length fifty characters.

Note also the Index List box in the Table Structure dialog. When you add records to a table, they're just added one after the other, and if you want to look for a particular value in a field, you have to search each record until you find it. Adding an index to a table, on the other hand, makes it easy to search for particular values, and we'll see how to create and work with indexes when we start programming databases.

Adding Data to a Table

I'm ready to create the new table, so I click the Build the Table item in the Table Structure window to build the new table with the two new fields. This creates the students table with two fields: Name and Grade, and opens that table in the Visual Data Manager's Database Window, as you see in Figure 2.5.

The next step is to enter data into a table, so right-click the students table in the Visual Data Manager's window and select the Open item, or just double-click the students table. Doing so opens the Table: students di-

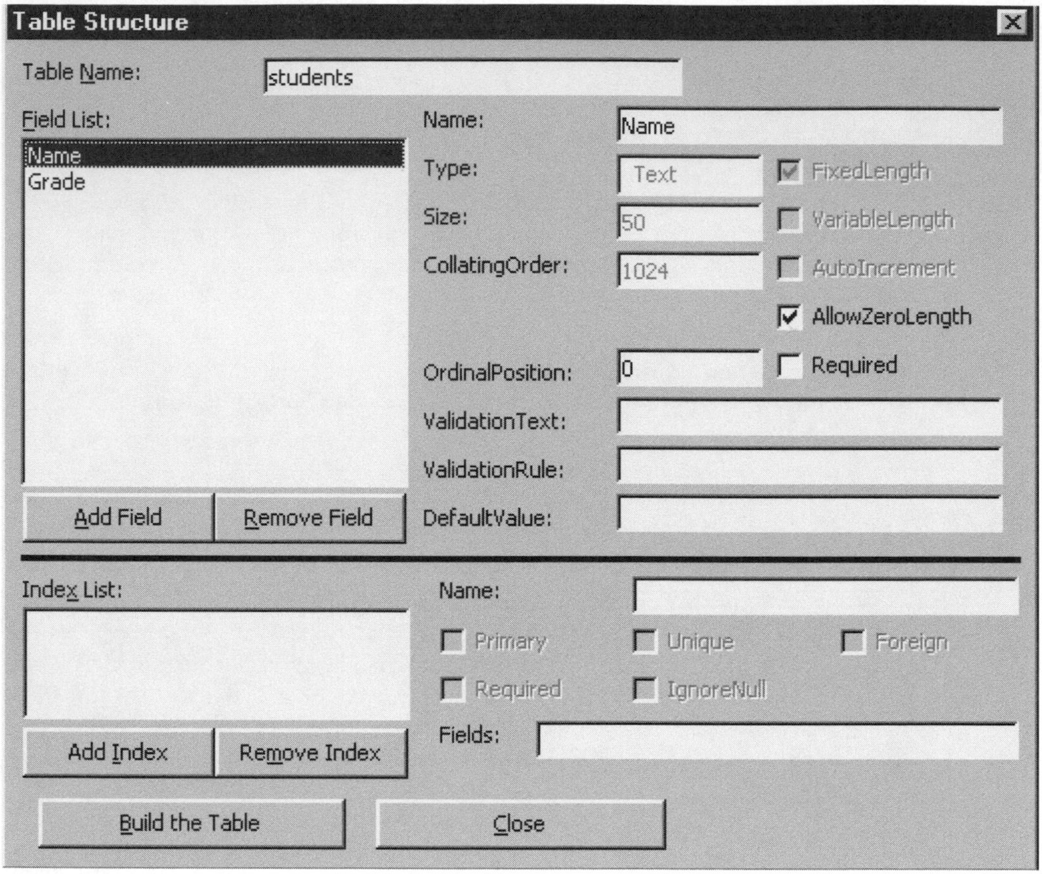

FIGURE 2.4 New table fields.

alog you see in Figure 2.6. I'll use this dialog to enter data into this database, but I could also use it to edit data.

To start, enter the name Ann and the grade C for the first student in the labeled boxes in the Table dialog box. Then, click Update to add that new record to the database; when the Visual Data Manager displays a message box asking if you want to save the new record to the database, click Yes.

To add a new record, click the Add button and add the name Mark and the grade B, and click Update, answering Yes when the Visual Data Manager asks if you want to save the new record to the database. Keep going with any other records you want to add.

That's how you usually work with tables in the Visual Data Manager—one record at a time. When you're done entering your records, click the Close button in the Table dialog box and close the database with the

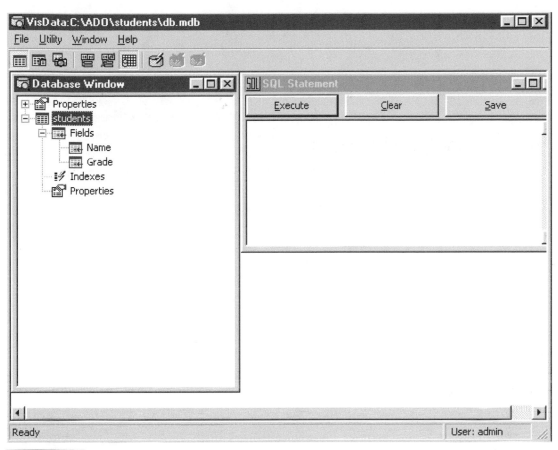

FIGURE 2.5   A new database table.

Close item in the Visual Data Manager's File menu. And that's it—you've just created a new database. The new file, db.mdb, is a full database file that you can use in Visual Basic applications or in Microsoft Access.

Editing a Database

Now that you've created a new database file, you can edit that file by opening it in the Visual Data Manager. To open a file, just select the Open Data-Base item in the Visual Data Manager's File menu. This menu opens to display these submenu items, indicating the types of databases you can work with:

- Microsoft Access
- Dbase
- FoxPro

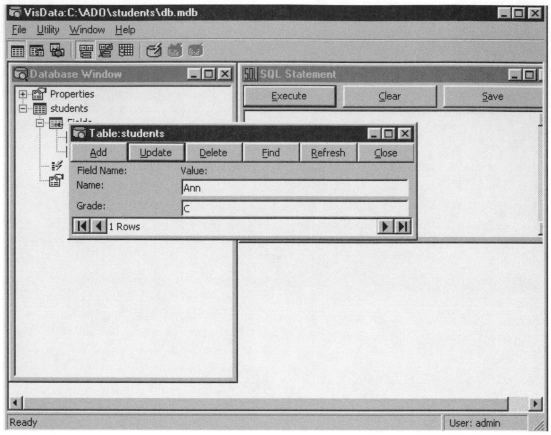

FIGURE 2.6 Entering data into a database.

- Paradox
- Excel
- Text Files
- ODBC

To open the db.mdb file we just created, select Microsoft Access, browse to db.mdb, and click the Open button to open the file.

If you want to open a table, like the students table we created, in the Visual Data Manager, just double-click it. The table's fields will be displayed just as when you added records to the students table, and you can move record by record through the table. As you see in Figure 2.6, the Visual Data Manager gives you these buttons when you're editing a database:

- **Add**—Adds a new record.
- **Update**—Updates the database with the new or edited record.

- **Delete**—Deletes the current record.
- **Find**—Finds a record by searching for a value.
- **Refresh**—Refreshes the current record from the database.
- **Close**—Closes the table.

The control you see at the bottom of Figure 2.6 is the DAO data control, which lets you move through the items in a table. However, you don't need to use a DAO control at all; you can let the Visual Data Manager add code to the table editing form to display a set of buttons that you can use to navigate through the table. To do that, click the button with the tooltip (a tooltip is one of those small yellow windows with explanatory text that appears when you let the mouse hover over a control) Don't Use Data Control on New Form; this button is shown in Figure 2.7.

When you double-click a table to edit it now, you get the table editing form you see in Figure 2.8, with these buttons:

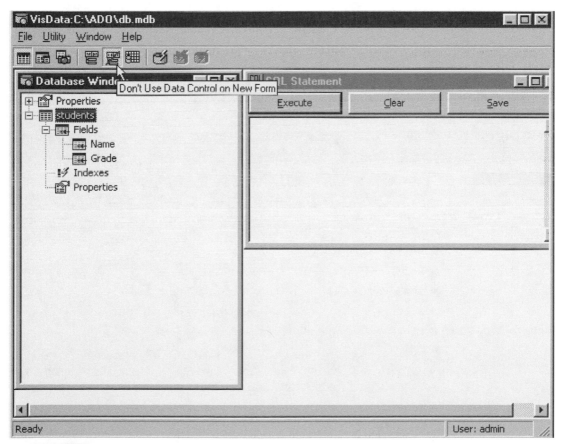

FIGURE 2.7   Selecting the Don't Use Data Control on New Form button.

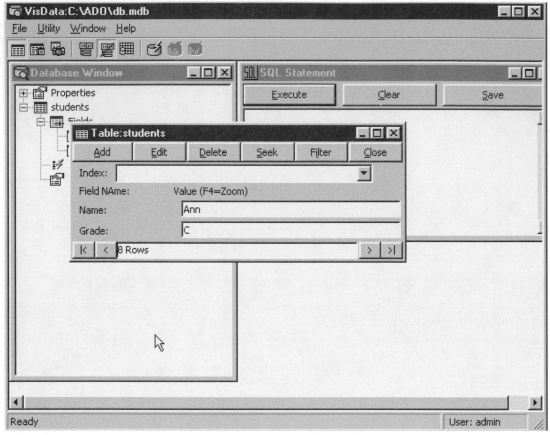

FIGURE 2.8 A table editing form without a DAO data control.

- **Add**—Adds a new record.
- **Edit**—Edits a record.
- **Delete**—Deletes the current record.
- **Seek**—Finds a record by searching for a value.
- **Filter**—Selects records that match particular criteria.
- **Close**—Closes the table.

In fact, you can also use a Visual Basic DBGrid control in the table editing form presented by the Visual Data Manager, and that can be useful, because with a grid control, you can see the contents of the whole table at once.

To use a DBGrid control, click the Use DBGrid Control on New Form button, which appears immediately to the right of the Don't Use Data Control on New Form button in Figure 2.7. The result appears in

Figure 2.9—as you can see, the whole `students` table appears at once in this form, making it easy to see what's going on at a glance. To edit the fields of a record, just enter the new data and use the mouse to move to another record.

Besides creating and editing databases in the Visual Data Manager, you can also execute SQL queries on databases. One of the powerful tools built into the Visual Data Manager is the Query Builder, which lets you design and execute SQL queries, and I'll take a look at that utility now. The Query Builder lets you cheat if you don't want to write the SQL for a particular database query—it'll write the SQL for you.

Using the Query Builder

To open the Query Builder in the Visual Data Manager, right-click a table and select the `New Query` item, or select the `Query Builder` item in the `Utility` menu, opening the Query Builder as you see in Figure 2.10.

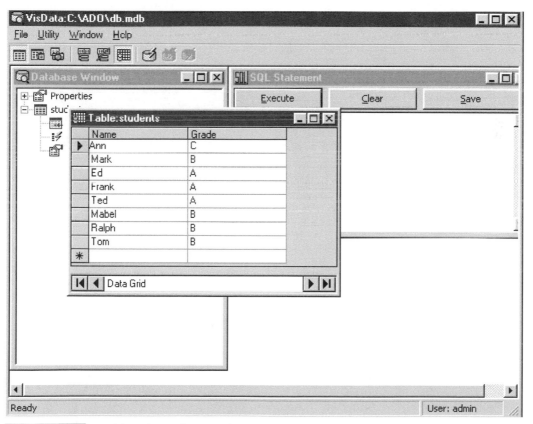

FIGURE 2.9   A table editing form with a DBGrid control.

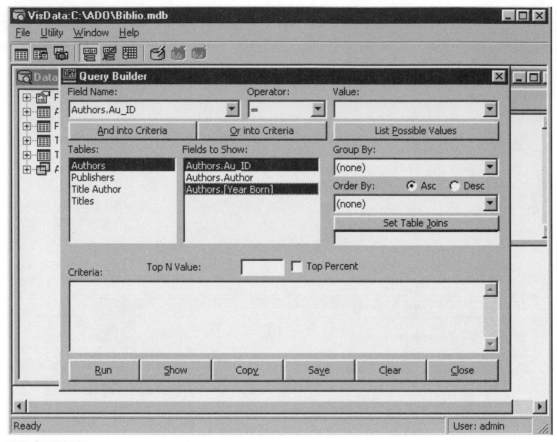

FIGURE 2.10 The Query Builder.

You can create complex SQL queries using the Query Builder. As an example, I'll work with the Biblio.mdb database that comes with Visual Basic and execute SQL queries on it. The Biblio.mdb database holds tables with information on authors, books, and publishers, and in this example, I'll create an SQL query that will select only authors born later than 1945.

Open Biblio.mdb now in the Visual Data Manager and open the Query Builder, as shown in Figure 2.10. Select the Authors table in the Tables box. In the Fields to Show box, select Authors.[Year Born] and Authors.Author (you can select multiple fields just by clicking them).

Now, using the controls at the top of the Query Builder, select the [Year Born] field in the table in the Field Name box. (In SQL, you enclose field names with spaces in them in square brackets, which is why this field's name is [Year Born].) In the Operator box, select the > operator, and in the `Value` box, type `1945`. You can add this requirement, that the author was born later than 1945, to other SQL clauses in an SQL statement you're creating in two ways—by ANDing it or by ORing it. When you connect two clauses with AND, both must be true for the associated record to be returned by the SQL statement; when you connect them with OR, either clause can be true. In this case, click the `And into Criteria` button.

Doing so gives you the results you see in Figure 2.10, where you see the generated SQL at the bottom of the Query Builder: `Authors.[Year Born] > 1945`. You can copy and paste the query into the rest of your code and, of course, elaborate it with other criteria. The results so far appear in the Query Builder in Figure 2.11.

You can run the SQL query now by clicking the `Run` button. The Query Builder will ask if this is an SQLPassThrough Query (an SQL pass-through query will bypass the Jet database engine and pass the SQL statement directly

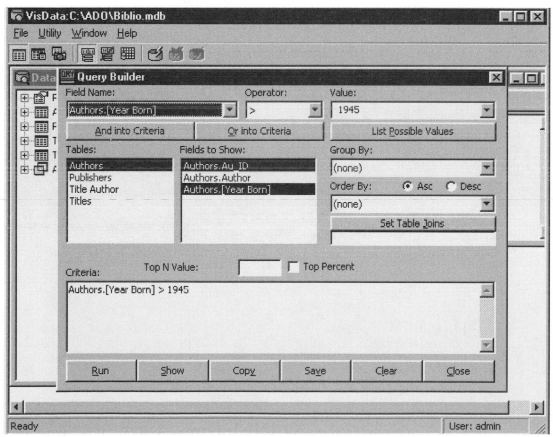

FIGURE 2.11   Creating a query in the Query Builder.

to a server that you specify); click No. When you do, the Query Builder creates a new recordset and opens it, showing the fields you've asked it to show, as you see in Figure 2.12, where I'm using a DBGrid to display the results.

Let's try another example. Say, for instance, that you want to list all the books published by publishers in Boston. The problem with that is that there are two different tables we'll need to use here—the Publishers table, which holds the names of the publishers, and the Titles table, which holds the names of the books.

These two tables can be tied together because each has a PubID field, which holds the ID of the publisher. You can tie these tables together by clicking the Set Table Joins button in Query Builder, opening the Join Tables dialog you see in Figure 2.13.

To connect records for the same publisher across the two tables Publishers and Titles using the PubID field, select those tables in the Se-

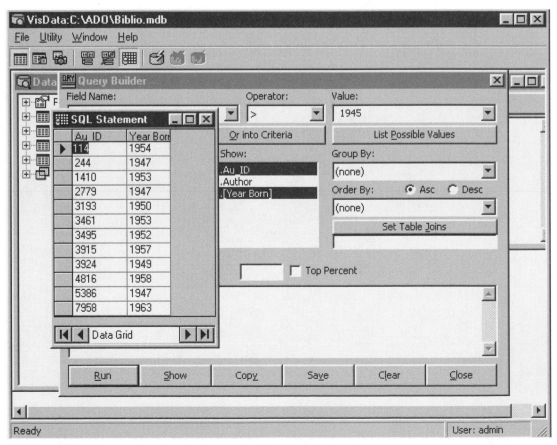

FIGURE 2.12   Running an SQL query in the Query Builder.

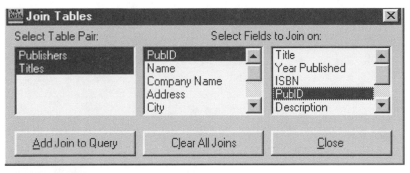

FIGURE 2.13   Creating a table join in the Query Builder.

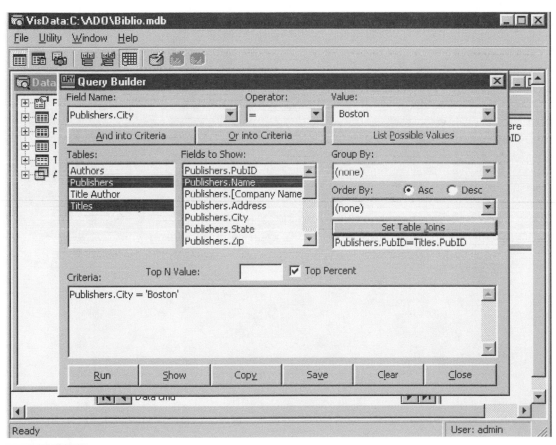

FIGURE 2.14   Selecting publishers in the Query Builder.

lect Table box in the Join Table dialog, as shown in Figure 2.13, and select PubID in the two list boxes to the right of the Select Table box, as also shown in Figure 2.13. Then, click the Add Join to Query button to add the table join to the SQL query we're building, and click Close to close the Join Table dialog. When you've closed the Join Table dialog, the Query Builder adds this clause to the SQL statement we're building: Publishers.PubID=Titles.PubID.

To make sure we only display data from publishers in Boston, specify that the City field in the Publishers table must equal Boston, as shown in Figure 2.14. To fill the Value drop-down list with the possible values—which, in this case, are all the cities of the publishers in the Biblio.mdb database—you can click the List Possible Values button in the Query Builder. After you've filled the Value drop-down list with all the possible cities, select Boston, then click the And into Criteria button to add this new requirement to the SQL query we're building.

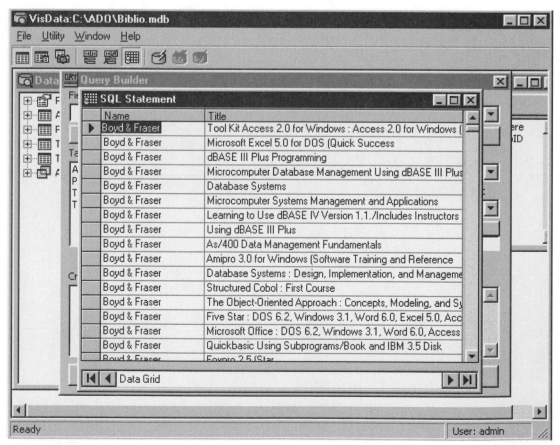

FIGURE 2.15   Running a query on the Publishers table in the Query Builder.

Finally, select the fields you want to see in the Fields to Show box; in this case, I'll show the Publishers.Name and Titles.Title fields. And that's it; click the Run button to execute the SQL query. The results appear in Figure 2.15, where you can see the publishers in Boston and the titles of their books.

If you close the Query Builder, you'll see the actual SQL query that it built displayed in the SQL statement window, as shown in Figure 2.16. Here's what that SQL statement looks like:

```
Select Publishers.Name,Titles.Title From

Publishers,Titles Where (Publishers.City =

'Boston') And Publishers.PubID=Titles.PubID
```

As you can see, you can indeed use the Query Builder to build simple SQL statements.

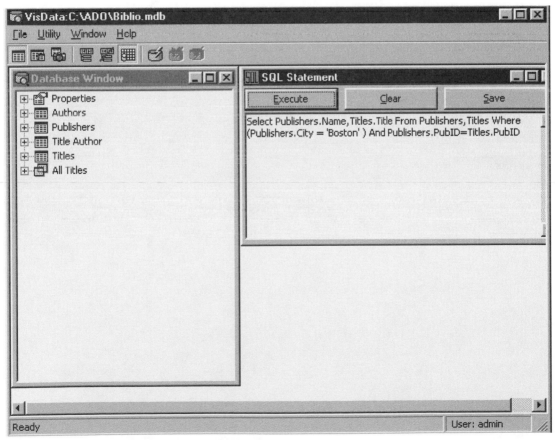

FIGURE 2.16 An SQL statement created by the Query Builder.

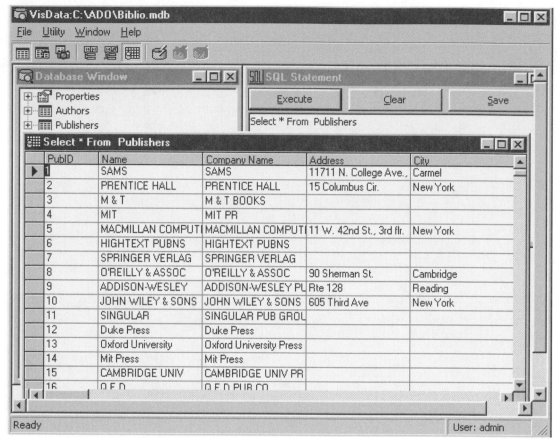

FIGURE 2.17   Executing SQL in the Visual Data Manager.

Note that you can also enter your own SQL directly into the SQL Statement window, which is great if you just want to test something out. For example, I've entered the SQL statement Select * From Publishers in the SQL Statement window in Figure 2.17 to see all the fields in the Publishers table, and you can see the results in that figure.

Now you've created a database—so how do you show it in a Visual Basic program? There are many options in Visual Basic, and one is the Data Form Wizard.

The Data Form Wizard

The Data Form Wizard will create a form that lets you navigate through the fields in a database using an ADO data control. This is useful if you just want to work with a database in a simplistic way and provides a quick solution if you just want to let the user navigate through a database.

You start the Data Form Wizard in one of three ways:

- Select the `VB Data Form Wizard` item in the `Add Form` dialog that opens when you select the `Add Form` item in the `Project` menu.
- Use the Add-In Manager to add the Data Form Wizard to the `Tools` menu and select the `Data Form Wizard` from the `Add-Ins` menu.
- Select the `Utility` menu's `Data Form Designer` item in the Visual Data Manager. (This does not actually launch the Data Form Wizard, but the resulting form is very much the same.)

The first page of the Visual Basic Data Form Wizard, the `Introduc-tion` page, appears in Figure 2.18.

As with many other Visual Basic wizards, you can save the settings to use when creating a data form in a profile; I won't use a profile here, so I click the `Next` button to see the database formats the Data Form Wizard sup-ports—Access and ODBC—in the `Database Type` page.

Select `Access` for this example and click the `Next` button again to open the `Database` page to select the database you want to make a data form from, as in Figure 2.19, where I'm selecting the `Biblio.mdb` database that comes with Visual Basic.

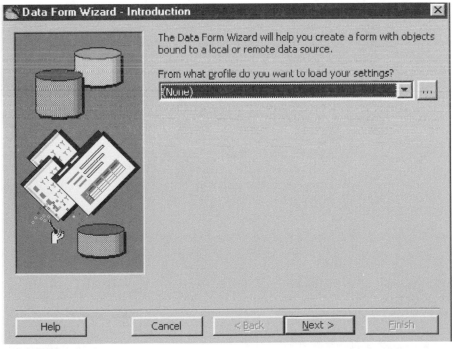

FIGURE 2.18 The Visual Basic Data Form Wizard, `Introduction` page.

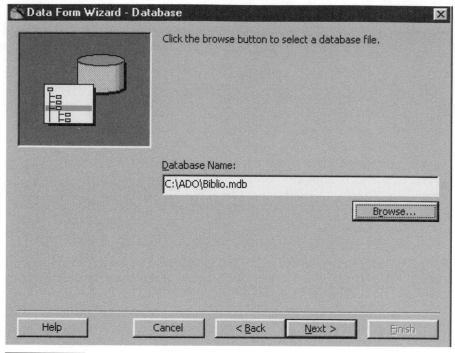

FIGURE 2.19 The Visual Basic Data Form Wizard, Database page.

Now click Next to bring up the Form dialog, as shown in Figure 2.20.

In the Form dialog, you design the appearance of the form that will show the database. You can specify a name for the form, and I'll use the name DataForm here, as shown in Figure 2.20.

Now take a look at the Form Layout box at the bottom left of the page. The Single Record option lets you show single records, the Grid, HFlexGrid, and Chart options let you specify what controls to use in the data form, and the Master/Detail option lets you work through an overview of the database and view details in additional controls.

Note that you can also indicate the binding support you want here: ADO Data Control, ADO Code, or Class (i.e., a Visual Basic class that acts as a data source). Each of these can be data sources, and we'll see them all in this book. In this case, I'll select the ADO Data Control and the Master/Detail options here and click Next.

In the next page, the Master Record Source page, you select a record source in the box labeled Record Source—select the Authors table now—and the fields you want in the master control in the Selected Fields box, as shown in Figure 2.21; here, I'll select all the fields in the Authors table.

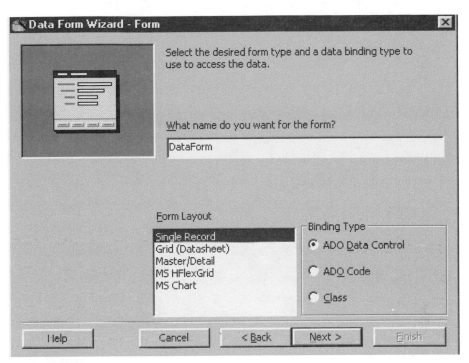

FIGURE 2.20 Designing a form in the Visual Basic Data Form Wizard.

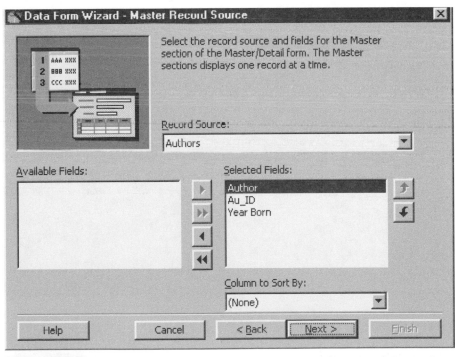

FIGURE 2.21 Designing the master record source in the Visual Basic Data Form Wizard.

Click the Next button to bring up the Detail Record Source dialog now; select the Title Author table and add all the fields to the Selected Fields box, as shown in Figure 2.22.

Now you have to tie the master and detail information together; click Next to bring up the Record Source Relation dialog, as shown in Figure 2.23.

Select the author ID, that is, AU_ID, field to relate the two record sources, as shown in Figure 2.23, and click Next, bringing up the Control Selection dialog as shown in Figure 2.24.

You can see the possible buttons the Data Form Wizard will add to the new data form here: an Add button, an Update button, a Delete button, a Refresh button, and a Close button. In this case, I'll just click Next to accept all the default controls the wizard usually creates. This brings up the Finished! page, so click the Finish button to create the new form (you can also save the settings you specified in a profile at this point). The Data Form Wizard adds the new data form, DataForm, to the current project when you click the Finish button.

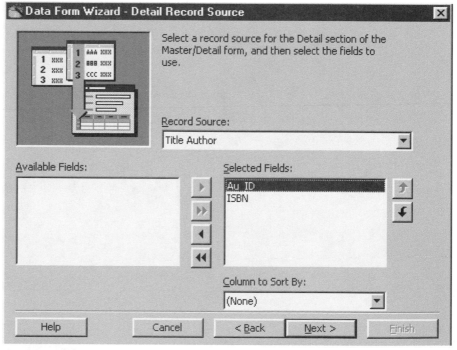

FIGURE 2.22 Designing the detail record source in the Visual Basic Data Form Wizard.

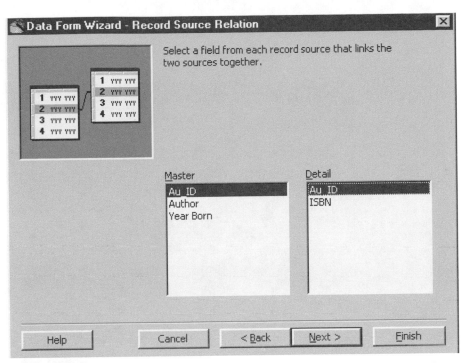

FIGURE 2.23 Designing the record relation in the Visual Basic Data Form Wizard.

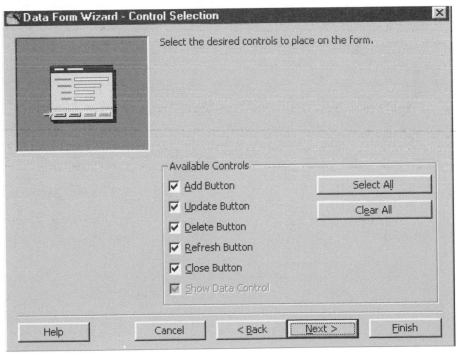

FIGURE 2.24 Setting the control selection in the Visual Basic Data Form Wizard.

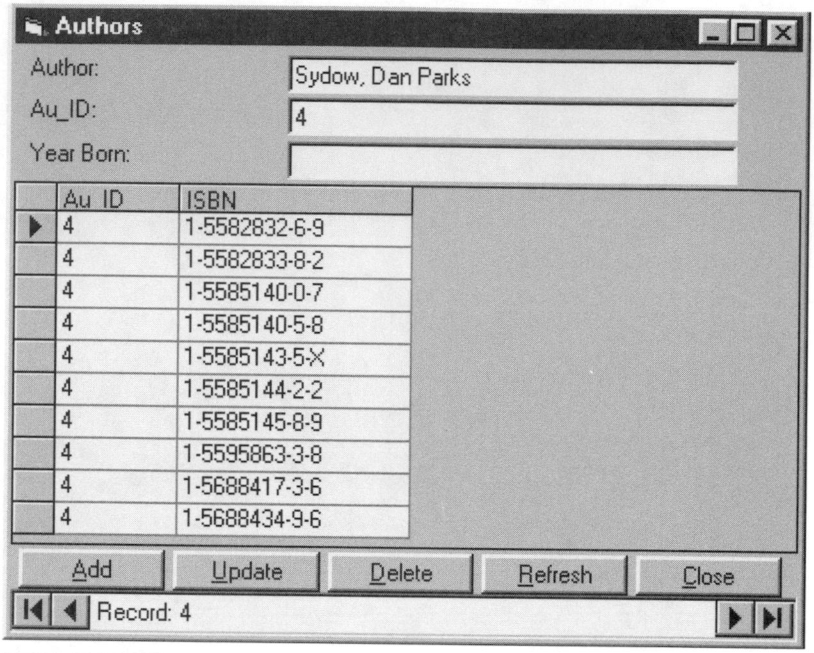

FIGURE 2.25 Designing the record relation in the Visual Basic Data Form Wizard.

This new form appears in Figure 2.25. As you can see there, the user can now move through the `Title Author` table to see the titles of an author, and at the same time, see more information about the author whose ID is selected; this is valuable because the `Title Author` table only displays the author ID, not the author name. In this way, you can tie two relational databases together and view the data in both at the same time, using a field in one database as a key into another.

For the sake of reference, the actual code produced by the Data Form Wizard appears in Listing 2.1. If you're curious, take a look at that listing; we'll be developing similar code soon.

LISTING 2.1   *Dataform.frm Code*

```
Private Sub Form_Load()
   Set grdDataGrid.DataSource =
datPrimaryRS.Recordset("ChildCMD").UnderlyingValue
End Sub

Private Sub Form_Resize()
  On Error Resume Next
  'This will resize the grid when the form is
resized
```

```
  grdDataGrid.Width = Me.ScaleWidth
  grdDataGrid.Height = Me.ScaleHeight -
grdDataGrid.Top - datPrimaryRS.Height - 30 -
picButtons.Height
End Sub

Private Sub Form_Unload(Cancel As Integer)
  Screen.MousePointer = vbDefault
End Sub

Private Sub datPrimaryRS_Error(ByVal ErrorNumber As
Long, Description As String, ByVal Scode As Long,
ByVal Source As String, ByVal HelpFile As String,
ByVal HelpContext As Long, fCancelDisplay As
Boolean)
  'This is where you would put error handling code
  'If you want to ignore errors, comment out the
next line
  'If you want to trap them, add code here to handle
them
  MsgBox "Data error event hit err:" & Description
End Sub

Private Sub datPrimaryRS_MoveComplete(ByVal adReason
As ADODB.EventReasonEnum, ByVal pError As
ADODB.Error, adStatus As ADODB.EventStatusEnum,
ByVal pRecordset As ADODB.Recordset)
  'This will display the current record position for
this recordset
  datPrimaryRS.Caption = "Record: " &
CStr(datPrimaryRS.Recordset.AbsolutePosition)
End Sub

Private Sub datPrimaryRS_WillChangeRecord(ByVal
adReason As ADODB.EventReasonEnum, ByVal cRecords As
Long, adStatus As ADODB.EventStatusEnum, ByVal
pRecordset As ADODB.Recordset)
  'This is where you put validation code
  'This event gets called when the following actions
occur
  Dim bCancel As Boolean

  Select Case adReason
  Case adRsnAddNew
  Case adRsnClose
  Case adRsnDelete
  Case adRsnFirstChange
  Case adRsnMove
  Case adRsnRequery
  Case adRsnResynch
  Case adRsnUndoAddNew
```

```
      Case adRsnUndoDelete
      Case adRsnUndoUpdate
      Case adRsnUpdate
      End Select

      If bCancel Then adStatus = adStatusCancel
   End Sub

   Private Sub cmdAdd_Click()
      On Error GoTo AddErr
      datPrimaryRS.Recordset.AddNew

      Exit Sub
   AddErr:
      MsgBox Err.Description
   End Sub

   Private Sub cmdDelete_Click()
      On Error GoTo DeleteErr
      With datPrimaryRS.Recordset
        .Delete
        .MoveNext
        If .EOF Then .MoveLast
      End With
      Exit Sub
   DeleteErr:
      MsgBox Err.Description
   End Sub

   Private Sub cmdRefresh_Click()
      'This is only needed for multi user apps
      On Error GoTo RefreshErr
      datPrimaryRS.Refresh
      Set grdDataGrid.DataSource =
   datPrimaryRS.Recordset("ChildCMD").UnderlyingValue
      Exit Sub
   RefreshErr:
      MsgBox Err.Description
   End Sub

   Private Sub cmdUpdate_Click()
      On Error GoTo UpdateErr

      datPrimaryRS.Recordset.UpdateBatch adAffectAll
      Exit Sub
   UpdateErr:
      MsgBox Err.Description
   End Sub

   Private Sub cmdClose_Click()
      Unload Me
   End Sub
```

The tools we've used so far take you about as far as you can go without creating an actual connection to a database with a data source. Many different types of objects can act as data sources in Visual Basic—data source controls like the DAO, RDO, and ADO data controls; the DAO, RDO, and ADO objects in code; ActiveX controls; data source classes that you can create with tools like the Data Object Wizard; and Visual Basic Data Environments. Data Environments are particularly important in Visual Basic because they've been designed to be the data source you use most.

Data Environments

Data Environments are designed to be the basis of design-time and run-time data access in your applications. They give you a way of working with ADO `Connection` and `Command` objects at both design-time and at run-time.

It's helpful to get the concept down here first: Data Environments make data available to the forms and modules in your application as part of the development *environment*, which is to say that you don't add a Data Environment to a form as you would a data control like the ADO data control. Instead, a Data Environment can provide data to any of the forms and modules in a project, or even to the projects in a project group. You can refer to a Data Environment from any code in the current Visual Basic session by name, such as `DataEnvironment1`.

Data Environments at Design-Time

Data Environments are useful at design-time; here are some of the things you can do with them:

- Separate the relative complexity of handling database connections from the rest of your code.
- Organize and group `Command` objects.
- Create `Command` objects for use with databases.
- Set up access rights for each connection.
- Drag and drop `Connection` objects onto forms and data reports.
- Allow multiple forms to access data from the same source, in the same way.

At design-time, you set property values for `Connection` and `Command` objects in a Data Environment, write code to respond to ADO events, and execute commands. You can also drag fields from a Data Environment directly to a form or data report, creating data-bound text boxes instantly, as we'll see in this chapter.

Although you can access the properties of `Connections` and `Commands` in a Data Environment at design-time, what you're really accessing is

`DEConnection` and `DECommand` objects, not `Connection` and `Command` objects. The `DEConnection` and `DECommand` objects contain the design-time properties of `Connection` and `Command` objects. Here are the significant properties of `DEConnection` objects (they have no methods or events):

- **`Attributes`**—Any extra attributes needed for the connection string associated with a `DEConnection` object.
- **`CommandTimeout`**—The time, in seconds, that the provider waits for a command to return from the server.
- **`ConnectionSource`**—Source of the `DEConnection` object.
- **`ConnectionTimeout`**—Time, in seconds, for which the provider attempts to connect to the server specified in the `DEConnection` object.
- **`CursorLocation`**—Location of the cursor library for the `DEConnection` or `DECommand` object.
- **`DesignPassword`**—Password for the user at design-time.
- **`DesignPromptBehavior`**—Design-time prompting behavior, such as when to request logon information.
- **`DesignSaveAuthentication`**—Specifies whether the authentication information is saved with the design-time class.
- **`DesignUserName`**—User name that is used when connecting to the data source at design-time.
- **`DisplayName`**—Description of the connection, including the database and user name, displayed in a Data View.
- **`RunSaveAuthentication`**—Specifies whether the authentication information is saved with the run-time class.
- **`RunPassword`**—Password for the user at run-time.
- **`RunPromptBehavior`**—Run-time prompting behavior by the `DEConnection` object, such as when to request logon information.
- **`RunUserName`**—Run-time user name.
- **`SourceOfData`**—Source of the object definition.

Here are the significant properties of the `DECommand` object:

- **`CacheSize`**—Number of records that are cached in local memory.
- **`CallSyntax`**—Call syntax used to send the `CommandText` property to the ADO `Command` object.
- **`CommandText`**—Actual command text.
- **`CommandTimeout`**—Whether timeout is allowed for the command.
- **`CommandType`**—Lets the provider know what the `CommandText` property holds, which can include the type of the command; using this property can optimize command execution.

- **ConnectionName**—Name of the DEConnection object associated with the Command object.

- **CursorLocation**—Location of the cursor.

- **CursorType**—Type of the cursor.

- **GrandTotalName**—Name used for a grand total recordset when the DE-Command object has an associated grand total DEAggregate object defined.

- **LockType**—Specifies the lock type desired.

- **MaxRecords**—Maximum number of records that can be fetched from the data source.

- **ParentCommandName**—Used in relationship hierarchies; the name of an existing parent DECommand object to which you are linking the child DECommand object.

- **Prepared**—Indicates if the source of the DECommand object is prepared before the DECommand object is executed.

- **RecordSetReturning**—Indicates if the command returns a recordset.

- **RelateToParent**—Indicates if this DECommand object is related to a parent DECommand object.

- **ShapeText**—SHAPE string generated by the DataEnvironment object for a Command hierarchy.

- **SummaryCommandName**—The summary recordset (created when the DE-Command object is grouped).

- **DEAggregates**—Reference to the DEAggregates collection.

- **DEGroupingFields**—Reference to the DEGroupingFields collection.

- **DEParameters**—Reference to the DEParameters collection.

- **DERelationConditions**—Reference to the DERelationConditions collection.

The DECommand object also has two methods (but no events):

- **BeginQueryEdit**—The DECommand object that the Query designer will begin to edit.

- **EndQueryEdit**—The DECommand object that the query edit has completed editing.

Data Environments at Run-Time

You can use a Data Environment as an ADO run-time data source in your code. Here's how that works, step by step:

1. Create a new Data Environment (we'll see how below).

2. Configure the DEConnection object (which corresponds to the design-time properties of the ADO Connection object) in the Data Environment to connect to a database.

3. Add a DECommand object (which corresponds to the design-time properties of the ADO Command object) to the Connection object that returns a recordset.

4. Bind the Data Environment to the various controls in your forms by setting each control's DataSource property to the Data Environment, DataEnvironment1, and their DataMember property to the Command object you created, Command1.

5. If applicable, set the bound control's other bound properties, like DataField.

6. Run the application.

In addition, you can access the ADO recordset that a command creates directly from your code so the Data Environment can provide you with recordsets at run-time.

With all this going for them, then, you can see that Data Environments are serious contenders in Visual Basic applications—serious enough, in fact, that Microsoft expects them to take over the role of data source in Visual Basic applications eventually, instead of data source controls or data source object libraries.

note Note that when Data Environments act as data sources in your application, the user is not presented with navigation arrow buttons as they are with data controls like the ADO data control. You'll have to implement your own navigation interface, and you do that by getting a recordset from the Data Environment and using that recordset's **Move** methods, like **MoveFirst**, **MoveNext**, and so on. We'll see how that works soon.

Creating a Data Environment

To create a Data Environment, you select the Add Data Environment item in the Project menu, creating a new Data Environment like the one you see in Figure 2.26. This new Data Environment, DataEnvironment1, is an object that is accessible throughout that application, which is a big advantage over localized data controls. The Data Environ**ment contains Commands, Connections, and Recordsets collections that hold the corresponding ADO objects.

When a Data Environment is first created, you'll see a Connection object, Connection1, in the pane under the toolbar. To access data using your Data Environment, you must create a Connection object, and that object represents a connection to a database. Every Data Environment should include at least one Connection object.

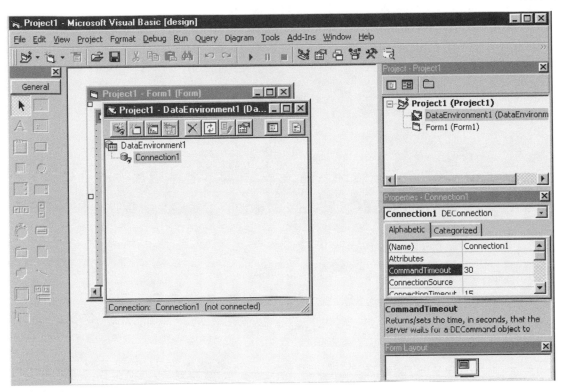

FIGURE 2.26   A new Data Environment.

I'll take a quick look at creating a connection with a Data Environment now, and I'll go into more depth in Chapter 5. To create a connection, right-click a `Connection` object in the Data Environment and select the `Properties` item, opening the `Data Link Properties` dialog to the `Provider` page you see in Figure 2.27, which allows you to create a new data link.

In this case, I'm going to connect to a database using SQL Server 7, because you can do some powerful things with Data View windows (coming up next) using SQL Server 7. To make this connection, I select `Microsoft OLE DB Provider for SQL Server` in the `Data Link Properties` dialog and click `Next` to open the `Connection` page in the same dialog box you see in Figure 2.28.

You use the `Connection` page to specify a data source. In this case, I'm going to use the default SQL Server installation on my machine, so I'll leave the box labeled `Select or enter a server name` blank. However, if your server is named or on a network, this is where you enter that server's name, including the network path, if applicable.

Since I'm the system administrator for my installation of SQL Server 7, I use `sa` as the user name for the database I want to open and no password, as

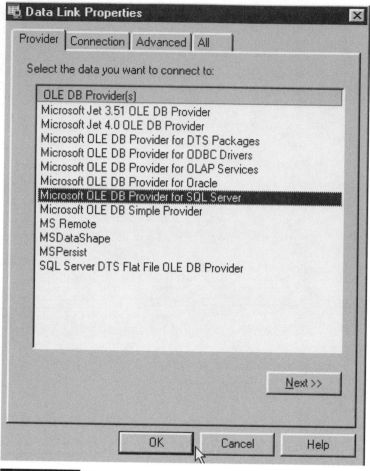

FIGURE 2.27 The Data Link Properties dialog, Provider page.

you see in Figure 2.28, but if you need both a user name and a password to log onto a database, this is where you enter those items.

All that's left to do here is to choose a database in the drop-down list labeled Select the database on the server. When you click the arrow button at the right in the drop-down list, you'll see a list of the databases registered on the server. In this case, I'll choose the Northwind database on my server, as you see in Figure 2.28.

You can test the connection with the Test Connection button; you should see the message Test connection succeeded when you click this button—otherwise, something's not working right.

After specifying the connection I want, I close the Data Link Properties dialog by clicking the OK button.

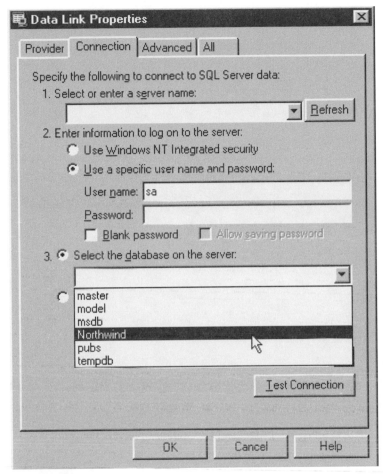

FIGURE 2.28 The Data Link Properties dialog, Connection page.

Now I'm connected to a database, but that's not enough—I have to indicate what records I actually want to extract from the database, and I do that with a Command object. To create a new Command object, right-click the current Connection object and select the Add Command menu item, creating a new Command object right under the Connection icon in the Data Environment.

The command you create specifies how you want to extract records from the database. A Connection object can have multiple Command objects. A Command object can be an SQL statement that does complex things like select records from a number of tables, or a stored procedure in the server, or a number of other database constructs as we'll see later.

In this case, I'll just extract the `Customers` table from the `Nwind` database. To do that, right-click the `Connection` object in the Data Environment and select the `Properties` menu item, opening the `Command1 Properties` dialog you see in Figure 2.29.

As you can see in Figure 2.29, you can create a command using an SQL statement, or a database object such as a table. To connect to a table, I click the arrow button in the `Database Object` drop-down list and select the `Table` item. To indicate what table I want to connect to, I click the arrow button in the `Object Name` drop-down list and Visual Basic, helpful as ever, displays a list of the tables in the database. All I have to do is select the `Customers` table, as shown in Figure 2.29, then click `OK` to close the dialog.

The result appears in Figure 2.30, where you can see the fields of the `Customers` table in the `Command` object. You can get the details on a field (e.g., its type and size) by right-clicking it and selecting the `Properties` item. If you double-click the `Command` object itself, a code window will open, and you can apply ADO `Recordset` methods to the `Command` object.

Now that I've set up a `Connection` object with a `Command` object in it, the Data Environment can function as a data source. To get an idea of how that works, I'll bind a text box to the Data Environment now—more details on this process will be given in Chapter 5.

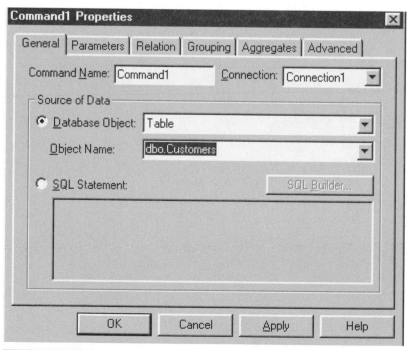

FIGURE 2.29 The `Command1` Properties dialog.

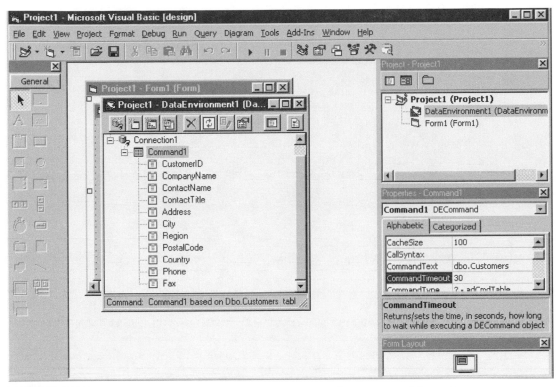

FIGURE 2.30   A data environment with `Connection` and `Command` objects.

Add a text box to a form now and clear the text in it. When you click the arrow button in the text box's `DataSource` property entry in the Properties window, you'll see `DataEnvironment1` listed; select that Data Environment as the text box's data source.

Because Data Environments can support many `Command` objects, there's a new data property associated with controls you can bind to data sources—the `DataMember` property. Select `Command1` in the `DataMember` property's entry in the `Properties` window now. Finally, I'll select an individual field to display from the `Customers` table that the `Command1` object returns. In this case, I'll select the `ContactName` field by selecting that item in the `DataField` property's drop-down list in the `Properties` window. That's it; at this point, the properties of the text box we've set up are:

- `DataSource: DataEnvironment1`
- `DataMember: Command1`
- `DataField: ContactName`

Now run the program. As you see in Figure 2.31, the text box is connected, via the Data Environment, to the database, and is displaying the first

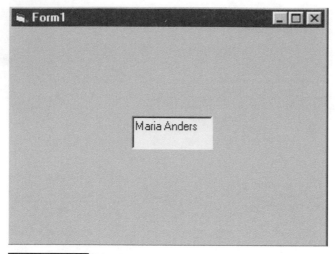

FIGURE 2.31 Using a Data Environment to connect to a database.

name in the ContactName field of the Customers table. Note that there's no data control that you can use to navigate through the Customers table here—if you want to navigate using a Data Environment connection, you'll have to do it yourself, as we'll see later.

Data Environments act as data sources in Visual Basic, and your project can support multiple Data Environments, each of which can have multiple connections and commands. How do you keep track of all that? With another Visual Basic database tool, of course—Data Views.

Data Views

Data Views give you an overview of the database objects you have in a project, such as Data Environments, connections, data links, commands, and the tables and fields in them. By double-clicking, dragging and dropping, and using the right-click feature, you can open, create, and edit your database objects easily. If you have a number of Data Environments in your project, the connections of those Data Environments appear in the Data View, and you can manipulate their Command objects there as well.

You open a Data View by selecting the Data View Window item in the View menu, or by clicking the Data View button in the toolbar. A Data View appears in Figure 2.32; as you can see in that figure, the Data View presents a hierarchy of data connections.

Data Views like the one in Figure 2.32 give you a graphical way of organizing database objects, including tables, stored procedures, and triggers. As you can see in Figure 2.32, the idea behind Data Views is that they

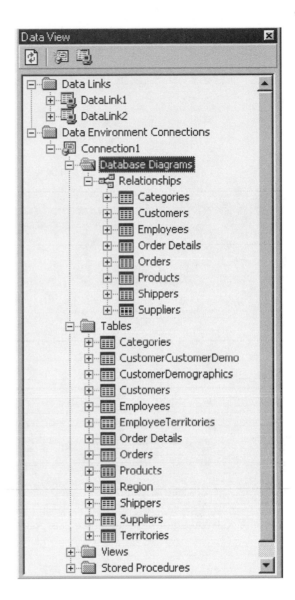

FIGURE 2.32 A
Data View window.

give you an overview of what's happening with data access in your project or project group. Data Views let you organize and configure your data connections.

You can automatically create Connection objects by dragging a connection from the Data View window to your Data Environment designer. This is an easy and efficient way to create Connection objects that already exist in your Data View. The Data View window is also closely connected to the Visual Database tools—the Database Designer and Query Designer.

As you can see in Figure 2.32, there are four folders in the Data View window for the `Nwind` connection we created in the last topic:

- `Database Diagrams`
- `Tables`
- `Views`
- `Stored Procedures`

I'll take a look at all of these items now.

Database Diagrams and the Database Designer

Database diagrams represent the tables in a database graphically. In a database diagram, tables display the columns they contain, the relationships between tables, and their indexes and constraints; the relations between tables are indicated with lines called relationship lines. Database diagrams are displayed in the Visual Basic Database Designer tool.

With database diagrams, you can change the actual structure of a database; here's an overview of what's possible:

- Manipulate databases without using SQL.
- Make the structure of database tables and their relationships visible.
- Change views of databases.
- Experiment with databases without modifying the stored data.
- Create new tables, indices, and relationships.
- Change the structure of a database.

When you modify a database object in a database diagram, those modifications are not saved in the database until you save the table or the database diagram. In fact, you can save a *change script* instead of saving your changes to the database. You can edit the change script and then apply the modified script to a database.

When you open the `Database Diagrams` folder for a connection in a Data View, you'll see the tables in that connection and an icon labeled `Relationships`. Double-clicking the `Relationships` item opens a database diagram in the Database Designer, showing the relationships between the tables, as you see in Figure 2.33.

note Database diagrams will not work with Jet engine databases, but they will work with other types, such as SQL Server databases.

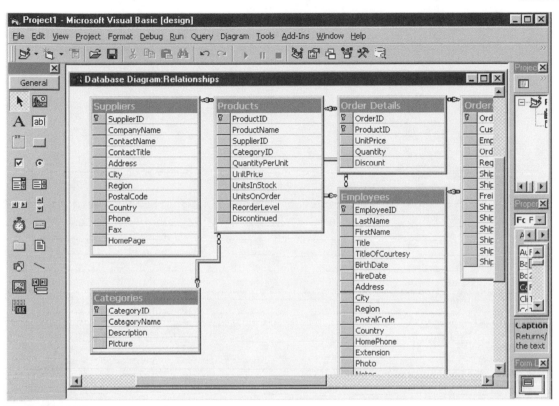

FIGURE 2.33 A database diagram

You can see the relationships between the tables in the Nwind database illustrated in Figure 2.33. If a field in one table acts as a key into another table, that relationship is displayed with a connecting line, as you see in Figure 2.33. Note that the actual fields themselves are not connected by this line visually; however, if you let the mouse hover over a connection line, the database diagram will display the names of the fields involved. You can also add text annotations to database diagrams simply by typing the text directly onto the background.

To create a new database diagram, right-click the Database Diagrams folder in the Data View and choose New Diagram from the shortcut menu. A blank database diagram appears.

You add tables to the diagram by dragging a table or one of its columns into the diagram. When you release the mouse button, the table appears on your diagram and valid relationship lines to other tables in the diagram are automatically drawn. You can also create a new table in the diagram by right-clicking anywhere inside the diagram and then choosing New Table from the shortcut menu.

Note in addition that you can use the items in the Visual Basic `Diagram` menu to work with diagrams, as you can see in Figure 2.34 (plenty of Visual Basic programmers wonder why there's a `Diagram` menu in Visual Basic—it's there to work with Data View database diagrams, and the items in the menu aren't active unless a database diagram is selected in a Database Designer).

The next folder in the Data View window I'll take a look at is the `Tables` folder.

Tables

As you might expect, the `Tables` folder holds the available tables, as you see in Figure 2.32. You can open a table for editing by right-clicking it and selecting the `Open` item. For example, I'm editing the `Categories` table in the `Nwind` database in Figure 2.35. To change a value in the table, all you need to do is edit the appropriate field and then move to another record. Note that opening a table also gives you a great way of taking a look at all the data in the table at once, even if you don't want to edit it.

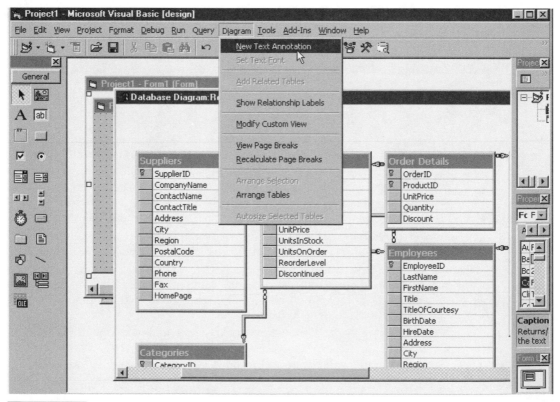

FIGURE 2.34   The Visual Basic `Diagram` menu.

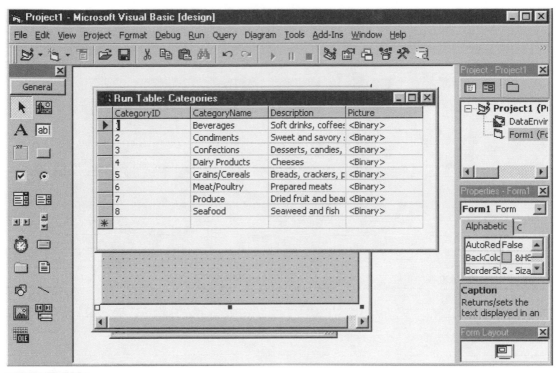

FIGURE 2.35   Editing a table.

You can also edit the *design* of a table with the Data View window. To work on a table's design, right-click it in the `Tables` folder and select the `Design` menu item, opening the designer you see in Figure 2.36.

As you can see in Figure 2.36, you can work field by field through a table when you design it, specifying what each field's type should be, what its length and precision should be, and more.

As with the Visual Data Manager, you can create new tables using the Data View window. To create a new table in the `Nwind` database that holds, say, telephone numbers, right-click the `Tables` folder and select the `New Table` item. The Data View window asks you for the name of the new table, then opens the `New Table` designer you see in Figure 2.37.

You can design the structure of the new table, field by field, using the `New Table` designer. For example, you can see that I've added a new field, [`Phone Numbers`] to the table in Figure 2.37, making this field a text field 10 characters long. If you're unsure what possibilities there are for each of the columns in the `New Table` designer—like `Datatype`—just click the cell you're about to enter data in, and a drop-down list will appear, listing the various options you can select.

The next Data View folder I'll take a look at is the `Views` folder.

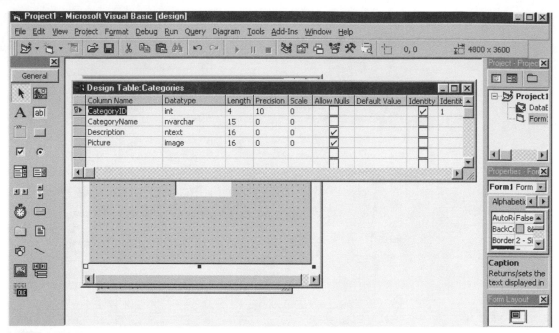

FIGURE 2.36 Designing a database table.

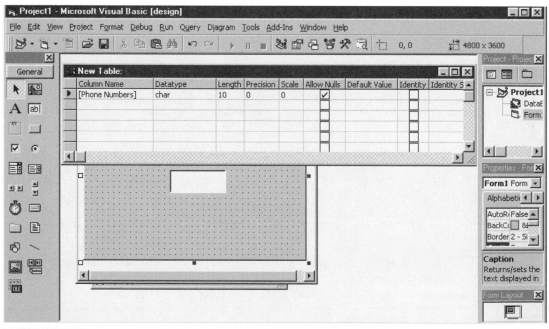

FIGURE 2.37 Creating a new table.

Views and the Query Designer

What is a view? A view is a *virtual*, not actual, table whose contents are defined by a pre-compiled query that is stored on the database server. Even though a view is a virtual table, it looks like a real table, with columns and rows. Note, though, that a view does not really exist as a stored table in a database. Instead, it is a query-based recordset that is created on the server and updated each time you open the view. You can use a view to extract and combine just the information you need from one or more existing tables.

The `Nwind` database already has a number of views defined, as you can see in Figure 2.32. I'll take a look at the `Sales by Category` view in the `Nwind` database by right-clicking that view and selecting the `Open` item, opening that view as you see in Figure 2.38.

When you open a view, you can modify the data that appears inside it. When you modify the data you see in a view, you are changing data in the underlying database.

You can create views using most ODBC-compliant databases. You create a new view into a database by right-clicking the `Views` folder and selecting the `New View` item (for SQL Server databases, you can also create, edit, and delete views with the SQL Enterprise Manager), which opens the Query Designer that you see in Figure 2.39.

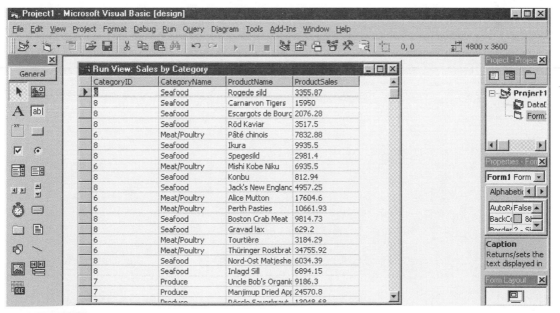

FIGURE 2.38   A database view.

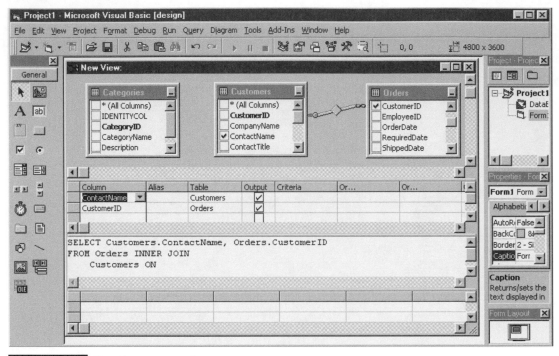

FIGURE 2.39   Creating a new view.

 You can also open the Query Designer using `Connection` objects in a Data Environment. If you click the `SQL Statement` option button in the `General` page of a `Command` object's `Property Pages` and then click the `SQL Builder` button, the Query Designer will open. Or, if you've already given a `Command` object an SQL statement in its `Property Pages`, you can also open the Query Designer by right-clicking the `Command` object in the Data Environment and selecting the `Design` item.

The Query Designer is one of Visual Basic's Visual Database tools (the other one is the Database Designer), and it's organized into a series of panes in which you can design, edit, and test an SQL query. The panes are synchronized so that changes you make in one are reflected in the others, which gives you both a graphical and text version of your SQL query.

In the Data View window, you can select tables, views, or individual columns and drag them to the Diagram pane of the Query Designer (you can't drag such items from a Data Environment to the Query Designer). Note that you can also manipulate queries from the Visual Basic `Query` menu, which only appears in the Query Designer, as shown in Figure 2.40. Plenty of Visual Basic programmers wonder why, (like the `Diagram` menu, there's a `Query` menu in

Visual Basic—it's there to work with SQL queries, and the items in the menu aren't active unless the Query Designer is selected.)

Using the Query Designer, you can:

- Create queries to retrieve data.
- Specify which elements, such as tables, to display, how to order query results, and what values to search for.
- Preview query results in the Results pane.
- Join tables to create relational queries.
- Edit databases by updating, inserting, or deleting records.
- Create queries that modify databases.
- Create parameterized queries where the parameter values are typed in when the query is executed.

In overview, here are the parts of the Query Designer, pane by pane; these panes appear in order (starting at the top) in the Query Designer, which appears in Figure 2.39:

- **Diagram pane**—Displays the database objects, such as tables or views, which you are constructing the query for. Each window here shows an

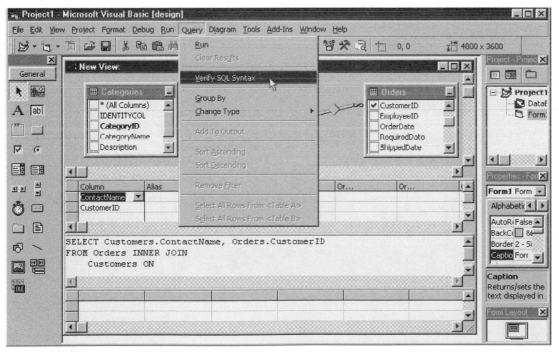

FIGURE 2.40   The Visual Basic Query menu.

input source and includes the data columns and icons to show how each column is used in the query.

- **Grid pane**—A spreadsheet-like grid in which you specify query options, such as which data columns to display, what rows to select, how to group rows, and more.

- **SQL pane**—The SQL statement for the current query. You can edit the SQL statement created by the Query Designer, or you can enter your own SQL statement.

- **Results pane**—A grid with the results of the most recently executed query. You can modify the database by changing values in the cells, and you can also add or delete rows.

The Diagram, Grid, and SQL panes are coordinated—when you make a change in one pane, the Query Designer updates the other panes to take the change into account.

Constructing a query in the Query Designer is a lot like constructing a query in the Visual Data Manager's Query Builder. For example, to add a field to a query, you drag that field from its table (you can drag all the fields in the table by selecting the All Columns item) in the Diagram pane to a cell in the first column in the Grid pane.

You can set the SQL options for a field, such as whether a query sorts on the field, in the other columns in the Grid pane. When you add fields this way and set SQL options, the SQL Designer creates the SQL statement that does what you want in the SQL pane. To run a query, you just right-click the Query Designer and select the Run item. The results appear at the bottom, in the Results pane. When you've tested your SQL statement, you can copy it from the Query Designer and paste it where it's needed in your application.

The next folder in the data view I'll take a look at is the Stored Procedure folder.

Stored Procedures

Stored procedures are made up of precompiled SQL statements stored under one name. They allow user-declared variables, conditional execution, and other powerful programming features. These procedures are stored within a database and can be executed with one call from an application.

 Stored procedures will not work with the Jet engine, but they will work with other providers, such as SQL Server.

note

Stored procedures can contain program flow, logic, and queries on a database. They can accept parameters, return single or multiple result sets, and return values. You can use stored procedures for any purpose for which you would use SQL statements, with these advantages:

- You can execute a number of SQL statements in a single stored procedure.

- You can refer to other stored procedures from a stored procedure.

- Stored procedures execute faster than individual SQL statements, because they are compiled on the server when created.

To create a new stored procedure, right-click the `Stored Procedures` folder or any stored procedure in that folder in the Data View. Doing so opens the SQL Editor, and you can create a new procedure, as you see in Figure 2.41.

After you create a stored procedure, that procedure appears in the `Stored Procedures` folder in the Data View window. You can expand a stored procedure in the Data View window to see a list of the parameters it contains.

You can also edit a stored procedure by right-clicking it in the Data View window and selecting the `Design` menu item. As an example, I'm editing the `CustOrderHist` stored procedure in the `Nwind` database in Figure 2.42.

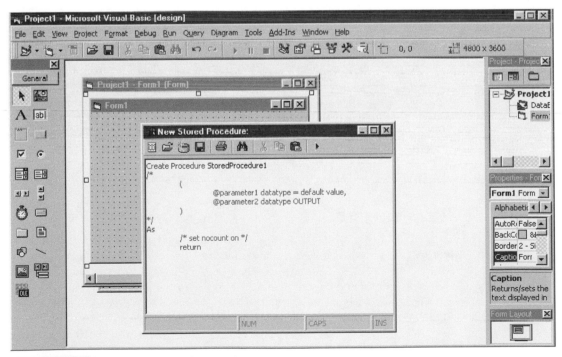

FIGURE 2.41   Creating a stored procedure.

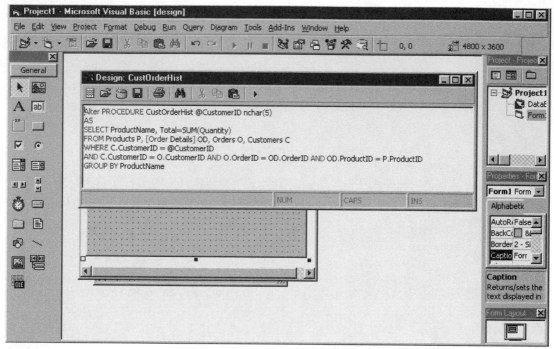

FIGURE 2.42   Editing a stored procedure.

You can also run a stored procedure on your database from the Design window. To do that, click the right-facing arrow on the toolbar in the Design window, which appears in Figure 2.42. The Data View asks you for the value of any parameters that are needed to run the stored procedure, and then opens the SQL debugger, as shown in Figure 2.43. You can run the stored procedure in the SQL debugger by selecting the Go item in the Debug menu. And, as with any other debugger, you can single-step through your code using the SQL debugger.

Triggers

A trigger is a special kind of stored procedure that is run when you modify data in a specified table using one or more of these SQL operations: UPDATE, INSERT, or DELETE. Triggers can query other tables and can include complex SQL statements; they're useful for enforcing business rules. For example, you might use a trigger to decide whether or not to ship an order after checking a customer's account status.

You can use the Data View to create, open, copy, and delete triggers in your database. Because triggers are associated with specific tables, each trigger can be found in the Tables folder with the table the trigger belongs to.

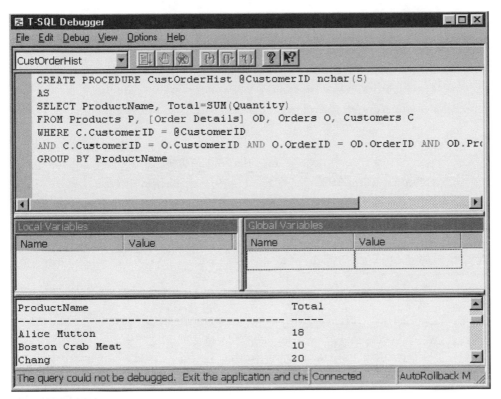

FIGURE 2.43   Running a stored procedure in the T-SQL debugger.

That's it for Data Views for the moment; as you can see, there's a tremendous amount of database power in this tool. Next, I'll take a look at Data Report Designers.

Data Report Designer

The Data Report Designer is new in Visual Basic 6, although previous versions included various data report tools. When you have a data source in an application, you can create a data report at design-time using the Data Report Designer. This designer lets you present all the data from the data source at once in a printable report.

Here are some of the features of the Data Report Designer:

■ **Drag-and-Drop**—You can drag fields from the Data Environment to the Data Report Designer, which will automatically create a text box on the data report and set the `DataMember` and `DataField` properties. You can also drag a `Command` object from the Data Environment Designer to the Data Report Designer, and for each of the fields contained by the Command object, a text box is created on the data report.

- **Toolbox Controls**—The Data Report Designer has its own set of controls in the toolbox.
- **Print Preview**—You can preview the report by using the Show method.
- **Print Reports**—You can now print a report under program control by calling the PrintReport method.
- **File Export**—You can export the data report information using the ExportReport method, including into HTML or text.
- **Export Templates**—You can create a collection of file templates to be used with the ExportReport method (useful for exporting reports in a number of formats, each customized to the report type).

When you add a Data Report Designer to a project, the data report controls are automatically added to the toolbox in a new page, which you reach by clicking the DataReport button in the toolbox.

The new controls are similar to the Visual Basic intrinsic controls, and include a Label, Shape, Image, TextBox, and Line control. The last data report control, the Function control, supports four functions: Sum, Average, Minimum, and Maximum.

To create a new data report, select the Add Data Report item in the Project menu, adding a Data Report Designer to the project, as shown in Figure 2.44.

The new data report is divided into *bands* on the page, as you see in Figure 2.44. These bands include a header and footer, and the detail section.

To create a data report, you set the report's DataSource and DataMember properties to the table in the Data Environment you want to use (you can also use data controls as data sources) and drag a Command object, Command1, from the Data Environment to the detail section of the data report; doing so will add all the items returned by the Command object to the data report. You can also drag individual fields from a Command object to a data report.

I'll construct an example now; the Data Environment I'll use is connected to the Nwind.mdb database, and I will connect Command1 to the Customers table in Nwind. Next, I will drag the Command1 object to the detail section of the data report so each field in the Customers table is displayed in the data report's detail section, as you see in Figure 2.44.

That's all it takes to create a simple data report. You can show the data report at run-time using DataReport1's Show method, as you would for any other form, like this:

```
Private Sub Command1_Click()

    DataReport1.Show

End Sub
```

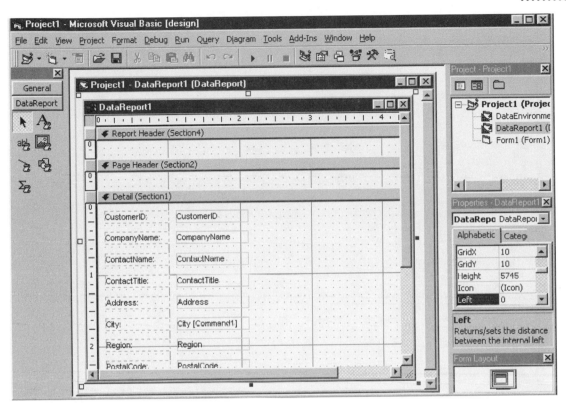

FIGURE 2.44　The Data Report Designer.

When you show the data report form, you see a preview that indicates what the report will look like when you print it. That appears in Figure 2.45. Notice that each record in the table is displayed in full, one after the other.

You can use the `DataReport1` object's `PrintReport` method to actually print the report.

You can also construct data reports manually, using the various controls in the toolbox. Each of the fields in Figure 2.45 is displayed in a `Rpt-TextBox`, and you can add and bind those controls (using the `DataMember` and `DataField` properties) to fields in a database yourself. You can use the `RptLabel`, `RptLine`, `RptShape`, and `RptImage` controls to customize the display of your data report (but these controls cannot be data-bound). You can also use the `Sum`, `Average`, `Minimum`, and `Maximum` functions to summarize your data.

Data reports can be useful if you need a quick way of presenting all the data in a table or a database and, in fact, Visual Basic provides you with a way of easily creating projects with a built-in Data Environment and Data Report Designer—data projects.

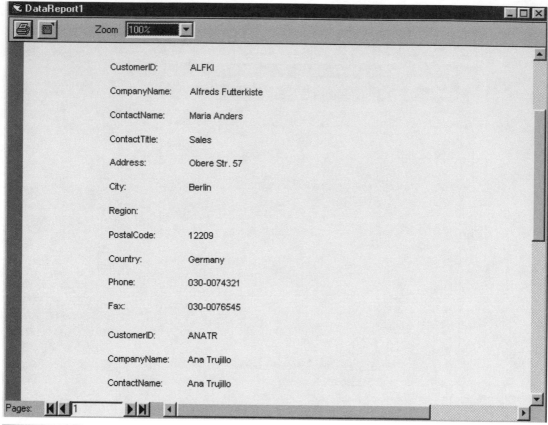

FIGURE 2.45 A data report.

Data Projects

Visual Basic data projects come with built-in Data Environments and Data Report Designers, and you create them from the New Project dialog—just select the Data Project icon in that dialog and click OK. This creates a new project with a form, Data Report Designer, and Data Environment, as shown in Figure 2.46.

Data projects can be useful if you want to create a data report, but they really only save a step or two—there's not much that's special here.

Next, I'll take a look at two powerful design tools that are very powerful, but are not truly Visual Basic-specific—the Microsoft Application Performance Explorer and the Microsoft Visual Modeler.

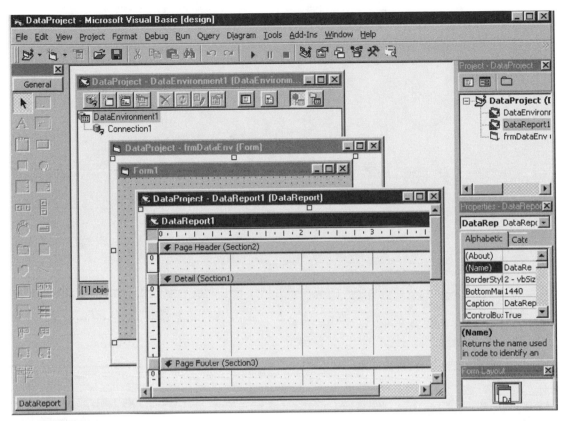

FIGURE 2.46   A data project.

Modeling Multi-Tier Database Architectures

Visual Basic comes with two tools that help in planning multi-tiered applications: the Application Performance Explorer, `AeManagr.exe` (which you can find in the `Common\Tools\APE` folder), as shown in Figure 2.47, and the Visual Modeler, `Msvm.exe` (in the `Common\Tools\VS-Ent98\vmodeler` folder), as shown in Figure 2.48.

Both of these tools help you design and plan various multi-tiered applications, letting you test out the possibilities and get some indication of what's right for your application. For example, in Figure 2.47, I'm setting up a test scenario using ADO to connect to SQL Server using server and client machines. In Figure 2.48, I'm modeling a three-tiered database system using Visual Basic 6 objects.

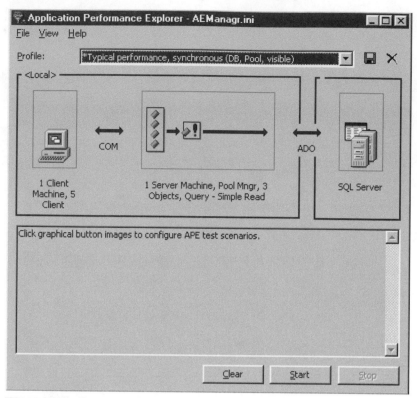

FIGURE 2.47 The Microsoft Application Performance Explorer.

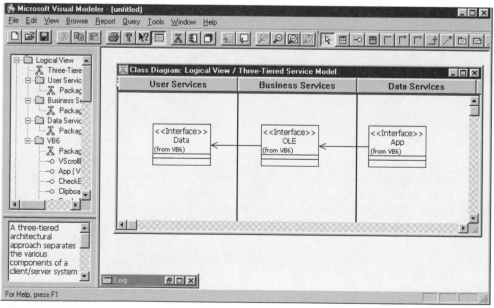

FIGURE 2.48 The Microsoft Visual Modeler.

I'm not going to go into these two tools in-depth, because they're beyond the scope of this book, but they're worth knowing about. If you want to plan multi-tiered database applications, give them a try.

That completes the Visual Basic database tools I'll take a look at in this chapter; but, there is one more item I'll discuss here—the Microsoft Transaction Server.

The Microsoft Transaction Server

The Microsoft Transaction Server (MTS) is a run-time environment made up of components that allow you to perform tasks using transactions. These components implement business rules and usually run from the middle tier of a three-tier application.

The MTS helps coordinate transactions in a three-tier application, making the application more modular. In fact, MTS is becoming very important as developers start insisting on data integrity across the various tiers of an application, and dividing operations up into transactions supports data integrity extremely well.

Note in particular that Visual Basic class modules, which we'll see more about later in this book, have a new MTSTransactionMode property. This property can take these values:

- **NotAnMTSObject**—0 (the default), doesn't support Microsoft Transaction Server.

- **NoTransactions**—1, does not support transactions.

- **RequiresTransaction**—2, must execute within the scope of a transaction. When a new object of this type is created, the object context inherits the transaction from the context of the client. Note that if the client does not have any transactions, MTS will create a new transaction for the object.

- **UsesTransaction**—3, can execute within the scope of the client's transactions. When a new object of this type is created, the object context inherits the transaction from the context of the client. Note that if the client does not have any transactions, MTS creates the new context without one.

- **RequiresNewTransaction**—4, must execute within its own transactions. When a new object is created, MTS automatically creates a new transaction for the object.

And that rounds off our introduction to the database tools in Visual Basic. We'll be using these tools throughout the book, and as you can see, there's a lot of information here. In fact, there's so much power here that it'll take some time to get used to what's going on—it's a good idea to try these tools out and see what they have to offer you. When you see what they have to offer and how they work, you'll find yourself relying on them more and more.

Now it's time to start actually using ADO with the ADO data control. On to the next chapter . . .

Using the ADO
Data Control

In this chapter, I'll take a look at the ADO data control, and in the next chapter, I'll take a look at how to bind this control to data-bound controls. The ADO data control is the new king of data controls as far as Microsoft is concened; you use this control to connect to data with the ADO protocol if you want a simple, quick data access solution using ADO. Putting this control to work will give us an easy start with ADO.

I'll start this chapter with an overview of the ADO data control.

ADO Data Control Overview

The ADO data control appears in Figure 3.1, under the text box. As you can see in that figure, the ADO data control presents a number of buttons to the user. The user can click those buttons to move through a recordset, and from the user's point of view, that's what ADO data controls are all about—navigating through records. From left to right, these buttons are named First, Previous, Next, and Last.

The recordset used by the ADO data control is internal to the control, and it's managed by that control. In fact, the ADO data control maintains a cache of records from the data source, and you can adjust

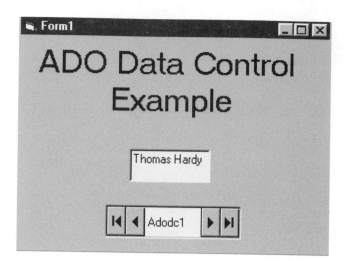

FIGURE 3.1   An ADO data control at work.

the size of that cache using the CacheSize property, as we'll see in this chapter.

You can bind controls to the ADO data control to display fields from the records in the ADO data control's internal recordset—that's the way the ADO data control is designed to be used. Using the ADO data control, you can define your own user interface by binding the control to the Visual Basic controls you want to display, such as text boxes, list boxes, and grid controls. The actual number of fields you display depends on the control you use—a text box, for example, can only display one field of the current record in the ADO data control, while a list box can display an entire column from a table, and a grid control can display a whole table at once. When the user clicks the navigation buttons in the ADO data control, the bound controls are updated automatically to display the new current record in the ADO data control (controls that can display more than one field or record at the same time still give a visual indication of which is the current record; for example, grid controls display a small black triangle in the left-most column next to the current record's row).

As far as the user is concerned, the ADO data control is there to provide a way to move from record to record, but behind the scenes, there's a lot more going on. The ADO data control automatically initiates and manages the connection to an OLE DB provider, using the parameters you've set for it (such as an ADO connection string, which indicates what data source to connect to and what data to retrieve). It reads and stores data from the data source. When the user edits the data in bound controls and then moves to a new record, the ADO data control will update the underlying data source—subject to your validation, as we'll see.

Overall, the ADO data control gives you a quick and easy solution to using ADO in your programs, and that's what Microsoft designed it for. You add an ADO data control to a project using the `Components` item in the Visual Basic `Project` menu, set its `ConnectionString`, `RecordSource`, and `CommandType` properties, then bind it to bound controls like text boxes using the properties of those controls like `DataSource` and `DataField`. That's all it takes, and you're in business, letting the user display and edit data from an OLE DB data provider.

This chapter covers the ADO data control in-depth, including all its properties, methods, events, how to use the control, and even how to reach the recordset inside the control. The first place to start is with the properties of the ADO data control.

Properties of the ADO Data Control

I'll cover the properties of the ADO data control here, one by one, starting with the `Align` property. You use these properties to configure the ADO data control—especially the connection properties like `ConnectionString` and `RecordSource`, which you have to set before using the control with bound controls. It's not necessary to know all these properties by heart—because they're listed here, you can always check back as needed.

Align

This property sets the alignment of the control in a form (for example, you can align the control to the top of a form). The possible values are:

- **VbAlignNone**—No alignment specified.
- **VbAlignTop**—Align to the top of the form.
- **VbAlignBottom**—Align to the bottom of the form.
- **VbAlignLeft**—Align to the left of the form.
- **VbAlignRight**—Align to the right of the form.

This property is useful if you want to use the ADO data control as a toolbar, or align and stretch it to the bottom of a form.

Appearance

The `Appearance` property makes the ADO data control appear flat or three-dimensional. Here are the possible values for this property:

- **0**—Flat. Paints controls and forms without visual effects.
- **1**—(default) 3D. Paints controls with three-dimensional effects.

BackColor, ForeColor

You use the BackColor property to set the control's background color and the ForeColor property to set its foreground color. There are four ways to set colors in Visual Basic:

- Use the RGB function.
- Use the QBColor function to choose one of 16 Microsoft QuickBasic colors.
- Use one of the intrinsic Visual Basic color constants.
- Enter a color value directly.

The RGB function takes three colors values, 0-255, to specify the red, green, and blue values in the color you want like this: RGB(RRR, GGG, BBB), where RRR, GGG, and BBB are the red, green, and blue color values, respectively. Here are some examples showing how to use this function and the color created:

```
RGB(255, 0, 0)          'Red
RGB(0, 255, 0)          'Green
RGB(0, 0, 255)          'Blue
RGB(0, 0, 0)            'Black
RGB(255, 255, 255)      'White
RGB(128, 128, 128)      'Gray
```

The QBColor function returns one of these colors when you pass it the matching numbers, 0-15:

- Black: 0.
- Blue: 1.
- Green: 2.
- Cyan: 3.
- Red: 4.
- Magenta: 5.
- Yellow: 6.
- White: 7.
- Gray: 8.
- Light Blue: 9.
- Light Green: 10.
- Light Cyan: 11.
- Light Red: 12.

- Light Magenta: 13.
- Light Yellow: 14.
- White: 15.

You can also use one of the built-in Visual Basic color constants, like **vbRed**, to specify a color. Here are the standard Visual Basic color constants:

- **vbBlack** (&H0): Black.
- **vbRed** (&HFF): Red.
- **vbGreen** (&HFF00): Green.
- **vbYellow** (&HFFFF): Yellow.
- **vbBlue** (&HFF0000): Blue.
- **vbMagenta** (&HFF00FF): Magenta.
- **vbCyan** (&HFFFF00): Cyan.
- **vbWhite** (&HFFFFFF): White.

You can also use the built-in system colors of Visual Basic, such as vbScrollBars or vbDesktop.

BOFAction

The BOFAction property specifies the action the control should take when the user moves to the very beginning of the current recordset, as when they press the Previous button in the ADO data control, even though they are already at the beginning of the recordset. The possible actions are:

- **adDoMoveFirst**—(default) Move to the first record.
- **adStayBOF**—Stay at the beginning of the file (before the first record).

Note that if you set this property to adStayBOF, the control will stay at the beginning of the recordset, *before* the first record, and all bound controls will appear blank.

CacheSize

This property returns or sets the number of records that are cached in local memory for the ADO data control. The default is 50; for better performance, at a cost of more memory usage, you can increase this value.

Caption

You use the Caption property to set the text that appears in the center of the ADO data control. By default, the control's name, such as Adodc1, appears in the control. To change that, for example, you might want to display the name of a table the ADO data control is connected to, using this property.

This is one of the properties that you usually set when working with an ADO data control rather than accepting the default.

CausesValidation

This property returns or sets a value that determines whether the `Validate` event will occur when the user tries to shift the focus from another control to the ADO data control. If you want the data in bound controls to be checked when the user clicks the ADO data control, set this property to True and add code to the bound control's `Validate` event. See Chapter 1 for more on data validation.

CommandTimeout

The `CommandTimeout` property sets the timeout, in seconds, for command execution. This is the amount of time the ADO data control will allow for commands to be executed on the server. The default is 30 seconds; if you're on a slow network, you might increase this value.

CommandType

The `CommandType` property holds the type of command used to generate the recordset, and may be one of these values:

- **adCmdText**—1. SQL statement.
- **adCmdTable**—2. Table.
- **adCmdStoredProc**—4. Stored procedure.
- **adCmdUnknown**—8. Unknown.

You usually don't set this connection property directly in code, but rather when you set the `RecordSource` property at design-time, after creating a connection string. However, if you are configuring an ADO data control at run-time, this is one of the properties you should set, as well as others like `ConnectionString` and `RecordSource` (some OLE DB providers do not require you to set this property).

ConnectionString

The `ConnectionString` property holds the ADO connection string the ADO data control will use to connect to a data source. You must set this property before using the ADO data control, or you'll get an error.

ADO uses connection strings to connect to data sources; here's a typical connection string that uses the Microsoft Jet 4.0 OLE DB provider to connect to the `Nwind.mdb` database:

```
Provider=Microsoft.Jet.OLEDB.4.0;Persist Security
Info=False;Data Source=C:\ADO\Nwind.mdb
```

Probably the easiest way to create a connection string is to let Visual Basic build it for you; just click the ellipsis button that appears when you click the ConnectionString property in the Properties window, then click the Build button in the Property Pages that open and follow the on-screen directions. I'll do this later in the chapter when putting the ADO data control to work. You can also use the Data Form Wizard to create connection strings.

Note that besides setting the ConnectionString property, you must also set the RecordSource property to indicate how you want to extract records from the data source.

ConnectionTimeout

This property sets the timeout, in seconds, for making the connection. The default is 15 seconds; if you're on a slow network and have connection time-out problems, this is the property to change.

Container

The Container property holds a reference to the ADO data control's container. As you can guess from the name, a container holds controls, and ADO data controls can be contained by forms, frame controls, picture boxes, and SSTabStrip controls.

CursorLocation

You can use the CursorLocation property to set the location of the ADO cursor (a cursor manages a recordset as far as the code in your program goes; see Chapter 1 for more details). You can maintain the cursor on the client or the server; here are the possibilities:

- **adUseServer**—2. Use server cursors.
- **adUseClient**—3 (default). Use Microsoft client batch cursors.

To improve cursor performance, you can use a server-side cursor if your OLE DB provider supports it (e.g., SQL Server does, Microsoft Jet does not). Note that you cannot use server-side cursors if you're creating a disconnected or multiple recordset.

CursorType

This property sets the type of cursor the ADO data control uses (see Chapter 1 for more on cursors), and may be one of the following:

- **adOpenDynamic**—*Dynamic cursor.* This cursor type lets you view additions, changes, and deletions by other users, and allows all types of movement through the recordset.

- **adOpenKeyset**—*Keyset cursor.* This cursor behaves like a dynamic cursor, except that it prevents you from seeing records that other users add, and prevents access to records that other users delete. Data changes by other users will still be visible.

- **adOpenStatic**—*Static cursor* (default). This cursor provides a static copy of a set of records for you to use to find data or generate reports. Note that additions, changes, or deletions by other users will not be visible.

Note that ForwardOnly cursors are not available for the ADO data control.

DragIcon

This property returns or sets the icon to be used when the control is dragged.

DragMode

This property returns or sets a value that determines whether manual or automatic drag mode is used in drag-and-drop operations. Here are the possible settings:

- **VbManual**—0 (default), Manual. This setting requires using the Drag method to start a drag-and-drop operation on the control.

- **VbAutomatic**—1, Automatic. This setting means that clicking the control automatically initiates a drag-and-drop operation.

Enabled

This property indicates whether or not the control is enabled (i.e., accessible to the user). When disabled, the control appears grayed out. Setting this property to True enables the control; setting it to False disables the control.

You can use the ADO data control's Enabled property to avoid program problems; for example, when a user is finished with a database, you can disable the associated ADO data control.

Note that when the ADO data control is not connected to a database, it's disabled automatically.

EOFAction

This property specifies the action the control takes when the user tries to move past the end of the recordset. Here are the possible values:

- **adDoMoveLast**—0 (default). Move to last record.
- **adStayEOF**—1. Stay at end of file.
- **adDoAddNew**—2. Add a new record.

Note that the default action is to stay at the last record in the recordset. However, you can set the control to create a new record each time the user clicks the Next button at the end of the recordset by setting the EOFAction property to adDoAddNew.

Font

This property sets the font used in the ADO data control's caption. You can set this property at design-time by clicking the ellipsis button that appears when you click the Font property in the Properties window, or at run-time by setting this property to a Font object.

Height, Width

The Height and Width properties hold the height and width of the ADO data control. By default, these settings are in twips (1/1440ths of an inch), but you can set the measurement units to other values using the ScaleMode property of the ADO data control's container.

Index

You use the Index property to make the ADO data control part of an array of such controls. To create an ADO data control array, you simply give two ADO data controls the same name, and Visual Basic will ask you if you want to create a control array. Click Yes. You can add other ADO data controls to the control array by giving them the same name.

When you have a control array, you can refer to the controls in that array by index (0-based), letting you handle multiple controls in code in an easy way. All event procedures for controls in a control array are automatically passed an index value as a parameter to indicate which control in the array caused the event.

Left, Top

The Left and Top properties set the left edge and top edge positions of the ADO data control in its container. By default, these properties are measured in twips (1/1440ths of an inch), but you can change that by setting the container's ScaleMode property.

LockType

This property sets the the locking type the control will use with the records in the recordset, and may be one of the following:

- **adLockReadOnly**—(default), Read-only. You cannot alter the data.
- **adLockPessimistic**—Pessimistic locking, record by record. The data provider does what is necessary to ensure successful editing of the

records, usually by locking records at the data source immediately when you start editing the data in the recordset's fields.

- **adLockOptimistic**—Optimistic locking, record by record. The provider uses optimistic locking, locking records only when you call the Update method.

- **adLockBatchOptimistic**—Optimistic batch updates. Required for batch update mode as opposed to immediate update mode.

See Chapter 1 for more on locking types.

MaxRecords

This property sets the maximum number of records to fill a recordset with. The default setting is 0, which actually means that there is no limit. However, if you want to limit the number of records a user can get at one time—to restrict network traffic, for example—set this property to a specific value.

Mode

This property sets the connection mode of the control to the data source. Here are the possibilities:

- **adModeUnknown**—0 (default). Unknown.
- **adModeRead**—1. Read only.
- **adModeWrite**—2. Write only.
- **adModeReadWrite**—3. Read/Write.
- **adModeShareDenyRead**—4. Deny others read permission.
- **adModeShareDenyWrite**—8. Deny others write permission.
- **adModeShareExclusive**—12. Deny others from opening a connection.
- **adModeShareDenyNone**—16. Deny no other users.

If you're unsure, leave this property set to the default, adModeUnknown, and let the OLE DB provider use its default connection mode.

If you're going to set this property, set it before connecting to a data source, because you can't set it on an open connection.

Negotiate

This property determines whether a control that can be aligned will be displayed or not when an active object on the form displays one or more toolbars. The default is False.

Orientation

You use the Orientation property to set the ADO data control's visual orientation, horizontal or vertical. Here are the possible settings:

- **adHorizontal**—0. Horizontal orientation.
- **adVertical**—1. Vertical orientation.

Password

The Password property sets the password used during the creation of an ADO Recordset object with OLE DB providers that require passwords. Note that the password and user name can both be set in the connection string (and usually are) when you create the connection string. You can also set the password and user name in the Authentication tab of the ADO data control's Property Pages.

Recordset

You can gain access to the underlying ADO Recordset object that the ADO data control uses, and I'll do that later in this chapter. When you work with the ADO data control's Recordset object, you can use the methods and properties of that object.

For example, here's how I use the MoveNext method of the Recordset object of an ADO data control named Adodc1 to move to the next record when the user clicks the button Command1:

```
Private Sub Command1_Click()
    Adodc1.Recordset.MoveNext
End Sub
```

This property is read/write at run-time.

RecordSource

This is an important property; the RecordSource property holds an SQL statement or query that returns a recordset or other record source, such as a table name. After you set the control's ConnectionString property to connect to a database, you must also set the RecordSource property to indicate how you intend to get records from that data source.

For example, if you've connected to the Nwind database using a connection string, you still need to indicate how to get records from that database. Say you've decided to use the Customers table as a record source; in that case, you click the ellipsis button that appears when you click the ADO data control's RecordSource property in the Properties window, opening the RecordSource Property Pages you see in Figure 3.2.

You can specify the command type to use for extracting data from the data source. In this case, I've set the command type (which will be stored in the CommandType property) to adCmdTable, and specified the table I want to use in the Table or Stored Procedure box in Figure 3.2.

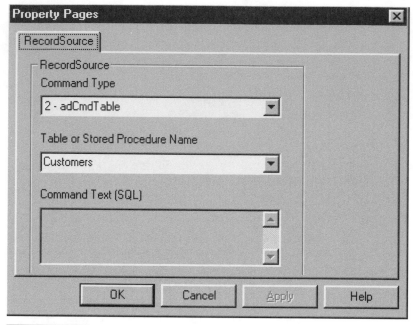

FIGURE 3.2 Setting the RecordSource property.

If you use other command types, like adCmdText, you can use an SQL statement to extract data from the data source. In that case, you'd place the SQL you want to use in the Command Text (SQL) box in Figure 3.2.

Tag

You use the Tag property to associate some text with a control. You normally use this property to store data that lets you distinguish between the controls in a control array, if using the control array's Index property is not enough.

ToolTipText

This property holds the text that appears in a tool tip, the small yellow window that appears when the mouse hovers over the control. Place text into this property if you want to give some kind of prompt or instruction to the user; using this property is usually a good idea in finished applications that you release for general use.

UserName

This property holds the user name for use with OLE DB data sources that require user name and password verification.

Note that you can (and usually do) set the user name when you're building the connection string—see the `ConnectionString` property for more information. You can also set the password and user name in the Authentication tab of the ADO data control's `Property Pages`.

Visible

The `Visible` property indicates whether or not the ADO data control is visible; by default, this property is set to True. If clicking a button in the control is going to cause a problem—as when the control is not connected to a database that you have yet to update—it can be a good idea to make the control invisible so users don't try to work with it.

WhatsThisHelpID

The `WhatsThisHelpID` property returns or sets a help context number for a help topic in a help file associated with an application (as with the `App` object's `HelpFile` property). When the user clicks a What's This Help button and clicks a control, the help topic will be displayed.

That's it for the properties of the ADO data control. I'll take a look at its methods next.

Methods of the ADO Data Control

I'll cover the methods of the ADO data control next, starting with the `Drag` method. You use the methods of this control when you want to perform some operation in your program, and you can call these methods directly from your code.

Drag

This method begins, ends, or cancels a drag operation of the ADO data control. You don't usually drag an ADO data control around, but if you want to, you can use this method, passing it one of these values:

- **vbCancel**—0. Cancels drag operation.
- **vbBeginDrag**—1. Begins dragging the control.
- **vbEndDrag**—2. Ends dragging and drops the control.

Move

You can use the `Move` method to move the ADO data control. You pass the new location and, optionally, the new size of the control to this method like this:

```
ADOcontrol.Move left [, top [, width [, height]]]
```

For example, here's how I move an ADO data control to the top left of a form:

```
Private Sub Command1_Click()
    Adodc1.Move 0, 0
End Sub
```

Refresh

You use the Refresh method to refresh the data in the ADO data control's internal recordset. You use this method if the data in the data source has been updated by some other user or application and you want to get a fresh copy of the revised data set.

SetFocus

Calling the ADO data control's SetFocus method gives the control the focus. This can be useful if you have multiple ADO data controls and want to select one after the user has indicated what type of data operation they want to perform.

ShowWhatsThis

You use this method to display the What's This Help topic associated with the control in a What's This Help pop-up window.

Zorder

You set the ADO data control's z-order with the Zorder property. A control's z-order indicates how it stacks with other controls. You can pass an optional value to this method, indicating the position of the ADO data control relative to other controls. If this value is 0 or omitted, the control is positioned at the front of the z-order. If the value is 1, the control is positioned at the back of the z-order.

That's it for the methods of the ADO data control; next I'll take a look at the events of this control.

Events of the ADO Data Control

To handle events in Visual Basic, you use event handlers, which are Sub procedures that are called when the corresponding event occurs. The ADO data control event handlers are passed objects of various types, and it's worth taking a look at those types before working through the events in detail. The ADODB.Recordset class is the ADO recordset class. The ADODB.Error class is the ADO error class. I'll cover both these classes thoroughly later in this book.

ADODB.EventReason is an enumeration type that indicates the reason an event occurred. It can take these possible values:

- **adRsnAddNew**—1. New record to be added.
- **adRsnDelete**—2. Record deleted.
- **adRsnUpdate**—3. Record to be updated.
- **adRsnUndoUpdate**—4. Undo update.
- **adRsnUndoAddNew**—5. Undo add new record.
- **adRsnUndoDelete**—6. Undo delete.
- **adRsnRequery**—7. Requery.
- **adRsnResynch**—8. Resynchronize.
- **adRsnClose**—9. Close.
- **adRsnMove**—10. Move.
- **adRsnMoveFirst**—12. Move first.
- **adRsnMoveNext**—13. Move next.
- **adRsnMovePrevious**—14. Move previous.
- **adRsnMoveLast**—15. Move last.

ADODB.EventStatus is an enumeration type that indicates the current status of the control. It can take these possible values:

- **adStatusOK**—1. OK.
- **adStatusErrorsOccurred**—2. Errors occurred.
- **adStatusCantDeny**—3. Can't deny change.
- **adStatusCancel**—4. Cancel.
- **adStatusUnwantedEvent**—5. Prevent future notifications.

If an operation was successful, you'll see the value adStatusOK passed to you in the adStatus parameter that is passed to event handlers—in general, event handlers are passed a number of parameters by Visual Basic, as in this case, where the Error event handler for an ADO data named Adodc1 gets seven parameters:

```
Private Sub Adodc1_Error(ByVal ErrorNumber As Long,
Description As String, ByVal Scode As Long, ByVal
Source As String, ByVal HelpFile As String, ByVal
HelpContext As Long, fCancelDisplay As Boolean)


End Sub
```

You can use the parameters passed to the event handler in the Sub procedure itself, as in this case, where I'm using a message box to indicate to the user that an error has occurred:

```
Private Sub Adodc1_Error(ByVal ErrorNumber As Long,
Description As String, ByVal Scode As Long, ByVal
Source As String, ByVal HelpFile As String, ByVal
HelpContext As Long, fCancelDisplay As Boolean)
    MsgBox "There's been an error: " & Description
End Sub
```

As I list the ADO data control events, I'll also list what parameters are passed to their event handlers, and what those parameters mean.

Data Validation with the ADO Data Control

Earlier in this book, I took a look at client-side field validation using the Validate event and various other techniques. The ADO data control object also provides the means to validate data on the client by using these events:

- **WillChangeField**—Current field will change.
- **WillMove**—Current row position in a recordset will change.
- **WillChangeRecord**—Something in the current row of the recordset will change.
- **WillChangeRecordset**—Something in the current recordset will change.

You can find out about a pending change using the parameters passed to the event handler. For example, here are the parameters passed to the WillChangeField event handler:

- **cFields**—Number of Field objects in Fields.
- **Fields**—Field objects with pending changes.
- **pError**—Describes the error that occurred if the value of adStatus is adStatusErrorsOccurred; otherwise not set.
- **adStatus**—Status value; see below.
- **pRecordset**—The recordset that caused the event.

If you want to cancel the pending change, check the adStatus parameter; if it's not set to adStatusCantDeny, then you can cancel the change by setting it to adStatusCancel before returning.

Here's an example showing how to use the WillChangeField event:

```
Private Sub adoRecordset_WillChangeField(ByVal _
    cFields As Long, ByVal Fields As Variant, _
    adStatus As ADODB.EventStatusEnum, ByVal _
    pRecordset As ADODB.Recordset)
    If adStatus <> adCantDeny Then
        If MsgBox("Do you really want to change " _
            & Fields(0) & "?", vbYesNo) = vbNo Then
            adStatus = adStatusCancel
        End If
    End If
End Sub
```

That's it for the overview—it's time to start working with the ADO data control events, starting with DragDrop.

DragDrop

The DragDrop event occurs when a drag-and-drop operation is completed as a result of dragging a control over the ADO data control and releasing the mouse button, or using the Drag method with its action argument set to 2 to drop an object.

Here is what the event handler looks like for this event:

```
Private Sub Adodc1_DragDrop(Source As Control, x As
Single, y As Single)

End Sub
```

Here are the parameters passed to this event's handler:

- **Source**—The control being dragged.
- **x**—The current x coordinate of the mouse.
- **y**—The current y coordinate of the mouse.

DragOver

The DragOver event occurs when a drag-and-drop operation is in progress. You can use this event to monitor the mouse pointer as it enters, leaves, or hovers directly over a valid target. The mouse pointer position determines the target object that receives this event.

Here is what the event handler looks like for this event:

```
Private Sub Adodc1_DragOver(Source As Control, x As
Single, y As Single, State As Integer)

End Sub
```

Here are the parameters passed to this event's handler:

- **Source**—The control being dragged.
- **x**—The current x coordinate of the mouse.
- **y**—The current y coordinate of the mouse.

EndOfRecordset

This event occurs when there was an attempt to move to a row past the end of the recordset.

Here is what the event handler looks like for this event:

```
Private Sub Adodc1_EndOfRecordset(fMoreData As
Boolean, adStatus As ADODB.EventStatusEnum, ByVal
pRecordset As ADODB.Recordset)

End Sub
```

Here are the parameters passed to this event's handler:

- **fMoreData**—You can append new records to pRecordset while processing this event. Add your data, then set this parameter to True to indicate that there is a new end to the recordset before exiting the event handler.
- **adStatus**—The current status value.
- **pRecordset**—The Recordset object for which this event occurred.

Note that you can use this event to add more data to the end of a recordset if the user tries to move past the end of the recordset.

Error

This event occurs if there's been an error, which can come from the objects in the ADO library or the OLE DB provider.

Here is what the event handler looks like for this event:

```
Private Sub Adodc1_Error(ByVal ErrorNumber As Long,
Description As String, ByVal Scode As Long, ByVal
Source As String, ByVal HelpFile As String, ByVal
HelpContext As Long, fCancelDisplay As Boolean)


End Sub
```

Here are the parameters passed to this event's handler:

- **ErrorNumber**—Number of the error that occurred.
- **Description**—Description of the error.
- **Scode**—Status code of the error.
- **Source**—The query or command that caused the error.
- **HelpFile**—The application's help file.
- **HelpContext**—The help context for the control.

In addition to errors from the OLE DB data provider, ADO itself defines a number of errors that can occur in the ADO data control, which you'll find in Table 3.1.

Note that this event fires only as the result of a data access error that occurs when no Visual Basic code is being executed.

FieldChangeComplete

This event fires after the value in a field of the current record has been changed, such as when the user edits the data in a bound control and then moves to another record.

Here is what the event handler looks like for this event:

```
Private Sub Adodc1_FieldChangeComplete(ByVal cFields
As Long, Fields As Variant, ByVal pError As
ADODB.Error, adStatus As ADODB.EventStatusEnum,
ByVal pRecordset As ADODB.Recordset)


End Sub
```

Here are the parameters passed to this event's handler:

- **cFields**—The number of fields in the `Fields` array.
- **Fields**—An array of variants that holds the fields that will be changed.

TABLE 3.1	ADO data control error codes	
Constant name	**Number**	**Description**
adErrInvalidArgument	3001	Your code is using arguments that are of the wrong type, are out of acceptable range, or are in conflict with one another.
adErrNoCurrentRecord	3021	Either you are at the beginning or end of the file, or the current record has been deleted; the operation requested by the application requires a current record.
adErrIllegalOperation	3219	The operation you requested is not allowed in this context.
adErrInTransaction	3246	You cannot explicitly close a Connection object while in the middle of a transaction.
adErrFeatureNotAvailable	3251	The operation you requested is not supported by the OLE DB provider.
adErrItemNotFound	3265	ADO could not find the object in the collection corresponding to the name or ordinal reference you requested.
adErrObjectInCollection	3367	The object is already in the collection and so can't be appended.
adErrObjectNotSet	3420	The object you referenced no longer points to a valid object.
adErrDataConversion	3421	You are using a value of the wrong type for the current operation.
adErrObjectClosed	3704	The operation you requested is not allowed if the object is closed.
adErrObjectOpen	3705	The operation you requested is not allowed if the object is open.
adErrProviderNotFound	3706	ADO could not find the provider you specified.
adErrBoundToCommand	3707	You cannot change the ActiveConnection property of a Recordset object with a Command object as its source.
adErrInvalidParamInfo	3708	You defined a Parameter object improperly.
adErrInvalidConnection	3709	You requested an operation on an object with a reference to a closed or invalid Connection object.

- **pError**—Describes the error that occurred when the value of ad-Status is adStatusErrorsOccurred; otherwise not set.
- **adStatus**—The current status value.
- **pRecordset**—The Recordset object for which this event occurred.

You can check what the original value of a changed field was using the Fields array, which is an array of the fields that were changed (you can change multiple fields with batch updates, as we'll see later). For example, say you added this code to the FieldChangeComplete event handler for the ADO data control Adodc1:

```
Private Sub Adodc1_FieldChangeComplete(ByVal cFields
As Long, Fields As Variant, ByVal pError As
ADODB.Error, adStatus As ADODB.EventStatusEnum,
ByVal pRecordset As ADODB.Recordset)
    MsgBox Fields(0)
End Sub
```

Now say you connected this ADO data control to the students table developed in the previous chapter and connected the Name field in that table to a text box. When you run the program, you should see the name of the first student in the text box, Ann. If you were to change that name to Anne, you'd see a message box displayed by the above code—and the name you'd see in the message box would be Ann, the original value, not Anne, the new value.

You can also check the values in fields *before* they are changed—see the WillChangeField event coming up.

MouseDown

This event fires when a mouse button is pressed. Here is what the event handler looks like for this event:

```
Private Sub Adodc1_MouseDown(Button As Integer,
Shift As Integer, x As Single, y As Single)


End Sub
```

Here are the parameters passed to this event's handler:

- **Button**—Identifies the button that was pressed. The *Button* argument is a bit field with bits corresponding to the left button (bit 0), right button (bit 1), and middle button (bit 2). These bits correspond to the values 1, 2, and 4, respectively. Only one of the bits is set, indicating the button that caused the event.

- **Shift**—The state of the SHIFT, CTRL, and ALT keys when the button specified in the *Button* argument was pressed or released. A bit is set if the key is down. The *Shift* argument is a bit field with the least-significant bits corresponding to the SHIFT key (bit 0), the CTRL key (bit 1), and the ALT key (bit 2). These bits correspond to the values 1, 2, and 4, respectively. The *Shift* argument indicates the state of these keys. Some, all, or none of the bits can be set, indicating that some, all, or none of the keys are pressed.

- **x**—Horizontal location of the mouse when the event occurred (in twips, by default).

- **y**—Vertical location of the mouse when the event occurred (in twips, by default).

MouseMove

This event fires when the mouse is moved across the ADO data control. Here is what the event handler looks like for this event:

```
Private Sub Adodc1_MouseMove(Button As Integer,
Shift As Integer, x As Single, y As Single)


End Sub
```

Here are the parameters passed to this event's handler:

- **Button**—Identifies the button that was pressed. The *Button* argument is a bit field with bits corresponding to the left button (bit 0), right button (bit 1), and middle button (bit 2). These bits correspond to the values 1, 2, and 4, respectively. Only one of the bits is set, indicating the button that caused the event.

- **Shift**—The state of the SHIFT, CTRL, and ALT keys when the button specified in the *Button* argument was pressed. A bit is set if the key is down. The *Shift* argument is a bit field with the least-significant bits corresponding to the SHIFT key (bit 0), the CTRL key (bit 1), and the ALT key (bit 2). These bits correspond to the values 1, 2, and 4, respectively. The *Shift* argument indicates the state of these keys. Some, all, or none of the bits can be set, indicating that some, all, or none of the keys are pressed.

- **x**—Horizontal location of the mouse when the event occurred (in twips, by default).

■ **y**—Vertical location of the mouse when the event occurred (in twips, by default).

MouseUp

This event fires when the mouse button is released. Here is what the event handler looks like for this event:

```
Private Sub Adodc1_MouseUp(Button As Integer, Shift
As Integer, x As Single, y As Single)


End Sub
```

Here are the parameters passed to this event's handler:

■ **Button**—An integer that identifies the button that was released to cause the event. The *Button* argument is a bit field with bits corresponding to the left button (bit 0), right button (bit 1), and middle button (bit 2). These bits correspond to the values 1, 2, and 4, respectively. Only one of the bits is set, indicating the button that caused the event.

■ **Shift**—The state of the SHIFT, CTRL, and ALT keys when the button specified in the *Button* argument was pressed or released. A bit is set if the key is down. The *Shift* argument is a bit field with the least-significant bits corresponding to the SHIFT key (bit 0), the CTRL key (bit 1), and the ALT key (bit 2). These bits correspond to the values 1, 2, and 4, respectively. The *Shift* argument indicates the state of these keys. Some, all, or none of the bits can be set, indicating that some, all, or none of the keys are pressed.

■ **x**—Horizontal location of the mouse when the event occurred (in twips, by default).

■ **y**—Vertical location of the mouse when the event occurred (in twips, by default).

MoveComplete

This event occurs when the current position in the recordset has changed. Here is what the event handler looks like for this event:

```
Private Sub Adodc1_MoveComplete(ByVal adReason As
```

```
ADODB.EventReasonEnum, ByVal pError As ADODB.Error,

adStatus As ADODB.EventStatusEnum, ByVal pRecordset

As ADODB.Recordset)


End Sub
```

Here are the parameters passed to this event's handler:

- **adReason**—The reason this event occurred.
- **pError**—describes the error that occurred when the value of adStatus is adStatusErrorsOccurred; otherwise not set.
- **adStatus**—The current status value.
- **pRecordset**—The Recordset object for which this event occurred.

The adReason parameter is set to adStatusOK if the operation that caused the event was successful, or adStatusErrorsOccurred if the operation failed. You can set this value to adStatusUnwantedEvent to prevent further notifications.

To catch moves before they occur, take a look at the WillMove event coming up.

RecordChangeComplete

This event fires when one or more records have changed. Here is what the event handler looks like for this event:

```
Private Sub Adodc1_RecordChangeComplete(ByVal

adReason As ADODB.EventReasonEnum, ByVal cRecords As

Long, ByVal pError As ADODB.Error, adStatus As

ADODB.EventStatusEnum, ByVal pRecordset As

ADODB.Recordset)


End Sub
```

Here are the parameters passed to this event's handler:

- **adReason**—The reason this event occurred.
- **cRecords**—The number of records that were changed.
- **pError**—Describes the error that occurred when the value of adStatus is adStatusErrorsOccurred; otherwise not set.
- **adStatus**—The current status value.
- **pRecordset**—The Recordset object for which this event occurred.

When `RecordChangeComplete` is called, the `adReason` parameter is set to `adStatusOK` if the operation that changed the record worked successfully, or `adStatusErrorsOccurred` if the operation failed. Note that you can set this parameter to `adStatusUnwantedEvent` to prevent further notifications.

To catch record changes before they occur, take a look at the `WillChangeRecord` event coming up.

RecordsetChangeComplete

As you can guess from its name, this event occurs after the ADO data control's recordset has changed. Here is what the event handler looks like for this event:

```
Private Sub Adodc1_RecordsetChangeComplete(ByVal
adReason As ADODB.EventReasonEnum, ByVal pError As
ADODB.Error, adStatus As ADODB.EventStatusEnum,
ByVal pRecordset As ADODB.Recordset)


End Sub
```

Here are the parameters passed to this event's handler:

- **adReason**—The reason this event occurred.
- **pError**—Describes the error that occurred when the value of ad-Status is `adStatusErrorsOccurred`; otherwise not set.
- **adStatus**—The current status value.
- **pRecordset**—The Recordset object for which this event occurred.

When `RecordsetChangeComplete` is called, the `adStatus` parameter is set to `adStatusOK` if the operation that changed the recordset was successful, `adStatusErrorsOccurred` if the operation failed, or `adStatus-Cancel` if the operation associated with the previous `WillChangeRecord-set` event was canceled.

Note that you can set `adStatus` to `adStatusUnwantedEvent` to prevent further notifications.

WillChangeField

This event occurs when the ADO data control is about to change the value in a field, and you can use this event for data validation, canceling the change if you want to. Here is what the event handler looks like for this event:

```
Private Sub Adodc1_WillChangeField(ByVal cFields As
```

```
Long, Fields As Variant, adStatus As
ADODB.EventStatusEnum, ByVal pRecordset As
ADODB.Recordset)


End Sub
```

Here are the parameters passed to this event's handler:

- **cFields**—Number of Field objects in Fields.
- **Fields**—Field objects with pending changes.
- **pError**—Describes the error that occurred when the value of ad-Status is adStatusErrorsOccurred; otherwise not set.
- **adStatus**—Status value; see below.
- **pRecordset**—The recordset that caused the event.

You can determine what data will be changed by looking at the field(s) in the Fields array; each element in this array is the data in a field that will change. To cancel a change, you set the adStatus parameter to adStatusCancel.

For example, here's how I cancel all changes to the fields in a record-set—by setting the adStatus parameter to adStatusCancel every time the WillChangeField event fires:

```
Private Sub Adodc1_WillChangeField(ByVal cFields As
Long, Fields As Variant, adStatus As
ADODB.EventStatusEnum, ByVal pRecordset As
ADODB.Recordset)
    adStatus = adStatusCancel
End Sub
```

The result when the user tries to change the value in a field appears in Figure 3.3; as you can see, the user is notified with a message box that no changes were made. Note that the FieldChangeComplete event occurs after a change has been made to a field.

There's a problem with the above code, however; when the user makes a change to the data in a field and the above code cancels the update to the data source, the ADO data control still knows that the field has been changed, so every time the user tries to move away from the current record, they'll get the same message box and won't be able to move to a new record.

To change that, I update the data in all bound controls with the ADO data control's Refresh method, which refreshes the data from the data

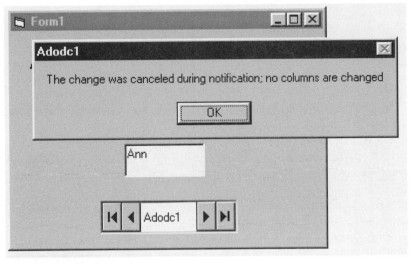

FIGURE 3.3   Canceling a field change.

source (the DAO and RDO data controls include an UpdateControls method to update the data in bound controls without refreshing the recordset, but the ADO data control does not support that method yet):

```
Private Sub Adodc1_WillChangeField(ByVal cFields As
Long, Fields As Variant, adStatus As
ADODB.EventStatusEnum, ByVal pRecordset As
ADODB.Recordset)
    adStatus = adStatusCancel
    Adodc1.Refresh
End Sub
```

WillChangeRecord

This event fires when the ADO data control is about to change a record in the underlying data source, as when the user edits the data in a bound control and moves to a new record. You can review and cancel the change if you wish, performing data validation. Here is what the event handler looks like for this event:

```
Private Sub Adodc1_WillChangeRecord(ByVal adReason
As ADODB.EventReasonEnum, ByVal cRecords As Long,
```

```
adStatus As ADODB.EventStatusEnum, ByVal pRecordset
As ADODB.Recordset)

End Sub
```

Here are the parameters passed to this event's handler:

- **adReason**—The reason this event occurred.
- **cRecords**—The number of records that will change.
- **adStatus**—The current status value.
- **pRecordset**—The Recordset object for which this event occurred.

Here's an example in which the code asks the user if he really want to update a record when it's about to be changed. If the user answers no, the change is canceled. Note that as before, I also use the ADO data control's Refresh method here to refresh the data in the bound controls to its original state—otherwise, the user wouldn't be able to move away from the current record, because the data in that record has been edited, and the code would keep asking him if they really want to update:

```
Private Sub Adodc1_WillChangeRecord(ByVal adReason
As ADODB.EventReasonEnum, ByVal cRecords As Long,
adStatus As ADODB.EventStatusEnum, ByVal pRecordset
As ADODB.Recordset)
    If adStatus <> adCantDeny Then
        If MsgBox("Do you really want to update?" _
            , vbYesNo) = vbNo Then
            adStatus = adStatusCancel
            Adodc1.Refresh
        End If
    End If
End Sub
```

Note that the RecordChangeComplete event fires after a change to a record is complete.

WillChangeRecordset

The WillChangeRecordset event fires before changes are written to a recordset, and you can use this event to validate data entered by the user before committing those changes to the data source. Here is what the event handler looks like for this event:

```
Private Sub Adodc1_WillChangeRecordset(ByVal
adReason As ADODB.EventReasonEnum, adStatus As
ADODB.EventStatusEnum, ByVal pRecordset As
ADODB.Recordset)


End Sub
```

Here are the parameters passed to this event's handler:

- **adReason**—The reason this event occurred.
- **adStatus**—The current status value.
- **pRecordset**—The Recordset object for which this event occurred.

Note that the RecordsetChangeComplete event fires after the change to the recordset is complete.

WillMove

This event fires before the ADO data control moves to a new record. Here is what the event handler looks like for this event:

```
Private Sub Adodc1_WillMove(ByVal adReason As
ADODB.EventReasonEnum, adStatus As
ADODB.EventStatusEnum, ByVal pRecordset As
ADODB.Recordset)


End Sub
```

Here are the parameters passed to this event's handler:

- **adReason**—The reason this event occurred.
- **adStatus**—The current status value.
- **pRecordset**—The Recordset object for which this event occurred.

This event can be useful if, for example, you want the user to do something with the current record before moving on to a new one. After a successful move, the MoveComplete event fires.

That finishes our look at the ADO data control's properties, methods, and events. It's time to put this control to work.

Using the ADO Data Control

I'll put the ADO data control to work now, in all its glory. I'll connect the control to a text box, displaying data from the `Customers` table in the `Nwind` database that comes with Visual Basic. This whole process starts by adding the control to a form.

Adding an ADO Data Control to a Form

Create a new standard EXE project now in Visual Basic. To add an ADO data control to the default form, `Form1`, in the project, start by selecting the `Components` item in the Visual Basic `Project` menu, opening the `Components` dialog you see in Figure 3.4. Select the `Microsoft ADO Data Control 6.0 (OLE DB)` box in this dialog, as also shown in Figure 3.4, then click `OK`.

    This adds the ADO data control tool to the toolbox, as shown in Figure 3.5, where you see that its tooltip is `Adodc`. Double-click that tool now to

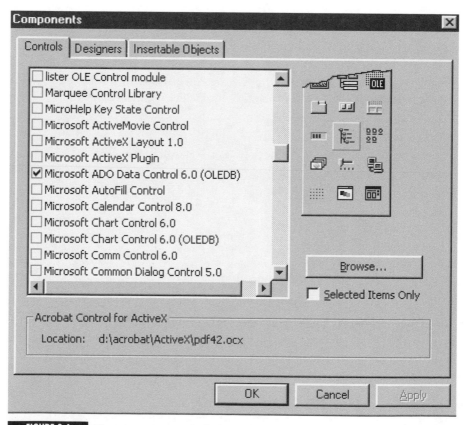

FIGURE 3.4   The `Components` dialog.

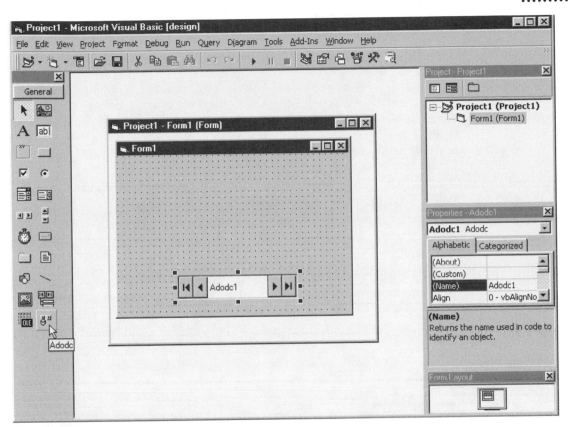

FIGURE 3.5   Adding an ADO data control to a form.

add an ADO data control to the form, and use the mouse to size and move it as shown in the figure.

Now change the `Caption` property of the ADO data control to `Customers` in the `Properties` window to reflect the fact that we're using it with the `Customers` table in the `Nwind` database.

The next step is to connect the ADO data control to a data source.

Connecting an ADO Data Control to a Data Source

You can connect an ADO data control to a data source at design-time or run-time; I'll take a look at working with the control at design-time first.

To connect an ADO data control to a database, you typically use the `ConnectionString` property to specify a database and provider, and set the `RecordSource` property to specify the record source, such as the table you want to use or an SQL statement that creates a recordset. The three properties you should set at a minimum to establish a connection are: `Connection-`

String, RecordSource, and CommandType (you can set the CommandType
property when you click the ellipsis button next to the RecordSource property's entry in the Properties window; note that not all OLE DB providers
require you to set this property).

Here's how the process of connecting an ADO data control goes; first,
click the ConnectionString property for the ADO data control, Adodc1, in
the Properties window, then click the ellipsis button that appears (you can
type a connection string directly into the Properties window, but I'll build
a connection string here). This opens the ADO data control's Property
Pages to the General tab, as you see in Figure 3.6.

As you can see in this figure, there are three ways to connect to a data
source using the ADO data control:

- If you've created a data link file with the extension .udl, click the Use
  Data Link File button and browse to the data link file you want to
  use.

- To connect to a registered ODBC data source (see Chapter 1 for more
  information), click the button labeled Use ODBC Data Source Name
  and enter the ODBC's DSN in the text box.

- To use a connection string, click the button marked Use Connection
  String and enter the connection string in the corresponding text box.
  To build a connection string, click the Build button.

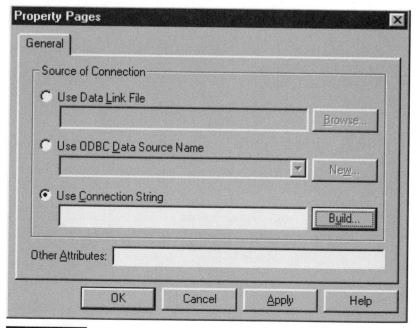

FIGURE 3.6   The ADO data control's Property Pages General tab.

In this case, I'll build a connection string, so I click the Build button, opening the Data Link Properties dialog to the Provider tab, as you see in Figure 3.7.

Here, you select the OLE DB provider to use with the ADO data control. In this case, I'll use the Microsoft Jet 4.0 OLE DB Provider. Click the Next button to move to the Connection tab in the Data Link Properties dialog, as shown in Figure 3.8.

In this property page, you select a database to connect to and specify your password and user name, if applicable. Click the ellipsis button to browse to the database you want to use; in this case, I'll use Nwind.mdb. You can also include a network path, if applicable.

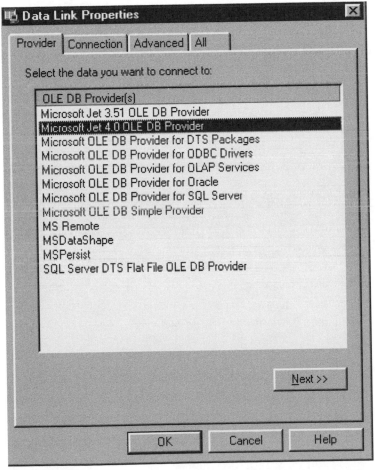

FIGURE 3.7   The Data Link Properties dialog, Provider tab.

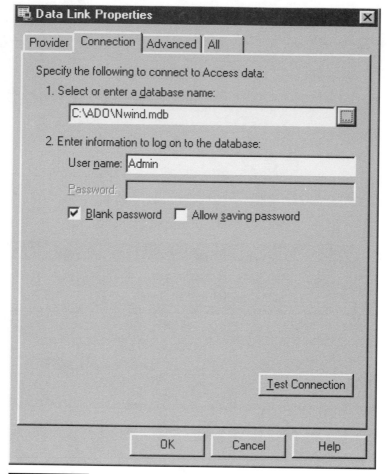

FIGURE 3.8   The Data Link Properties dialog, Connection tab.

Note that the Connection page's appearance will vary by OLE DB provider; for example, the Connection page for SQL Server 7 appears in Figure 3.9. There, you don't browse to a database name; instead, you select a database already registered on a server.

The Connection page for Oracle databases appears in Figure 3.10.

Even though they vary in appearance by provider, all Connection pages have one thing in common—the Test Connection button you see at the lower right. After you've specified all that the ADO data control needs to connect to a database, click the Test Connection button, and if the connection works, you'll see a message box showing the message Test connection succeeded. If there was an error, you'll get a description of what went wrong.

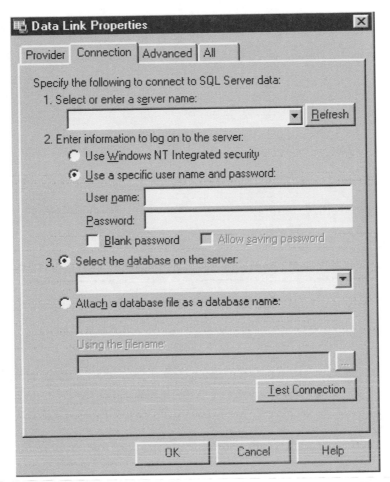

FIGURE 3.9 The Data Link Properties dialog, Connection tab for SQL Server.

You can work with additional properties of the connection in the Advanced property page of the Data Link Properties dialog. If you're using the MS Jet OLE DB provider and click the Advanced tab in the Data Link Properties dialog, you'll see something like Figure 3.11. Here you can set access to the database for other users, as you see in that figure. Note that since the capabilities of various OLE DB providers are very different for each provider, what you'll see on this page will also vary by provider.

Now click OK in the Data Link Properties dialog and then click OK in the ADO data control's Property Pages to close those pages. You've set the ADO data control's connection to a database—next, you have to indicate how to get records from that database.

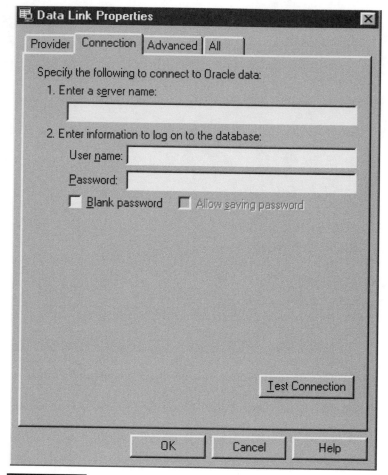

FIGURE 3.10 The Data Link Properties dialog, Connection tab for Oracle.

Setting the Record Source

To set the way you want to extract records from the record source, click the ellipsis button that appears when you click the RecordSource property in the Properties window for the ADO data control, opening the ADO data control's Property Pages to the RecordSource page, as shown in Figure 3.12.

To extract records from the data source, you create a command. You can use several types of commands here, as you see by clicking the arrow box in the Command Type drop-down list box. The possibilities are:

■ **adCmdUnknown**—(default) Lets the OLE DB provider interpret the record source type.

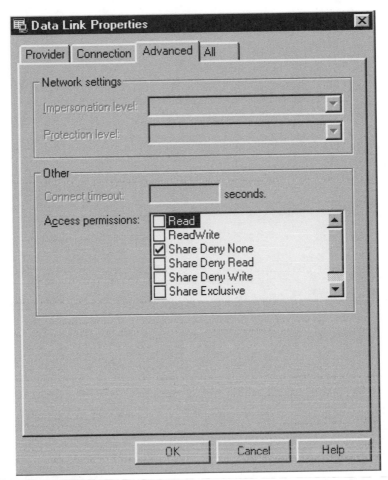

FIGURE 3.11   The Data Link Properties dialog, Advanced tab for Microsoft Jet.

- **adCmdText**—Lets you specify an SQL statement in the Command Text (SQL) text box.
- **adCmdTable**—Lets you specify a table in the Table or Stored Procedure drop-down list box.
- **adCmdStoredProc**—Lets you specify a stored procedure in the Table or Stored Procedure drop-down list box.

In this case, I'll select adCmdTable and specify the Customers table in the Table or Stored Procedure drop-down list box, but I could also have selected adCmdText and entered an SQL statement like this in the Command Text (SQL) text box:

```
SELECT * From Customers
```

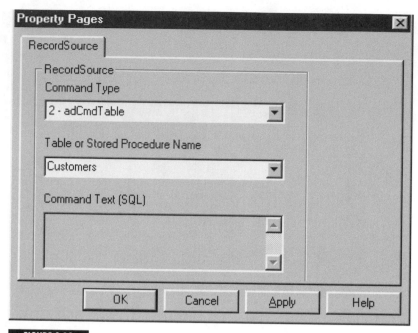

The ADO data control's `Property Pages`, `RecordSource` page.

After selecting `Customers` in the `Table or Stored Procedure` drop-down list box, I click `OK` to close the ADO data control's `Property Pages`. That's it—the ADO data control will connect to the data source automatically when the program starts. However, to actually see any data from the database, you have to connect the ADO data control to data-bound controls. I'll take a look at that in detail in the next chapter, but will give a quick overview of the process here.

Binding to Text Boxes

I'll start taking a look at binding controls to an ADO data control by binding the control to a text box. To do that, I add a new text box to the ADO data control project developed in the previous topic, as shown in Figure 3.13. I'll bind this text box to the `City` field of the `Nwind Customer` table. I'll also add a label with the caption `Customer City:` to label the text box, as shown in Figure 3.13.

To bind the text box to the ADO data control, use the drop-down list box that appears when you click the text box's `DataSource` property, and select the `Adodc1` control in the drop-down list.

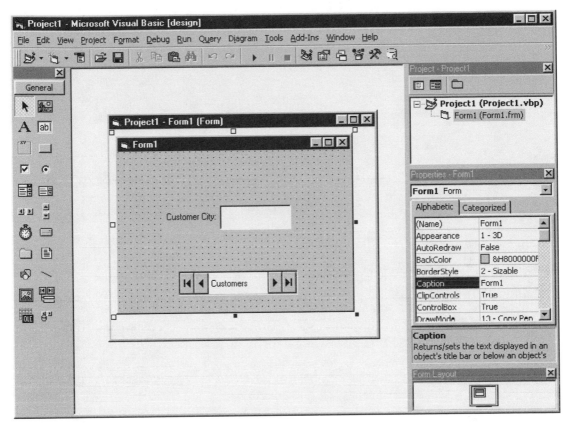

FIGURE 3.13   Adding a text box to the ADO data control project.

After you've set the text box's DataSource property, you can set the data field that will be displayed in the text box by clicking the drop-down list in the DataField property. Doing so lists all the available fields in the Customers table, as shown in Figure 3.14; select the City field now.

That's all it takes—you've bound the text box to the ADO data control. When you run the program, you can see the various cities in the Customers table in the bound text box, as shown in Figure 3.15. When you click the buttons in the ADO data control, you can navigate through the Customers table, and if you edit the data in the text field and move to a new record, the new data will be written to the underlying database.

The code for the main form in this project, Form1, appears in Listing 3.1.

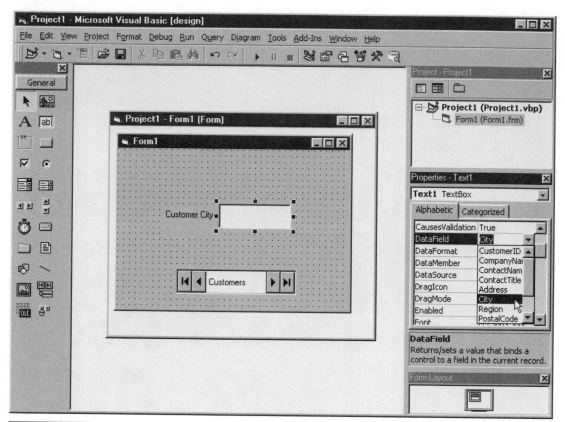

FIGURE 3.14 Selecting a field to display.

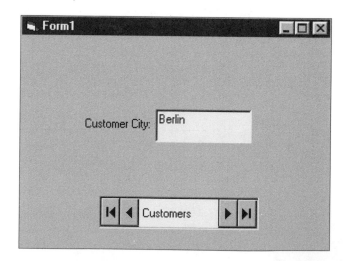

FIGURE 3.15 Binding a text box to an ADO data control.

LISTING 3.1 *Adocontrol.frm Code*

```
VERSION 5.00
Object = "{67397AA1-7FB1-11D0-B148-00A0C922E820}#6.0#0"; "MSADODC.OCX"
Begin VB.Form Form1
    Caption         =    "Form1"
    ClientHeight    =    3195
    ClientLeft      =    60
    ClientTop       =    345
    ClientWidth     =    4680
    LinkTopic       =    "Form1"
    ScaleHeight     =    3195
    ScaleWidth      =    4680
    StartUpPosition =    3    'Windows Default
    Begin VB.TextBox Text1
        DataField       =    "City"
        DataSource      =    "Adodc1"
        Height          =    495
        Left            =    2040
        TabIndex        =    0
        Top             =    1080
        Width           =    1455
    End
    Begin MSAdodcLib.Adodc Adodc1
        Height          =    495
        Left            =    1200
        Top             =    2400
        Width           =    2415
        _ExtentX        =    4260
        _ExtentY        =    873
        ConnectMode     =    0
        CursorLocation  =    3
        IsolationLevel  =    -1
        ConnectionTimeout=    15
        CommandTimeout  =    30
        CursorType      =    3
        LockType        =    3
        CommandType     =    2
        CursorOptions   =    0
        CacheSize       =    50
        MaxRecords      =    0
        BOFAction       =    0
        EOFAction       =    0
        ConnectStringType=    1
        Appearance      =    1
        BackColor       =    -2147483643
        ForeColor       =    -2147483640
        Orientation     =    0
        Enabled         =    -1
        Connect         =    "Provider=Microsoft.Jet.OLEDB.3.51Persist
```

```
Security Info=False;Data Source=C:\ADO\Nwind.mdb"
      OLEDBString       =   "Provider=Microsoft.Jet.OLEDB.3.51;Persist
Security Info=False;Data Source=C:\ADO\Nwind.mdb"
      OLEDBFile         =   ""
      DataSourceName    =   ""
      OtherAttributes   =   ""
      UserName          =   ""
      Password          =   ""
      RecordSource      =   "Customers"
      Caption           =   "Customers"
      BeginProperty Font
{0BE35203-8F91-11CE-9DE3-00AA004BB851}
         Name           =   "MS Sans Serif"
         Size           =   8.25
         Charset        =   0
         Weight         =   400
         Underline      =   0      'False
         Italic         =   0      'False
         Strikethrough  =   0      'False
      EndProperty
      _Version          =   393216
   End
   Begin VB.Label Label1
      Caption           =   "Customer City:"
      Height            =   495
      Left              =   960
      TabIndex          =   1
      Top               =   1200
      Width             =   1095
   End
End
Attribute VB_Name = "Form1"
Attribute VB_GlobalNameSpace = False
Attribute VB_Creatable = False
Attribute VB_PredeclaredId = True
Attribute VB_Exposed = False
```

Binding Controls from Code

Besides binding controls at design-time, you can also bind controls to an ADO data control at run-time. Here's an example; in this case, I'll connect the ADO data control in the previous example to the data source when the user clicks a button labeled `Connect`.

I add that button, `Command1`, to the project now and set the ADO data control's `ConnectionString`, `CommandType` (it's actually not necessary to set `CommandType` here, but it's a good idea with more complex OLE DB providers), and `RecordSource` properties when the button is clicked:

```
Private Sub Command1_Click()
    Adodc1.ConnectionString = _
"Provider=Microsoft.Jet.OLEDB.4.0;Persist " & _
"Security Info=False;Data Source=C:\ADO\Nwind.mdb"
    Adodc1.CommandType = adCmdTable
    Adodc1.RecordSource = "Customers"
        .
        .
        .
End Sub
```

Starting in Visual Basic 6.0, you can bind controls at run-time, not just at design-time, so I'll take advantage of that and bind the text box's Data-Source and DataField properties like this—note that the DataSource property holds an object, Adodc1, so I need to use the Set keyword here:

```
Private Sub Command1_Click()
    Adodc1.ConnectionString = _
"Provider=Microsoft.Jet.OLEDB.4.0;Persist " & _
"Security Info=False;Data Source=C:\ADO\Nwind.mdb"
    Adodc1.CommandType = adCmdTable
    Adodc1.RecordSource = "Customers"
```

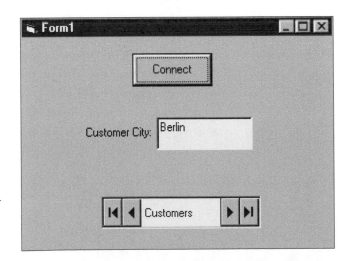

FIGURE 3.16 Binding a text box to an ADO data control from code.

```
Set Text1.DataSource = Adodc1
Text1.DataField = "City"
```
End Sub

And that's it—the results appear in Figure 3.16. When the user clicks the Connect button, the ADO data control connects to the data source and binds to the text box, as also shown in that figure. The project is a success.

Besides connecting an ADO data control in code, you can also access its Recordset object directly, and I'll take a look at that next.

Using the ADO Data Control's Recordset Object

You can access the Recordset object in an ADO data control with its Recordset property, giving direct control over the records in the control. Any changes you make to that recordset are reflected in the controls bound to the ADO data control, including navigating to new records.

We'll take a look at Recordset objects in detail in this book, but I'll take a look at them here in overview so we can put the Recordset object in the ADO data control to work. Here are the significant properties of the ADO Recordset object which is in the ADO data control:

- **AbsolutePage**—Page where the current record resides.
- **AbsolutePosition**—Position of a Recordset object's current record.
- **ActiveConnection**—Connection object the Recordset object belongs to.
- **BOF**—True if the current record position is before the first record.
- **Bookmark**—Unique identifier for the current record in a Recordset object.
- **CacheSize**—Number of records from a Recordset object that are cached locally in memory.
- **CursorLocation**—Location of the cursor.
- **CursorType**—Type of cursor used.
- **EditMode**—Indicates if editing is in progress.
- **EOF**—True if the current record position is after the last record.
- **Filter**—Filter for the data in the recordset.
- **LockType**—Type of locking used.
- **MarshalOption**—Specifies which records are to be marshaled back to the server.
- **MaxRecords**—Maximum number of records to return to a recordset from a query.

- **PageCount**—Number of pages of data the recordset contains.
- **PageSize**—Number of records that make up one page.
- **RecordCount**—Number of records in the recordset.
- **Sort**—One or more field names the recordset is sorted on.
- **Source**—Source for the data in the recordset; might be a `Command` object, SQL statement, table name, or stored procedure.
- **State**—State of the object, open or closed.
- **Status**—Status of the current record with respect to batch updates.

Note in particular the `AbsolutePosition` property, which holds the 1-based position of the current record. Here are the significant methods of the ADO `Recordset` object:

- **AddNew**—Adds a new record if the recordset is updateable.
- **Cancel**—Cancels execution of a pending `Execute` or `Open` method call.
- **CancelBatch**—Cancels a pending batch operation.
- **CancelUpdate**—Cancels a pending update.
- **Clone**—Creates a duplicate `Recordset` object.
- **Delete**—Deletes the current record or a group of records.
- **Move**—Moves the position of the current record.
- **MoveFirst, MoveLast, MoveNext, MovePrevious**—Navigate to various locations in the recordset.
- **NextRecordset**—Clears the current `Recordset` object and returns the next recordset by advancing through a series of commands.
- **Open**—Opens a cursor.
- **Requery**—Re-executes the query that created the recordset.
- **Resync**—Refreshes the data in the recordset.
- **Save**—Saves the recordset in a file.
- **Update**—Saves changes to the database.
- **UpdateBatch**—Performs a multiple-record update to the database.

I'll put these methods to work now in an example.

The example I'll create to use the methods of the ADO data control's `Recordset` object is called `adomethods`, and it appears in the folder of that name on the CD. You can see this application at work in Figure 3.17, where it's displaying the `Publisher` and `Address` fields of the `Publishers` table in the database file `Biblio.mdb`, which comes with Visual Basic. It uses an ADO data control, `Adodc1`, which is bound to the two text boxes.

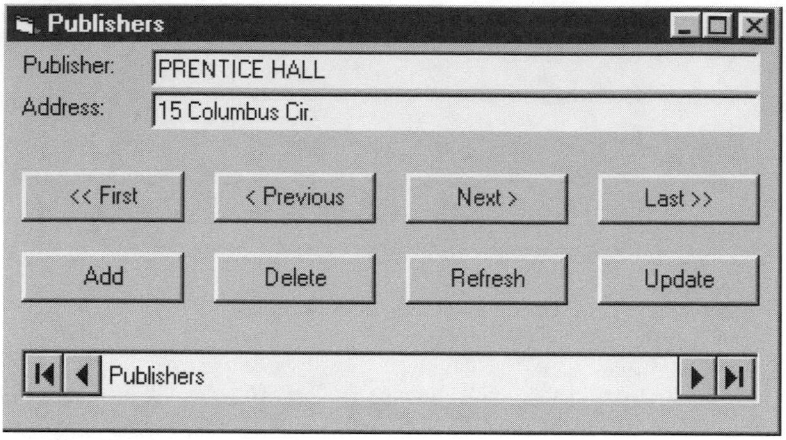

FIGURE 3.17 The adomethods project at work.

As you can see in that figure, you can use the buttons in the application to navigate through the Publishers table, as well as add, delete, refresh, and update records in that table.

The buttons in this application have names that match their function, such as cmdNext to move to the next record, cmdLast to move to the last record, and so on. To make those buttons active, we'll use the ADO data control's Recordset methods.

Moving to the Next Record

You move to the next record in a recordset with the Recordset object's MoveNext method, and I'll use that method to implement the cmdNext button in the adomethods project. First, I'll put error handling in place:

```
Private Sub cmdNext_Click()
    On Error GoTo ErrLabel
    .
    .
    .
```

Next we'll move to the next record—if we're not already at the end of the recordset, which you can test with the EOF property:

```
Private Sub cmdNext_Click()
    On Error GoTo ErrLabel
```

```
If Not Adodc1.Recordset.EOF Then
    Adodc1.Recordset.MoveNext
End If
```

.

.

.

If this leaves us at the end of the recordset, this code will move us back to the last record (note that the code also checks to make sure there *is* a last record with the RecordCount property):

```
Private Sub cmdNext_Click()
    On Error GoTo ErrLabel

    If Not Adodc1.Recordset.EOF Then
            Adodc1.Recordset.MoveNext
    End If
```

```
If Adodc1.Recordset.EOF And _
    Adodc1.Recordset.RecordCount > 0 Then
    Adodc1.Recordset.MoveLast
End If
```

.

.

.

All that's left is to add the error-handling code:

```
Private Sub cmdNext_Click()
    On Error GoTo ErrLabel

    If Not Adodc1.Recordset.EOF Then
        Adodc1.Recordset.MoveNext
    End If

    If Adodc1.Recordset.EOF And _
```

```
        Adodc1.Recordset.RecordCount > 0 Then
        Adodc1.Recordset.MoveLast
    End If
```

```
    Exit Sub
```

```
ErrLabel:
    MsgBox Err.Description
End Sub
```

And that's it—now the user can move to the next record in the recordset.

Moving to the Previous Record

Moving to the previous record is much like moving to the next record, except that you use the MovePrevious method and check if the user is trying to move to a location before the beginning of the recordset. That looks like this in code:

```
Private Sub cmdPrevious_Click()
    On Error GoTo ErrLabel

    If Not Adodc1.Recordset.BOF Then
        Adodc1.Recordset.MovePrevious
    End If

    If Adodc1.Recordset.BOF And _
        Adodc1.Recordset.RecordCount > 0 Then
        Adodc1.Recordset.MoveFirst
    End If

    Exit Sub

ErrLabel:
    MsgBox Err.Description
End Sub
```

Moving to the First Record

As you might expect, you use the MoveFirst method to move to the first record in the recordset. When the user clicks the First button in the adomethod application, the application moves to the first record this way:

```
Private Sub cmdFirst_Click()
    On Error GoTo ErrLabel

    If Adodc1.Recordset.RecordCount > 0 Then
        Adodc1.Recordset.MoveFirst
    End If

    Exit Sub


ErrLabel:
    MsgBox Err.Description
End Sub
```

Moving to the Last Record

As you've probably guessed, you use the MoveLast method to move to the last record in a recordset. When the user clicks the Last button in the adomethods application, you can move to the last record like this:

```
Private Sub cmdLast_Click()
    On Error GoTo ErrLabel

    If Adodc1.Recordset.RecordCount > 0 Then
        Adodc1.Recordset.MoveLast
    End If

    Exit Sub


ErrLabel:
    MsgBox Err.Description
End Sub
```

That completes the navigation techniques in the adomethod application. It's time to start working on modifying the underlying database itself now, beginning by adding new records.

Adding Records

To add a new record to a Recordset object, you can use the AddNew method. In the adomethods application, I'll let the user add a new record by clicking the Add button, cmdAdd.

When the user clicks that button, the code adds a new record to the end of the recordset with the AddNew method and clears the text in the two text boxes that hold the Publisher and Address fields:

```
Private Sub cmdAdd_Click()
    On Error GoTo ErrLabel

    Adodc1.Recordset.AddNew

    Text1.Text = ""
    Text2.Text = ""

    Exit Sub

ErrLabel:
    MsgBox Err.Description
End Sub
```

The new record becomes the current record, and the user can enter data into the new record's fields. When they click the Update button or move away from the record, the new data is sent to the underlying database automatically.

Deleting Records

You can use the Delete method to delete the current record in a recordset. In the adomethods application, the user does this by navigating to the record they want to delete and clicking the Delete button.

Here's how that button is implemented in code—note that after deleting a record, you should move to the next record so the user isn't left staring at a blank record (if you're already at the end of the recordset, you should move to the last record):

```
Private Sub cmdDelete_Click()
    On Error GoTo ErrLabel

    Adodc1.Recordset.Delete

    Adodc1.Recordset.MoveNext
    If Adodc1.Recordset.EOF Then
        Adodc1.Recordset.MoveLast
    End If

    Exit Sub

ErrLabel:
    MsgBox Err.Description
End Sub
```

Refreshing the ADO Data Control

If other users are working with the same database you are, at the same time, you might want to refresh your copy of that data from time to time. You can do this with the Requery method, which recreates the current recordset using the original query used to create it in the first place.

The user can refresh the recordset in the adomethods application by clicking the Refresh button. The code for that button looks like this:

```
Private Sub cmdRefresh_Click()

    On Error GoTo ErrLabel
        Adodc1.Recordset.Requery
    Exit Sub

ErrLabel:
    MsgBox Err.Description
End Sub
```

Updating a Database

After changing the fields in a record by editing or entering new text, the user can update a database with the UpdateRecord method of the ADO data control. (Note that the database is automatically updated if the user moves to a new record.)

When the user clicks the Update button in the adomethods application, you can update the database with the new record with this code:

```
Private Sub cmdUpdate_Click()
    On Error GoTo ErrLabel


    Adodc1.Recordset.Update


    Exit Sub


ErrLabel:
    MsgBox Err.Description
End Sub
```

That's all it takes. Now the user can add or delete records, update and refresh the database, and navigate through the records of the database—more than what's possible with just using the ADO data control by itself—all by using the buttons in the adomethods application. For reference, that application's code appears in Listing 3.2.

LISTING 3.2   *Adomethods.frm Code*

```
Private Sub cmdAdd_Click()
    On Error GoTo ErrLabel
    Adodc1.Recordset.AddNew

    Text1.Text = ""
    Text2.Text = ""

    Exit Sub

ErrLabel:
    MsgBox Err.Description
End Sub
```

```
Private Sub cmdDelete_Click()
    On Error GoTo ErrLabel

    Adodc1.Recordset.Delete

    Adodc1.Recordset.MoveNext

    If Adodc1.Recordset.EOF Then
        Adodc1.Recordset.MoveLast
    End If

    Exit Sub

ErrLabel:
    MsgBox Err.Description
End Sub

Private Sub cmdRefresh_Click()

    On Error GoTo ErrLabel
    Adodc1.Recordset.Requery
    Exit Sub

ErrLabel:
    MsgBox Err.Description
End Sub

Private Sub cmdUpdate_Click()
    On Error GoTo ErrLabel

    Adodc1.Recordset.Update

    Exit Sub

ErrLabel:
    MsgBox Err.Description
End Sub

Private Sub cmdFirst_Click()
    On Error GoTo ErrLabel

    If Adodc1.Recordset.RecordCount > 0 Then
        Adodc1.Recordset.MoveFirst
    End If

    Exit Sub

ErrLabel:
    MsgBox Err.Description
End Sub
```

```
Private Sub cmdLast_Click()
    On Error GoTo ErrLabel

    If Adodc1.Recordset.RecordCount > 0 Then
        Adodc1.Recordset.MoveLast
    End If

    Exit Sub

ErrLabel:
    MsgBox Err.Description
End Sub

Private Sub cmdNext_Click()
    On Error GoTo ErrLabel

    If Not Adodc1.Recordset.EOF Then
            Adodc1.Recordset.MoveNext
    End If

    If Adodc1.Recordset.EOF And _
Adodc1.Recordset.RecordCount > 0 Then
        Adodc1.Recordset.MoveLast
    End If

    Exit Sub

ErrLabel:
    MsgBox Err.Description
End Sub

Private Sub cmdPrevious_Click()
    On Error GoTo ErrLabel

    If Not Adodc1.Recordset.BOF Then
Adodc1.Recordset.MovePrevious
    If Adodc1.Recordset.BOF And _
Adodc1.Recordset.RecordCount > 0 Then
        Adodc1.Recordset.MoveFirst
    End If

    Exit Sub

ErrLabel:
    MsgBox Err.Description
End Sub

Private Sub cmdClose_Click()
    Unload Me
End Sub
```

Note that this simple example points out a useful technique—you can use the simple interface of the ADO data control to connect to and manage updates from bound controls to a data source, while keeping the control invisible by setting its `Visible` property to False. You can then customize the navigation actions the user takes through the recordset by providing your own navigation buttons, or by using code to automatically move to the next record after finishing with the current one.

In fact, you can use the ADO data control as a quick way of gaining access to ADO recordsets, using the ADO data control to set up the connection and provide access to a database object, while keeping the control itself invisible. This is a great time-saving technique that lets you avoid setting up the connection in code, but it comes at a significant cost—the ADO data control is a memory-heavy control, using many system resources.

That's it for the ADO data control itself. As you can see, this control is a powerful one, but it relies on you to use bound controls to create the actual user interface—and so the next chapter is going to be all about how to use the data-bound controls in Visual Basic.

Using
Data-Bound
Controls

This chapter is all about using data-bound controls in Visual Basic. In previous chapters, we looked at creating Data Environments and the ADO data control. In this chapter, we'll see how to use those objects as data sources for data-bound controls. Later in this chapter, we'll also see how to bind controls to databases in code without using either Data Environments or the ADO data control.

Being able to specify what controls you want to bind to a data source was an inspired addition to Visual Basic because you can use the standard Visual Basic controls to design your user interface, and there are additional controls that are specifically designed to be used as bound controls. Since you can choose what controls you use, rather than having to accept the defaults in some hypothetical database control, you can tailor your application to your database. For example, if each record in your database holds two text fields and an image, you can use two text boxes and a picture box to display that data, adding an ADO data control to let the user move through the database.

I'll start this chapter by taking a look at the data binding process in overview.

·················

Data Binding Overview

Data sources and bound controls have long been a popular pairing in Visual Basic. For example, you might display the titles and publishers of books from the `Biblio.mdb` database that comes with Visual Basic in text boxes that you have bound to those fields. Binding data from a database in bound controls makes that data visible and accessible to the user (behind the scenes, data binding is handled by the Visual Basic Data Binding Manager), so as you navigate through the database, the text boxes you have bound to those fields will be continually updated with the successive values of the book titles and publishers in `Biblio.mdb`. In this way, you can make your data visible to the user and, by selecting and configuring the controls you use, design exactly how that data is made visible.

Besides the standard Visual Basic controls, there is a set of controls expressly made to be data-bound, and there's an additional set to be used only with ADO.

Data-bound controls need an intermediary between them and the database (clearly, if each control had to handle the database connection itself, it would use a prohibitively large amount of memory). That intermediary is a data source. There are four standard data sources in ADO programming in Visual Basic:

- ADO data controls.
- Data Environments.
- ADO library objects.
- Data objects.

We'll see all of these data sources in this book; this chapter covers how to bind to data controls and Data Environments.

After you've set up your data source, such as a data control or Data Environment, you're ready to bind the data from that data source to bound controls, which will display the data in the fields of the underlying database.

Data Binding Properties

In Visual Basic, the data-bound controls use these properties to tie to a database through a data source:

- **DataSource**—Points to a data control or Data Environment.
- **DataField**—The field from the data control or Data Environment.
- **DataMember**—If you're using a Data Environment, this property holds the command in the Data Environment you want to use.
- **DataFormat**—Specifies the display format of fields (note that it's often not necessary to use this field).

The `DataSource`, `DataField`, and `DataMember` properties are all ones we've seen before, and we'll see them in more depth in this chapter. The `DataFormat` property lets you indicate to Visual Basic how it should interpret the data in a particular field. Here are the possible formats:

- General (no formatting).
- Number.
- Currency.
- Date.
- Time.
- Scientific.
- Boolean.
- Check box.
- Picture.
- Custom.

When you click the `DataFormat` property's entry in the `Properties` window, an ellipsis button appears, and clicking that button displays the control's `Property Pages`, set to the `Format` tab, as you see in Figure 4.1. If you wish, you can set the formatting Visual Basic will use for a specific field using this dialog.

Note that Visual Basic usually will be able to figure out what kind of data is in a field and display it, but that display may be quite plain. For example, the Currency type displays as a simple floating point number unless you format it; if you format it as a Currency data type, on the other hand, you can set the number of decimal places the value is displayed to, as well as a currency symbol, like $, to use in front of the number. The same goes for other formats, like Date and Time formats—data in these formats are displayed using default settings, which are quite plain, unless you format them specifically. When you format dates and times, there's quite a wide variety of formats you can choose from—66 formats for dates (from 06/09/00 to Wednesday, June 09, 2000) and 33 for times.

As we'll see, some controls add other properties to the above list, like the DataCombo control, which also supports the `RowSource`, `ListField`, `BoundText`, and `BoundColumn` properties.

In fact, some controls support properties complex enough to support data bindings themselves, like the `BoundText` property of the DataCombo control. Those properties are supported through the control's `DataBindings` property, which holds a `DataBindings` collection. Here are the controls that have a `DataBindings` property:

- Slider.
- TabStrip.

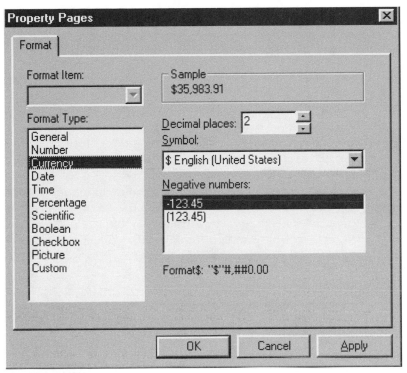

FIGURE 4.1   Setting a data binding format.

- Toolbar.
- DateTimePicker.
- MonthView.
- DataRepeater.
- DataCombo.
- DataList.
- DBCombo.
- DBList.
- Masked Edit.
- Multimedia.
- MCI.
- MSChart.
- MSFlexGrid.
- MSHFlexGrid.
- SSTab.

- RichTextBox.
- VBControlExtender object.
- Extender object.

You can use the DataBindings collection of the control at design- and run-time to bind to the properties in that collection. If you click the ellipsis button in the DataBindings entry in the Properties window for the control, the Data Bindings dialog box opens, showing the control's bindable properties that are available, and drop-down list boxes for the DataSource, DataField, DataMember, and DataFormat values, so that you can set those values for each bindable property.

For example, the Data Bindings dialog for a DataCombo control appears in Figure 4.2, and to set up the DataSource, DataField, Data-Member, and DataFormat values for the BoundText property of a Data-Combo control, you place values in the corresponding drop-down list boxes, as I'll do in an example in this chapter.

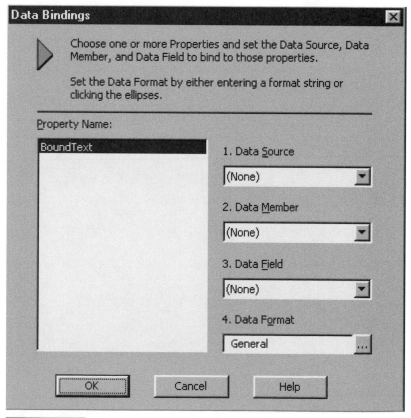

FIGURE 4.2   The Data Bindings dialog for a DataCombo control.

Besides binding properties at design-time, you can bind properties at run-time in code like this:

```
Set Text1.DataSource = adoRecordset
Text1.DataField = "Name"
Set Text2.DataSource = adoRecordset
Text2.DataField = "Address"
```

At the end of the chapter, I'll also take a look at how to use a control's DataBindings collection at run-time.

That sums up what's going on, then—to bind controls, you use the properties of both the data source and the bound control. There are many controls that may be bound in Visual Basic, and it's time to take a look at them in detail now.

Text Boxes, RichTextBoxes, Masked Edit Controls, and Labels

Controls like text boxes and labels that display text directly are among the most popular of bound controls, because they can display the text from an individual field of a table, which means you can tailor your application's data display field by field.

You can use the data in any of these controls to update a database (note that a label may not be changed directly by the user, of course, but you can change the contents of a label under programmatic control).

To use these controls, you just work with the DataSource and DataField properties and, optionally, the DataFormat property, as well as the DataMember property if you're using Data Environments. We've already seen examples of binding text boxes to data sources.

Check Boxes

You can bind check boxes to Boolean (True/False) fields in databases, and the check box will be checked or unchecked to match the value in that field. (Note that technically, check boxes actually have three states: checked, unchecked, and disabled.)

Check boxes have the standard data binding properties: DataSource, DataField, DataMember, and DataFormat. By default, the DataFormat property is set to Checkbox, which sets the check box properly when it's bound to a Boolean field.

Picture Boxes, Image Controls, and OLE Controls

Picture boxes, image controls, and OLE controls can view Binary Large Objects (BLOBs) from a database. You can use picture boxes and image controls only with the usual Visual Basic-acceptable graphic formats: `.bmp`, `.wmf`, `.gif.`, `.jpg`, `.ico`, and so on. OLE controls, on the other hand, can display actual OLE items stored in databases.

List Boxes and Combo Boxes

You can bind both standard list boxes and combo boxes to data sources, however, it's usually easier to use the data-handling equivalents of these controls, DBList and DBCombo, or the ADO equivalents, DataList and Data-Combo.

When you bind a list box or combo box to a data source, you specify the `DataSource` and `DataField` properties, and the field you've referenced appears in the text associated with the control. However, to populate the list part of the control, you have to do it yourself.

That's the advantage of using DBList, DBCombo, DataList, and Data-Combo controls: They populate the list part of the control automatically. For that reason, I'll stick to using the DBList, DBCombo, DataList, and Data-Combo controls for data binding here.

DateTimePickers and MonthViews

These two controls are some of the ActiveX controls that come with Visual Basic that are also data-bound. You use DateTimePickers to let the user select dates and times, and MonthViews present the user with a small calendar.

DataRepeaters

The DataRepeater control, new in Visual Basic 6.0, functions as a scrollable container of data-bound user controls. Each control appears in its own row as a "repeated" control, allowing the user to view several data-bound controls at once. For example, if you want to display all the authors in the `Biblio.mdb` database's `Authors` table, you can you display a set of rich text boxes, one for each record in the table, each displaying the value in the record's `Author` field.

You populate this control using the `RepeatedControlName` property, setting that property to a type of control that can accept ADO data bindings. You then set the `DataSource` of the DataRepeater to the name of the data source you want to use, which must be an ADO data control or Data Environment. You also set the `DataMember` property if you're binding to a Data Environment.

In the DataRepeater's `Property Pages`, you can click the `RepeaterBindings` tab, select a property of the repeated control you want to bind to, such as `TextRTF` in a rich text box or `BoundText` in a DataCombo, select the field in the data source you want to bind to by specifying the `DataField` property, and click the `Add` button. One bound control appears in the DataRepeater for each record in the database, giving you an easy way to see all the records at once. Note that the user can edit the data in each control, if the control allows editing, at run-time.

For example, I've bound the `Biblio.mdb` database's `Authors` table's `Author` field to rich text boxes in Figure 4.3.

Charts

You can bind the MSChart control to a data source, which is very handy, because you can then graph the data in a database directly. Note, however, that your data should be in numeric format.

In addition, there are special controls that are designed to be used as bound controls, and I'll take a look at them now.

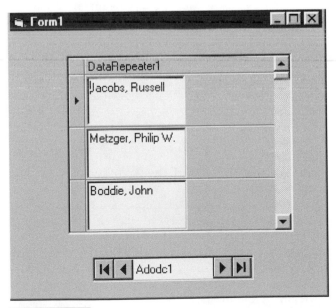

FIGURE 4.3   A DataRepeater control.

DBLists and DBCombos

The DBList and DBCombo controls are different from the list and combo controls because they automatically populate their lists—you don't have to use the `AddItem` method (in fact, they don't have one). You can also use DBList and DBCombo controls with relational databases.

Here are the special properties of these controls that support working with relational databases; only these and the DataList and DataCombo controls support these properties:

- **RowSource**—The data control used as a source for the list part of the control.
- **ListField**—Field in the recordset given by `RowSource` that supplies items for the list.
- **BoundColumn**—Field in the recordset given by `RowSource` that is passed back to the `DataField` once a selection is made.
- **BoundText**—Text in the `BoundColumn` field. When a selection is made, this value is passed back to update the recordset given by the `DataSource` and `DataField` properties.

You can search the DBCombo control by entering text into the text box of the control. That value is located in the list, and the current list item is set to that item if it is found. If the item is not found, the `BoundText` property is set to null. The DBList control also has an automated search mode.

Note, however, that you cannot use an ADO data source as the row source with the DBList and DBCombo controls, which means that you cannot automatically populate these controls from ADO data sources. To populate list and combo controls from an ADO data source like an ADO data control or Data Environment, use the DataList or DataCombo controls, which are coming up in a few pages.

Hierarchical FlexGrids

The Hierarchical FlexGrid (MSH FlexGrid) control is the successor to Visual Basic 5's FlexGrid control (which you can't use with the ADO data control or Data Environments). The Hierarchical FlexGrid control can only be used with ADO data sources and provides you with advanced features for displaying data in a grid. It's similar to the Microsoft data-bound grid (DataGrid) control, which is coming up in a few pages, but with the difference that the Hierarchical FlexGrid control does not allow the user to edit data bound to, or contained within, it.

What's hierarchical about the Hierarchical FlexGrid? It can handle hierarchical databases, which are databases in which a field can itself contain a whole new table. That is to say, Hierarchical FlexGrids can handle databases where tables have a parent-child relationship, as we'll see later in the book.

The user can drag columns around in a Hierarchical FlexGrid and re-arrange them just by dragging the column headers, as shown in Figure 4.4, where I'm using a Hierarchical FlexGrid to display the Visual Basic Nwind.mdb database. We'll see how to do this later in the chapter.

You can use the Col and Row properties to determine the number of columns and rows in an MSHFlexGrid. Here are some of the significant properties of Hierarchical FlexGrids:

- **Row**—The current row.
- **Col**—The current column.
- **Rows**—The total number of rows.
- **Cols**—The total number of columns.
- **Text**—The text in the cell at (Row, Col).

Hierarchical FlexGrids also have FixedCols and FixedRows properties, which specify the number of header columns and rows in the control.

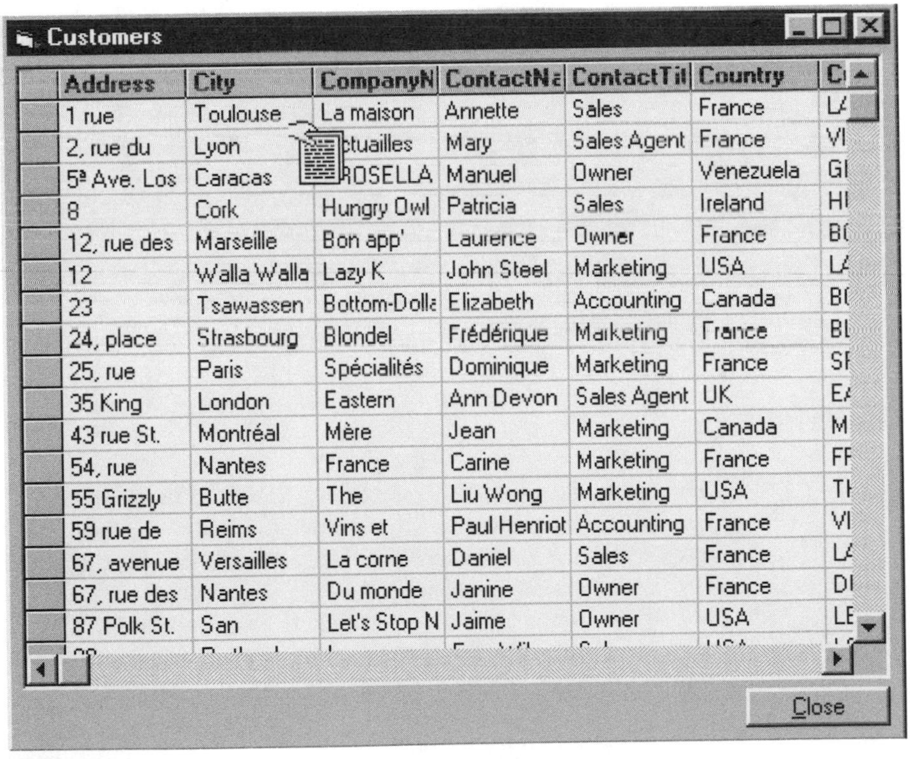

FIGURE 4.4 A Hierarchical Flexgrid Control.

These columns and rows are meant to label the other columns and rows, and they appear in gray by default (the other cells are white by default). Both `FixedCols` and `FixedRows` are set to 1 by default.

Hierarchical FlexGrids have a number of display options when bound to a hierarchy of recordsets. For example, you can display grouped and related recordsets, including arranging them into bands. You use the control's `Band` properties like `BandDisplay`, `BandIndent`, `BandExpandable`, and others to specify the style of the bands used.

We'll see how to use the Hierarchical FlexGrid with hieracrhical recordsets in Chapter 13.

There are three data-bound controls that are specially optimized for use with the ADO data control: DataGrid controls, DataCombo controls, and DataList controls (don't confuse these controls with the non-ADO, optimized, data-bound controls like the DBCombo and DBList controls). These controls are specifically designed to work with ADO data controls and won't work with standard controls like the data control. I'll take a brief look at them in overview now (a more detailed look is coming up in this chapter).

DataLists and DataCombos

You can use the DataList and DataCombo controls like the DBList and DBCombo controls, but these new controls are specifically optimized to work only with ADO data sources, such as the ADO data control or Data Environments.

Like the DBList and DBCombo controls, the DataList and DataCombo controls support the `RowSource`, `BoundColumn`, `BoundText`, and `ListField` properties that make it possible to work with relational databases, as we'll see later in this chapter. Unlike the DBList and DBCombo controls, however, the DataList and DataCombo controls automatically populate the list part of the control when used with ADO data sources, so I'll use the DataList and DataCombo controls with ADO data sources here.

DataGrids

The DataGrid control is much like a Hierarchical FlexGrid, except that you can write to it, it doesn't support hierarchical databases, and it's optimized for use with ADO. It's an OLE DB-aware form of the DBGrid control that shipped with Visual Basic 5.0.

This control has a `DataSource` property, but, because it displays whole tables, no `DataField` property. The cells in a DataGrid control can hold text values, but not linked or embedded objects. You can specify the current cell in code, or the user can select a cell using the mouse or arrow keys. You can edit the contents of a cell interactively, and you can select cells individually or by row.

Sometimes, the text in a cell can be too long to be displayed on one line, so the text will wrap to the next line. If the wrapped text is not visible, you can increase the Column object's Width property, or the DataGrid's RowHeight property.

The columns in a DataGrid are stored in the control's Columns collection, and you can find out how many columns there are with that collection's Count property (you can have up to 32767 columns). You can find out how many rows there are by checking the Recordset object's RecordCount property (there is no maximum number of rows).

The DataGrid uses the idea of a current cell to let you work with the cell that's selected, if any. When a cell is selected, the ColIndex property holds the column number of the selected cell. The Text and Value properties of the Column object refer to the contents of the current cell. In addition, note that the data in the entire current row can be accessed using the Bookmark property, which gives you access to the Recordset object's current record. We'll see an example of how to use this control later in this chapter.

That's it for the DataGrid control, and that's it for the overview of the bound controls; it's time to start putting them to work, connecting them to data sources.

Using Standard Data Binding

As you can see from the material I've already covered in this chapter, different controls can connect to data sources using different protocols in Visual Basic. Perhaps one day all Visual Basic controls will be able to use ADO data sources, but that day hasn't arrived yet—for example, although you can set the DataSource property of DBList and DBCombo controls to an ADO data source, you can't set those controls' RecordSource property to an ADO data source. On the other hand, Hierarchical FlexGrids can't be used with data sources other than ADO data sources like the ADO data control, so as you can see, it's quite a zoo.

Because so many controls don't support ADO data sources yet, you might find yourself binding to controls using DAO or RDO when you develop your own database applications. I'll take a quick look at an example binding the DAO data control to a database table here.

To create this example, I just add a DAO data control from the toolbox to a form, then set its DatabaseName property to the name of the database I'm using. In this case, I'll use the students table we put together earlier in this book, so I set the DatabaseName property to C:\ADO\db.mdb. Next, I set the DAO data control's RecordSource property to the students table.

After that, I'm free to bind controls to the DAO data control. Here I'll use the text box, combo box, label, DBList, DBCombo, and FlexGrid controls, setting the DataSource property to the DAO data control, Data1; the DataField property to Name; and the RowSource property to Data1 as well. The result appears in Figure 4.5.

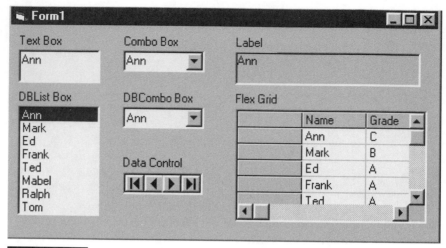

FIGURE 4.5   Binding controls in Visual Basic.

When the user clicks the navigation buttons in the DAO data control, he can move through the records in the `students` table, and the data in the bound controls is automatically updated to match. Note that this example would not have been possible using the ADO data control, because you can't set the `RowSource` property of DBList and DBCombo controls to an ADO data control, which means you can't populate the DBList and DBCombo controls with data from the `students` table (unlike standard list and combo controls, DBList and DBCombo controls don't have an `AddItem` method, because you usually just connect them to a data source). In addition, you can't use the Microsoft FlexGrid control with an ADO data source—you use a Hierarchical FlexGrid control instead.

The code for this example, `dbcontrols.frm`, appears in Listing 4.1. You'll find this example in the `dbcontrols` folder on the CD.

LISTING 4.1   *Dbcontrols.frm Code*

```
VERSION 5.00
Object = "{FAEEE763-117E-101B-8933-08002B2F4F5A}#1.1#0"; "DBLIST32.OCX"
Object = "{5E9E78A0-531B-11CF-91F6-C2863C385E30}#1.0#0"; "MSFLXGRD.OCX"
Begin VB.Form Form1
   Caption        =    "Form1"
   ClientHeight   =    3120
   ClientLeft     =    1350
   ClientTop      =    1530
   ClientWidth    =    6390
```

```
LinkTopic          =     "Form1"
PaletteMode        =     1    'UseZOrder
ScaleHeight        =     3120
ScaleWidth         =     6390
Begin MSFlexGridLib.MSFlexGrid MSFlexGrid1
   Bindings        =     "dbcontrols.frx":0000
   Height          =     1695
   Left            =     3360
   TabIndex        =     12
   Top             =     1200
   Width           =     2895
   _ExtentX        =     5106
   _ExtentY        =     2990
   _Version        =     393216
End
Begin VB.ComboBox Combo1
   DataField       =     "Name"
   DataSource      =     "Data1"
   Height          =     315
   Left            =     1680
   TabIndex        =     1
   Text            =     "Combo1"
   Top             =     360
   Width           =     1215
End
Begin VB.TextBox Text1
   DataField       =     "Name"
   DataSource      =     "Data1"
   Height          =     495
   Left            =     120
   TabIndex        =     0
   Text            =     "Text1"
   Top             =     360
   Width           =     1215
End
Begin VB.Data Data1
   Caption         =     "Data1"
   Connect         =     "Access"
   DatabaseName    =     "C:\ADO\db.mdb"
   DefaultCursorType=    0    'DefaultCursor
   DefaultType     =     2    'UseODBC
   Exclusive       =     0    'False
   Height          =     300
   Left            =     1680
   Options         =     0
   ReadOnly        =     0    'False
   RecordsetType   =     1    'Dynaset
   RecordSource    =     "students"
   Top             =     2160
   Width           =     1215
End
```

```
Begin MSDBCtls.DBCombo DBCombo1
    Bindings        =       "dbcontrols.frx":0014
    DataField       =       "Name"
    DataSource      =       "Data1"
    Height          =       315
    Left            =       1680
    TabIndex        =       4
    Top             =       1200
    Width           =       1215
    _ExtentX        =       2143
    _ExtentY        =       556
    _Version        =       393216
    ForeColor       =       0
    ListField       =       "Name"
    BoundColumn     =       "Name"
    Text            =       "DBCombo1"
End
Begin MSDBCtls.DBList DBList1
    Bindings        =       "dbcontrols.frx":0028
    DataField       =       "Name"
    DataSource      =       "Data1"
    Height          =       1620
    Left            =       120
    TabIndex        =       3
    Top             =       1200
    Width           =       1215
    _ExtentX        =       2143
    _ExtentY        =       2858
    _Version        =       393216
    BackColor       =       -2147483643
    ForeColor       =       -2147483640
    ListField       =       "Name"
    BoundColumn     =       "Name"
End
Begin VB.Label Label8
    Caption         =       "Data Control"
    Height          =       255
    Left            =       1680
    TabIndex        =       11
    Top             =       1920
    Width           =       1215
End
Begin VB.Label Label7
    Caption         =       "Flex Grid"
    Height          =       255
    Left            =       3360
    TabIndex        =       10
    Top             =       960
    Width           =       1215
End
Begin VB.Label Label6
```

```
      Caption         =     "DBCombo Box"
      Height          =     255
      Left            =     1680
      TabIndex        =     9
      Top             =     960
      Width           =     1215
   End
   Begin VB.Label Label5
      Caption         =     "DBList Box"
      Height          =     255
      Left            =     120
      TabIndex        =     8
      Top             =     960
      Width           =     1095
   End
   Begin VB.Label Label4
      Caption         =     "Label"
      Height          =     255
      Left            =     3360
      TabIndex        =     7
      Top             =     120
      Width           =     615
   End
   Begin VB.Label Label3
      Caption         =     "Combo Box"
      Height          =     255
      Left            =     1680
      TabIndex        =     6
      Top             =     120
      Width           =     1215
   End
   Begin VB.Label Label2
      Caption         =     "Text Box"
      Height          =     255
      Left            =     120
      TabIndex        =     5
      Top             =     120
      Width           =     1215
   End
   Begin VB.Label Label1
      BorderStyle     =     1    'Fixed Single
      Caption         =     "Label1"
      DataField       =     "Name"
      DataSource      =     "Data1"
      Height          =     495
      Left            =     3360
      TabIndex        =     2
      Top             =     360
      Width           =     2775
   End
End
```

....

```
Attribute VB_Name = "Form1"
Attribute VB_GlobalNameSpace = False
Attribute VB_Creatable = False
Attribute VB_PredeclaredId = True
Attribute VB_Exposed = False
```

Although I didn't include standard list or combo boxes in this example, I could have. In that case, I'd have to populate the list part of those controls myself in code, and I could do that with code like this—this example illustrates some of the kind of code we'll see in Chapter 8 when working directly with recordsets; it uses the DAO data control:

```
Private Sub Form_Load()

    Adodc1.Recordset.MoveFirst

    For loop_index = 1 To _
        Adodc1.Recordset.RecordCount
        StudentName = _
            Adodc1.Recordset.Fields(0).Value
        List1.AddItem StudentName
        Adodc1.Recordset.MoveNext
    Next loop_index

End Sub
```

Now it's time to take a look at some of the controls specifically designed to be used with ADO.

Using ADO Data Binding

Although you can bind most controls to ADO data sources, there are three controls that are specially designed to work only with ADO data sources: the DataList, DataCombo, and DataGrid controls.

I'll create an example here using these controls. To do that, I just create a new standard EXE project and add an ADO data control to the default form in the project, Form1. I connect the ADO data control to the same database I used in the previous example—the db.mdb database—and set the ADO data control's RecordSource property to the students table.

Now I'm ready for the DataList, DataCombo, and DataGrid controls, and to use these controls, I select the Components item in the Project menu,

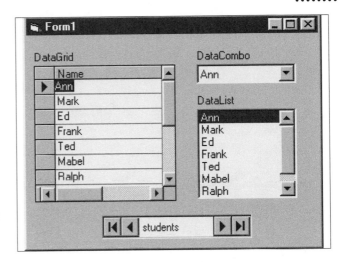

FIGURE 4.6 Binding the DataList, DataCombo, and DataGrid controls to an ADO data source.

opening the Components dialog. In that dialog, I select the Microsoft DataList controls (which include the DataList and DataCombo controls) and the Microsoft DataGrid control, and click OK. Then I add those controls to Form1 and set their DataSource property to Adodc1, their DataField property to Name, and their RecordSource property to Adodc1.

That's all it takes; the result appears in Figure 4.6, and you can see the data from the Name field of the students table displayed there. The user can move through the records in the students table, and the bound controls are updated to match. This program is a success; we'll be using these controls in more depth in a few pages.

The code for this example, dbcontrols2.frm, appears in Listing 4.2. You'll find this example in the dbcontrols2 folder on the CD.

LISTING 4.2 *Dbcontrols2.frm Code*

```
VERSION 5.00
Object =
"{CDE57A40-8B86-11D0-B3C6-00A0C90AEA82}#1.0#0";
"MSDATGRD.OCX"
Object =
"{67397AA1-7FB1-11D0-B148-00A0C922E820}#6.0#0";
"MSADODC.OCX"
Object =
"{F0D2F211-CCB0-11D0-A316-00AA00688B10}#1.0#0";
"MSDATLST.OCX"
Begin VB.Form Form1
   Caption         =   "Form1"
   ClientHeight    =   3375
   ClientLeft      =   60
   ClientTop       =   345
```

```
ClientWidth        =    4680
LinkTopic          =    "Form1"
ScaleHeight        =    3375
ScaleWidth         =    4680
StartUpPosition =       3   'Windows Default
Begin MSDataListLib.DataList DataList1
   Bindings        =    "dbcontrols2.frx":0000
   DataField       =    "Name"
   DataSource      =    "Adodc1"
   Height          =    1425
   Left            =    2760
   TabIndex        =    2
   Top             =    1200
   Width           =    1575
   _ExtentX        =    2778
   _ExtentY        =    2514
   _Version        =    393216
   ListField       =    "Name"
End
Begin MSDataListLib.DataCombo DataCombo1
   Bindings        =    "dbcontrols2.frx":0015
   DataField       =    "Name"
   DataSource      =    "Adodc1"
   Height          =    315
   Left            =    2760
   TabIndex        =    1
   Top             =    480
   Width           =    1575
   _ExtentX        =    2778
   _ExtentY        =    556
   _Version        =    393216
   ListField       =    "Name"
   BoundColumn     =    "Name"
   Text            =    "DataCombo1"
End
Begin MSDataGridLib.DataGrid DataGrid1
   Bindings        =    "dbcontrols2.frx":002A
   Height          =    2175
   Left            =    120
   TabIndex        =    0
   Top             =    480
   Width           =    2295
   _ExtentX        =    4048
   _ExtentY        =    3836
   _Version        =    393216
   HeadLines       =    1
   RowHeight       =    15
   BeginProperty HeadFont
{0BE35203-8F91-11CE-9DE3-00AA004BB851}
      Name         =    "MS Sans Serif"
      Size         =    8.25
      Charset      =    0
```

```
        Weight             =    400
        Underline          =    0    'False
        Italic             =    0    'False
        Strikethrough      =    0    'False
     EndProperty
     BeginProperty Font
{0BE35203-8F91-11CE-9DE3-00AA004BB851}
        Name               =    "MS Sans Serif"
        Size               =    8.25
        Charset            =    0
        Weight             =    400
        Underline          =    0    'False
        Italic             =    0    'False
        Strikethrough      =    0    'False
     EndProperty
     ColumnCount        =    2
     BeginProperty Column00
        DataField          =    ""
        Caption            =    ""
        BeginProperty DataFormat
{6D835690-900B-11D0-9484-00A0C91110ED}
           Type               =    0
           Format             =    ""
           HaveTrueFalseNull=    0
           FirstDayOfWeek  =    0
           FirstWeekOfYear =    0
           LCID               =    1033
           SubFormatType   =    0
        EndProperty
     EndProperty
     BeginProperty Column01
        DataField          =    ""
        Caption            =    ""
        BeginProperty DataFormat
{6D835690-900B-11D0-9484-00A0C91110ED}
           Type               =    0
           Format             =    ""
           HaveTrueFalseNull=    0
           FirstDayOfWeek  =    0
           FirstWeekOfYear =    0
           LCID               =    1033
           SubFormatType   =    0
        EndProperty
     EndProperty
     SplitCount         =    1
     BeginProperty Split0
        BeginProperty Column00
        EndProperty
        BeginProperty Column01
        EndProperty
     EndProperty
  End
```

....

```
    Begin MSAdodcLib.Adodc Adodc1
       Height            =   375
       Left              =   1200
       Top               =   2880
       Width             =   2415
       _ExtentX          =   4260
       _ExtentY          =   661
       ConnectMode       =   0
       CursorLocation    =   3
       IsolationLevel    =   -1
       ConnectionTimeout=   15
       CommandTimeout    =   30
       CursorType        =   3
       LockType          =   3
       CommandType       =   2
       CursorOptions     =   0
       CacheSize         =   50
       MaxRecords        =   0
       BOFAction         =   0
       EOFAction         =   0
       ConnectStringType=   1
       Appearance        =   1
       BackColor         =   -2147483643
       ForeColor         =   -2147483640
       Orientation       =   0
       Enabled           =   -1
       Connect           =   "Provider=Microsoft.Jet.OLEDB.3.51;Persist
    Security
Info=False;Data Source=C:\ADO\db.mdb"
       OLEDBString       =
"Provider=Microsoft.Jet.OLEDB.3.51;Persist Security
Info=False;Data Source=C:\ADO\db.mdb"
       OLEDBFile         =   ""
       DataSourceName    =   ""
       OtherAttributes   =   ""
       UserName          =   ""
       Password          =   ""
       RecordSource      =   "students"
       Caption           =   "students"
       BeginProperty Font
{0BE35203-8F91-11CE-9DE3-00AA004BB851}
          Name           =   "MS Sans Serif"
          Size           =   8.25
          Charset        =   0
          Weight         =   400
          Underline      =   0        'False
          Italic         =   0        'False
          Strikethrough  =   0        'False
       EndProperty
       _Version          =   393216
    End
    Begin VB.Label Label3
```

```
        Caption         =    "DataList"
        Height          =    255
        Left            =    2760
        TabIndex        =    5
        Top             =    960
        Width           =    1215
    End
    Begin VB.Label Label2
        Caption         =    "DataCombo"
        Height          =    255
        Left            =    2760
        TabIndex        =    4
        Top             =    240
        Width           =    1215
    End
    Begin VB.Label Label1
        Caption         =    "DataGrid"
        Height          =    255
        Left            =    120
        TabIndex        =    3
        Top             =    240
        Width           =    1215
    End
End
Attribute VB_Name = "Form1"
Attribute VB_GlobalNameSpace = False
Attribute VB_Creatable = False
Attribute VB_PredeclaredId = True
Attribute VB_Exposed = False
```

Note that we haven't really explored the DataCombo, DataList, and DataGrid controls very thoroughly yet; these controls can use additional properties to bind, such as BoundColumn and ListField. I'll take a look at these properties next.

Using the DataCombo Control

Imagine that you've been asked to use the Biblio.mdb database as the basis of a database application for a bookstore. The manager that uses this database wants to see both the book titles in the database and the phone numbers of the publishers so he can call and order the titles.

The only problem is that the book titles are stored in the Titles table in the Biblio.mdb database, but the publisher's phone numbers are not in that table—they're in the Publishers table. Sounds like you'll be doing a lot of coding to match the two up—unless you use a DataCombo or DataList control, which can work with relational databases. I'll look at the DataCombo control first and the DataList control next.

Like other bound controls, the DataCombo control has `DataSource` and `DataField` properties. I'll connect the `DataSource` to the primary database here, the `Titles` database; this way, when the manager moves through the `Titles` database, the DataCombo will be kept up-to-date.

Setting the `DataField` property takes a little more thought. In this case, we want to coordinate between the `Titles` and `Publishers` tables. These tables have one field in common that can act as a key: `PubID`. To get the phone number for a publisher that's printed a certain book, you get the `PubID` value from the book's record in the `Titles` table, use that to locate the record with the same `PubID` value in the `Publishers` table, and then retrieve the phone number from the new record in the `Publishers` table.

DataCombos are set up to handle just such operations. First, connect the DataCombo's `DataField` property to the key we'll need from the `Titles` table: `PubID` (i.e., just select `PubID` from the drop-down list that appears in the `DataField` property's entry in the `Properties` window).

Next, connect the `RowSource` property of the DataCombo to a new ADO data control that is connected to the `Publishers` table in the `Biblio.mdb` database. We need some way of indicating what key we want to use in the `Publishers` table, so set the `BoundColumn` property of the Data-Combo to the `PubID` field in the `Publishers` table (i.e., just select `PubID` from the drop-down list that appears in the `BoundColumn` property's entry in the `Properties` window).

n·o·t·e When the user makes a selection with a DataList or DataCombo control, the `BoundText` property contains the field value of the `BoundColumn` property.

Now the DataCombo indexes records in the `Publishers` table using the `PubID` value provided from the `Titles` table. We've set up the key connection now and so we can reference the correct record in the `Publishers` table—all that's left is to display the phone number from that record. You do that by setting the DataCombo's `ListField` property to the `Telephone` field in the `Publishers` table.

In this way, Microsoft has produced a bound control that works with relational databases. To make sure that the title of the book also appears in the application, add a text box to the form now and bind it to the `Title` field of the `Titles` table as represented by the ADO control bound to that table.

The result appears in Figure 4.7, where you can see the title of a book in the top text box and the phone number of the corresponding publisher below in the DataCombo (note that not all publishers listed in the `Nwind.mdb` database have phone numbers in that database; you might have to click the right arrow button in the ADO control a few times before you see a phone number appear).

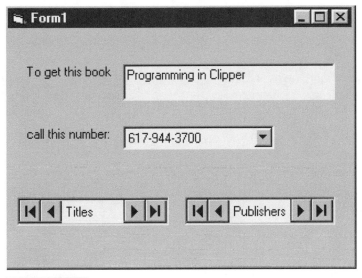

FIGURE 4.7   Using a DataCombo control with a relational database.

To keep things straight, here are the various property settings for the controls in this project, starting with the first ADO control, `Adodc1`:

- **ConnectionString**—Points to `Nwind.mdb`.
- **RecordSource**—`Titles` table.

Here's the second ADO control, `Adodc2`:

- **ConnectionString**—Points to `Nwind.mdb`.
- **RecordSource**—`Publishers` table.

The DataCombo control, `DataCombo1`, is connected like this:

- **DataSource**—`Adodc1`.
- **DataField**—`PubID`.
- **RowSource**—`Adodc2`.
- **BoundColumn**—`PubID`.
- **ListField**—`Telephone`.

The text box, `Text1`, has these bindings:

- **DataSource**—`Adodc1`.
- **DataField**—`Title`.

This project appears on the CD in the `datcombo` folder, and the code for this example, `datcombo.frm`, appears in Listing 4.3.

....

LISTING 4.3   *Datcombo.frm Code*

```
VERSION 5.00
Object = "{67397AA1-7FB1-11D0-B148-00A0C922E820}#6.0#0";  "MSADODC.OCX"
Object = "{F0D2F211-CCB0-11D0-A316-00AA00688B10}#1.0#0";  "MSDATLST.OCX"
Begin VB.Form Form1
   Caption          =    "Form1"
   ClientHeight     =    3195
   ClientLeft       =    60
   ClientTop        =    345
   ClientWidth      =    4680
   LinkTopic        =    "Form1"
   ScaleHeight      =    3195
   ScaleWidth       =    4680
   StartUpPosition  =    3    'Windows Default
   Begin MSDataListLib.DataCombo DataCombo1
      Bindings       =    "datcombo.frx":0000
      DataField      =    "PubID"
      DataSource     =    "Adodc1"
      Height         =    315
      Left           =    1560
      TabIndex       =    1
      Top            =    1320
      Width          =    2055
      _ExtentX       =    3625
      _ExtentY       =    556
      _Version       =    393216
      ListField      =    "Telephone"
      BoundColumn    =    "PubID"
      Text           =    "DataCombo1"
   End
   Begin MSAdodcLib.Adodc Adodc2
      Height         =    375
      Left           =    2400
      Top            =    2280
      Width          =    2055
      _ExtentX       =    3625
      _ExtentY       =    661
      ConnectMode    =    0
      CursorLocation =    3
      IsolationLevel =    -1
      ConnectionTimeout=   15
      CommandTimeout =    30
      CursorType     =    3
      LockType       =    3
      CommandType    =    2
      CursorOptions  =    0
      CacheSize      =    50
      MaxRecords     =    0
      BOFAction      =    0
```

```
        EOFAction        =    0
        ConnectStringType=    1
        Appearance       =    1
        BackColor        =    -2147483643
        ForeColor        =    -2147483640
        Orientation      =    0
        Enabled          =    -1
        Connect          =
"Provider=Microsoft.Jet.OLEDB.3.51;Persist Security Info=False;Data
    Source=C:\ADO\Biblio.mdb"
        OLEDBString      =
"Provider=Microsoft.Jet.OLEDB.3.51;Persist Security Info=False;Data
    Source=C:\ADO\Biblio.mdb"
        OLEDBFile        =    ""
        DataSourceName   =    ""
        OtherAttributes  =    ""
        UserName         =    ""
        Password         =    ""
        RecordSource     =    "Publishers"
        Caption          =    "Publishers"
        BeginProperty Font {0BE35203-8F91-11CE-9DE3-00AA004BB851}
            Name         =    "MS Sans Serif"
            Size         =    8.25
            Charset      =    0
            Weight       =    400
            Underline    =    0    'False
            Italic       =    0    'False
            Strikethrough =   0    'False
        EndProperty
        _Version         =    393216
    End
    Begin MSAdodcLib.Adodc Adodc1
        Height           =    375
        Left             =    120
        Top              =    2280
        Width            =    2055
        _ExtentX         =    3625
        _ExtentY         =    661
        ConnectMode      =    0
        CursorLocation   =    3
        IsolationLevel   =    -1
        ConnectionTimeout=    15
        CommandTimeout   =    30
        CursorType       =    3
        LockType         =    3
        CommandType      =    2
        CursorOptions    =    0
        CacheSize        =    50
        MaxRecords       =    0
        BOFAction        =    0
        EOFAction        =    0
        ConnectStringType=    1
```

```
        Appearance       =    1
        BackColor        =    -2147483643
        ForeColor        =    -2147483640
        Orientation      =    0
        Enabled          =    -1
        Connect          =
"Provider=Microsoft.Jet.OLEDB.3.51;Persist Security Info=False;Data
    Source=C:\ADO\Biblio.mdb"
        OLEDBString      =
"Provider=Microsoft.Jet.OLEDB.3.51;Persist Security Info=False;Data
    Source=C:\ADO\Biblio.mdb"
        OLEDBFile        =    ""
        DataSourceName   =    ""
        OtherAttributes  =    ""
        UserName         =    ""
        Password         =    ""
        RecordSource     =    "Titles"
        Caption          =    "Titles"
        BeginProperty Font {0BE35203-8F91-11CE-9DE3-00AA004BB851}
            Name         =    "MS Sans Serif"
            Size         =    8.25
            Charset      =    0
            Weight       =    400
            Underline    =    0     'False
            Italic       =    0     'False
            Strikethrough =   0     'False
        EndProperty
        _Version         =    393216
    End
    Begin VB.TextBox Text1
        DataField        =    "Title"
        DataSource       =    "Adodc1"
        Height           =    495
        Left             =    1560
        TabIndex         =    0
        Text             =    "Text1"
        Top              =    480
        Width            =    2895
    End
    Begin VB.Label Label2
        Caption          =    "call this number:"
        Height           =    375
        Left             =    240
        TabIndex         =    3
        Top              =    1320
        Width            =    1215
    End
    Begin VB.Label Label1
        Caption          =    "To get this book"
        Height           =    255
        Left             =    240
        TabIndex         =    2
        Top              =    480
```

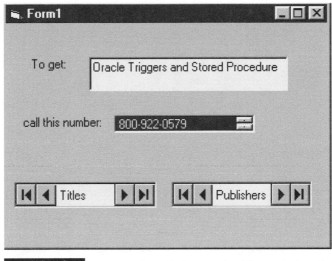

FIGURE 4.8 Using a DataList control with a relational database.

```
        Width               =       1215
    End
End
Attribute VB_Name = "Form1"
Attribute VB_GlobalNameSpace = False
Attribute VB_Creatable = False
Attribute VB_PredeclaredId = True
Attribute VB_Exposed = False
```

Besides using the DBCombo and DataCombo controls to handle relational databases, you can also use the DBList and DataList controls.

Using the DataList Control

You can create the same application that we created in the last topic using the DataList control instead of the DataCombo control. To do so, just recreate the project using a DataList instead of a DataCombo; the property settings are the same. The results appear in Figure 4.8.

This project is on the CD in the `datalist` folder.

The DataCombo and DataList controls are two of the new Visual Basic 6.0 data-bound controls designed expressly to work with ADO; the third such control is the DataGrid control, and that merits a look as well.

Using the DataGrid Control

The DataGrid control is a powerful one, letting you display and manipulate a database's table directly. Like other grid controls, data handling in DataGrid controls is based on the concept of the current cell, which is specified by the Row and Col properties. Unlike other grid controls, the DataGrid is especially optimized to work with ADO. You can also split the DataGrid's window into a number of panes, much like Microsoft Word, each of which is held in a Split object.

This control is a massive one, as you can see by this list of its significant properties (this control has far more properties, methods, and events than the ADO Recordset object itself):

- **RightToLeft**—Can be used to configure the display for Middle Eastern users.

- **Bookmark**—Returns or sets a bookmark for the specified row.

- **AddNewMode**—Describes the location of the current cell with respect to the grid's AddNew row.

- **AllowArrows**—Determines whether the control uses the arrow keys for grid navigation.

- **ApproxCount**—Approximate number of rows in the grid.

- **CurrentCellModified**—Modification status of the current cell.

- **CurrentCellVisible**—True if the current cell is visible.

- **EditActive**—Editing status of the current cell.

- **MarqueeStyle**—The marquee effect's style for the DataGrid control or Split object.

- **Split**—Index of the current split.

- **Splits**—Collection of Split objects.

- **TabAcrossSplits**—Behavior of the TAB and arrow keys at split borders.

- **WrapCellPointer**—If True, the cell pointer will move from one split to the next before wrapping occurs.

- **AllowAddNew**—Indicates whether the user can add new records to the Recordset object.

- **AllowDelete**—Indicates whether the user can delete records from the Recordset object.

- **AllowRowSizing**—Indicates if the user can resize rows at run-time.

- **AllowUpdate**—Indicates whether the user can modify data in the control.

- **ColumnHeaders**—Indicates whether column headers are displayed.

- **Columns**—Collection of Column objects.

- **DataChanged**—Indicates that the data in the control has been changed by some process other than that of retrieving data from the current record.

- **DefColWidth**—Default column width.

- **FirstRow**—Value containing the bookmark for the first visible row.
- **HeadLines**—Number of lines of text displayed in the column headers.
- **LeftCol**—Integer representing the leftmost visible column of the control.
- **RecordSelectors**—Indicates if record selectors are displayed in the DataGrid control or Split object.
- **RowDividerStyle**—Specifies the style of border drawn between rows.
- **VisibleCols**—Number of visible columns.
- **VisibleRows**—Number of visible rows.
- **Col, Row**—Row and column of the current cell.
- **DataSource**—The data source the control is bound to.

Here are the control's significant methods:

- **CaptureImage**—A captured image of the grid's display.
- **ClearFields**—Restores the default state of the control.
- **ClearSelCols**—De-selects all columns in a split.
- **HoldFields**—Sets the current column/field layout as the customized layout.
- **SplitContaining**—Index of the split containing the specified coordinate pair.
- **ColContaining**—ColIndex value of the DataGrid control column containing the specified x coordinate.
- **GetBookmark**—Value containing a bookmark for a row relative to the current row.
- **RowContaining**—Value corresponding to the row number of the specified y coordinate.
- **RowTop**—Value containing the y coordinate of the top of a specified row of a DataGrid control.
- **Scroll**—Scrolls the control.
- **Refresh**—Refreshes the control.

And here are the control's significant events:

- **AfterColEdit**—Fires after a column edit.
- **BeforeColEdit**—Fires before a column edit.
- **ButtonClick**—Fires when the current cell's built-in button is clicked.
- **ColEdit**—Fires when a user enters Edit mode (by typing a character in a cell).
- **OnAddNew**—Fires when the AddNew operation starts.
- **SelChange**—Fires when the current selection is changed.
- **SplitChange**—Fires when the user moves to a different split.

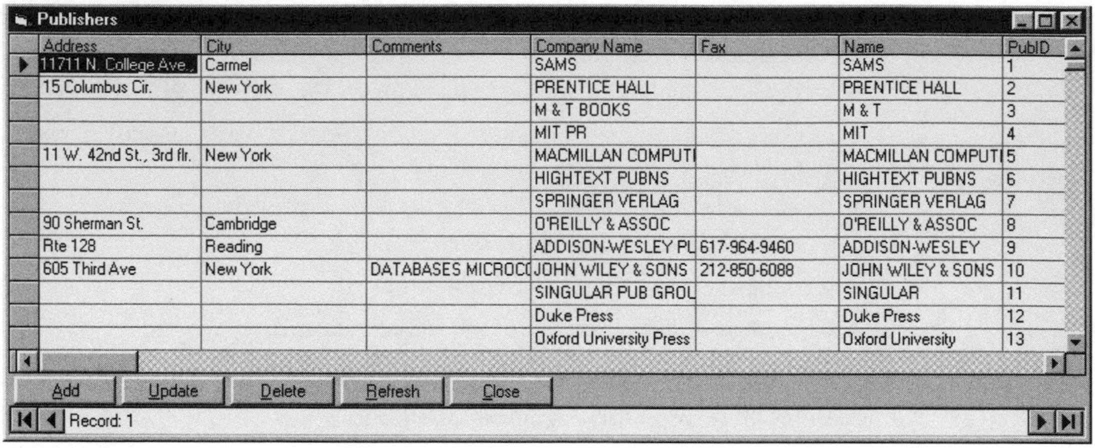

Address	City	Comments	Company Name	Fax	Name	PubID
11711 N. College Ave.,	Carmel		SAMS		SAMS	1
15 Columbus Cir.	New York		PRENTICE HALL		PRENTICE HALL	2
			M & T BOOKS		M & T	3
			MIT PR		MIT	4
11 W. 42nd St., 3rd flr.	New York		MACMILLAN COMPUTI		MACMILLAN COMPUTI	5
			HIGHTEXT PUBNS		HIGHTEXT PUBNS	6
			SPRINGER VERLAG		SPRINGER VERLAG	7
90 Sherman St.	Cambridge		O'REILLY & ASSOC		O'REILLY & ASSOC	8
Rte 128	Reading		ADDISON-WESLEY PL	617-964-9460	ADDISON-WESLEY	9
605 Third Ave	New York	DATABASES MICROCC	JOHN WILEY & SONS	212-850-6088	JOHN WILEY & SONS	10
			SINGULAR PUB GROU		SINGULAR	11
			Duke Press		Duke Press	12
			Oxford University Press		Oxford University	13

FIGURE 4.9 A DataGrid control at work.

- **`AfterColUpdate`**—Fires after a column is updated.
- **`AfterDelete`**—Fires after a delete operation.
- **`AfterInsert`**—Fires after an insert operation.
- **`AfterUpdate`**—Fires after an update operation.
- **`BeforeColUpdate`**—Fires before a column is updated.
- **`BeforeDelete`**—Fires before a delete operation.
- **`BeforeInsert`**—Fires before an insert operation.
- **`BeforeUpdate`**—Fires before an update operation.
- **`ColResize`**—Fires when a column is resized.
- **`HeadClick`**—Fires when a column header is clicked.
- **`RowResize`**—Fires when a row is resized.
- **`Change`**—Fires when the contents of the control have changed.
- **`Click`**—Standard `Click` event.
- **`Scroll`**—Fires when a scroll operation takes place.
- **`DblClick`**—Standard `Double-Click` event.

You can see a DataGrid bound to the `Biblio.mdb` database in Figure 4.9.

There's another powerful grid control that you can use as well—the Hierarchical FlexGrid control.

Using the Hierarchical FlexGrid Control

As mentioned earlier in this chapter, Hierarchical FlexGrid controls let you bind (using the ADO control or a Data Environment) to hierarchical databases in which tables have a parent-child relationship by using bands in the control.

How do you create hierarchical databases? You use the SHAPE language in SQL, specifying the relationship of various tables, as we'll do in Chapter 13.

You can also drag and drop columns in a Hierarchical FlexGrid. To see how this works, create a new project now and add the Hierarchical FlexGrid control to the toolbox using the Components item of the Project menu, selecting the Microsoft Hierarchical FlexGrid Control entry and clicking OK. Add a Hierarchical FlexGrid to a form now, and make sure its DragMode property is set to vbManual. In addition, set its DragIcon property to the icon graphics\icons\dragdrop\drag1pg.ico to give it the standard column-dragging icon.

To implement column dragging, you store the column number that the user is trying to drag and use the Drag method to start the dragging operation by adding code to the MouseDown event (the MouseCol property specifies the column position of the mouse):

```
Dim intDragCol As Integer


Private Sub MSHFlexGrid1_MouseDown(Button As _
    Integer, Shift As Integer, X As Single, Y As _
    Single)


    intDragCol = MSHFlexGrid1.MouseCol
    MSHFlexGrid1.Drag 1


End Sub
```

Then, in the DragDrop event, you use the control's ColPosition method to reposition the column like this:

```
Private Sub MSHFlexGrid1_DragDrop(Source As _
    VB.Control, X As Single, Y As Single)


    MSHFlexGrid1.ColPosition(intDragCol) = _
        MSHFlexGrid1.MouseCol


End Sub
```

That's all it takes—now the user can drag columns around by the column headers, as shown in Figure 4.4.

There's one thing we've left out of our study of binding controls—binding to Data Environments—and I'll take a look at that now.

Binding to a Data Environment

Binding a Data Environment to a control is simple. To start, you simply set the control's `DataSource` property to the name of the Data Environment, such as `DataEnvironment1`. With ADO data controls, you can set the `RecordSource` property to an individual property in the database, and all controls you bind to the ADO control are bound to that table. However, a Data Environment can contain many such record sources—that is, many `Command` objects. You specify which `Command` object you want to connect a bound control to by using the control's `DataMember` property.

After setting a bound control's `DataSource` and `DataMember` properties, you can keep going and set the control's other data binding properties, such as `DataField` and so forth as appropriate. As you might expect, you can also bind data-bound properties using a control's `DataBindings` collection when you've bound that control to a Data Environment.

As you can see, binding to a Data Environment is very much like binding to a data control, except that you must also set the `DataMember` property of bound controls. And as with data controls, you can access the `Recordset` object in a Data Environment directly. To access the `Recordset` object returned by a command in a Data Environment, you just preface the command's name with the letters "`rs`".

I'll write a brief example showing how to bind to a Data Environment and use the Data Environment's underlying `Recordset` object. You can see this example at work in Figure 4.10, where it's displaying all the fields of the `Customers` table in the `Nwind.mdb` database. Note also the buttons that let the user navigate through the database.

To create this example, just add a Data Environment, `DataEnvironment1`, to a standard EXE project, connect the default connection, `Connection1`, to `Nwind.mdb`, add a `Command` object named `CustomersTable`, and connect that `Command` object to the `Customers` table in the Data Environment.

If you want to, you can now add the labels and text boxes individually that you see in Figure 4.10, setting the `DataSource` property of each text box to `DataEnvironment1`, the `DataMember` of each text box to the `Command` object `CustomersTable`, and the `DataField` of each text box to match its label in the figure. However, the Data Environment can do all this for you: Just drag the `CustomersTable` `Command` object from the data control to the form, `Form1`, and all the text boxes and labels you see in Figure 4.10 will be added to the form automatically. The text boxes' `DataSource`, `DataMember`, and `DataField` properties are set at the same time. Note that you can open the `Command` object in the Data Environment and drag individual fields to the form one by one if you prefer.

You can also implement the buttons in the application using the `CustomersTable` command's `Recordset` object, which is called `rsCustomersTable` in this case, because the recordset corresponding to a `Command` object in a Data Environment uses the same name as the `Command` object

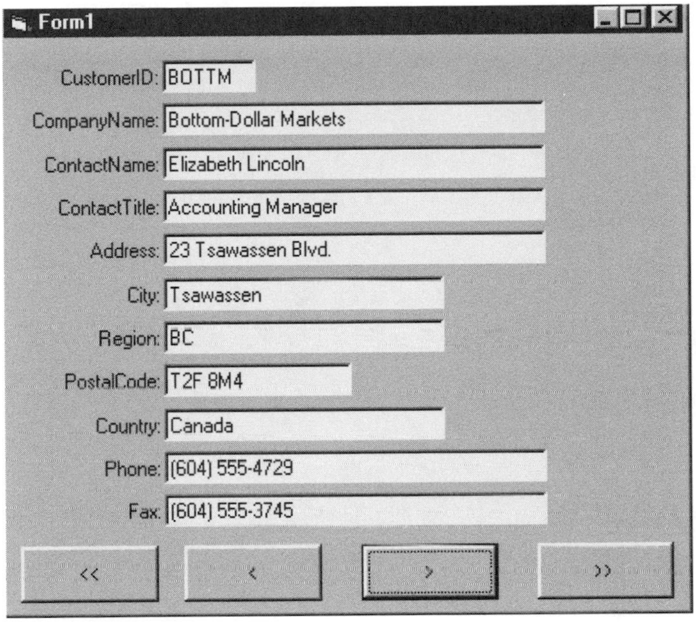

FIGURE 4.10 Binding to a Data Environment.

prefaced with the letters "rs" (for recordset). Here's how to implement the cmdFirst button, which moves the Data Environment to the first record (note that I check the RecordCount property of the recordset to make sure there are records in the recordset before moving to the first record). (All the properties and methods of Recordset objects appear in Chapter 7.)

```
Private Sub cmdFirst_Click()
  On Error GoTo ErrLabel


  If DataEnvironment1.rsCustomersTable.RecordCount _
    > 0 Then
      DataEnvironment1.rsCustomersTable.MoveFirst
  End If


  Exit Sub


ErrLabel:
  MsgBox Err.Description
End Sub
```

You can implement the other buttons in the same way, just as we did earlier for the `Recordset` object we obtained from the ADO control directly. That's all it takes; the code for this example appears in Listing 4.3. You can find this project on the CD in the `decontrols` folder.

LISTING 4.3   *Decontrols.frm Code*

```
VERSION 5.00
Begin VB.Form Form1
   Caption         =   "Form1"
   ClientHeight    =   5010
   ClientLeft      =   60
   ClientTop       =   345
   ClientWidth     =   6000
   LinkTopic       =   "Form1"
   ScaleHeight     =   5010
   ScaleWidth      =   6000
   StartUpPosition =   3   'Windows Default
   Begin VB.CommandButton cmdLast
      Caption      =   ">>"
      Height       =   495
      Left         =   4680
      TabIndex     =   25
      Top          =   4440
      Width        =   1215
   End
   Begin VB.CommandButton cmdNext
      Caption      =   ">"
      Height       =   495
      Left         =   3120
      TabIndex     =   24
      Top          =   4440
      Width        =   1215
   End
   Begin VB.CommandButton cmdPrevious
      Caption      =   "<"
      Height       =   495
      Left         =   1560
      TabIndex     =   23
      Top          =   4440
      Width        =   1215
   End
   Begin VB.CommandButton cmdFirst
      Caption      =   "<<"
      Height       =   495
      Left         =   120
      TabIndex     =   22
      Top          =   4440
      Width        =   1215
   End
```

```
Begin VB.TextBox txtFax
    DataField       =   "Fax"
    DataMember      =   "CustomersTable"
    DataSource      =   "DataEnvironment1"
    Height          =   285
    Left            =   1395
    TabIndex        =   21
    Top             =   3995
    Width           =   3375
End
Begin VB.TextBox txtPhone
    DataField       =   "Phone"
    DataMember      =   "CustomersTable"
    DataSource      =   "DataEnvironment1"
    Height          =   285
    Left            =   1395
    TabIndex        =   19
    Top             =   3615
    Width           =   3375
End
Begin VB.TextBox txtCountry
    DataField       =   "Country"
    DataMember      =   "CustomersTable"
    DataSource      =   "DataEnvironment1"
    Height          =   285
    Left            =   1395
    TabIndex        =   17
    Top             =   3235
    Width           =   2475
End
Begin VB.TextBox txtPostalCode
    DataField       =   "PostalCode"
    DataMember      =   "CustomersTable"
    DataSource      =   "DataEnvironment1"
    Height          =   285
    Left            =   1395
    TabIndex        =   15
    Top             =   2855
    Width           =   1650
End
Begin VB.TextBox txtRegion
    DataField       =   "Region"
    DataMember      =   "CustomersTable"
    DataSource      =   "DataEnvironment1"
    Height          =   285
    Left            =   1395
    TabIndex        =   13
    Top             =   2475
    Width           =   2475
End
Begin VB.TextBox txtCity
    DataField       =   "City"
```

```
      DataMember       =     "CustomersTable"
      DataSource       =     "DataEnvironment1"
      Height           =     285
      Left             =     1395
      TabIndex         =     11
      Top              =     2095
      Width            =     2475
   End
   Begin VB.TextBox txtAddress
      DataField        =     "Address"
      DataMember       =     "CustomersTable"
      DataSource       =     "DataEnvironment1"
      Height           =     285
      Left             =     1395
      TabIndex         =     9
      Top              =     1715
      Width            =     3375
   End
   Begin VB.TextBox txtContactTitle
      DataField        =     "ContactTitle"
      DataMember       =     "CustomersTable"
      DataSource       =     "DataEnvironment1"
      Height           =     285
      Left             =     1395
      TabIndex         =     7
      Top              =     1335
      Width            =     3375
   End
   Begin VB.TextBox txtContactName
      DataField        =     "ContactName"
      DataMember       =     "CustomersTable"
      DataSource       =     "DataEnvironment1"
      Height           =     285
      Left             =     1395
      TabIndex         =     5
      Top              =     955
      Width            =     3375
   End
   Begin VB.TextBox txtCompanyName
      DataField        =     "CompanyName"
      DataMember       =     "CustomersTable"
      DataSource       =     "DataEnvironment1"
      Height           =     285
      Left             =     1395
      TabIndex         =     3
      Top              =     575
      Width            =     3375
   End
   Begin VB.TextBox txtCustomerID
      DataField        =     "CustomerID"
      DataMember       =     "CustomersTable"
```

```
    DataSource      =    "DataEnvironment1"
    Height          =    285
    Left            =    1395
    TabIndex        =    1
    Top             =    195
    Width           =    825
End
Begin VB.Label lblFieldLabel
    Alignment       =    1    'Right Justify
    AutoSize        =    -1   'True
    Caption         =    "Fax:"
    Height          =    255
    Index           =    10
    Left            =    -450
    TabIndex        =    20
    Top             =    4035
    Width           =    1815
End
Begin VB.Label lblFieldLabel
    Alignment       =    1    'Right Justify
    AutoSize        =    -1   'True
    Caption         =    "Phone:"
    Height          =    255
    Index           =    9
    Left            =    -450
    TabIndex        =    18
    Top             =    3660
    Width           =    1815
End
Begin VB.Label lblFieldLabel
    Alignment       =    1    'Right Justify
    AutoSize        =    -1   'True
    Caption         =    "Country:"
    Height          =    255
    Index           =    8
    Left            =    -450
    TabIndex        =    16
    Top             =    3285
    Width           =    1815
End
Begin VB.Label lblFieldLabel
    Alignment       =    1    'Right Justify
    AutoSize        =    -1   'True
    Caption         =    "PostalCode:"
    Height          =    255
    Index           =    7
    Left            =    -450
    TabIndex        =    14
    Top             =    2895
    Width           =    1815
End
```

```
Begin VB.Label lblFieldLabel
    Alignment          =    1  'Right Justify
    AutoSize           =    -1   'True
    Caption            =    "Region:"
    Height             =    255
    Index              =    6
    Left               =    -450
    TabIndex           =    12
    Top                =    2520
    Width              =    1815
End
Begin VB.Label lblFieldLabel
    Alignment          =    1  'Right Justify
    AutoSize           =    -1   'True
    Caption            =    "City:"
    Height             =    255
    Index              =    5
    Left               =    -450
    TabIndex           =    10
    Top                =    2145
    Width              =    1815
End
Begin VB.Label lblFieldLabel
    Alignment          =    1  'Right Justify
    AutoSize           =    -1   'True
    Caption            =    "Address:"
    Height             =    255
    Index              =    4
    Left               =    -450
    TabIndex           =    8
    Top                =    1755
    Width              =    1815
End
Begin VB.Label lblFieldLabel
    Alignment          =    1  'Right Justify
    AutoSize           =    -1   'True
    Caption            =    "ContactTitle:"
    Height             =    255
    Index              =    3
    Left               =    -450
    TabIndex           =    6
    Top                =    1380
    Width              =    1815
End
Begin VB.Label lblFieldLabel
    Alignment          =    1  'Right Justify
    AutoSize           =    -1   'True
    Caption            =    "ContactName:"
    Height             =    255
    Index              =    2
    Left               =    -450
```

```
        TabIndex        =    4
        Top             =    1005
        Width           =    1815
    End
    Begin VB.Label lblFieldLabel
        Alignment       =    1    'Right Justify
        AutoSize        =    -1   'True
        Caption         =    "CompanyName:"
        Height          =    255
        Index           =    1
        Left            =    -450
        TabIndex        =    2
        Top             =    615
        Width           =    1815
    End
    Begin VB.Label lblFieldLabel
        Alignment       =    1    'Right Justify
        AutoSize        =    -1   'True
        Caption         =    "CustomerID:"
        Height          =    255
        Index           =    0
        Left            =    -450
        TabIndex        =    0
        Top             =    240
        Width           =    1815
    End
End
Attribute VB_Name = "Form1"
Attribute VB_GlobalNameSpace = False
Attribute VB_Creatable = False
Attribute VB_PredeclaredId = True
Attribute VB_Exposed = False

Private Sub cmdFirst_Click()
    On Error GoTo ErrLabel

    If DataEnvironment1.rsCustomersTable.RecordCount _
        > 0 Then
        DataEnvironment1.rsCustomersTable.MoveFirst
    End If

    Exit Sub

ErrLabel:
    MsgBox Err.Description
End Sub

Private Sub cmdLast_Click()
    On Error GoTo ErrLabel

    If DataEnvironment1.rsCustomersTable.RecordCount _
```

```
            > 0 Then
            DataEnvironment1.rsCustomersTable.MoveLast
        End If

        Exit Sub

ErrLabel:
        MsgBox Err.Description
End Sub

Private Sub cmdNext_Click()
        On Error GoTo ErrLabel

        If Not DataEnvironment1.rsCustomersTable.EOF Then
                DataEnvironment1.rsCustomersTable.MoveNext
        End If

        If DataEnvironment1.rsCustomersTable.EOF And _
           DataEnvironment1.rsCustomersTable.RecordCount _
           > 0 Then
            DataEnvironment1.rsCustomersTable.MoveLast
        End If

        Exit Sub

ErrLabel:
        MsgBox Err.Description
End Sub

Private Sub cmdPrevious_Click()
        On Error GoTo ErrLabel

        If Not DataEnvironment1.rsCustomersTable.BOF Then
            DataEnvironment1.rsCustomersTable.MovePrevious
        End If

        If DataEnvironment1.rsCustomersTable.BOF And _
           DataEnvironment1.rsCustomersTable.RecordCount _
           > 0 Then
            DataEnvironment1.rsCustomersTable.MoveFirst
        End If

        Exit Sub

ErrLabel:
        MsgBox Err.Description
End Sub
```

The last topic I'll take a look at in this chapter is data binding in code.

Data Binding at Run-Time

Although the examples in this chapter have bound data sources to bound controls at design-time, it's also possible, as of Visual Basic 6.0, to bind controls at run-time. All you need to do to bind a control at run-time is to set the control's binding properties correctly. For example, here's how to bind a text box, Text1, to an ADO data control, Adodc1, at run-time:

```
Set Text1.DataSource = Adodc1
Text1.DataField = "ContactName"
```

Here's how to bind the same text box to a Data Environment—note that I'm also setting the text box's DataMember property here because I'm working with a Data Environment and must specify a Command object:

```
Set Text1.DataSource = DataEnvironment1
Text1.DataMember = "Command1"
Text1.DataField = "ContactName"
```

That's fine for simple controls, but what if you're working with a control that supports complex properties, such as the BoundText property of the DataCombo control? Such properties can require you to set a Data Source, Data Field, and other properties, and you can reach those properties from the control's DataBindings collection. Here's an example where I set the BoundText property's DataSource property to an ADO data control, Adodc1, and its DataField property to "PubID" (note that as usual, I have to use the Set keyword when assigning Adodc1 to anything, because Adodc1 is an object):

```
Set _
DataCombo1.DataBindings("BoundText").DataSource _
= Adodc1
DataCombo1.DataBindings("BoundText").DataField = _
"PubID"
```

Now that we've put ADO to work the easy way—with ADO data controls and Data Environments—it's time to dig into the ADO library of objects that makes all this work, starting by examining how to really put ADO connections to use.

Connecting
to Databases

The first step in working with a database in ADO is to connect to that database using an OLE DB provider, and this chapter is all about how you make that connection. There are three ways of connecting to databases using ADO: using the ADO data control, Data Environments, and connecting in code using the ADO Connection object. In fact, all three of these techniques are based on the ADO object library's Connection object, and this chapter is largely an exploration of that object.

A Connection object represents a connection to a database, and directly or indirectly, working with a Connection object is the first thing you do when you're working in ADO. Up to this point, we've let the ADO data control and Data Environments handle the connection behind the scenes, but in this chapter, we'll also see how to use Connection objects directly in code. In the next chapter, I'll take a look at associating Command objects with Connection objects, and you can use those Command objects to extract records from databases, insert records, delete records, and more.

That's all the overview we need—we'll start by creating connections with the ADO data control now.

Connecting with an ADO Data Control

We've already seen how to connect to an ADO data source using the ADO data control. This control handles a `Connection` object behind the scenes and provides an easy interface to that object.

At design-time, you create a connection with an ADO data control either by right-clicking the ADO data control and selecting the `Properties` item, or by clicking the `ConnectionString` property in the `Properties` window and clicking the ellipsis button that appears. Doing so opens the ADO data control's `Property Pages General` tab, as shown in Figure 5.1.

As we've seen already in this book, there are three ways to create a connection using this page. You can use a data link file with the extension `.udl`, a registered ODBC source, or an ADO connection string. You can either type an ADO connection string in directly, or click the `Build` button to create a connection string, as we've done before. Clicking the `Build` button opens the `Data Link Properties` dialog box to the `Provider` tab, as shown in Figure 5.2.

You select the OLE DB provider you want to use in the `Provider` page and click the `Next` button to open the `Connection` page, as shown in Figure 5.3.

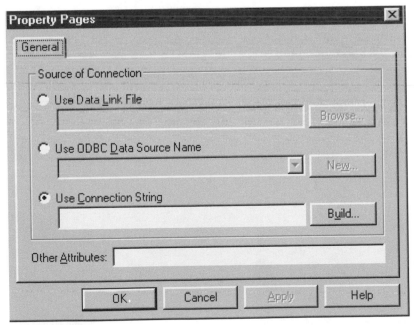

FIGURE 5.1   The ADO data control's `Property Pages`, `General` tab.

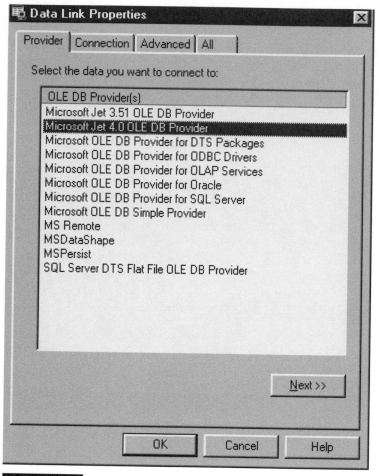

FIGURE 5.2 The Data Link Properties dialog, Provider page.

As we've seen, the Connection page varies by OLE DB provider. The Connection page for the Microsoft Jet OLE DB provider appears in Figure 5.3, and you can select the database file you want to work with in that page. Clicking the Test Connection button in this page tests the connection to the database.

When you click the OK button to close the Data Link Properties page and then click the OK button to close the Property Pages, the new connection string is placed in the ADO data control's ConnectionString property:

```
Provider=Microsoft.Jet.OLEDB.4.0;Persist

Security Info=False;Data Source=C:\ADO\Nwind.mdb
```

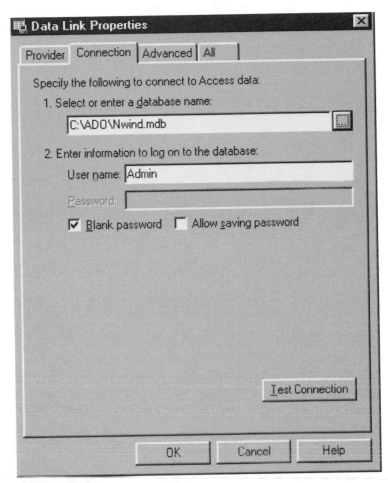

The Data Link Properties dialog, Connection page.

In addition, you set the ADO data control's RecordSource property to indicate how you want to extract records from the data source. Clicking the ellipsis button in the control's RecordSource property entry in the Properties window opens the control's Property Pages to the RecordSource page, as you see in Figure 5.4.

As we saw earlier, in the RecordSource page, you can select the type of command that will be stored in the ADO data control's CommandType property. Here are the possibilities:

- **adCmdText**—1. SQL statement.
- **adCmdTable**—2. Table.
- **adCmdStoredProc**—4. Stored procedure.
- **adCmdUnknown**—8. Unknown.

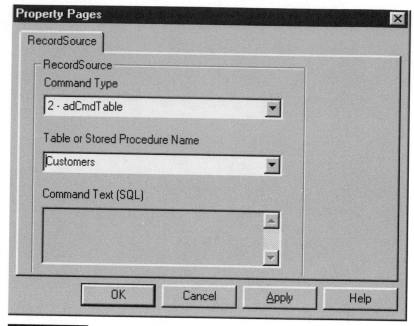

FIGURE 5.4 The ADO data control's `Property Pages`, `RecordSource` page.

We'll see more about these various options in the next chapter, which covers ADO commands.

Creating a connection as I've done above at design-time is one way of connecting an ADO data control, but you can also connect an ADO data control in code. To do that, you only need to set the ADO data control's `ConnectionString`, as here where I'm using the connection string we built above:

```
Private Sub Command1_Click()
    Adodc1.ConnectionString = _
"Provider=Microsoft.Jet.OLEDB.4.0;Persist " & _
"Security Info=False;Data Source=C:\ADO\Nwind.mdb"
    .
    .
    .
End Sub
```

You can also connect to an ODBC source using the ADO data control's `ConnectionString` property; to do so, you just set the connection string parameter DSN to the DSN of the ODBC data source, as in this example, where I've registered the db.mdb database we created with "DSN db":

```
Private Sub Command1_Click()
    Adodc1.ConnectionString = "DSN=db"
    .
    .
    .
End Sub
```

That's how connecting to a database with the ADO data control works. Besides connecting with an ADO data control, you can also connect to an ADO data source using a Data Environment, and I'll take a look at that now.

Connecting with a Data Environment

You use the Add Data Environment item in the Visual Basic Project menu to add a Data Environment to a project or project group. When you create a Data Environment, it's created with one default Connection object, Connection1, as you see in Figure 5.5. You can add other connections by clicking the Add Connection button at the extreme left on the Data Environment toolbar, or you can right-click the Data Environment and select Add Connection from the shortcut menu.

You can also, of course, change the name of the connection in the Visual Basic Properties window if you want, giving it a more meaningful name, such as CustomerDatabase instead of Connection1.

To set up an actual connection, you right-click the Connection object and choose the Properties item to open the Data Link Properties dialog, Provider page, as shown in Figure 5.2, and so create a new data link. You follow the same steps as with the ADO data control to create a connection.

Note that in some cases, you might have to supply login information too (this information only needs to be supplied if the provider you're accessing demands authentication information).

If you want to, you can specify a different set of login information to be used at design-time and run-time for the Data Environment. As an example, you might develop your application using a system administrator user ID and password, but give a guest user ID to test the application when you run it. You can supply different design-time and run-time authentication by selecting the Connection object and setting the DesignPassword and Design-UserName in the Properties window for the design-time authentication, and RunPassword and RunUserName for the run-time authentication.

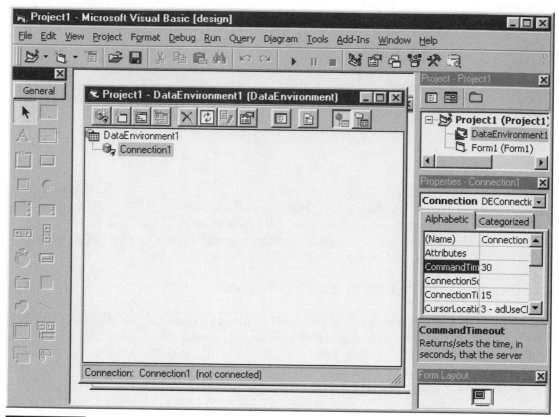

FIGURE 5.5 A Connection object in a Data Environment.

You have more access to the Connection object in a Data Environment than you do to the Connection object in an ADO data control. While you interact with the Connection object in an ADO data control through the ADO data control's properties (e.g., ConnectionString), you can reach the Connection object in a Data Environment directly in code, like this: DataEnvironment1.Connection1, which means you have complete access to that Connection object's properties, methods, and events. For example, here's how to set the ConnectionString of the Connection object, Connection1:

```
Private Sub Command1_Click()
    DataEnvironment1.Connection1.ConnectionString _
= "Provider=Microsoft.Jet.OLEDB.4.0;Persist " & _
"Security Info=False;Data Source=C:\ADO\Nwind.mdb"
```

```
          .
          .
          .

End Sub
```

As you can see, referring to a connection object as `DataEnviron-ment1.Connection1` lets you use that `Connection` object's properties and methods in code—but, how do you add code to the events of a `Connection` object in a Data Environment? You just double-click the `Connection` object in the Data Environment itself to open a code window, as shown in Figure 5.6, and you can add code directly to all the Data Environment's `Connec-tion` objects this way.

Now that you've created a `Connection` object in a Data Environment, you should give the `Connection` object a `Command` object, because connections usually use commands to work with a database and so return a

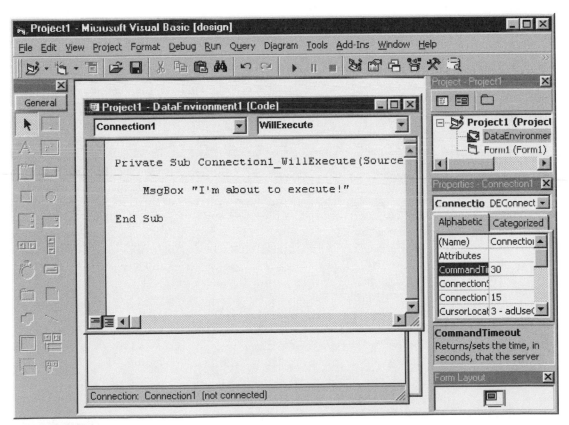

FIGURE 5.6   Adding code to a `Connection` object in a Data Environment.

Recordset object. We'll see how to create and use Command objects in the next chapter. In the meantime, it's time to start working with Connection objects directly in code.

Connecting with a Connection Object

I'll take a more detailed look at Connection objects in ADO now. As mentioned at the beginning of the chapter, a Connection object represents a unique session with a data source. In the case of a client/server database system, it may be equivalent to an actual network connection to the server. Access from your application to the data source is through this connection, which provides the environment necessary for exchanging data. The Connection object is used to specify a particular data provider and any parameters.

As you know, you specify a connection string to connect to a data source, and that string specifies not only the database to use, but also the OLE DB provider, passwords, if any, and other options, such as what security protocol you want to use with the SQL Server. You can use the Connection object's Open method to open a connection.

When you're connected, you can execute SQL queries on the data source with the Connection object's Execute method, which can return a recordset (or you can use other methods, such as the Recordset object's Open method, to open a recordset).

Note that you can also manage database *transactions* using the Connection object. Using transactions, you can group what may be many different individual actions into one coherent whole, so if one action fails, they all do. In this way, you don't end up with only partial updates to your database if there's a problem during update operations.

The Connection object supports methods to work with transactions like BeginTrans (begin a transaction), CommitTrans (update a database), and RollbackTrans (restore the state before the transaction began). Once you call the BeginTrans method, the provider will not commit changes to the database until you call CommitTrans or RollbackTrans and so end the transaction. I'll take a look at transactions later in this chapter.

Using the collections, methods, and properties of a Connection object, you can do quite a lot, including the following:

- Configure a connection before opening it, using the Connection-String, ConnectionTimeout, and Mode properties.
- Specify the default database for the connection with the DefaultDatabase property.
- Specify the level of isolation for the transactions opened on the connection with the IsolationLevel property.

- Specify the `CursorLocation` property to use the Client Cursor Provider (which supports batch updates).
- Specify an OLE DB provider with the `Provider` property.
- Establish a connection to the data source with the `Open` method.
- Break the connection to the data source with the `Close` method.
- Execute a command with the `Execute` method.
- Configure command execution with the `CommandTimeout` property.
- Manage transactions with the `BeginTrans`, `CommitTrans`, and `RollbackTrans` methods and the `Attributes` property.
- Read the version of ADO in use with the `Version` property.
- Get schema information about a database with the `OpenSchema` method.

To get all the details on the `Connection` object, I'll take a look at all of its properties, methods, and events, starting with its properties. After working through what's available, I'll put the `Connection` object to work in examples in the remainder of this chapter.

Connection Object Properties

You use the properties of a `Connection` object to configure that object, and we'll see all the possibilities here, beginning with the `Attributes` property.

Attributes

This property configures the connection, such as whether rolling back a transaction starts a new transaction. Here are the possible settings for this property:

- **`adXactCommitRetaining`**—This setting makes the connection perform "retaining" commits: for example, calling `CommitTrans` automatically starts a new transaction. Note that not all providers support retaining commits.
- **`adXactAbortRetaining`**—This setting makes the connection perform "retaining" aborts: for example, calling `RollbackTrans` automatically starts a new transaction. Note that not all providers support retaining aborts.

CommandTimeout

This property holds the timeout, in seconds, of a command. The default setting of this property is 30 seconds; if you're on a slow network, consider increasing that time. Working with very large resultsets or very complex queries may also require an increase in the timeout.

ConnectionString

ADO connections use connection strings to hold the connection parameters needed for the connection itself, and using a connection string is usually the biggest aspect of ADO programming developers have to get used to when making connections.

This property, `ConnectionString`, holds the actual connection string in a `Connection` object. We've already built a number of connection strings in this book, and I'll cover the connection string parameters used in this string for each OLE DB provider later in this chapter.

ConnectionTimeout

This property holds the timeout, in seconds, for a connection. The default is 15 seconds, which can be quite short on networks; so, if your connections are timing out and they shouldn't be, this is the setting to change.

CursorLocation

You can use the `CursorLocation` property to set the location of the ADO cursor (a cursor manages a recordset as far as the code in your program goes; see Chapter 1 for more details). You can maintain the cursor on the client or the server; here are the possibilities:

- **adUseServer**—2. Use server cursors.
- **adUseClient**—3 (default). Use Microsoft client batch cursors.

If you want to improve cursor performance, you can use a server-side cursor if your OLE DB provider supports it (e.g., SQL Server does, Microsoft Jet does not). Note that you cannot use server-side cursors if you're creating a disconnected recordset or a multiple recordset. However, server-side cursors are also expensive as far as server resources are concerned: They require more round trips, and could present scalability problems.

DefaultDatabase

When you set a default database, you can make unqualified references to it in SQL. That is, if no database is specified, the default database, if there is one, will be used. Note that some data sources and providers may not support this property.

For example, here's how to make the `Northwind` database the default database in the SQL Server:

```
ConnectionObject.DefaultDatabase = "Northwind"
RecordsetObject.Open "Customers", _
```

```
ConnectionObject,    adOpenKeyset, adLockReadOnly, _
adCmdTable
```

IsolationLevel

The level of isolation of your transactions indicates how other transactions will influence yours, if they can see the changes you make, and if you can see theirs. Here are the possible settings for this property:

- **adXactUnspecified**—This setting indicates that a provider is using a different isolation level than specified, but that the level cannot be determined.
- **adXactChaos**—This setting indicates that you cannot overwrite pending changes from more highly isolated transactions.
- **adXactBrowse**—This setting indicates that you can view uncommitted changes in other transactions.
- **adXactReadUncommitted**—Same as adXactBrowse.
- **adXactCursorStability**—(default) This setting indicates that you can view changes in other transactions only after they've been committed.
- **adXactReadCommitted**—Same as adXactCursorStability.
- **adXactRepeatableRead**—This setting indicates that you cannot see changes made in other transactions, but that requerying can bring new recordsets.
- **adXactIsolated**—This setting indicates that transactions will be conducted in isolation of other transactions.
- **adXactSerializable**—Same as adXactIsolated.

Mode

This property holds available permissions for modifying data in a Connection object. Here are the possible values:

- **adModeUnknown**—(default) This setting indicates that the permissions have not yet been set or cannot be determined.
- **adModeRead**—This setting indicates read-only permissions.
- **adModeWrite**—This setting indicates write-only permissions.
- **adModeReadWrite**—This setting indicates read/write permissions.
- **adModeShareDenyRead**—This setting prevents others from opening the connection with read permissions.
- **adModeShareDenyWrite**—This setting prevents others from opening the connection with write permissions.

- **adModeShareExclusive**—This setting prevents others from opening the connection.

- **adModeShareDenyNone**—This setting prevents others from opening the connection with any permissions.

You can use this property to set the connection mode before opening the connection; note that you cannot set this property for open connections.

Provider

This property holds the name of the OLE DB data provider. You usually set the name of the OLE DB provider in the connection string, but you can also specify it here. Note that Microsoft warns against using different providers in the connection string and in `Provider` property. I put the OLE DB provider name in the ADO connection string in this book, but here are the possible values for the `Provider` property:

- **ADSDSOObject**—For Microsoft Active Directory.
- **DTSFlatFile**—For DTS flat-file providers.
- **DTSPackageDSO**—For DTS packages.
- **Microsoft.Jet.OLEDB.3.51**—For Microsoft Jet 3.51.
- **Microsoft.Jet.OLEDB.4.0**—For Microsoft Jet 4.0.
- **MS Remote**—For remote providers.
- **MSDAORA**—For Oracle.
- **MSDAOSP**—For simple OLE DB providers.
- **MSDASQL**—(default) For ODBC data sources.
- **MSDataShape**—For the Microsoft data shape provider; see Chapter 13 for more details.
- **MSIDXS**—For the Microsoft Index Server.
- **MSOLAP**—For the Microsoft OLAP provider.
- **MSPersist**—For the Microsoft Persist OLE DB provider.
- **SQLOLEDB**—For Microsoft SQL Server.

Note also that Visual Basic adds a version number (optional), if the OLE DB provider does not specify a version number, to the end of the OLE DB provider name. This version is 1 by default, like this: `MSDASQL.1` or `MSIDXS.1`.

State

You check the `State` property of a `Connection` object to see if the object is open, closed, or connecting. Here are the possible values:

- **adStateClosed**—(default) This setting indicates that the object is closed.

- **adStateOpen**—This setting indicates that the object is open.
- **adStateConnecting**—This setting indicates that the `Recordset` object is connecting.
- **adStateExecuting**—This setting indicates that the `Recordset` object is executing a command.
- **adStateFetching**—This setting indicates that the rows of the `Recordset` object are being fetched.

Here's an example where I check to make sure that a `Connection` object is open before using its `Execute` method to open a recordset:

```
If ConnectionObject.State = adStateOpen Then
    Set adoRecordset = ConnectionObject.Execute( _
    "SELECT * FROM Publishers")
End If
```

That's it for the `Connection` object's properties—now it's time to take a look at this object's methods.

Connection Object Methods

Now that we've covered the properties of the `Connection` object, I'll take a look at all its methods, starting with `BeginTrans`, which starts a transaction.

Transactions are a big feature of the `Connection` object, because they allow you a way to wrap database operations into one single unit. That's important—imagine a case where you start changing a database and the network server goes down in the middle of your changes; how can you tell what's actually been changed? Or what if, after making some changes, the user wants to revoke those changes and restore the database to the way it was?

You can take care of problems like these with transactions and transaction methods: `BeginTrans`, which starts a transaction; `CommitTrans`, which commits the changes made to the database so they take effect; and `RollbackTrans`, which revokes, or rolls back, the changes so they are not made to the database.

I'll take a look at a transaction example later in this chapter. In the meantime, here are the details concerning the `Connection` object's methods, starting with `BeginTrans`.

BeginTrans

This method starts a transaction. You call this method (`BeginTrans` takes no parameters) to start a transaction, then perform the operations you want on the database, and finally call `CommitTrans` to commit the changes all at once to the database, or `RollbackTrans` to roll the changes back.

This method returns the current level of the transaction (starting with 1), which you use to keep track of nested transactions. A nested transaction can itself contain other transactions, often nested to arbitrary depth. Note that not all OLE DB providers support transactions, and of those that do, not all support nested transactions. See the transactions example later in this chapter for more details.

Cancel

You use the `Cancel` method to cancel the execution of a pending, asynchronous `Execute` or `Open` method call; this method takes no parameters. For example, you could display a `Cancel` button in your application to use if the connection is taking too long to complete.

Note that if you use this method when a connection is not asynchronous, an error is generated. I'll take a look at making asynchronous connections later in this chapter.

Close

You use the `Close` method to close an open connection; this method takes no parameters. This is the method you typically call when finished with a connection. Note that `Close` also closes any `Recordset` or other objects associated with the connection.

Here's an example:

```
If ConnectionObject.State = adStateOpen Then

    Set adoRecordset = ConnectionObject.Execute( _

    "SELECT * FROM Publishers")

    [Work with and close the Recordset object]

    ConnectionObject.Close

End If
```

One thing to realize is that just closing a `Connection` object does not remove it from memory. To do that, you must set it to `Nothing` in Visual Basic, like this:

```
If ConnectionObject.State = adStateOpen Then

    Set adoRecordset = ConnectionObject.Execute( _

    "SELECT * FROM Publishers")

    [Work with and close the Recordset object]
```

```
ConnectionObject.Close
```
`    Set ConnectionObject = Nothing`
```
End If
```

Note that any pending operations on the database will be rolled back if they have not been executed when you close the connection.

CommitTrans

The `CommitTrans` method commits a transaction in the data source for those data sources that support transactions, or commits the most recent level of a nested transaction for those data sources that support nested transactions.

When you commit a transaction, the data source performs any pending changes to the underlying data set and ends the current transaction. That is, all the changes made since the corresponding `BeginTrans` call was made are committed to the data set.

Note also that if the `Connection` property's `Attributes` property is set to `adXactCommitRetaining`, the data source starts a new transaction automatically after completing this one. If you don't want to commit the current changes to the data set, call `RollbackTrans` instead of `CommitTrans`.

Execute

You use the `Execute` method to execute a query, SQL statement, stored procedure, or OLE DB provider-specific command. Here's how you use this method:

```
ConnectionObject.Execute [CommandText [, _

RecordsAffected [, Options ]]]
```

Here are the parameters you pass to `Execute`:

- **CommandText**—SQL statement, table name, stored procedure, or provider-specific text to execute.

- **RecordsAffected**—Variable in which the provider returns the number of records that the operation affected.

- **Options**—Indicates how the provider should evaluate the `Command-Text` argument. See below for more information.

Here are the possible values for the `Options` argument:

- **adCmdText**—Provider should evaluate `CommandText` as a textual definition of a command.

- **adCmdTable**—ADO should generate an SQL query to return all rows from the table named in `CommandText`.

- **adCmdTableDirect**—Provider should return all rows from the table named in `CommandText`.

- **adCmdStoredProc**—Provider should evaluate `CommandText` as a stored procedure.

- **adCmdUnknown**—Type of command in the `CommandText` argument is not known.

- **adExecuteAsync**—Command should execute asynchronously.

- **adFetchAsync**—Remaining rows after the initial quantity specified in the `CacheSize` property should be fetched asynchronously.

This method can be used to return an ADO `Recordset` object, and in fact, even if there are no records in the recordset, a `Recordset` object is still returned (since the return value is an object, don't forget to use the `Set` keyword if you want to assign that object to a variable). Usually, however, this method is used to execute SQL statements that don't result in a return set of data, like `INSERT` and `DELETE`, while recordsets are usually obtained with the `Open` method of a `Recordset` object. How you use this method is up to you.

If you want to find out how many records were affected by this call, pass a variable as the `RecordAffected` argument, and that variable will be filled with the number of records affected. Note that you can also execute commands asynchronously using the asynchronous options shown above.

When the `Execute` call is finished, the `ExecuteComplete` event fires, and you can add code to that event to handle the completion of asynchronous `Execute` calls.

Note that the `Recordset` object returned by the `Execute` method is always a forward-only, read-only recordset. To get different types of recordsets, use another method, such as the `Open` method of a `Recordset` object.

Open

You use the `Open` method to open a connection to a data source. Here's how you use this method:

```
ConnectionObject.Open [ConnectionString [, UserID _
[, Password [, Options]]]]
```

Here are the parameters you pass to `Open`:

- **ConnectionString**—The connection string for the `Connection` object.

- **UserID**—A string containing a user name to use when establishing the connection.

- **Password**—A string containing a password to use when establishing the connection.
- **Options**—A ConnectOptionEnum value that determines whether this method should return after (synchronously) or before (asynchronously) the connection is established.

If you pass a user ID and password to this method, those values override the values in the connection string. The Options parameter can be set to one of the following:

- **adConnectUnspecified**—(default) Opens the connection synchronously.
- **adAsyncConnect**—Opens the connection asynchronously. The ConnectionComplete event may be used to determine when the connection is available.

Here's an example showing how to open a connection to the Biblio.mdb database that comes with Visual Basic:

```
Private adoConnect As Connection
Private Sub Form_Load()
    Set adoConnect = New Connection

    adoConnect.Open _
        "PROVIDER=Microsoft.Jet.OLEDB.3.51;Data " & _
        "Source=C:\ADO\Biblio.mdb;"

    .
    .
    .

End Sub
```

When you're finished with the connection, use the Connection object's Close method to close it. We'll use this method in examples later in this chapter.

OpenSchema

You use OpenSchema to get database schema information from the provider, which lets you query the structure of tables, columns, and more in a database. Here's how you use OpenSchema:

```
ConnectionObject.OpenSchema QueryType, _
Criteria, SchemaID
```

This method returns a `Recordset` object that contains schema information. The recordset will be opened as a read-only, static cursor; note that because this return value is an object, you should use the `Set` keyword when assigning the return value of this method to a variable. Here are the parameters you pass to `OpenSchema`:

- **QueryType**—The type of schema query to run. Can be any of the constants listed in Table 5.1.
- **Criteria**—An array of query constraints for each `QueryType` option, as listed in Table 5.1.
- **SchemaID**—The GUID for a provider-schema query not defined by the OLE DB specification. This parameter is required if `QueryType` is set to `adSchemaProviderSpecific`; otherwise, it is not used.

You'll find the possible `QueryType` and `Criteria` values in Table 5.1. Note the term "catalog" in that table; a catalog contains a list of schemas and other data. Catalogs always contain at least one schema named INFORMATION_SCHEMA, which holds information about the catalog. In applications like Microsoft Access and SQL Server, a catalog is a database. Schemas themselves are collections of informational database objects that are owned or were created by a particular user, and let you examine the structure of a data set.

As an example, I'll take a look at the `adSchemaTables` query. The TABLE_TYPE criteria for that query can be one of these: ALIAS, TABLE, SYNONYM, SYSTEM TABLE, or VIEW. You can find all the tables in a particular connection and add them to a list box, `List1`, as in this example:

```
Private Sub Form_Load()
    Set SchemaRecordset = _
        ConnectionObject.OpenSchema(adSchemaTables)
    While Not SchemaRecordset.EOF
        If SchemaRecordset("TABLE_TYPE") = "TABLE" _
            Then
            List1.AddItem _
                SchemaRecordset("TABLE_NAME")
        End If
        SchemaRecordset.MoveNext
    Wend
End Sub
```

TABLE 5.1	Criteria Values for OpenSchema

QueryType Values	Criteria Values
adSchemaAsserts	CONSTRAINT_CATALOG
	CONSTRAINT_SCHEMA
	CONSTRAINT_NAME
adSchemaCatalogs	CATALOG_NAME
adSchemaCharacterSets	CHARACTER_SET_CATALOG
	CHARACTER_SET_SCHEMA
	CHARACTER_SET_NAME
adSchemaCheckConstraints	CONSTRAINT_CATALOG
	CONSTRAINT_SCHEMA
	CONSTRAINT_NAME
adSchemaCollations	COLLATION_CATALOG
	COLLATION_SCHEMA
	COLLATION_NAME
adSchemaColumnDomainUsage	DOMAIN_CATALOG
	DOMAIN_SCHEMA
	DOMAIN_NAME
	COLUMN_NAME
adSchemaColumnPrivileges	TABLE_CATALOG
	TABLE_SCHEMA
	TABLE_NAME
	COLUMN_NAME
	GRANTOR
	GRANTEE
adSchemaColumns	TABLE_CATALOG
	TABLE_SCHEMA
	TABLE_NAME
	COLUMN_NAME
adSchemaConstraintColumnUsage	TABLE_CATALOG
	TABLE_SCHEMA
	TABLE_NAME
	COLUMN_NAME
adSchemaConstraintTableUsage	TABLE_CATALOG
	TABLE_SCHEMA
	TABLE_NAME
adSchemaForeignKeys	PK_TABLE_CATALOG
	PK_TABLE_SCHEMA
	PK_TABLE_NAME
	FK_TABLE_CATALOG
	FK_TABLE_SCHEMA
	FK_TABLE_NAME

TABLE 5.1	(*Continued*)
QueryType Values	**Criteria Values**
adSchemaIndexes	TABLE_CATALOG
	TABLE_SCHEMA
	INDEX_NAME
	TYPE
	TABLE_NAME
adSchemaKeyColumnUsage	CONSTRAINT_CATALOG
	CONSTRAINT_SCHEMA
	CONSTRAINT_NAME
	TABLE_CATALOG
	TABLE_SCHEMA
	TABLE_NAME
	COLUMN_NAME
adSchemaPrimaryKeys	PK_TABLE_CATALOG
	PK_TABLE_SCHEMA
	PK_TABLE_NAME
adSchemaProcedureColumns	PROCEDURE_CATALOG
	PROCEDURE_SCHEMA
	PROCEDURE_NAME
	COLUMN_NAME
adSchemaProcedureParameters	PROCEDURE_CATALOG
	PROCEDURE_SCHEMA
	PROCEDURE_NAME
	PARAMETER_NAME
adSchemaProcedures	PROCEDURE_CATALOG
	PROCEDURE_SCHEMA
	PROCEDURE_NAME
	PROCEDURE_TYPE
adSchemaProviderSpecific	See remarks.
adSchemaProviderTypes	DATA_TYPE
	BEST_MATCH
adSchemaReferentialConstraints	CONSTRAINT_CATALOG
	CONSTRAINT_SCHEMA
	CONSTRAINT_NAME
adSchemaSchemata	CATALOG_NAME
	SCHEMA_NAME
	SCHEMA_OWNER
adSchemaSQLLanguages	None.
adSchemaStatistics	TABLE_CATALOG
	TABLE_SCHEMA
	TABLE_NAME

TABLE 5.1 *(Continued)*

QueryType Values	Criteria Values
adSchemaTableConstraints	CONSTRAINT_CATALOG
	CONSTRAINT_SCHEMA
	CONSTRAINT_NAME
	TABLE_CATALOG
	TABLE_SCHEMA
	TABLE_NAME
	CONSTRAINT_TYPE
adSchemaTablePrivileges	TABLE_CATALOG
	TABLE_SCHEMA
	TABLE_NAME
	GRANTOR
	GRANTEE
adSchemaTables	TABLE_CATALOG
	TABLE_SCHEMA
	TABLE_NAME
	TABLE_TYPE
adSchemaTranslations	TRANSLATION_CATALOG
	TRANSLATION_SCHEMA
	TRANSLATION_NAME
adSchemaUsagePrivileges	OBJECT_CATALOG
	OBJECT_SCHEMA
	OBJECT_NAME
	OBJECT_TYPE
	GRANTOR
	GRANTEE
adSchemaViewColumnUsage	VIEW_CATALOG
	VIEW_SCHEMA
	VIEW_NAME
adSchemaViewTableUsage	VIEW_CATALOG
	VIEW_SCHEMA
	VIEW_NAME
adSchemaViews	TABLE_CATALOG
	TABLE_SCHEMA
	TABLE_NAME

RollbackTrans

You use the `RollbackTrans` method to cancel the changes in a pending transaction and to end that transaction. The most recent transaction is affected if the OLE DB provider supports nested transactions. When you use the `RollbackTrans` method, the changes made since the most recent `BeginTrans` method call will be canceled.

Note that if the `Attributes` property of the `Connection` object is set to adXactAbortRetaining, the provider automatically starts a new transaction after the `RollbackTrans` call.

That's it for the `Connection` object's methods; next, I'll take a look at the `Connection` object's events.

Connection Object Events

Events were first introduced for the `Connection` object in ADO 2.0, and currently, there are nine such events. I'll take a look at all of them here, starting with `BeginTransComplete`

BeginTransComplete

This event fires when a `BeginTrans` method call is complete. Here's what the event handler for this event looks like:

```
Private Sub Connection1_BeginTransComplete(ByVal _
TransactionLevel As Long, ByVal pError As _
ADODB.Error, adStatus As ADODB.EventStatusEnum, _
ByVal pConnection As ADODB.Connection)


End Sub
```

Here are the parameters passed to this method:

- **TransactionLevel**—The current transaction level for nested transactions; starts with 1 for the outermost transaction.
- **pError**—Describes the error that occurred when the value of adStatus is adStatusErrorsOccurred; otherwise not set. See Table 3.1 for a listing of errors.
- **adStatus**—The status of the operation. See Chapter 3 for all the possible values for this parameter.
- **pConnection**—The `Connection` object in which this event fired.

You can use this event to start other operations in a transaction, because this event's handler is called after the transaction has begun.

CommitTransComplete

This event fires when a `CommitTrans` call is completed. Here is what the event handler for this event looks like:

```
Private Sub Connection1_CommitTransComplete(ByVal _
pError As ADODB.Error, adStatus As _
ADODB.EventStatusEnum, ByVal pConnection As _
ADODB.Connection)


End Sub
```

Here are the parameters passed to this method:

- **pError**—Describes the error that occurred when the value of `adStatus` is `adStatusErrorsOccurred`; otherwise not set. See Table 3.1 for a listing of errors.
- **adStatus**—The status of the operation. See Chapter 3 for all the possible values for this parameter.
- **pConnection**—The `Connection` object in which this event fired.

This event fires when the current transaction is committed in the data source, and it's a good one to use if you have operations you want to undertake when changes have been written to the data source and you're ready to begin a new transaction.

ConnectComplete

The `ConnectComplete` event fires when the `Connection` object has made a connection. Here is what the event handler for this event looks like:

```
Private Sub Connection1_ConnectComplete(ByVal _
pError As ADODB.Error, adStatus As _
ADODB.EventStatusEnum, ByVal pConnection As _
ADODB.Connection)


End Sub
```

Here are the parameters passed to this method:

- **pError**—Describes the error that occurred when the value of `adSta-tus` is `adStatusErrorsOccurred`; otherwise not set. See Table 3.1 for a listing of errors.
- **adStatus**—The status of the operation. See Chapter 3 for all the possible values for this parameter.
- **pConnection**—The `Connection` object in which this event fired.

This event is a very useful one, especially if you're making asynchronous connections, and I'll write an example of that later in the chapter. Since this event fires when the connection is made, you can tell that the `Connection` object has completed the asynchronous connection process by placing code in this event's handler.

Disconnect

The `Disconnect` event fires when a connection has ended. Here is what the event handler for this event looks like:

```
Private Sub Connection1_Disconnect(adStatus As _

ADODB.EventStatusEnum, ByVal pConnection As _

ADODB.Connection)


End Sub
```

Here are the parameters passed to this method:

- **adStatus**—The status of the operation. See Chapter 3 for all the possible values for this parameter.
- **pConnection**—The `Connection` object in which this event fired.

You can use this event to record when a connection was terminated, or to warn users if a connection closes unexpectedly and ask if they want to reconnect.

ExecuteComplete

The `ExecuteComplete` event fires when a call to the `Execute` method is completed. Here is what the event handler for this event looks like:

```
Private Sub Connection1_ExecuteComplete(ByVal _

RecordsAffected As Long, ByVal pError As _

ADODB.Error, adStatus As ADODB.EventStatusEnum, _

ByVal pCommand As ADODB.Command, ByVal pRecordset _
```

```
As ADODB.Recordset, ByVal pConnection As _
ADODB.Connection)

End Sub
```

Here are the parameters passed to this method:

- **RecordsAffected**—A long variable in which the provider has stored the number of records affected by the operation.
- **pError**—Describes the error that occurred when the value of adStatus is adStatusErrorsOccurred; otherwise not set. See Table 3.1 for a listing of errors.
- **adStatus**—The status of the operation. See Chapter 3 for all the possible values for this parameter.
- **pCommand**—The Command object that was executed; note that if no Command object was used, this parameter will be empty.
- **pRecordset**—The Recordset object on which the command was executed. Note that this parameter may be empty if the command was a non-recordset-returning command.
- **pConnection**—The Connection object in which this event fired.

You can check the status returned in the adStatus parameter of this event's handler to see if an operation was successfully executed (adStatus will be set to adStatusOK if so). You can also use this event to check when asynchronous execution requests are completed.

InfoMessage

The InfoMessage event fires when a warning occurs as the Connection object is connecting to a data source. Here is what the event handler for this event looks like:

```
Private Sub Connection1_InfoMessage(ByVal pError _
As ADODB.Error, adStatus As ADODB.EventStatusEnum, _
ByVal pConnection As ADODB.Connection)

End Sub
```

Here are the parameters passed to this method:

- **pError**—Describes the error that occurred when the value of adStatus is adStatusErrorsOccurred; otherwise not set. See Table 3.1 for a listing of errors.

- **adStatus**—The status of the operation. See Chapter 3 for all the possible values for this parameter.
- **pConnection**—The Connection object in which this event fired.

If something is going wrong with your connections, this is one of the places to search for error messages.

RollbackTransComplete

The RollbackTransComplete event fires when a RollbackTrans call has finished executing. Here's what the event handler for this event looks like:

```
Private Sub Connection1_RollbackTransComplete(_
ByVal pError As ADODB.Error, adStatus As _
ADODB.EventStatusEnum, ByVal pConnection As _
ADODB.Connection)


End Sub
```

Here are the parameters passed to this method:

- **pError**—Describes the error that occurred when the value of adStatus is adStatusErrorsOccurred; otherwise not set. See Table 3.1 for a listing of errors.
- **adStatus**—The status of the operation. See Chapter 3 for all the possible values for this parameter.
- **pConnection**—The Connection object in which this event fired.

This event is useful when you've rolled back a transaction and want to wait until the rollback is complete before starting a new transaction. Also note that some OLE DB providers may roll back transactions because of errors, and the only notification you get may be in this event.

WillConnect

The WillConnect event fires when the Connection object is about to connect to a data source. Here is what the event handler for this event looks like:

```
Private Sub Connection1_WillConnect( _
ConnectionString As String, UserID As String, _
Password As String, Options As Long, adStatus As _
ADODB.EventStatusEnum, ByVal pConnection As _
```

```
ADODB.Connection)

End Sub
```

Here are the parameters passed to this method:

- **ConnectionString**—The connection string that will be used to open the connection
- **UserID**—The user ID that will be used to open the connection.
- **Password**—The password that will be used to open the connection.
- **Options**—The connection options that were passed to the Open method.
- **adStatus**—The status of the operation. See Chapter 3 for all the possible values for this parameter.
- **pConnection**—The Connection object in which this event fired.

You can use this event to monitor how users are attempting to create connections. For example, if you don't want users to try to log on as the system administrator, you can cancel the operation by setting adStatus to ad StatusCancel like this:

```
Private Sub Connection1_WillConnect( _
ConnectionString As String, UserID As String, _
Password As String, Options As Long, adStatus As _
ADODB.EventStatusEnum, ByVal pConnection As _
ADODB.Connection)
    If UserID = "sa" Then
        adStatus = adStatusCancel
    End If
End Sub
```

WillExecute

The WillExecute event fires when the Execute method of a Connection object has been called. Here's what the event handler for this event looks like:

```
Private Sub Connection1_WillExecute(Source As _
String, CursorType As ADODB.CursorTypeEnum, _
LockType As ADODB.LockTypeEnum, Options As Long, _
```

```
adStatus As ADODB.EventStatusEnum, ByVal pCommand _

As ADODB.Command, ByVal pRecordset As _

ADODB.Recordset, ByVal pConnection As _

ADODB.Connection)


End Sub
```

Here are the parameters passed to this method:

- **Source**—The SQL command or stored procedure that will be executed.
- **CursorType**—The type of cursor for the recordset that will be created.
- **LockType**—The lock type for the recordset that will be created.
- **Options**—The options placed in the Options parameter of the Execute call.
- **adStatus**—The status of the operation. See Chapter 3 for all the possible values for this parameter.
- **pCommand**—The Command object for this event.
- **pRecordset**—The Recordset object for this event.
- **pConnection**—The Connection object in which this event fired.

If you want to cancel the execution of a command, set adStatus to adStatusCancel. Using this event, you can watch what commands users are trying to execute. For example, you can examine SQL statements before they are executed with this event, and warn about actions likely to change a database in common usage.

Connection Object Collections

The Connection object has two collections:

- **Errors**—Collection of Parameter objects.
- **Properties**—All the Property objects for this Command object.

For more on these collections, see Chapter 9.

Creating Connection Strings

This chapter covers creating ADO connections, and I'll take a look at creating connection strings next. Note that Visual Basic provides an automated way to build connection strings—just click the ellipsis button in the ConnectionString property and click the Build button in the Property Pages that appear—but, it's worth knowing what should go into connection strings, because as you know, connection strings vary by provider.

For example, here's a connection string for Microsoft Jet for the Nwind.mdb database:

```
Provider=Microsoft.Jet.OLEDB.4.0;Persist Security
Info=False;Data Source=C:\ADO\Nwind.mdb
```

Here's how the connection string would look if I were using the Microsoft SQL Server:

```
Provider=SQLOLEDB.1;Persist Security Info=False;User
ID=sa;Initial Catalog=Northwind
```

In general, the ConnectionString property of the Connection object formally supports only these parameters:

- **Provider**—Name of a data provider to use for the connection.
- **File Name**—Name of a provider-specific file containing preset connection information.
- **Remote Provider**—Name of a provider to use when opening a client-side connection. (This applies to the Remote Data Services only.)
- **Remote Server**—Path name of the server to use when opening a client-side connection. (This applies to the Remote Data Services only.)

Here are the possible options for the Provider parameter:

- **ADSDSOObject**—For Microsoft Active Directory.
- **DTSFlatFile**—For DTS flat file providers.
- **DTSPackageDSO**—For DTS packages.
- **Microsoft.Jet.OLEDB.3.51**—For Microsoft Jet 3.51.
- **Microsoft.Jet.OLEDB.4.0**—For Microsoft Jet 4.0.
- **MS Remote**—For remote providers.
- **MSDAORA**—For Oracle.
- **MSDAOSP**—For simple OLE DB providers.
- **MSDASQL** —(default) For ODBC data sources.
- **MSDataShape**—For the Microsoft data shape provider; see Chapter 13 for more details.
- **MSIDXS**—For the Microsoft Index Server.
- **MSOLAP**—For the Microsoft OLAP provider.
- **MSPersist**—For the Microsoft Persist OLE DB provider.

- **SQLOLEDB**—for Microsoft SQL Server.

Note that Visual Basic adds a version number (which is optional), if the OLE DB provider does not specify a version number, to the end of the OLE DB provider name. This version is 1 by default, like this: `MSDASQL.1` or `MSIDXS.1`.

In an effort to simplify and standardize connection strings, ADO defines some additional connection string parameters that are interpreted and sent on to the OLE DB provider:

- **Data Source**—Data source (type depends on the OLE DB provider).
- **Initial Catalog**—The database name for servers that support catalogs.
- **Password**—The user's password.
- **Persist Security Info**—Security information.
- **User ID**—The user's ID.

For example, when you specify a value for the ODBC OLE DB provider using the `Data Source` parameter, that value can be a DSN; when you use Microsoft Jet, `Data Source` holds the name of a database file; when you use SQL Server, `Data Source` holds the name of a server. When you build connection strings using the `Build` button in the `Property Pages`, these ADO-defined parameters are the parameters that Visual Basic uses.

There are plenty of additional provider-specific connection string parameters, such as `Network Library`, `Packet Size`, and `Trusted Connection` for the SQL Server, and I'll take a look at those below. The provider-specific parameters are passed on to the OLE DB provider directly. If a provider-specific parameter is a synonym for an ADO-defined one (such as the ADO-defined `User ID` parameter and the ODBC-defined parameter `UID`) and you include both parameters in a connection string, the ADO-defined parameter takes precedence.

I'll work through the connection string parameters for the more popular OLE DB providers here, starting with the default provider, the Microsoft OLE DB Provider for ODBC.

Microsoft OLE DB Provider for ODBC

To connect to this provider, you set the `Provider` argument of the `ConnectionString` property to `MSDASQL`. This is the default provider for ADO, so if you omit the `Provider` parameter from the connection string, ADO will try to establish a connection to this provider.

The ODBC provider will pass any non-ADO connection parameters to the ODBC driver manager directly, and here are the parameters you can use:

- **Database**—Default database name.
- **DBQ**—Database qualifier or name.

- **DefaultDir**—Default directory for database drivers.
- **Driver**—Non-DSN ODBC server driver.
- **DSN**—ODBC DSN value.
- **FileDSN**—ODBC file DSN entry.
- **PWD**—Password.
- **Server**—Non-DSN database server.
- **UID**—User ID.

 note Because you can omit the **Provider** parameter, you can create an ADO connection string that is the same as an ODBC connection string for the same data source, using the same parameter names, values, and syntax as you would when creating an ODBC connection string.

You can connect with or without a predefined data source name. Here's what the connection string looks like when you use a DSN (note that if you also specify the ADO-defined User ID and Password connection string parameters, the ADO-defined parameters take precedence over the ODBC UID and PWD parameters):

```
"[Provider=MSDASQL;] DSN=name; [DATABASE=database;]
UID=user; PWD=password"
```

Here's how the connection string looks without a DSN (creating a DSN-less ODBC connection):

```
"[Provider=MSDASQL;] DRIVER=driver;
SERVER=server_name; DATABASE=database;
UID=user; PWD=password"
```

Note that you should enclose the driver name in braces; this name is the full name that you select for the driver when you create the DSN (in the Create New Data Source dialog), such as {Microsoft Access Driver (*.mdb)}.

Although a DSN definition already specifies a database, you can specify a DATABASE parameter in addition to a DSN to connect to a different database. This changes the DSN definition to include the specified database. Some programmers consider it a good idea to always include the DATABASE parameter when you use a DSN, because that ensures you will connect to the proper database (that is, another user may have changed the default database parameter since you last checked the DSN).

Microsoft OLE DB Provider for Microsoft Index Server

To connect to this provider, set the `Provider` argument to `MSIDXS` and the `Data Source` connection string parameter to the name of the catalog you want to open. You handle other operations in the `CommandText` property of the `Command` object.

Connection String Parameters for OLE DB Provider for Microsoft Jet

To connect to this provider, set the `Provider` argument of the `ConnectionString` property to `Microsoft.Jet.OLEDB.3.51` or `Microsoft.Jet.OLEDB.4.0`.

The OLE DB Provider for Microsoft Jet supports several provider-specific connection string parameters in addition to those defined by ADO. Here are the settings you'd use for the Microsoft Jet OLE DB provider:

- **Jet OLEDB:System Database**—Path and file name for the workgroup information file.
- **Jet OLEDB:Registry Path**—Registry key that contains values used by the Microsoft Jet database engine.
- **Jet OLEDB:Database Password**—Database password.

Microsoft OLE DB Provider for SQL Server

To connect to this provider, set the `Provider` argument of the `ConnectionString` property to `SQLOLEDB`. This provider supports several provider-specific connection parameters in addition to those defined by ADO. Here are the connection parameters you can use with the SQL Server:

- **Application Name**—Client application name.
- **Auto Translate**—OEM/ANSI character conversion. If this property is set to True, then SQLOLEDB performs OEM/ANSI character conversion on multi-byte character strings.
- **Current Language**—SQL Server language name. Identifies the language used for system message selection and formatting.
- **Data Source**—Server name.
- **Network Address**—Network address of the SQL Server specified by the `Location` property.
- **Network Library**—Name of the net-library (DLL) used to communicate with the SQL Server. The name should not include the path or the `.dll` file name extension. The default is provided by the SQL Server client configuration.

- **Packet Size**—Network packet size in bytes. The packet size property value must be between 512 and 32767. The default SQLOLEDB network packet size is 4096.
- **Trusted Connection**—User authentication mode. If this property is set to True, then SQL Server uses Windows NT authentication. If this property is set to False (the default), then it uses mixed mode to authorize user access. The SQL Server login and password are specified in the User ID and Password properties.
- **Use Procedure for Prepare**—Specifies the use of SQL Server temporary stored procedures when commands are prepared.
- **Workstation ID**—String identifying the workstation.

That completes the reference part of the chapter—it's time to get to the code now, starting with creating and using a Connection object.

Programming with the ADO Library in Code

To create and work with Connection objects and other ADO objects in code, you start by adding a reference to the ADO library to your project. To add a reference to the ADO library—and so gain access to the ADO library of objects—you select the References item in the Project menu and select the Microsoft ActiveX Data Objects Library item in the References dialog that opens, as shown in Figure 5.7. Click OK to add the reference to your project.

Make sure you add a reference to the Microsoft ActiveX Data Objects Library, not the Microsoft ActiveX Data Objects Recordset Library, which is the library used by the Internet Explorer to support recordsets only.

After adding a reference to the ADO library, you're free to use those objects in code, and the first step is to use the Connection object to open a connection to a database. To do that, I declare a new Connection object like this:

```
Private adoConnect As Connection
```

Then I create the new Connection object when the main form loads:

```
Private adoConnect As Connection
Private Sub Form_Load()
```

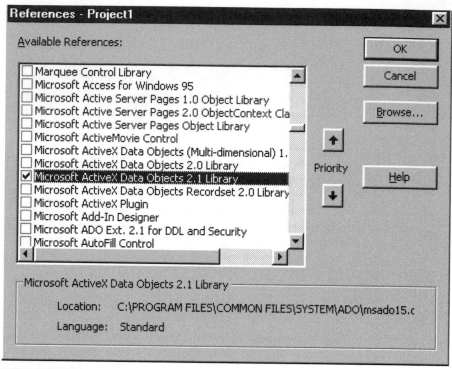

FIGURE 5.7   The References dialog.

```
Set adoConnect = New Connection
    .
    .
    .

End Sub
```

Now we've created a new `Connection` object. The next step is to open the actual connection.

Opening ADO Connections

We'll see plenty of examples in this book, and the one that illustrates basic ADO programming over the next few chapters is the `adodb` project, which appears in the folder of that name on the CD. This application shows how to open and work with databases in ADO—in particular, the `Biblio.mdb` database that comes with Visual Basic. You can see it running in Figure 5.8. This

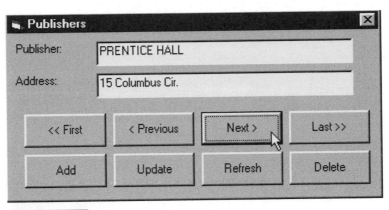

FIGURE 5.8 The adodb application.

application is just like the one we developed in the previous chapter to show how to use the ADO control—but note that there's no ADO control here; we're doing it all with ADO library methods.

To open an ADO connection, you use the `Connection` object's `Open` method:

```
connection.Open [ConnectionString [, UserID _

    [, Password [, OpenOptions]]]]
```

Here are the arguments to this method:

- **ConnectionString**—String containing connection information.
- **UserID**—User name to use when establishing the connection.
- **Password**—Password to use when establishing the connection.
- **OpenOptions**—If you specify a value for this argument and set it to adConnectAsync, the connection will be opened asynchronously. Note that a `ConnectComplete` event will fire when the connection is available.

The first parameter you pass to the `Open` method is the connection string to use. As an example of showing how to open a connection, here's how the adodb project does it when its form loads, opening the database `Biblio.mdb`.

I use the `Open` method like this, using the connection we created above:

```
Private adoConnect As Connection

Private Sub Form_Load()
```

```
         Set adoConnect = New Connection


         adoConnect.Open _

              "PROVIDER=Microsoft.Jet.OLEDB.3.51;Data " & _

              "Source=C:\ADO\Biblio.mdb;"

              .

              .

              .

End Sub
```

That's all it takes—now the connection is open. Note that opening connections can be error-prone, so in applications you release, you'd usually add error-handling code (with the On Error GoTo statement) when opening a connection like this:

```
Private adoConnect As Connection

Private Sub Form_Load()

    On Error GoTo ErrHandler


    Set adoConnect = New Connection


    adoConnect.Open _

       "PROVIDER=Microsoft.Jet.OLEDB.3.51;Data " & _

       "Source=C:\ADO\Biblio.mdb;"

          .

          .

          .

          Exit Sub

ErrorHandler:

          MsgBox Err.Description

End Sub
```

After the connection is open, you can execute commands on the connection and open a recordset; I'll open a recordset in the adodb project later.

Opening a Connection Asynchronously

Because ADO is designed to work with networks and the Internet, both of which can be slow data providers, the `Open` methods can also support asynchronous open operations, which means that you don't have to wait for a connection to be made. If you set the `OpenOptions` argument in the `Connection` object's `Open` method to `adConnectAsync`, the object opens a connection asynchronously:

```
Private Sub Form_Load()
    Set adoConnect = New Connection

    adoConnect.Open _
        "PROVIDER=Microsoft.Jet.OLEDB.3.51;Data" & _
        " Source=C:\ADO\Biblio.mdb;", , , _
        adConnectAsync
            .
            .
            .
```

There are two ways to determine if an asynchronous connection has been made. First, you can use the `Connection` object's `State` property, which can take two values, depending on whether the connection is open or closed:

- **adStateClosed**—(default) The connection is closed.
- **adStateOpen**—The connection is open.

For example, here's how to use the `State` property to make the application do something really significant until the connection is made, like beep:

```
Private Sub Form_Load()
    Set adoConnect = New Connection

    adoConnect.Open _
        "PROVIDER=Microsoft.Jet.OLEDB.3.51;Data" & _
        " Source=C:\ADO\Biblio.mdb;", , , _
        adConnectAsync
```

```
Do Until adoConnect.State And adStateOpen
        Beep
    Loop
```

The second way of determining when a connection is made is to use the `ConnectComplete` event, which fires when the connection is available.

To use that event, you must first make sure you declare the `Connection` object using the `WithEvents` keyword:

```
Private WithEvents adoConnect As Connection
adoConnect.Open _
    "PROVIDER=Microsoft.Jet.OLEDB.3.51;Data" & _
    "Source=C:\ADO\Biblio.mdb;", , , _
    AdConnectAsync
```

The `WithEvents` keyword is new in Visual Basic, and it indicates that you want to support the events of the object you're creating in code (before `WithEvents` was added to Visual Basic, you could only use an object's properties and methods). Then, in the `ConnectComplete` event handler, you can take an action when the connection is complete:

```
Private Sub adoConnect_ConnectComplete(ByVal pError _
    As ADODB.Error, adStatus As _
    ADODB.EventStatusEnum, ByVal pConnection As _
    ADODB.Connection)
    MsgBox "Connection is complete."
End Sub
```

 The counterpart of the `ConnectComplete` event is the `Disconnect` event, which fires when the connection ends.

Note also that you can cancel a pending asynchronous request like the `Open` request with the `Cancel` method like this, if you want to:

```
adoConnect.Cancel
```

Setting Cursor Location

Note that one thing you don't specify in a connection's `Open` method is where you want to set the cursor, on the client side or the server side. By default, ADO uses server-side cursors, but you can specify client-side cursors by setting the `CursorLocation` property of the `Connection` object to `adUse-Client`. The default setting is `adUseServer`.

Server-side cursors are usually faster, so you may wonder why you'd ever want to use a client-side cursor if your server supports server-side cursors. It turns out that several data operations—such as batch updates, recordset persistence, or working with the ADO recordset library, ADOR (not the full ADO library)—need client-side cursors.

Closing Connections

To close a connection, you use the `Connection` object's `Close` method. This method takes no parameters. Note that, like any other Visual Basic object, the `Connection` object will hang around in memory, even if you've closed it. To remove it from memory, you do what you'd do with any object—you set it to `Nothing`:

```
adoConnect.Close
Set adoConnect = Nothing
```

That's it for making and breaking the ADO connection. After you have an open connection to a database, you can open a recordset from that database, and I'll take a look at that next.

Opening Recordsets with Connections

The operations you undertake in ADO usually involve working with recordsets, which are supported with the ADO `Recordset` object.

Once you have an open connection to a database, you can use three methods to open a recordset: the `Connection` object's `Execute` method, the `Recordset` object's `Open` method, and the `Command` object's `Execute` method. I'll take a look at the `Connection` object's `Execute` method in this chapter.

 note Note that the three methods mentioned above all can be used to open recordsets. To simply execute a command that does not return any records, you can use either the `Connection` object's `Execute` method or the `Command` object's `Execute` method.

Using the Connection Object's Execute Method

You can use the `Connection` object's `Execute` method to execute a query, SQL statement, stored procedure, or provider-specific command without using a `Command` object (however, you need to use a `Command` object if you want to persist the command text and re-execute it, or use query parameters). We saw how to use the `Execute` method earlier in this chapter:

```
ConnectionObject.Execute [CommandText [, _
RecordsAffected [, Options ]]]
```

Here's an example showing how to use the `Connection` object's `Execute` method; in this case, I'm opening the `Publishers` table in the `Biblio.mdb` database:

```
Set adoRecordset = adoConnect.Execute( _
    "SELECT * FROM Publishers")
```

Once the `Recordset` object is created, you can work with the properties and methods of that object, as I'll do in the next topic (and a great deal more in Chapters 7 and 8).

Using Transactions

`Connection` objects provide the `BeginTrans`, `CommitTrans`, and `RollbackTrans` methods to let you wrap multiple operations into single transactions. Note that not all data providers support transactions. You can check if your provider does by seeing if the provider-defined property `Transaction DDL` appears in the `Connection` object's `Properties` collection.

Here's an example that uses transactions in the Microsoft SQL Server. In the example, I'll let the user work with the `Nwind` database that comes with Visual Basic and roll back their changes if they don't want to preserve them.

I start by adding a reference to the ADO library, then create a new connection to the `Northwind` database:

```
Private Sub Form_Load()
    Dim adoConnect As ADODB.Connection
    Dim rsCustomers As ADODB.Recordset
    Dim strPrompt As String

    Set adoConnect = New ADODB.Connection
    adoConnect.Open _
        "Provider=SQLOLEDB.1;Persist " & _
        "Security Info=False;User ID=sa;Initial" & _
```

```
" Catalog=Northwind"

    .

    .

    .
```

Next, I'll open the Customers table and move to the first record like this—we'll see how to work with Recordset objects like this in Chapter 7:

```
Set rsCustomers = New ADODB.Recordset

rsCustomers.CursorType = adOpenDynamic

rsCustomers.LockType = adLockPessimistic

rsCustomers.Open "Customers", adoConnect, , , _
    adCmdTable


rsCustomers.MoveFirst

    .

    .

    .
```

Now I begin the transaction with BeginTrans:

```
adoConnect.BeginTrans

    .

    .

    .
```

In this next part, I'll loop over each name in the ContactName field of the Customers table and ask the user if they want to change that name to "undefined"; if so, I'll change the name accordingly and update the recordset:

```
Do Until rsCustomers.EOF
    strPrompt = "Current contact name = " & _
        rsCustomers!ContactName & _
        ". Change to undefined?"

    If MsgBox(strPrompt, vbYesNo) = vbYes Then
            rsCustomers!ContactName = _
                "undefined"
```

```
                          rsCustomers.Update
                End If


                    rsCustomers.MoveNext
            Loop

                .

                .

                .
```

After looping through the whole table, I'll ask the user if they want to save their changes. If they answer yes, I'll commit the changes to the database with `CommitTrans`; otherwise, I'll roll the changes back with `RollbackTrans`:

```
If MsgBox("Save your changes?", vbYesNo) = _
    vbYes Then
        adoConnect.CommitTrans
Else
        adoConnect.RollbackTrans
End If


rsCustomers.Close
adoConnect.Close


End Sub
```

And that's all there is to it. The code for this example, `transactions.frm`, appears in Listing 5.1.

LISTING 5.1   *Transactions.frm Code*

```
VERSION 5.00
Begin VB.Form Form1
    Caption         =   "Form1"
    ClientHeight    =   3195
    ClientLeft      =   60
    ClientTop       =   345
    ClientWidth     =   4680
    LinkTopic       =   "Form1"
```

```
    ScaleHeight    =    3195
    ScaleWidth     =    4680
    StartUpPosition =   3   'Windows Default
End
Attribute VB_Name = "Form1"
Attribute VB_GlobalNameSpace = False
Attribute VB_Creatable = False
Attribute VB_PredeclaredId = True
Attribute VB_Exposed = False
Private Sub Form_Load()
    Dim adoConnect As ADODB.Connection
    Dim rsCustomers As ADODB.Recordset
    Dim strPrompt As String

    Set adoConnect = New ADODB.Connection
    adoConnect.Open _
    "Provider=SQLOLEDB.1;Persist " & _
    "Security Info=False;User " & _
    "ID=sa;Initial Catalog=Northwind"

    Set rsCustomers = New ADODB.Recordset
    rsCustomers.CursorType = adOpenDynamic
    rsCustomers.LockType = adLockPessimistic
    rsCustomers.Open "Customers", adoConnect, , , adCmdTable

    rsCustomers.MoveFirst

    adoConnect.BeginTrans

    Do Until rsCustomers.EOF
        strPrompt = "Current contact name - " & _
        rsCustomers!ContactName & ". Change to undefined?"

        If MsgBox(strPrompt, vbYesNo) = vbYes Then
                rsCustomers!ContactName - "undefined"
                rsCustomers.Update
        End If

        rsCustomers.MoveNext
    Loop

    If MsgBox("Save your changes?", vbYesNo) = vbYes Then
        adoConnect.CommitTrans
    Else
        adoConnect.RollbackTrans
    End If

    rsCustomers.Close
    adoConnect.Close

End Sub
```

Connection Pooling

Connecting to databases is a time-consuming process in ADO, so Microsoft created connection pooling. In connection pooling, ADO will not destroy a connection unless it needs to, as set by a timeout value—if the connection has not been reused in a certain amount of time, ADO destroys it. In other words, if you close a connection, it is really closed from your point of view, but ADO keeps it around in case you want to re-open it.

To reuse a connection, you must specify the exact same parameters you used to open the connection earlier (this is done for security reasons—that is, other users won't be able to use the connections you've been using), so connection pooling only really helps when you're connecting and disconnecting to the same data source a great deal of the time.

If you're not connecting and disconnecting to the same data source a lot, you may want to turn off connection pooling to be able to reclaim the large amount of memory connection pooling can use. You can turn off connection pooling by adding `OLE DB Services = -2` at the end of the connection string, or by executing this line of code: `ConnectionObject.Properties("OLE DB Services") = -2` (see Chapter 9 for more on the `Properties` collection).

Using ADO Commands

In the previous chapter, I took a look at the process of connecting to data sources using ADO `Connection` objects; in this chapter, I'll take a look at the next step—executing commands on those data sources. A connection is just that—a connection to a data source; to work with the data source, you execute an ADO command. Commands are usually associated with `Connection` objects (although you actually can place a connection string into a `Command` object's `ActiveConnection` property without using a `Connection` object—Visual Basic will create a `Connection` object for you in this case). In fact, a `Connection` object can have several different `Command` objects associated with it, which makes sense, because you may want to work with multiple tables or views in a database.

There are various ways to work with commands; for example, the ADO data control works with commands behind the scenes and simply exposes a few properties that let you configure its internal `Command` object to some extent. Using Data Environments, however, you have full access to the `Command` objects of a connection, and so can use the properties and methods of that object. And, you can also work with `Command` objects directly in code, creating and executing commands as you require.

253

Command objects can perform a great many tasks; the most common task is to return a recordset, often after executing an SQL statement, but commands can also perform many non-recordset-returning tasks like deleting or inserting records. Command objects can be of several different types, as set by the CommandType property; for example, a command can be configured simply to return a table, to execute an SQL statement, or to run a stored procedure. We'll see all of these techniques and more in this chapter.

In addition, you can configure commands at run-time by passing them parameters in Parameter objects. For example, you may have a command that executes SQL to find the total number of orders a particular customer made in the previous year, and you'd pass the customer's name or ID as an input parameter to this command. Parameters can also be output parameters, in which case, they'd return information from a command, as we'll see.

Later in this book, we'll also take a look at hierarchical recordsets, which you can create using parent and child commands. That's it for the introduction; I'll start taking a look at Command and Parameter objects now, starting with the ADO data control.

Using Commands in ADO Data Controls

You interact with the Command object in the ADO data control, to the limited extent that the control allows you, with its RecordSource property. For example, to connect to the Customers table in the Nwind database, you first create a connection string to the Nwind database using the control's ConnectionString property, then click the ellipsis button in the RecordSource property's entry in the Properties window, opening the ADO data control's Property Pages to the RecordSource tab, as you see in Figure 6.1.

To configure the ADO data control's Command object, you select the command type first, as shown in Figure 6.1 (this property is also available as the control's CommandType property). Here are the possibilities for the ADO data control:

- **adCmdUnknown**—Unknown command type (i.e., the data provider will determine the type).
- **adCmdText**—Text type command, usually SQL.
- **adCmdTable**—Table type command that returns a table.
- **adCmdStoredProc**—Stored procedure type command that executes a stored procedure.

We'll see how to use the text, table, and stored procedure command types in this chapter; in this case, I set the command type to adCmdTable, as you see in Figure 6.1, and enter the name of the table in the Table or Stored Procedure Name box, as also shown in that figure. If I had made this a command of type adCmdText, I could have stored an SQL statement to

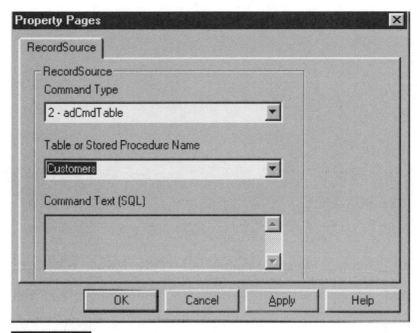

FIGURE 6.1 The ADO data control's `Property Pages`, `RecordSource` tab.

execute in this command in the `Command Text (SQL)` box you see in Figure 6.1.

Besides the `RecordSource` property, you can also set the `Command-Timeout` property in the ADO data control, but that's about all the power you have to work with the ADO `Command` object in the ADO data control; the actual `Command` object is not exposed for use. However, the situation is different with Data Environments.

Using Commands in Data Environments

As you know, you can add commands directly to `Connection` objects in Data Environments; just right click the connection and select the `Add Command` menu item that appears. You can have multiple commands for each connection, as shown in Figure 6.2, where I've given `Connection1` two commands, `Command1` and `Command2`.

To configure a new `Command` object, just right-click it in the Data Environment and select the `Properties` menu item, opening the `Command` object's `Property Pages`, as you see in Figure 6.3.

The `Command` object's `Property Pages` give you full access to the properties of the command. As you see in Figure 6.3, you can set the command's type, active connection, SQL, database object type (e.g., `Table` or `View`), and

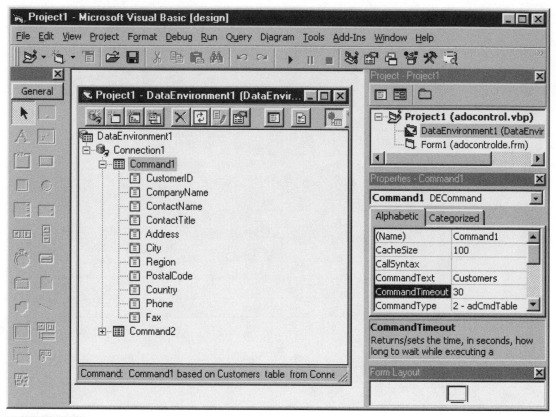

FIGURE 6.2 Using `Connection` objects in a Data Environment.

the actual database object (e.g., the table's name or the name of the view), all in the `General` tab of the `Property Pages`. As an example, I'm using the `Sales By Category` view in the `Nwind` database in Figure 6.3.

If you click the `Parameters` tab in the `Command` object's `Property Pages`, you can set all the properties of the parameters required by the command (we'll see how to use parameters in a few pages), including the parameter's `Name`, `Direction` (input or output), and `DataType` properties, as well as others.

The `Relation`, `Grouping`, and `Aggregates` tabs in the command's `Property Pages` are used when creating child commands, which we'll see more of later in the book. The `Advanced` tab gives you even more control, as you see in Figure 6.4, letting you set the cursor location, lock type, command timeout, and more.

After you've given the `Command` object the properties you want, you click `OK` to close the `Property Pages`.

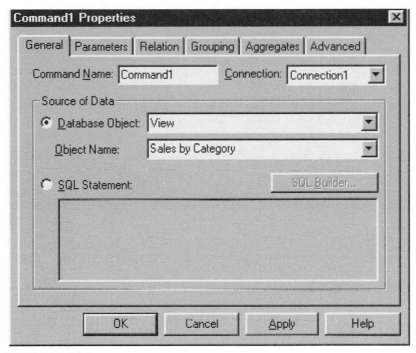

FIGURE 6.3 A `Connection` object's `Property Pages`, `General` tab.

You can also reach the commands in a Data Environment in code, using the Data Environment's `Commands` collection, which holds all the commands in a Data Environment indexed by number and name (note that all the commands in a Data Environment should have unique names since they all appear in the `Commands` collection). Here's an example where I set the `CommandText` property of `Command1` in the Data Environment `DataEnvironment1`:

```
Private Sub Form_Load()
DataEnvironment1.Commands("Command1").CommandText _
= "Select * From Publishers"
    .
    .
    .
End Sub
```

If `Command1` is the first command in the Data Environment, I could do the same thing referring to the command by numeric index this way:

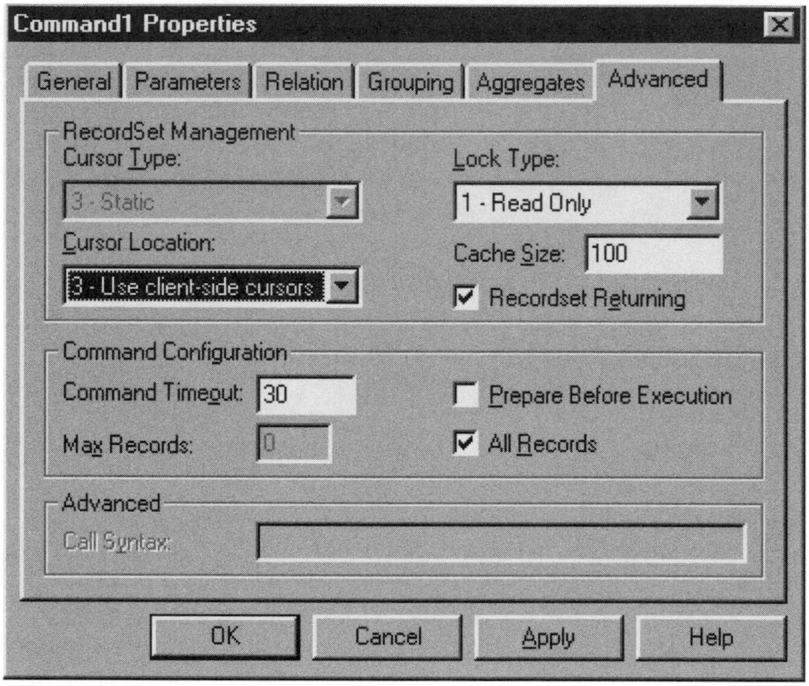

FIGURE 6.4 A Connection object's Property Pages, Advanced tab.

```
Private Sub Form_Load()
DataEnvironment1.Commands(0).CommandText _
= "Select * From Publishers"
      .
      .
      .
End Sub
```

You also use the Commands collection to execute the methods of commands in a Data Environment from code. For example, here I'm calling the Execute method of Command1 in DataEnvironment1:

```
Private Sub Form_Load()
DataEnvironment1.Commands("Command1").CommandText _
= "Select * From Publishers"
DataEnvironment1.Commands("Command1").Execute
End Sub
```

There's a shorthand way of executing commands associated with a
`Connection` object or Data Environment; you can just use the command's
name as a method of the `Connection` object or Data Environment. Here's
how that looks using Data Environments (we'll see more about this later in
the chapter):

```
Private Sub Form_Load()

DataEnvironment1.Commands("Command1").CommandText _

= "Select * From Publishers"

DataEnvironment1.Command1

End Sub
```

In many ways, Data Environments treat recordset-returning commands
as recordsets themselves. For example, you can see fields in the recordset returned by `Command1` in the Data Environment in Figure 6.2. You can also
treat recordset-returning commands in Data Environments as recordsets by
adding the letters "rs" to the front of the command's name in code. Here's an
example where I'm using the recordset returned by `Command1` as `rsCom-
mand1`:

```
Private Sub cmdFirst_Click()
    On Error GoTo ErrLabel


    If DataEnvironment1.rsCommand1.RecordCount > _
        0 Then
        DataEnvironment1.rsCommand1.MoveFirst
    End If


    Exit Sub


ErrLabel:
    MsgBox Err.Description
End Sub
```

Note that you can add code to a recordset-returning command in a Data
Environment directly by double-clicking the command in the Data Environment, or by right-clicking the command and selecting the `View Code` menu
item that appears. Doing so lets you add code directly to the recordset object
returned by the command (e.g., the recordset `rsCommand1` returned by the

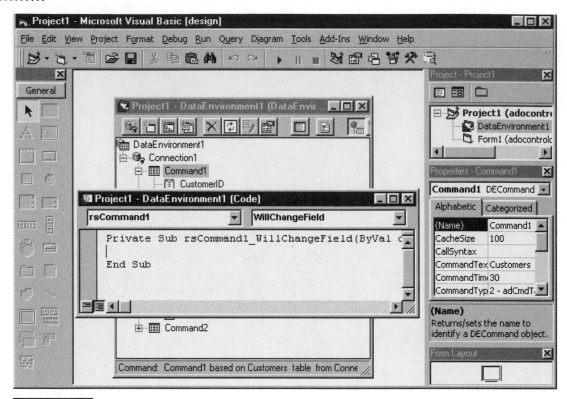

FIGURE 6.5 Adding code to the recordset returned by a command in a Data Environment.

command Command1), as shown in Figure 6.5. By default, the Data Environment opens the rsCommand1_WillChangeField event handler.

We'll see more about using Data Environment commands as recordsets in Chapter 8.

As you can see, you have full access to the Command objects in a Data Environment, both at design-time and at run-time. That being so, it's time to take a look at how Command objects themselves work.

Using ADO Command Objects

Formally, a Command object stores and executes instructions issued across a connection to manipulate a data source, typically through SQL. You use Command objects to query a database and return records in a Recordset object, to execute multiple operations, or to manipulate the structure of a database.

Using the methods and properties of a Command object, you can do the following:

- Specify the executable text of the command, like an SQL statement, using the CommandText property.
- Set up parameterized queries or stored-procedure arguments with Parameter objects and the Parameters collection.
- Execute a command and possibly return a Recordset object using the Execute method.
- Specify the type of command with the CommandType property.
- Specify whether or not the provider saves a compiled version of the command before execution using the Prepared property.
- Specify the number of seconds providers will wait for commands to execute using the CommandTimeout property.
- Associate an open connection with a Command object by setting its ActiveConnection property.
- Use the name of the command, as stored in the Name property, as a method of the associated Connection object.
- Pass Command objects to the Source property of a recordset to get data.

Note that you can execute a command without using a Command object—you can pass command text to the Execute method of a Connection object or to the Open method of a Recordset object directly. However, you need a Command object when you want to persist the command text and re-execute it, or to use query parameters.

To execute a command, you call its Execute method, or simply call it by name (as stored in its Name property) as a method of the associated Connection object. Note that before executing a command, the command must have its ActiveConnection property set to the Connection object. If the command has parameters, you can pass their values as arguments to the method.

I'll take a look at the properties, methods, and collections of Command objects now, starting with Command object properties.

Command Object Properties

You configure a Command object using its properties, and I'll start with one of the most important Command object properties: the ActiveConnection property.

ActiveConnection

The ActiveConnection property holds the current connection the Command object is part of. This property must be set before you try to execute the command. If you want to disconnect the command from a connection, set the ActiveConnection property to Nothing.

You usually set the ActiveConnection property to an open Connection object, and I'll do that in this chapter. However, you can also set the

`ActiveConnection` property to a valid connection string. ADO still creates a `Connection` object behind the scenes.

CommandText

The `CommandText` property holds the actual text of a `Command` object. Usually, this text is an SQL statement, but can also be any other type of command statement that the provider recognizes, such as a stored procedure call.

Note also that if the `Prepared` property of the `Command` object is set to True and the `Command` object is associated with an open connection when you set the `CommandText` property, ADO prepares the query, which means that a compiled form of the query is stored by the provider when you call the command's `Execute` or `Open` methods.

note You should know that, depending on the `CommandType` property setting, ADO may change the `CommandText` property. You can check the `CommandText` property at run-time or design-time to see the actual command text that ADO will use.

I'll take a look at the different kinds of commands you can place in the `CommandText` property for different OLE DB providers later in this chapter.

CommandTimeout

This property holds the timeout length of the command in seconds; the default is 30 seconds. If your commands are timing out, due to heavy server use or network traffic, this is the setting to change.

CommandType

This property holds the type of the command; the default is `adCmdUnknown`. There are several different types of commands available, and you indicate which type you're using. Here are the possible command types (note that not all providers will support all command types, and the ADO data control only supports `adCmdunknown`, `adCmdText`, `adCmdTable`, and `adCmdStoredProc`):

- **adCmdText**—This setting makes ADO evaluate `CommandText` as a command or stored procedure call.
- **adCmdTable**—This setting makes ADO evaluate `CommandText` as a table name whose columns are all returned by an internally generated SQL query.
- **adCmdTableDirect**—This setting makes ADO evaluate `CommandText` as a table name whose columns are all returned.

- **adCmdStoredProc**—This setting makes ADO evaluate CommandText as a stored procedure name.

- **adCmdUnknown**—(default)This setting indicates that the type of command in the CommandText property is not known. In this case, it's up to the provider to interpret the command.

- **adCmdFile**—This setting makes ADO evaluate CommandText as the file name of a persisted recordset.

- **adExecuteNoRecords**—This setting specifies that CommandText is a command or stored procedure that does not return rows. If any rows are retrieved, they are discarded and not returned. Note that this setting is always combined with adCmdText or adCmdStoredProc.

Prepared

This property indicates whether or not to save a compiled version of a command before execution. Note that setting this property to True will probably make a command's first execution slower, but once the provider compiles a command, the provider will use the compiled version of the command from then on, which should make execution faster. On the other hand, if you set this property to False, the provider executes the Command object without compiling it.

Note that if the provider does not support preparation, the compiler will usually return an error when you set this property to True (if it does not return an error, it will probably ignore the prepare request and set the Prepared property to False).

State

This property indicates whether the Command object is open or closed with these settings:

- **adStateClosed**—(default) Indicates that the Command object is closed.

- **adStateOpen**—Indicates that the Command object is open.

You can use the State property to determine the current state of a given object at design-time or run-time.

That's it for the Command object's properties; now I'll take a look at the methods of this object.

Command Object Methods

You use the methods of the Command object to execute or cancel commands, or to create new parameters. I'll take a look at all the methods of this object here.

Cancel

You use this method to cancel a pending, asynchronous Execute call (you can make an Execute call asynchronous by using the adAsyncExecute or adAsyncFetch parameters). This is useful if an asynchronous command is taking a long time to execute and you want to provide the user with a way of stopping the operation, such as by providing a Cancel button. The Cancel method takes no parameters.

CreateParameter

You use the CreateParameter method to create a new Parameter object for a Command object. Here's how you use this method:

```
CommandObject.CreateParameter [Name _
[, Type [, Direction [, Size [, Value]]]]
```

This method will return a Parameter object (to assign that object to a variable, use the Set keyword). Here are the parameters you pass to this method:

- **Name**—The name of the Parameter object.
- **Type**—The data type of the Parameter object. See the Parameter object's Type property below for valid settings.
- **Direction**—The type of Parameter object. See the Parameter object's Direction property below for valid settings.
- **Size**—The maximum length for the parameter value in characters or bytes.
- **Value**—The value for the Parameter object.

You use the CreateParameter method to create a new Parameter object with the given name, type, direction, size, and value. The values you pass to this method are placed in the corresponding Parameter object's properties.

Note that this method does not add a Parameter object to the Parameters collection of a Command object—you have to do that yourself with the Parameters collection's Append method.

Note also that if you specify a variable-length data type in the Type argument, you must either pass a Size argument to CreateParameter or set the Size property of the Parameter object before adding it to the Parameters collection. If you don't, ADO generates an error.

Execute

You can use the Command object's Execute method to open a Recordset object:

```
CommandObject.Execute [RecordsAffected
[, Parameters [, Options]]]
```

Here are what the arguments to this method mean:

- **RecordsAffected**—Variable in which the provider returns the number of records that the operation affected.

- **Parameters**—Variant array of parameter values passed with an SQL statement.

- **Options**—Specifies how the provider should evaluate the Command-Text property of the Command object.

The Options argument can hold any of these values:

- **adCmdText**—Provider should evaluate CommandText as a textual definition of a command.

- **adCmdTable**—ADO should generate an SQL query to return all rows from the table named in CommandText.

- **adCmdTableDirect**—Provider should return all rows from the table named in CommandText.

- **adCmdStoredProc**—Provider should evaluate CommandText as a stored procedure.

- **adCmdUnknown**—Type of command in the CommandText argument is not known.

- **adAsyncExecute**—Command should execute asynchronously.

- **adAsyncFetch**—Remaining rows after the initial quantity specified in the CacheSize property should be fetched asynchronously.

I'll put the methods of the Command object to work in this chapter. In the meantime, I'll take a look at the Command object's collections.

Command Object Collections

The Command object has two collections: Parameters and Properties. I'll give an overview of these collections here, and take a closer look at them in the chapter on ADO collections, Chapter 9.

Parameters

The Parameters collection holds a collection of Parameter objects for an object. You append Parameter objects to Command objects that require them using this collection. The Parameters collection has one property: the Count property, which holds the number of the parameters in the collection. Here are the methods of the Parameters collection:

- **Append**—Appends a new parameter to the `Parameters` collection.
- **Delete**—Deletes a parameter from the `Parameters` collection.
- **Item**—Returns a `Parameter` object.
- **Refresh**—Refreshes the `Parameters` collection.

Properties

The `Properties` collection of the `Command` object holds the `Property` objects for the object. For example, to check if the current provider makes output parameters available as soon as a command is executed, you can check its `Output Parameter Availability` property like this:

```
DataEnvironment1.OrdersByEmployee("Jones", Status)
If ConnectionObject.Properties( _
"Output Parameter Availability") = _
DBPROPVAL_OA_ATEXECUTE Then
    If Status = "OK" Then
        MsgBox "The command succeeded."
    End If
End If
```

As we've seen, parameters are a big part of using commands, and I'll take a look at the `Parameter` object next—we'll see how to use commands and parameters together later in this chapter.

Parameter Objects

`Parameter` objects hold all the parameters that you need to use with a command. You use parameters with commands where the actual command is defined once, but the variables (that is, the parameters) are used to specify the values used in the command. For example, you could use a parameter with an SQL `SELECT` statement to specify the criteria of a `WHERE` clause.

Using the collections, methods, and properties of a `Parameter` object, you can do the following:

- Set or get the name of a parameter with the `Name` property.
- Set or get the value of a parameter with the `Value` property.
- Set or get the characteristics of a parameter with properties like `Attributes`, `Direction`, `Precision`, `NumericScale`, `Size`, and `Type`.

• Store long binary or character data to a parameter with the Append-Chunk method.

I'll take a look at the properties and methods of the Parameter object here and put that object to work later in this chapter.

Parameter Object Properties

You use the properties of the Parameter object to configure that object; I'll now take a look at all the properties of this object, starting with the Attributes property.

Attributes

You set a Parameter object's attributes using the Attributes property. The value of this property can be the sum of any one or more of these values:

- **adParamSigned**—(default) Specifies that the parameter accepts signed values.
- **adParamNullable**—Specifies that the parameter accepts null values.
- **adParamLong**—Specifies that the parameter accepts long binary data.

Direction

This property specifies whether a Parameter object is an input parameter (the default), an output parameter—or both—or if the parameter is the return value from a stored procedure. Here are the possible values:

- **adParamUnknown**—The parameter direction is unknown.
- **adParamInput**—(default) The parameter is an input parameter.
- **adParamOutput**—The parameter is an output parameter.
- **adParamInputOutput**—The parameter is both an input and output parameter.
- **adParamReturnValue**—The parameter is a return value.

You use the Direction property to specify how a parameter is passed to or from a command. Note that not all providers can determine the direction of parameters in their stored procedures, and in such cases, you should set the Direction property before you execute a command.

Here's an example using output parameters in a stored procedure named GetValue. This stored procedure takes one input parameter and one output parameter—note that the procedure specifies that the @Data parameter is an output parameter explicitly with the OUTPUT keyword:

```
Create PROCEDURE GetValue
@CustomerID nchar(5)
@Data integer OUTPUT
AS
SELECT ProductName, Total=SUM(Quantity)
    .

    .

    .
```

You can create an output parameter to pass to this stored procedure like this; note that I'm making this an output parameter by specifying the adParamOutput type:

```
CommandObject.CreateParameter ("Data", _
adVarInteger, adParamOutput)
    .

    .

    .
```

Now if I call the GetValue stored procedure, specifying a variable for the output parameter, the stored procedure will place the value of the output parameter in that variable:

```
DataEnvironment1.GetValue("JONES", Data)
MsgBox "The output parameter was:" & Data
    .

    .

    .
```

Name

This property holds the name of the parameter, as referenced in the Command object's CommandText or stored procedure. You use this property to give a name to a parameter. For example, here's a command of the type we'll see how to create in a few pages, which uses one parameter, Name; note that I specify the value of this parameter with a question mark, which means it'll be filled in at run-time—we'll see more about exactly how to create commands that use parameters like this in a few pages:

```
adoCommand.CommandType = adCmdText
```

```
adoCommand.CommandText = "SELECT * from "& _
Publishers WHERE Name = ?"
```

When you create a `Parameter` object for this parameter, you specify the name of the parameter like this:

```
Set adoParam = New Parameter
adoParam.Name = "Name"
    .
    .
    .
```

After appending the new `Parameter` object to the command's `Parameters` collection, you can execute the command and ADO will know what parameter to use for the `Name` parameter by searching that collection.

NumericScale

The `NumericScale` property contains the scale of numeric objects in the `Parameter` object, which indicates how many decimal places to the right of the decimal numeric values will use.

Precision

The `Precision` property of a `Parameter` object holds the degree of precision for numeric values in the `Parameter` object. This property holds a value indicating the maximum total number of digits used to represent values. You use the `Precision` property to determine the maximum number of digits used to represent values for a numeric `Parameter` object.

Size

The `Size` property gives the maximum size, in bytes, of the `Parameter` object. Note that if your parameter contains variable-length data, such as variable-length strings, you should bear in mind that such data can grow in length.

Also bear in mind that the OLE DB provider may require you to use specific maximum sizes for the parameter; for example, when you create a parameter with an image in it, which I'll discuss later in this chapter, using SQL Server, you must specify the `Size` property as the maximum size SQL Server can handle for images—2,147,483,647 bytes.

Type

The `Type` property of a `Parameter` object specifies the type of the parameter. Table 6.1 lists the possible settings for this property:

TABLE 6.1	*Parameter type values*
Constant	**Description**
adArray	Joined in a logical OR together with another type to indicate that the data is a safe array of that type (DBTYPE_ARRAY).
adBigInt	An 8-byte signed integer (DBTYPE_I8).
adBinary	A binary value (DBTYPE_BYTES).
adBoolean	A Boolean value (DBTYPE_BOOL).
adByRef	Joined in a logical OR together with another type to indicate that the data is a pointer to data of the other type (DBTYPE_BYREF).
adBSTR	A null-terminated character string (Unicode) (DBTYPE_BSTR).
adChar	A string value (DBTYPE_STR).
adCurrency	A currency value (DBTYPE_CY). Currency is a fixed-point number with 4 digits to the right of the decimal point. It is stored in an 8-byte signed integer scaled by 10,000.
adDate	A date value (DBTYPE_DATE). A date is stored as a double, the whole part of which is the number of days since December 30, 1899, and the fractional part of which is the fraction of a day.
adDBDate	A date value (*yyyymmdd*) (DBTYPE_DBDATE).
adDBTime	A time value (*hhmmss*) (DBTYPE_DBTIME).
adDBTimeStamp	A date-time stamp (*yyyymmddhhmmss,* plus a fraction in billionths) (DBTYPE_DBTIMESTAMP).
adDecimal	An exact numeric value with a fixed precision and scale (DBTYPE_DECIMAL).
adDouble	A double-precision floating point value (DBTYPE_R8).
adEmpty	No value was specified (DBTYPE_EMPTY).
adError	A 32-bit error code (DBTYPE_ERROR).
adGUID	A globally unique identifier (GUID) (DBTYPE_GUID).
adIDispatch	A pointer to an IDispatch interface on an OLE object (DBTYPE_IDISPATCH).
adInteger	A 4-byte signed integer (DBTYPE_I4).
adIUnknown	A pointer to an IUnknown interface on an OLE object (DBTYPE_IUNKNOWN).
adLongVarBinary	A long binary value.
adLongVarChar	A long string value.
adLongVarWChar	A long null-terminated string value.
adNumeric	An exact numeric value with a fixed precision and scale (DBTYPE_NUMERIC).
adSingle	A single-precision floating point value (DBTYPE_R4).
adSmallInt	A 2-byte signed integer (DBTYPE_I2).
adTinyInt	A 1-byte signed integer (DBTYPE_I1).
adUnsignedBigInt	An 8-byte unsigned integer (DBTYPE_UI8).

TABLE 6.1	(Continued)
Constant	**Description**
adUnsignedInt	A 4-byte unsigned integer (DBTYPE_UI4).
adUnsignedSmallInt	A 2-byte unsigned integer (DBTYPE_UI2).
adUnsignedTinyInt	A 1-byte unsigned integer (DBTYPE_UI1).
adUserDefined	A user-defined variable (DBTYPE_UDT).
adVarBinary	A binary value.
adVarChar	A string value.
adVariant	An automation variant (DBTYPE_VARIANT).
adVector	Joined in a logical OR together with another type to indicate that the data is a DBVECTOR structure, as defined by OLE DB, that contains a count of elements and a pointer to data of the other type (DBTYPE_VECTOR).
adVarWChar	A null-terminated Unicode character string (Parameter object only).
adWChar	A null-terminated Unicode character string (DBTYPE_WSTR).

For example, here's how I specify that a parameter is a string:

```
adoCommand.CommandType = adCmdText
adoCommand.CommandText = "SELECT * from "& _
Publishers WHERE Name = ?"


Set adoParam = New Parameter
adoParam.Name = "Name"
adoParam.Type = adVarChar

    .

    .

    .

adoCommand.Parameters.Append adoParam
Set adoCommand.ActiveConnection = adoConnect


Set adoRecordset = adoCommand.Execute
```

Value

The Value property of a Parameter object is a very important one. As you can guess from its name, this property holds the actual value of the parameter that will be used in the command.

Here's an example where I'm setting a parameter's `Value` property to "PRENTICE HALL":

```
adoCommand.CommandType = adCmdText
adoCommand.CommandText = "SELECT * from "& _
Publishers WHERE Name = ?"

Set adoParam = New Parameter
adoParam.Name = "Name"
adoParam.Type = adVarChar
adoParam.Value = "PRENTICE HALL"
    .
    .
    .

adoCommand.Parameters.Append adoParam
Set adoCommand.ActiveConnection = adoConnect

Set adoRecordset = adoCommand.Execute
```

We'll see how to use the `Value` property when we create parameterized commands. That completes the properties of the `Parameter` object; I'll take a look at this object's methods next.

Parameter Object Methods

`Parameter` objects support two methods: `AppendChunk` and `Delete`, and I'll take a look at those methods here.

AppendChunk

The `AppendChunk` method lets you add long or binary data to a parameter. Here's how you use this method:

ParameterObject.AppendChunk *Data*

Here, `Data` is a variant that holds the data you want to append to the `Parameter` object.

You use this method when you've got some additional data to store in a parameter; the most common use for `AppendChunk` is to store images in parameters, and I'll take a look at that process later in this chapter. The first `AppendChunk` call on a `Parameter` object writes data to the parameter, overwriting any existing data. Further `AppendChunk` calls on a `Parameter` object add to existing parameter data. Note also that an `AppendChunk` call with a null value clears the parameter's data.

Parameter Object Collections

`Parameter` objects have one collection—the `Properties` collection.

Properties

The `Properties` collection of the `Parameter` object holds the `Property` objects for the `Parameter` object. I'll cover the `Properties` collections in detail in Chapter 9.

We've now finished the properties, methods, and collections of the `Parameter` object. So far in this chapter, I've taken a look at both the `Command` and `Parameter` objects, but there's one more topic I'll take a look at before putting these objects to work—how to specify an actual command, which varies by OLE DB provider.

Command Text By OLE DB Provider

You specify an actual command in the `CommandText` property, which can be a table name, SQL statement, or provider-specific command. I'll take a look at how to create the text for commands for the popular OLE DB providers here, starting with the default OLE DB provider, the Microsoft OLE DB Provider for ODBC.

Microsoft OLE DB Provider for ODBC

How you can use commands with an ODBC provider depends on what type of commands it will accept, and that's up to the provider. However, ODBC provides a specific syntax for calling stored procedures. Here's how you set the `CommandText` property of a `Command` object:

```
{[ ? = ] call procedure [ (? [, ? [ , ... ]])]}
```

In this case, each question mark, ?, refers to a parameter in the `Parameters` collection. The first ? refers to `Parameters(0)`, the next ? refers to `Parameters(1)`, and so on. For example, to call a stored procedure that has no parameters, you could use this command text:

```
{call stored_procedure}
```

If you have three command parameters, your string would look like this:

```
{call stored_procedure(?, ?, ?)}
```

Stored procedures can return values, in which case, the return value is treated as another parameter. For example, if a procedure takes no parameters but returns a value, the command text would look like this:

```
{? = call stored_procedure}
```

If a stored procedure has a return value and takes three parameters, the command text would look like this:

```
{? = call stored_procedure(?, ?, ?)}
```

Microsoft OLE DB Provider for Microsoft Index Server

The Index Server provider does not support stored procedure calls or table names; here, the CommandType property will always be adCmdText. The Index Server SQL query syntax is made up of extensions to the SQL92 SELECT statement. The results of the command are interpreted by ADO and returned as Recordset objects.

Microsoft OLE DB Provider for Microsoft Active Directory Service

This provider supports command text strings with four parts:

```
Root; Filter; Attributes[; Scope]
```

Here's what the parts of this command text string are:

- **Root**—The root object from which the search should start.
- **Filter**—The search filter.
- **Attributes**—A list of attributes to be returned.
- **Scope**—A string specifying the scope of the search.

Here are the possible values for the Scope parameter:

- **Base**—Search only the root object.
- **OneLevel**—Search just one level.
- **Subtree**—Search the whole sub-tree.

OLE DB Provider for Microsoft Jet

The command text in `Command` objects you use with the Jet provider uses Jet SQL. There's a great deal you can do with Jet SQL—you can place row-returning queries, action queries, and table names in the command text. Note, however, that stored procedures are not supported by the Jet OLE DB provider.

Microsoft OLE DB Provider for SQL Server

The SQL Server OLE DB provider, SQLOLEDB, can handle quite a mix of ODBC, ANSI, and Transact-SQL (SQL Server's own version of SQL), and this topic itself could make up a book.

When you execute a stored procedure in the SQL Server, you should use the ODBC procedure call in the command text. If you do, the SQL Server provider uses the remote procedure call mechanism of the SQL Server to optimize processing of the command. For example, here's the preferred ODBC-type SQL statement for a stored procedure call:

```
{call Stored_Procedure('Johnson', '2001')}
```

And here's the Transact-SQL form of the same command:

```
EXECUTE Stored_Procedure 'Johnson', '2001'
```

Executing Commands

There are plenty of ways of executing commands in ADO programming. You can use the command's `Execute` method, you can use the `Execute` method with parameters, you can add parameters to a command's `Parameters` collection and then use `Execute`, you can treat the command as a method of a `Connection` object, you can pass parameters to the command when you treat it as a method of a `Connection` object, and so on. In addition, there are different types of commands—`adCmdTable` commands that just open a table, `adCmdText` commands that execute SQL, `adCmdStoredProc` commands that execute stored procedures, and so on. There are also various types of parameters—input parameters, output parameters, and return values. I'll take a look at the various possibilities here.

To start, I'll take a look at executing commands using the `Command` object's `Execute` method:

```
Execute [RecordsAffected [, Parameters [, Options]]]
```

Here are what the arguments to this method mean:

- **RecordsAffected**—Variable in which the provider returns the number of records that the operation affected.
- **Parameters**—Variant array of parameter values passed with an SQL statement.
- **Options**—Specifies how the provider should evaluate the `Command-Text` property of the `Command` object.

The `Options` argument can hold any of these values:

- **adCmdText**—Provider should evaluate `CommandText` as a textual definition of a command.
- **adCmdTable**—ADO should generate an SQL query to return all rows from the table named in `CommandText`.
- **adCmdTableDirect**—Provider should return all rows from the table named in `CommandText`.
- **adCmdStoredProc**—Provider should evaluate `CommandText` as a stored procedure.
- **adCmdUnknown**—Type of command in the `CommandText` argument is not known.
- **adExecuteAsync**—Command should execute asynchronously.
- **adFetchAsync**—Remaining rows after the initial quantity specified in the `CacheSize` property should be fetched asynchronously.

As you can see, there are all kinds of commands that you can execute; I'll start by opening tables.

Opening Tables

In the first `Execute` method example, I'll use the `Command` object's `Execute` method to open the `Publishers` recordset in the `Biblio.mdb` recordset and tie the `Name` and `Address` fields to two text boxes. I start by creating a new connection object, `adoConnect`:

```
Private Sub Form_Load()
    Dim adoConnect As Connection
    Set adoConnect = New Connection
    .
    .
    .
```

Next, I open the connection to `Biblio.mdb`:

```
Private Sub Form_Load()
    Dim adoConnect As Connection
```

```
Set adoConnect = New Connection
```

```
adoConnect.Open _
"PROVIDER=Microsoft.Jet.OLEDB.4.0;" & _
    "Data Source=C:\ado\biblio.mdb;"
```

        .
        .
        .

At this point, I'm ready to create a new Command object and set its CommandType property to adCmdTable, its CommandText property to the table to open, Publishers, and its ActiveConnection property to ado-Connect:

```
Private Sub Form_Load()
    Dim adoConnect As Connection
    Set adoConnect = New Connection

    adoConnect.Open _
    "PROVIDER=Microsoft.Jet.OLEDB.4.0;" & _
        "Data Source=C:\ado\biblio.mdb;"
```

```
    Set adoCommand = New Command
```

```
    adoCommand.CommandType = adCmdTable
    adoCommand.CommandText = "Publishers"
    adoCommand.ActiveConnection = adoConnect
```

        .
        .
        .

All that's left is to execute the command using the Execute method and bind the resulting Recordset object to two text boxes that will display the Name and Address fields like this:

```
    Set adoRecordset = adoCommand.Execute
```

```
Set Text1.DataSource = adoRecordset
Text1.DataField = "Name"
Set Text2.DataSource = adoRecordset
Text2.DataField = "Address"


End Sub
```

The result of this code appears in Figure 6.6, where I've added some code to let the user navigate through the recordset using navigation buttons. This project appears in the adotable folder on the CD, and the code for this project, adotable.frm, appears in Listing 6.1.

LISTING 6.1   *Adotable.frm Code*

```
VERSION 5.00
Begin VB.Form Form1
    BorderStyle       =   3   'Fixed Dialog
    Caption           =   "Publishers"
    ClientHeight      =   2550
    ClientLeft        =   1095
    ClientTop         =   330
    ClientWidth       =   5550
    LinkTopic         =   "Form3"
    MaxButton         =   0   'False
    MinButton         =   0   'False
    ScaleHeight       =   2550
    ScaleWidth        =   5550
    ShowInTaskbar     =   0   'False
```

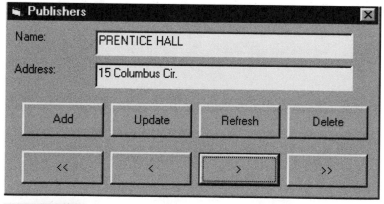

FIGURE 6.6   Executing a command to open a database table

```
Begin VB.CommandButton cmdLast
   Caption          =     ">>"
   Height           =     495
   Left             =     4200
   TabIndex         =     11
   Top              =     1920
   Width            =     1215
End
Begin VB.CommandButton cmdNext
   Caption          =     ">"
   Height           =     495
   Left             =     2880
   TabIndex         =     10
   Top              =     1920
   Width            =     1215
End
Begin VB.CommandButton cmdPrevious
   Caption          =     "<"
   Height           =     495
   Left             =     1560
   TabIndex         =     9
   Top              =     1920
   Width            =     1215
End
Begin VB.CommandButton cmdFirst
   Caption          =     "<<"
   Height           =     495
   Left             =     240
   TabIndex         =     8
   Top              =     1920
   Width            =     1215
End
Begin VB.CommandButton cmdRefresh
   Caption          =     "Refresh"
   Height           =     495
   Left             =     2880
   TabIndex         =     6
   Top              =     1200
   Width            =     1215
End
Begin VB.CommandButton cmdUpdate
   Caption          =     "Update"
   Height           =     495
   Left             =     1560
   TabIndex         =     5
   Top              =     1200
   Width            =     1215
End
Begin VB.CommandButton cmdDelete
   Caption          =     "Delete"
   Height           =     495
```

```
            Left            =     4200
            TabIndex        =     4
            Top             =     1200
            Width           =     1215
         End
         Begin VB.CommandButton cmdAdd
            Caption         =     "Add"
            Height          =     495
            Left            =     240
            TabIndex        =     3
            Top             =     1200
            Width           =     1215
         End
         Begin VB.TextBox Text2
            Height          =     375
            Left            =     1320
            TabIndex        =     2
            Text            =     "Text2"
            Top             =     600
            Width           =     3855
         End
         Begin VB.TextBox Text1
            Height          =     375
            Left            =     1320
            TabIndex        =     1
            Text            =     "Text1"
            Top             =     120
            Width           =     3855
         End
         Begin VB.Label lblLabels
            Caption         =     "Name:"
            Height          =     255
            Index           =     0
            Left            =     120
            TabIndex        =     7
            Top             =     120
            Width           =     1095
         End
         Begin VB.Label lblLabels
            Caption         =     "Address:"
            Height          =     255
            Index           =     1
            Left            =     120
            TabIndex        =     0
            Top             =     600
            Width           =     1095
         End
      End
Attribute VB_Name = "Form1"
Attribute VB_GlobalNameSpace = False
Attribute VB_Creatable = False
Attribute VB_PredeclaredId = True
```

```
Attribute VB_Exposed = False
Private adoRecordset As Recordset
Attribute adoRecordset.VB_VarHelpID = -1

Private Sub Form_Load()
    Dim adoConnect As Connection
    Set adoConnect = New Connection

    adoConnect.Open _
    "PROVIDER=Microsoft.Jet.OLEDB.4.0;" & _
        "Data Source=C:\ado\biblio.mdb;"

    Set adoCommand = New Command

    adoCommand.CommandType = adCmdTable
    adoCommand.CommandText = "Publishers"
    adoCommand.ActiveConnection = adoConnect

    Set adoRecordset = adoCommand.Execute

    Set Text1.DataSource = adoRecordset
    Text1.DataField = "Name"
    Set Text2.DataSource = adoRecordset
    Text2.DataField = "Address"

End Sub


Private Sub cmdAdd_Click()
    On Error GoTo ErrLabel
    adoRecordset.AddNew

    Text1.Text = ""
    Text2.Text = ""

    Exit Sub

ErrLabel:
    MsgBox Err.Description
End Sub

Private Sub cmdDelete_Click()
    On Error GoTo ErrLabel

    adoRecordset.Delete

    adoRecordset.MoveNext
    If adoRecordset.EOF Then
        adoRecordset.MoveLast
    End If

    Exit Sub
```

••••••••••••••••

```
ErrLabel:
    MsgBox Err.Description
End Sub

Private Sub cmdRefresh_Click()

    On Error GoTo ErrLabel
    adoRecordset.Requery
    Exit Sub

ErrLabel:
    MsgBox Err.Description
End Sub

Private Sub cmdUpdate_Click()
    On Error GoTo ErrLabel

    adoRecordset.Update

    Exit Sub

ErrLabel:
    MsgBox Err.Description
End Sub

Private Sub cmdFirst_Click()
    On Error GoTo ErrLabel

    adoRecordset.MoveFirst

    Exit Sub

ErrLabel:
    MsgBox Err.Description
End Sub

Private Sub cmdLast_Click()
    On Error GoTo ErrLabel

    adoRecordset.MoveLast

    Exit Sub

ErrLabel:
    MsgBox Err.Description
End Sub

Private Sub cmdNext_Click()
    On Error GoTo ErrLabel

    If Not adoRecordset.EOF Then
            adoRecordset.MoveNext
```

```
    End If

    If adoRecordset.EOF And adoRecordset.RecordCount > 0 Then
        adoRecordset.MoveLast
    End If

    Exit Sub

ErrLabel:
    MsgBox Err.Description
End Sub

Private Sub cmdPrevious_Click()
    On Error GoTo ErrLabel

    If Not adoRecordset.BOF Then adoRecordset.MovePrevious
    If adoRecordset.BOF And adoRecordset.RecordCount > 0 Then
        adoRecordset.MoveFirst
    End If

    Exit Sub

ErrLabel:
    MsgBox Err.Description
End Sub
```

There are other types of commands besides the `adCmdTable` type, of course; for example, you can execute SQL with the `adCmdText` type of command.

Executing SQL

You can execute text commands—usually SQL—when you set the `Command-Type` of a `Command` object to `adCmdText`. Here's an example in which I'm using the `Command` object's `Execute` method to open the `Publishers` recordset in the `Biblio.mdb` recordset and using SQL to select `Prentice Hall`:

```
Private Sub Form_Load()
    Dim adoConnect As Connection
    Set adoConnect = New Connection

    adoConnect.Open _
    "PROVIDER=Microsoft.Jet.OLEDB.3.51;" & _
    "Data Source=C:\ado\biblio.mdb;"

    Set adoCommand = New Command
```

```
adoCommand.CommandType = adCmdText
adoCommand.CommandText = "SELECT * from " & _
"Publishers WHERE Name = 'PRENTICE HALL'"

    adoCommand.ActiveConnection = adoConnect

    Set adoRecordset = adoCommand.Execute

    Set Text1.DataSource = adoRecordset
    Text1.DataField = "Name"
    Set Text2.DataSource = adoRecordset
    Text2.DataField = "Address"


End Sub
```

Besides using the `Execute` method directly, you can also call `Command` objects by name as methods of a `Connection` object.

Commands as Connection Methods

One convenient technique in ADO is to use commands as connection methods. For example, say that you have a command named `Command1` that's associated with a `Connection` object, `Connection1`:

```
Private Sub Form_Load()
    Connection1.Commands("Command1").CommandText _
    = "Select * From Publishers"
    .
    .
    .
```

You can call `Command1` as a method of `Connection1` like this:

```
Private Sub Form_Load()
    Connection1.Commands("Command1").CommandText _
    = "Select * From Publishers"
    .
    .
    .
```

```
    Connection1.Command1
```

End Sub

This also works in Data Environments:


```
Private Sub Form_Load()
DataEnvironment1.Commands("Command1").CommandText _
= "Select * From Publishers"
    .

    .

    .
```

```
DataEnvironment1.Command1
```

End Sub

There's a full example using command objects as methods with parameters coming up in a few pages—and that introduces the topic of using parameters with Command objects, which I'll take a look at now.

Using Parameters

You can use parameters to supply the values used in commands. To show how this works, I'll use parameters with a command to select Prentice Hall from the Publishers table in the Biblio.mdb database.

To use a parameter in an SQL statement, you use question marks as placeholders, like this:

```
adoConnect.Open _
"PROVIDER=Microsoft.Jet.OLEDB.3.51;Data
Source=C:\ado\biblio.mdb;"


Set adoCommand = New Command
adoCommand.CommandType = adCmdText
adoCommand.CommandText = "SELECT * from Publishers
WHERE Name = ?"
    .

    .

    .
```

In this case, the command uses one parameter to specify the name of the publisher to search for. Now you need to supply a parameter that will hold that name when this command is run. Here's how I create and configure a new parameter, adoParam, to hold the name of a publisher to search for:

```
Set adoParam = New Parameter
adoParam.Name = "Name"
adoParam.Type = adVarChar
adoParam.Size = 20
adoParam.Value = "PRENTICE HALL"

     .

     .

     .
```

You append the parameters you want to use in a command using its Parameters collection's Append method, and then you execute the command as usual like this:

```
adoCommand.Parameters.Append adoParam
Set adoCommand.ActiveConnection = adoConnect


Set adoRecordset = adoCommand.Execute
```

This code produces the same results you see in Figure 6.6—now we've opened a recordset using a command with parameters. This project is in the adocommand folder on the CD, and the code for this example, adocommand.frm, appears in Listing 6.2.

LISTING 6.2   *Adocommand.frm Code*

```
VERSION 5.00
Begin VB.Form Form1
    BorderStyle     =   3  'Fixed Dialog
    Caption         =   "students"
    ClientHeight    =   2550
    ClientLeft      =   1095
    ClientTop       =   330
    ClientWidth     =   5550
    LinkTopic       =   "Form3"
    MaxButton       =   0   'False
    MinButton       =   0   'False
```

```
ScaleHeight      =    2550
ScaleWidth       =    5550
ShowInTaskbar    =    0      'False
Begin VB.CommandButton cmdLast
   Caption         =     ">>"
   Height          =     495
   Left            =     4200
   TabIndex        =     11
   Top             =     1920
   Width           =     1215
End
Begin VB.CommandButton cmdNext
   Caption         =     ">"
   Height          =     495
   Left            =     2880
   TabIndex        =     10
   Top             =     1920
   Width           =     1215
End
Begin VB.CommandButton cmdPrevious
   Caption         =     "<"
   Height          =     495
   Left            =     1560
   TabIndex        =     9
   Top             =     1920
   Width           =     1215
End
Begin VB.CommandButton cmdFirst
   Caption         =     "<<"
   Height          =     495
   Left            =     240
   TabIndex        =     8
   Top             =     1920
   Width           =     1215
End
Begin VB.CommandButton cmdRefresh
   Caption         =     "Refresh"
   Height          =     495
   Left            =     2880
   TabIndex        =     6
   Top             =     1200
   Width           =     1215
End
Begin VB.CommandButton cmdUpdate
   Caption         =     "Update"
   Height          =     495
   Left            =     1560
   TabIndex        =     5
   Top             =     1200
   Width           =     1215
End
```

```
      Begin VB.CommandButton cmdDelete
         Caption         =   "Delete"
         Height          =   495
         Left            =   4200
         TabIndex        =   4
         Top             =   1200
         Width           =   1215
      End
      Begin VB.CommandButton cmdAdd
         Caption         =   "Add"
         Height          =   495
         Left            =   240
         TabIndex        =   3
         Top             =   1200
         Width           =   1215
      End
      Begin VB.TextBox Text2
         Height          =   375
         Left            =   1320
         TabIndex        =   2
         Text            =   "Text2"
         Top             =   600
         Width           =   3855
      End
      Begin VB.TextBox Text1
         Height          =   375
         Left            =   1320
         TabIndex        =   1
         Text            =   "Text1"
         Top             =   120
         Width           =   3855
      End
      Begin VB.Label lblLabels
         Caption         =   "Name:"
         Height          =   255
         Index           =   0
         Left            =   120
         TabIndex        =   7
         Top             =   120
         Width           =   1095
      End
      Begin VB.Label lblLabels
         Caption         =   "Address:"
         Height          =   255
         Index           =   1
         Left            =   120
         TabIndex        =   0
         Top             =   600
         Width           =   1095
      End
   End
End
Attribute VB_Name = "Form1"
```

```
Attribute VB_GlobalNameSpace = False
Attribute VB_Creatable = False
Attribute VB_PredeclaredId = True
Attribute VB_Exposed = False
Private adoRecordset As Recordset
Attribute adoRecordset.VB_VarHelpID = -1
Private cmd As Command
Private prm As Parameter

Private Sub Form_Load()
    Dim adoConnect As Connection
    Set adoConnect = New Connection

    adoConnect.Open _
    "PROVIDER=Microsoft.Jet.OLEDB.4.0;Data " & _

    Source=C:\ado\biblio.mdb;"

    Set adoCommand = New Command

    adoCommand.CommandType = adCmdText
    adoCommand.CommandText = "SELECT * from "& _
    Publishers WHERE Name = ?"

    Set adoParam = New Parameter
    adoParam.Name = "Name"
    adoParam.Type = adVarChar
    adoParam.Size = 20
    adoParam.Value = "PRENTICE HALL"
    adoCommand.Parameters.Append adoParam
    Set adoCommand.ActiveConnection = adoConnect

    Set adoRecordset = adoCommand.Execute

    Set Text1.DataSource = adoRecordset
    Text1.DataField = "Name"
    Set Text2.DataSource = adoRecordset
    Text2.DataField = "Address"

End Sub

Private Sub cmdAdd_Click()
    On Error GoTo ErrLabel
    adoRecordset.AddNew

    Text1.Text = ""
    Text2.Text = ""

    Exit Sub

ErrLabel:
    MsgBox Err.Description
```

```
End Sub

Private Sub cmdDelete_Click()
    On Error GoTo ErrLabel

    adoRecordset.Delete

    adoRecordset.MoveNext
    If adoRecordset.EOF Then
        adoRecordset.MoveLast
    End If

    Exit Sub

ErrLabel:
    MsgBox Err.Description
End Sub

Private Sub cmdRefresh_Click()

    On Error GoTo ErrLabel
    adoRecordset.Requery
    Exit Sub

ErrLabel:
    MsgBox Err.Description
End Sub

Private Sub cmdUpdate_Click()
    On Error GoTo ErrLabel

    adoRecordset.Update

    Exit Sub

ErrLabel:
    MsgBox Err.Description
End Sub

Private Sub cmdFirst_Click()
    On Error GoTo ErrLabel

    adoRecordset.MoveFirst

    Exit Sub

ErrLabel:
    MsgBox Err.Description
End Sub

Private Sub cmdLast_Click()
```

```
    On Error GoTo ErrLabel
    adoRecordset.MoveLast

    Exit Sub

ErrLabel:
    MsgBox Err.Description
End Sub

Private Sub cmdNext_Click()
    On Error GoTo ErrLabel

    If Not adoRecordset.EOF Then
            adoRecordset.MoveNext
    End If

    If adoRecordset.EOF And adoRecordset.RecordCount > 0 Then
        adoRecordset.MoveLast
    End If

    Exit Sub

ErrLabel:
    MsgBox Err.Description
End Sub

Private Sub cmdPrevious_Click()
    On Error GoTo ErrLabel

    If Not adoRecordset.BOF Then adoRecordset.MovePrevious
    If adoRecordset.BOF And adoRecordset.RecordCount > 0 Then
        adoRecordset.MoveFirst
    End If

    Exit Sub

ErrLabel:
    MsgBox Err.Description
End Sub
```

Note that you don't have to use the Execute method when you execute commands with parameters—you can also call a Command object by name as a method of a Connection object, passing the parameters you want to it.

Using Parameters with Commands as Connection Methods

In the next example, I'll re-create the previous example in which I used a command with parameters to open a recordset of entries to find Prentice

Hall in the Publishers table of Biblio.mdb—but in this case, I'll use the command as a method of the Connection object.

I start by creating a new connection, adoConnect, and a new command, adoCommand, and connecting to the command like this—note that you must specify a name for the Command object, using the Name property, before you can call the command as a method:

```
Private Sub Form_Load()
    Dim adoConnect As Connection
    Set adoRecordset = New ADODB.Recordset
    Set adoConnect = New Connection

    adoConnect.Open _
    "PROVIDER=Microsoft.Jet.OLEDB." & _
    "4.0;Data "Source=C:\ado\biblio.mdb;"


    Set adoCommand = New Command
    adoCommand.CommandType = adCmdText
    adoCommand.CommandText = _
    "SELECT * from Publishers WHERE Name = ?"
    adoCommand.Name = "adoCommand"


    Set adoCommand.ActiveConnection = adoConnect
        .

        .

        .
```

Now I call the command as a method of the Connection object, passing the value I want the parameter to have, "PRENTICE HALL". If you have multiple parameters, you pass them in order. If the command returns a Recordset object, as the one here does, you don't assign the return result of the command to a Recordset object; instead, you pass a variable of type Recordset as the last parameter to the Command method like this (note that I've declared adoRecordset as a variable of type ADODB.Recordset at the beginning of the code):

```
    adoConnect.adoCommand "PRENTICE HALL", _
    adoRecordset
```

That fills the `Recordset` object appropriately, and now I can tie that `Recordset` object to the two text controls as before:

```
Set Text1.DataSource = adoRecordset
Text1.DataField = "Name"
Set Text2.DataSource = adoRecordset
Text2.DataField = "Address"


End Sub
```

And that's it—the result is in the previous example. You can also use this same technique on `Command` objects in Data Environments.

Note that if your `Command` object uses multiple parameters, and you want to pass only some of those parameters, you must set the value of the parameters explicitly in the `Parameters` collection instead of calling the `Command` object by name. To execute the command, you use the `Command` object's `Execute` method.

Besides creating your own parameterized commands in code, you can also execute stored procedures using parameters, and I'll take a look at that next.

Using Stored Procedures

As an example of showing how to call stored procedures with parameters, I'll call the `CustOrderHist` stored procedure in the `Nwind` database, which looks like this:

```
Alter PROCEDURE CustOrderHist
@CustomerID nchar(5)
AS
SELECT ProductName, Total=SUM(Quantity)
FROM Products P, [Order Details] OD, Orders O,
Customers C
WHERE C.CustomerID = @CustomerID
AND C.CustomerID = O.CustomerID AND O.OrderID =
OD.OrderID AND OD.ProductID = P.ProductID
GROUP BY ProductName
```

You pass this stored procedure the ID of a customer (IDs are stored as five-character strings in this database), and the procedure returns the customer's orders as a recordset with two fields, `ProductName`—the name of a product—and `Total`—the total number of that product ordered.

I'll let the user provide the customer ID to work with in a text box, `Text1`, and when the user clicks a button with the caption `Execute stored procedure`, I'll connect to the `Nwind` database using SQL Server and execute the `CustOrderHist` stored procedure, passing it a `Parameter` object that holds the customer ID the user has specified. I'll also tie the returned recordset to two text boxes so the fields of the first record in the recordset will be visible.

When the user clicks the `Execute stored procedure` button, `Command1`, I connect to the `Nwind` database using SQL Server:

```
Private Sub Command1_Click()
    Dim adoConnect As Connection
    Set adoRecordset = New ADODB.Recordset
    Set adoConnect = New Connection

    adoConnect.Open "Provider=SQLOLEDB.1;" & _
    "Persist Security Info=False;User " & _
    "ID=sa;Initial Catalog=Northwind"
    .
    .
    .
```

Next, I set up the `Command` object I'll use to execute the stored procedure, setting the `CommandType` property to `adCmdStoredProc` and the `CommandText` property to the name of the stored procedure to execute, `CustOrderHist`:

```
    Set adoCommand = New Command
    adoCommand.CommandText = "CustOrderHist"
    adoCommand.CommandType = adCmdStoredProc
    adoCommand.Name = "adoCommand"
    .
    .
    .
```

At this point, I'm ready to create the parameter the stored procedure will use, which I do like this, using the customer ID the user specified in Text1:

```
Set adoParam = New Parameter
adoParam.Name = "@CustomerID"
adoParam.Type = adVarChar
adoParam.Size = 5
adoParam.Value = Text1.Text
    .
    .
    .
```

Finally, I append the new parameter to the command's `Parameters` collection and execute the command, creating a new recordset:

```
adoCommand.Parameters.Append adoParam
Set adoCommand.ActiveConnection = adoConnect

Set adoRecordset = adoCommand.Execute
    .
    .
    .
```

All that's left is to tie the new recordset to two text boxes to display the fields in the first record:

```
Set Text2.DataSource = adoRecordset
Text2.DataField = "ProductName"
Set Text3.DataSource = adoRecordset
Text3.DataField = "Total"
```

```
End Sub
```

And that's it—the result appears in Figure 6.7. When the user enters the ID of a customer—ANTON, in this case—and clicks the `Execute stored procedure` button, the code executes the stored procedure and displays the

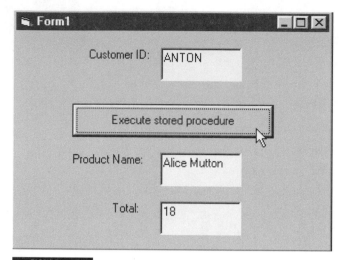

FIGURE 6.7 Executing a stored procedure with parameters using SQL Server.

fields of the first record returned. This project appears in the `storedproce-dure` folder on the CD, and the code for this example, `storedproce-dure.frm`, appears in Listing 6.3.

LISTING 6.3 *Storedprocedure.frm Code*

```
VERSION 5.00
Begin VB.Form Form1
   Caption         =    "Form1"
   ClientHeight    =    3195
   ClientLeft      =    60
   ClientTop       =    345
   ClientWidth     =    4680
   LinkTopic       =    "Form1"
   ScaleHeight     =    3195
   ScaleWidth      =    4680
   StartUpPosition =    3    'Windows Default
   Begin VB.CommandButton Command1
      Caption         =    "Execute stored procedure"
      Height          =    495
      Left            =    840
      TabIndex        =    3
      Top             =    1080
      Width           =    3015
   End
   Begin VB.TextBox Text3
      Height          =    495
      Left            =    2160
```

```vb
      TabIndex        =    2
      Top             =    2520
      Width           =    1215
   End
   Begin VB.TextBox Text2
      Height          =    495
      Left            =    2160
      TabIndex        =    1
      Top             =    1800
      Width           =    1215
   End
   Begin VB.TextBox Text1
      Height          =    495
      Left            =    2160
      TabIndex        =    0
      Top             =    240
      Width           =    1215
   End
   Begin VB.Label Label3
      Caption         =    "Total:"
      Height          =    255
      Left            =    1440
      TabIndex        =    6
      Top             =    2520
      Width           =    495
   End
   Begin VB.Label Label2
      Caption         =    "Product Name:"
      Height          =    375
      Left            =    840
      TabIndex        =    5
      Top             =    1800
      Width           =    1215
   End
   Begin VB.Label Label1
      Caption         =    "Customer ID:"
      Height          =    495
      Left            =    1080
      TabIndex        =    4
      Top             =    240
      Width           =    1095
   End
End
Attribute VB_Name = "Form1"
Attribute VB_GlobalNameSpace = False
Attribute VB_Creatable = False
Attribute VB_PredeclaredId = True
Attribute VB_Exposed = False
Private Sub Command1_Click()
    Dim adoConnect As Connection
    Set adoRecordset = New ADODB.Recordset
```

```
Set adoConnect = New Connection

adoConnect.Open "Provider=SQLOLEDB.1;" & _
"Persist Security Info=False;User " & _
"ID=sa;Initial Catalog=Northwind"

Set adoCommand = New Command
adoCommand.CommandText = "CustOrderHist"
adoCommand.CommandType = adCmdStoredProc
adoCommand.Name = "adoCommand"

Set adoParam = New Parameter
adoParam.Name = "@CustomerID"
adoParam.Type = adVarChar
adoParam.Size = 5
adoParam.Value = Text1.Text
adoCommand.Parameters.Append adoParam
Set adoCommand.ActiveConnection = adoConnect

Set adoRecordset = adoCommand.Execute

Set Text2.DataSource = adoRecordset
Text2.DataField = "ProductName"
Set Text3.DataSource = adoRecordset
Text3.DataField = "Total"
```

End Sub

Using Stored Procedures as Connection Methods

Just as you can with commands, you can call a stored procedure by name as a method of a Connection object. For example, here's how I call the CustOrderHist stored procedure, passing a customer ID to that procedure directly, as well as a Recordset object to fill with data:

```
Private Sub Form_Load()
    Dim adoConnect As Connection
    Set adoRecordset = New ADODB.Recordset
    Set adoConnect = New Connection

    adoConnect.Open "Provider=" & _
    "SQLOLEDB.1;Persist Security " & _
    "Info=False;User ID=sa;" & _
    "Initial Catalog=Northwind"
```

```
Set adoCommand = New Command
adoCommand.CommandText = "CustOrderHist"
adoCommand.CommandType = adCmdStoredProc
adoCommand.Name = "adoCommand"


Set adoCommand.ActiveConnection = adoConnect
```

```
adoConnect.adoCommand "ANTON", adoRecordset
```

```
Set Text1.DataSource = adoRecordset
Text1.DataField = "ProductName"
Set Text2.DataSource = adoRecordset
Text2.DataField = "Total"
```


```
End Sub
```

Note that you can also execute a stored procedure by setting the CommandText of a Command object like this:

```
{call CustOrderHist('ANTON')}
```

So far, I've just taken a look at text parameters, but of course there are other kinds, and for the most part, they're straightforward to handle, like numeric values. One kind of parameter that takes a little discussion, however, is the image type.

Adding Images to Parameters

You can use the AppendChunk method of the Parameter object to store images and other binary data in a parameter. To do that, I first open and store an image, converting it to the Unicode format that SQL Server uses, like this:

```
Dim TempData As Byte


Open "c:\figure.bmp" For Binary As #1
ReDim TempData(LOF(1))
bmpData = StrConv(TempData, vbUnicode)
```

.

.

Then I create a new parameter, naming it Image, giving it the size required by SQL Server for images, and appending it to a command's Parameters collection:

```
Set adoParam = adoCommand.CreateParameter("Image", _
adVarBinary, adParamInput, 2147483647)


adoCommand.Parameters.Append adoParam
```

.

.

.

Now I append the image data to the parameter with the AppendChunk method like this:

```
adoCommand.Parameters("Image").AppendChunk bmpData


Close #1
```

Command Object Return Values

When working with commands, as we've seen, you can use input parameters and output parameters—but, you can also handle return values. Here's an example where a stored procedure, SortedData, accessed with a Data Environment, takes an input parameter, places data in an output parameter, and also returns a value:

```
NumberRecords = _
DataEnvironment1.SortedData("JONES", _
Status)
If Status = "OK" Then
    DataEnvironment1.rsSortedData.MoveFirst
    MsgBox "The number of returned was: ", _
    NumberRecords
End If
```

In this case, I store the return value in the variable `NumberRecords`. To return a value from a stored procedure, you use the `RETURN` statement at the end of a stored procedure like this: `RETURN 100` to return a value of 100. If your procedure returns a value, and you want to pass parameters to the procedure using the `Parameters` collection, you should make the first parameter in the `Parameters` collection the return value, giving it the name RETURN_VALUE, like this:

```
adoCommand.CreateParameter("RETURN_VALUE", _
adVarInteger, adParamReturnValue, 0)
```

Note also that for some OLE DB providers, output parameters are not available until the recordset is closed. You can check when output parameters will be available by checking the property "`Output Parameter Availability`" in the `Connection` object's `Properties` collection (i.e., as `adoConnect.Properties("Output Parameter Availability")`). Here are the possible values for this property:

- **DBPROPVAL_OA_ATEXECUTE**—2. Indicates that the values of output parameters are available when a command is finished executing.
- **DBPROPVAL_OA_ATROWRELEASE**—4. Indicates that the values of output parameters are available when the recordset has been closed.
- **DBPROPVAL_OA_NOTSUPPORTED**—1. Output parameters are not supported.

Note finally that if more than one `Command` object is executed on the same connection, and one of these `Command` objects is a stored procedure with output parameters, an error occurs. To execute each `Command` object, use separate connections or disconnect all other `Command` objects from the connection.

That completes our look at `Command` and `Parameter` objects for the moment; in the next chapter, I'll take a look at ADO `Recordset` and `Field` objects.

The ADO Recordset Object

Recordsets hold the data you work with in ADO programming, so they're the favorite ADO object of many programmers. This chapter is all about the Recordset object, which has a great many properties and methods, which we'll explore here. There is so much going on with recordsets that the next chapter will also be about Recordset objects, and we'll put those objects to work sorting, searching, and filtering recordsets in that chapter.

The columns of each record in a recordset are its fields, and as you might expect, you treat fields as objects in ADO programming as well. For that reason, I'll take a look at the ADO Field object here, as well as the Recordset object. Using the Field object, you can manipulate, store, and retrieve data and, in fact there are a variety of ways of using Field objects with Recordset objects, as we'll see here.

When you work with the data in a data source, you execute a command on that data source that returns a Recordset object, so you can see the importance of this object in ADO programming. I'll start by taking a look at using recordsets in ADO data controls.

Using ADO Recordsets in ADO Data Controls

Unlike the internal Connection and Command objects, you have full access to the Recordset object in an ADO data control, and you can reach it using the Recordset property of the control. For example, here's how I emulate the Next record button in an ADO data control using the properties and methods of the Recordset object in the control. Before moving to the next record, I first check whether we're at the end of the recordset with the Recordset object's EOF property and, if not, I move to the next record with the MoveNext method:

```
Private Sub cmdNext_Click()
    On Error GoTo ErrLabel


    If Not Adodc1.Recordset.EOF Then
            Adodc1.Recordset.MoveNext
    End If
    .
    .
    .
```

If this operation moves us past the last record to the actual end of the recordset, we should move back to the last record, which I do like this—first checking to make sure there's at least one record to work with by examining the RecordCount property:

```
Private Sub cmdNext_Click()
    On Error GoTo ErrLabel


    If Not Adodc1.Recordset.EOF Then
            Adodc1.Recordset.MoveNext
    End If

    If Adodc1.Recordset.EOF And _
            Adodc1.Recordset.RecordCount > 0 Then
        Adodc1.Recordset.MoveLast
    End If


    Exit Sub
```

```
ErrLabel:

    MsgBox Err.Description
End Sub
```

In fact, you can do more than just mimic the navigation buttons in an ADO data control using the properties and methods of the control's `Recordset` object—you can also let the user add new records, edit records, and delete records. Take a look at Figure 7.1 where I'm doing just that in an application named `adocontrolrecordset`, which you'll find in a folder on the CD with the same name. The code for this project, `adocontrolrecordset.frm`, appears in Listing 7.1, and we'll see how to put programs like this together after we take a look at the properties and methods of the `Recordet` object in more detail.

LISTING 7.1   *Adocontrolrecordset.frm Code*

```
VERSION 5.00
Object = "{67397AA1-7FB1-11D0-B148-00A0C922E820}#6.0#0"; "MSADODC.OCX"
Begin VB.Form Form1
    BorderStyle     =    3   'Fixed Dialog
    Caption         =    "Publishers"
    ClientHeight    =    3030
    ClientLeft      =    1095
    ClientTop       =    330
    ClientWidth     =    5550
```

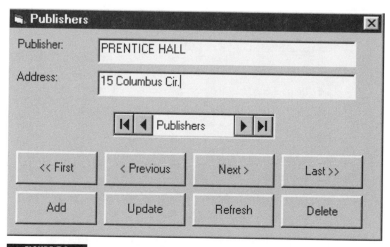

FIGURE 7.1   Using the properties and methods of the `Recordset` object in an ADO data control

```
LinkTopic          =    "Form3"
MaxButton          =    0    'False
MinButton          =    0    'False
ScaleHeight        =    3030
ScaleWidth         =    5550
ShowInTaskbar      =    0    'False
Begin MSAdodcLib.Adodc Adodc1
    Height            =    375
    Left              =    1560
    Top               =    1200
    Width             =    2415
    _ExtentX          -    4260
    _ExtentY          =    661
    ConnectMode       =    0
    CursorLocation    =    3
    IsolationLevel    =    -1
    ConnectionTimeout=    15
    CommandTimeout    =    30
    CursorType        =    3
    LockType          =    3
    CommandType       =    2
    CursorOptions     =    0
    CacheSize         =    50
    MaxRecords        =    0
    BOFAction         =    0
    EOFAction         -    0
    ConnectStringType=    1
    Appearance        =    1
    BackColor         =    -2147483643
    ForeColor         =    -2147483640
    Orientation       =    0
    Enabled           =    -1
    Connect           =
    "Provider=Microsoft.Jet.OLEDB.4.0;Persist Security
   Info=False;Data Source=C:\ADO\Biblio.mdb"
    OLEDBString       =
    "Provider=Microsoft.Jet.OLEDB.4.0;Persist Security
   Info=False;Data Source=C:\ADO\Biblio.mdb"
    OLEDBFile         =    ""
    DataSourceName    =    ""
    OtherAttributes   =    ""
    UserName          =    ""
    Password          =    ""
    RecordSource      =    "Publishers"
    Caption           =    "Publishers"
    BeginProperty Font
{0BE35203-8F91-11CE-9DE3-00AA004BB851}
        Name          =    "MS Sans Serif"
        Size          =    8.25
        Charset       =    0
        Weight        =    400
```

```
            Underline       =    0    'False
            Italic          =    0    'False
            Strikethrough   =    0    'False
         EndProperty
         _Version        =    393216
      End
      Begin VB.CommandButton cmdLast
         Caption         =    "Last >>"
         Height          =    495
         Left            =    4080
         TabIndex        =    11
         Top             =    1800
         Width           =    1215
      End
      Begin VB.CommandButton cmdNext
         Caption         =    "Next >"
         Height          =    495
         Left            =    2760
         TabIndex        =    10
         Top             =    1800
         Width           =    1215
      End
      Begin VB.CommandButton cmdPrevious
         Caption         =    "< Previous"
         Height          =    495
         Left            =    1440
         TabIndex        =    9
         Top             =    1800
         Width           =    1215
      End
      Begin VB.CommandButton cmdFirst
         Caption         =    "<< First"
         Height          =    495
         Left            =    120
         TabIndex        =    8
         Top             =    1800
         Width           =    1215
      End
      Begin VB.CommandButton cmdRefresh
         Caption         =    "Refresh"
         Height          =    495
         Left            =    2760
         TabIndex        =    6
         Top             =    2400
         Width           =    1215
      End
      Begin VB.CommandButton cmdUpdate
         Caption         =    "Update"
         Height          =    495
         Left            =    1440
         TabIndex        =    5
         Top             =    2400
```

```
      Width               =     1215
   End
   Begin VB.CommandButton cmdDelete
      Caption             =     "Delete"
      Height              =     495
      Left                =     4080
      TabIndex            =     4
      Top                 =     2400
      Width               =     1215
   End
   Begin VB.CommandButton cmdAdd
      Caption             =     "Add"
      Height              =     495
      Left                =     120
      TabIndex            =     3
      Top                 =     2400
      Width               =     1215
   End
   Begin VB.TextBox Text2
      DataField           =     "Address"
      DataSource          =     "Adodc1"
      Height              =     375
      Left                =     1320
      TabIndex            =     2
      Top                 =     600
      Width               =     3855
   End
   Begin VB.TextBox Text1
      DataField           =     "Name"
      DataSource          =     "Adodc1"
      Height              =     375
      Left                =     1320
      TabIndex            =     1
      Top                 =     120
      Width               =     3855
   End
   Begin VB.Label lblLabels
      Caption             =     "Publisher:"
      Height              =     255
      Index               =     0
      Left                =     120
      TabIndex            =     7
      Top                 =     120
      Width               =     1095
   End
   Begin VB.Label lblLabels
      Caption             =     "Address:"
      Height              =     255
      Index               =     1
      Left                =     120
      TabIndex            =     0
      Top                 =     600
```

```
        Width          =    1095
    End
End
Attribute VB_Name = "Form1"
Attribute VB_GlobalNameSpace = False
Attribute VB_Creatable = False
Attribute VB_PredeclaredId = True
Attribute VB_Exposed = False
Private Sub cmdAdd_Click()
    On Error GoTo ErrLabel
    Adodc1.Recordset.AddNew

    Text1.Text = ""
    Text2.Text = ""

    Exit Sub

ErrLabel:
    MsgBox Err.Description
End Sub

Private Sub cmdDelete_Click()
    On Error GoTo ErrLabel

    Adodc1.Recordset.Delete

    Adodc1.Recordset.MoveNext
    If Adodc1.Recordset.EOF Then
        Adodc1.Recordset.MoveLast
    End If

    Exit Sub

ErrLabel:
    MsgBox Err.Description
End Sub

Private Sub cmdRefresh_Click()

    On Error GoTo ErrLabel
    Adodc1.Recordset.Requery
    Exit Sub

ErrLabel:
    MsgBox Err.Description
End Sub

Private Sub cmdUpdate_Click()
    On Error GoTo ErrLabel

    Adodc1.Recordset.Update
```

```
    Exit Sub
ErrLabel:
    MsgBox Err.Description
End Sub

Private Sub cmdFirst_Click()
    On Error GoTo ErrLabel

    Adodc1.Recordset.MoveFirst

    Exit Sub

ErrLabel:
    MsgBox Err.Description
End Sub

Private Sub cmdLast_Click()
    On Error GoTo ErrLabel

    Adodc1.Recordset.MoveLast

    Exit Sub

ErrLabel:
    MsgBox Err.Description
End Sub

Private Sub cmdNext_Click()
    On Error GoTo ErrLabel

    If Not Adodc1.Recordset.EOF Then
            Adodc1.Recordset.MoveNext
    End If

    If Adodc1.Recordset.EOF And _
        Adodc1.Recordset.RecordCount > 0 Then
        Adodc1.Recordset.MoveLast
    End If

    Exit Sub

ErrLabel:
    MsgBox Err.Description
End Sub

Private Sub cmdPrevious_Click()
    On Error GoTo ErrLabel

    If Not Adodc1.Recordset.BOF Then _
        Adodc1.Recordset.MovePrevious
```

```
If Adodc1.Recordset.BOF And _
    Adodc1.Recordset.RecordCount > 0 Then
    Adodc1.Recordset.MoveFirst
End If

Exit Sub

ErrLabel:
    MsgBox Err.Description
End Sub
```

Besides using the properties and methods of the `Recordset` object in an ADO data control, most `Recordset` object events (except asynchronous ones), such as `MoveComplete` and `WillChangeRecordset`, are also methods of the ADO data control, and you can access them directly.

Using ADO Recordsets in Data Environments

As you might expect, you have full access to `Recordset` objects in Data Environments, just as you do in the ADO data control. In fact, we've already

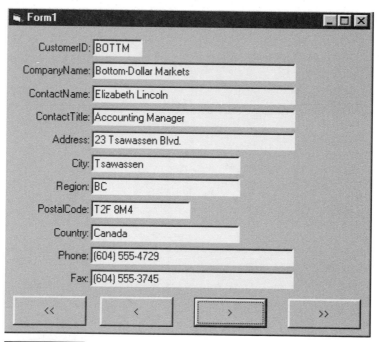

FIGURE 7.2   Using the properties and methods of a `Recordset` object in a Data Environment.

seen how this looks earlier when writing the decontrols project you see at work in Figure 7.2, which uses a Data Environment to create a recordset.

Unlike the ADO data control, you are responsible for navigating through the recordset in a Data Environment yourself, because Data Environments are not visible controls that expose navigation buttons. Instead, you use recordset properties and methods to interact with recordsets in the Data Environment.

If a command in a Data Environment returns a recordset, you can refer to that recordset in code using the name of the command, prefixed with the letters "rs." As we saw in Chapter 4, that means that if you have a Command object in a Data Environment named CustomersTable, you can refer to the Recordset object the command returns as rsCustomersTable. For example, here's how to write the cmdNext_Click Sub procedure that we started the chapter out with, this time using Data Environments instead of ADO data controls:

```
Private Sub cmdNext_Click()
    On Error GoTo ErrLabel


    If Not DataEnvironment1.rsCustomersTable.EOF _
    Then
            DataEnvironment1.rsCustomersTable.MoveNext
    End If


    If DataEnvironment1.rsCustomersTable.EOF And _
    DataEnvironment1.rsCustomersTable.RecordCount _
        > 0 Then
        DataEnvironment1.rsCustomersTable.MoveLast
    End If


    Exit Sub

ErrLabel:
    MsgBox Err.Description
End Sub
```

How do you add code to the events of the Recordset objects in a Data Environment? Just double-click the Connection object that creates the recordset, or right-click it and select the View Code item in the menu that appears to open the code window for the corresponding Recordset object's events.

As you can see, you have complete access to Recordset objects in both ADO data controls and Data Environments—it's time to take a look at working with those objects in code.

ADO Recordset Objects

When you use ADO, you manipulate data almost entirely using Recordset objects. All Recordset objects are constructed using records (rows) and fields (columns). I'll take a look at the properties, methods, and events of the Recordset object in detail here. Here's an overview of the Recordset object's properties before we dig into these in detail:

- **AbsolutePage**—Page where the current record resides.
- **AbsolutePosition**—Position of a Recordset object's current record.
- **ActiveCommand**—Command object for the Recordset object.
- **ActiveConnection**—Connection object the Recordset object belongs to.
- **BOF**—True if the current record position is before the first record.
- **Bookmark**—Unique identifier for the current record in a Recordset object.
- **CacheSize**—Number of records from a Recordset object that are cached locally in memory.
- **CursorLocation**—Location of the cursor.
- **CursorType**—Type of cursor used.
- **DataMember**—Visual Basic (not ADO) property indicating a Data Environment command that created the recordset.
- **DataSource**—Visual Basic (not ADO) property indicating the data that will become the recordset.
- **EditMode**—Indicates if editing is in progress.
- **EOF**—True if the current record position is after the last record.
- **Filter**—Filter for the data in the recordset.
- **LockType**—Type of locking used.
- **MarshalOption**—Specifies which records are to be marshaled back to the server.
- **MaxRecords**—Maximum number of records to return to a recordset from a query.
- **PageCount**—Number of pages of data the recordset contains.

- **PageSize**—Number of records that make up one page.
- **RecordCount**—Number of records in the recordset.
- **Sort**—One or more field names the recordset is sorted on.
- **Source**—Source for the data in the recordset; might be a Command object, SQL statement, table name, or stored procedure.
- **State**—State of the object, open or closed.
- **Status**—Status of the current record with respect to batch updates.
- **StayInSync**—Indicates if a hierarchical recordset should stay in contact with the data source.

Here are the methods of the ADO Recordset object in overview:

- **AddNew**—Adds a new record if the recordset can be updated.
- **Cancel**—Cancels execution of a pending execute or open.
- **CancelBatch**—Cancels a pending batch operation.
- **CancelUpdate**—Cancels a pending update.
- **Clone**—Creates a duplicate recordset.
- **Close**—Closes a recordset.
- **Delete**—Deletes the current record (or group of records).
- **Find**—Searches the recordset.
- **GetRows**—Fetches records to an array.
- **GetString**—Gets the recordset as a string.
- **Move**—Moves the position of the current record.
- **MoveFirst, MoveLast, MoveNext, MovePrevious** Navigate to various locations in the recordset.
- **NextRecordset**—Clears the current Recordset object and returns the next recordset.
- **Open**—Opens a cursor.
- **Requery**—Re-executes the query that created the recordset.
- **Resync**—Refreshes the data in the recordset.
- **Save**—Saves the recordset in a file.
- **Supports**—Indicates the features the recordset supports.
- **Update**—Saves changes to the database.
- **UpdateBatch**—Performs a multiple-record update to the database.

Here are the events you can use with Recordsets in overview:

- **FetchProgress**— Progress of a data retrieval operation.
- **FetchComplete**—Retrieval operation has completed.
- **WillChangeField**— Current field will change.

- **FieldChangeComplete**—Current field has changed.
- **WillMove**—Current row position in a recordset will change.
- **MoveComplete**—Current row position in a recordset has changed.
- **EndOfRecordset**—Reached the end of the recordset.
- **WillChangeRecord**—Something in the current row of the recordset will change.
- **RecordChangeComplete**—Something in the current row of the recordset has changed.
- **WillChangeRecordset**—Something in the current recordset will change.
- **RecordsetChangeComplete**—Something in the current recordset has changed.

I'll take a look at each of these in more detail now, starting with the properties of the `Recordset` object.

Recordset Properties

You use the properties of the `Recordset` object to configure that object and determine its current configuration. The important thing to know before dissecting this object is that it works much like a cursor in your data, and the record you work with at any one time is the *current record*. When you move to a new record, that record becomes the current record. Many of the properties and methods of this object work specifically on the current record, and only on that record. I'll examine the properties of the `Recordset` object here now, beginning with the `AbsolutePage` property.

AbsolutePage

You can divide a recordset into pages that are used for display purposes; to divide a recordset into pages, you use the `PageSize` property, which sets the number of records on a page, then you can work page by page through a recordset, using some providers (as, for example, when you want to return records in a Web page of limited length).

The `Absolute` page property holds the page number where the current record resides. The `AbsolutePage` property is 1-based and is 1 when the current record is the first record in the recordset. You set this property to move to the first record of a particular page, and you can get the total number of pages with the `PageCount` property. You can set `AbsolutePage` to a page number or to one of these constants:

- **adPosUnknown**—Indicates that the recordset is empty, the current position is unknown, or the OLE DB provider does not support the AbsolutePage property.

- **adPosBOF**—Indicates that the current record pointer is at the beginning of the recordset.

- **adPosEOF**—Indicates that the current record pointer is at the end of the recordset.

AbsolutePosition

This property holds the position of the current record in the recordset, starting with 1 and ranging up to the total number of records in the recordset (which you can determine with the RecordCount property). When you set this property, the corresponding record becomes the current record, which means you can use this property to move through a recordset; however, keep in mind that if the user deletes or adds records, the AbsolutePosition property of a record may change, so don't count on this property to always be able to locate a particular record (a better choice is the Bookmark property).

The AbsolutePosition property holds the number of the current record, or you can set it to the number of a record or these constants:

- **adPosUnknown**—Indicates that the recordset is empty, the current position is unknown, or the OLE DB provider does not support the AbsolutePosition property.

- **adPosBOF**—Indicates that the current record pointer is at the beginning of the recordset.

- **adPosEOF**—Indicates that the current record pointer is at the end of the recordset.

ActiveCommand

The ActiveCommand property holds the Command object that created the recordset. This can be useful if you want to reach that command's text and parameters when they've not been supplied to you, as when working with ADO data controls or Data Environments:

```
DataEnvironment1.rsCommand.ActiveCommand.CommandText
```

Note that this property will be set to a null object reference if the recordset was not created with a command.

ActiveConnection

The ActiveConnection object holds the Connection object that the Recordset object was created using. You can disconnect a recordset from a connection by setting this property to Nothing; you can reconnect the recordset to the connection at some later time.

You can use this property to set a recordset's connection as long as the recordset isn't open, or its Source property hasn't already been set to a valid

Connection object. When you set this property to a valid Connection object or to a valid connection string, the provider creates a new Connection object using this definition and opens the connection.

BOF

This property is set to True if the current record position is before the first record in a recordset. Novice database programmers often think that the beginning of a recordset corresponds to the first record in a recordset, but in fact, that's not true. The beginning of a recordset corresponds to a location before the first record, so if BOF is True, there is no current record.

Note that BOF is always True if a recordset is empty, so simply noting that BOF is True may be misleading unless you also check if there are any records in the Recordset object (using, for example, the RecordCount property). Note also that if you delete the last record in a Recordset object, BOF may remain False until you try to reposition the current record. Here's an example where I check the BOF property when moving to the previous record in a recordset:

```
Private Sub cmdPrevious_Click()
    On Error GoTo ErrLabel

    If Not adoRecordset.BOF Then _
        adoRecordset.MovePrevious
    If adoRecordset.BOF And _
        adoRecordset.RecordCount > 0 Then
        adoRecordset.MoveFirst
    End If

    Exit Sub

ErrLabel:
    MsgBox Err.Description
End Sub
```

Bookmark

The Bookmark property holds a unique identifier for a record in a Recordset object. You can use bookmarks to mark a specific record and return to it later. You store the current record's bookmark in a variant:

```
varBookmark = adoRecordset.Bookmark
```

Then you can move to a new location in the recordset:

```
adoRecordset.MoveNext
adoRecordset.MoveNext
```

And, when you set the recordset's Bookmark property to the bookmark you've stored, the bookmarked record becomes the current record:

```
adoRecordset.Bookmark = varBookmark
```

We'll see more about the Bookmark property in the next chapter. Usually, bookmarks are only supported when you're using keyset and static cursors, but some providers support them with dynamic cursors; to check, examine the adBookmark value of the Supports method.

CacheSize

This property holds the number of records from a Recordset object that are cached locally in memory; the default is 1. If your connection is over a slow network, you may want to increase this number so more records will be cached locally. In general, the larger the cache size, the more efficiently ADO can work with your records, but bear in mind that more memory is used as well. However, a cache size of 1 means that ADO must fetch records from the data store each time you want to move to a new record, which can slow things up considerably if you jump around a lot.

Note that when you cache records, those records are local, which means that they won't reflect changes made by other users on the same data store. To synchronize the records in the cache with those in the data store, use the Resync method.

Note that when you change the cache size, that change only takes effect when there's a new fetch of records to the cache. Also note that the cache size cannot be set to 0 without generating an error.

CursorLocation

You use this property to set the location of the cursor, which manages the recordset (see Chapter 1 for more discussion of cursors). Local cursors are often faster and allow many features that driver-supplied cursors may not, so using this setting may provide an advantage. Server-side cursors can be very flexible and can respond to changes others make to the data source. However, some features of the Microsoft Client Cursor Provider (such as disassociated recordsets) cannot be simulated with server-side cursors and these features are unavailable with this setting.

Here are the possible settings for this property:

- **adUseNone**—No cursor services are used. (Note that this constant is obsolete and appears for backward compatibility.)
- **adUseClient**—Uses client-side cursors supplied by a local cursor library. For backward compatibility, the synonym adUseClientBatch is also supported.
- **adUseServer**—(default) Uses data provider or driver-supplied cursors.

CursorType

The CursorType property holds the type of cursor the recordset uses. Here are the four possible options:

- **adOpenDynamic**—*Dynamic cursor.* This cursor type lets you view additions, changes, and deletions by other users, and allows all types of movement through the recordset.
- **adOpenKeyset**—*Keyset cursor.* This cursor behaves like a dynamic cursor, except that it prevents you from seeing records that other users add, and prevents access to records that other users delete. Data changes by other users will still be visible.
- **adOpenStatic**—*Static cursor.* This cursor provides a static copy of a set of records for you to use to find data or generate reports. Note that additions, changes, or deletions by other users will not be visible.
- **adOpenForwardOnly**—*Forward-only cursor.* This cursor behaves the same as a dynamic cursor, except that it allows you to only scroll forward through records. This can improve performance when you only need to make a single pass through the data in a recordset.

Note that some providers will not support all cursor types. For example, when you request a dynamic cursor from the Jet provider, it returns a keyset cursor and resets the CursorType property. For that reason, it's a good idea to check the CursorType property after a recordset has been opened to see if it's set to the cursor type you've requested.

Here's a summary of some of the different types of cursors various providers support when you ask for server-side cursors (client-side cursors for these providers will always be static when you ask for a client-side cursor):

- The SQL Server OLE DB provider supports all four cursor types, except when you request a static cursor with pessimistic, optimistic, or batch optimistic locking, in which case, the server uses a dynamic cursor.
- The Jet OLE DB provider always uses a keyset cursor when you use pessimistic, optimistic, or batch optimistic locking, no matter what type of cursor you request. If you request read-only locking, however, Jet will support all four cursor types, except the dynamic type, in which case, it uses a static cursor instead.

■ The ODBC OLE DB provider supports all four types of cursors, no matter what locking type you request.

I'll discuss cursors more when discussing recordset properties and methods by OLE DB provider later in this chapter.

DataMember

This property holds the value that you use when binding controls to Data Environments to specify a command object.

DataSource

This property holds the object that you use when binding controls to Data Environments.

EditMode

The EditMode property indicates if an editing operation is in progress. Here are the possible settings of this property:

■ **adEditNone**—Indicates that no editing operation is in progress.

■ **adEditInProgress**—Indicates that data in the current record has been modified but not saved.

■ **adEditAdd**—Indicates that the AddNew method has been invoked, and the current record in the copy buffer is a new record that hasn't been saved in the database.

■ **adEditDelete**—Indicates that the current record has been deleted.

ADO uses an editing buffer for the current record, and the EditMode property indicates whether changes have been made to this buffer, or if a new record has been created. You can use the EditMode property to determine the editing status of the current record, such as checking for pending changes if an editing process has been interrupted to determine if you need to use the Update or CancelUpdate method. This property is read-only, so you cannot set the editing mode.

Note that when the user moves to a new record, the current edits made to a record (as when the user edits the values in bound controls) are automatically stored to the data store. If you want to check with the user before updating the data store, check if this property is set to adEditInProgress, and if so, query the user if they want to save the changes; if not, call the CancelUpdate method.

EOF

This property is set to True if the current position is after the last record in a recordset (*not* at the last record). If this property is True, there is no current record.

Note that `EOF` will also be True if a recordset contains no records, so before assuming you're at the end of a recordset, check to make sure the recordset contains records by examining the `RecordCount` property. Note also that this property may remain False after you delete the last record in a recordset until you try to move to a new record.

Here's an example in which I use `EOF` to check for the end of the recordset when moving to the next record:

```
Private Sub cmdNext_Click()
    On Error GoTo ErrLabel


    If Not adoRecordset.EOF Then
            adoRecordset.MoveNext
    End If


    If adoRecordset.EOF And _
        adoRecordset.RecordCount > 0 Then
        adoRecordset.MoveLast
    End If


    Exit Sub


ErrLabel:
    MsgBox Err.Description
End Sub
```

Filter

This property holds the *filter* for the data in the recordset. You can use a filter to specify criteria that you want records to match when creating a recordset, and we'll see how to use filters in the next chapter. You can set this property to a filter string, an array of bookmarks, or one of these constants:

- **adFilterNone**—Removes the current filter and restores all records.
- **adFilterPendingRecords**—Allows you to view only records that have changed, but have not yet been sent to the server. Note that this is applicable only for batch update mode.
- **adFilterAffectedRecords**—Allows you to view only records affected by the last `Delete`, `Resync`, `Updatebatchm`, or `Cancelbatch` call.

- **adFilterFetchedRecords**—Allows you to view records in the current cache—that is, the results of the last call to retrieve records from the database.

- **adFilterConflictingRecords**—Allows you to view the records that failed the last batch update attempt.

When you apply a filter, the current record becomes the first record in the filtered view. To cancel filtering, you can use adFilterNone or set this property to an empty string, "". We'll put filtering to work in the next chapter.

LockType

When you open a Recordset object, you can specify the lock type using the LockType argument. This argument specifies how you lock records that are being updated. To update a record, you edit the data in a record's fields (by changing a Field object's Value property, or by editing the data in a bound control), which puts the recordset in Edit mode (as indicated in the Edit-Mode property, which is set to adEditInProgress), then call the Update method. Various types of locking can occur when you edit or update records. Here are the possibilities; note in particular the difference between optimistic and pessimistic locking:

- **adLockReadOnly**—(default) Read-only, you cannot alter the data.

- **adLockPessimistic**—Pessimistic locking, record by record. The data provider does what is necessary to ensure successful editing of the records, usually by locking records at the data source immediately when you start editing the data in the recordset's fields.

- **adLockOptimistic**—Optimistic locking, record by record. The provider uses optimistic locking, locking records only when you call the Update method.

- **adLockBatchOptimistic**—Optimistic batch updates, required for batch update mode as opposed to immediate update mode.

Pessimistic locking is the safest, since it locks the record when you start editing the record, but it relies on a continuous connection to the data source, which can be impractical. (Note that you can't use pessimistic locking on client cursors.)

Optimistic locking makes lighter use of system resources, but only locks the record when it's actually being updated, so note that someone else may have changed the record since you've read it.

Batch locking can be used with server-side cursors, but it's also very useful when working with disconnected recordsets, where you edit the data and make your changes in batches.

MarshalOptions

This property specifies which records are to be *marshalled* back to the server. You use this property when using disconnected, client-side recordsets.

When using a client-side recordset, records that have been modified on the client are written back to the middle tier or Web server through a technique called *marshalling*, the process of packaging and sending interface method parameters across thread or process boundaries. Setting the `MarshalOptions` property can improve performance when modified remote data is marshalled for updating back to the middle tier or Web server.

Using marshalling, you can specify that all records be sent to the server, or just those that were modified; here are the valid settings for this property:

- **adMarshalAll**—(default) Indicates that all rows will be returned to the server.
- **adMarshalModifiedOnly**—Indicates that only modified rows are returned to the server.

MaxRecords

This property holds the maximum number of records to return to a recordset from a command. The default value is 0, which actually means all records will be returned; however, you can restrict the number of records returned, such as when you want to display those records in a Web page or restrict network traffic.

Note that you can set this property only before you've opened a `Recordset` object.

PageCount

The `PageCount` property is the number of pages of data the recordset contains. You can divide a recordset into pages using the `PageSize` property, and the number of pages that results appears in the `PageCount` property.

Note that if the `PageSize` property is not set (and not all providers support pages), `PageCount` will be –1. There's an easy way to move to the last page in a recordset using `PageCount`—just set the `AbsolutePage` property to `PageCount`.

PageSize

To divide a recordset into pages, you set the number of records that make up one page in `PageSize` (note that not all providers support pages, and note that page size is not related to cache size—see the `CacheSize` property above).

You can use pages when you want to limit the number of records displayed at once, as with the Microsoft Index Server, for example, if you want to display those records in a Web page.

RecordCount

The RecordCount property is an important one, because it holds the number of records in the recordset. When you want to loop over all records in a recordset, for example, you can use this property to set up the loop.

Use the RecordCount property to find out how many records are in a recordset object. The property returns −1 when ADO cannot determine the number of records or whether the provider or cursor type does not support RecordCount. Reading the RecordCount property on a closed recordset causes an error.

If the Recordset object supports approximate positioning or bookmarks, this value will be the exact number of records in the recordset, regardless of whether it has been filled with records. If the Recordset object does not support approximate positioning, all records have to be retrieved and counted to return an accurate RecordCount value (you can do this by executing the MoveLast method).

The cursor type of the Recordset object affects whether the number of records can be determined. The RecordCount property will return −1 for a forward-only cursor, the actual count for a static or keyset cursor, and either −1 or the actual count, depending on the data source, for a dynamic cursor.

Sort

This property specifies one or more field names to use to sort the recordset. You can set this property to a string of comma-separated field names to sort on, where each name is a field in the recordset, and is optionally followed by a blank and the keyword ASC or DESC, to specify the field sort order.

If you want to sort on one column, you just set this property to that column name:

```
adoRecordset.Sort = "Name"
```

If you want to sort on more than one column, you can set this property to a list of columns:

```
adoRecordset.Sort = "Name, Grade"
```

We'll put this property to work in the next chapter.

Source

The Source property holds the source for the data in the recordset, which might be a Command object, SQL statement, table name, or stored procedure. This property is useful if you want to identify the actual way the recordset was created.

State

The State property holds the state of the recordset, open or closed. Here are the possible settings for this property:

- **adStateClosed**—(default) Indicates the object is closed.
- **adStateOpen**—Recordset is open.
- **adStateConnecting**—Recordset object is connecting.
- **adStateExecuting**—Recordset object is executing a command.
- **adStateFetching**—Rows of the Recordset object are being fetched.

For a Recordset object executing an asynchronous method, this property indicates whether the object is connecting, executing, or fetching. You can use the State property to determine the current state of a given object at any time; note that this property is read-only.

Note also that the Recordset object's State property can have a combination of values. For example, if a statement is executing, this property will have a value of adStateOpen ANDed with adStateExecuting.

Status

This property holds the status of the current record with respect to batch updates. Here are the possible values this property can hold:

- **adRecOK**—The record was successfully updated.
- **adRecNew**—The record is new.
- **adRecModified**—The record was modified.
- **adRecDeleted**—The record was deleted.
- **adRecUnmodified**—The record was not modified.
- **adRecInvalid**—The record was not saved because its bookmark is invalid.
- **adRecMultipleChanges**—The record was not saved because it would have affected multiple records.
- **adRecPendingChanges**—The record was not saved because it refers to a pending insert.
- **adRecCanceled**—The record was not saved because the operation was canceled.
- **adRecCantRelease**—The new record was not saved because of existing record locks.
- **adRecConcurrencyViolation**—The record was not saved because optimistic concurrency was in use.
- **adRecIntegrityViolation**—The record was not saved because the user violated integrity constraints.

- **adRecMaxChangesExceeded**—The record was not saved because there were too many pending changes.
- **adRecObjectOpen**—The record was not saved because of a conflict with an open storage object.
- **adRecOutOfMemory**—The record was not saved because the computer has run out of memory.
- **adRecPermissionDenied**—The record was not saved because the user has insufficient permissions.
- **adRecSchemaViolation**—The record was not saved because it violates the structure of the underlying database.
- **adRecDBDeleted**—The record has already been deleted from the data source.

StayInSync

This property applies to hierarchical recordsets of the kind we'll see later in the book, and must be set on the parent recordset before the child recordset is retrieved.

This property indicates, in a hierarchical Recordset object, whether the reference to the underlying child records changes when the parent row position changes, and it simplifies navigating hierarchical recordsets.

The StayInSync property is a Boolean value, and the default value is True. If True, the child recordset will be updated if the parent Recordset object changes row position; if False, the child recordset will not be updated.

That completes the Recordset object's properties; I'll take a look at this object's methods next.

Recordset Methods

There is quite a number of methods for the Recordset object, and we'll take a look at all of them here, starting with AddNew.

AddNew

You use the AddNew method to add a new record to a recordset (if the Recordset object can be updated). Here's how you use this method:

```
adoRecordset.AddNew [FieldList [, Values]]
```

Here are the parameters for this method:

- **FieldList**—A single name, or an array of names or ordinal positions, of the fields in the new record.

■ **Values**—A single value, or an array of values, for the fields in the new record. (If FieldList is an array, Values must also be an array with the same number of members; otherwise, an error occurs. The order of field names must match the order of field values in each array.)

You can use AddNew without any parameters, in which case, a new record is added to the recordset and becomes the current record. You can then add data to the field and use the Update or UpdateBatch methods to write the record to the data store.

You can also pass a field and a value, or an array of fields and values. Here's how to create a new record with one field:

```
adoRecordset.AddNew "employees", "Robert"
```

Here's how to use AddNew with arrays, creating a new record with two fields:

```
Fields = Array("Employees", "ID")
Values = Array("Robert", 1234)
adoRecordset.AddNew Fields, Values
```

When you pass parameters to this method, you don't need to call Update or UpdateBatch; the changes are made at once.

To make sure your provider supports AddNew, you can use the Supports method; see that method's description later in this chapter. I'll put AddNew to work in the next chapter.

Cancel

The Cancel method cancels execution of pending Open operations. This method takes no parameters. You can use this method to let users cancel queries made on a data source if they are taking too long to execute; for example, you might provide the user with a Cancel button.

Note that an error is generated if you did not open the recordset asynchronously before using Cancel (see the Open method coming up in a few pages).

CancelBatch

The CancelBatch method cancels a pending batch operation when you're executing a batch update. Here's how you use this method:

```
recordset.CancelBatch AffectRecords
```

Here is the parameter you pass to this method:

■ **AffectRecords**—An AffectEnum value that determines how many records the CancelBatch method will affect.

The AffectRecords value can be one of these constants:

■ **adAffectCurrent**—Cancels pending updates only for the current record.

■ **adAffectGroup**—Cancels pending updates for records that satisfy the current Filter property setting. You must set the Filter property to one of the valid pre-defined constants to use this option.

■ **adAffectAll**—(default) Cancels pending updates for all the records in the Recordset object, including any hidden by the current Filter property setting.

CancelUpdate

This method cancels a pending update after the current record has been edited. This method takes no parameters. After the user has edited the data in a field, you can ask them if they want to update the database with the new value; if so, call Update, if not, call CancelUpdate.

You can also use CancelUpdate to cancel the automatic updating that takes place when the user moves to a new record if they've edited the data in the current record (as in bound controls). You can use this method to cancel the addition of a new record as well.

Clone

The Clone method creates a duplicate recordset from the current recordset. Here's how you use Clone:

```
rstOriginal.Clone [LockType]
```

This method returns a Recordset object reference; to assign that recordset to a variable, use the Set keyword. Here is the parameter you pass to this method:

■ **LockType**—A LockTypeEnum value that specifies either the lock type of the original recordset, or a read-only recordset.

Here are the lock types you can use:

■ **adLockUnspecified**—(default) The clone is created with the same lock type as the original.

■ **adLockReadOnly**—The clone is created as read-only.

What you should know here is that cloning a recordset does not create a new recordset, despite the name of this method. Instead, it creates a new Recordset object, but both the new and old Recordset objects point to the same underlying data. The reason you clone recordsets is that you can move to locations in the new recordset without affecting the old recordset. If that's the kind of operation you want to undertake, you should consider cloning, because round trips to the server can take a long time. On the other hand, if you really want a new recordset, you must open a new recordset manually.

Close

The Close method, as you can guess, closes a Recordset object, making its properties and methods unavailable. Note that pending changes will be discarded when in Batch Update mode, and when in Immediate Update mode, an error will occur if there were pending changes.

Simply closing a Recordset object does not remove it from memory; for that, you should set it to Nothing like this: adoRecordset = Nothing. In addition, before closing a Recordset object, you might check to make sure it's really open (using the State property) before you try to close it; otherwise, closing it when it's already closed will generate an error.

CompareBookmarks

This method compares two bookmarks and indicates how they stand in relation to each other. Here's how you use this method:

```
recordset.CompareBookmarks Bookmark1, Bookmark2
```

This method returns one of the following values:

- **adCompareLessThan**—The first bookmark is before the second.
- **adCompareEqual**—The bookmarks are equal.
- **adCompareGreaterThan**—The first bookmark is after the second.
- **adCompareNotEqual**—The bookmarks are not equal and not ordered.
- **adCompareNotComparable**—The bookmarks cannot be compared.

Note that this method only compares bookmarks, not the data the bookmarks point to, and that the bookmarks must be in the same Recordset object.

Delete

The Delete method deletes the current record (or group of records). Here's how you use this method:

```
adoRecordset.Delete [AffectRecords]
```

The AffectRecords parameter you can pass to this method can be one of the following constants:

- **adAffectCurrent**—(default) Deletes only the current record.
- **adAffectGroup**—Deletes the records that satisfy the current `Filter` property setting. You must set the `Filter` property to one of the valid pre-defined constants in order to use this option.
- **adAffectAll**—Deletes all records.
- **adAffectAllChapters**—Deletes all chapter records (hierarchical recordsets).

Note that when you're operating in Batch Update mode, records are only marked for deletion and not actually deleted until you call `Update-Batch`.

Find

You use the `Find` method to search a recordset, and I'll use `Find` in the next chapter. Here's how you use `Find` in general:

```
Find criteria [, SkipRows  [, searchDirection
[, start]]]
```

Here are the parameters you pass to this method:

- **criteria**—A string containing a statement that specifies the column name, comparison operator, and value to use in the search.
- **SkipRows**—A value, whose default value is zero, that specifies the offset from the current row or start bookmark to begin the search.
- **searchDirection**—A value that specifies whether the search should begin on the current row or the next available row in the direction of the search. Its value can be `adSearchForward` or `adSearchBackward`. The search stops at the start or end of the recordset, depending on the value of `searchDirection`.
- **start**—A variant bookmark to use as the starting position for the search.

Note that the comparison operator in criteria may be `">"` (greater than), `"<"` (less than), `"="` (equal), `">="` (greater than or equal), `"<="` (less than or equal), `"<>"` (not equal), or `"like"` (to use pattern matching). The value in criteria may be a string, floating point number, or date. You delimit string values with single quotes (for example, `"state = 'MA'"`) and date values with `"#"` (for example, `"start_date > #1/1/2001#"`).

Note also that if the comparison operator is `like`, the string value may contain * (which stands for one or more occurrences of any character) or _ (which stands for one occurrence of any character).

GetRows

This method is a useful one because it returns records from a recordset in a two-dimensional array of rows and columns. Here's how you use this method:

```
recordset.GetRows([Rows [, Start [, Fields]]])
```

This method returns a two-dimensional array. Here are the parameters you pass to this method:

- **Rows**—Indicates the number of records to retrieve. The default is ad-GetRowsRest (-1).
- **Start**—Bookmark for the record from which the GetRows operation should begin. You can also use one of the following BookmarkEnum values: adBookmarkCurrent, adBookmarkFirst, or adBookmark-Last.
- **Fields**—Field name or position, or an array of field names or positions. ADO returns only the data in these fields.

Note that the columns are stored in the first dimension of the returned array, and the rows are stored in the second, which is the reverse of what you might expect.

Also note that when you're working with large recordsets, it is usually more efficient to retrieve multiple arrays than trying to get the whole record-set at once. For example, if you have a recordset of 10,000 lines, try retrieving the records as ten arrays of 1,000 lines each, or breaking the recordset up into even smaller ranges.

GetString

This method returns a Recordset object as a string. Here's how you use this method in general:

```
recordset.GetString([StringFormat [, NumRows
[, ColumnDelimiter [, RowDelimiter [, NullExpr]]]]])
```

Here are the parameters you pass to GetString:

- **StringFormat**—Specifies that the recordset should be converted to a particular format. The only possible value currently is adClipString in which rows are delimited by RowDelimiter, columns by Column-Delimiter, and null values by NullExpr (note that these parameters are valid only with adClipString).

- **NumRows**—The number of rows in the recordset to convert. If NumRows is not specified or if it is greater than the total number of rows in the recordset, then all the rows in the recordset are converted.
- **ColumnDelimiter**—Delimiter used between columns, if specified, otherwise the TAB character.
- **RowDelimiter**—Delimiter used between rows, if specified, otherwise the RETURN character.
- **NullExpr**—Expression used in place of a null value, if specified; otherwise, the empty string.

One good use for this method is to format tables for display in ASP Web pages, using HTML table tags like <TR> and <TD> for delimiters.

Move

This method moves to the given position in a recordset. Here's how you use Move:

```
adoRecordset.Move NumRecords [, Start]
```

Here are the parameters you pass to this method:

- **NumRecords**—Number of records the current record position moves.
- **Start**—A bookmark, including the Bookmark enumeration values for this parameter; see below.

Here are Bookmark values you can use for the Start value:

- **adBookmarkCurrent**—(default) Starts at the current record.
- **adBookmarkFirst**—Starts at the first record.
- **adBookmarkLast**—Starts at the last record.

This method lets you move around freely in a recordset, selecting the record that will become the current record. Note that if the data in the current record has been changed and Update has not yet been called, then moving to a new record will automatically call Update.

Note also that you can use a negative number to move backward from the current position, like this (note that you cannot move backward in a forward-only recordset):

```
adoRecordset.Move -10
```

If you move past the beginning or end of a recordset, the BOF or EOF property will be set to True; if you try to move past the beginning or end of the recordset again, an error will be generated.

MoveFirst

The `MoveFirst` method moves to the first record in the recordset, and this method takes no parameters. Note that calling this method in a forward-only recordset will probably result in an error.

After executing this method successfully, the first record in the recordset will be the current record. As with all moves, if there were pending changes to the current record before the move, the `Update` method is called before the move is made.

MoveLast

The `MoveLast` method moves to the last record in the recordset, and this method takes no parameters. Note that calling this method in a forward-only recordset will probably result in an error, because you're only supposed to move forward one record at a time in such recordsets.

After executing this method successfully, the last record in the recordset will be the current record. As with all moves, if there were pending changes to the current record before the move, the `Update` method is called before the move is made.

MoveNext

The `MoveNext` method moves to the next record in the recordset, and this method takes no parameters. If you try to move past the end of the recordset, the `EOF` property is set to True.

After executing this method successfully, the next record in the record-set will become the current record. As with all moves, if there were pending changes to the current record before the move, the `Update` method is called before the move is made.

MovePrevious

The `MovePrevious` method moves to the previous record in the recordset, and this method takes no parameters. You can check if this method is supported by using the `Supports` method. If you try to move past the beginning of the recordset, the `BOF` property is set to True.

After executing this method successfully, the previous record in the recordset will become the current record. As with all moves, if there were pending changes to the current record before the move, the `Update` method is called before the move is made.

NextRecordset

This method clears the current `Recordset` object and returns the next recordset when you're working with multiple recordsets. Here's how you use this method:

```
recordset1.NextRecordset([RecordsAffected])
```

This method returns a `Recordset` object. Here is the parameter you can pass to this method:

- **RecordsAffected**—A variable in which the provider returns the number of records that the current operation affected.

You use the `NextRecordset` method to return the results of either the next command in a compound command statement or a stored procedure that returns multiple results. If you open a `Recordset` object using a compound command statement (for example, `"SELECT * FROM First Table;SELECT * FROM SecondTable"`) using the `Execute` method on a command or the `Open` method on a recordset, ADO executes only the first command and returns the results. To access the results of additional commands in the statement, you call the `NextRecordset` method.

Open

You use the `Open` method to open a recordset. Here's how you use this method:

```
recordset.Open [Source [, ActiveConnection
[, CursorType [, LockType [, Options]]]]]
```

Here are the parameters you can pass to this method:

- **Source**—A valid `Command` object variable name, an SQL statement, a table name, a stored procedure call, or the file name of a persisted recordset.
- **ActiveConnection**—A valid `Connection` object variable name or a string containing `ConnectionString` parameters.
- **CursorType**—The type of cursor that the provider should use when opening the recordset. Can be one of the following constants: `adOpenForwardOnly` (default), `adOpenKeyset`, `adOpenDynamic`, or `adOpenStatic`. (See the `CursorType` property for more information.)
- **LockType**—Specifies what type of locking the provider should use when opening the recordset. Can be one of the following constants: `adLockReadOnly` (default), `adLockPessimistic`, `adLockOptimistic`, or `adLockBatchOptimistic`. (See the `LockType` property for more information.)
- **Options**—Indicates how the provider should evaluate the `Source` argument if it represents something other than a `Command` object, or that the recordset should be restored from a file where it was previously saved.

Here are the possible values for the Options parameter:

- **adCmdText**—Indicates that the provider should evaluate Source as a textual definition of a command.
- **adCmdTable**—Indicates that ADO should generate an SQL query to return all rows from the table named in Source.
- **adCmdTableDirect**—Indicates that the provider should return all rows from the table named in Source.
- **adCmdStoredProc**—Indicates that the provider should evaluate Source as a stored procedure.
- **adCmdUnknown**—Indicates that the type of command in the Source argument is not known.
- **adCmdFile**—Indicates that the persisted (saved) recordset should be restored from the file named in Source.
- **adAsyncExecute**—Indicates that the Source should be executed asynchronously.
- **adAsyncFetch**—Indicates that after the initial quantity specified in the Initial Fetch Size property is fetched, any remaining rows should be fetched asynchronously. If a row is required that has not been fetched, execution is blocked until the requested row becomes available.
- **adAsyncFetchNonBlocking**—Indicates that the main thread never blocks (i.e., waits) while fetching. If the requested row has not been fetched, the current row automatically moves to the end of the file.

Here's an example in which I open a recordset using the Open method:

```
Private Sub Form_Load()
    Dim adoConnect As Connection
    Set adoConnect = New Connection

    adoConnect.Open _
        "PROVIDER=Microsoft.Jet.OLEDB.3.51;Data " & _
        "Source=C:\ado\biblio.mdb;"

    Set adoRecordset = New Recordset
    adoRecordset.Open "select * from Publishers", _
        adoConnect, adOpenStatic, adLockOptimistic

    Set Text1.DataSource = adoRecordset
```

```
Set Text2.DataSource = adoRecordset

Text1.DataField = "Name"

Text2.DataField = "Address"


adoRecordset.Find "Name LIKE 'P*'"
End Sub
```

To open a recordset asynchronously, use a client-side cursor, as I'll do in the next chapter, and use OR to combine an asynchronous constant like adAsyncFetch to the other options you want to use, like adCmdStored-Procedure OR adAsyncFetch. With adAsyncFetch, ADO will wait until the records are available, and with adAsyncFetchNonBlocking, ADO will not wait, but EOF will be True until the records are available.

Note also that if you set ActiveConnection to a connection string, ADO will create a new connection to the data store automatically. You can also use a Command object as the Source parameter, and if you do, you should not pass an ActiveConnection parameter.

We'll see more about the Open method in the next chapter.

Requery

The Requery method re-executes the query that created the recordset. Here's how you use this method:

```
recordset.Requery [Options]
```

Here is the parameter you can pass to this method:

- **Options**—A bitmask indicating options affecting this operation. If this parameter is set to adAsyncExecute, this operation will execute asynchronously and a RecordsetChangeComplete event will fire when it concludes.

You use the Requery method to refresh the entire contents of a Recordset object from the data source by re-executing the original command and so retrieving the data a second time. Calling this method is the same as using the Close and then the Open methods. If you are editing the current record or adding a new record, an error occurs.

Resync

This method refreshes the data in the recordset. Here's how you use this method:

```
recordset.Resync [AffectRecords [, ResyncValues]]
```

Here are the parameters you can pass to this method:

- **AffectRecords**—A value that determines how many records the Re-sync method will affect.
- **ResyncValues**—A value that specifies whether underlying values are overwritten.

The AffectRecords parameter can be one of the following constants:

- **adAffectCurrent**—Refreshes only the current record.
- **adAffectGroup**—Refreshes the records that satisfy the current Filter property setting. You must set the Filter property to one of the valid pre-defined constants to use this option.
- **adAffectAll**—(default) Refreshes all the records in the Recordset object, including any hidden by the current Filter property setting.
- **adAffectAllChapters**—Refreshes all the chapter records.

The ResyncValues parameter can be one of the following constants:

- **adResyncAllValues**—(default) Data is overwritten and pending updates are canceled.
- **adResyncUnderlyingValues**—Data is not overwritten and pending updates are not canceled.

Use the Resync method to resynchronize records in the current record-set with the underlying database. This is useful if you are using either a static or forward-only cursor but you want to see any changes in the underlying database.

If you set the CursorLocation property to adUseClient, Resync is only available for non-read-only Recordset objects.

Save

The Save method saves the recordset to a file. Here's how you use this method:

```
recordset.Save [FileName [, PersistFormat]]
```

Here are the parameters you can use with this method:

- **FileName**—Complete path and name of the file where the recordset is to be saved.
- **PersistFormat**—A value that specifies the format in which the recordset is to be saved.

The `PersistFormat` parameter can be one of the following constants:

- **adPersistADTG**—(default) Saves in proprietary advanced data table-gram format.
- **adPersistXML**—Saves in XML format.

The first time you save a recordset, you specify the file name. If you use `Save` again, you omit the file name or a run-time error will occur (if you call `Save` with a new file name after the first time, the recordset is saved to the new file).

Note that the `Save` method does not close the recordset, so you can continue to work with the recordset and save your most recent changes. The file remains open until the recordset is closed; you use the `Open` method to restore the recordset from the file at a later time.

Supports

You can use the `Supports` method to query a `Recordset` object to see what features it supports. Here's how you use this method:

```
recordset.Supports( CursorOptions )
```

The `CursorOptions` parameter can be one or more of these values:

- **adAddNew**—You can use the `AddNew` method to add new records.
- **adApproxPosition**—You can read and set the `AbsolutePosition` and `AbsolutePage` properties.
- **adBookmark**—You can use the `Bookmark` property to gain access to specific records.
- **adDelete**—You can use the `Delete` method to delete records.
- **adHoldRecords**—You can retrieve more records or change the next retrieve position without committing all pending changes.
- **adMovePrevious**—You can use the `MoveFirst` and `MovePrevious` methods, and `Move` or `GetRows` methods, to move the current record position backward without requiring bookmarks.
- **adResync**—You can update the cursor with the data visible in the underlying database using the `Resync` method.
- **adUpdate**—You can use the `Update` method to modify existing data.
- **adUpdateBatch**—You can use batch updating (`UpdateBatch` and `CancelBatch` methods) to transmit groups of changes to the provider.
- **adIndex**—You can use the `Index` property to name an index.
- **adSeek**—You can use the `Seek` method to locate a row in a recordset.

You can use the Supports method to determine what types of functionality a Recordset object supports. If the Recordset object supports the features whose corresponding constants are in CursorOptions, the Supports method returns True; otherwise, it returns False.

Here's an example in which I check if a Recordset object supports the MovePrevious method before using that method:

```
Private Sub cmdPrevious_Click()
    If adoRecordset.Supports(adMovePrevious) Then

        On Error GoTo ErrLabel

        If Not adoRecordset.BOF Then _
            adoRecordset.MovePrevious
        If adoRecordset.BOF And _
            adoRecordset.RecordCount > 0 Then
            adoRecordset.MoveFirst
        End If

        Exit Sub

ErrLabel:
    MsgBox Err.Description

    End If
End Sub
```

Update

This method saves changes to the database. Here's how to use this method:

```
recordset.Update [Fields [, Values]]
```

Here are the parameters you can use with this method:

- **Fields**—A single name or a variant array representing names or ordinal positions of the field(s) you wish to modify.
- **Values**—A single value or a variant array representing values for the field(s) in the new record.

You use the Update method to save any changes you make to the current record of a Recordset object since calling the AddNew method or since changing any field values in an existing record. Note that the Recordset object must support updates.

If the Recordset object supports batch updating, you can cache a number of changes to one or more records until you call the Updatebatch method. Note that if you are editing the current record or adding a new record when you call the UpdateBatch method, ADO will automatically call the Update method to save any pending changes to the current record before transmitting the batched changes to the provider.

If you move from the record you are adding or editing before calling the Update method, ADO will automatically call it to save the changes. You must call the CancelUpdate method to cancel any changes made to the current record or to delete a newly added record.

UpdateBatch

You use this method to perform multiple-record updates to a database.

```
recordset.UpdateBatch AffectRecords
```

The AffectRecords parameter determines how many records the UpdateBatch method will affect and can be one of the following constants:

- **adAffectCurrent**—Writes pending changes only for the current record.
- **adAffectGroup**—Writes pending changes for the records that satisfy the current Filter property setting.
- **adAffectAll**—(default) Writes pending changes for all the records in the Recordset object, including any hidden by the current Filter property setting.
- **adAffectAllChapters**—Writes pending changes for all chapters.

You use the UpdateBatch method when modifying a Recordset object in Batch Update mode to send all changes made in the Recordset object back to the database. If the Recordset object supports batch updating, you can cache multiple changes to one or more records until you call the UpdateBatch method. If you are editing the current record or adding a new record when you call the UpdateBatch method, ADO will automatically call the Update method to save any pending changes to the current record before transmitting the batched changes to the provider. Note that you should use batch updating only with either a keyset or static cursor.

That completes the methods of the Recordset object; I'll take a look at this object's events next.

Recordset Events

You use recordset events to determine when the provider is about to perform certain actions and when it has performed them, such as changing the data in a field. To use the events of an ADO `Recordset` object, you declare the object using the `WithEvents` keyword, as I'll do in the next chapter.

ADO recordset events use certain enumeration types, such as the `ADODB.EventReason`, which indicates the reason an event occurred. It can take these possible values:

- **adRsnAddNew**—1. New record to be added.
- **adRsnDelete**—2. Record deleted.
- **adRsnUpdate**—3. Record to be updated.
- **adRsnUndoUpdate**—4. Undo update.
- **adRsnUndoAddNew**—5. Undo add new record.
- **adRsnUndoDelete**—6. Undo delete.
- **adRsnRequery**—7. Requery.
- **adRsnResynch**—8. Resynchronize.
- **adRsnClose**—9. Close.
- **adRsnMove**—10. Move.
- **adRsnFirstChange**—11. First change..
- **adRsnMoveFirst**—12. Move first.
- **adRsnMoveNext**—13. Move next.
- **adRsnMovePrevious**—14. Move previous.
- **adRsnMoveLast**—15. Move last.

`ADODB.EventStatus` is an enumeration type that indicates the current status of the control. It can take these possible values:

- **adStatusOK**—1. OK.
- **adStatusErrorsOccurred**—2. Errors occurred.
- **adStatusCantDeny**—3. Can't deny change.
- **adStatusCancel**—4. Cancel.
- **adStatusUnwantedEvent**—5. Prevent future notifications.

`ADODB.Error` is an enumeration that holds the ADO or provider-specific error that occurred; the ADO errors appear in Table 7.1 for reference. I'll turn to the recordset events now, starting with `EndOfRecordset`.

EndOfRecordset

The `EndOfRecordset` event fires when you try to move past the end of a recordset. Here's how the event handler for this event looks:

TABLE 7.1 ADO error codes

Constant Name	Number	Description
adErrInvalidArgument	3001	Your code is using arguments that are of the wrong type, out of acceptable range, or in conflict with one another.
adErrNoCurrentRecord	3021	Either you are at the beginning or end of the file, or the current record has been deleted; the operation requested by the application requires a current record.
adErrIllegalOperation	3219	The operation you requested is not allowed in this context.
adErrInTransaction	3246	You cannot explicitly close a Connection object while in the middle of a transaction.
adErrFeatureNotAvailable	3251	The operation you requested is not supported by the OLE DB provider.
adErrItemNotFound	3265	ADO could not find the object in the collection corresponding to the name or ordinal reference you requested.
adErrObjectInCollection	3367	The object is already in the collection and so can't be appended.
adErrObjectNotSet	3420	The object you referenced no longer points to a valid object.
adErrDataConversion	3421	You are using a value of the wrong type for the current operation.
adErrObjectClosed	3704	The operation you requested is not allowed if the object is closed.
adErrObjectOpen	3705	The operation you requested is not allowed if the object is open.
adErrProviderNotFound	3706	ADO could not find the provider you specified.
adErrBoundToCommand	3707	You cannot change the ActiveConnection property of a Recordset object with a Command object as its source.
adErrInvalidParamInfo	3708	You improperly defined a Parameter object.
adErrInvalidConnection	3709	You requested an operation on an object with a reference to a closed or invalid Connection object.

```
Private Sub adoRecordset_EndOfRecordset(fMoreData As
Boolean, adStatus As ADODB.EventStatusEnum, ByVal
pRecordset As ADODB.Recordset)


End Sub
```

Here are the parameters passed to this event's handler:

- **fMoreData**—You can append new records to pRecordset while processing this event. Add your data, then set this parameter to True to indicate that there is a new end to the recordset before exiting the event handler.
- **adStatus**—The current status value.
- **pRecordset**—The Recordset object for which this event occurred.

Note that you can use this event to add more data to the end of a recordset if the user tries to move past the end of the recordset.

FetchComplete

The FetchComplete event fires when a retrieval operation has completed. Here's what the event handler for this event looks like:

```
Private Sub adoRecordset_FetchComplete(ByVal pError
As ADODB.Error, adStatus As ADODB.EventStatusEnum,
ByVal pRecordset As ADODB.Recordset)


End Sub
```

Here are the parameters for this event handler:
- **pError**—Describes the error that occurred when the value of adStatus is adStatusErrorsOccurred; otherwise, not set.
- **adStatus**—The status of the event.
- **pRecordset**—The Recordset object this event is for.

This event is a useful one when you're executing an asynchronous fetch and don't want to keep having to check the State property—instead, you can just add code to this event that will run when the fetch is complete.

FetchProgress

This event lets you monitor the progress of a data retrieval operation. Here's what the event handler for this event looks like:

```
Private Sub adoRecordset_FetchProgress(ByVal
Progress As Long, ByVal MaxProgress As Long,
adStatus As ADODB.EventStatusEnum, ByVal pRecordset
As ADODB.Recordset)



End Sub
```

Here are the parameters passed to this event handler:

- **Progress**—Number of rows that have been retrieved so far.
- **MaxProgress**—Maximum number of rows ADO expects to retrieve.
- **adStatus**—The status of the event.
- **pRecordset**—The Recordset object this event is for.

You use this event to monitor the status of a row-fetching operation, and it's useful for updating a control like a Visual Basic progress bar on the screen to keep the user informed of the operation's progress.

FieldChangeComplete

This event fires when the value in a field(s) has changed. Here's what the event handler for this event looks like:

```
Private Sub adoRecordset_FieldChangeComplete(ByVal
cFields As Long, ByVal Fields As Variant, ByVal
pError As ADODB.Error, adStatus As
ADODB.EventStatusEnum, ByVal pRecordset As
ADODB.Recordset)



End Sub
```

Here are the parameters passed to this event's handler:

- **cFields**—The number of fields in the Fields array.
- **Fields**—An array of variants that holds the fields that will be changed.
- **pError**—Describes the error that occurred when the value of adStatus is adStatusErrorsOccurred; otherwise, not set.
- **adStatus**—The current status value.
- **pRecordset**—The Recordset object for which this event occurred.

You can check what the original value of the changed field was using the `Fields` array, which is an array of the fields that were changed (you can change multiple fields with batch updates, as we'll see later). For example, say you added this code to the `FieldChangeComplete` event handler for an ADO recordset, adoRecordset:

```
Private Sub adoRecordset_FieldChangeComplete(ByVal
cFields As Long, Fields As Variant, ByVal pError As
ADODB.Error, adStatus As ADODB.EventStatusEnum,
ByVal pRecordset As ADODB.Recordset)
    MsgBox Fields(0)
End Sub
```

Now say you connect this recordset to the `students` table developed earlier in this book and connect the `Name` field in that table to a text box. When you run the program, you'll see the name of the first student in the text box, Ann. If you were to change that name to Annie, you'd see a message box displayed by the above code—and the name you'd see in the message box is Ann, the original value, not Annie, the new value.

You can also check the values in fields *before* they are changed—see the `WillChangeField` event coming up.

MoveComplete

This event fires when the current row position in a recordset has changed. Here's what the event handler for this event looks like:

```
Private Sub adoRecordset_MoveComplete(ByVal adReason
As ADODB.EventReasonEnum, ByVal pError As
ADODB.Error, adStatus As ADODB.EventStatusEnum,
ByVal pRecordset As ADODB.Recordset)

End Sub
```

Here are the parameters passed to this event's handler:

- **adReason**—The reason why this event occurred.
- **pError**—Describes the error that occurred when the value of adStatus is adStatusErrorsOccurred; otherwise, not set.
- **adStatus**—The current status value.
- **pRecordset**—The Recordset object for which this event occurred.

The adReason parameter is set to adStatusOK if the operation that caused the event was successful, or adStatusErrorsOccurred if the operation failed. You can set this value to adStatusUnwantedEvent to prevent further notifications. Here are the possible values for adReason:

- adRsnMoveFirst
- adRsnMoveLast
- adRsnMoveNext
- adRsnMovePrevious
- adRsnMove
- adRsnRequery

To catch moves before they take place, look at the WillMove event, coming up soon.

RecordChangeComplete

This event fires when one or more records in the recordset have changed. Here's what the event handler for this event looks like:

```
Private Sub adoRecordset_RecordChangeComplete(ByVal
adReason As ADODB.EventReasonEnum, ByVal cRecords As
Long, ByVal pError As ADODB.Error, adStatus As
ADODB.EventStatusEnum, ByVal pRecordset As
ADODB.Recordset)


End Sub
```

Here are the parameters passed to this event's handler:

- **adReason**—The reason why this event occurred.
- **cRecords**—The number of records that were changed.
- **pError**—Describes the error that occurred when the value of adStatus is adStatusErrorsOccurred; otherwise, not set.
- **adStatus**—The current status value.
- **pRecordset**—The Recordset object for which this event occurred.

When RecordChangeComplete is called, the adReason parameter is set to adStatusOK if the operation that changed the record worked successfully, or adStatusErrorsOccurred if the operation failed. Note that you can set this parameter to adStatusUnwantedEvent to prevent further notifications. Here are the possible values for adReason:

- adRsnAddNew
- adRsnDelete
- adRsnUpdate
- adRsnUndoUpdate
- adRsnUndoAddNew
- adRsnUndoDelete
- adRsnFirstChange

This is a useful event to use if you want to keep track of what records a user has changed, such as when you create an audit log.

To catch record changes before they occur, take a look at the WillChangeRecord event coming up.

RecordsetChangeComplete

This event fires when the recordset has changed. Here's what the event handler for this event looks like:

```
Private Sub
adoRecordset_RecordsetChangeComplete(ByVal adReason
As ADODB.EventReasonEnum, ByVal pError As
ADODB.Error, adStatus As ADODB.EventStatusEnum,
ByVal pRecordset As ADODB.Recordset)


End Sub
```

Here are the parameters passed to this event's handler:

- **adReason**—The reason why this event occurred.
- **pError**—Describes the error that occurred when the value of adStatus is adStatusErrorsOccurred; otherwise, not set.
- **adStatus**—The current status value.
- **pRecordset** The Recordset object for which this event occurred.

When RecordsetChangeComplete is called, the adStatus parameter is set to adStatusOK if the operation that changed the recordset was successful, adStatusErrorsOccurred if the operation failed, or adStatusCancel if the operation associated with the previous WillChangeRecordset event was canceled. Here are the possible values for adReason:

- adRsnReQuery
- adRsnReSynch

- adRsnClose
- adRsnOpen

You can keep track of overall changes to a recordset with this event. Note that you can set adStatus to adStatusUnwantedEvent to prevent further notifications.

WillChan geField

This event fires when the value in a field(s) will change. Here's what the event handler for this event looks like:

```
Private Sub adoRecordset_WillChangeField(ByVal
cFields As Long, ByVal Fields As Variant, adStatus
As ADODB.EventStatusEnum, ByVal pRecordset As
ADODB.Recordset)


End Sub
```

Here are the parameters passed to this event's handler:

- **cFields**—Number of Field objects in Fields.
- **Fields**—Field objects with pending changes.
- **pError**—Describes the error that occurred when the value of adStatus is adStatusErrorsOccurred; otherwise, not set.
- **adStatus**—Status value, see below.
- **pRecordset**—The recordset that caused the event.

You can determine what data will be changed by looking at the field(s) in the Fields array; each element in this array is the data in a field that will change. To cancel a change, you set the adStatus parameter to adStatus-Cancel. Note also that the FieldChangeComplete event occurs after a change has been made to a field.

WillChangeRecord

This event fires when the current row of the recordset will change. Here's what the event handler for this event looks like:

```
Private Sub adoRecordset_WillChangeRecord(ByVal
adReason As ADODB.EventReasonEnum, ByVal cRecords As
Long, adStatus As ADODB.EventStatusEnum, ByVal
```

```
pRecordset As ADODB.Recordset)
End Sub
```

Here are the parameters passed to this event's handler:

- **adReason**—The reason why this event occurred.
- **cRecords**—The number of records that will change.
- **adStatus**—The current status value.
- **pRecordset**—The Recordset object for which this event occurred.

You can use this event to monitor the changes a user makes to a record. Here are the possible values for adReason:

- adRsnAddNew
- adRsnDelete
- adRsnUpdate
- adRsnUndoUpdate
- adRsnUndoAddNew
- adRsnUndoDelete
- adRsnFirstChange

Note that the RecordChangeComplete event fires after a change to a record is complete.

WillChangeRecordset

This event fires when a recordset will change. Here is the event handler for this event:

```
Private Sub adoRecordset_WillChangeRecordset(ByVal
adReason As ADODB.EventReasonEnum, adStatus As
ADODB.EventStatusEnum, ByVal pRecordset As
ADODB.Recordset)

End Sub
```

Here are the parameters passed to this event's handler:

- **adReason**—The reason why this event occurred.
- **adStatus**—The current status value.
- **pRecordset**—The Recordset object for which this event occurred.

Here are the possible values for adReason:

- adRsnReQuery
- adRsnReSynch
- adRsnClose
- adRsnOpen

Note that the RecordsetChangeComplete event fires after the change to the recordset is complete.

WillMove

This event fires when the current row position in a recordset will change. Here's what the event handler for this event looks like:

```
Private Sub adoRecordset_WillMove(ByVal adReason As
ADODB.EventReasonEnum, adStatus As
ADODB.EventStatusEnum, ByVal pRecordset As
ADODB.Recordset)


End Sub
```

Here are the parameters passed to this event's handler:

- **adReason**—The reason why this event occurred.
- **adStatus**—The current status value.
- **pRecordset**—The Recordset object for which this event occurred.

And here are the possible values for adReason:

- adRsnMoveFirst
- adRsnMoveLast
- adRsnMoveNext
- adRsnMovePrevious
- adRsnMove
- adRsnRequery

This event can be useful if, for example, you want the user to do something with the current record before moving on to a new one. After a successful move, the MoveComplete event fires.

That completes the events of the Recordset object; I'll take a look at the collections of this object next.

Recordset Collections

The `Recordset` object has two collections: `Fields` and `Properties`.

Fields

The `Fields` collection holds the fields in the current record. There are a variety of ways of using the `Fields` collection, and we'll see them all later in this chapter and in the next chapter.

Properties

The `Properties` collection holds the dynamic properties of the `Recordset` object, including provider-specific properties. I'll take a look at collections in general in the chapter on collections, Chapter 9. In the meantime, I'll examine some of the characteristics of the behavior of `Recordset` objects by provider now.

Recordset Properties and Methods by OLE DB Provider

The properties and methods of recordsets will differ by OLE DB provider. For example, the Jet OLE DB provider cannot provide all the functionality of the SQL Server OLE DB provider.

You can determine what methods the provider you're using supports with the `Recordset` object's `Supports` method, passing it constants like `adUpdateBatch`, `adBookmark`, `adMovePrevious`, `adDelete`, and others to see if the provider supports the corresponding methods and properties. You can also enumerate the `Properties` collection of the recordset to determine what provider-specific properties are present. In this way, you can get a lot of information about the provider you're working with at run-time.

I'll take a look at some of the recordset characteristics of the most popular providers here.

Microsoft ODBC OLE DB Provider

The recordset properties that the ODBC OLE DB provider, the default ADO provider, supports appear in Table 7.2, and the recordset methods it supports appear in Table 7.3.

Microsoft OLE DB Provider for Microsoft Index Server

Only the static cursor type is available for the Microsoft Index Server. Table 7.4 gives the properties available with a `Recordset` object opened with this provider, and Table 7.5 gives the methods.

TABLE 7.2   Microsoft ODBC OLE DB recordset properties by cursor type

Property	ForwardOnly	Dynamic	Keyset	Static
AbsolutePage	Not Available	Not Available	Read/Write	Read/Write
AbsolutePosition	Not Available	Not Available	Read/Write	Read/Write
ActiveConnection	Read/Write	Read/Write	Read/Write	Read/Write
BOF	Read-Only	Read-Only	Read-Only	Read-Only
Bookmark	Not Available	Not Available	Read/Write	Read/Write
CacheSize	Read/Write	Read/Write	Read/Write	Read/Write
CursorLocation	Read/Write	Read/Write	Read/Write	Read/Write
CursorType	Read/Write	Read/Write	Read/Write	Read/Write
EditMode	Read-Only	Read-Only	Read-Only	Read-Only
EOF	Read-Only	Read-Only	Read-Only	Read-Only
Filter	Read/Write	Read/Write	Read/Write	Read/Write
LockType	Read/Write	Read/Write	Read/Write	Read/Write
MarshalOptions	Read/Write	Read/Write	Read/Write	Read/Write
MaxRecords	Read/Write	Read/Write	Read/Write	Read/Write
PageCount	Not Available	Not Available	Read-Only	Read-Only
PageSize	Read/Write	Read/Write	Read/Write	Read/Write
RecordCount	Not Available	Not Available	Read-Only	Read-Only
Source	Read/Write	Read/Write	Read/Write	Read/Write
State	Read-Only	Read-Only	Read-Only	Read-Only
Status	Read-Only	Read-Only	Read-Only	Read-Only

Microsoft OLE DB Provider for Microsoft Active Directory Service

Only the static cursor type is available for the Microsoft Active Directory Service. Table 7.6 gives the properties available with a `Recordset` object opened with this provider, and Table 7.7 gives the methods.

OLE DB Provider for Microsoft Jet

The Microsoft Jet database engine does not support dynamic cursors, so the OLE DB Provider for Microsoft Jet does not support the `adLockDynamic` cursor type. When you request a dynamic cursor, this provider returns a keyset cursor and resets the `CursorType` property.

In addition, if you request an updatable recordset, setting `LockType` to `adLockOptimistic`, `adLockBatchOptimistic`, or `adLockPessimistic`, this provider will also return a keyset cursor and reset the `CursorType` property.

TABLE 7.3 Microsoft ODBC OLE DB recordset methods by cursor type

Method	ForwardOnly	Dynamic	Keyset	Static
AddNew	Yes	Yes	Yes	Yes
CancelBatch	Yes	Yes	Yes	Yes
CancelUpdate	Yes	Yes	Yes	Yes
Clone	No	No	Yes	Yes
Close	Yes	Yes	Yes	Yes
Delete	Yes	Yes	Yes	Yes
GetRows	Yes	Yes	Yes	Yes
Move	Yes	Yes	Yes	Yes
MoveFirst	Yes	Yes	Yes	Yes
MoveLast	No	Yes	Yes	Yes
MoveNext	Yes	Yes	Yes	Yes
MovePrevious	No	Yes	Yes	Yes
NextRecordset	Yes	Yes	Yes	Yes
Open	Yes	Yes	Yes	Yes
Requery	Yes	Yes	Yes	Yes
Resync	No	No	Yes	Yes
Supports	Yes	Yes	Yes	Yes
Update	Yes	Yes	Yes	Yes
UpdateBatch	Yes	Yes	Yes	Yes

TABLE 7.4 Microsoft Index Server OLE DB recordset properties

Property	Availability
AbsolutePage	Read/Write
AbsolutePosition	Read/Write
ActiveConnection	Read-Only
BOF	Read-Only
Bookmark	Read/Write
CacheSize	Read/Write
CursorLocation	Always adUseServer
CursorType	Always adOpenStatic
EditMode	Always adEditNone
EOF	Read-Only
Filter	Read/Write
LockType	Read/Write
MarshalOptions	Not Available
MaxRecords	Read/Write
PageCount	Read-Only
PageSize	Read/Write
RecordCount	Read-Only
Source	Read/Write
State	Read-Only
Status	Read-Only

TABLE 7.5	Microsoft Index Server OLE DB recordset methods
Method	**Availability**
AddNew	No
Cancel	No
CancelBatch	No
CancelUpdate	No
Clone	Yes
Close	Yes
Delete	No
GetRows	Yes
Move	Yes
MoveFirst	Yes
MoveLast	Yes
MoveNext	Yes
MovePrevious	Yes
NextRecordset	Yes
Open	Yes
Requery	Yes
Resync	Yes
Supports	Yes
Update	No
UpdateBatch	No

Microsoft OLE DB Provider for SQL Server

The Microsoft OLE DB Provider for SQL Server, SQLOLEDB, cannot use SQL Server cursors to support multiple-rowsets results. That means that when you request a recordset requiring SQL Server cursor support, an error occurs if the command text used generates more than a single recordset as its result.

SQL Server cursors support scrollable SQLOLEDB recordsets, although SQL Server has some limitations on cursors that are sensitive to changes made by other users. In particular, the rows in some cursors cannot be ordered, so attempting to use an SQL ORDER BY clause may fail.

As we'll see in the next chapter, to access the data in a record in a recordset, you use Field objects. For that reason, I'll take a look at the Field object here.

TABLE 7.6 Microsoft Active Directory Service OLE DB recordset properties	
Property	**Availability**
AbsolutePage	Read/Write
AbsolutePosition	Read/Write
ActiveConnection	Read-Only
BOF	Read-Only
Bookmark	Read/Write
CacheSize	Read/Write
CursorLocation	Always adUseServer
CursorType	Always adOpenStatic
EditMode	Always adEditNone
EOF	Read-Only
Filter	Read/Write
LockType	Read/Write
MarshalOptions	Not Available
MaxRecords	Read/Write
PageCount	Read-Only
PageSize	Read/Write
RecordCount	Read-Only
Source	Read/Write
State	Read-Only
Status	Read-Only

ADO Field Objects

A Field object represents a field in a table; that is, a column of data. You access the fields in the current record in a Recordset object with the Fields collection (see Chapter 9 for more on collections). Here are some examples using Field objects that we'll see more about in the next chapter:

```
adoRecordset.Fields(1).Value = "Steve"

adoRecordset("Name") = "Steve"

adoRecordset.Fields(1) = "Steve"

adoRecordset.Fields("Name") = "Steve"

adoRecordset!Name = "Steve"
```

As you can see, there is a variety of ways of referring to a field in the current record in the recordset; we'll see more in the next chapter. Here,

TABLE 7.7	Microsoft Active Directory Service OLE DB recordset methods	
Method		**Availability**
AddNew		No
Cancel		No
CancelBatch		No
CancelUpdate		No
Clone		Yes
Close		Yes
Delete		No
GetRows		Yes
Move		Yes
MoveFirst		Yes
MoveLast		Yes
MoveNext		Yes
MovePrevious		Yes
NextRecordset		Yes
Open		Yes
Requery		Yes
Resync		Yes
Supports		Yes
Update		No
UpdateBatch		No

I'll take a look at all the members of the Field object, starting with its properties.

Field Properties

You use the properties of the Field object to configure it. I'll take a look at all the properties of this object now, starting with the ActualSize property.

ActualSize

The ActualSize property holds the actual length of a field's value. The maximum possible size of the field is stored in the DefinedSize property, but for variable-length fields, the actual size appears in this property. For fixed-length data types, the DefinedSize and ActualSize properties should hold the same value. You can set the actual size of a field by assigning a value to this property.

Attributes

As its name indicates, this property holds the attributes of a field, such as whether or not the field can hold a null value. Here are the possible settings for this property:

- **adFldMayDefer**—Indicates that the field is deferred—that is, the field values are not retrieved from the data source with the whole record, but only when you access them specifically.

- **adFldUpdatable**—Indicates that you can write to the field.

- **adFldUnknownUpdatable**—Indicates that the provider cannot determine if you can write to the field.

- **adFldFixed**—Indicates that the field contains fixed-length data.

- **adFldIsNullable**—Indicates that the field accepts null values.

- **adFldMayBeNull**—Indicates that you can read null values from the field.

- **adFldLong**—Indicates that the field is a long binary field. Also indicates that you can use the AppendChunk and GetChunk methods.

- **adFldRowID**—Indicates that the field contains a persistent row identifier that cannot be written to.

- **adFldRowVersion**—Indicates that the field contains a time- or date-stamp used to track updates.

- **adFldCacheDeferred**—Indicates that the provider caches field values and that future read operations may be done from the cache.

Note that the Attributes property may hold a combination of the above constants. Here's an example where I check to see if a field has a fixed length:

```
If adoRecordset.Fields(1).Attributes And _
adFldFixed = adFldFixed Then
    MsgBox "This field has a fixed length."
End If
```

DataFormat

The DataFormat property is one that Visual Basic supports for fields, not ADO. Here are the possible values for the data format of a field:

- **General** (no formatting).
- **Number.**
- **Currency.**
- **Date.**

- **Time.**
- **Scientific.**
- **Boolean.**
- **Checkbox.**
- **Picture.**
- **Custom.**

For more on the `DataFormat` property, see Chapter 3.

DefinedSize

This property holds the size the `Field` object was defined with—that is, the maximum possible size of the field. For example, if you declare an SQL Server column as varchar(80), it'll have a defined size of 80. Note that this property is read-only when the recordset is open.

Name

The `Name` property holds the name of the field. There are two ways to refer to a field in a record: by position in the `Fields` collection, or by name. Here's how I give a field a name:

```
adoRecordset.Fields(1).Name = "Employee"
```

Now I can refer to that field by name, as in these examples (note that the `Value` property is the default property of the `Field` object):

```
adoRecordset("Employee").Value = "Tina"
adoRecordset("Employee") = "Tina"
adoRecordset.Fields("Employee") = "Tina"
adoRecordset!Employee = "Tina"
```

NumericScale

This property holds the number of digits to the right of the decimal point that will be used in the field. This property is useful when formatting your fields. Note that this property becomes read-only when the recordset is open.

OriginalValue

This property holds the original value that was in a field before changes were made, and it's good to use when the user decides to cancel changes (it's the property ADO uses to restore a field's value when you call the `CancelUpdate` method).

Precision

This property holds the numeric precision for the `Field` object, which is the maximum number of digits that will be used. Note that this property becomes read-only when the recordset is open.

Type

The `Type` property holds the data type of the `Field` object. The possible types appear in Table 7.8. Note that not all providers will support all data types listed in that table.

UnderlyingValue

The `UnderlyingValue` property holds a `Field` object's current value in the underlying database. This property is not quite the same as the `Original-Value` property, because this property reflects the current value for the field in the database, which some other user may have changed.

Using this property is much like resynching with the database; when you call the `Resync` method, you can think of the value in this property as coming from its `UnderlyingValue` property. Note that this value is read-only when a recordset is open.

TABLE 7.8	Parameter type values
Constant	**Description**
adArray	Joined in a logical OR together with another type to indicate that the data is a safe array of that type (DBTYPE_ARRAY).
adBigInt	An 8-byte signed integer (DBTYPE_I8).
adBinary	A binary value (DBTYPE_BYTES).
adBoolean	A Boolean value (DBTYPE_BOOL).
adByRef	Joined in a logical OR together with another type to indicate that the data is a pointer to data of the other type (DBTYPE_BYREF).
adBSTR	A null-terminated character string (Unicode) (DBTYPE_BSTR).
adChar	A string value (DBTYPE_STR).
adCurrency	A currency value (DBTYPE_CY). Currency is a fixed-point number with 4 digits to the right of the decimal point. It is stored in an 8-byte signed integer scaled by 10,000.
adDate	A date value (DBTYPE_DATE). A date is stored as a double, the whole part of which is the number of days since December 30, 1899, and the fractional part of which is the fraction of a day.

TABLE 7.8	(Continued)

Constant	Description
adDBDate	A date value (*yyyymmdd*) (DBTYPE_DBDATE).
adDBTime	A time value (*hhmmss*) (DBTYPE_DBTIME).
adDBTimeStamp	A date-timestamp (*yyyymmddhhmmss*, plus a fraction in billionths) (DBTYPE_DBTIMESTAMP).
adDecimal	An exact numeric value with a fixed precision and scale (DBTYPE_DECIMAL).
adDouble	A double-precision, floating-point value (DBTYPE_R8).
adEmpty	No value was specified (DBTYPE_EMPTY).
adError	A 32-bit error code (DBTYPE_ERROR).
adGUID	A globally unique identifier (GUID) (DBTYPE_GUID).
adIDispatch	A pointer to an IDispatch interface on an OLE object (DBTYPE_IDISPATCH).
adInteger	A 4-byte signed integer (DBTYPE_I4).
adIUnknown	A pointer to an IUnknown interface on an OLE object (DBTYPE_IUNKNOWN).
adLongVarBinary	A long binary value.
adLongVarChar	A long string value.
adLongVarWChar	A long, null-terminated string value.
adNumeric	An exact numeric value with a fixed precision and scale (DBTYPE_NUMERIC).
adSingle	A single-precision, floating-point value (DBTYPE_R4).
adSmallInt	A 2-byte signed integer (DBTYPE_I2).
adTinyInt	A 1-byte signed integer (DBTYPE_I1).
adUnsignedBigInt	An 8-byte unsigned integer (DBTYPE_UI8).
adUnsignedInt	A 4-byte unsigned integer (DBTYPE_UI4).
adUnsignedSmallInt	A 2-byte unsigned integer (DBTYPE_UI2).
adUnsignedTinyInt	A 1-byte unsigned integer (DBTYPE_UI1).
adUserDefined	A user-defined variable (DBTYPE_UDT).
adVarBinary	A binary value.
adVarChar	A string value.
adVariant	An automation variant (DBTYPE_VARIANT).
adVector	Joined in a logical OR together with another type to indicate that the data is a DBVECTOR structure, as defined by OLE DB, that contains a count of elements and a pointer to data of the other type (DBTYPE_VECTOR).
adVarWChar	A null-terminated Unicode character string (`Parameter` object only).
adWChar	A null-terminated Unicode character string (DBTYPE_WSTR).

Value

The `Value` property is the big property for `Field` objects, because it represents the actual value of the data in the field. For example, here's how I set the value in a `Field` object:

```
adoRecordset("Employee").Value = "Tina"
```

The `Value` property is the default property for `Field` objects, so you don't even have to refer to it by name in this code:

```
adoRecordset("Employee") = "Tina"
```

Here are some additional examples using the `Value` property:

```
adoRecordset.Fields("Employee").Value = "Tina"
adoRecordset.Fields("Employee") = "Tina"
adoRecordset!Employee = "Tina"
```

That completes the properties of the `Field` object; it's time to take a look at this object's methods next.

Field Methods

There are only two methods for the `Field` object: `AppendChunk` and `GetChunk`, which let you work with longer data in fields. I'll take a look at these methods now.

AppendChunk

The `AppendChunk` method adds long data to the field. Here's how you use `AppendChunk`:

```
FieldObject.AppendChunk Data
```

Here, *Data* is a variant that holds the data. You can use this method to store images or other long data in a field.

The first call to a `Field` object's `AppendChunk` method writes data to the field, overwriting any existing data. Succeeding `AppendChunk` calls add to that data. Note that if you append data to one field and then you set or read the value of another field in the current record, ADO assumes that you are done appending data to the first field. If you call the `AppendChunk` method on the first field again, ADO will interpret your action as a new AppendChunk operation and overwrite the existing data.

To retrieve the stored data, you use GetChunk, coming up next.

GetChunk

You use the GetChunk method to retrieve long data stored in a field. Here's how you use GetChunk:

```
variable = FieldObject.GetChunk(Size)
```

This method returns a variant holding the data you've requested. Here is the parameter you pass to GetChunk:

- **Size**—Number of bytes or characters you want to retrieve.

You can use this method to retrieve data from a field object, such as an image or long text data.

Field Collections

The Field object has one collection: Properties.

Properties

The Properties collection holds the dynamic properties of the Field object, including provider-specific properties. I'll take a look at collections in general in Chapter 9.

That completes the Field object, and that completes our look at the Recordset object as well—it's time to put these two objects to work, and I'll do that in the next chapter.

Using
Recordsets
in Code

The previous chapter introduced the `Recordset` object and `Field` objects—I'll put those objects to use in this chapter. The previous chapter also covered a great deal of material, mostly in reference form, and this is the chapter in which we'll see that material at work.

I'll start by opening recordsets in code. We've seen how to use `Recordset` objects in ADO data controls and Data Environments already—you just use the `Recordset` property of an ADO data control (as in `Adodc1.Recordset`) and refer to the `Recordset` object returned by a command in a Data Environment by prefacing the name of the command with the letters "rs" (as in `DataEnvironment1.rsCommand1`). Here, I'll take a look at the three ways of opening recordsets in code.

I'll also take a look at setting the various lock types and cursor options in this chapter. Most of the examples here use server-side cursors, but when I write an example using disconnected recordsets, I'll use a client-side cursor along with batch updating, and set the marshalling options accordingly.

I'll also take a look at working with recordsets asynchronously, how to let the user navigate through them, bind them to controls in code, let the user edit the fields in the current record, close recordsets, persist them to disk, search them, sort them, and filter them (that is, create a new recordset from the records that match the criteria you specify). I'll also cover how to create a recordset entirely in code, including adding and populating it with fields and field data.

As you can see, there's a lot coming up in this chapter. I'll start with the three ways of opening recordsets in ADO programming.

Opening Recordsets

We've already seen how to use the Recordset objects in ADO data controls and Data Environments; here, I'll take a look at opening them in code. Once you have an open connection to a database, you can use three methods to open a recordset: the Connection object's Execute method, the Recordset object's Open method, and the Command object's Execute method. I'll take a look at using each of these methods now.

 Note that the three methods we're about to examine all can be used to open recordsets. If you want to simply execute a command that does not return any records, you can use either the Connection object's Execute method or the Command object's Execute method.

Connection Execute

You can use the Connection object's Execute method to execute a query, SQL statement, stored procedure, or provider-specific command. Here's how you use the Execute method:

```
connection.Execute [CommandText [, RecordsAffected _
[, Options ]]]
```

Here are the arguments to Execute:

- **CommandText**—SQL statement, table name, stored procedure, or provider-specific text to execute.
- **RecordsAffected**—Variable in which the provider returns the number of records that the operation affected.
- **Options**—Indicates how the provider should evaluate the Command-Text argument. See below for more information.

Here are the possible values for the Options argument:

- **adCmdText**—Provider should evaluate CommandText as a textual definition of a command.
- **adCmdTable**—ADO should generate an SQL query to return all rows from the table named in CommandText.

- **adCmdTableDirect**—Provider should return all rows from the table named in CommandText.

- **adCmdStoredProc**—Provider should evaluate CommandText as a stored procedure.

- **adCmdUnknown**—Type of command in the CommandText argument is not known.

- **adExecuteAsync**—Command should execute asynchronously.

- **adFetchAsync**—Remaining rows after the initial quantity specified in the CacheSize property should be fetched asynchronously.

Note that there are two asynchronous Open options here: adExecute-Async and adFetchAsync.

Here's an example showing how to use the Connection object's Execute method:

```
Set adoRecordset = adoConnect.Execute( _
    "SELECT * FROM Publishers")
```

Recordset Open

You can also use the ADO Recordset object's Open method to open a recordset. Here's how that method works:

```
recordset.Open [Source [, ActiveConnection [, _
CursorType [, LockType [, Options]]]]]
```

The Source argument points to a valid Command object variable name, an SQL statement, a table name, a stored procedure call, or the file name of a recordset on disk (called a persisted recordset).

The ActiveConnection argument is a Connection object variable name, or a string containing ConnectionString parameters.

The CursorType argument specifies the type of cursor that the provider should use when opening the recordset. This value can be one of the following constants:

- **adOpenForwardOnly**—(default) Opens a forward-only-type cursor.

- **adOpenKeyset**—Opens a keyset-type cursor.

- **adOpenDynamic**—Opens a dynamic-type cursor.

- **adOpenStatic**—Opens a static-type cursor.

The LockType argument determines what type of locking the provider should use when opening the recordset. This can be one of the following constants:

- **adLockReadOnly** (default)—Read-only, you cannot alter the data.
- **adLockPessimistic**—Pessimistic locking, record by record. The provider does what is necessary so editing of records is successful, usually by locking records at the data source upon editing.
- **adLockOptimistic**—Optimistic locking, record by record. The provider uses optimistic locking, locking records only when you call the Update method.
- **adLockBatchOptimistic**—Optimistic batch updates, required for Batch Update mode as opposed to Immediate Update mode.

The Options argument indicates how the provider should evaluate the Source argument if it represents something other than a Command object, or that the recordset should be restored from a file where it was previously saved. This can be one of the following constants:

- **adCmdText**—Provider should evaluate Source as a command.
- **adCmdTable**—ADO should generate an SQL query to return all records in the table named in Source.
- **adCmdTableDirect**—Provider should return all rows from the table named in Source.
- **adCmdStoredProc**—Provider should evaluate Source as a stored procedure.
- **adCmdUnknown**—Type of command in the Source argument is not known.
- **adCommandFile**—Persisted (saved) recordset should be restored from the file named in Source.
- **adExecuteAsync**—Source should be executed asynchronously.
- **adFetchAsync**—After the initial quantity specified in the CacheSize property is fetched, remaining rows should be fetched asynchronously.

The adodb project on the CD uses the Recordset object's Open method to open the Publishers table in the Biblio.mdb database this way:

```
Private Sub Form_Load()
    Set adoConnect = New Connection

    adoConnect.Open _
        "PROVIDER=Microsoft.Jet.OLEDB.3.51;" & _
        "Data Source=C:\ado\Biblio.mdb;"
```

```
Set adoRecordset = New Recordset
adoRecordset.Open "SELECT * FROM Publishers", _
       adoConnect, adOpenStatic, adLockOptimistic
```

Command Execute

You can also use the Command object's Execute method to open a recordset object:

```
Execute [RecordsAffected [, Parameters [, Options]]]
```

Here is what the arguments to this method mean:

- **RecordsAffected**—Variable in which the provider returns the number of records that the operation affected.
- **Parameters**—Variant array of parameter values passed for use with an SQL statement.
- **Options**—Specifies how the provider should evaluate the CommandText property of the Command object.

The Options argument can hold any of these values:

- **adCmdText**—Provider should evaluate CommandText as a textual definition of a command.
- **adCmdTable**—ADO should generate an SQL query to return all rows from the table named in CommandText.
- **adCmdTableDirect**—Provider should return all rows from the table named in CommandText.
- **adCmdStoredProc**—Provider should evaluate CommandText as a stored procedure.
- **adCmdUnknown**—Type of command in the CommandText argument is not known.
- **adExecuteAsync**—Command should execute asynchronously.
- **adFetchAsync**—Remaining rows after the initial quantity specified in the CacheSize property should be fetched asynchronously.

Here's an example in which I'm using the Command object's Execute method to open the Publishers recordset in the Biblio.mdb recordset:

```
Dim adoConnect As Connection
Set adoConnect = New Connection
```

```
adoConnect.Open _
"PROVIDER=Microsoft.Jet.OLEDB.3.51;Data" & _
"Source=C:\ado\biblio.mdb;"
```

```
Set adoCommand = New Command
adoCommand.CommandText = "SELECT * from Publishers _
WHERE Name = 'PRENTICE HALL'"
Set adoRecordset = adoCommand.Execute
```

Using Parameters

As we saw in the previous chapter, you can also use parameters in commands. To use a parameter in an SQL statement, you use question marks as placeholders, like this:

```
adoConnect.Open _
"PROVIDER=Microsoft.Jet.OLEDB.3.51;Data " &
"Source=C:\ado\db.mdb;"
```

```
Set adoCommand = New Command
adoCommand.CommandText = "SELECT * from students
WHERE Name = ?"
```

Here's how you create and configure a new parameter, adoParam, to hold the name of a publisher to search for:

```
Set adoParam = New Parameter
adoParam.Name = "Name"
adoParam.Type = adVarChar
adoParam.Size = 20
adoParam.Value = "Ted"
```

You append the parameters you want to use in a command using its Parameters collection's Append method, and then you can execute the command as usual:

```
adoCommand.Parameters.Append adoParam
Set adoCommand.ActiveConnection = adoConnect
Set adoRecordset = adoCommand.Execute
```

Working with Recordsets Asynchronously

Like other ADO operations, you can work with recordsets asynchronously. For example, if you set the `Option` argument of the `Recordset` object's `Open` method to `adExecuteAsync`, the SQL statement or `Command` object in the `Source` argument is executed asynchronously. You can keep track of the state of asynchronous recordset operations with the recordset's `State` property, which can take these values:

- **adStateClosed**—(default) Indicates the object is closed.
- **adStateOpen**—Recordset is open.
- **adStateConnecting**—Recordset object is connecting.
- **adStateExecuting**—Recordset object is executing a command.
- **adStateFetching**—Rows of the `Recordset` object are being fetched.

You can also keep track of asynchronous recordset operations with these recordset events:

- **FetchProgress**—Progress of a data retrieval operation.
- **FetchComplete**—Retrieval operation has completed.
- **WillChangeField**—Current field will change.
- **FieldChangeComplete**—Current field has changed.
- **WillMove**—Current row position in a recordset will change.
- **MoveComplete**—Current row position in a recordset has changed.
- **EndOfRecordset**—Reached the end of the recordset.
- **WillChangeRecord**—Something in the current row of the recordset will change.
- **RecordChangeComplete**—Something in the current row of the recordset has changed.
- **WillChangeRecordset**—Something in the current recordset will change.
- **RecordsetChangeComplete**—Something in the current recordset has changed.

Closing Recordsets

To close a recordset, you just use the `Close` method. As with the `Connection` object, you must set the `Recordset` object to `Nothing` if you want to remove it from memory:

```
adoRecordset.Close
Set adoRecordset = Nothing
```

Navigating in a Recordset

Now that you have an open recordset, you can work with the methods of the recordset, such as Move, AddNew, Delete, MoveFirst, and so on, as we did in the previous chapter. For example, here's how the adodb project implements the Next button that lets the user move to the next record:

```
Private Sub cmdNext_Click()
    On Error GoTo ErrLabel

    If Not adoRecordset.EOF Then
            adoRecordset.MoveNext
    End If

    If adoRecordset.EOF And _
    adoRecordset.RecordCount > 0 Then
        adoRecordset.MoveLast
    End If

    Exit Sub

ErrLabel:
    MsgBox Err.Description
End Sub
```

You can see the navigation buttons in the adodb project in Figure 8.1.

Note that although you can use the MoveFirst, MoveLast, MoveNext, and MovePrevious methods in a recordset, you can also use the Move method to move directly to a particular record. Here are the methods you can use to move around in a recordset:

- **Move**—Moves to a specified record.
- **MoveFirst**—Moves to the first record.
- **MoveLast**—Moves to the last record.
- **MoveNext**—Moves to the next record.
- **MovePrevious**—Moves to the previous record.
- **Find**—Finds a record.

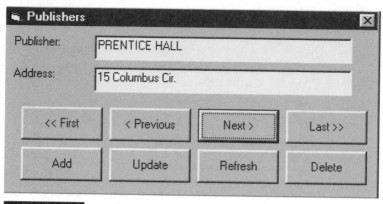

FIGURE 8.1 The navigation buttons in the adodb project.

- **AddNew**—Adds a new record and makes it the current record.
- **NextRecordset**—Moves to the next recordset.

  Here are the properties you can set to move around in a recordset:

- **AbsolutePage**—Sets the absolute page.
- **AbsolutePosition**—Sets the absolute position.
- **Bookmark**—Moves to a bookmark.

  Note in particular the Bookmark property, which I'll take a look at in more detail next.

Using Bookmarks for Navigation

You can set bookmarks in an ADO recordset using the Bookmark property. To store a bookmark for the current record, you store the recordset's Bookmark property in a variant variable:

```
varBookmark1 = adoRecordset.Bookmark
```

Then you can move to a new location in the recordset and undertake as many recordset operations as you like:

```
adoRecordset.Move 10
MsgBox "The data is: " & adoRecordset.Fields(1)
adoRecordset.Move 20
adoRecordset.Fields(1) = NewData
adoRecordset.MoveNext
```

However, when you set the recordset's `Bookmark` property to the bookmark you've stored, the bookmarked record becomes the current record once again:

```
adoRecordset.Bookmark = varBookmark1
```

In this way, you can use bookmarks to mark a record and return to that record later, which is a more reliable way of returning to a record than using its `AbsolutePosition` property, because the user may have inserted or deleted records, changing the record's absolute position in the recordset.

You can use arrays of bookmarks to filter a recordset, and only the bookmarked records will appear in the filtered version. You can also use these pre-defined bookmarks with the `Move` method:

- **adBookmarkCurrent**—Starts at the current record.
- **adBookmarkFirst**—Starts at the first record.
- **adBookmarkLast**—Starts at the last record.

Here's how to move to the first record in the recordset with the `Move` method and the `adBookmarkFirst` pre-defined bookmark:

```
adoRecordset.Move 0, adBookmarkFirst
```

Modifying Field Data

There are two ways of modifying data in the fields of the current record in a `Recordset` object: using bound controls and accessing fields directly in code.

Binding Controls to a Recordset in Code

After a recordset is open, you can bind it to controls dynamically (new in Visual Basic 6.0) just by setting the binding properties of the controls you want to bind. For example, here's how I bind the `Name` and `Address` fields of the recordset named `adoRecordset`, which holds the `Biblio.mdb` Publishers table in the `adodb` project, to text boxes:

```
Set Text1.DataSource = adoRecordset
Text1.DataField = "Name"
```

```
Set Text2.DataSource = adoRecordset
Text2.DataField = "Address"
  .

  .

  .
```

You can also edit fields in code, which is a far more powerful technique.

Editing Fields in Code

There are three ways to edit the values in fields in code:

- Assign values to a `Field` object's `Value` property and call the `Update` method.
- Pass a field name and a value as arguments when you call `Update`.
- Pass an array of field names and an array of values when you call `Update`.

I'll take a look at the `Update` method in more detail in the next topic. When you change a field's data using its `Value` property, the recordset's `EditMode` property will become `adEditInProgress`. Here are all the possible values for this property:

- **adEditNone**—Indicates that no editing operation is in progress.
- **adEditInProgress**—Indicates that data in the current record has been modified but not saved.
- **adEditAdd**—Indicates that the `AddNew` method has been invoked, and the current record in the copy buffer is a new record that hasn't been saved in the database.
- **adEditDelete**—Indicates that the current record has been deleted.

When you're done editing, you use the `Update` method to update the database or the `CancelUpdate` method to cancel the update and return the `EditMode` property to `adEditNone`.

So, how do you actually modify the data in a field? You can access the data in the fields of the current record of an ADO recordset using the `Fields` collection to reach the individual `Field` object, and you set a new value in its `Value` property like this, where I'm setting the value in the first field in the current record:

```
adoRecordset.Fields(1).Value = "12773.00"
  .
```

To update the database with the new value, you can call Update like this:

```
adoRecordset.Fields(1).Value = "12773.00"
adoRecordset.Update
```

On the other hand, to cancel the Update and end the edit operation, you can call CancelUpdate like this:

```
adoRecordset.Fields(1).Value = "12773.00"
adoRecordset.CancelUpdate
```

The Value property is the default property for the Field object, so you can refer to that property even when you omit its name, like this:

```
adoRecordset.Fields(1) = "12773.00"
```

If you've set a Field object's Name property in the Fields collection, you can also refer to the field by name in the Fields collection like this:

```
adoRecordset.Fields("Cost") = "12773.00"
```

In fact, using the Fields collection is the default when referring to recordsets, so you can write code this way:

```
adoRecordset("Cost") = "12773.00"
```

And there's even one more shortcut you can take; you can use ! to specify a field by name like this:

```
adoRecordset!Cost = "12773.00"
```

You will see more about editing fields in code when creating recordsets in code near the end of the chapter. As we've seen, you can use the `Update` or `CancelUpdate` methods to update the database or cancel the update, and I'll take a closer look at those methods now.

Updating Databases

In DAO programming, you used to have to use the `Edit` method to place a control in Edit mode. After you made your changes to a record, you would call the `Update` method to update the recordset.

In ADO programming, you don't need to call a `Recordset` object's `Edit` method (in fact, there isn't one). However, if you change the value of one of the current record's `Field` objects, the recordset automatically enters Edit mode. After you've made changes to the fields of a record, you can call the `Update` method to write the new data to the database:

```
Update [Fields [, Values]]
```

Here are the arguments for this method:

- **Fields**—Variant holding a name or a variant array representing names or ordinal positions of the field(s) to update.
- **Values**—Variant holding a value or a variant array holding values for the field(s) in the updated record.

It's important to note that if you change the fields of a record and then move to a new record, ADO will perform an automatic update by calling `Update` for you. In addition, if you change a record and then call `AddNew`, ADO will also perform an automatic update by calling `Update`.

Here's how the `Update` button is implemented in the `adodb` project; after the user edits the data in the bound controls and clicks the `Update` button, the new data is written to the database:

```
Private Sub cmdUpdate_Click()
    On Error GoTo ErrLabel


    adoRecordset.Update


    Exit Sub
```

```
ErrLabel:

    MsgBox Err.Description
End Sub
```

You can see the Update button in the adodb project in Figure 8.1. In general, you use the Update method to save any changes you make to the current record of a Recordset object since calling the AddNew method or since changing any field values in an existing record.

Note that you can also cancel any pending changes with the Cancel-Update method; here's how you use this method, which takes no parameters:

```
adoRecordset.Update
```

Besides working with single records, you can also update a number of records with batch updating; I'll take a look at that here and put it to use later in the chapter.

Batch Updating

You can make a number of changes at once with a technique called batch updating. To support batch updating, you use the UpdateBatch method:

```
UpdateBatch [AffectRecords]
```

The AffectRecords argument determines how many records the UpdateBatch method will affect and can be one of the following constants:

- **adAffectCurrent**—Writes pending changes only for the current record.
- **adAffectGroup**—Writes pending changes for the records that satisfy the current Filter property setting.
- **adAffectAll**—(default) Writes pending changes for all records, including any that have been hidden by the current Filter property setting.

Note that to use batch updating, you must set the LockType to ad-LockBatchOptimistic when you open the recordset.

Here's an example in which I change all the publishers named in the Biblio.mdb database to Prentice Hall and then call UpdateBatch to make all the changes at once to the database:

```
adoConnect.Open "Provider=MSDASQL.1;Persist
        Security Info=False;Data Source=Biblio"
```

```
Set adoRecordset = New Recordset
adoRecordset.Open "select * from Publishers", _
    adoConnect, adOpenKeyset, _
    adLockBatchOptimistic


Do Until (adoRecordset.EOF)
    With adoRecordset
        'MsgBox .RecordCount
        .Fields("Name") = "Prentice Hall"
        .MoveNext
    End With
Loop


adoRecordset.BatchUpdate
```

Note that you can also cancel pending batch updates with the Cancel-Batch method.

Deleting Records

You can delete records using the Delete method:

adoRecordset.Delete [*AffectRecords*]

The AffectRecords parameter you pass to this method can be one of the following constants:

- **adAffectCurrent** (default)—Deletes only the current record.
- **adAffectGroup**—Deletes the records that satisfy the current Filter property setting. You must set the Filter property to one of the valid pre-defined constants to use this option.
- **adAffectAll**—Deletes all records.
- **adAffectAllChapters**—Deletes all chapter records (hierarchical recordsets).

Here's how the adodb project lets the user delete the current record—note that I move to the next record to stop displaying the deleted record (and moving to the next record also updates the database, removing the deleted record):

```
Private Sub cmdDelete_Click()
    On Error GoTo ErrLabel

    adoRecordset.Delete

    adoRecordset.MoveNext
    If adoRecordset.EOF Then
        adoRecordset.MoveLast
    End If

    Exit Sub

ErrLabel:
    MsgBox Err.Description
End Sub
```

Adding New Records

You can add new records to a recordset using the AddNew method:

```
adoRecordset.AddNew [FieldList [, Values]]
```

IIere are the parameters for this method:

- **FieldList**—A single name, or an array of names, or ordinal positions of the fields in the new record.
- **Values**—A single value, or an array of values, for the fields in the new record. (If Fields is an array, Values must also be an array with the same number of members; otherwise, an error occurs. The order of field names must match the order of field values in each array.)

This method inserts a new record and makes that new, empty record the current record. Here's how I let the user add a new record in the adodb project:

```
Private Sub cmdAdd_Click()
    On Error GoTo ErrLabel
    adoRecordset.AddNew
```

```
                        Text1.Text = ""
                        Text2.Text = ""


                        Exit Sub


                  ErrLabel:

                        MsgBox Err.Description
                  End Sub
```

The user can use the Add button in the adodb project, which appears in Figure 8.1, to add a new record.

That completes the adodb project, which has given us the basics of ADO programming and which appears in the adodb folder on the CD. That project's code appears in Listing 8.1.

LISTING 8.1   *Adodb.frm Code*

```
VERSION 5.00
Begin VB.Form Form1
   BorderStyle     =     3   'Fixed Dialog
   Caption         =     "Publishers"
   ClientHeight    =     2460
   ClientLeft      =     1095
   ClientTop       =     330
   ClientWidth     =     5550
   LinkTopic       =     "Form3"
   MaxButton       =     0     'False
   MinButton       =     0     'False
   ScaleHeight     =     2460
   ScaleWidth      =     5550
   ShowInTaskbar   =     0     'False
   Begin VB.CommandButton cmdLast
      Caption      =     "Last >>"
      Height       =     495
      Left         =     4200
      TabIndex     =     11
      Top          =     1200
      Width        =     1215
   End
   Begin VB.CommandButton cmdNext
      Caption      =     "Next >"
      Height       =     495
      Left         =     2880
      TabIndex     =     10
      Top          =     1200
      Width        =     1215
```

```
End
Begin VB.CommandButton cmdPrevious
   Caption           =    "< Previous"
   Height            =    495
   Left              =    1560
   TabIndex          =    9
   Top               =    1200
   Width             =    1215
End
Begin VB.CommandButton cmdFirst
   Caption           =    "<< First"
   Height            =    495
   Left              =    240
   TabIndex          =    8
   Top               =    1200
   Width             =    1215
End
Begin VB.CommandButton cmdRefresh
   Caption           =    "Refresh"
   Height            =    495
   Left              =    2880
   TabIndex          =    6
   Top               =    1800
   Width             =    1215
End
Begin VB.CommandButton cmdUpdate
   Caption           =    "Update"
   Height            =    495
   Left              =    1560
   TabIndex          =    5
   Top               =    1800
   Width             =    1215
End
Begin VB.CommandButton cmdDelete
   Caption           =    "Delete"
   Height            =    495
   Left              =    4200
   TabIndex          =    4
   Top               =    1800
   Width             =    1215
End
Begin VB.CommandButton cmdAdd
   Caption           =    "Add"
   Height            =    495
   Left              =    240
   TabIndex          =    3
   Top               =    1800
   Width             =    1215
End
Begin VB.TextBox Text2
   Height            =    375
   Left              =    1320
```

```
            TabIndex        =    2
            Text            =    "Text2"
            Top             =    600
            Width           =    3855
        End
        Begin VB.TextBox Text1
            Height          =    375
            Left            =    1320
            TabIndex        =    1
            Text            =    "Text1"
            Top             =    120
            Width           =    3855
        End
        Begin VB.Label lblLabels
            Caption         =    "Publisher:"
            Height          =    255
            Index           =    0
            Left            =    120
            TabIndex        =    7
            Top             =    120
            Width           =    1095
        End
        Begin VB.Label lblLabels
            Caption         =    "Address:"
            Height          =    255
            Index           =    1
            Left            =    120
            TabIndex        =    0
            Top             =    600
            Width           =    1095
        End
    End
Attribute VB_Name = "Form1"
Attribute VB_GlobalNameSpace = False
Attribute VB_Creatable = False
Attribute VB_PredeclaredId = True
Attribute VB_Exposed = False
Private WithEvents adoRecordset As ADODB.Recordset
Attribute adoRecordset.VB_VarHelpID = -1
Private WithEvents adoConnect As Connection
Attribute adoConnect.VB_VarHelpID = -1


Private Sub Form_Load()

    Set adoConnect = New Connection

    adoConnect.Open "PROVIDER=Microsoft.Jet.OLEDB.3.51;" & _
    Data Source=C:\ado\Biblio.mdb;", , , adConnectAsync

    Set adoRecordset = New Recordset
```

```
    adoRecordset.Open "select * from Publishers", _
    adoConnect, adOpenStatic, adLockOptimistic

    Set Text1.DataSource = adoRecordset
    Text1.DataField = "Name"
    Set Text2.DataSource = adoRecordset
    Text2.DataField = "Address"

End Sub

Private Sub cmdAdd_Click()
    On Error GoTo ErrLabel
    adoRecordset.AddNew

    Text1.Text = ""
    Text2.Text = ""

    Exit Sub

ErrLabel:
    MsgBox Err.Description
End Sub

Private Sub cmdDelete_Click()
    On Error GoTo ErrLabel

    adoRecordset.Delete

    adoRecordset.MoveNext
    If adoRecordset.EOF Then
        adoRecordset.MoveLast
    End If

    Exit Sub

ErrLabel:
    MsgBox Err.Description
End Sub

Private Sub cmdRefresh_Click()

    On Error GoTo ErrLabel
    adoRecordset.Requery
    Exit Sub

ErrLabel:
    MsgBox Err.Description
End Sub

Private Sub cmdUpdate_Click()
    On Error GoTo ErrLabel
```

```
        adoRecordset.Update

        Exit Sub

ErrLabel:
        MsgBox Err.Description
End Sub

Private Sub cmdFirst_Click()
        On Error GoTo ErrLabel

        adoRecordset.MoveFirst

        Exit Sub

ErrLabel:
        MsgBox Err.Description
End Sub

Private Sub cmdLast_Click()
        On Error GoTo ErrLabel

        adoRecordset.MoveLast

        Exit Sub

ErrLabel:
        MsgBox Err.Description
End Sub

Private Sub cmdNext_Click()
        On Error GoTo ErrLabel

        If Not adoRecordset.EOF Then
                adoRecordset.MoveNext
        End If

        If adoRecordset.EOF And adoRecordset.RecordCount _
            > 0 Then
                adoRecordset.MoveLast
        End If

        Exit Sub

ErrLabel:
        MsgBox Err.Description
End Sub

Private Sub cmdPrevious_Click()
        On Error GoTo ErrLabel
```

```
    If Not adoRecordset.BOF Then adoRecordset.MovePrevious
    If adoRecordset.BOF And adoRecordset.RecordCount _
        > 0 Then
        adoRecordset.MoveFirst
    End If

    Exit Sub

ErrLabel:
    MsgBox Err.Description
End Sub
```

Using Recordset Events

One new aspect of ADO programming is the ability to use recordset events. Here are the events of the Recordset object:

- **FetchProgress**—Progress of a data retrieval operation.
- **FetchComplete**—Retrieval operation has completed.
- **WillChangeField**—Current field will change.
- **FieldChangeComplete**—Current field has changed.
- **WillMove**—Current row position in a recordset will change.
- **MoveComplete**—Current row position in a recordset has changed.
- **EndOfRecordset**—Reached the end of the recordset.
- **WillChangeRecord**—Something in the current row of the recordset will change.
- **RecordChangeComplete**—Something in the current row of the recordset has changed.
- **WillChangeRecordset**—Something in the current recordset will change.
- **RecordsetChangeComplete**—Something in the current recordset has changed.

In code, you must declare a recordset using the WithEvents keyword if you want to use its events:

```
Private WithEvents adoRecordset As ADODB.Recordset
```

When you declare an object using WithEvents, you can assign code to the events of the object in the Visual Basic code window, as you see in Figure 8.2, where I'm adding code to the events of a Recordset object.

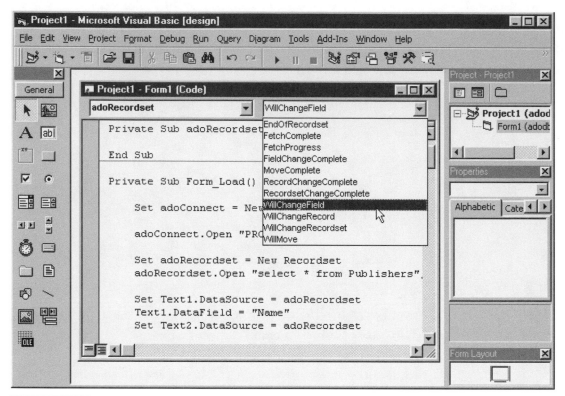

FIGURE 8.2 Assigning code to a recordset's events.

Here's an example where I'm connecting code to the `WillMove` event of a recordset, informing the user that the current record is about to change:

```
Private WithEvents adoRecordset As ADODB.Recordset


Private Sub adoRecordset_WillMove(ByVal adReason As
ADODB.EventReasonEnum, adStatus As
ADODB.EventStatusEnum, ByVal pRecordset As
ADODB.Recordset)
    MsgBox "I'm about to move!"
End Sub
```

Validating Data

Earlier in this book, I took a look at client-side field validation using the `Validate` event. The ADO `Recordset` object also provides the means to validate data on the client by using these events:

- **WillChangeField**—Current field will change.
- **WillMove**—Current row position in a recordset will change.
- **WillChangeRecord**—Something in the current row of the recordset will change.
- **WillChangeRecordset**—Something in the current recordset will change.

You can find out about pending changes using the parameters passed to the event handler. For example, here are the parameters passed to the `WillChangeField` event handler:

- **cFields**—Number of `Field` objects in `Fields`.
- **Fields**—`Field` objects with pending changes.
- **pError**—Describes the error that occurred when the value of `adStatus` is `adStatusErrorsOccurred`; otherwise not set.
- **adStatus**—Status value, see below.
- **pRecordset**—The recordset that caused the event.

Here are the possible values of the `adStatus` parameter as passed to this event handler:

- **adStatusOK**—Operation executed successfully.
- **adStatusErrorsOccurred**—Operation that caused the event occurred unsuccessfully, or a `Will` event canceled the operation.
- **adStatusCantDeny**—`Will` event cannot request cancellation of the operation about to occur.

If you want to cancel the pending change, check the `adStatus` parameter; if it's not set to `adStatusCantDeny`, then you can cancel the change by setting it to `adStatusCancel` before returning.

Here's an example showing how to use the `WillMove` event to make sure the user placed a numeric value in a certain field:

```
Private Sub adoRecordset_WillMove(ByVal adReason _
As ADODB.EventReasonEnum, adStatus As _
ADODB.EventStatusEnum, ByVal pRecordset As _
ADODB.Recordset)
    If Not IsNumeric(pRecordset.Fields(0)) Then
```

```
        MsgBox "Please enter a numeric value."
        adStatus = adStatusCancel
    End If
End Sub
```

I'll take a look at some of the methods of recordsets next, starting with the Find method.

Searching a Recordset

You can use the Find method to search a recordset (or you can, of course, create a new recordset using the SQL statement you want to select new records). Here's how you use Find:

```
Find (Criteria, [SkipRows [, SearchDirection [, _
Start]]])
```

Here is what the arguments to this method mean:

- **Criteria**—Statement that specifies the column name, comparison operator, and value to use in the search.
- **SkipRows**—Offset from the current row or start bookmark to begin the search; default value is 0.
- **SearchDirection**—Can be adSearchForward (the default) or adSearchBackward. Note that the search stops at the start or end of the recordset, depending on the value of searchDirection.
- **Start**—Variant bookmark to use as the starting location for the search.

It's worth taking apart the Criteria argument here. The value you specify in Criteria may be a string, floating point number, or date. Note that string values are delimited with single quotes (like this: "Name = 'Phoebe'"). You must delimit date values with "#" (for example: "Date < #1/1/1900#"). The comparison operator you use in the Criteria argument can be >, <, =, or LIKE. If the comparison operator is LIKE, the string value may contain these wildcards: * (one or more of any character) or _ or % (one of any character). You can only use a wildcard as the first and last character of a Criteria string, or as the last character. Also note that if the field name you specify has spaces, you must enclose it in square brackets, [and].

If the Find operation doesn't find any matches, it'll leave the recordset at EOF or BOF, depending on the search direction.

Here's an example showing how to search the Biblio.mdb database for publishers whose name starts with "P":

```
Private Sub Form_Load()
    Dim adoConnect As Connection
    Set adoConnect = New Connection


    adoConnect.Open _
        "PROVIDER=Microsoft.Jet.OLEDB.3.51;" & _
        "Data Source=C:\ado\biblio.mdb;"


    Set adoRecordset = New Recordset
    adoRecordset.Open "select * from Publishers", _
        adoConnect, adOpenStatic, adLockOptimistic


    Set Text1.DataSource = adoRecordset
    Set Text2.DataSource = adoRecordset
    Text1.DataField = "Name"
    Text2.DataField = "Address"


    adoRecordset.Find "Name LIKE 'P*'"
End Sub
```

There's a way to speed up operations like Find—you can use the Op-timize property to create an index.

Using the Optimize Property

You can use an index to improve the performance of operations that find or sort values in a recordset. To create an index for a field, you use the Field object's Optimize property. The Optimize property is a dynamic property; it is not a part of the Field object interface, which is to say that it exists only in a Field object's Properties collection. To use it, you must set the CursorLocation property to adUseClient.

note The index is internal to ADO, which means that you cannot explicitly access or use it in your application.

To create an index on a field, set the Optimize property to True, and to delete the index, set this property to False. Note that if some operation implicitly creates an index on this field, then the operation will set the Opti-mize property to True automatically.

Here's an example showing how to create an index for a field and so optimize search and sort operations using this field:

```
set adoField = adoRecordset.Fields(0)
adoField.Properties("Optimize") = TRUE

    .

    .

    .
```

Besides searching a recordset, it's also possible to sort one, and I'll take a look at that next.

Sorting a Recordset

You can use the Recordset object's Sort property to sort recordsets. You specify the field(s) to sort on as in this example, where I'm sorting on the Name field of the Publishers table in Biblio.mdb:

```
Private Sub Form_Load()
    Dim adoConnect As Connection
    Set adoConnect = New Connection

    adoConnect.Open _
        "PROVIDER=Microsoft.Jet.OLEDB.3.51;Data " & _
        "Source=C:\ado\biblio.mdb;"
    adoConnect.CursorLocation = adUseClient

    Set adoRecordset = New Recordset
    adoRecordset.Open "select * from Publishers", _
        adoConnect, adOpenStatic, adLockOptimistic

    Set Text1.DataSource = adoRecordset
    Text1.DataField = "Name"
    Set Text2.DataSource = adoRecordset
    Text2.DataField = "Address"
```

```
adoRecordset.Sort = "Name"
```

```
End Sub
```

After the sort operation is finished, all the records in the recordset will be sorted in the order you've specified. Note that the recordset is not actually reordered—the cursor simply presents the records in the new order.

You can sort on multiple fields, like this, where I'm sorting on the Name field first, and, in case two publishers have the same name (not too likely), I specify the next level of sorting to be on the Address field:

```
adoRecordset.Sort = "Name, Address"
        .
        .
        .
```

By default, sorts are ordered by ascending value, but you can change that by adding the keyword DESC after any field you want to sort in descending order:

```
adoRecordset.Sort = "Name DESC, Address"
        .
        .
        .
```

To explicitly sort in ascending order, you can use the ASC keyword (note that you can't sort fields named ASC or DESC because those names conflict with the ordering keywords):

```
adoRecordset.Sort = "Name ASC, Address"
        .
        .
        .
```

You can also restore a recordset to its original sort order by setting the Sort property to an empty string:

```
adoRecordset.Sort = ""
        .
        .
        .
```

Besides searching and sorting recordsets, you can also filter them.

Filtering a Recordset

You use the `Filter` property to screen out records in a `Recordset` object temporarily (the filtered-out records are still in the underlying recordset). The filtered recordset becomes the current cursor.

 Note that filtering affects other properties such as `AbsolutePosition`, `AbsolutePage`, `RecordCount`, and `PageCount` that return values based on the current cursor. In addition, filtering to a specific value will move the current record to the first record that satisfies the filter.

You can set the `Filter` property to these values:

- **Criteria string**—A string made up of one or more individual clauses concatenated with `AND` or `OR` operators.
- **Array of bookmarks**—An array of unique bookmark values that point to records in the `Recordset` object.
- A **FilterGroupEnum value**—See below for the possible values.

Here are the allowed `FilterGroupEnum` values:

- **adFilterNone**—Removes the current filter and restores all records to view.
- **adFilterPendingRecords**—Displays only records that have changed but have not yet been sent to the server. Applicable only for `Batch Update` mode.
- **adFilterAffectedRecords**—Displays only records affected by the last `Delete`, `Resync`, `UpdateBatch`, or `CancelBatch` call.
- **adFilterFetchedRecords**—Displays records in the current cache— that is, the results of the last call to retrieve records from the database.
- **adFilterConflictingRecords**—Displays the records that failed during the last batch update attempt.

The criteria string is just like the criteria string you use with the `Find` method. However, when filtering, you can also create compound clauses by joining individual clauses with `AND` or `OR`. You can group clauses with parentheses too, but the only operator you can use between groups of parentheses is `OR`.

To restore the recordset to its unfiltered state, use a criteria string of `""` or `adFilterNone`.

Here's an example in which I filter the Publishers table to get only the records where the publisher name is Prentice Hall or MIT:

```
Private Sub Form_Load()
    Dim adoConnect As Connection
    Set adoConnect = New Connection

    adoConnect.Open _
        "PROVIDER=Microsoft.Jet.OLEDB.3.51;" & _
        "Data Source=C:\ado\biblio.mdb;"

    Set adoRecordset = New Recordset
    adoRecordset.Open "select * from Publishers", _
        adoConnect, adOpenStatic, adLockOptimistic

    Set Text1.DataSource = adoRecordset
    Text1.DataField = "Name"
    Set Text2.DataSource = adoRecordset
    Text2.DataField = "Address"

    adoRecordset.Filter = "Name = 'PRENTICE HALL' _
        OR Name = 'MIT'"
End Sub
```

Using filters, you can create a subset of a recordset without having to query the underlying database.

Server Synchronization

You can determine if other users have modified the data in fields by staying synchronized with the server. One way of doing this is with the Original-Value property, which holds the original value in a field. If this value is different from the current value in the field, that value has been changed by your application or another user.

You can also use the UnderlyingValue property of a field. This property is set to the current value of the field in the underlying database. If this value is not the same as the value you have in your recordset, that value may have been changed by another user.

So how do you stay in sync with a database dynamically? You can use the `Recordset` object's `Resync` method, which refreshes the data in the current recordset from the underlying database:

```
Recordset.Resync [AffectRecords [, ResyncValues]]
```

The `AffectRecords` argument is an `AffectEnum` value that determines how many records the `Resync` method will affect, and can be set to these constants:

- **adAffectCurrent**—Refreshes only the current record.
- **adAffectGroup**—Refreshes the records that satisfy the current `Filter` property setting. Note that you must set the `Filter` property to one of the valid pre-defined constants to use this option.
- **adAffectAll**—(default) Refreshes all the records in the `Recordset` object, including any hidden by the current `Filter` property setting.

The `ResyncValues` arguments specifies whether underlying values are overwritten, and can be one of the following constants.

- **adResyncAllValues**—(default) Data is overwritten and pending updates are canceled.
- **adResyncUnderlyingValues**—Data is not overwritten and pending updates are not canceled.

You can identify which fields have conflicting values in your recordset and the database by comparing the `OriginalValue` property to the `UnderlyingValue` property before executing the `Update` method. You can also use the `UpdateBatch` method to try updating all records with pending changes, and then use the `adFilterConflictingRecords` filter to see which records failed the `UpdateBatch` operation.

Note that not all providers will support the `Resync` method.

Using Disconnected Recordsets

Another new aspect of ADO programming is that you can use *disconnected recordsets*, working with them in the client and reconnecting to the server when needed. Using disconnected recordsets, you can cut down on network traffic and get better response from your program when network connections are slow.

I'll write an example to examine how disconnected recordsets work; this example will modify the `adodb` example from earlier in this chapter into a new version that uses a disconnected recordset. You'll find this example in the disconnected folder on the CD.

I'll start by creating a remote recordset when the main form first loads. In this example, I'll use the students table in the db.mdb database we created earlier in this book (and which is on the CD). Here, I open that database using a client recordset, which is necessary for disconnected recordsets—note that I'm using the Recordset object's Open method to connect to the data source, not a Connection object, and using a lock type of adLock-BatchOptimistic:

```
Private WithEvents adoRecordset As ADODB.Recordset


Private Sub Form_Load()

    Set adoRecordset = New Recordset

    adoRecordset.CursorType = adOpenKeyset
    adoRecordset.LockType = adLockBatchOptimistic
    adoRecordset.CursorLocation = adUseClient

    adoRecordset.Open "select * from students", _
    "PROVIDER=Microsoft.Jet.OLEDB.3.51;Data " & _
    "Source=C:\ado\temp\db.mdb;"
        .
        .
        .
```

I'll set the marshalling option to adMarshalModifiedOnly so only the modified records will be updated:

```
    adoRecordset.MarshalOptions = _
        adMarshalModifiedOnly
        .
        .
        .
```

After creating the recordset, I set the recordset's ActiveConnection property to Nothing to disconnect it:

```
Set adoRecordset.ActiveConnection = Nothing

    .

    .

    .
```

Now there's no connection to any outside data in the program, but the Recordset object is active. I bind the fields in that recordset to two text boxes, Text1 and Text2, like this:

```
Set Text1.DataSource = adoRecordset
Text1.DataField = "Name"
Set Text2.DataSource = adoRecordset
Text2.DataField = "Grade"
```

```
End Sub
```

And that completes the Form_Load event; now we have a working disconnected recordset. The user can work with that recordset as they like— the only tricky point comes when it's time to update the underlying data source.

When the user clicks the Update button in this project, we should update the actual database with the changes the user has made. You can do that by first creating a Connection object, then setting the Recordset object's ActiveConnection property to that object, and finally, using an Update method. Here's how that works when the user clicks the Update button; first, I create the new connection:

```
Private Sub cmdUpdate_Click()

    Set adoConnect = New Connection

    adoConnect.Open _
    "PROVIDER=Microsoft.Jet.OLEDB.3.51;Data " & _
    Source=C:\ado\db.mdb;", , , adConnectAsync

    .

    .

    .
```

Then I set the `ActiveConnection` property of the recordset to this new connection:

```
adoRecordset.ActiveConnection = adoConnect
    .
    .
    .
```

Now we're connected again and ready to update the database using batch updating, which looks like this:

```
adoRecordset.UpdateBatch
    .
    .
    .
```

That updates the database with the changes the user has made. I disconnect the recordset again by setting the `ActiveConnection` property to `Nothing`, closing the `Connection` object, and removing the `Connection` object from memory like this:

```
adoRecordset.ActiveConnection = Nothing

adoConnect.Close

Set adoConnect = Nothing

Exit Sub


ErrLabel:
    MsgBox Err.Description
End Sub
```

The rest of the code is the same as in the `adodb` project, except when the user clicks the `Refresh` button to refill the recordset from the underlying database. In that case, I just reconnect and refresh the recordset like this:

```
Private Sub cmdRefresh_Click()
    Set adoRecordset = New Recordset
```

```
adoRecordset.CursorType - adOpenKeyset
adoRecordset.LockType = adLockBatchOptimistic
adoRecordset.CursorLocation = adUseClient

adoRecordset.Open "select * from students", _
"PROVIDER=Microsoft.Jet.OLEDB.3.51;Data " & _
"Source=C:\ado\temp\db.mdb;"

adoRecordset.MarshalOptions = _
adMarshalModifiedOnly

Set adoRecordset.ActiveConnection = Nothing

Set Text1.DataSource = adoRecordset
Text1.DataField = "Name"
Set Text2.DataSource = adoRecordset
Text2.DataField = "Grade"


End Sub
```

And that's it; the results appear in Figure 8.3. As you can see in that figure, all the buttons that the `adodb` project supports are supported by this project also, except that this project uses a disconnected recordset. The code for this example appears in the `disconnected` folder on the CD, and in Listing 8.2.

LISTING 8.2   *Disconnected.frm Code*

```
VERSION 5.00
Begin VB.Form Form1
   BorderStyle     =    3   'Fixed Dialog
   Caption         =    "Students"
   ClientHeight    =    2460
   ClientLeft      =    1095
   ClientTop       =    330
   ClientWidth     =    5550
   LinkTopic       =    "Form3"
   MaxButton       =    0    'False
```

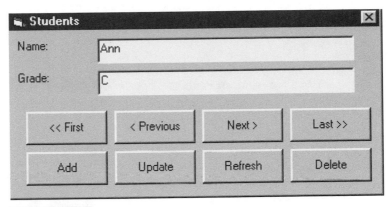

FIGURE 8.3 Using a disconnected recordset.

```
MinButton         =    0    'False
ScaleHeight       =    2460
ScaleWidth        =    5550
ShowInTaskbar     =    0    'False
Begin VB.CommandButton cmdLast
   Caption         =    "Last >>"
   Height          =    495
   Left            =    4200
   TabIndex        =    11
   Top             =    1200
   Width           =    1215
End
Begin VB.CommandButton cmdNext
   Caption         =    "Next >"
   Height          =    495
   Left            =    2880
   TabIndex        =    10
   Top             =    1200
   Width           =    1215
End
Begin VB.CommandButton cmdPrevious
   Caption         =    "< Previous"
   Height          =    495
   Left            =    1560
   TabIndex        =    9
   Top             =    1200
   Width           =    1215
End
Begin VB.CommandButton cmdFirst
   Caption         =    "<< First"
   Height          =    495
```

```
            Left            =    240
            TabIndex        =    8
            Top             =    1200
            Width           =    1215
         End
         Begin VB.CommandButton cmdRefresh
            Caption         =    "Refresh"
            Height          =    495
            Left            =    2880
            TabIndex        =    6
            Top             =    1800
            Width           =    1215
         End
         Begin VB.CommandButton cmdUpdate
            Caption         =    "Update"
            Height          =    495
            Left            =    1560
            TabIndex        =    5
            Top             =    1800
            Width           =    1215
         End
         Begin VB.CommandButton cmdDelete
            Caption         =    "Delete"
            Height          =    495
            Left            =    4200
            TabIndex        =    4
            Top             =    1800
            Width           =    1215
         End
         Begin VB.CommandButton cmdAdd
            Caption         =    "Add"
            Height          =    495
            Left            =    240
            TabIndex        =    3
            Top             =    1800
            Width           =    1215
         End
         Begin VB.TextBox Text2
            Height          =    375
            Left            =    1320
            TabIndex        =    2
            Top             =    600
            Width           =    3855
         End
         Begin VB.TextBox Text1
            Height          =    375
            Left            =    1320
            TabIndex        =    1
            Top             =    120
            Width           =    3855
         End
```

```
   Begin VB.Label lblLabels
      Caption         =    "Name:"
      Height          =    255
      Index           =    0
      Left            =    120
      TabIndex        =    7
      Top             =    120
      Width           =    1095
   End
   Begin VB.Label lblLabels
      Caption         =    "Grade:"
      Height          -    255
      Index           =    1
      Left            =    120
      TabIndex        =    0
      Top             =    600
      Width           =    1095
   End
End
Attribute VB_Name = "Form1"
Attribute VB_GlobalNameSpace = False
Attribute VB_Creatable = False
Attribute VB_PredeclaredId = True
Attribute VB_Exposed = False
Private WithEvents adoRecordset As ADODB.Recordset
Attribute adoRecordset.VB_VarHelpID = -1
Private WithEvents adoConnect As Connection
Attribute adoConnect.VB_VarHelpID = -1

Private Sub Form_Load()

    Set adoRecordset = New Recordset

    adoRecordset.CursorType = adOpenKeyset
    adoRecordset.LockType = adLockBatchOptimistic
    adoRecordset.CursorLocation = adUseClient

    adoRecordset.Open "select * from students", _
    "PROVIDER=Microsoft.Jet.OLEDB.3.51;Data " & _
    "Source=C:\ado\temp\db.mdb;"

    adoRecordset.MarshalOptions = adMarshalModifiedOnly

    Set adoRecordset.ActiveConnection = Nothing

    Set Text1.DataSource = adoRecordset
    Text1.DataField = "Name"
    Set Text2.DataSource = adoRecordset
    Text2.DataField = "Grade"

End Sub
```

```
Private Sub cmdAdd_Click()
    On Error GoTo ErrLabel
    adoRecordset.AddNew

    Text1.Text = ""
    Text2.Text = ""

    Exit Sub

ErrLabel:
    MsgBox Err.Description
End Sub

Private Sub cmdDelete_Click()
    On Error GoTo ErrLabel

    adoRecordset.Delete

    adoRecordset.MoveNext
    If adoRecordset.EOF Then
        adoRecordset.MoveLast
    End If

    Exit Sub

ErrLabel:
    MsgBox Err.Description
End Sub

Private Sub cmdRefresh_Click()

    Set adoRecordset = New Recordset

    adoRecordset.CursorType = adOpenKeyset
    adoRecordset.LockType = adLockBatchOptimistic
    adoRecordset.CursorLocation = adUseClient

    adoRecordset.Open "select * from students", _
    "PROVIDER=Microsoft.Jet.OLEDB.3.51;Data " & _
    "Source=C:\ado\temp\db.mdb;"

    adoRecordset.MarshalOptions = adMarshalModifiedOnly

    Set adoRecordset.ActiveConnection = Nothing

    Set Text1.DataSource = adoRecordset
    Text1.DataField = "Name"
    Set Text2.DataSource = adoRecordset
    Text2.DataField = "Grade"

End Sub
```

```
Private Sub cmdUpdate_Click()

    Set adoConnect = New Connection

    adoConnect.Open "PROVIDER=Microsoft.Jet.OLEDB.3.51;" & _
    "Data Source=C:\ado\temp\db.mdb;", , , adConnectAsync

    adoRecordset.ActiveConnection = adoConnect

    adoRecordset.UpdateBatch

    adoRecordset.ActiveConnection = Nothing

    adoConnect.Close

    Set adoConnect = Nothing

    Exit Sub

ErrLabel:
    MsgBox Err.Description
End Sub

Private Sub cmdFirst_Click()
    On Error GoTo ErrLabel

    adoRecordset.MoveFirst

    Exit Sub

ErrLabel:
    MsgBox Err.Description
End Sub

Private Sub cmdLast_Click()
    On Error GoTo ErrLabel

    adoRecordset.MoveLast

    Exit Sub

ErrLabel:
    MsgBox Err.Description
End Sub

Private Sub cmdNext_Click()
    On Error GoTo ErrLabel

    If Not adoRecordset.EOF Then
            adoRecordset.MoveNext
    End If
```

```
    If adoRecordset.EOF And adoRecordset.RecordCount _
        > 0 Then
        adoRecordset.MoveLast
    End If

    Exit Sub

ErrLabel:
    MsgBox Err.Description
End Sub

Private Sub cmdPrevious_Click()
    On Error GoTo ErrLabel

    If Not adoRecordset.BOF Then adoRecordset.MovePrevious
    If adoRecordset.BOF And adoRecordset.RecordCount _
        > 0 Then
        adoRecordset.MoveFirst
    End If

    Exit Sub

ErrLabel:
    MsgBox Err.Description
End Sub
```

Next, I'll take a look at saving recordsets to disk, another way of working with data on the client.

Persisting Recordsets

A major part of ADO has to do with working on networks and the Internet, which means that not only have the Remote Data Services (RDS) become important, but so has working with local, downloaded copies of data, as we've seen in the previous topic on disconnected recordsets. Another way of working with local data is to store the current recordset in a file and work with it offline. You do that with the Recordset object's Save method:

```
Recordset.Save [FileName [, PersistFormat]]
```

- **FileName**—Path and name of the file where the recordset is to be saved.

- **PersistFormat**—Format in which the recordset is to be saved. Currently, the default—and only valid—value is adPersistADTG.

Here's an example in which I save, close, and reload—using the Open method—the Publishers table from Biblio.mdb. First I open and store that table in a recordset, binding the Address and Name fields to text boxes:

```
Private Sub Command1_Click()

    Dim adoConnect As Connection
    Set adoConnect = New Connection

    adoConnect.Open _
        "PROVIDER=Microsoft.Jet.OLEDB.3.51;" & _
        "Data Source=C:\ado\Biblio.mdb;"

    adoConnect.CursorLocation = adUseClient

    Set adoRecordset = New Recordset
    adoRecordset.Open "select * from Publishers", _
        adoConnect, adOpenStatic, adLockOptimistic

    Set Text1.DataSource = adoRecordset
    Text1.DataField = "Name"
    Set Text2.DataSource = adoRecordset
    Text2.DataField = "Address"
    .
    .
    .
```

To save this recordset to disk, you use the Save method like this and then close it:

```
    adoRecordset.Save "c:\ado\Table", _
        adPersistADTG

    adoRecordset.Close
```

To open the recordset again, you use the Open method, specifying the MSPersist OLE DB provider like this:

```
adoRecordset.Open "c:\ado\Table", _
    "Provider=MSPersist", , , adCommandFile


Set Text1.DataSource = adoRecordset
Text1.DataField = "Name"
Set Text2.DataSource = adoRecordset
Text2.DataField = "Address"
    .
    .
    .


End Sub
```

And that's all it takes—now you've persisted a recordset and read it back in.

Creating an ADO Recordset in Code

As with other database connectivity protocols, you can create new recordsets on-the-fly with ADO. I'll create an example to do that right now. To start, you create a new Recordset object:

```
Private adoRecordset As ADODB.Recordset


Private Sub Form_Load()


    Set adoRecordset = New ADODB.Recordset
    .
    .
    .
```

Then you use the Fields collection's Append method to append a new field:

```
Fields.Append Name, Type, [DefinedSize [, Attrib]]
```

Here are the arguments to this method:

- **Name**—Name of the new Field object, which must not be the same name as any other object in Fields.
- **Type**—Data type of the new field, which must be a DataTypeEnum value like adBigInt, adChar, adDouble, adInteger, adSingle, or adVarChar (for strings). The default is adEmpty.
- **DefinedSize**—Defined size of the new field in characters or bytes. The default value is derived from the Type parameter.
- **Attrib**—Attributes for the new field, which must be a FieldAttributeEnum value such as adFldUpdatable, adFldIsNullable, adFldFixed, and so on; the default value is adFldDefault. If you don't specify this value, it will be derived from Type.

In this case, I'll add two string fields, Name and Address, to the Fields collection:

```
Private adoRecordset As ADODB.Recordset


Private Sub Form_Load()


    Set adoRecordset = New ADODB.Recordset


    adoRecordset.Fields.Append "Name", adVarChar, _
        60
    adoRecordset.Fields.Append "Address", _
        adVarChar, 200
        .
        .
        .
```

To work with the new recordset, you must open it like this:

```
adoRecordset.Open , , adOpenKeyset, _
    adLockOptimistic
        .
        .
        .
```

Now you're free to create new records and populate the fields of those records with data:

```
adoRecordset.AddNew
adoRecordset.Fields("Name") = "Ted"
adoRecordset.Fields("Address") = _
    "121 Mars Place"
adoRecordset.Update

adoRecordset.AddNew
adoRecordset.Fields("Name") = "Tina"
adoRecordset.Fields("Address") = "133 Jupiter
    Street"
adoRecordset.Update

adoRecordset.AddNew
adoRecordset.Fields("Name") = "Nancy"
adoRecordset.Fields("Address") = _
"16 Earth Square"
adoRecordset.Update
    .
    .
    .
```

Your new recordset is ready. You can bind it to controls like this:

```
Set Text1.DataSource = adoRecordset
Text1.DataField = "Name"

Set Text2.DataSource = adoRecordset
Text2.DataField = "Address"

adoRecordset.MoveFirst
```

```
End Sub
```

Note that after you add records to a recordset, you end up positioned at the last record added, so I move back to the first record with `MoveFirst` in the above code. You can also add navigation buttons, such as a button to move to the next record, like this:

```
Private Sub cmdNext_Click()
    On Error GoTo ErrLabel

    If Not adoRecordset.EOF Then
            adoRecordset.MoveNext
    End If

    If adoRecordset.EOF And _
        adoRecordset.RecordCount > 0 Then
        adoRecordset.MoveLast
    End If

    Exit Sub

ErrLabel:
    MsgBox Err.Description
End Sub
```

The results appear in Figure 8.4, where I've added navigation buttons; you see the current record displayed in that figure. Congratulations, you're now creating recordsets on-the-fly!

This project appears in the adocreate folder on the CD and in Listing 8.3.

LISTING 8.3   *Adocreate.frm Code*

```
VERSION 5.00
Begin VB.Form Form1
    Caption         =   "Form1"
    ClientHeight    =   3195
    ClientLeft      =   60
    ClientTop       =   345
    ClientWidth     =   5385
    LinkTopic       =   "Form1"
    ScaleHeight     =   3195
```

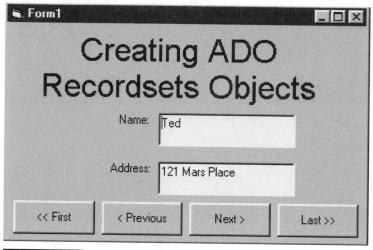

FIGURE 8.4   Creating a recordset in code.

```
ScaleWidth      =    5385
StartUpPosition =    3    'Windows Default
Begin VB.CommandButton cmdlast
   Caption      =    "Last >>"
   Height       =    495
   Left         =    4080
   TabIndex     =    8
   Top          =    2640
   Width        =    1215
End
Begin VB.CommandButton cmdNext
   Caption      =    "Next >"
   Height       =    495
   Left         =    2760
   TabIndex     =    7
   Top          =    2640
   Width        =    1215
End
Begin VB.CommandButton cmdPrevious
   Caption      =    "< Previous"
   Height       =    495
   Left         =    1440
   TabIndex     =    6
   Top          =    2640
   Width        =    1215
End
Begin VB.CommandButton cmdFirst
   Caption      =    "<< First"
   Height       =    495
```

```
   Left                =    120
   TabIndex            =    5
   Top                 =    2640
   Width               =    1215
End
Begin VB.TextBox Text2
   Height              =    495
   Left                =    2280
   TabIndex            =    1
   Text                =    "Text2"
   Top                 =    2040
   Width               =    2055
End
Begin VB.TextBox Text1
   Height              =    495
   Left                =    2280
   TabIndex            =    0
   Text                =    "Text1"
   Top                 =    1320
   Width               =    2055
End
Begin VB.Label Label3
   Caption             =    "Address:"
   Height              =    495
   Left                =    1560
   TabIndex            =    4
   Top                 =    2040
   Width               =    735
End
Begin VB.Label Label2
   Caption             =    "Name:"
   Height              =    495
   Left                =    1680
   TabIndex            =    3
   Top                 =    1320
   Width               =    495
End
Begin VB.Label Label1
   Alignment           =    2    'Center
   Caption             =    "Creating ADO Recordsets Objects in code"
   BeginProperty Font
      Name             =    "Arial"
      Size             =    24
      Charset          =    0
      Weight           =    400
      Underline        =    0    'False
      Italic           =    0    'False
      Strikethrough    =    0    'False
   EndProperty
   Height              =    1095
   Left                =    360
```

```
        TabIndex        =    2
        Top             =    120
        Width           =    4575
    End
End
Attribute VB_Name = "Form1"
Attribute VB_GlobalNameSpace = False
Attribute VB_Creatable = False
Attribute VB_PredeclaredId = True
Attribute VB_Exposed = False
Private adoRecordset As ADODB.Recordset
Attribute adoRecordset.VB_VarHelpID = -1

Private Sub Form_Load()

    Set adoRecordset = New ADODB.Recordset

    adoRecordset.Fields.Append "Name", adVarChar, 60
    adoRecordset.Fields.Append "Address", adVarChar, 200

    adoRecordset.Open , , adOpenKeyset, adLockOptimistic

    adoRecordset.AddNew
    adoRecordset.Fields("Name") = "Ted"
    adoRecordset.Fields("Address") = "121 Mars Place"
    adoRecordset.Update

    adoRecordset.AddNew
    adoRecordset.Fields("Name") = "Tina"
    adoRecordset.Fields("Address") = "133 Jupiter Street"
    adoRecordset.Update

    adoRecordset.AddNew
    adoRecordset.Fields("Name") = "Nancy"
    adoRecordset.Fields("Address") = "16 Earth Square"
    adoRecordset.Update

    Set Text1.DataSource = adoRecordset
    Text1.DataField = "Name"

    Set Text2.DataSource = adoRecordset
    Text2.DataField = "Address"

    adoRecordset.MoveFirst

End Sub

Private Sub cmdFirst_Click()
    On Error GoTo ErrLabel

    adoRecordset.MoveFirst
```

```
    Exit Sub

ErrLabel:
    MsgBox Err.Description
End Sub

Private Sub cmdLast_Click()
    On Error GoTo ErrLabel

    adoRecordset.MoveLast

    Exit Sub

ErrLabel:
    MsgBox Err.Description
End Sub

Private Sub cmdNext_Click()
    On Error GoTo ErrLabel

    If Not adoRecordset.EOF Then
            adoRecordset.MoveNext
    End If

    If adoRecordset.EOF And adoRecordset.RecordCount > 0 Then
        adoRecordset.MoveLast
    End If

    Exit Sub

ErrLabel:
    MsgBox Err.Description
End Sub

Private Sub cmdPrevious_Click()
    On Error GoTo ErrLabel

    If Not adoRecordset.BOF Then adoRecordset.MovePrevious
    If adoRecordset.BOF And adoRecordset.RecordCount > 0 Then
        adoRecordset.MoveFirst
    End If

    Exit Sub

ErrLabel:
    MsgBox Err.Description
End Sub
```

Exporting Recordsets

One of the most important parts of database programming is working with other databases and other formats; this is one of the most common topics one runs into in commercial database programming. I'll take a look at how to export a recordset to Microsoft Excel in two ways in this chapter: using a .csv (command-separated value) file and accessing Excel directly through OLE automation.

Exporting to CSV Format

One very basic, but very popular, technique for exporting data is with the comma-separated value (CSV) format for plain text files. This format just stores one record on a separate line of a plain text file, and separates the values in the fields with commas (note that you can use the Visual Basic CStr function to convert various data types to string).

For example, here's how the students table of the db.mdb database would look in CSV format:

```
Ann,C

Mark,B

Ed,A

Frank,A

Ted,A

Mabel,B

Ralph,B

Tom,B
```

Many applications, such as Microsoft Access and Excel, can read and convert .csv files into tables. For that reason, I'll write an example now to convert the students table into the above .csv file. That application, export, appears in Figure 8.5. When the user clicks the Export button in that figure, I'll export the table to a file named export.csv.

The students table is rcad into the Recordset object, adoRecordset, by this program when the main form loads. When the user clicks the Export button, I'll store the current location in the recordset, move to the first record, and create the file export.csv:

```
Private Sub cmdExport_Click()
    On Error GoTo ErrLabel
```

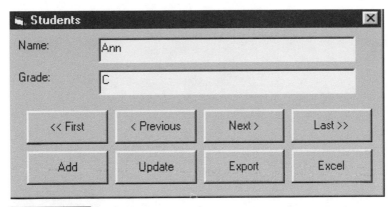

FIGURE 8.5 Letting the user export a recordset.

```
OldPosition = adoRecordset.AbsolutePosition

adoRecordset.MoveFirst

Open "c:\ado\export\export.csv" For Output As #1
.
.
.
```

Next, I loop over all the records and fields in the students table like this, printing them out to the export.csv file:

```
Do Until adoRecordset.EOF
    For loop_index = 0 To
        adoRecordset.Fields.Count - 1
        If loop_index <> _
        adoRecordset.Fields.Count - 1 Then
         Print #1, _
         Trim(adoRecordset.Fields(loop_index)) _
         & ",";
        Else
          Print #1, _
          Trim(adoRecordset.Fields(loop_index))
        End If
```

```
      Next loop_index
      adoRecordset.MoveNext
   Loop
```

All that's left is to close `export.csv` and return the recordset to the record it was on before looping over it:

```
   Close #1

   adoRecordset.AbsolutePosition = OldPosition

   Exit Sub


ErrLabel:
   MsgBox Err.Description
End Sub
```

And that's it; now when the user clicks the `Export` button, this program will create the file `export.csv`, and you can open that file in Excel, as shown in Figure 8.6.

There's another way to export data to applications like Excel; you can do it directly with OLE automation.

Exporting to Microsoft Excel

To let the user export the `students` table directly to Microsoft Excel, I'll add the `Excel` button you see in Figure 8.5. When the user clicks that button, the program will open Excel and populate a worksheet with the data in the `students` table.

To work with an application from Visual Basic using OLE automation, you must first add a reference to that application's object library. So, I add a reference to the Microsoft Excel Object Library using the `References` item in the Visual Basic `Project` menu now.

When the user clicks the `Excel` button, I'll record the current location in the recordset and create a new `Excel` object like this:

```
Private Sub cmdExportToExcel_Click()
   On Error GoTo ErrLabel
```

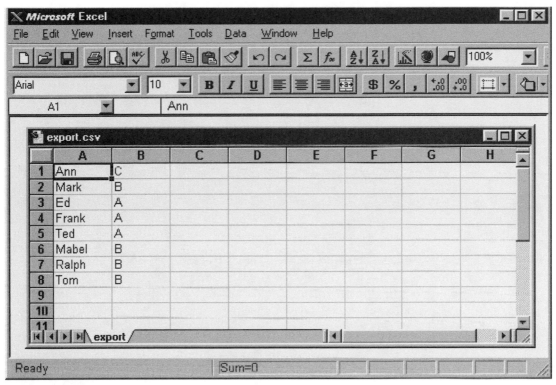

FIGURE 8.6 Opening the students table in Excel.

```
OldPosition = adoRecordset.AbsolutePosition

Dim objExcel As Object
Set objExcel = CreateObject("Excel.Application")
objExcel.Workbooks.Add
   .
   .
   .
```

Next, I loop over all the records and fields in the `students` table, using the `Excel` object's `Cells` method to populate the cells of the worksheet:

```
For record_loop_index = 0 To _
    adoRecordset.RecordCount - 1
```

```
                        For field_loop_index = 0 To _
                            adoRecordset.Fields.Count - 1
                                objExcel.Cells(record_loop_index + _
                                1, field_loop_index + 1).Value = _
                        Trim(adoRecordset.Fields(field_loop_index))
                        Next field_loop_index
                        adoRecordset.MoveNext
                    Next record_loop_index

                    .

                    .

                    .
```

All that's left is to make Excel visible and to restore the recordset to its original location:

```
        objExcel.Visible = True


        adoRecordset.AbsolutePosition = OldPosition


        Exit Sub


    ErrLabel:
        MsgBox Err.Description
    End Sub
```

And that's it—the result appears in Figure 8.6, where you can see the data from the `students` table in Excel. The code for this example appears in Listing 8.4.

LISTING 8.4   *Export.frm Code*

```
VERSION 5.00
Begin VB.Form Form1
    BorderStyle     =   3   'Fixed Dialog
    Caption         =   "Students"
    ClientHeight    =   2460
    ClientLeft      =   1095
    ClientTop       =   330
    ClientWidth     =   5550
```

```
LinkTopic          =    "Form3"
MaxButton          =    0    'False
MinButton          =    0    'False
ScaleHeight        =    2460
ScaleWidth         =    5550
ShowInTaskbar      =    0    'False
Begin VB.CommandButton cmdLast
    Caption        =    "Last >>"
    Height         =    495
    Left           =    4200
    TabIndex       =    11
    Top            =    1200
    Width          =    1215
End
Begin VB.CommandButton cmdNext
    Caption        =    "Next >"
    Height         =    495
    Left           =    2880
    TabIndex       =    10
    Top            =    1200
    Width          =    1215
End
Begin VB.CommandButton cmdPrevious
    Caption        =    "< Previous"
    Height         =    495
    Left           =    1560
    TabIndex       =    9
    Top            =    1200
    Width          =    1215
End
Begin VB.CommandButton cmdFirst
    Caption        =    "<< First"
    Height         =    495
    Left           =    240
    TabIndex       =    8
    Top            =    1200
    Width          =    1215
End
Begin VB.CommandButton cmdExport
    Caption        =    "Export"
    Height         =    495
    Left           =    2880
    TabIndex       =    6
    Top            =    1800
    Width          =    1215
End
Begin VB.CommandButton cmdUpdate
    Caption        =    "Update"
    Height         =    495
    Left           =    1560
    TabIndex       =    5
```

```
         Top            =    1800
         Width          =    1215
      End
      Begin VB.CommandButton cmdExportToExcel
         Caption        =    "Excel"
         Height         =    495
         Left           =    4200
         TabIndex       =    4
         Top            =    1800
         Width          =    1215
      End
      Begin VB.CommandButton cmdAdd
         Caption        =    "Add"
         Height         =    495
         Left           =    240
         TabIndex       =    3
         Top            =    1800
         Width          =    1215
      End
      Begin VB.TextBox Text2
         Height         =    375
         Left           =    1320
         TabIndex       =    2
         Top            =    600
         Width          =    3855
      End
      Begin VB.TextBox Text1
         Height         =    375
         Left           =    1320
         TabIndex       =    1
         Top            =    120
         Width          =    3855
      End
      Begin VB.Label lblLabels
         Caption        =    "Name:"
         Height         =    255
         Index          =    0
         Left           =    120
         TabIndex       =    7
         Top            =    120
         Width          =    1095
      End
      Begin VB.Label lblLabels
         Caption        =    "Grade:"
         Height         =    255
         Index          =    1
         Left           =    120
         TabIndex       =    0
         Top            =    600
         Width          =    1095
      End
```

```
End
Attribute VB_Name = "Form1"
Attribute VB_GlobalNameSpace = False
Attribute VB_Creatable = False
Attribute VB_PredeclaredId = True
Attribute VB_Exposed = False
Private WithEvents adoRecordset As ADODB.Recordset
Attribute adoRecordset.VB_VarHelpID = -1
Private WithEvents adoConnect As Connection
Attribute adoConnect.VB_VarHelpID = -1

Private Sub Form_Load()

    Set adoRecordset = New Recordset

    adoRecordset.CursorType = adOpenKeyset
    adoRecordset.LockType = adLockBatchOptimistic
    adoRecordset.CursorLocation = adUseClient

    adoRecordset.Open "select * from students", _
    "PROVIDER=Microsoft.Jet.OLEDB.3.51;Data " & _
    "Source=C:\ado\db.mdb;"

    Set Text1.DataSource = adoRecordset
    Text1.DataField = "Name"
    Set Text2.DataSource = adoRecordset
    Text2.DataField = "Grade"

End Sub

Private Sub cmdAdd_Click()
    On Error GoTo ErrLabel
    adoRecordset.AddNew

    Text1.Text = ""
    Text2.Text = ""

    Exit Sub

ErrLabel:
    MsgBox Err.Description
End Sub

Private Sub cmdExportToExcel_Click()
    On Error GoTo ErrLabel

    OldPosition = adoRecordset.AbsolutePosition

    Dim objExcel As Object
    Set objExcel = CreateObject("Excel.Application")
    objExcel.Workbooks.Add
```

```
    For record_loop_index = 0 To adoRecordset.RecordCount - 1
        For field_loop_index = 0 To _
            adoRecordset.Fields.Count - 1
                objExcel.Cells(record_loop_index + 1, _
                field_loop_index + 1).Value = _
                Trim(adoRecordset.Fields(field_loop_index))
        Next field_loop_index
        adoRecordset.MoveNext
    Next record_loop_index

    objExcel.Visible = True

    adoRecordset.AbsolutePosition = OldPosition

    Exit Sub

ErrLabel:
    MsgBox Err.Description
End Sub

Private Sub cmdExport_Click()
    On Error GoTo ErrLabel

    OldPosition = adoRecordset.AbsolutePosition

    adoRecordset.MoveFirst

    Open "c:\ado\export\export.csv" For Output As #1

    Do Until adoRecordset.EOF
        For loop_index = 0 To adoRecordset.Fields.Count - 1
            If loop_index <> adoRecordset.Fields.Count - 1 _
                Then
                Print #1, _
                Trim(adoRecordset.Fields(loop_index)) & ",";
            Else
                Print #1, _
                Trim(adoRecordset.Fields(loop_index))
            End If
        Next loop_index
        adoRecordset.MoveNext
    Loop

    Close #1

    adoRecordset.AbsolutePosition = OldPosition

    Exit Sub

ErrLabel:
    MsgBox Err.Description
```

```
End Sub

Private Sub cmdUpdate_Click()

    Set adoConnect = New Connection

    adoConnect.Open "PROVIDER=Microsoft.Jet.OLEDB.3.51;" & _
    "Data Source=C:\ado\temp\db.mdb;", , , adConnectAsync

    adoRecordset.ActiveConnection = adoConnect

    adoRecordset.UpdateBatch

    adoRecordset.ActiveConnection = Nothing

    adoConnect.Close

    Set adoConnect = Nothing

    Exit Sub

ErrLabel:
    MsgBox Err.Description
End Sub

Private Sub cmdFirst_Click()
    On Error GoTo ErrLabel

    adoRecordset.MoveFirst

    Exit Sub

ErrLabel:
    MsgBox Err.Description
End Sub

Private Sub cmdLast_Click()
    On Error GoTo ErrLabel

    adoRecordset.MoveLast

    Exit Sub

ErrLabel:
    MsgBox Err.Description
End Sub

Private Sub cmdNext_Click()
    On Error GoTo ErrLabel

    If Not adoRecordset.EOF Then
```

```
                  adoRecordset.MoveNext
        End If

        If adoRecordset.EOF And adoRecordset.RecordCount > 0 Then
            adoRecordset.MoveLast
        End If

        Exit Sub

ErrLabel:
    MsgBox Err.Description
End Sub

Private Sub cmdPrevious_Click()
    On Error GoTo ErrLabel

    If Not adoRecordset.BOF Then adoRecordset.MovePrevious
    If adoRecordset.BOF And adoRecordset.RecordCount > 0 Then
        adoRecordset.MoveFirst
    End If

    Exit Sub

ErrLabel:
    MsgBox Err.Description
End Sub
```

That's it for our `Recordset` object work for the moment—we've seen a lot in this chapter, from creating a recordset in code to binding it to controls, from searching recordsets to sorting them, from using disconnected recordsets to using recordset events. In the next chapter, I'll keep digging into what ADO has to offer when I turn to the ADO collections.

ADO
Collections

This chapter is on the ADO collections, and here they are:

- **Parameters**—The `Command` object's collection of `Parameter` objects.
- **Fields**—The `Recordset` object's collection of `Field` objects.
- **Errors**—The `Connection` object's collection of `Error` objects.
- **Properties**—The `Connection`, `Command`, `Recordset`, and `Field` objects' collection of `Property` objects.

In this chapter, I'll take a look at each of these collections. We've seen all the objects in these collections before, except the ADO `Error` and `Property` objects, which we'll see in this chapter.

Collections are more than just useful in ADO programming—they're essential. For example, we've already seen the `Fields` collection, which holds the collection of fields in a record, as in this case, where I'm setting the value of a field to 1556:

```
adoRecordset.Fields(1).Value = 1556
```

In this chapter, I'll take a detailed look at the ADO collections' properties and methods, starting with an overview of those properties and methods now.

The ADO Collections in Overview

The `Parameters` collection belongs to the `Command` object.

The Parameters Collection

You store parameters in `Parameter` objects to use in a command in the `Parameters` collection. This collection has one property:

- **Count**—Count of items.

    The `Parameters` collection also has these methods:

- **Append**—Appends a new item.
- **Delete**—Deletes an item.
- **Refresh**—Refreshes items.
- **Item**—Gets an item.

The Fields Collection

The `Fields` collection is part of the `Recordset` object, and you store `Field` objects, each representing a field in a record, in this collection. This collection has one property:

- **Count**—Count of items.

    This collection also has these methods:

- **Append**—Appends a new item.
- **Delete**—Deletes an item.
- **Refresh**—Refreshes items.
- **Item**—Gets an item.

The Errors Collection

The `Errors` collection belongs to the `Connection` object, and it holds provider-specific errors. (Note that in addition to these errors, ADO has its own error set that you can trap with the `On Error GoTo` statement; you'll find these errors listed in Table 3.1.) When you start an error-prone operation, clear the `Errors` collection with the `Clear` method; after the operation, check the `Count` property of the `Errors` collection—if it's non-zero, errors occurred, and you can get them from this collection.

The `Errors` collection is a collection of `Error` objects, and we'll take a look at the objects in this chapter. This collection has one property:

- **Count**—Count of items.

  This collection has these methods:

- **Clear**—Clears the collection.
- **Refresh**—Refreshes items.
- **Item**—Gets an item.

The Properties Collection

The `Properties` collection is a collection of the `Connection`, `Command`, `Recordset`, and `Field` objects. This is the biggest collection in this chapter, because it holds the dynamic properties for these objects. Dynamic properties are provider-specific, so they vary by provider. For example, the `Maximum Rows` dynamic property holds the maximum number of rows you can use, which varies greatly by provider. In fact, what dynamic properties are available also varies greatly by provider. We'll see the possibilities in this chapter.

The `Properties` collection is a collection of `Property` objects, and we'll see those objects in this chapter. This collection itself has one property:

- **Count**—Count of items.

  The `Properties` collection has these methods:

- **Refresh**—Refreshes items.
- **Item**—Gets an item.

That's what these collections look like in overview; it's time to get to the details now, starting with the `Parameters` collection.

The Parameters Collection

The `Parameters` collection is a 0-based collection that holds the parameters you use with ADO commands. We first saw the `Parameters` collection back in Chapter 6. Here's an example where I'm configuring a `Command` object by creating a `Parameter` object and appending the `Parameter` object to the `Command` object's `Parameters` collection:

```
adoConnect.Open _
"PROVIDER=Microsoft.Jet.OLEDB.3.51;Data
Source=C:\ado\db.mdb;"
```

```
Set adoCommand = New Command
adoCommand.CommandType = adCmdText
adoCommand.CommandText = "SELECT * from Students
WHERE Name = ?"
Set adoParam = New Parameter
adoParam.Name = "Name"
adoParam.Type = adVarChar
adoParam.Size = 20
adoParam.Value = "Tom"
```

```
adoCommand.Parameters.Append adoParam
```

```
Set adoCommand.ActiveConnection = adoConnect
Set adoRecordset = adoCommand.Execute
```

I'll take a look at the property of the `Parameters` collection now.

Parameters Collection Property

The `Parameters` collection has only one property: `Count`.

Count

The `Count` property holds the number of `Parameter` objects in the collection. Note that when you append `Parameter` objects to this collection using its `Append` method, the `Count` property is incremented.

Parameters Collection Methods

The `Parameters` collection has four methods: `Append`, `Delete`, `Item`, and `Refresh`.

Append

You use the `Parameters` collection's `Append` method to append a new parameter to the collection. Here's how you use this method:

```
Parameters.Append ParameterObject
```

You pass only one item to this method: the `Parameter` object you want to append to the `Parameters` collection.

Delete

You use the `Delete` method to delete a `Parameter` object in the `Parameters` collection. Here's how you use this method:

```
Parameters.Delete Index
```

The `Index` parameter can hold either the numeric index of the parameter to delete, or the name of the parameter (as specified by its `Name` property).

Item

The `Item` method returns a `Parameter` object from the `Parameters` collection. Here's how you use this method:

```
Set ParameterObject = Parameters.Item (Index)
```

The `Index` parameter can hold either the numeric index of the parameter to get, or the name of the parameter (as specified by its `Name` property).

Refresh

The `Refresh` method refreshes the `Parameter` objects in the `Parameters` collection. This method takes no parameters. This method actually queries the data source for parameters, so keep in mind that it can take time to complete the round trip to the server.

That's it for the `Parameters` collection; I'll take a look at the `Fields` collection in detail next.

The Fields Collection

The `Fields` collection holds a 0-based collection of all the `Field` objects of a `Recordset` object. We've already seen that there are a variety of ways of working with the `Field` objects in the `Fields` collection, like this:

```
adoRecordset.Fields(1).Value = "Nancy"
adoRecordset("Name") = "Nancy"
adoRecordset.Fields(1) = "Nancy"
adoRecordset.Fields("Name") = "Nancy"
adoRecordset!Name = "Nancy"
```

. . . .

I'll take a look at the `Fields` collection's property first.

Fields Collection Property

The `Fields` collection has one property: `Count`.

Count

As with other collections, the `Count` property holds the number of items in the collection; in this case, the number of `Field` objects in the `Fields` collection.

Fields Collection Methods

The `Fields` collection has four methods: `Append`, `Delete`, `Item`, and `Refresh`.

Append

You use the `Append` method to append a `Field` object to the `Fields` collection when creating a recordset. Here's how you use this method:

`Fields.Append Name, Type [, DefinedSize [, Attrib]]`

Here are the parameters you pass to this method:

- **Name**—The name of the new `Field` object, which must not be the same name as any other object in the `Fields` collection.
- **Type**—A `DataType` enumeration value (see below), whose default value is `adEmpty`. This specifies the data type of the new field.
- **DefinedSize**—The defined size, in characters or bytes, of the new field. The default value for this parameter is derived from `Type`.
- **Attrib**—A `FieldAttribute` enumeration value (see below), whose default value is `adFldDefault`. Specifies attributes for the new field.

Here are the possible values for the `Type` parameter:

- **adArray**—Joined in a logical OR together with another type to indicate that the data is a safe array of that type (`DBTYPE_ARRAY`).
- **adBigInt**—An 8-byte signed integer (`DBTYPE_I8`).
- **adBinary**—A binary value (`DBTYPE_BYTES`).
- **adBoolean**—A Boolean value (`DBTYPE_BOOL`).
- **adByRef**—Joined in a logical OR together with another type to indicate that the data is a pointer to data of the other type (`DBTYPE_BYREF`).

- **adBSTR**—A null-terminated character string (Unicode) (DBTYPE_BSTR).

- **adChar**—A string value (DBTYPE_STR).

- **adCurrency**—A currency value (DBTYPE_CY). Currency is a fixed-point number with 4 digits to the right of the decimal point. It is stored in an 8-byte signed integer scaled by 10,000.

- **adDate**—A date value (DBTYPE_DATE). A date is stored as a double, the whole part of which is the number of days since December 30, 1899, and the fractional part of which is the fraction of a day.

- **adDBDate**—A date value (*yyyymmdd*) (DBTYPE_DBDATE).

- **adDBTime**—A time value (*hhmmss*) (DBTYPE_DBTIME).

- **adDBTimeStamp**—A date- and timestamp (*yyyymmddhhmmss,* plus a fraction in billionths) (DBTYPE_DBTIMESTAMP).

- **adDecimal**—An exact numeric value with a fixed precision and scale (DBTYPE_DECIMAL).

- **adDouble**—A double-precision, floating point value (DBTYPE_R8).

- **adEmpty**—(default) No value was specified (DBTYPE_EMPTY).

- **adError**—A 32-bit error code (DBTYPE_ERROR).

- **adGUID**—A globally unique identifier (GUID) (DBTYPE_GUID).

- **adIDispatch**—A pointer to an IDispatch interface on an OLE object (DBTYPE_IDISPATCH).

- **adInteger**—A 4-byte signed integer (DBTYPE_I4).

- **adIUnknown**—A pointer to an IUnknown interface on an OLE object (DBTYPE_IUNKNOWN).

- **adLongVarBinary**—A long binary value.

- **adLongVarChar**—A long string value.

- **adLongVarWChar**—A long, null-terminated string value.

- **adNumeric**—An exact numeric value with a fixed precision and scale (DBTYPE_NUMERIC).

- **adSingle**—A single-precision, floating point value (DBTYPE_R4).

- **adSmallInt**—A 2-byte signed integer (DBTYPE_I2).

- **adTinyInt**—A 1-byte signed integer (DBTYPE_I1).

- **adUnsignedBigInt**—An 8-byte unsigned integer (DBTYPE_UI8).

- **adUnsignedInt**—A 4-byte unsigned integer (DBTYPE_UI4).

- **adUnsignedSmallInt**—A 2-byte unsigned integer (DBTYPE_UI2).

- **adUnsignedTinyInt**—A 1-byte unsigned integer (DBTYPE_UI1).

- **adUserDefined**—A user-defined variable (DBTYPE_UDT).

- **adVarBinary**—A binary value.

- **adVarChar**—A string value.

- **adVariant**—An automation variant (DBTYPE_VARIANT).
- **adVector**—Joined in a logical OR together with another type to indicate that the data is a DBVECTOR structure, as defined by OLE DB, that contains a count of elements and a pointer to data of the other type (DBTYPE_VECTOR).
- **adVarWChar**—A null-terminated, Unicode character string (Parameter object only).
- **adWChar**—A null-terminated, Unicode character string (DBTYPE_WSTR).

Here are the possible values for the Attrib parameter:

- **adCacheDeferred**—Can defer operations.
- **adFixed**—Field is fixed.
- **adIsNullable**—Field may be set to null.
- **adKeyColumn**—Field is a key column.
- **adLong**—Field is a long integer.
- **adMayBeNull**—Field may be null.
- **adMayDefer**—May defer operations.
- **adNegativeScale**—Field can use a negative scale.
- **adRowID**—Field is a row ID field.
- **adRowVersion**—Field is a row version field.
- **adUnknown**—Field is an unknown type.
- **adUnknownUpdatable**—Field is an unknown, updatable type.
- **adUnspecified**—Field is unspecified.

We've already seen how to use the Fields collection's Append method in the previous chapter when building a recordset, like this:

```
Set adoRecordset = New ADODB.Recordset


adoRecordset.Fields.Append "Name", adVarChar, _
    60
adoRecordset.Fields.Append "Address", _
    adVarChar, 200
    .
    .
    .
```

Note that you cannot use this method on an open Recordset object unless you're using a client-side cursor.

Delete

You use the `Delete` method to remove a `Field` object from the `Fields` collection. Here's how you use this method:

```
Fields.Delete Index
```

The `Index` parameter can hold either the numeric index of the field to delete, or the name of the field (as specified by its `Name` property).

Item

The `Item` method returns a `Field` object from the `Fields` collection. Here's how you use this method:

```
Set FieldObject = Fields.Item (Index)
```

The `Index` parameter can hold either the numeric index of the field to get, or the name of the field (as specified by its `Name` property).

Refresh

The `Refresh` method refreshes the `Field` objects in the `Fields` collection. This method takes no parameters. Note that this method may not work well with all providers; if you don't get any results using `Refresh`, try `Requery` instead.

That's it for the `Fields` collection. Next, I'll take a look at `Error` objects and the `Errors` collection.

The Error Object

The `Error` object holds the details about data access errors involving the provider. You use `On Error GoTo` statements to handle ADO errors (see Table 3.1 for a list of ADO errors); `Error` objects are for provider-specific errors.

When a provider error occurs, it is placed in the `Errors` collection of the `Connection` object. ADO supports the return of multiple errors by a single ADO operation to allow for error information specific to the provider. To obtain this information in an error handler, you use loops to loop over the properties of each `Error` object in the `Errors` collection. Note that if there is no valid `Connection` object, you will need to retrieve error information from the Visual Basic `Err` object.

I'll go over the properties of the `Error` object first (it has no methods or events), followed by the properties and methods of the `Errors` collection, and then I'll put them both to work.

Error Object Properties

The `Error` object has seven properties: `Description`, `HelpContext`, `HelpFile`, `NativeError`, `Number`, `Source`, and `SQLState`. I'll take a look at each one here.

Description

The `Description` property is the default property for the `Error` object, which means you can omit it. This property holds a description of the error that occurred. I'll put this property to work in an example in a few pages.

HelpContext

The `HelpContext` property holds the ContextID in the Help file, or 0 if there is no Help context. You use this property if you open the Help file for the application, passing this value to the Help functions.

HelpFile

This property holds the name of the Help file, if there is one. You use this property if you open the Help file for the application, passing this value to the Help functions.

NativeError

This property holds the provider-specific error code for the error. This property can often provide more detailed information than the corresponding ADO error. For example, if there's an error in a stored procedure, this property can let you know exactly what happened.

Number

This property holds the ADO error number. For a list of the ADO errors by number, see Table 3.1. Note that if ADO can't figure the error out, you'll just find a generic error number stored here.

Source

This property holds the name of the object or application that originally generated an error. If the error was an ADO error, this name will be of the form `ADODB.Object`.

SQLState

This property holds a five-character error code that the provider returns when an error occurs during the processing of an SQL statement. These codes are standardized by groups like the SQL Access Group.

That finishes the `Error` object's properties; next, I'll take a look at the `Errors` collection.

The Errors Collection

Because a provider can return multiple errors, you usually work with the `Errors` collection, a collection of `Error` objects. Usually, you call the `Errors` collection's `Clear` method to clear the collection, then undertake sensitive operations. After each such operation, you can check the `Errors` collection's `Count` property to see if any errors were generated.

I'll take a look at the `Errors` collection's property and methods next.

Errors Collection Property

The `Errors` collection has one property: `Count`.

Count

As with other collections, the `Count` property holds the number of items in the collection; in this case, the number of `Error` objects in the `Errors` collection. You can use this property to loop over all the errors in the collection. This is the property to check if an operation has generated any errors in the `Errors` collection.

Errors Collection Methods

The `Errors` collection has two methods: `Clear` and `Item`.

Clear

You use the `Clear` method to clear the `Errors` collection of any `Error` objects. This method takes no parameters. You should use this method before undertaking sensitive operations, because you can check if any errors have been added to the collection after the operation.

Item

The `Item` method returns an `Error` object from the `Errors` collection. Here's how you use this method:

```
Set ErrorObject = Errors.Item (Index)
```

The `Index` parameter holds the numeric index of the `Error` object to get.

That's it for the details of the `Error` object and the `Errors` collection. I'll put these two to work in an example next.

Using the Errors Collection

Here's an example showing how to use `Error` objects and the `Errors` collection. First, I'll start by turning error handling on:

```
Private Sub Form_Load()


    On Error GoTo ErrHandler

    .

    .

    .


```

Next, I create a new `Connection` object and clear its `Errors` collection, then connect to a database, `Biblio.mdb`:

```
Set adoConnect = New Connection

adoConnect.Errors.Clear

adoConnect.Open _
"PROVIDER=Microsoft.Jet.OLEDB.3.51;" & _
"Data Source=C:\ado\Biblio.mdb;", , , _
adConnectAsync

    .

    .

    .

```

Now I connect to the `Publishers` table in the `Biblio` database:

```
Set adoRecordset = New Recordset

adoRecordset.Open "select * from Publisher", &
adoConnect, adOpenStatic, adLockOptimistic
```

```
Set Text1.DataSource = adoRecordset

Text1.DataField = "Name"

Set Text2.DataSource = adoRecordset

Text2.DataField = "Address"


Exit Sub

.

.

.
```

You may not have noticed it, but I asked ADO to connect to the Publisher table (not Publishers), which doesn't exist. I handle errors like this by looping over the Errors collection and displaying errors in a message box from the error handler, like this:

```
ErrHandler:


If adoConnect.Errors.Count > 0 Then

    For Each objError In adoConnect.Errors

        MsgBox "Error: " & _

        adoConnect.Errors(0).Description

    Next

End If

End


End Sub
```

The result appears in Figure 9.1, where you can see the error returned by the Jet engine, indicating that it could not find the table I specified.

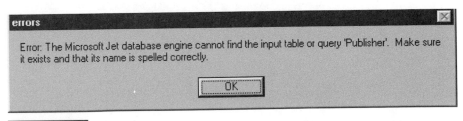

errors

Error: The Microsoft Jet database engine cannot find the input table or query 'Publisher'. Make sure it exists and that its name is spelled correctly.

OK

FIGURE 9.1   Catching errors.

The code for this example, `errors.frm`, appears in Listing 9.1. This example appears in the `errors` folder on the CD.

LISTING 9.1 *Errors.frm Code*

```
VERSION 5.00
Begin VB.Form Form1
    BorderStyle     =   3   'Fixed Dialog
    Caption         =   "Publishers"
    ClientHeight    =   1935
    ClientLeft      =   1095
    ClientTop       =   330
    ClientWidth     =   5550
    LinkTopic       =   "Form3"
    MaxButton       =   0   'False
    MinButton       =   0   'False
    ScaleHeight     =   1935
    ScaleWidth      =   5550
    ShowInTaskbar   =   0   'False
    Begin VB.CommandButton cmdLast
        Caption     =   "Last >>"
        Height      =   495
        Left        =   4200
        TabIndex    =   7
        Top         =   1200
        Width       =   1215
    End
    Begin VB.CommandButton cmdNext
        Caption     =   "Next >"
        Height      =   495
        Left        =   2880
        TabIndex    =   6
        Top         =   1200
        Width       =   1215
    End
    Begin VB.CommandButton cmdPrevious
        Caption     =   "< Previous"
        Height      =   495
        Left        =   1560
        TabIndex    =   5
        Top         =   1200
        Width       =   1215
    End
    Begin VB.CommandButton cmdFirst
        Caption     =   "<< First"
        Height      =   495
        Left        =   240
        TabIndex    =   4
        Top         =   1200
        Width       =   1215
    End
```

```
    Begin VB.TextBox Text2
        Height          =       375
        Left            =       1320
        TabIndex        =       2
        Text            =       "Text2"
        Top             =       600
        Width           =       3855
    End
    Begin VB.TextBox Text1
        Height          =       375
        Left            =       1320
        TabIndex        =       1
        Text            =       "Text1"
        Top             =       120
        Width           =       3855
    End
    Begin VB.Label lblLabels
        Caption         =       "Publisher:"
        Height          =       255
        Index           =       0
        Left            =       120
        TabIndex        =       3
        Top             =       120
        Width           =       1095
    End
    Begin VB.Label lblLabels
        Caption         =       "Address:"
        Height          =       255
        Index           =       1
        Left            =       120
        TabIndex        =       0
        Top             =       600
        Width           =       1095
    End
End
Attribute VB_Name = "Form1"
Attribute VB_GlobalNameSpace = False
Attribute VB_Creatable = False
Attribute VB_PredeclaredId = True
Attribute VB_Exposed = False
Private adoRecordset As ADODB.Recordset
Attribute adoRecordset.VB_VarHelpID = -1
Private adoConnect As Connection
Attribute adoConnect.VB_VarHelpID = -1
Private adoCommand As Command
Attribute adoCommand.VB_VarHelpID = -1

Private Sub Form_Load()

    On Error GoTo ErrHandler

    Set adoConnect = New Connection
```

```
        adoConnect.Errors.Clear

        adoConnect.Open _
        "PROVIDER=Microsoft.Jet.OLEDB.3.51;" & _
        "Data Source=C:\ado\Biblio.mdb;", , , adConnectAsync

        Set adoRecordset = New Recordset

        adoRecordset.Open "select * from Publisher", &
        adoConnect, adOpenStatic, adLockOptimistic

        Set Text1.DataSource = adoRecordset
        Text1.DataField = "Name"
        Set Text2.DataSource = adoRecordset
        Text2.DataField = "Address"

        Exit Sub
    ErrHandler:

        If adoConnect.Errors.Count > 0 Then
            For Each objError In adoConnect.Errors
                MsgBox "Error: " & _
                adoConnect.Errors(0).Description
            Next
        End If
        End

End Sub

Private Sub cmdFirst_Click()
    On Error GoTo ErrLabel

    adoRecordset.MoveFirst

    Exit Sub

ErrLabel:
    MsgBox Err.Description
End Sub

Private Sub cmdLast_Click()
    On Error GoTo ErrLabel

    adoRecordset.MoveLast

    Exit Sub

ErrLabel:
    MsgBox Err.Description
End Sub

Private Sub cmdNext_Click()
```

```
      On Error GoTo ErrLabel

   If Not adoRecordset.EOF Then
           adoRecordset.MoveNext
   End If

   If adoRecordset.EOF And adoRecordset.RecordCount > 0 Then
       adoRecordset.MoveLast
   End If

   Exit Sub

ErrLabel:
   MsgBox Err.Description
End Sub

Private Sub cmdPrevious_Click()
   On Error GoTo ErrLabel

   If Not adoRecordset.BOF Then adoRecordset.MovePrevious
   If adoRecordset.BOF And adoRecordset.RecordCount > 0 Then
       adoRecordset.MoveFirst
   End If

   Exit Sub

ErrLabel:
   MsgBox Err.Description
End Sub
```

Note that some operations return warnings that appear as `Error` objects in the `Errors` collection, but do not stop a program from executing. For example, before you call the `Resync`, `UpdateBatch`, or `CancelBatch` methods on a `Recordset` object, the `Open` method on a `Connection` object, or set the `Filter` property on a `Recordset` object, you should call the `Clear` method on the `Errors` collection, so you can check the `Count` property of the `Errors` collection to test for warnings.

Now I'll start taking a look at the big collection in this chapter—the `Properties` collection, which supports dynamic properties in ADO programming.

ADO Dynamic Properties

ADO objects have two types of properties: built-in and dynamic. Built-in properties are implemented in ADO and immediately available in any new object, using the `Object.Property` syntax. They do not appear as

Property objects in an object's Properties collection, so although you can change their values, you cannot modify their characteristics.

Dynamic properties are defined by the underlying data provider, and appear in the Properties collection for the appropriate ADO object. For example, a property specific to a provider may indicate if a Recordset object supports transactions or updating. These additional properties will appear as Property objects in that Recordset object's Properties collection. Dynamic properties can be referenced only through the collection, using the syntax Object.Properties(0) or Object.Properties("Name"). ADO Connection, Recordset, Command, Field, and Parameter objects all have a Properties collection.

Some dynamic properties hold strings, some hold Boolean values, some hold long values, some hold special enumeration values, and so on. For example, to check if you can compare bookmarks in a recordset directly, you can examine the Literal Bookmarks Boolean dynamic property, like this:

```
If DataEnvironment1.rsCommand1.Properties( _
    "Literal Bookmarks") Then
    strMsg = strMsg & "Literal bookmarks " & _
        are supported" & vbCrLf
Else
    strMsg = strMsg & "Literal bookmarks " & _
        are not supported" & vbCrLf
End If


MsgBox strMsg
```

Each dynamic property is accessed using a Property object in the Properties collection, and I'll take a look at the Property object first.

The Property Object

A Property object represents a dynamic property of an ADO object defined by the provider. A dynamic Property object has four built-in properties of its own: Attributes, Name, Type, and Value. I'll take a look at these properties here.

Attributes

As you might expect, this property holds attributes about a property; for example, whether or not the property is supported by the provider. The

`Attributes` property is read-only, and its value can be the sum of any one or more of these values:

- **adPropNotSupported**—Indicates that the provider does not support the property.
- **adPropRequired**—Indicates that the user must specify a value for this property before the data source is initialized.
- **adPropOptional**—Indicates that the user does not need to specify a value for this property before the data source is initialized.
- **adPropRead**—Indicates that the user can read the property.
- **adPropWrite**—Indicates that the user can set the property.

Type

The `Type` property holds the data type of the property (that is, some dynamic properties hold string values, some hold Boolean values, and so on). Here are the possible settings for this property:

- **adArray**—Joined in a logical OR together with another type to indicate that the data is a safe array of that type (DBTYPE_ARRAY).
- **adBigInt**—An 8-byte signed integer (DBTYPE_I8).
- **adBinary**—A binary value (DBTYPE_BYTES).
- **adBoolean**—A Boolean value (DBTYPE_BOOL).
- **adByRef**—Joined in a logical OR together with another type to indicate that the data is a pointer to data of the other type (DBTYPE_BYREF).
- **adBSTR**—A null-terminated character string (Unicode) (DBTYPE_BSTR).
- **adChar**—A string value (DBTYPE_STR).
- **adCurrency**—A currency value (DBTYPE_CY). Currency is a fixed-point number with 4 digits to the right of the decimal point. It is stored in an 8-byte signed integer scaled by 10,000.
- **adDate**—A date value (DBTYPE_DATE). A date is stored as a double, the whole part of which is the number of days since December 30, 1899, and the fractional part of which is the fraction of a day.
- **adDBDate**—A date value (*yyyymmdd*) (DBTYPE_DBDATE).
- **adDBTime**—A time value (*hhmmss*) (DBTYPE_DBTIME).
- **adDBTimeStamp**—A date- and timestamp (*yyyymmddhhmmss,* plus a fraction in billionths) (DBTYPE_DBTIMESTAMP).
- **adDecimal**—An exact numeric value with a fixed precision and scale (DBTYPE_DECIMAL).
- **adDouble**—A double-precision, floating point value (DBTYPE_R8).
- **adEmpty**—No value was specified (DBTYPE_EMPTY).

- **adError**—A 32-bit error code (DBTYPE_ERROR).

- **adGUID**—A globally unique identifier (GUID) (DBTYPE_GUID).

- **adIDispatch**—A pointer to an IDispatch interface on an OLE object (DBTYPE_IDISPATCH).

- **adInteger**—A 4-byte signed integer (DBTYPE_I4).

- **adIUnknown**—A pointer to an IUnknown interface on an OLE object (DBTYPE_IUNKNOWN).

- **adLongVarBinary**—A long binary value (Parameter object only).

- **adLongVarChar**—A long string value (Parameter object only).

- **adLongVarWChar**—A long, null-terminated string value (Parameter object only).

- **adNumeric**—An exact numeric value with a fixed precision and scale (DBTYPE_NUMERIC).

- **adSingle**—A single-precision, floating point value (DBTYPE_R4).

- **adSmallInt**—A 2-byte signed integer (DBTYPE_I2).

- **adTinyInt**—A 1-byte signed integer (DBTYPE_I1).

- **adUnsignedBigInt**—An 8-byte unsigned integer (DBTYPE_UI8).

- **adUnsignedInt**—A 4-byte unsigned integer (DBTYPE_UI4).

- **adUnsignedSmallInt**—A 2-byte unsigned integer (DBTYPE_UI2).

- **adUnsignedTinyInt**—A 1-byte unsigned integer (DBTYPE_UI1).

- **adUserDefined**—A user-defined variable (DBTYPE_UDT).

- **adVarBinary**—A binary value (Parameter object only).

- **adVarChar**—A string value (Parameter object only).

- **adVariant**—An automation variant (DBTYPE_VARIANT).

- **adVector**—Joined in a logical OR together with another type to indicate that the data is a DBVECTOR structure, as defined by OLE DB, that contains a count of elements and a pointer to data of the other type (DBTYPE_VECTOR).

- **adVarWChar**—A null-terminated, Unicode character string (Parameter object only).

- **adWChar**—A null-terminated, Unicode character string (DBTYPE_WSTR).

Name

The Name property holds the name of the property. For example, here's how to display a message box indicating the name of the first dynamic property in the Properties collection:

```
MsgBox DataEnviron1.rsCommand1.Properties(0).Name
```

Value

This property holds the actual setting of the dynamic property. This is the default property of the `Property` object, so these two lines of code do the same thing—assign a value of True to the first property in the `Properties` collection:

```
DataEnviron1.rsCommand1.Properties(0).Value = True
DataEnviron1.rsCommand1.Properties(0) = True
```

That's it for the `Property` object; I'll take a look at the `Properties` collection next.

The Properties Collection

The `Properties` collection is a 0-based collection of `Property` objects, each of which supports a dynamic property. ADO `Connection`, `Recordset`, `Command`, `Field`, and `Parameter` objects all have a `Properties` collection. This collection itself has properties and methods, such as the `Count` property, which holds the number of `Property` objects in the `Properties` collection. I'll take a look at the property of this collection first.

Properties Collection Property

The `Properties` collection has one property: `Count`.

Count

As with other collections, the `Count` property holds the number of items in the collection; in this case, the number of `Property` objects in the Properties collection.

Properties Collection Methods

The `Properties` collection has two methods: `Item` and `Refresh`.

Item

The `Item` method returns a `Property` object from the `Properties` collection. Here's how you use this method:

```
Set PropertyObject = Properties.Item (Index)
```

The `Index` parameter can hold either the numeric index of the `Property` object to get, or the name of the `Property` object (as specified by its `Name` property).

Refresh

The `Refresh` method refreshes the `Property` objects in the `Properties` collection. This method takes no parameters.

That completes the `Property` object and `Properties` collection in overview. I'll take a look at the current dynamic properties in ADO next, starting with the `Connection` object. There are a lot of dynamic properties, so some pretty big tables are coming up. After taking a look at what dynamic properties there are, I'll put them to work in an example.

Connection Object Dynamic Properties

The list of dynamic properties for the `Connection` object is being added to all the time, but you'll find the current ones in Table 9.1. Note that the enumeration values in Table 9.1, like `DBPROPVAL_ASYNCH`, are listed in Table 9.4.

Recordset Object Dynamic Properties

The current recordset dynamic properties appear in Table 9.2 (note that there are more being added all the time, so this list is probably already incomplete). Besides the dynamic properties in Table 9.2, the `Recordset` object also supports the names of COM interfaces like `IColumnsRowset` as Boolean dynamic properties; if one of these properties is set to True, the corresponding interface is supported. Note also that the enumeration values in Table 9.2, like `DBPROPVAL_ASYNCH`, are listed in Table 9.4.

Field Object Dynamic Properties

The current dynamic properties for the `Field` object appear in Table 9.3 (note that more are being added all the time). These dynamic properties look a little different than the ones we've seen, because they're all one word and in capital letters. The values for the `DB_SEARCHABLE` enumeration that appears in Table 9.3 are listed in Table 9.4.

Dynamic Property Enumeration Values

As you can see in Tables 9.1, 9.2, and 9.3, many dynamic properties store and return enumerated values. Those enumerated types and their possible values appear in Table 9.4.

TABLE 9.1	Connection object dynamic properties
Property	**Description**
Accessible Procedures	Boolean specifying accessible procedures.
Accessible Tables	Boolean specifying accessible tables.
Active Sessions	Long specifying maximum number of sessions.
Active Statements	Long specifying maximum number of statements.
Application Name	String holding the application name.
Asynchable Abort	Boolean indicating if transactions can be aborted asynchronously.
Asynchable Commit	Boolean indicating if transactions can be committed asynchronously.
Asynchronous Processing	DBPROPVAL_ASYNCH value indicating asynchronous processing on a rowset.
Auto Translate	Boolean specifying if OEM/ANSI character translation will be used.
Autocommit Isolation Level	DBPROPVAL_OS value specifying the isolation level while in auto-commit.
Cache Authentication	Boolean indicating if the cache can hold authentication information.
Catalog Location	DBPROPVAL_CL value specifying the position of the catalog name in a table name in text commands.
Catalog Term	String holding the name the provider uses for a catalog.
Catalog Usage	DBPROPVAL_CU value specifying how catalog names are used in commands.
Column Definition	DBPROPVAL_CD value specifying valid clauses for column definition.
Connect Timeout	Long holding the number of seconds to wait before the connection times out.
Connection Status	DBPROPVAL_CS specifying the current status.
Current Catalog	String holding the name of the current catalog.
Current Language	Boolean specifying language used for system messages.
Data Source	String holding the name of the data source to connect to.
Data Source Name	String holding a data source's ODBC DSN.
Data Source Object Threading Model	DBPROPVAL_RT value indicating the threading model.
DBMS Name	String holding the name of the database application the provider interfaces to.
DBMS Version	String holding the version of the database application the provider interfaces to.
Driver Name	String specifying the ODBC driver.
Driver ODBC Version	String holding the driver version.

TABLE 9.1   *(Continued)*

Property	Description
Driver Version	String holding the driver version.
Encrypt Password	Boolean specifying if the provider requires encrypted passwords.
Extended Properties	String holding provider-specific extended information.
File Usage	Long specifying the usage count of the ODBC driver.
GROUP BY Support	DBPROPVAL_BG value specifying the relationship of columns in a GROUP BY clause and non-aggregated columns.
Heterogenous Table Support	DBPROPVAL_HT value specifying if the provider allows joins from different catalogs.
Identifier Case	DBPROPVAL_IC value specifying how identifiers handle case sensitivity.
Initial Catalog	String holding the name of the initial catalog to connect to.
Integrated Security	String holding the name of the authentication service the provider uses.
Integrity Enhancement Facility	Boolean specifying if the provider supports the Integrity Enhancement Facility.
Isolation Levels	DBPROPVAL_TI value specifying supported levels of isolation.
Isolation Retention	DBPROPVAL_TR value specifying the supported levels of isolation retention.
Jet OLEDB:Compact Without Replica Repair	Boolean specifying if compact operations should use replica repair.
Jet OLEDB:Create System Database	Boolean specifying creation of the system database.
Jet OLEDB:Database Password	String holding the password for the database.
Jet OLEDB:Don't Copy Locale on Compact	Boolean specifying if the locale should be copied during compact operations.
Jet OLEDB:Encrypt Database	Boolean specifying if the database should use encryption.
Jet OLEDB:Engine Type	String holding the Jet engine type.
Jet OLEDB:Global Bulk Transactions	Boolean specifying if global bulk transactions are supported.
Jet OLEDB:Global Partial Bulk Ops	Boolean specifying if partial values are allowed in bulk operations.
Jet OLEDB:New Database Password	String holding new database password.
Jet OLEDB:Registry Path	String holding the Jet engine's Registry key.
Jet OLEDB:System Database	String holding the path and name of the Jet workgroup file.
LIKE Escape Clause	String specifying the SQL LIKE escape clause.
Locale Identifier	Long specifying the locale ID.

TABLE 9.1	(Continued)

Property	Description
Location	String holding the location of the data source.
Log Text And Image Writes	Boolean specifying whether text and image writes are logged.
Mask Password	Boolean specifying if password should be sent in masked form.
Max Columns in GROUP BY	Long specifying the maximum number of columns in a GROUP BY clause.
Max Columns in Index	Long specifying the maximum number of columns in an index.
Max Columns in ORDER BY	Long specifying the maximum number of columns in an ORDER BY clause.
Max Columns in SELECT	Long specifying the maximum number of columns in a SELECT clause.
Max Columns in Table	Long specifying the maximum number of columns in a table.
Maximum Blob Length	Long specifying the maximum BLOB (binary long object, such as an image) field size.
Maximum Index Size	Long specifying the maximum number of bytes in an index.
Maximum Open Chapters	Long specifying the maximum number of open chapters.
Maximum OR Conditions	Long specifying the maximum number of conditions in an OR clause.
Maximum Row Size	Long specifying the maximum size of a row.
Maximum Row Size Includes BLOB	Long specifying the maximum row size, including BLOBs.
Maximum Sort Columns	Long specifying the maximum number of columns that may be used in a view sort.
Maximum Tables in SELECT	Long specifying the maximum number of tables you can use in a SELECT statement.
Mode	DB_MODE value specifying access permissions.
Multiple Connections	Boolean specifying if the provider supports multiple connections.
Multiple Parameter Sets	Boolean indicating if the provider supports multiple parameter sets.
Multiple Results	DBPROPVAL_MR value specifying if the provider supports multiple result objects.
Multiple Storage Objects	Boolean specifying if the provider supports multiple storage objects.
Multi-Table Update	Boolean specifying if the provider supports multi-table updates.
Network Address	String holding the network address of SQL Server.
Network Library	String specifying the Net-Library DLL used to connect to SQL Server.
NULL Collation Order	DBPROPVAL_NC value specifying the NULL collation order.
NULL Concatenation Behavior	DBPROPVAL_CB value specifying how the provider handles concatenation of NULL columns.

TABLE 9.1	*(Continued)*
Property	**Description**
Numeric Functions	SQL_FN_NUM value specifying the numeric functions supported.
OLE DB Services	DBPROPVAL_OS value specifying OLE DB services.
OLE DB Version	String holding the OLE DB version used by the provider.
OLE Object Support	DBPROPVAL_OO value specifying the provider's OLE object support.
ORDER BY Columns in SELECT List	Boolean specifying if the columns used in an ORDER BY clause must be in the SELECT list.
Outer Join Capabilities	SQL_OJ value specifying the support for outer joins.
Outer Joins	Boolean specifying if the provider supports outer joins.
Output Parameter Availability	DBPROPVAL_OA specifying when output parameters will be available.
Packet Size	Long specifying the size of network packets.
Pass By Ref Accessors	Boolean specifying if the provider supports the DBACCESSOR_PASSBYREF flag.
Password	String holding the connection password.
Persist Encrypted	Boolean specifying if the provider should persist encrypted authentication information.
Persist Security Info	Boolean specifying if the provider should persist encrypted security information.
Persistent ID Type	DBPROPVAL_PT value specifying the type of DBID the provider uses.
Prepare Abort Behavior	DBPROPVAL_CB value specifying how aborts affect prepared (compiled) commands.
Prepare Commit Behavior	DBPROPVAL_CB value spcifying how commits affect prepared (compiled) commands.
Procedure Term	String holding the name the provider uses for procedures.
Prompt	DBPROMPT value specifying if the provider should prompt during initialization.
Protection Level	DB_PROT_LEVEL value specifying the level of protection.
Provider Friendly Name	String holding the provider's friendly name.
Provider Name	String holding the provider file name.
Provider Version	String holding the provider version.
Quoted Identifier Sensitivity	DBPROPVAL_IC value specifying how quoted identifiers handle case.
Read-Only Data Source	Boolean specifying if the data source is read-only.
Reset Data Source	DBPROPVAL_RD value specifying the data source state you want to reset.
Rowset Conversions on Command	Boolean specifying if callers can query on conversions.

TABLE 9.1 *(Continued)*	
Property	**Description**
Schema Term	String holding the name the provider uses for the term schema.
Schema Usage	DBPROPVAL_SU specifies how you can use schemas.
Server Name	String holding the server's name.
Sort on Index	Boolean specifying if the provider only supports sorting on index columns.
Special Characters	String holding the special characters in the data source.
SQL Grammar Support	Long identifying the SQL grammar support (0 = none, 1 = level 1, 2 = level 2).
SQL Support	DBPROPVAL_SQL value specifying the SQL support.
SQLOLE Execute a SET TEXTLENGTH	Boolean specifying if the provider executes a SET TEXTLENGTH command before using BLOBs.
Stored Procedures	Boolean indicating if stored procedures are supported.
String Functions	SQL_FN_STR value indicating if string functions are supported.
Structured Storage	DBPROPVAL_SS value specifying what structured storage is available.
Subquery Support	DBPROPVAL_SQ value specifying the level of subquery support.
System Functions	SQL_FN_SYS value specifying the system functions.
Table Term	String holding the name the provider uses for tables.
Time/Date Functions	SQL_SDF_CURRENT value specifying the supported time/date functions.
Transaction DDL	DBPROPVAL_TC value specifying if Data Definition Language statements are supported.
Use Procedure for Prepare	SSPROPVAL_UP value specifying if the provider uses temporary stored procedures for prepared statements.
User Authentication Mode	Boolean specifying if Windows NT authentication is used with SQL Server.
User ID	String holding the user's ID.
User Name	String holding the user name.
Window Handle	Long holding the window handle the provider should use for prompts.
Workstation ID	String holding the workstation ID.

TABLE 9.2	Recordset object dynamic properties
Property	**Description**
Access Order	DBPROPVAL_AO specifying the order in which columns must be accessed.
Append Only Rowset	Boolean specifying if you can create append-only rowsets.
Asynchronous Rowset Processing	DBPROPVAL_ASYNCH value specifying asynchronous processing on the recordset.
Auto Recalc	Integer specifying if chaptered recordsets using COMPUTE automatically recalculate results.
Background Thread Priority	Integer holding the priority of background threads.
Batch Size	Integer holding the number of rows in a batch.
BLOB Accessibility on Forward-Only Cursor	Boolean specifying if BLOB columns can be accessed no matter what their column position.
Blocking Storage Objects	Boolean specifying if storage objects may prevent some methods from operating.
Bookmark Information	DBPROPVAL_BI value that specifies additional bookmark information.
Bookmark Type	DBPROPVAL_BMK value that specifies the bookmark type supported.
Bookmarkable	Boolean specifying if bookmarks are supported.
Bookmarks Ordered	Boolean specifying if you can compare bookmarks based on ordering.
Bulk Operations	DBPROPVAL_BO value specifying bulk operation optimizations.
Cache Child Rows	Boolean specifying whether child rows in a chapter are cached.
Cache Deferred Columns	Boolean specifying if the provider caches deferred columns.
Change Inserted Rows	Boolean specifying if you can update or delete new rows.
Column Privileges	Boolean specifying if access privileges are granted column by column.
Column Set Notification	DBPROPVAL_NP value specifying if you can cancel changing a column set.
Column Writable	Boolean specifying if a column is writeable.
Command Timeout	Long specifying the command timeout.
Concurrency Control Method	SSPROPVAL_CONCUR value specifying method used for concurrency for server-based cursors.
Cursor Engine Version	String specifying the cursor engine's version.
Defer Column	Boolean specifying if column data is not fetched until requested.
Delay Storage Object Updates	Boolean specifying if storage objects are used in Delayed Update mode.
Fetch Backward	Boolean specifying if a provider can fetch backward.
Filter Operations	DBPROPVAL_CO value specifying what filter operations are supported.

TABLE 9.2	*(Continued)*
Property	**Description**
Find Operations	DBPROPVAL_CO value specifying what find operations are supported.
For BROWSE Versioning Columns	Boolean specifying a rowset containing a primary key or timestamp field.
Force No Command Preparation When Executing A Parameterized Command	Boolean specifying if the provider creates stored procedures for parameterized commands.
Force No Command Reexecution When Failure To Satisfy All Required Properties	Boolean specifying if the command is reexecuted if the property settings are invalid.
Force No Parameter Rebinding When Executing Command	Boolean specifying if parameters are rebound each time command is executed.
Force SQL Server Firehose Mode Cursor	Boolean specifying if forward-only, read-only cursors are all that are allowed.
Generate A Rowset That Can Be Marshalled	Boolean specifying if the rowset can be marshalled between processes.
Hidden Columns	Boolean specifying if hidden columns are supported.
Hold Rows	Boolean specifying if you can perform operations while holding rows with pending changes.
Immobile Rows	Boolean specifying if the provider will reorder rows upon insertion.
Include SQL_FLOAT, SQL_DOUBLE, and SQL_REAL In QBU Where Clauses	Boolean specifying if you want to include these types in Where clauses.
Initial Fetch Size	Long value specifying the initial cache size.
Jet OLDB:ODBC Pass-Through Statement	String holding a pass-through SQL statement.
Jet OLEDB:Partial Bulk Ops	Boolean specifying if bulk operations will succeed if some values fail.
Jet OLEDB:Pass-Through Query Connect String	String holding the connect string.
Literal Bookmarks	Boolean specifying if you can compare bookmarks literally.
Literal Row Identity	Boolean specifying if you can compare row handles literally.
Lock Mode	DBPROPVAL_LM value specifying the lock mode.
Maximum BLOB Length	Long specifying the maximum length of a BLOB (binary long object) field.
Maximum Open Rows	Long specifying the maximum number of open (active) rows.

TABLE 9.2 *(Continued)*

Property	Description
Maximum Pending Rows	Long specifying the maximum number of rows that can have pending changes.
Maximum Rows	Long specifying the maximum number of rows for a rowset.
Memory Usage	Long specifying the amount of memory used by the rowset.
Name	Specifies a name for the Recordset object (for use with client-side cursors).
Notification Granularity	DBPROPVAL_NT value specifying when notifications occur for multiple row operations.
Notification Phases	DBPROPVAL_NP value specifying supported notification phases.
Objects Transacted	Boolean specifying if objects created are transacted.
ODBC Concurrency Type	Integer specifying the ODBC concurrency type.
ODBC Cursor Type	Integer specifying the ODBC cursor type.
Others' Changes Visible	Boolean specifying if you can see changes made by other users.
Others' Inserts Visible	Boolean specifying if you can see insertions made by other users.
Own Changes Visible	Boolean specifying if you can see your own changes.
Own Inserts Visible	Boolean specifying if you can see your own rowset insertions.
Position On The Last Row After Insert	Boolean specifying if the cursor moves to the last row after an insertion.
Preserve On Abort	Boolean specifying that a rowset will be active after a transaction is aborted.
Preserve On Commit	Boolean specifying that a rowset will be active after a transaction is committed.
Query-Based Updates/ Deletes/Inserts	Boolean specifying if you can use queries for updates/deletes/inserts.
Quick Restart	Boolean specifying if RestartPosition may be executed quickly.
Reentrant Events	Boolean specifying if calbacks are reentrant.
Remove Deleted Rows	Boolean specifying if the provider removes deleted rows.
Report Multiple Changes	Boolean specifying if multiple changes are reported.
Resync Command	String holding the Resync command.
Return Pending Inserts	Boolean indicating if pending inserts are returned.
Row Delete Notification	DBPROPVAL_NP value specifying if you can cancel deleting a row.
Row First Change Notification	DBPROPVAL_NP value specifying if changes to the first row can be cancelled.
Row Insertion Notification	DBPROPVAL_NP value specifying if you can cancel a row insertion.
Row Privileges	Boolean indicating if you can get access privileges by row.

TABLE 9.2 *(Continued)*	
Property	**Description**
Row Synchronization Notification	DBPROPVAL_NP value specifying if resynchronizing a row can be cancelled.
Row Threading Model	DBPROPVAL_RT value specifying supported threading models.
Row Undo Change Notification	DBPROPVAL_NP value specifying if you can cancel undoing a change.
Row Undo Delete Notification	DBPROPVAL_NP value specifying if you can cancel undoing a delete operation.
Row Undo Insertion Notification	DBPROPVAL_NP value specifying if you can cancel undoing an insertion operation.
Row Update Notification	DBPROPVAL_NP value specifying if you can cancel updating a row.
Rowset Fetch Position Change Notification	DBPROPVAL_NP value specifying if you can cancel changing the fetch position.
Rowset Release Notification	DBPROPVAL_NP value specifying if you can cancel releasing a rowset.
Scroll Backward	Boolean specifying if you can scroll backward.
Server Cursor	Boolean specifying if the cursor must be on the server.
Server Data On Insert	Boolean specifying if the provider updates the row cache on insertions
Skip Deleted Bookmarks	Boolean specifying if you can position a rowset if bookmarks were deleted.
Strong Row Identity	Boolean specifying if you can compare new rows' handles.
Unique Catalog	Specifies the catalog, or name, of the database containing the table.
Unique Rows	Boolean specifying if each row is uniquely identified by field values.
Unique Schema	Specifies the schema, or name, of the owner of the table.
Unique Table	Specifies the name of the one base table upon which updates, insertions, and deletions are allowed.
Updatability	DBPROPVAL_UP value specifying the supported update methods.
Update Criteria	String holding requery criteria for chaptered recordsets.
Update Operation	String holding the operation to be executed on chaptered recordsets for requeries.
Update Resync	Specifies whether the UpdateBatch method is followed by an implicit Resync method operation, and if so, the scope of that operation.
Use Bookmarks	Boolean specifying if the rowset supports bookmarks.

• • • • • • • • • • • • • • • •

TABLE 9.3	Field object dynamic properties
Property	**Description**
BASECATALOGNAME	String holding the name of the catalog.
BASECOLUMNNAME	String holding the name of the column.
BASESCHEMANAME	String holding the name of the schema.
BASETABLENAME	String holding the table name.
CALCULATIONINFO	Binary value specifying calculations for chaptered recordsets.
DATETIMEPRECISION	Long holding the number of digits in the fractional seconds of date/time fields.
ISAUTOINCREMENT	Boolean specifying if the field is an auto-increment field.
ISCASESENSITIVE	Boolean specifying if the field is case-sensitive (as when you search fields).
ISSEARCHABLE	DB_SEARCHABLE value specifying if the field is searchable.
KEYCOLUMN	Boolean specifying if the field is a key.
OCTETLENGTH	Long holding the maximum field length in bytes.
OPTIMIZE	Boolean specifying if the field's column is indexed internally in ADO.
RELATIONCONDITIONS	Binary value specifying relations between chaptered recordsets.

TABLE 9.4	Dynamic property enumeration values
Enumeration	**Members**
DB_MODE	DB_MODE_READ = 1
	DB_MODE_SHARE_EXCLUSIVE = 12
	DB_MODE_SHARE_DENY_NONE = 16
	DB_MODE_WRITE = 2
	DB_MODE_READWRITE = 3
	DB_MODE_SHARE_DENY_READ = 4
	DB_MODE_SHARE_DENY_WRITE = 8
DB_PROT_LEVEL	DB_PROT_LEVEL_NONE = 0
	DB_PROT_LEVEL_CONNECT = 1
	DB_PROT_LEVEL_CALL = 2
	DB_PROT_LEVEL_PKT = 3
	DB_PROT_LEVEL_PKT_INTEGRITY = 4
	DB_PROT_LEVEL_PKT_PRIVACY = 5
DB_SEARCHABLE	DB_UNSEARCHABLE = 1
	DB_LIKE_ONLY = 2
	DB_ALL_EXCEPT_LIKE = 3
	DB_SEARCHABLE = 4
DBPROPVAL_AO	DBPROPVAL_AO_SEQUENTIAL = 0
	DBPROPVAL_AO_SEQUENTIALSTORAGEOBJECTS = 1
	DBPROPVAL_AO_RANDOM = 2

Enumeration	Members
TABLE 9.4 *(Continued)*	
DBPROPVAL_ASYNCH	DBPROPVAL_ASYNCH_INITIALIZE = 1
	DBPROPVAL_ASYNCH_PREPOPULATE = 16
	DBPROPVAL_ASYNCH_SEQUENTIALPOPULATION = 2
	DBPROPVAL_ASYNCH_POPULATEONDEMAND = 32
	DBPROPVAL_ASYNCH_RANDOMPOPULATION = 4
	DBPROPVAL_ASYNCH_BACKGROUNDPOPULATION = 8
DBPROPVAL_BG	DBPROPVAL_BG_NOT_SUPPORTED = 1
	DBPROPVAL_BG_COLLATE = 16
	DBPROPVAL_BG_EQUALS_SELECT = 2
	DBPROPVAL_BG_CONTAINS_SELECT = 4
	DBPROPVAL_GB_NO_RELATION = 8
DBPROPVAL_BI	DBPROPVAL_BI_CROSSROWSET = 1
DBPROPVAL_BMK	DBPROPVAL_BMK_NUMERIC = 1
	DBPROPVAL_BMK_KEY = 2
DBPROPVAL_BO	DBPROPVAL_BO_NOLOG = 0
	DBPROPVAL_BO_NOINDEXUPDATE = 1
	DBPROPVAL_BO_REFINTEGRITY = 2
DBPROPVAL_CB	DBPROPVAL_CB_NULL = 1
	DBPROPVAL_CB_DELETE = 1
	DBPROPVAL_CB_NON_NULL = 2
	DBPROPVAL_CB_PRESERVE = 2
DBPROPVAL_CD	DBPROPVAL_CD_NOTNULL = 1
DBPROPVAL_CL	DBPROPVAL_CL_START = 1
	DBPROPVAL_CL_END = 2
DBPROPVAL_CO	DBPROPVAL_CO_EQUALITY = 1
	DBPROPVAL_CO_CONTAINS = 16
	DBPROPVAL_CO_STRING = 2
	DBPROPVAL_CO_BEGINSWITH = 32
	DBPROPVAL_CO_CASESENSITIVE = 4
	DBPROPVAL_CO_CASEINSENSITIVE = 8
DBPROPVAL_CS	DBPROPVAL_CS_UNINITIALIZED = 0
	DBPROPVAL_CS_INITIALIZED = 1
	DBPROPVAL_CS_COMMUNICATIONFAILURE = 2
DBPROPVAL_CU	DBPROPVAL_CU_DML_STATEMENTS = 1
	DBPROPVAL_CU_TABLE_DEFINITION = 2
	DBPROPVAL_CU_INDEX_DEFINITION = 4
	DBPROPVAL_CU_PRIVILEGE_DEFINITION = 8

TABLE 9.4 *(Continued)*

Enumeration	Members
DBPROPVAL_DF	DBPROPVAL_DF_INITIALLY_DEFERRED = 1
	DBPROPVAL_DF_INITIALLY_IMMEDIATE = 2
	DBPROPVAL_DF_NOT_DEFERRABLE = 3
DBPROPVAL_DST	DBPROPVAL_DST_TDP = 1
	DBPROPVAL_DST_MDP = 2
	DBPROPVAL_DST_TDPANDMDP = 3
DBPROPVAL_HT	DBPROPVAL_HT_DIFFERENT_CATALOGS = 1
	DBPROPVAL_HT_DIFFERENT_PROVIDERS = 2
DBPROPVAL_IC	DBPROPVAL_IC_UPPER = 1
	DBPROPVAL_IC_LOWER = 2
	DBPROPVAL_IC_SENSITIVE = 4
	DBPROPVAL_IC_MIXED = 8
DBPROPVAL_IN	DBPROPVAL_IN_DISALLOWNULL = 1
	DBPROPVAL_IN_IGNORENULL = 2
	DBPROPVAL_IN_IGNOREANYNULL = 4
DBPROPVAL_IT	DBPROPVAL_IT_BTREE = 1
	DBPROPVAL_IT_HASH = 2
	DBPROPVAL_IT_CONTENT = 3
	DBPROPVAL_IT_OTHER = 4
DBPROPVAL_LM	DBPROPVAL_LM_NONE = 1
	DBPROPVAL_LM_READ = 2
	DBPROPVAL_LM_SINGLEROW = 2
	DBPROPVAL_LM_INTENT = 4
	DBPROPVAL_LM_RITE = 8
DBPROPVAL_MR	DBPROPVAL_MR_NOTSUPPORTED = 0
	DBPROPVAL_MR_SUPPORTED = 1
	DBPROPVAL_MR_CONCURRENT = 2
DBPROPVAL_NC	DBPROPVAL_NC_END = 1
	DBPROPVAL_NC_HIGH = 2
	DBPROPVAL_NC_LOW = 4
	DBPROPVAL_NC_START = 8
DBPROPVAL_NP	DBPROPVAL_NP_OKTODO = 1
	DBPROPVAL_NP_DIDEVENT = 16
	DBPROPVAL_NP_ABOUTTODO = 2
	DBPROPVAL_NP_SYNCHAFTER = 4
	DBPROPVAL_NP_FAILEDTODO = 8
DBPROPVAL_NT	DBPROPVAL_NT_SINGLEROW = 1
	DBPROPVAL_NT_MULTIPLEROWS = 2

Enumeration	Members
TABLE 9.4 *(Continued)*	
DBPROPVAL_OA	DBPROPVAL_OA_NOTSUPPORTED = 1
	DBPROPVAL_OA_ATEXECUTE = 2
	DBPROPVAL_OA_ATROWRELEASE = 4
DBPROPVAL_OO	DBPROPVAL_OO_BLOB = 1
	DBPROPVAL_OO_IPERSIST = 2
DBPROPVAL_OS	DBPROPVAL_OS_ENABLEALL = -1
	DBPROPVAL_OS_RESOURCEPOOLING = 1
	DBPROPVAL_OS_TXNENLISTMENT = 2
DBPROPVAL_PT	DBPROPVAL_PT_GUID_NAME = 1
	DBPROPVAL_PT_PROPID = 16
	DBPROPVAL_PT_GUID_PROPID = 2
	DBPROPVAL_PT_PGUID_NAME = 32
	DBPROPVAL_PT_NAME = 4
	DBPROPVAL_PT_PGUID_PROPID = 64
	DBPROPVAL_PT_GUID = 8
DBPROPVAL_RD	DBPROPVAL_RD_RESETALL = -1
DBPROPVAL_RT	DBPROPVAL_RT_FREETHREAD = 1
	DBPROPVAL_RT_APTMTTHREAD = 2
	DBPROPVAL_RT_SINGLETHREAD = 4
DBPROPVAL_SQ	DBPROPVAL_SQ_CORRELATEDSUBQUERIES = 1
	DBPROPVAL_SQ_QUANTIFIED = 16
	DBPROPVAL_SQ_COMPARISON = 2
	DBPROPVAL_SQ_EXISTS = 4
	DBPROPVAL_SQ_IN = 8
DBPROPVAL_SQL	DBPROPVAL_SQL_NONE = 0
	DBPROPVAL_SQL_ODBC_MINIMUM = 1
	DBPROPVAL_SQL_MINIMUM = 1
	DBPROPVAL_SQL_ANSI92_FULL = 128
	DBPROPVAL_SQL_ANSI92_ENTRY = 16
	DBPROPVAL_SQL_ODBC_CORE = 2
	DBPROPVAL_SQL_CORE = 2
	DBPROPVAL_SQL_ESCAPECLAUSES = 256
	DBPROPVAL_SQL_FIPS_TRANSITIONAL = 32
	DBPROPVAL_SQL_ODBC_EXTENDED = 4
	DBPROPVAL_SQL_EXTENDED = 4
	DBPROPVAL_SQL_SUBMINIMUM = 512
	DBPROPVAL_SQL_ANSI92_INTERMEDIATE = 64
	DBPROPVAL_SQL_ANDI89_IEF = 8

TABLE 9.4	(*Continued*)
Enumeration	**Members**
DBPROPVAL_SS	DBPROPVAL_SS_ISEQUENTIALSTREAM = 1
	DBPROPVAL_SS_ISTREAM = 2
	DBPROPVAL_SS_ISTORAGE = 4
	DBPROPVAL_SS_ILOCKBYTES = 8
DBPROPVAL_SU	DBPROPVAL_SU_DML_STATEMENTS = 1
	DBPROPVAL_SU_TABLE_DEFINITION = 2
	DBPROPVAL_SU_INDEX_DEFINITION = 4
	DBPROPVAL_SU_PRIVILEGE_DEFINITION = 8
DBPROPVAL_TC	DBPROPVAL_TC_NONE = 0
	DBPROPVAL_TC_DML = 1
	DBPROPVAL_TC_DDL_COMMIT = 2
	DBPROPVAL_TC_DDL_IGNORE = 4
	DBPROPVAL_TC_ALL = 8
DBPROPVAL_TI	DBPROPVAL_TI_SERIALIZABLE = 1048576
	DBPROPVAL_TI_ISOLATED = 1048576
	DBPROPVAL_TI_CHAOS = 16
	DBPROPVAL_TI_READUNCOMMITTED = 256
	DBPROPVAL_TI_BROWSE = 256
	DBPROPVAL_TI_CURSORSTABILITY = 4096
	DBPROPVAL_TI_READCOMMITTED = 4096
	DBPROPVAL_TI_REPEATABLEREAD = 65536
DBPROPVAL_TR	DBPROPVAL_TR_COMMIT_DC = 1
	DBPROPVAL_TR_BOTH = 128
	DBPROPVAL_TR_ABORT = 16
	DBPROPVAL_TR_COMMIT = 2
	DBPROPVAL_TR_NONE = 256
	DBPROPVAL_TR_ABORT_NO = 32
	DBPROPVAL_TR_COMMIT_NO = 4
	DBPROPVAL_TR_OPTIMISTIC = 512
	DBPROPVAL_TR_DONTCARE = 64
	DBPROPVAL_TR_ABORT_DC = 8
DBPROPVAL_UP	DBPROPVAL_UP_CHANGE = 1
	DBPROPVAL_UP_DELETE = 2
	DBPROPVAL_UP_INSERT = 4

That completes our look at dynamic properties in general; I'll take a look at the specific dynamic properties of some popular providers next.

Dynamic Properties by Provider

As an example of what dynamic properties are available for what providers, I'll take a look at some of these properties for the Microsoft Jet and SQL Server OLE DB providers.

Microsoft Jet Dynamic Properties

You can always check what dynamic properties a particular ADO object supports just by looping over the Name property of the Property objects in the Properties collection. To give an indication of what kinds of properties some providers support, I'll take a look at those properties for the Microsoft Jet provider first. The Connection object dynamic properties for the Microsoft Jet 4.0 OLE DB provider appear in Table 9.5, and the Recordset object dynamic properties for this provider appear in Table 9.6.

SQL Server Dynamic Properties

The Connection object dynamic properties for the SQL Server OLE DB provider appear in Table 9.7, and the Recordset object dynamic properties for this provider appear in Table 9.8.

Up to this point, we've seen quite a lot about dynamic properties in theory—now it's time to put them to work.

TABLE 9.5 Microsoft Jet connection object dynamic properties

Cache Authentication	Prompt	Jet OLEDB:Global Partial Bulk Ops
Encrypt Password	Extended Properties	Jet OLEDB:Global Bulk Transactions
Mask Password	Locale Identifier	Jet OLEDB:New Database Password
Password	OLE DB Services	Jet OLEDB:Create System Database
Persist Encrypted	Jet OLEDB:System database	Jet OLEDB:Encrypt Database
Persist Security Info	Jet OLEDB:Registry Path	Jet OLEDB:Don't Copy Locale on
User ID	Jet OLEDB:Database Password	Compact
Data Source	Jet OLEDB:Engine Type	Jet OLEDB:Compact Without Replica
Window Handle	Jet OLEDB:Database Locking	Repair
Mode	Mode	

TABLE 9.6   Microsoft Jet recordset object dynamic properties

IAccessor	Hold Rows	Row Update Notification
IChapteredRowset	Scroll Backwards	Bookmarks Ordered
IColumnsInfo	Change Inserted Rows	Others' Inserts Visible
IColumnsRowset	Column Privileges	Others' Changes Visible
IConnectionPointContainer	Command Time Out	Own Inserts Visible
IConvertType	Preserve on Commit	Own Changes Visible
ILockBytes	Defer Column	Quick Restart
IRowset	Delay Storage Object Updates	Reentrant Events
IDBAsynchStatus	Private1	Remove Deleted Rows
IParentRowset	Filter Operations	Report Multiple Changes
IRowsetChange	Find Operations	Return Pending Inserts
IRowsetExactScroll	Hidden Columns	Row Privileges
IRowsetFind	Immobile Rows	Asynchronous Rowset Processing
IRowsetIdentity	Literal Bookmarks	Row Threading Model
IRowsetInfo	Literal Row Identity	Server Cursor
IRowsetLocate	Maximum Open Rows	Strong Row Identity
IRowsetRefresh	Maximum Pending Rows	Objects Transacted
IRowsetResynch	Maximum Rows	Unique Rows
IRowsetScroll	Column Writable	Updatability
IRowsetUpdate	Memory Usage	Batch Size
IRowsetView	Notification Granularity	Update Criteria
IRowsetIndex	Notification Phases	Background Fetch Size
ISequentialStream	Column Set Notification	Initial Fetch Size
IStorage	Row Delete Notification	Background Thread Priority
IStream	Row First Change Notification	Cache Child Rows
ISupportErrorInfo	Row Insert Notification	Maintain Change Status
Preserve on Abort	Row Resynchronization Notifi-	Auto Recalc
Access Order	cation	Unique Table
Append-Only Rowset	Rowset Release Notification	Unique Schema
Blocking Storage Objects	Rowset Fetch Position Change	Unique Catalog
Use Bookmarks	Notification	Resync Command
Skip Deleted Bookmarks	Row Undo Change Notifica-	Cursor Engine Version
Bookmark Type	tion	Reshape Name
Cache Deferred Columns	Row Undo Delete Notification	Update Resync
Fetch Backwards	Row Undo Insert Notification	Bookmarkable

TABLE 9.7   SQL server connection object dynamic properties

Integrated Security	Window Handle	Current Language	Application Name
Password	Locale Identifier	Network Address	Workstation ID
Persist Security Info	Prompt	Network Library	Initial File Name
User ID	Extended Properties	Use Procedure for Prepare	
Initial Catalog	Connect Timeout	Auto Translate	
Data Source	OLE DB Services	Packet Size	

TABLE 9.8   SQL server recordset object dynamic properties

IAccessor	Scroll Backwards	Others' Inserts Visible
IChapteredRowset	Change Inserted Rows	Others' Changes Visible
IColumnsInfo	Column Privileges	Own Inserts Visible
IColumnsRowset	Command Time Out	Own Changes Visible
IConnectionPointContainer	Preserve on Commit	Quick Restart
IConvertType	Defer Column	Reentrant Events
ILockBytes	Delay Storage Object Updates	Remove Deleted Rows
IRowset	Private1	Report Multiple Changes
IDBAsynchStatus	Filter Operations	Return Pending Inserts
IParentRowset	Find Operations	Row Privileges
IRowsetChange	Hidden Columns	Asynchronous Rowset Pro-
IRowsetExactScroll	Immobile Rows	cessing
IRowsetFind	Literal Bookmarks	Row Threading Model
IRowsetIdentity	Literal Row Identity	Server Cursor
IRowsetInfo	Maximum Open Rows	Strong Row Identity
IRowsetLocate	Maximum Pending Rows	Objects Transacted
IRowsetRefresh	Maximum Rows	Unique Rows
IRowsetResynch	Column Writable	Updatability
IRowsetScroll	Memory Usage	Batch Size
IRowsetUpdate	Notification Granularity	Update Criteria
IRowsetView	Notification Phases	Background Fetch Size
IRowsetIndex	Column Set Notification	Initial Fetch Size
ISequentialStream	Row Delete Notification	Background Thread Priority
IStorage	Row First Change Notification	Cache Child Rows
IStream	Row Insert Notification	Maintain Change Status
ISupportErrorInfo	Row Resynchronization Noti-	Auto Recalc
Preserve on Abort	fication	Unique Table
Access Order	Rowset Release Notification	Unique Schema
Append-Only Rowset	Rowset Fetch Position	Unique Catalog
Blocking Storage Objects	Change Notification	Resync Command
Use Bookmarks	Row Undo Change Notifica-	Cursor Engine Version
Skip Deleted Bookmarks	tion	Reshape Name
Bookmark Type	Row Undo Delete Notification	Update Resync
Cache Deferred Columns	Row Undo Insert Notification	Bookmarkable
Fetch Backwards	Row Update Notification	
Hold Rows	Bookmarks Ordered	

·················

Using Dynamic Properties

To work with dynamic properties, you use the `Properties` collection; for example, to store all the names of the dynamic properties in a `Recordset` object in a Data Environment, you can use code like this:

```
Open "c:\ado\rs.txt" For Output As #1
For Each objProp In _
    DataEnvironment1.rsCommand1.Properties
    Print #1, objProp.Name
Next
Close #1
```

I'll put together an example here that checks some dynamic properties of the Microsoft Jet 4.0 OLE DB provider. This example is easy enough; it just checks the settings for various dynamic properties and displays the result in a message box. For example, here's how I check the `Row Threading Model` property:

```
Private Sub Command1_Click()
    On Error GoTo ErrHandler

    Select Case _
        DataEnvironment1.rsCommand1.Properties( _
            "Row Threading Model")
        Case 1
            strMsg =
            "Row threading model: free threading" _
            & vbCrLf
        Case 2
            strMsg =
            "Row threading model: apartment " & _
            threading" & vbCrLf
        Case 4
            strMsg =
            "Row threading model: single " & _
            "threading" & vbCrLf
```

```
End Select

        .

        .

        .
```

And here's how I check whether or not the provider supports a Resync command (which the Jet OLE DB provider does not):

```
If DataEnvironment1.rsCommand1.Properties(_
    "Resync Command") <> "" Then
    strMsg = strMsg & "Resync command: " &
    DataEnvironment1.rsCommand1.Properties( _
    "Resync Command") & vbCrLf
Else
    strMsg = strMsg & "There is no resync " & _
    "command" & vbCrLf
End If

        .

        .

        .
```

The actual code for this example, dynamicproperties.frm, appears in Listing 9.2, and the results of running this code appear in Figure 9.2. As you can see in that figure, working with the dynamic property set is not difficult. And as you can see from the list of available dynamic properties in Tables 9.1, 9.2, and 9.3, these properties offer a rich resource for ADO programmers.

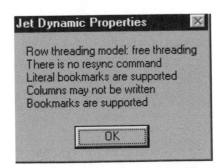

FIGURE 9.2 Reporting dynamic properties.

. . . .

LISTING 9.2 *Dynamicproperties.frm Code*

```
VERSION 5.00
Begin VB.Form Form1
   Caption         =    "Form1"
   ClientHeight    =    3195
   ClientLeft      =    60
   ClientTop       =    345
   ClientWidth     =    4680
   LinkTopic       =    "Form1"
   ScaleHeight     =    3195
   ScaleWidth      =    4680
   StartUpPosition =    3    'Windows Default
   Begin VB.CommandButton Command1
      Caption      =    "Examine dynamic properties"
      Height       =    855
      Left         =    1080
      TabIndex     =    0
      Top          =    1320
      Width        =    2775
   End
End
Attribute VB_Name = "Form1"
Attribute VB_GlobalNameSpace = False
Attribute VB_Creatable = False
Attribute VB_PredeclaredId = True
Attribute VB_Exposed = False
Private Sub Command1_Click()
    On Error GoTo ErrHandler

    Select Case _
        DataEnvironment1.rsCommand1.Properties(_
            "Row Threading Model")
        Case 1
            strMsg =
            "Row threading model: free threading" & vbCrLf
        Case 2
            strMsg =
            "Row threading model: apartment threading" & _
            vbCrLf
        Case 4
            strMsg = _
            "Row threading model: single threading" & vbCrLf
    End Select

    If DataEnvironment1.rsCommand1.Properties(_
        "Resync Command") <> "" Then
        strMsg = strMsg & "Resync command: " &
        DataEnvironment1.rsCommand1.Properties( _
        "Resync Command") & vbCrLf
    Else
```

```
        strMsg = strMsg & "There is no resync command" & _
        vbCrLf
    End If

    If DataEnvironment1.rsCommand1.Properties( _
        "Literal Bookmarks") Then
        strMsg = strMsg & "Literal bookmarks are supported" _
            & vbCrLf
    Else
        strMsg = strMsg & "Literal bookmarks are not " & _
        "supported" & vbCrLf
    End If

    If DataEnvironment1.rsCommand1.Properties( _
        "Column Writable") Then
        strMsg = strMsg & "Columns may be written" & vbCrLf
    Else
        strMsg = strMsg & "Columns may not be written" & _
        vbCrLf
    End If

    If DataEnvironment1.rsCommand1.Properties( _
        "Use Bookmarks") Then
        strMsg = strMsg & "Bookmarks are supported" & vbCrLf
    Else
        strMsg = strMsg & "Bookmarks are not supported" & _
        vbCrLf
    End If

    MsgBox strMsg, vbOKOnly, "Jet Dynamic Properties"

    Exit Sub

ErrHandler:

    MsgBox "Errors occurred."

    If DataEnvironment1.Connection1.Errors.Count > 0 Then
        For Each objError In _
            DataEnvironment1.Connection1.Errors
            MsgBox "Error: " & _
            DataEnvironment1.Connection1.Errors(0).Description
        Next
    End If
End Sub
```

That completes our look at the ADO collections: `Parameters`, the `Command` object's collection of `Parameter` objects; `Fields`, the `Recordset` object's collection of `Field` objects; `Errors`, the `Connection` object's collection of `Error` objects; and `Properties`, the collection of dynamic properties belonging to the `Connection`, `Recordset`, `Command`, `Field`, and `Parameter` objects.

In the next chapter, I'll take a look at some in-depth Visual Basic ADO programming as we create data objects and data-aware ActiveX controls.

Creating Data-Aware Objects and ActiveX Controls

This is the chapter on creating data-aware objects and ActiveX controls in Visual Basic. We'll see how to create ActiveX controls that can be used as data-bound controls, and other ActiveX controls that can be used as data sources. We'll also see how to create data objects using Visual Basic object-oriented programming (OOP), creating the classes and objects needed to handle databases.

Creating ActiveX controls itself is quite a topic, and I'll spend the first part of this chapter covering that. After creating some working ActiveX controls, I'll create some data-aware ActiveX controls that can be bound to data sources, or function themselves as data sources. Finally, I'll use the Visual Basic Data Object Wizard to create data objects.

ActiveX controls created in Visual Basic are based on the `User-Control` object, and that object makes life a lot easier for the programmer. In fact, all you have to do is to create a new ActiveX control project and the `UserControl` placed in your project is already viable and you can compile it into an `.ocx` file, ready to go—not that the control will do anything more than display a blank space when embedded in other programs, of course. The ActiveX controls you develop in Visual Basic are full ActiveX controls, and you can embed them in other applications and Web pages as you would any other ActiveX control.

There's a lot coming up in this chapter: creating ActiveX controls, the built-in properties, methods, and events of UserControl objects; supporting properties, methods, and events in your own controls; determining the control's environment; storing and restoring property settings; making an ActiveX control a data-bound control or data source, data objects, and more. It's time to get to work.

ActiveX Control Overview

The ActiveX controls you create in Visual Basic are based on the Visual Basic UserControl object. Here are the significant properties of that object:

- **DataMembers**—Returns a reference to the DataMembers collection. (A control that is a data source can support multiple sets of data that a data consumer can bind to. Each set of data is called a data member and is identified by a string.)

- **AccessKeys**—String that contains the keys that will act as the access keys (or hot keys) for the control.

- **Ambient**—Returns an AmbientProperties object, which holds the ambient properties of the container.

- **Extender**—Returns the Extender object for this control, which holds those properties of the control that are maintained by the container.

- **ControlContainer**—True if the control can act as a control container.

- **ContainedControls**—Returns a collection of the controls that were added to the control by the developer or user at run-time.

- **EventsFrozen**—Determines if a control can become active during the developer's design-time.

- **ParentControls**—Returns a collection of the other controls in the control's container.

- **Alignable**—Specifies if the control can be aligned in its container.

- **PropertyPages**—Name(s) of a property page(s) associated with the control.

- **ClipBehavior**—Clipping behavior of the HitTest event on a windowless UserControl.

- **HitBehavior**—Hit testing behavior of the HitTest event on a windowless UserControl object.

- **Controls**—Reference to a collection of Control objects.

- **Hyperlink**—Reference to a Hyperlink object.

- **Parent**—Reference to the container object on which the control is sited.

- **InvisibleAtRuntime**—Specifies if the control is invisible at run-time.
- **EditAtDesignTime**—Specifies if the control may be edited at design-time.
- **ParentControlsType**—Determines whether the ParentControls collection contains references to controls incorporating the container's Extender object, or to controls without the Extender object.
- **MaskPicture**—Bitmap that, combined with the MaskColor property, determines the transparent and visible regions of a UserControl object whose BackStyle property is set to transparent.
- **Picture**—The standard Picture property.
- **Enabled**—The standard Enabled property.

Here are the UserControl's significant methods:

- **Print**—Prints text in the control.
- **AsyncRead**—Starts the asynchronous reading of data from a file or URL by the control.
- **CancelAsyncRead**—Cancels an asynchronous data request.
- **CanPropertyChange**—Queries the container if a property bound to a data source can have its value changed.
- **PaintPicture**—Draws the contents of a graphics file (.bmp, .wmf, .emf, .cur, .ico, or .dib formats supported).
- **PopupMenu**—Displays a pop-up menu.

And here are the UserControl's significant events:

- **AccessKeyPress**—Fires when the user of the control presses one of the control's access keys.
- **AmbientChanged**—Fires when an ambient property's value changes.
- **AsyncReadComplete**—Fires when the container has completed an asynchronous read request.
- **EnterFocus**—Fires when the focus enters the control.
- **ExitFocus**—Fires when the focus leaves the object.
- **Hide**—Fires when the object's Visible property changes to False.
- **InitProperties**—Fires when a new instance of an object is created.
- **LostFocus**—Fires in the object or constituent control when the focus leaves it.
- **ReadProperties**—Fires when loading an old instance of an object that has a saved state.
- **Show**—Fires when the object's Visible property changes to True.
- **WriteProperties**—Signals to the object that the properties of the control need to be saved, so they can be restored later.

- **AsyncReadProgress**—Fires when more data is available as a result of an `AsyncRead` method.

- **HitTest**—Fires when the user moves the mouse over a `UserControl` object.

- **GetDataMember**—Fires when a data consumer requests a new data source.

- **Initialize**—Fires when an application creates an instance of the control.

- **Terminate**—Fires when all references to the control are removed from memory (by setting all variables that refer to the control to `Nothing`) or when the last reference to the control goes out of scope.

There are some additional points to consider when creating ActiveX controls, such as the lifetime of such controls, which is coming up next.

Lifetime of an ActiveX Control

ActiveX controls actually run at design-time as well as at run-time, so Visual Basic creates instances of your control at both times. That means your control will be created and destroyed frequently during the design process:

- It's created when the developer creates a control and places it in its container.

- It's destroyed when the developer closes the designer containing the control.

- It's destroyed when the developer runs the application from the Integrated Development Environment (IDE)—that is, the design-time instance of the control is destroyed.

- It's created when a program runs and sites the control in its container.

- It's destroyed when the control's container is destroyed, for example, when the application stops running.

- It's created when the IDE returns to design-time.

- It's destroyed when the developer closes the project.

When the developer switches from design-time to run-time, the design-time instance of a control is destroyed and the run-time instance is created. When the application switches back to design-time, the reverse process occurs.

It's important to know when ActiveX controls are created and destroyed, because you should make the property settings of the controls *persist* between instantiations. You handle that process by reading persisted properties when the control is created and storing them when the control is destroyed. You do this even when the control switches from design-time to run-time, because the settings the developer made at design-time should persist to run-time. I'll cover this process in some detail in this chapter.

The Ambient and Extender Properties

There are two useful properties that are built into `UserControls`: `Ambient` and `Extender`.

The `Ambient` property returns an `AmbientProperties` object that holds ambient information from the control's container to suggest behavior to the control. Using this object, you can tailor your control to match what's going on in the container. The `AmbientProperties` object has several standard properties:

- **BackColor**—Suggested interior color of the contained control. The default if the container does not support this property is 0x80000005 (the system color for a window background).

- **DisplayAsDefault**—Boolean that specifies if the control is the default control.

- **DisplayName**—Name that the control should display for itself. The default if the container does not support this property is an empty string: "".

- **Font**—Font object that contains the suggested font information of the contained control. The default if the container does not support this property is MS Sans Serif 8.

- **ForeColor**—Suggested foreground color of the contained control. The default if the container does not support this property is 0x80000008 (the system color for window text).

- **LocaleID**—Value that indicates the target language and country.

- **MessageReflect**—Boolean that specifies if the container supports message reflection.

- **Palette**—A Picture object whose palette specifies the suggested palette for the contained control.

- **RightToLeft**—Boolean that indicates the text display direction and controls the visual appearance on bi-directional systems.

- **ScaleUnits**—Name of the coordinate units being used by the container.

- **ShowGrabHandles**—Boolean which specifies if the container supports the showing of grab handles.

- **ShowHatching**—Boolean that specifies if the container supports the showing of hatching.

- **SupportsMnemonics**—Boolean that specifies if the container supports access keys for the control.

- **TextAlign**—Enumeration that specifies how text is to be aligned.

- **UserMode**—Boolean that specifies if the environment is in Design mode or Run mode.

- **UIDead**—Boolean that specifies if the user interface is not responding.

note Note in particular the **UserMode** property of the **AmbientProperties** object, which lets you know if your control is operating at design-time or run-time.

An `Extender` object supports properties, methods, and events that come built into your `UserControl` for free. The `Extender` object has these properties, methods, and events (note that not all are guaranteed to exist in all situations):

- **Name**—Read-only string holding the user-defined name of the control.
- **Visible**—Boolean that specifies if the control is visible or not.
- **Parent**—Read-only object that represents the container of the control.
- **Cancel**—Boolean indicating if the control is the default `Cancel` button for the container.
- **Default**—Boolean indicating if the control is the default button for the container.
- **Container**—Read-only object that represents the visual container of the control.
- **DragIcon**—`Picture` object that specifies the icon to use when the control is dragged.
- **DragMode**—Specifies if the control can be automatically dragged, or if the control must call the `Drag` method in code.
- **Enabled**—Boolean that specifies if the control is enabled. (This `Extender` property is not present unless the control also has an `Enabled` property with the correct procedure ID.)
- **Height**—Specifies the height of the control in the container's scale units.
- **HelpContextID**—Specifies the context ID to use when the `F1` key is pressed.
- **Index**—Specifies the control's position in a control array.
- **Left**—Specifies the position of the left edge of the control to the left edge of the container, in the container's scale units.
- **TabIndex**—Specifies the position of the control in the tab order of the container's controls.
- **TabStop**—Boolean that specifies if the user can tab to the control.
- **Tag**—Standard `Tag` property.
- **ToolTipText**—Standard `ToolTipText` property.
- **Top**—Position of the top edge of the control to the top edge of the container, given in the container's scale units.

- **WhatThisHelpID**—Context ID to use when the What's This pop-up is used on the control.

- **Width**—Specifies the width of the control in the container's scale units.

- **Drag**—Method to begin, end, or cancel a drag operation of the control.

- **Move**—Standard Move method.

- **SetFocus**—Standard SetFocus method.

- **ShowWhatsThis**—Method to display a topic in a Help file using the What's This pop-up.

- **ZOrder**—Method to place the control at the front or back of the Z-order.

- **DragDrop**—Event that fires when another control on the form is dropped on this control.

- **DragOver**—Event that fires when another control on the form is dragged over this control.

- **GotFocus**—Event that fires when this control gets the focus.

- **LostFocus**—Event that fires when this control loses the focus.

Asynchronous Reading

The control's AsyncRead method can return byte arrays, files, or pictures from a file or URL. You can track the progress of a download with the Async-ReadProgress event. And, when the data is available, the AsyncReadComplete event is fired. An asynchronous read can be canceled before it is completed by calling the UserControl's CancelAsyncRead method.

Note that AsyncRead is used more often in active documents, but it is available in UserControls as well.

The Initialize, InitializeProperties, and Terminate Events

The Initialize and Terminate events are much like a form's Load and Unload events in that you use them for initialization and cleanup. The Initialize event is the default event for UserControl objects (i.e., Visual Basic creates the event handler for this event when you double-click the control at design-time).

Note that you shouldn't assign default values to your properties in the Initialize event; you should use the InitializeProperties event. This event, InitializeProperties, fires only once during the lifetime of a control—when the control is first sited in its container, which is the perfect time to set default property values.

After setting property defaults once, however, you shouldn't reset them the next time the `UserControl` is created, because the developer may have changed those properties' settings.

Persisting Properties

When a developer sets a control's properties at design-time, you want those new settings to be available at run-time as well. You add code to the `Read-Properties` and `WriteProperties` events to handle the cases when you need to read and write properties.

A `PropertyBag` object is passed to these events, and you use that object's `ReadProperties` and `WriteProperties` methods to do the actual reading and writing.

In addition, you can trigger a `WriteProperties` event yourself with the `UserControl PropertyChanged` method.

We'll see how to use property bags later in the chapter.

Design-Time and Run-Time

As noted above, you can determine if a control is operating at design-time or run-time using the `AmbientProperties` object's `UserMode` property. Here's the order of events that occur when you switch from design-time to run-time:

- `WriteProperties`.
- `Terminate`.
- `ReadProperties`.

And here's the order of events that occur when you switch from run-time to design-time:

- `Initialize`.
- `ReadProperties`.

That completes the overview we'll need on `UserControls`. It's time to start coding.

Creating an ActiveX Control

Here are the basic steps for creating an ActiveX control:

1. Add a `UserControl` to a project, or create an ActiveX control project. When you add a `UserControl` to a project, you can use the ActiveX Control Interface Wizard to design your control, if you wish; when you create an ActiveX control project, the `UserControl` object is blank and it's up to you to configure it.

2. If you want to implement a user-drawn control, add the code you want to the `UserControl`'s `Paint` event; leave the control's `AutoRedraw` property False.

3. If you want to use constituent controls (embedded controls, including standard Visual Basic controls), add them to your control.

4. Add the custom properties, methods, and events you want to support in your control.

5. If you have constituent controls, you may want to add delegated properties, methods, and events to give the host application access to those properties, methods, and events.

6. Add any additional code you want to the `UserControl`.

7. Add code to the control's `Initialize` and `Terminate` events.

8. Support persistent properties by using the `PropertyBag` object when it's time to read or write those properties.

9. Compile the control; Visual Basic will register it for you.

10. Register and use the control.

In this chapter, I'll create an ActiveX control project that implements these features named `CalculatorControl`. This control will let the user enter and multiply two integers, and you can find it in the `calculatorcontrol` folder on the CD. Before creating that control, however, I'll take a look at creating a control that handles all of the details itself, including drawing itself when necessary.

Designing a User-Drawn ActiveX Control

You can handle the drawing of your ActiveX control yourself if you wish. To do so, make sure the control's `AutoRedraw` property is False so the control's `Paint` event is called when the control needs to be redrawn.

 Note that if you want to draw in the control from the `Initialize` event, you must set `AutoRedraw` to True, just as you must to draw from a form's `Load` event.

As an example, I'll create an ActiveX control now that draws an ellipse using the `Paint` event. To create that ActiveX control project, start Visual Basic now or select the `New Project` item in the `File` menu to open the `New Project` dialog. In that dialog, select the ActiveX Control icon and click OK, creating the new ActiveX control project you see in Figure 10.1. The new `UserControl` appears in the designer in that figure, and when you save it to disk, it's stored in a `.ctl` file.

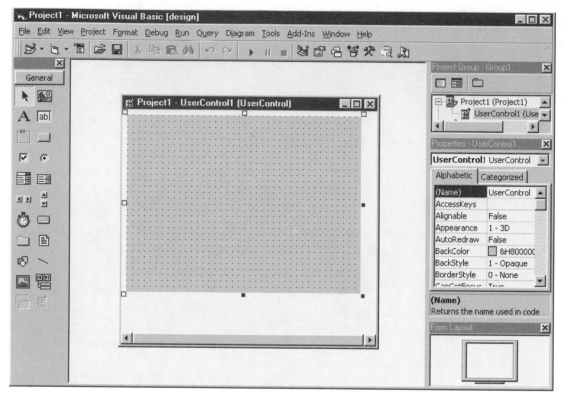

FIGURE 10.1 A new ActiveX control project.

As you can see, the new `UserControl` is blank, and it's up to us make something happen. The `AutoRedraw` property should be False by default, so add this code to the `Paint` event to display an ellipse in the control:

```
Private Sub UserControl_Paint()
    Dim intMinRadius As Integer

    intMinRadius = ScaleWidth / 2
    If intMinRadius > ScaleHeight / 2 Then
        intMinRadius = ScaleHeight / 2
    End If
    Circle (ScaleWidth / 2, ScaleHeight / 2), _
        intMinRadius, vbBlack, , , .8
End Sub
```

That's it; this control is ready to be tested.

Testing an ActiveX Control

There are three ways to test and debug an ActiveX control from the IDE:

- In a Web page.
- In-process.
- Out-of-Process.

Note that, much like when working with code components, debugging is interactive when you're working with ActiveX controls and their containers. You can set break points in the ActiveX control's code and you can execute statements like:

```
Debug.Print "In the Terminate event."
```

To actually test your code, you start the ActiveX control in one of the three ways listed above; I'll cover those ways now.

Testing a Control in a Web Page

You can simply select the Start item in the Run method to run a control. Since .ocx controls are actually special cases of dynamic link libraries, i.e., .dll files, they won't run by themselves. Instead, the Project Properties Debugging page appears, as you see in Figure 10.2.

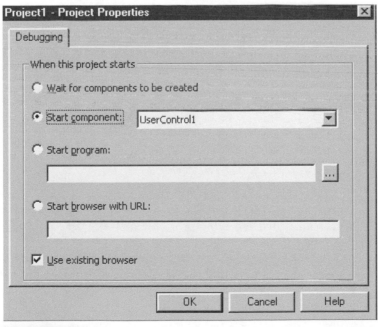

FIGURE 10.2   The Debugging page.

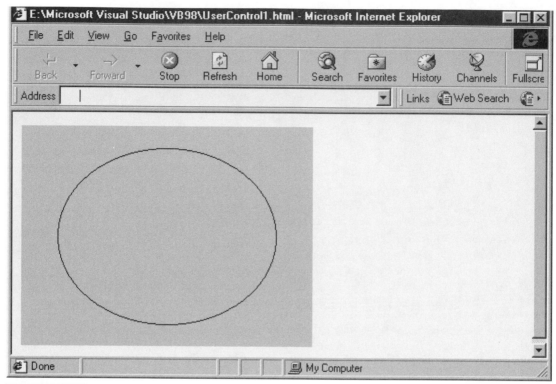

FIGURE 10.3   Running a control in Microsoft Internet Explorer.

Click the Start Component option button, make sure UserControl1 is selected, then click OK. When you do, Visual Basic starts the ActiveX control in your Web browser, as shown in Figure 10.3.

That's one way to test an ActiveX control. You can also test it in-process.

Testing a Control In-Process

You can run your new ActiveX control in a Visual Basic form and test it while it's running in-process (that is, as part of the same process as the form itself). With your ActiveX control's project open, select the Add Project item in the File menu. Make the new project—which I'll call Project2—a standard EXE project; Visual Basic will create a project group. You must make this new project the startup project in the group, which you do by right-clicking the project in the Project Explorer and selecting the Set as Startup item.

Now—and this is an important point—close the UserControl's designer. When you do, the control's icon in the toolbox will appear in its active state; if the `UserControl`'s designer is open, the control's icon will be grayed out in the toolbox.

When the control's icon is active in the toolbox, you can add that control to the form in `Project2`, as you see in Figure 10.4. Selecting the `Start` item in the `Run` menu will display the control in the form.

Besides testing an ActiveX control in-process, you can also test it out-of-process.

Testing a Control Out-of-Process

To test an ActiveX control out-of-process, you must create a stand-alone `.ocx` file for the control, and you do that by selecting the `Make Project-Name.ocx` item in the `File` menu (make sure you've set the project compatibility options as you want them to address version issues).

Visual Basic should register the control when it creates it. However, if it doesn't, or if you're testing the control on a different machine, you can register the control yourself with the Windows utility `regsvr32.exe`, passing the

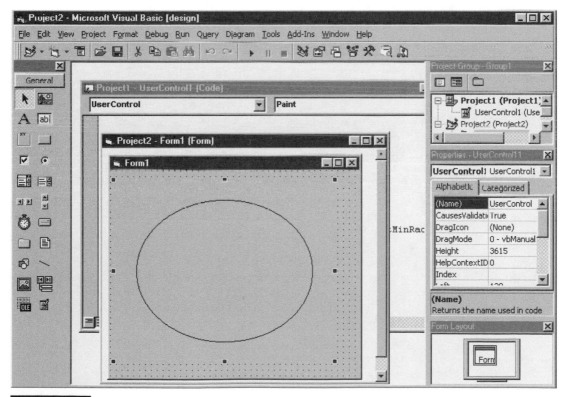

FIGURE 10.4   Running an ActiveX control in a project group.

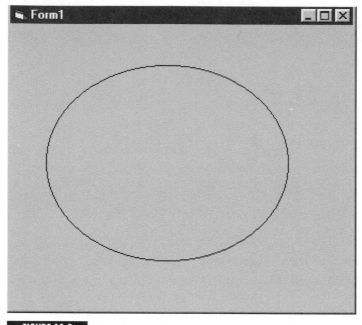

FIGURE 10.5   Running an ActiveX control out-of-process.

name of the `.ocx` file you want to register on the command line something like this:

```
C:\ado>\windows\system\regsvr32
calculatorcontrol.ocx
```

After the control is registered, you can place it in another Visual Basic project by adding it to the toolbox in that project as you would normally (i.e., using the `Components` item in the `Project` menu). Then you run that project, resulting in the form you see in Figure 10.5.

Those are your options for testing and debugging ActiveX controls, and that finishes the discussion on creating user-drawn controls. The next step up in complexity is to base your control on an existing Visual Basic control.

Basing ActiveX Controls on Existing Controls

You can base your ActiveX control on other Visual Basic controls, and programmers often do so to modify some aspect of a standard control and make the new control easily available to others.

In this case, you just stretch the standard control to cover the ActiveX control in the `Initialize` event (recall that the `Initialize` event also fires when the control is created at design-time, so the developer will also see the standard control stretched to fit the ActiveX control).

Here's a quick example—just add a text box, `Text1`, to a `UserControl`, and set its `ScrollBars` and `MultiLine` properties to True. In addition, add this code to the `Initialize` event to stretch that text box to cover the `UserControl` when the control is instantiated (you can place this code in the control's `Resize` event if you prefer):

```
Private Sub UserControl_Initialize()
    Text1.Left = 0
    Text1.Top = 0
    Text1.Width = UserControl.Width
    Text1.Height = UserControl.Height
End Sub
```

Now you add the code you want to modify the standard control's behavior. For example, you may hate celery and therefore want to remind the user that this is a celery-free zone whenever they type the word "celery."

You can handle that in the `Text1_Change` event, like this, where the code searches the text in the text box to make sure the word "celery" hasn't been typed:

```
Private Sub Text1_Change()
    If InStr(Text1.Text, "celery") <> 0 Then
        MsgBox "Sorry, this is a celery-free zone."
    End If
End Sub
```

You can add this new control to Visual Basic forms just as you can standard text boxes, but this control has the special behavior you've programmed into it. When the user tries to type the word "celery," a message box appears informing them of their error, as shown in Figure 10.6.

When you add controls to a `UserControl` like this, those controls are called *constituent controls*, and using constituent controls raises some new issues.

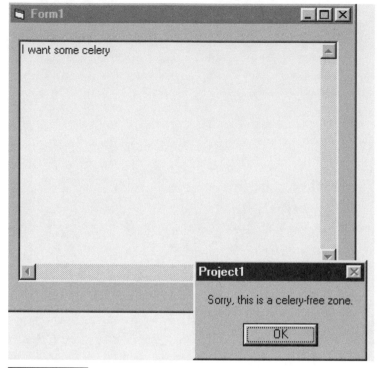

FIGURE 10.6   Basing an ActiveX control on a standard control.

Constituent Controls in ActiveX Controls

To show how to work with constituent controls, I'll create the multiplying calculator example here. This example is called `calculatorcontrol`; create it now as an ActiveX project, and change the name of the `UserControl` in it from `UserControl1` to `CalculatorControl`. In addition, change the project name in the `General` page of the `Project Properties` dialog to `calculator`, which is how other developers will see it listed in the `Components` dialog box when they add this control to their applications. Adding this control to a project will create a new control named `CalculatorControl1` the first time, `CalculatorControl2` the second time, and so on.

Now add three text boxes, a label with an X in it (X for multiplication), and a command button with an equals sign (=) in the caption, as you see in Figure 10.7.

The idea here is that the user can enter two integers in the first two text boxes, click the = button, and the control will multiply the two integers together and display the result in the third text box (note that in a real application, you might display the result in a label instead of a text box so the user can't modify it).

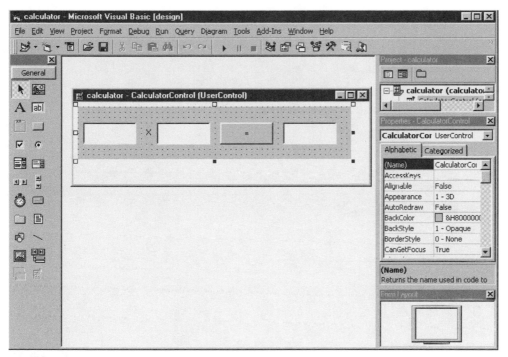

FIGURE 10.7 Basing an ActiveX control on a standard control.

Implementing this control is easy enough—just add this code to the = button's `Click` event handler (note that Visual Basic will convert the text in the operand text boxes, `Text1` and `Text2`, to numeric values automatically without using the `Str` and `Val` functions, because we're using those values in a numeric context):

```
Private Sub Command1_Click()
    Text3.Text = Text1.Text * Text2.Text
End Sub
```

That's all it takes to make this ActiveX control active. We'll need a way of testing this control, so create a new Visual Basic project (create a program group or open a new Visual Basic session) and name this new project `calculatorclient`, which is also the folder it appears in on the CD.

Just add the calculator control to this new project and draw `CalculatorControl1` in `Form1` now, then run the project as you see in Figure 10.8.

As you can see in that figure, the new calculator control appears in the test project—along with two buttons at the bottom that we'll use later—and is already working. So far, the project is a success.

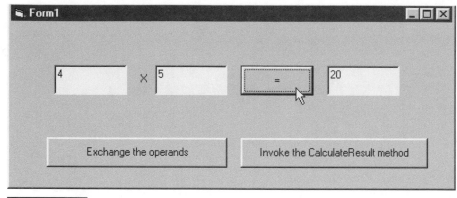

FIGURE 10.8   Running the calculator ActiveX control .

We have yet to add any properties, methods, or events to the control, however, and I'll get to that now.

Creating ActiveX Control Properties

Your ActiveX control can have properties that you create from scratch, or properties that access the inherent properties of the constituent controls in the ActiveX control.

ActiveX properties that expose the properties of constituent controls are called *delegated properties;* for example, properties that expose the values of the operands in the first two text boxes in the calculator control are delegated properties.

I'll implement those properties now, calling them Operand1 (which holds the text in Text1) and Operand2 (which holds the text in Text2). Using these properties, the developer will be able to refer to the two operands the calculator will multiply. You can add properties as public data members, or with Get/Let procedures; I'll use the more secure Get/Let technique here.

Server Side

To implement the Operand1 and Operand2 properties in the ActiveX control, just use the Tools menu's Add Procedure item to add those two new properties to the project. This creates Get and Let property procedures for these properties; just add code to read or write the text in the matching text box this way:

```
Public Property Get Operand1() As Variant
    Operand1 = Text1.Text
End Property
```

```
Public Property Let Operand1(ByVal vNewValue As _
    Variant)
    Text1.Text = vNewValue
End Property


Public Property Get Operand2() As Variant
    Operand2 = Text2.Text
End Property


Public Property Let Operand2(ByVal vNewValue _
    As Variant)
    Text2.Text = vNewValue
End Property
```

That's all it takes on the server side.

Client Side

In the client application, calculatorclient, you can find the new properties, Operand1 and Operand2, in the Properties window, and can set or read their values there. Note that if you set the properties to some new value, those new values will not be preserved when you run the client application, because new instances of the calculator control are created at design-time and run-time. We'll see how to preserve the values the developer sets in the control at run-time later; see the topic "Using Control Events to Save and Load Persistent Properties" coming up.

At run-time, you can access the operands in the two text boxes as Operand1 and Operand2, and I'll do that by adding a new command button, Command1, to let the user swap the two values in the text boxes. Give this new button the caption Exchange the operands, and add this code to the button's event handler:

```
Private Sub Command1_Click()
    Dim intTemp As Integer


    intTemp = CalculatorControl1.Operand1
    CalculatorControl1.Operand1 = _
        CalculatorControl1.Operand2
    CalculatorControl1.Operand2 = intTemp
End Sub
```

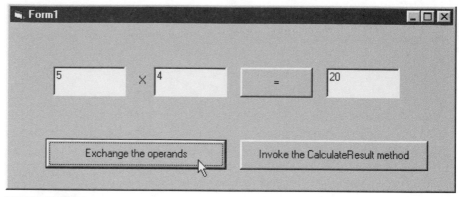

FIGURE 10.9   Using custom properties in an ActiveX control.

That's all it takes—now we've implemented custom properties in an ActiveX control. The new button with its caption, `Exchange the operands`, appears in Figure 10.9. When the user clicks this button, the two values in the operand text boxes are switched immediately.

Creating Read-Only Properties

You can make properties read-only if you want to. If you want to make a property read-only at all times, you can even remove its `Property Let` procedure. This means that, among other things, the property won't appear in the `Properties` window at design-time. But it will be available, and read-only, at run-time.

If you want a property to appear in the `Properties` window, leave the `Property Let` procedure implemented, but don't store the new value of the property. You can also make the property read-only selectively at run-time or design-time by checking the `UserMode` property of the `AmbientProperties` object.

Besides properties, you can add methods to an ActiveX control, and we're already familiar with that process.

Creating ActiveX Control Methods

You add methods to an ActiveX control as you do with other COM components: as public procedures. For example, I'll add a new method to the calculator control named `CalculateResult`. This method will do the same as clicking the = button—the two operands in the first two text boxes will be multiplied and the result displayed in the third text box.

Server Side

In the `calculatorcontrol` project, you just add a new public `Sub` procedure named `CalculateResult` and add the code to multiply the operands and display the result:

```
Public Sub CalculateResult()
    Text3.Text = Text1.Text * Text2.Text
End Sub
```

That's all you need on the server side, and implementing the client side is even easier.

Client Side

In the `calculateclient` project, you can test the new `CalculateResult` method by adding a new button, `Command2`, and giving it the caption `Invoke the CalculateResult method`. In that button's `Click` handler, just invoke the ActiveX control's `CalculateResult` method this way:

```
Private Sub Command2_Click()
    CalculatorControl1.CalculateResult
End Sub
```

Now run the `calculatorclient` application, as shown in Figure 10.10. When the user enters integers in the first two text boxes and clicks the `Invoke the CalculateResult` method, it's just as if they clicked the = button—the result is calculated and displayed in the third text box, as you see in that figure.

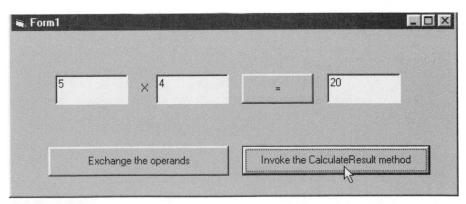

FIGURE 10.10 Using a custom method in an ActiveX control.

Creating ActiveX Control Events

You create ActiveX control events much as you do in code components—you just select the Tools menu's Add Procedure item, click the Event option button, give the event a name, and click OK.

As an example, I'll add a new event to the calculator control: CalculatorClick, which is fired each time the calculator control is clicked.

Server Side

On the server side, the calculatorcontrol project, you implement the CalculatorClick event with the Tools menu's Add Procedure item, as outlined above. Selecting the Event option button and clicking OK declares the new event:

```
Public Event CalculatorClick()
```

Now, when the user clicks the calculator control, you can fire this event with the RaiseEvent function:

```
Private Sub UserControl_Click()
    RaiseEvent CalculatorClick
End Sub
```

Now when the user clicks the calculator control, the CalculatorClick event fires. I'll make use of this by configuring the calculator to multiply its operands and display the result in the client program.

Client Side

Since we're not explicitly declaring the calculator control, you don't need to use the WithEvents keyword to be able to use the new CalculatorClick event. You just find the calculator control, CalculatorControl1, in the code window, and add this code to the control's CalculatorClick event handler, making the calculator control perform its multiplication when the user clicks it:

```
Private Sub CalculatorControl1_CalculatorClick()
    CalculatorControl1.CalculateResult
End Sub
```

Now when the user clicks the calculator control, it automatically multiplies its two operands and displays the result. That's all there is to it—we've added an event to an ActiveX control.

That completes the basics of creating properties, methods, and events. The next step is an important one: making properties persistent.

Creating Persistent Properties

As the calculator control stands, there's one issue yet to address. If the developer places some value in the Operand1 or Operand2 properties at design-time in the calculatorclient application and then runs the application, they'll find their values have not been retained, and both Operand1 and Operand2 have been reset to 0. Obviously, there's a problem here.

The solution is to write and read properties to a PropertyBag object, which will then store the data in the properties between instances. Here's how that works for Operand1 and Operand2; whenever you change the values of those properties—for example, in the Property Let procedures, you call the UserControl method PropertyChanged, passing the name of the property as a string (this method takes no other parameters)·

```
Public Property Let Operand1(ByVal vNewValue _
    As Variant)
    Text1.Text = vNewValue
    PropertyChanged "Operand1"
End Property


Public Property Let Operand2(ByVal vNewValue _
    As Variant)
    Text2.Text = vNewValue
    PropertyChanged "Operand2"
End Property
```

When you call PropertyChanged for a property, the UserControl's WriteProperties event fires, and you're passed a PropertyBag object, PropBag, that you can use to store your property or properties in at that time. You do that with the PropertyBag object's WriteProperty method:

```
PropertyBag.WriteProperty(PropertyName, Value _
    [, DefaultValue])
```

Here are the arguments to this method:

- **PropertyName**—String that represents the property to be stored in the property bag.
- **Value**—Data value to save in the property bag.
- **DefaultValue**—Default value for the data.

Here's how you store the values that Operand1 and Operand2 should have, using the UserControl's WriteProperties event handler (you can, of course, store only the changed values of properties here, and don't need to store every property's value every time):

```
Private Sub UserControl_WriteProperties(PropBag _
    As PropertyBag)
    PropBag.WriteProperty "Operand1", Text1.Text
    PropBag.WriteProperty "Operand2", Text2.Text
End Sub
```

When it's time to read the values stored for each property, a UserControl ReadProperties event fires, and you are passed a PropertyBag object named PropBag once again. This time, you use the PropertyBag ReadProperty method to read the values that should be in your properties:

PropertyBag.ReadProperty (*PropertyName*)

Here is the argument to this method:

- **PropertyName**—String that represents the property to be read from the property bag.

Here's how to use the ReadProperties event to read in the values for Operand1 and Operand2:

```
Private Sub UserControl_ReadProperties(PropBag _
    As PropertyBag)
    Text1.Text = PropBag.ReadProperty("Operand1")
    Text2.Text = PropBag.ReadProperty("Operand2")
End Sub
```

Where are the actual values stored? Where is the real "property bag"? In this case, it's the file for the form the calculator control is sited on, calculatorclient.frm. Here's how Operand1 and Operand2 are stored there (note that the data is stored as a string because we haven't changed the data types from the variant type that Visual Basic used in the `Property Get` and `Property Let` procedures):

```
Begin calculator.CalculatorControl
    CalculatorControl1
    Height          =    1215
    Left            =    600
    TabIndex        =    0
    Top             =    360
    Width           =    6255
    _ExtentX        =    11033
    _ExtentY        =    2143
    Operand1        =    "4"
    Operand2        =    "5"
End
```

Storing and retrieving property values makes properties persistent; when the developer sets properties at design-time and then runs the application, they'll find that the property values they set have been preserved.

Using InitProperties to Set Defaults

Note that you can use the `UserControl InitProperties` event to set defaults for properties. This event fires just once for an instance of a control—when the developer first sites it in an application. You set the defaults for properties in this event's handler, and since this event never fires again, the settings the developer made since originally creating the control are not overwritten.

Using the ActiveX Control Interface Wizard

You can let the Visual Basic ActiveX Control Interface Wizard set up a new control for you. Create a new ActiveX control project now. When you select the `Add User Control` item in the `Project` menu, the `Add User Control` dialog appears, as shown in Figure 10.11. To start the ActiveX Control Interface Wizard, select that item in the `Add User Control` dialog and click `Open`. The wizard will work with the `UserControl` already in your project.

You can also invoke the ActiveX Control Interface Wizard from the `Add-Ins` menu if you load it with the `Add-In Manager`, also available in that menu.

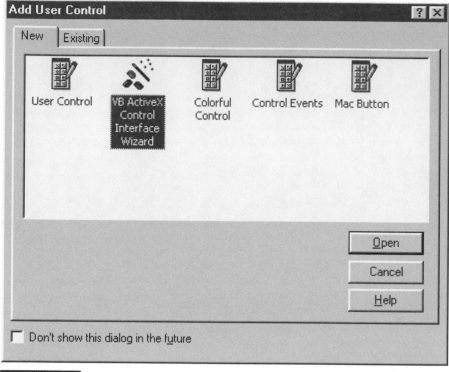

FIGURE 10.11   The Add User Control dialog.

The ActiveX Control Interface Wizard opens to its Introduction screen; click Next to start working on the properties, methods, and events in your control. When you click Next, the ActiveX Control Interface Wizard displays its Select Interface Members window, as shown in Figure 10.12.

You can choose from among a wide variety of already supported properties, methods, and events in the Select Interface Members window by adding them to the list box at the right. When you've added the items you want, click Next to bring up the Create Custom Interface Members window, as shown in Figure 10.13.

In the Create Custom Interface Members window, you can add support for the properties, methods, and events you want to add yourself. Just click the New button, type in the name of the item, and indicate whether it's a property, method, or event by clicking the appropriate option button.

After you've added the custom members you want, click Next to bring up the Set Mapping window, as shown in Figure 10.14.

In the Set Mapping window, you can map the properties, methods, and events to the various components in your control. For example, you may

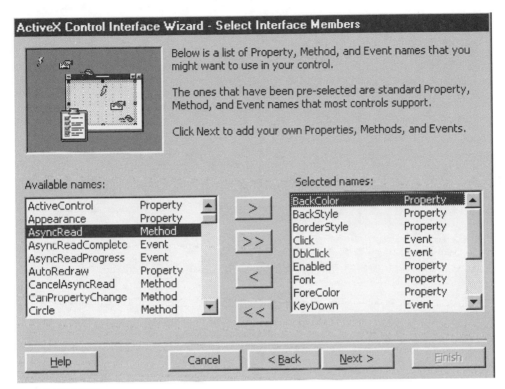

ActiveX Control Interface Wizard - Select Interface Members

Below is a list of Property, Method, and Event names that you might want to use in your control.

The ones that have been pre-selected are standard Property, Method, and Event names that most controls support.

Click Next to add your own Properties, Methods, and Events.

Available names:

ActiveControl	Property
Appearance	Property
AsyncRead	Method
AsyncReadComplete	Event
AsyncReadProgress	Event
AutoRedraw	Property
CancelAsyncRead	Method
CanPropertyChange	Method
Circle	Method

Selected names:

BackColor	Property
BackStyle	Property
BorderStyle	Property
Click	Event
DblClick	Event
Enabled	Property
Font	Property
ForeColor	Property
KeyDown	Event

> | >> | < | <<

| Help | | Cancel | < Back | Next > | Finish |

FIGURE 10.12   The ActiveX Control Interface Wizard, `Select Interface Members` window.

set the `BackColor` property of a text box, `Text1`, by mapping the Back-Color property in the left list box to `Text1`'s `BackColor` property in the `Maps to` frame after you've selected `Text1` in the `Control` drop-down list and `BackColor` in the `Member` drop-down list.

After mapping the items you want, click `Next` to bring up the `Set Attributes` window, as shown in Figure 10.15.

In this window, you set the attributes of properties, methods, and events. For example, you can set the default values for properties and specify whether they should be read/write or not at run-time or design-time. If you want to distinguish between design-time and run-time this way, the wizard will add code to check the `Ambient.UserMode` property automatically.

Click `Next` to bring up the `Finished!` window, and click the `Finish` button to let the wizard configure your `UserControl`.

The ActiveX Control Interface Wizard displays a summary of what it did, and allows you the option of saving the summary to disk; click the `Save` button to save it to disk, or the `Close` button to close the wizard. The wizard creates support for all that you asked it, using code like this:

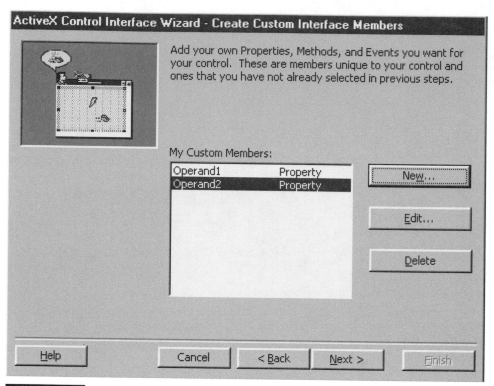

FIGURE 10.13 The ActiveX Control Interface Wizard, `Create Custom Interface Members` window.

```
'WARNING! DO NOT REMOVE OR MODIFY THE FOLLOWING _
    COMMENTED LINES!
'MappingInfo=UserControl,UserControl,-1,BackColor
Public Property Get BackColor() As OLE_COLOR
    BackColor = UserControl.BackColor
End Property


Public Property Let BackColor(ByVal New_BackColor _
    As OLE_COLOR)
    UserControl.BackColor() = New_BackColor
    PropertyChanged "BackColor"
End Property
```

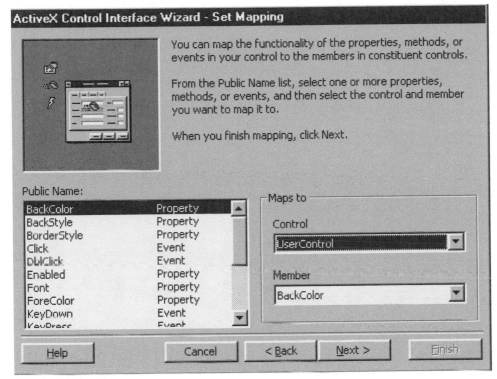

FIGURE 10.14 The ActiveX Control Interface Wizard, Set Mapping window.

The wizard also creates code to support property persistence automatically. As you can see, using the ActiveX Control Interface Wizard is an easy way to set up and configure ActiveX controls. The real way to get used to this tool, of course, is to put it to work—give it a try.

Experienced Visual Basic programmers usually find themselves using the code-generating Visual Basic wizards only rarely. However, if you're not familiar with a particular programming topic—like creating property pages, coming up next—the associated wizard gives you an easy introduction to the topic. Just run the wizard and take a look at the generated code to see what's possible.

Creating and Supporting Property Pages

In the early days of Visual Basic, you set properties for controls in the Properties window, and that was that. Since then, of course, controls have become much more complex, and property pages were born. Property pages can themselves become quite complex, but there's an easy way to create them: using the Property Page Wizard. You can also add property pages to

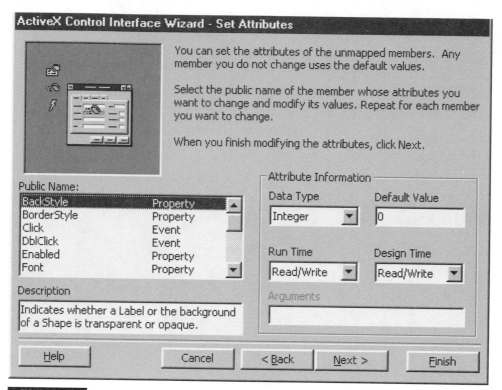

FIGURE 10.15 The ActiveX Control Interface Wizard, `Set Attributes` window.

your control directly using the `Add Property` page item in the `Project` menu; but, if you're new to creating property pages and working with `PropertyPage` objects, it's best to start with the Property Page Wizard.

The Property Page Wizard is an add-in, and you can make it appear in the `Add-Ins` menu by using the Add-In Manager. When you're working with a control that has properties, you start the Property Page Wizard by selecting it in that menu.

The Property Page Wizard first displays a window of introduction; click `Next` to bring up the `Select the Property Pages` window that you see in Figure 10.16.

Using this window, you create the property pages you want to support. Since the calculator control has two properties, `Operand1` and `Operand2`, I'll add two property pages, `PropertyPage1` and `PropertyPage2` (you can rename these pages by clicking the `Rename` button and typing in a new name).

Click the `Next` button to move to the `Add Properties` window, as shown in Figure 10.17. Here you'll find a tab for each new property page you've created, and a list of the available properties.

To add a property to a property page, you just click that page's tab and use the arrow buttons to add or remove properties from that page. I'll place

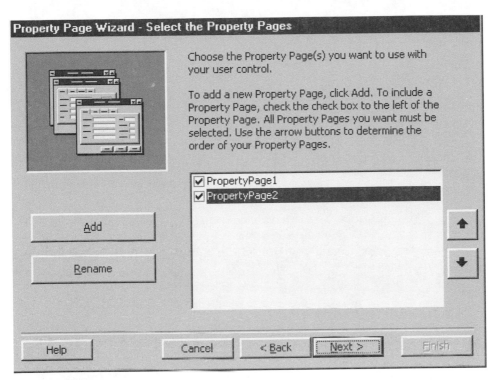

FIGURE 10.16 The Property Page wizard, `Select the Property Pages` window.

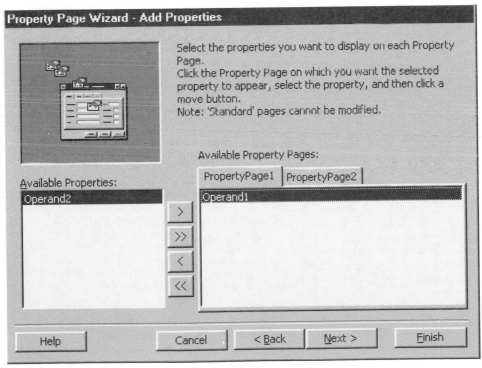

FIGURE 10.17 The Property Page Wizard, `Add Properties` window.

Operand1 on Page 1 and Operand2 on Page 2. Click Next after you've finished organizing your properties by page to bring up the Finished! window you see in Figure 10.18.

If you want a summary of what the Property Page Wizard did when creating your property pages, click the Yes option button, otherwise click No, then click the Finish button. If you clicked Yes, you'll see a summary report of the Property Page Wizard's actions; otherwise, the wizard just creates your pages and quits.

The new property pages are added to your control's project, and you store them in files with the extension .pag. At design-time, the developer can set the properties of your control using these pages, as shown in Figure 10.19, where I'm setting the value of Operand1 in the calculatorclient project to 4.

Customizing Property Pages

Note that the property pages that the Property Page Wizard creates are very simple. You can easily add more customization to those pages—just open them in their own designers by double-clicking them in the Project Explorer

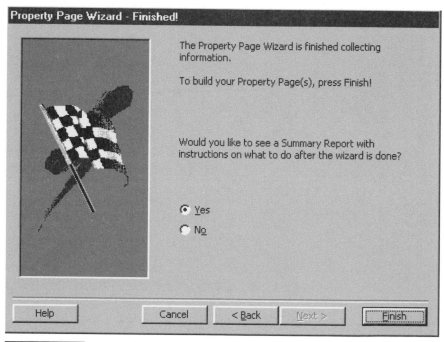

FIGURE 10.18 The Property Page Wizard, Finished! Window.

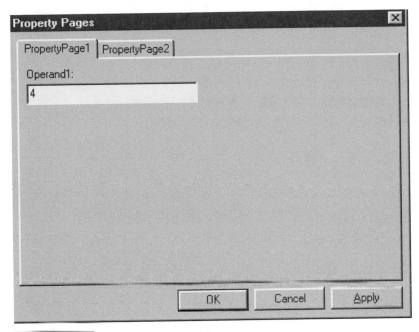

FIGURE 10.19   Using custom property pages.

(note that you don't need to use the Property Page Wizard at all after you become familiar with the process of creating property pages—just add them and code them).

For example, the first property page in the `calculatorcontrol` project appears in its designer in Figure 10.20.

Note that there is one text box, `txtOperand1`, in this property page, corresponding to the value the user wants to use for `Operand1`. To extend this page, you should know a little about how property pages work.

How Property Pages Work

Property pages are built on `PropertyPage` objects. When the user changes a setting of a property in a property page, you set the `Changed` property to True. When you set this property to True, you shouldn't necessarily update the property in the control—you should wait for the user to click an `Apply` button, if your page has one. If the `Changed` property is True, it's a signal to enable the `Apply` button.

Setting the `Changed` property to True also enables the `ApplyChanges` event, which occurs when the user clicks the `Apply` button that automatically appears under the `Property Pages` (not in the window). When this button

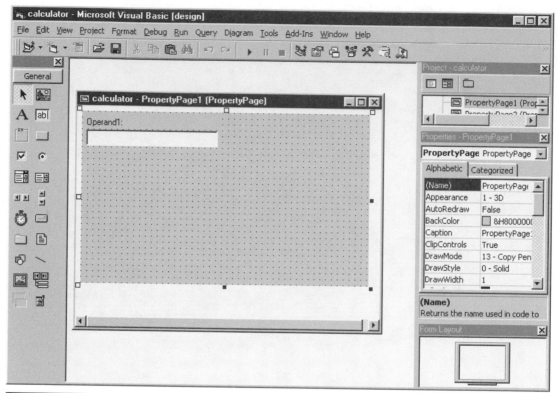

FIGURE 10.20   Using custom property pages.

is clicked, you take the new settings of the properties in the page and apply them to the control itself, which you access as `SelectedControls(0)` in the property page's `SelectedControls` property.

The `SelectedControls` property holds the controls that the user selected when opening the property page. This is an indexed property because the user can select more than one control. Note that when the user selects another control and the `Property Pages` window is still open, the `Property Pages` should display the new control's property settings, and you place code to do that in the property page's `SelectionChanged` event.

Here's how the Property Page Wizard has implemented the property page for `Operand1`:

```
Private Sub txtOperand1_Change()

    Changed = True

End Sub
```

```
Private Sub PropertyPage_ApplyChanges()
    SelectedControls(0).Operand1 = txtOperand1.Text
End Sub


Private Sub PropertyPage_SelectionChanged()
    txtOperand1.Text = SelectedControls(0).Operand1
End Sub
```

Now that you know how property pages function, you can elaborate this code to deal with more complex controls than simple text boxes, supplying list boxes, combo boxes, and more, as appropriate for the property you're working with.

That completes the calculatorcontrol and calculatorclient projects. For reference, the code from the calculatorcontrol project appears in Listing 10.1, and the code from the calculatorclient project appears in Listing 10.2. These two projects appear in folders with the same names on the CD.

LISTING 10.1   *Calculatorcontrol.ctl Code*

```
VERSION 5.00
Begin VB.UserControl CalculatorControl
   ClientHeight    =    1185
   ClientLeft      =    0
   ClientTop       =    0
   ClientWidth     =    6225
   PropertyPages   =    "calculatorcontrol.ctx":0000
   ScaleHeight     =    1185
   ScaleWidth      =    6225
   Begin VB.TextBox Text2
      Height       =    495
      Left         =    1800
      TabIndex     =    4
      Top          =    360
      Width        =    1215
   End
   Begin VB.CommandButton Command1
      Caption      =    "="
      Height       =    495
      Left         =    3240
      TabIndex     =    3
      Top          =    360
      Width        =    1215
   End
   Begin VB.TextBox Text3
      Height       =    495
```

```
      Left              =     4680
      TabIndex          =     1
      Top               =     360
      Width             =     1215
   End
   Begin VB.TextBox Text1
      Height            =     495
      Left              =     120
      TabIndex          =     0
      Top               =     360
      Width             =     1215
   End
   Begin VB.Label Label1
      Caption           =     "X"
      Height            =     255
      Left              =     1560
      TabIndex          =     2
      Top               =     480
      Width             =     255
   End
End
Attribute VB_Name = "CalculatorControl"
Attribute VB_GlobalNameSpace = False
Attribute VB_Creatable = True
Attribute VB_PredeclaredId = False
Attribute VB_Exposed = True
Attribute VB_Ext_KEY = "PropPageWizardRun" ,"Yes"
Public Event CalculatorClick()

Private Sub Command1_Click()
    Text3.Text = Text1.Text * Text2.Text
End Sub

Public Property Get Operand1() As Variant
Attribute Operand1.VB_ProcData.VB_Invoke_Property = _
    "PropertyPage1"
    Operand1 = Text1.Text
End Property

Public Property Let Operand1(ByVal vNewValue As Variant)
    Text1.Text = vNewValue
    PropertyChanged "Operand1"
End Property

Public Property Get Operand2() As Variant
Attribute Operand2.VB_ProcData.VB_Invoke_Property = _
    "PropertyPage2"
    Operand2 = Text2.Text
End Property

Public Property Let Operand2(ByVal vNewValue As Variant)
    Text2.Text = vNewValue
```

```
        PropertyChanged "Operand2"
End Property

Private Sub UserControl_Click()
    RaiseEvent CalculatorClick
End Sub

Private Sub UserControl_ReadProperties(PropBag As _
    PropertyBag)
    Text1.Text = PropBag.ReadProperty("Operand1")
    Text2.Text = PropBag.ReadProperty("Operand2")
End Sub

Private Sub UserControl_WriteProperties(PropBag As _
    PropertyBag)
    PropBag.WriteProperty "Operand1", Text1.Text
    PropBag.WriteProperty "Operand2", Text2.Text
End Sub

Public Sub CalculateResult()
    Text3.Text = Text1.Text * Text2.Text
End Sub
```

LISTING 10.2   *Calculatorclient.frm Code*

```
VERSION 5.00
Object = "{EC9FC239-D466-11D1-8881-E45E08C10000}#25.0#0";_
"calculatorcontrol.ocx"
Begin VB.Form Form1
    Caption         =    "Form1"
    ClientHeight    =    2715
    ClientLeft      =    60
    ClientTop       =    345
    ClientWidth     =    7380
    LinkTopic       =    "Form1"
    ScaleHeight     =    2715
    ScaleWidth      =    7380
    StartUpPosition =    3   'Windows Default
    Begin VB.CommandButton Command2
        Caption         =    "Invoke the CalculateResult method"
        Height          =    495
        Left            =    3840
        TabIndex        =    2
        Top             =    1920
        Width           =    3135
    End
    Begin VB.CommandButton Command1
        Caption         =    "Exchange the operands"
        Height          =    495
        Left            =    600
```

```
        TabIndex        =    1
        Top             =    1920
        Width           =    3015
    End
    Begin calculator.CalculatorControl CalculatorControl1
        Height          =    1215
        Left            =    600
        TabIndex        =    0
        Top             =    360
        Width           =    6255
        _ExtentX        =    11033
        _ExtentY        =    2143
        Operand1        =    "4"
        Operand2        =    "5"
    End
End
Attribute VB_Name = "Form1"
Attribute VB_GlobalNameSpace = False
Attribute VB_Creatable = False
Attribute VB_PredeclaredId = True
Attribute VB_Exposed = False
Private Sub CalculatorControl1_CalculatorClick()
    CalculatorControl1.CalculateResult
End Sub

Private Sub Command1_Click()
    Dim intTemp As Integer

    intTemp = CalculatorControl1.Operand1
    CalculatorControl1.Operand1 = CalculatorControl1.Operand2
    CalculatorControl1.Operand2 = intTemp
End Sub

Private Sub Command2_Click()
    CalculatorControl1.CalculateResult
End Sub
```

Now it's time to enable the data-aware capabilities of ActiveX controls, starting by making an ActiveX control into a data-bound control.

Making an ActiveX Control into a Data-Bound Control

You can enable the data binding capabilities of an ActiveX control easily. In this example, I'll create an ActiveX control named Bound that will display a text box. The developer can use the DataSource and DataField properties of the Bound control to connect a data source to this control, and the referenced data item will appear in Bound's text box. In this way, the Bound control will implement data binding.

Creating the Control

Create a new ActiveX control named Bound now, and place a text box, Text1, in the control. Set the control's BorderStyle property to Fixed Single so you'll be able to see it clearly in the client application. Now add a new property, intData, to the control. This property reflects the text in the text box, Text1, so you implement the property like this:

```
Public Property Get intData() As Variant
    intData = Text1.Text
End Property


Public Property Let intData(ByVal vNewValue _
    As Variant)
    Text1.Text = vNewValue
End Property
```

There's one issue to consider here: If this control is bound to a read-only database, we don't want to let the client change the data in the text box. You can check whether you're allowed to update the database or not with the CanPropertyChange method.

Using the CanPropertyChange Method

To use CanPropertyChange, you just pass this method the name of the property you want to update. If the database the control is bound to is not read-only, this method will return True, and before updating your data-bound property, you should check the result from this method. In fact, this method *always* returns True in Visual Basic 6.0 (if the database is really read-only, your changes will not be made to it), but Microsoft plans to implement this method at some point. Here's how using CanPropertyChange might look:

```
Public Property Let intData(ByVal vNewValue _
    As Variant)
    If CanPropertyChange("intData") Then
        Text1.Text = vNewValue
        PropertyChanged "intData"
    End If
End Property
```

To actually make this property data-bound, you select it in the `Proce-`
`dure Attributes` dialog from the `Tools` menu, as shown in Figure 10.21
(click the `Advanced` button to open the dialog fully).

Make sure the `intData` property is selected and click the `Property`
`is data bound` check box in the `Data binding` box at the bottom of the
dialog. This gives the control a `DataSource` property. Next, click the `This`
`property binds to DataField` check box, as also shown in Figure
10.21. This connects the `intData` property to the `DataField` property of
the control. Now close the `Procedure Attributes` dialog by clicking `OK`.

Creating the Client

We'll need a client to test the `Bound` control, so create a standard EXE project, `BoundClient`, now, and add the `Bound` control to `Form1` in this new
project. The `Bound` control, with its text box, appears.

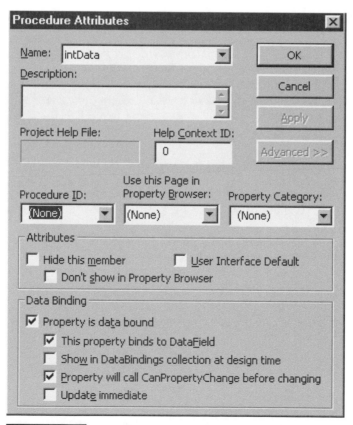

FIGURE 10.21   The `Procedure Attributes` dialog.

We'll also need a data source, so add an ADO data control, `Adodc1`, to `Form1`. Connect this data control to the database `Biblio.mdb` that comes with Visual Basic by setting the control's `ConnectionString` property. You also need to set the ADO data control's `RecordSource` property to one of the tables in the `Biblio.mdb` database, so open the drop-down list in that property's entry in the `Properties` window and select the `Authors` table.

Connect the `DataSource` property of the `Bound` control to `Adodc1`. Connect its `DataField` property to `Authors` in the drop-down list that appears in the property's entry in the `Properties` window.

Finally, run the application. When you do, you'll see the results in Figure 10.22, where the user can move through the authors stored in the `Biblio.mdb` database simply by using the arrow buttons in the data control. Congratulations—you've created a data-bound ActiveX control.

The DataBindings Collection

So far, I've implemented the `DataSource` and `DataField` properties of an ActiveX control, but some controls, like data-bound combo boxes, can have more data-aware properties. Only one property can be the `DataField` property of your control, but in fact, you can add any number of the properties of your ActiveX control to the data bindings collection and so make them bound properties as well.

Take another look at Figure 10.21—if you click the `Show in Data-Bindings collection at design time` check box, the property you're

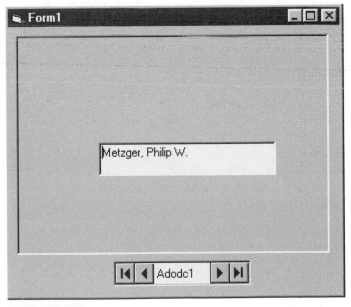

FIGURE 10.22   Creating a data-bound ActiveX control.

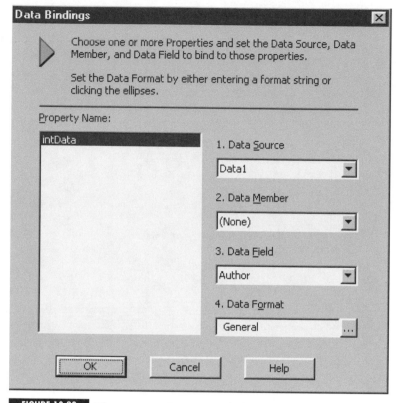

FIGURE 10.23   The Data Bindings dialog.

setting attributes for will appear in the control's data bindings collection, which means the developer can bind them to data sources as well.

To bind properties in the data bindings collection, you click the ellipsis button in the DataBindings property's entry in the Properties window at design-time, opening the Data Bindings dialog you see in Figure 10.23.

The developer can then use the Data Bindings dialog to bind the properties of your control to various data sources. In this way, you can bind multiple properties in an ActiveX control.

Besides binding properties to a data source, you can have an ActiveX control *become* a data source, and I'll take a look at that next.

Creating an ActiveX Control that is a Data Source

To make an ActiveX control (or any ActiveX component) a data source, you set its DataSourceBehavior to vbDataSource (the only other choice is vbNone, which is the default). Doing so adds a new event to your User-

Control: GetDataMember. This event fires when the client application wants to get the data that your control provides, and you'll usually pass a recordset back to the client; this recordset must be an ADO recordset (or, technically, a class that implements the OLEDBSimpleProvider interface).

I'll put this to work in an example now. In this case, I'll create an ActiveX control which is a data source for the Biblio.mdb database. I'll also include two buttons to let the user navigate forward and backward through the data in this database. This application is called datacontrol, and its client application is datacontrolclient. You'll find them on the CD in folders with those names.

Creating the Control

On the server side, create a new ActiveX control project now, naming the project DataControl in the Project Properties dialog. Set the User-Control's Name property to DataCtrl, its DataSourceBehavior property to vbDataSource, and add a label with the words Custom Data Control in it to the control. Next, make the control's BorderStyle property Fixed Single so it'll be clear in the client application, and add two command buttons, Command1 and Command2. We'll use these buttons to navigate through the database, so give Command1 a caption of < and Command2 a caption of >.

The actual data you return from a data source is an ADO recordset, so add a reference to the Microsoft ActiveX Data Objects library, giving the project the capability of working with ADO in code. We'll see more about ADO programming later, but the process is not difficult. First, you create a Recordset object, which I'll name rs:

```
Public rs As ADODB.Recordset
```

Next, in the control's Initialize event, you set up the recordset. First, you create an ADO Connection object, then use that object's Open method to open a connection to a database, which in our case is Biblio.mdb. After you've opened the database, you create a Recordset object and open that recordset with the Recordset object's Open method. It all looks like this:

```
Private Sub UserControl_Initialize()
    Dim db As Connection
    Set db = New Connection

    db.Open "PROVIDER=Microsoft.Jet.OLEDB.3.51;" & _
        "Data Source=C:\ado\Biblio.mdb;"
```

```
Set rs = New Recordset
rs.Open "select Author from Authors", db, _
    adOpenStatic, adLockOptimistic
```
End Sub

When the GetDataMember event fires, the client is asking for our data, and we can return the recordset, rs. That looks like this, where the DataMember parameter holds the name of the actual data member requested:

```
Private Sub UserControl_GetDataMember(DataMember _
    As String, Data As Object)
    Set Data = rs
```
End Sub

At this point, the data in the fields of the current record appear in the control bound to our ActiveX control.

You can also enable the < and > buttons to let the user move through the recordset by using the MoveNext, MovePrevious, MoveFirst, and Move-Last ADO methods. Here's how that works—note that I check to make sure the user isn't trying to move past the end of the database or before its beginning:

```
Private Sub Command1_Click()
    On Error GoTo ErrLabel


    If Not rs.BOF Then rs.MovePrevious
    If rs.BOF And rs.RecordCount > 0 Then
        rs.MoveFirst
    End If


    Exit Sub


ErrLabel:
    MsgBox Err.Description


End Sub


Private Sub Command2_Click()
    On Error GoTo ErrLabel
```

```
    If Not rs.EOF Then
            rs.MoveNext
    End If


    If rs.EOF And rs.RecordCount > 0 Then
        rs.MoveLast
    End If


    Exit Sub


ErrLabel:
    MsgBox Err.Description


End Sub
```

That's all it takes—the control is ready to go.

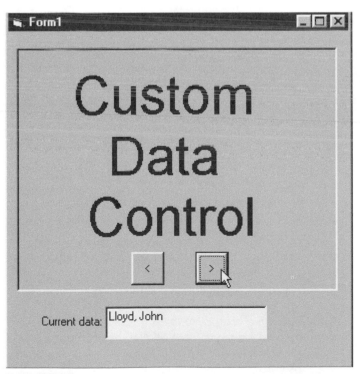

FIGURE 10.24 Creating a data source ActiveX control.

Creating the Client

When you embed the Data ActiveX control in a client application, you don't need any coding. You just set the DataSource property of a standard control you want to bind to the Data ActiveX control to the name of that control, DataCtrl1, and the DataField property of the standard control to the name of the database table we've used in the Data ActiveX control—Authors (this table will appear in the standard control's drop-down list in the DataField property's entry in the properties window).

Now run the application, as shown in Figure 10.24—the ActiveX control we created acts like a data source, supplying data to the text box you see in the figure. In addition, the user can use the < and > buttons to move through the database. Congratulations—you've created a data source ActiveX control.

Creating Invisible Data Controls, Control Containers, and Enumerated Properties

You might want to make your data source ActiveX control—or any other type of ActiveX control—invisible at run-time, much like timer controls. If so, there's a UserControl property you should set to True—not much chance for confusion here—the property is called InvisibleAtRunTime.

In addition, you can let your data-aware ActiveX control contain other controls, just as a picture box can contain other controls. To do so, you just set the ActiveX control's ControlContainer property to True.

There's one consideration you should bear in mind when supporting the Enabled property of your control, especially if you are drawing your own control. Although it might seem that you can just use the AmbientChanged event to check the UserControl's Enabled property, there's a little more to it. Your control must be able to redraw itself if its container is disabled; but, controls that are really disabled can't re-draw themselves.

Here's what you should do:

- Create a new, delegated Enabled property.
- Set this new property's ID to the Enabled property in the Procedure Attributes dialog
- If you're drawing the control yourself, check its Enabled property in the Paint event, and if it's disabled, draw the disabled representation of the control yourself.

You can also customize what the developer sees in the Properties window for a data-aware control. For example, you might want to let the developer only select from a certain list of possible settings for a property and display those properties in a drop-down list.

You do that by storing those values and their numeric equivalents in an enumerated list, like this:

```
Public Enum enmDay
    intSunday = 1
    intMonday = 2
    intTuesday = 3
    intWednesday = 4
    intThursday = 5
    intFriday = 6
    intSaturday = 7
End Enum
```

To store the value of the property internally, you must declare a variable of the enumeration's type:

```
Private intDay As enmDay
```

Then, in the `Property Get` and `Property Let` procedures, you set the data type to the enumeration, which tips Visual Basic off about what the possibilities are:

```
Public Property Get DayOfTheWeek() As enmDay
    DayOfTheWeek = intDay
End Property
```

```
Public Property Let DayOfTheWeek(ByVal vNewValue _
    As enmDay)
    intDay = vNewValue
End Property
```

Now when the developer accesses the new property in the `Properties` window for your data-aware ActiveX control, the possible values will appear, as shown in Figure 10.25. The developer can then select from among those values.

That's it for data-aware ActiveX controls. I'll take a look at creating data objects next.

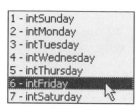

FIGURE 10.25 Set-
ting enumerated val-
ues for an ActiveX
control.

Creating and Using Data Objects

One of the powerful new aspects of database programming in Visual Basic is
the creation of data objects. We've seen how to create ActiveX controls that
are data sources, but it's also possible to create standard Visual Basic classes
that are data sources by setting their `DataSourceBehavior` property to `vb-
DataSource` and implementing the `GetDataMember` event handler.

You can use the Data Object Wizard add-in to create data objects, and
I'll create an example here. Create a new standard EXE project now and add
a Data Environment, `DataEnvironment1`, connected to the `Nwind.mdb`
database. Create a new command, `Command1`, that returns the `Customers`

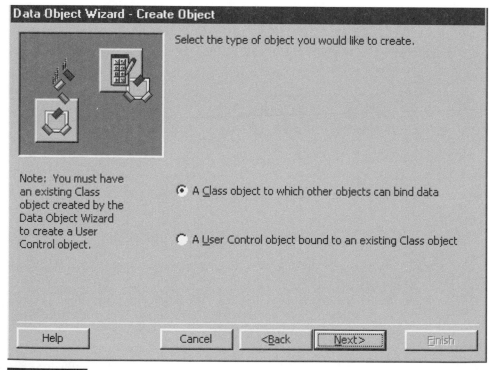

FIGURE 10.26 The Data Object Wizard `Create Object` page.

table from that database. Next, launch the `Data Object Wizard` from the `Add-Ins` menu (add it to that menu with the Add-In Manager if you have to).

The Data Object Wizard presents you with a window of introduction; click the `Next` button to bring up the `Create Object` page, as shown in Figure 10.26

As you can see in Figure 10.26, the Data Object Wizard allows you to create data classes and `UserControls`. We've already enabled `UserControls` as data sources, so select the `A class object to which other objects can bind data` option and click `Next`, bringing up the `Select Data Environment Command` page you see in Figure 10.27.

In this page, you select the `Command` object that acts as the data source, `Command1`, and click `OK`, bringing up the `Define Class Field Information` page you see in Figure 10.28.

In this page, you can indicate which fields can be set to null and which fields can act as primary keys. In this case, just accept the defaults. The next four pages let you indicate what Data Environment commands to use to perform lookup, insert, update, and delete operations. We won't use additional

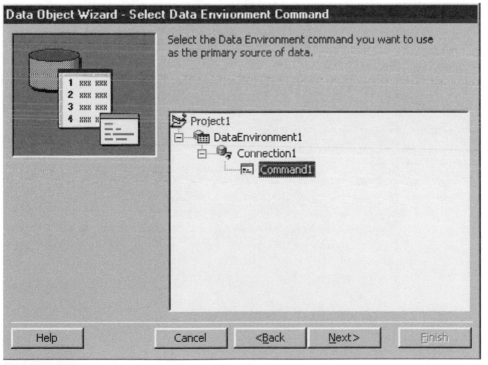

FIGURE 10.27 The Data Object Wizard, `Select Data Environment Command` page.

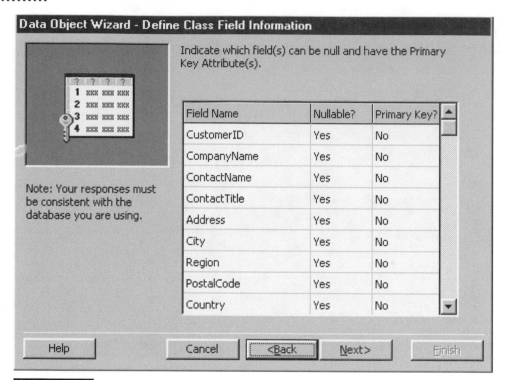

Data Object Wizard - Define Class Field Information

Indicate which field(s) can be null and have the Primary Key Attribute(s).

Note: Your responses must be consistent with the database you are using.

Field Name	Nullable?	Primary Key?
CustomerID	Yes	No
CompanyName	Yes	No
ContactName	Yes	No
ContactTitle	Yes	No
Address	Yes	No
City	Yes	No
Region	Yes	No
PostalCode	Yes	No
Country	Yes	No

[Help]   [Cancel]   [<Back]   [Next>]   [Finish]

FIGURE 10.28 The Data Object Wizard, `Define Class Field Information` page.

commands here, so just keep clicking `Next` until you get to the `Finished!` page you see in Figure 10.29.

Here, you give the new class a name—I'll just use `Nwind`—and click `Finish` to create the new data object. Doing so creates a new Visual Basic class, `rsclsNwind.cls`, which can act as a data source.

To bind to the data supplied by this class, create a new standard class, `Class1`, now, by selecting the `Add Class Module` item in the `Project` menu. I'll give this new class one property, `Name`, which we'll bind to the `ContactName` property in the `Customers` table exposed by the `rsclsNwind` class. Here's how I create this property:

```
Private varName


Public Property Get Name() As Variant
    Name = varName
End Property
```

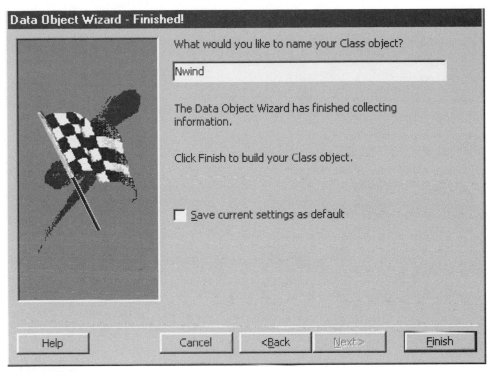

FIGURE 10.29 The Data Object Wizard, Finished! Page.

```
Public Property Let Name(ByVal vNewValue As Variant)
    varName = vNewValue
End Property
```

We'll create an object of the data source class, rsclsNwind, and an object of the data consumer class, Class1, and bind the Name property in the Class1 object to the ContactName field exposed in the data source. To do that, add this code to the Form_Load event of the project's default form, Form1. The code instantiates a data source object, objSource, and a data consumer object, objConsumer, like this:

```
Private objSource As rsclsNwind
Private objBinding As BindingCollection
Private objConsumer As Class1


Private Sub Form_Load()
```

```
Set objSource = New rsclsNwind
Set objConsumer = New Class1
    .
    .
    .
```

Now we can bind the ContactName field from objSource to the Name property of objConsumer by creating a new BindingCollection object, objBinding, and setting the objBinding object's DataSource property to objSource and its DataMember property to the command that exposes the Customers table, Command1:

```
Set objBinding = New BindingCollection
Set objBinding.DataSource = objSource
objBinding.DataMember = "Command1"
    .
    .
    .
```

Finally, you use the BindingCollection object's Add method to connect ContactName to Name. Here's how you use the Add method:

```
BindingCollection.Add object, PropertyName, _
DataField, [DataFormat [, Key]]
```

Here are the arguments of the Add method:

- **object**—Data consumer to be bound.
- **PropertyName**—Property of the data consumer to which the data field will be bound.
- **DataField**—Column of the data source that will be bound to the property specified in the PropertyName argument.
- **DataFormat**—A DataFormat object or a reference to a DataFormat variable that will be used to format the bound property.
- **Key**—Unique string that identifies the member of the collection.

In this case, you can use the Add method to bind objConsumer's Name property to the ContactName field exposed by objSource, and that ends the Form_Load event handler:

```
                 .

                 .

                 .

objBinding.Add objConsumer, "Name", _

    "ContactName"

End Sub
```

Now, objSource acts as a data source and objConsumer as its data consumer; the Name property of objConsumer is bound to the Contact-Name field exposed by objSource. To verify that, add a command button to Form1 and display the value in objConsumer's Name property, like this:

```
Private Sub Command1_Click()

    Text1.Text = objConsumer.Name

End Sub
```

The result appears in Figure 10.30. As you can see in that figure, we've bound objConsumer to objSource and displayed data from the underlying database. The project is a success. You can find it in the dataobject folder on the CD.

That finishes our work with data objects and ActiveX controls—as you can see, there's a great deal of power here. You can create ActiveX controls

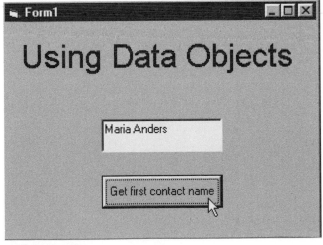

FIGURE 10.30   Using data objects.

that you can bind to data sources, and you can create ActiveX controls that are data sources. In addition, you can create data objects that can act as data sources in your code.

Now it's time to turn to something a little more exotic—using ADO programming with the Internet and Active Server Pages (ASP).

ADO and the Internet

One of the biggest aspects of ADO programming is working with the Internet, and I'll take a look at ADO and the Internet in this and the next chapter. Here, we'll see how to use the data source objects that ship with the Microsoft Internet Explorer, putting them to work in Web pages. The Internet Explorer ships with a number of data source objects (DSOs):

- MSHTML data source control.
- Tabular Data Control (TDC).
- XML data source control.
- JDBC data source applet.
- Remote Data Services (RDS, formerly named ADC).

We'll put the first four to work in this chapter, and work with RDS in the next chapter. Besides these DSOs, Microsoft has a gallery of data source objects; this gallery can be found currently at `www.microsoft.com/gallery/samples/default.asp` (note that things move around a lot on the Microsoft site, so this URL may be invalid when you try to use it; search for the word "gallery" if so).

With the exception of the JDBC data source applet, the DSOs above work with ADO to connect to data sources, using the ADOR library that comes with Internet Explorer (and which only supports `Record-set` objects). You can bind HTML tags to these data sources, and I'll start with an overview of those tags.

 Note that I'm assuming you're familiar with basic HTML in this and the next chapters. If not, you probably don't have to buy a book on HTML to see what's going on—just go to a Web search engine and search for the phrase "HTML tutorial". You're sure to find what you need on the Web, already freely available.

HTML-Bound Tags

In Microsoft's version of dynamic HTML, all HTML tags become active, with properties, methods, and sometimes events. Many tags in the Internet Explorer now support properties you can bind to data sources; to bind these tags to a data source, you use their `DATASRC` and `DATAFLD` attributes. Here's a list by HTML tag, showing what property is actually bound when you use the `DATASRC` and `DATAFLD` attributes:

- **A**—Binds to the `HREF` property; does not update data.
- **APPLET**—Binds to the `PARAM` property; updates data.
- **BUTTON**—Binds to the `innerText` and `innerHTML` properties; does not update data.
- **CHECKBOX**—Binds to the `checked` property; updates data.
- **DIV**—Binds to the `innerText` and `innerHTML` properties; does not update data.
- **FRAME**—Binds to the `src` property; does not update data.
- **HIDDEN**—Binds to the `value` property; updates data.
- **IFRAME**—Binds to the `src` property; does not update data.
- **IMG**—Binds to the `src` property; does not update data.
- **LABEL**—Binds to the `value` property; updates data.
- **MARQUEE**—Binds to the `innerText` and `innerHTML` properties; does not update data.
- **OBJECT**—Binds to the `PARAM` property; updates data.
- **PASSWORD**—Binds to the `value` property; updates data.
- **RADIO**—Binds to the `checked` property; updates data.
- **SELECT**—Binds to the `text` property of an option; updates data.
- **SPAN**—Binds to the `innerText` and `innerHTML` properties; does not update data.

· · · · · · · · · · · · · · ·

- **TABLE**—Constructs an entire table; does not update data.
- **TEXT**—Binds to the value property; updates data.
- **TEXTAREA**—Binds to the value property; updates data.

There are certain events that HTML tags have that you use with data bindings:

- **onbeforeupdate**—Fires when the data in the tag is sent to the DSO.
- **onafterupdate**—Fires after the data in the tag is sent to the DSO.
- **onerrorupdate**—Fires if there was an error that stopped data from being sent to the DSO.
- **onbeforeunload**—Fires before the page is unloaded.

I'll put a number of these tags to work in this chapter when we bind them to DSOs.

The MSHTML Data Source Control

The first Web page DSO I'll take a look at is the MSHTML data source control. Using this control as a DSO is easy; you just use the <OBJECT> tag in a Web page, giving the MSHTML data source control the ID you want to use to refer to it in the rest of the page, a height and width of 0, and set the tag's DATA attribute to the HTML page you want to use as the actual source of the data:

```
<OBJECT ID="dsoEmployees" DATA="employee.htm"
HEIGHT=0 WIDTH=0>
</OBJECT>
```

Here are the events of this control:

- **onDataAvailable**—Fires each time a batch of data is downloaded.
- **onDatasetChanged**—Fires when the data set was changed.
- **onDatasetComplete**—Fires when the data is downloaded and ready for use.
- **onReadyStateChange**—Fires when the ReadyState property changes.
- **onRowEnter**—Fires when a new record becomes the current one.
- **onRowExit**—Fires just before exiting the current record.

You can construct the Web page that holds the data in a free-form way, using all kinds of tags, as long as the type of tag you use has both an opening and closing tag (e.g., <H1> and </H1>), as well as an ID attribute. The MSHTML control will open and read through the data page, treating the ID attribute values as fields and successive groupings of fields as records. You can then treat the values you set for the ID attributes as fields in a database and bind them to other HTML tags using the DATAFLD attribute.

Here's an example that sets up a small database of employee records. In this case, I'm using the <SPAN> tag to define fields in records, but note that you can use any tag that has an ID attribute and a closing tag. Note also that the MSHTML control ignores tags that do not have their ID attribute set, so you can add other tags to the page as you like:

```
<HTML>
<HEAD>
<TITLE>Data Page</TITLE>
</HEAD>
<BODY>
<H1>This page holds data.</H1>
    Name: <SPAN ID="NAME">Tony</SPAN><BR>
    ID: <SPAN ID="ID">1234</SPAN><BR>
    Hire Date: <SPAN ID="HIRE_DATE">
        4-1-2001</SPAN><BR>
    Department: <SPAN ID="DEPARTMENT">
        Shipping</SPAN><BR>
    Title: <SPAN ID="TITLE">Packer</SPAN><BR>
    Name: <SPAN ID="NAME">Ed</SPAN><BR>
    ID: <SPAN ID="ID">1235</SPAN><BR>
    Hire Date: <SPAN ID="HIRE_DATE">
        4-1-2001</SPAN><BR>
    Department: <SPAN ID="DEPARTMENT">
        Programming</SPAN><BR>
    Title: <SPAN ID="TITLE">Programmer</SPAN><BR>
    Name: <SPAN ID="NAME">Francis</SPAN><BR>
    ID: <SPAN ID="ID">1236</SPAN><BR>
    Hire Date: <SPAN ID="HIRE_DATE">
        4-1-2001</SPAN><BR>
    Department: <SPAN ID="DEPARTMENT">
        Shipping</SPAN><BR>
    Title: <SPAN ID="TITLE">Packer</SPAN><BR>
```

```
Name: <SPAN ID="NAME">Linda</SPAN><BR>
ID: <SPAN ID="ID">1237</SPAN><BR>
Hire Date: <SPAN ID="HIRE_DATE">
    4-1-2001</SPAN><BR>
Department: <SPAN ID="DEPARTMENT">
    Shipping</SPAN><BR>
Title: <SPAN ID="TITLE">Packer</SPAN><BR>
Name: <SPAN ID="NAME">Louise</SPAN><BR>
ID: <SPAN ID="ID">1238</SPAN><BR>
Hire Date: <SPAN ID="HIRE_DATE">
    4-1-2001</SPAN><BR>
Department: <SPAN ID="DEPARTMENT">
    Shipping</SPAN><BR>
Title: <SPAN ID="TITLE">Packer</SPAN><BR>
</BODY>
</HTML>
```

This database page is called `employee.htm`, and as with the other HTML pages in this chapter, you'll find it in the HTML folder on the CD. Now that we have an HTML database, I'll put it to work with the MSHTML control.

Navigating with the MSHTML Control

Since the MSHTML control is built into the Internet Explorer, we can put it to work without any additional preparation, connecting it to the `employee.htm` data page developed above. I'll start by including a header for the new page, `mshtml1.htm`, using the `<OBJECT>` tag to point the MSHTML control at our data page, `employee.htm`, and naming this new control `dsoEmployees`:

```
<HTML>
<HEAD>
<TITLE>The MSHTML Data Source Control</TITLE>
</HEAD>


<BODY>


<CENTER>
```

```
<H1>Binding to buttons</H1>
```

```
<OBJECT ID="dsoEmployees" DATA="employee.htm"
HEIGHT=0 WIDTH=0>
</OBJECT>
```

.

.

.

Note that you can specify either a relative or absolute URL for the DATA attribute here, as long as it points to a data page that the MSHTML control can understand. That is, the DATA attribute does not have to point to a local page—you can retrieve the data from anywhere on the Web.

Now I'm ready to bind HTML tags to the MSHTML control. I'll start with two HTML text fields like this, binding their DATASRC properties to the DSO object dsoEmployees and their DATAFLD properties to NAME and ID:

```
Name: <INPUT TYPE="TEXT" DATASRC="#dsoEmployees"
DATAFLD="NAME" SIZE=10><P>
ID: <INPUT TYPE="TEXT" DATASRC="#dsoEmployees"
DATAFLD="ID" SIZE=5><P>
```

.

.

.

To display data in a Web page without visible controls like text fields, you can use tags like <SPAN> and <DIV>. Here's how to bind <SPAN> tags (I'll use <DIV> later in the chapter) to the HIRE_DATE and TITLE fields:

```
Hire date: <SPAN DATASRC="#dsoEmployees"
DATAFLD="HIRE_DATE"></SPAN><P>
Title: <SPAN DATASRC="#dsoEmployees"
DATAFLD="TITLE"></SPAN><P>
```

.

.

.

You can also bind involved controls, like SELECT controls, to a DSO. In this case, I'll bind a SELECT control to the DEPARTMENT field. If you set all the possible values for this field as options in the SELECT control, the control will display the setting of the field for the current record in the DSO:

```
Department: <SELECT DATASRC="#dsoEmployees"
DATAFLD="DEPARTMENT" SIZE=1>
            <OPTION VALUE="Shipping">Shipping
            <OPTION VALUE="Programming">Programming
            <OPTION VALUE="Editing">Editing
            <OPTION VALUE="Writing">Writing
            </SELECT><P>
               .

               .

               .
```

Having bound some controls to the MSHTML control, I'll add a few buttons to let the user navigate through the data. You gain access to the Recordset object in the DSO using that object's recordset property, which represents an ADO recordset. That means I can let the user navigate to the beginning of the recordset with the usual MoveFirst method like this when the user clicks a button with the caption <<:

```
<BUTTON
ONCLICK="dsoEmployees.recordset.MoveFirst()">
&lt;&lt;
</BUTTON>
        .

        .

        .
```

I can also let the user move to the previous record, if there is one, with a button like this, giving it the caption <:

```
<BUTTON
ONCLICK="if (!dsoEmployees.recordset.BOF)
dsoEmployees.recordset.MovePrevious()" >
&lt;
```

```
</BUTTON>
```

     .

     .

     .

And here's how to implement the other navigation buttons that let the user move to the next record and the last record:

```
<BUTTON
ONCLICK="if (!dsoEmployees.recordset.EOF)
dsoEmployees.recordset.MoveNext()">
&gt;
</BUTTON>


<BUTTON
ONCLICK="dsoEmployees.recordset.MoveLast()">
&gt;&gt;
</BUTTON>
</CENTER>


</BODY>
</HTML>
```

That's it; this page is called `mshtml1.htm`, and you'll find it in the HTML folder on the CD. When you open this page in the Internet Explorer, you see the result in Figure 11.1. As you can see in that figure, you can navigate through the recordset using the navigation buttons, just like the ADO data control, and the data in the recordset's fields appears in the bound tags. This first example is a success.

Besides using buttons to navigate through the recordset, you can also display all the data in a recordset at once, using tables, and I'll take a look at that next.

Creating Tables with the MSHTML Control

I'll create a new page here, named `mshtml2.htm` in the HTML folder on the CD, that will use the MSHTML control to display the data in `employee.htm` in an HTML table. I start by including the MSHTML control as before:

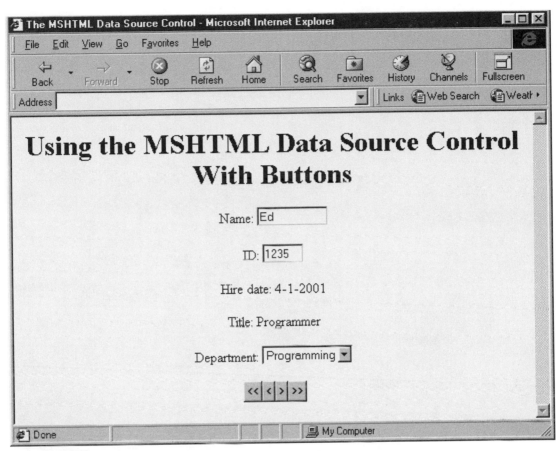

FIGURE 11.1   Using the MSHTML data source control with buttons.

```
<HTML>

<HEAD>

<TITLE>The MSHTML Data Source Control</TITLE>

</HEAD>

<BODY>


<CENTER>


<H1>Binding to a table</H1>


<OBJECT ID="dsoEmployees" DATA="employee.htm"
```

```
HEIGHT=0 WIDTH=0>
</OBJECT>
        .

        .

        .
```

Next, I bind a `<TABLE>` tag to the DSO I've named `dsoEmployees`:

```
<TABLE DATASRC="#dsoEmployees" CELLSPACING=10>
        .

        .

        .
```

I'll give this table a header, labelling the fields in each record, like this:

```
<TABLE DATASRC="#dsoEmployees" CELLSPACING=10>
<THEAD>
  <TR>
    <TH>Name</TH>
    <TH>ID</TH>
    <TH>Hire Date</TH>
    <TH>Department</TH>
  </TR>
</THEAD>
        .

        .

        .
```

Now I'll construct a table, using a `<SPAN>` tag in each cell and binding each cell to a data field (note that I don't have to specify the DATASRC attribute here, since I did that in the `<TABLE>` tag):

```
<TBODY>
  <TR>
      <TD><SPAN DATAFLD="NAME"
      DATAFORMATAS="HTML"></SPAN></TD>
```

```
      <TD><SPAN DATAFLD="ID"

      DATAFORMATAS="HTML"></SPAN></TD>

      <TD><SPAN DATAFLD="HIRE_DATE"

      DATAFORMATAS="HTML"></SPAN></TD>

      <TD><SPAN DATAFLD="DEPARTMENT"

      DATAFORMATAS="HTML"></SPAN></TD>

   </TR>

</TBODY>

</TABLE>


<CENTER>


</BODY>

</HTML>
```

And that's it; the result appears in Figure 11.2. As you can see in that figure, using HTML tables like this makes life very easy—all the data in the recordset is displayed at once for viewing. I'll take a look at another way of constructing HTML tables (using the `Recordset` object's `GetString` method) later in this chapter.

Besides the MSHTML control, another control that comes with the Internet Explorer is the Tabular Data Control (TDC).

The Tabular Data Control

The MSHTML control is great when you want to work with data stored in a Web page, but you can also work with data stored in text files using the Tabular Data Control (also, but incorrectly, called the Text Data Control). You can use this control to work with delimited text files (that is, text files where the fields are delimited with a certain character, such as a comma or semicolon) much like the `.csv` files created in Chapter 8. In fact, the TDC is a good choice if you don't want to give the user access to the data in your original database, since most database applications can produce `.csv` files. The data file used by the TDC is cached on the client and read off-line.

Here's how you place the TDC in a Web page using the `<OBJECT>` tag (the TDC is registered on your system when you install Internet Explorer):

```
<OBJECT
CLASSID="clsid:333C7BC4-460F-11D0-BC04-0080C7055A83"
```

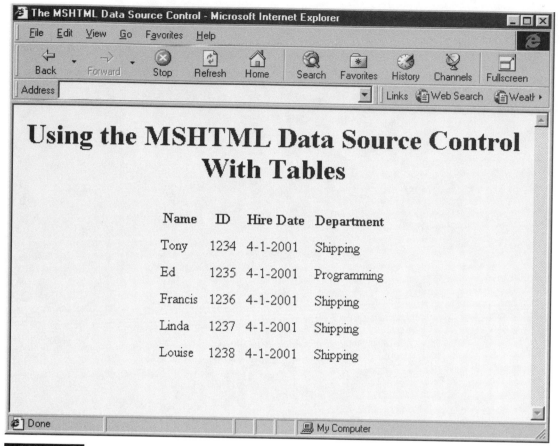

FIGURE 11.2
Using the MSHTML data source control with a table.

```
ID=dsoEmployees WIDTH=0 HEIGHT=0>
    <PARAM NAME="DataURL" VALUE="employees.csv">
</OBJECT>
```

Here, `DataURL` is a property specific to the TDC; you use this property to specify the data that should get loaded along with the page. I'll take a look at an example now. In this case, I'll store the employee data from `employee.htm` in a text file, `employee.text`. To name the fields in this database, I start with a header line like this, giving the names of each field and their types:

```
NAME:String;ID:Int;HIRE_DATE:Date;DEPARTMENT:String;
TITLE:String
```

.

.

.

Then I add the actual data to the file:

```
NAME:String;ID:Int;HIRE_DATE:Date;DEPARTMENT:String;
TITLE:String
Tony;1234;4-1-2001;Shipping;Packer
Ed;1235;4-1-2001;Programming;Programmer
Francis;1236;4-1-2001;Shipping;Packer
Linda;1237;4-1-2001;Shipping;Packer
Louise;1238;4-1-2001;Shipping;Packer
```

Now we're ready to use the TDC in a Web page.

Navigating with the TDC

This first example, which is named tdc1.htm and is in the HTML folder on the CD, will let the user move through the recordset using navigation buttons. I start by including a TDC in this page like this:

```
<HTML>
<HEAD>
<TITLE>The Tabular Data Control</TITLE>
</HEAD>
<BODY>

<CENTER>

<H1>
The Tabular Data Control
</H1>
```

```
<OBJECT
CLASSID="clsid:333C7BC4-460F-11D0-BC04-0080C7055A83"
ID="dsoEmployees" WIDTH=0 HEIGHT=0>
  <PARAM NAME="DataURL" VALUE="employee.txt">
  <PARAM NAME="FieldDelim" VALUE=";">
  <PARAM NAME="UseHeader" VALUE="True">
  <PARAM NAME="Sort" VALUE="ID">
</OBJECT>
```

.

.

.

Note that I use `<PARAMETER>` tags to configure the properties of the TDC. In this case, I'm specifying the location of the data text file with the `DataURL` parameter, the field delimiter character with the `FieldDelim` parameter, specifying whether or not to use a header in the text file with the `UseHeader` parameter, and indicating that the TDC should sort the data on the `ID` field. You can specify a URL in the `DataURL` parameter that points to files on Web servers; the data file need not be local.

Here are the properties you can use with the TDC:

- **AppendData**—Determines if new data is appended or replaces existing data.
- **CaseSensitive**—Indicates if the TDC distinguishes characters in the data set based upon their case.
- **CharSet**—Identifies the character set of the data file.
- **DataURL**—Specifies the location of the data file.
- **EscapeChar**—Specifies the character used to escape special characters.
- **FieldDelim**—Specifies the character used to mark the end of data fields.
- **Filter**—Specifies the criteria to use for filtering the data.
- **Language**—Specifies the language of the data file, including numerical and date formats.
- **Recordset**—Retrieves the recordset if the object is a data provider.
- **RowDelim**—Specifies the character used to mark the end of each row.
- **Sort**—Identifies the columns to be sorted, and ascending or descending sort order.
- **TextQualifier**—Specifies the optional character that surrounds a field.

- **UseHeader**—Specifies whether the first line of the data file contains header information.

The TDC has one method:

- **Reset**—Causes the control to filter or sort its data based on new settings.

The TDC also has the standard DSO events:

- **onDataAvailable**—Fires each time a batch of data is downloaded.
- **onDatasetChanged**—Fires when the data set is changed.
- **onDatasetComplete**—Fires when the data is downloaded and ready for use.
- **onReadyStateChange**—Fires when the ReadyState property changes.
- **onRowEnter**—Fires when a new record becomes the current one.
- **onRowExit**—Fires just before exiting the current record.

Using the TDC, I can bind HTML tags to the TDC as before:

```
Name: <INPUT TYPE="TEXT" DATASRC="#dsoEmployees"
DATAFLD="NAME" SIZE=10><P>
ID: <INPUT TYPE="TEXT" DATASRC="#dsoEmployees"
DATAFLD="ID" SIZE=5><P>
Department: <SELECT DATASRC="#dsoEmployees"
DATAFLD="DEPARTMENT"
SIZE=1>
            <OPTION VALUE="Shipping">Shipping
            <OPTION VALUE="Programming">Programming
            <OPTION VALUE="Editing">Editing
            <OPTION VALUE="Writing">Writing
            </SELECT><P>


Hire date: <SPAN DATASRC="#dsoEmployees"
DATAFLD="HIRE_DATE"></SPAN><P>
Title: <SPAN DATASRC="#dsoEmployees"
DATAFLD="TITLE"></SPAN><P>
    .

    .

    .
```

All that's left is to add navigation buttons, and that also works as before:

```
<BUTTON
ONCLICK="dsoEmployees.recordset.MoveFirst()">
&lt;&lt;
</BUTTON>

<BUTTON
ONCLICK="if (!dsoEmployees.recordset.BOF)
dsoEmployees.recordset.MovePrevious()">
&lt;
</BUTTON>

<BUTTON
ONCLICK="if (!dsoEmployees.recordset.EOF)
dsoEmployees.recordset.MoveNext()">
&gt;
</BUTTON>

<BUTTON
ONCLICK="dsoEmployees.recordset.MoveLast()">
&gt;&gt;
</BUTTON>

</CENTER>

</BODY>

</HTML>
```

This Web page appears in the Internet Explorer in Figure 11.3. As you can see in that figure, the user can navigate through the recordset using the buttons as before, and the field data in the recordset will appear in the bound HTML tags. The only difference here is that I'm using the TDC and storing the database in a text file.

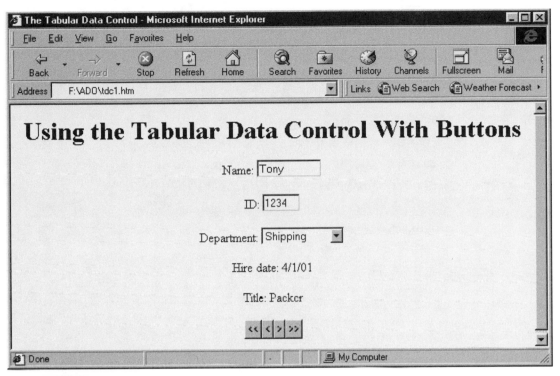

FIGURE 11.3 Using the TDC with buttons.

As with the MSHTML control, you can also present the data in a TDC in an HTML table.

Creating Tables with the TDC

Using the TDC to present data in a table is straightforward. I just add a TDC to a Web page:

```
<HTML>
<HEAD>
<TITLE>The Tabular Data Control</TITLE>
</HEAD>
<BODY>


<CENTER>


<H1>
```

Using the Tabular Data Control With Tables
</H1>

```
<OBJECT
CLASSID="clsid:333C7BC4-460F-11D0-BC04-0080C7055A83"
ID="dsoEmployees" WIDTH=0 HEIGHT=0>
  <PARAM NAME="DataURL" VALUE="employee.txt">
  <PARAM NAME="FieldDelim" VALUE=";">
  <PARAM NAME="UseHeader" VALUE="True">
  <PARAM NAME="Sort" VALUE="ID">
</OBJECT>
```

.

.

.

Then I bind that DSO to a table as before:

```
<TABLE DATASRC="#dsoEmployees" CELLSPACING=10>
<THEAD>
  <TR>
   <TH>Name</TH>
   <TH>ID</TH>
   <TH>Hire Date</TH>
   <TH>Department</TH>
  </TR>
</THEAD>
<TBODY>
  <TR>
   <TD><SPAN DATAFLD="NAME"
DATAFORMATAS="HTML"></SPAN></TD>
   <TD><SPAN DATAFLD="ID"
DATAFORMATAS="HTML"></SPAN></TD>
   <TD><SPAN DATAFLD="HIRE_DATE"
DATAFORMATAS="HTML"></SPAN></TD>
```

```
    <TD><SPAN DATAFLD="DEPARTMENT"
DATAFORMATAS="HTML"></SPAN></TD>

    </TR>

</TBODY>

</TABLE>


</CENTER>


</BODY>

</HTML>
```

That's all it takes; the result appears in Figure 11.4. As you can see, you can bind the TDC to tables just as easily as you can bind tables to the MSHTML control.

So far, we've seen the MSHTML and TDC controls; it's time to turn to XML.

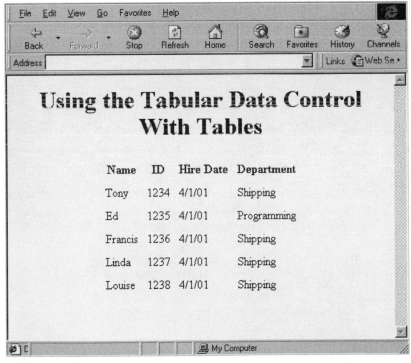

FIGURE 11.4   Using the TDC with tables.

The XML Data Source Control

You can use Extensible Markup Language (XML) to describe data in a structured way on the Web. XML DSOs have an advantage over other DSOs, because you can use XML to structure your data many levels deep, as I'll do in this chapter.

Internet Explorer 4 comes with an applet that lets you create an XML DSO like this:

```
<APPLET
    CODE="com.ms.xml.dso.XMLDSO.class"
    ID="dsoEmployees"
    WIDTH="0"
    HEIGHT="0"
    MAYSCRIPT="true">
    <PARAM NAME="URL" VALUE="employee.xml">
</APPLET>
```

In this case, you pass the XML page that holds the data using the URL parameter. The XML data source control supports the usual DSO events:

- **onDataAvailable**—Fires each time a batch of data is downloaded.
- **onDatasetChanged**—Fires when the data set is changed.
- **onDatasetComplete**—Fires when the data is downloaded and ready for use.
- **onReadyStateChange**—Fires when the ReadyState property changes.
- **onRowEnter**—Fires when a new record becomes the current one.
- **onRowExit**—Fires just before exiting the current record.

Internet Explorer 5 goes one step further, and integrates XML support directly by using XML *data islands*. You can use XML data islands to embed data in XML format in an HTML page.

As an example, I'll take a look at using the XML DSO here, and I'll translate the employee database—employee.htm—into an XML page, employee.xml. I start by giving the XML version:

```
<?xml version="1.0"?>
        .

        .

        .
```

Next, I create a new XML tag named `<EMPLOYEES>` (you define your own tags in XML; in more involved applications, you can also specify how those headers are to work, what tags can nest in other tags, and so on):

```
<?xml version="1.0"?>

<EMPLOYEES>

        .

        .

        .
```

I'll give each employee's record a NAME, ID, HIRE_DATE, DEPARTMENT, and TITLE tag like this:

```
<?xml version="1.0"?>

<EMPLOYEES>
    <ITEM>
        <NAME>Tony</NAME>
        <ID>1234</ID>
        <HIRE_DATE>4-1-2001</HIRE_DATE>
        <DEPARTMENT>Shipping</DEPARTMENT>
        <TITLE>Packer</TITLE>
    </ITEM>
    <ITEM>
        <NAME>Ed</NAME>
        <ID>1235</ID>
        <HIRE_DATE>4-1-2001</HIRE_DATE>
        <DEPARTMENT>Programming</DEPARTMENT>
        <TITLE>Programmer</TITLE>
    </ITEM>
    <ITEM>
        <NAME>Francis</NAME>
        <ID>1236</ID>
        <HIRE_DATE>4-1-2001</HIRE_DATE>
        <DEPARTMENT>Shipping</DEPARTMENT>
        <TITLE>Packer</TITLE>
    </ITEM>
```

```
<ITEM>
    <NAME>Linda</NAME>
    <ID>1237</ID>
    <HIRE_DATE>4-1-2001</HIRE_DATE>
    <DEPARTMENT>Shipping</DEPARTMENT>
<TITLE>Packer</TITLE>
</ITEM>
<ITEM>
    <NAME>Louise</NAME>
    <ID>1238</ID>
    <HIRE_DATE>4-1-2001</HIRE_DATE>
    <DEPARTMENT>Shipping</DEPARTMENT>
    <TITLE>Packer</TITLE>
</ITEM>
</EMPLOYEES>
```

That completes `employee.xml`, which you'll find on the CD in the HTML folder. It's time to put this XML file to work.

Navigating with the XML Data Source Control

In this first example, I'll use the XML data source control to bind to the `employee.xml` file, presenting the user with a set of navigation buttons. I start by adding the XML data source control to a Web page, `xml1.htm`, which you'll find in the HTML folder on the CD:

```
<HTML>
<HEAD>
<TITLE>XML Data Source Control</TITLE>
</HEAD>
<BODY>

<CENTER>

<H1>Using the XML Data Source Control With
Buttons</H1>
```

```
<APPLET CODE="com.ms.xml.dso.XMLDSO.class"
ID="dsoEmployees" WIDTH=0 HEIGHT=0
MAYSCRIPT=true>
  <PARAM NAME="URL" VALUE="employee.xml">
</APPLET>
    .
    .
    .
```

That's it—now all that's left is to bind the XML data source control to HTML tags and invoke recordset methods with buttons:

```
Name: <INPUT TYPE="TEXT" DATASRC="#dsoEmployees"
DATAFLD="NAME"
SIZE=10><P>
ID: <INPUT TYPE="TEXT" DATASRC="#dsoEmployees"
DATAFLD="ID" SIZE=5><P>
Hire date: <SPAN DATASRC="#dsoEmployees"
DATAFLD="HIRE_DATE"></SPAN><P>
Title: <SPAN DATASRC="#dsoEmployees"
DATAFLD="TITLE"></SPAN><P>
Department: <SELECT DATASRC="#dsoEmployees"
DATAFLD="DEPARTMENT" SIZE=1>
            <OPTION VALUE="Shipping">Shipping
            <OPTION VALUE="Programming">Programming
            <OPTION VALUE="Editing">Editing
            <OPTION VALUE="Writing">Writing
            </SELECT><P>

<BUTTON
ONCLICK="dsoEmployees.recordset.MoveFirst()">
&lt;&lt;
</BUTTON>

<BUTTON
```

```
ONCLICK="if (!dsoEmployees.recordset.BOF)
dsoEmployees.recordset.MovePrevious()">
&lt;
</BUTTON>

<BUTTON
ONCLICK="if (!dsoEmployees.recordset.EOF)
dsoEmployees.recordset.MoveNext()">
&gt;
</BUTTON>

<BUTTON
ONCLICK="dsoEmployees.recordset.MoveLast()">
&gt;&gt;
</BUTTON>

</CENTER>

</BODY>
</HTML>
```

And that's all it takes; the results appear in Figure 11.5. As you can see in that figure, the XML data source control can function just like other DSOs—but, there's more coming up.

Creating Tables with the XML Data Source Control

You can also use the XML data source control with tables, as you'd expect. For example, xml2.htm, which you'll find in the HTML folder on the CD, appears in Listing 11.1. This Web page uses the XML data source control to display the data in employee.xml in a table.

LISTING 11.1   *Xml2.htm Code*

```
<HTML>
<HEAD>
<TITLE>XML Data Source Control</TITLE>
</HEAD>
<BODY>
```

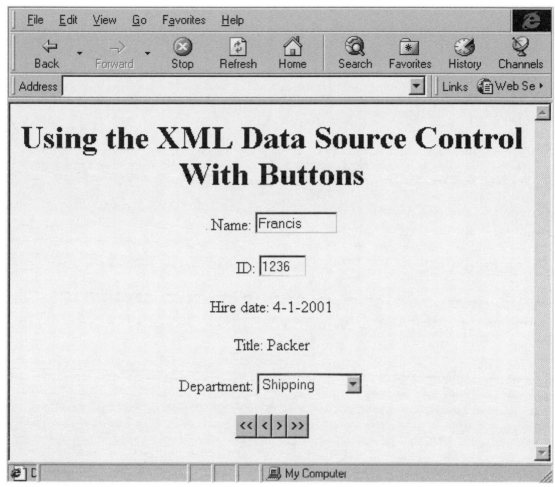

FIGURE 11.5 Using the XML data source control with buttons.

```
<CENTER>

<H1>Using the XML Data Source Control With Tables</H1>

<APPLET CODE="com.ms.xml.dso.XMLDSO.class"
  ID="dsoEmployees" WIDTH=0 HEIGHT=0 MAYSCRIPT=true>
  <PARAM NAME="URL" VALUE="employee.xml">
</APPLET>

<TABLE DATASRC="#dsoEmployees" CELLSPACING=10>
<THEAD>
  <TR>
   <TH>Name</TH>
```

```
    <TH>ID</TH>
    <TH>Hire Date</TH>
    <TH>Department</TH>
  </TR>
</THEAD>
<TBODY>
  <TR>
    <TD><SPAN DATAFLD="NAME"
    DATAFORMATAS="HTML"></SPAN></TD>
    <TD><SPAN DATAFLD="ID"
    DATAFORMATAS="HTML"></SPAN></TD>
    <TD><SPAN DATAFLD="HIRE_DATE"
    DATAFORMATAS="HTML"></SPAN></TD>
    <TD><SPAN DATAFLD="DEPARTMENT"
    DATAFORMATAS="HTML"></SPAN></TD>
  </TR>
</TBODY>
</TABLE>

</CENTER>

</BODY>
</HTML>
```

The results of xml2.htm appear in Figure 11.6. As you can see in that figure, you can use the XML data source control to create and populate HTML tables with data.

However, there's more that you can do with the XML data source control—you can also handle hierarchical data, and I'll take a look at that after the JDBC data source applet, coming up next.

JDBC Data Source Applet

As of this writing, the JDBC data source applet is available for download from msdn.microsoft.com/downloads/samples/Internet/author/data src/jdbcapplet/default.asp. When you install this applet on your hard disk, it's stored in a .cab file named jdc.cab, placed by default in the directory C:\Workshop\Samples\Internet\author\datasrc\jdbcapplet. This applet doesn't actually use ADO at all, but rather, it uses ODBC DSNs, so I'll just review it here.

You embed the JDBC data source applet in a Web page like this:

```
<HTML>

<HEAD>

<TITLE>The JDBC Data Source Control</TITLE>
```

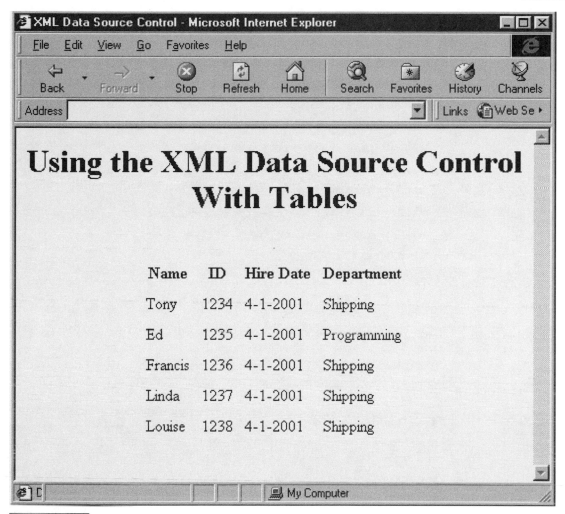

FIGURE 11.6 Using the XML data source control with tables.

```
</HEAD>
<BODY>

<CENTER>

<H1>Using the JDBC Data Source Control With
Buttons</H1>
```

```
<APPLET CODE=JDC.class NAME="dsoEmployees"
ID="dsoEmployees" WIDTH=0 HEIGHT=0>
    <PARAM NAME="cabbase" VALUE=
    "C:\Workshop\Samples\Internet\author\datasrc\
    jdbcapplet\jdc.cab">
    <PARAM NAME="dbURL" VALUE="jdbc:odbc:db">
    <PARAM NAME="showUI" VALUE="false">
    <PARAM NAME="sqlStatement"
    VALUE="SELECT * FROM students">
    <PARAM NAME="allowInsert" VALUE="true">
    <PARAM NAME="allowDelete" VALUE="true">
    <PARAM NAME="allowUpdate" VALUE="true">
</APPLET>
```

Note the large number of parameters you can pass to this applet; here are all the possibilities and what they mean:

- **allowDelete**—Indicates whether existing records can be deleted.
- **allowInsert**—Indicates whether new records can be inserted into the data set.
- **allowUpdate**—Indicates whether existing records can be updated.
- **cabbase**—The location of the code for the applet. The code will be downloaded to the client if not already installed.
- **dbURL**—The ODBC data source name (DSN) configured in the user's control panel.
- **password**—The user's password (optional).
- **showUI**—Indicates if a user interface should be displayed (optional).
- **sqlStatement**—SQL string identifying the table and columns to be selected from the database.
- **user**—User name (optional).

After you've added the JDBC data source control to a Web page using the <APPLET> tag, you can use it as you would any other DSO, binding it to controls and using the methods of its internal recordset.

That completes the overview of the four DSOs we'll take a look at in this chapter. In the rest of this chapter, I'll take a look at how to handle hierarchical data with the XML DSO, and how to work with DSOs in code.

Handling Hierarchical Data in XML

The big attraction of XML is that it lets you structure your data. XML can support hierarchical data, where records can themselves have multiple data items. To see how this works, I'll modify the employee.xml XML data file I created earlier to a new file, employee2.xml, which will include two supervisor evaluations for each employee.

The supervisor evaluations will themselves each store two items—a date and a letter report like this:

```
<?xml version="1.0"?>
<EMPLOYEES>
    <EMPLOYEE>
        <NAME>Tony</NAME>
        <RECORD>
            <ID>1234</ID>
            <HIRE_DATE>4-1-2001</HIRE_DATE>
            <DEPARTMENT>Shipping</DEPARTMENT>
            <TITLE>Packer</TITLE>
            <EVALUATION>
                <DATE>4-1-2002</DATE>
                <REPORT>B</REPORT>
            </EVALUATION>
            <EVALUATION>
                <DATE>5-1-2002</DATE>
                <REPORT>A</REPORT>
            </EVALUATION>
        </RECORD>
    </EMPLOYEE>
```

The whole document, employees2.xml, appears in Listing 11.2; as you can see in that listing, each employee's record now contains two evaluation records, giving this database a hierarchical structure. The XML data source control lets you handle this kind of structured data easily, and I'll put it to work next.

►•••••••••••••••

LISTING 11.2 *Employees2.xml Document*

```xml
<?xml version="1.0"?>
<EMPLOYEES>
    <EMPLOYEE>
        <NAME>Tony</NAME>
        <RECORD>
            <ID>1234</ID>
            <HIRE_DATE>4-1-2001</HIRE_DATE>
            <DEPARTMENT>Shipping</DEPARTMENT>
            <TITLE>Packer</TITLE>
            <EVALUATION>
                <DATE>4-1-2002</DATE>
                <REPORT>B</REPORT>
            </EVALUATION>
            <EVALUATION>
                <DATE>5-1-2002</DATE>
                <REPORT>A</REPORT>
            </EVALUATION>
        </RECORD>
    </EMPLOYEE>
    <EMPLOYEE>
        <NAME>Ed</NAME>
        <RECORD>
            <ID>1235</ID>
            <HIRE_DATE>4-1-2001</HIRE_DATE>
            <DEPARTMENT>Programming</DEPARTMENT>
            <TITLE>Programmer</TITLE>
            <EVALUATION>
                <DATE>4-1-2002</DATE>
                <REPORT>A</REPORT>
            </EVALUATION>
            <EVALUATION>
                <DATE>5-1-2002</DATE>
                <REPORT>A</REPORT>
            </EVALUATION>
        </RECORD>
    </EMPLOYEE>
    <EMPLOYEE>
        <NAME>Francis</NAME>
        <RECORD>
            <ID>1236</ID>
            <HIRE_DATE>4-1-2001</HIRE_DATE>
            <DEPARTMENT>Shipping</DEPARTMENT>
            <TITLE>Packer</TITLE>
            <EVALUATION>
                <DATE>4-1-2002</DATE>
                <REPORT>A</REPORT>
            </EVALUATION>
            <EVALUATION>
                <DATE>5-1-2002</DATE>
```

```
                <REPORT>A</REPORT>
            </EVALUATION>
        </RECORD>
    </EMPLOYEE>
    <EMPLOYEE>
        <NAME>Linda</NAME>
        <RECORD>
            <ID>1237</ID>
            <HIRE_DATE>4-1-2001</HIRE_DATE>
            <DEPARTMENT>Shipping</DEPARTMENT>
            <TITLE>Packer</TITLE>
            <EVALUATION>
                <DATE>4-1-2002</DATE>
                <REPORT>A</REPORT>
            </EVALUATION>
            <EVALUATION>
                <DATE>5-1-2002</DATE>
                <REPORT>C</REPORT>
            </EVALUATION>
        </RECORD>
    </EMPLOYEE>
    <EMPLOYEE>
        <NAME>Louise</NAME>
        <RECORD>
            <ID>1238</ID>
            <HIRE_DATE>4-1-2001</HIRE_DATE>
            <DEPARTMENT>Shipping</DEPARTMENT>
            <TITLE>Packer</TITLE>
            <EVALUATION>
                <DATE>4-1-2002</DATE>
                <REPORT>B</REPORT>
            </EVALUATION>
            <EVALUATION>
                <DATE>5-1-2002</DATE>
                <REPORT>C</REPORT>
            </EVALUATION>
        </RECORD>
    </EMPLOYEE>
</EMPLOYEES>
```

The Web page I'll develop to use XML hierarchical data is called `hier-arch.htm`, and you'll find it in the `HTML` folder on the CD. This page will display the data in `employees2.xml` in a series of tables. I'll start by adding the XML data source control and connecting it to `employee2.xml`:

```
<HTML>

<HEAD><TITLE></TITLE>
```

```
<BODY>

<CENTER>

<H1>The XML Data Source Control With Hierarchical
Records</H1>

<APPLET CODE=com.ms.xml.dso.XMLDSO.class
    WIDTH=0 HEIGHT=0
    ID=dsoEmployee mayscript=true>
   <PARAM NAME="url" VALUE="employee2.xml">
</APPLET>
    .
    .
    .
```

Next, I'll create a table using the XML DSO:

```
<TABLE DATASRC="#dsoEmployee" BORDER=1>
    <TR>
    .
    .
    .
```

Inside that table, I'll list the employee's name first:

```
<TABLE DATASRC="#dsoEmployee" BORDER=1>
    <TR>
        <TH><DIV DATAFLD="NAME"></DIV></TH>
    .
    .
    .
```

Now I'll create a new table inside the first table, binding it to the
<RECORD> field:

```
<TABLE DATASRC="#dsoEmployee" BORDER=1>
    <TR>
        <TH><DIV DATAFLD="NAME"></DIV></TH>
        <TD>
            <TABLE DATASRC="#dsoEmployee"
            DATAFLD="RECORD">

                .
                .
                .
```

Finally, I'll create a third table within this new table. This table will display the date and report values for each evaluation. To reach the <EVALU-ATION> items inside the <RECORD> items, I refer to them as RECORD.EVALU-ATION:

```
<TABLE DATASRC="#dsoEmployee" BORDER=1>
    <TR>
        <TH><DIV DATAFLD="NAME"></DIV></TH>
        <TD>
            <TABLE DATASRC="#dsoEmployee"
            DATAFLD="RECORD">
                <TR ALIGN = CENTER>
                    <TD>Evaluations</TD>
                </TR>
                <TR>
                    <TD>
                        <TABLE DATASRC="#dsoEmployee"
                        DATAFLD="RECORD.EVALUATION"
                        BORDER = 1>
                            <TR ALIGN = CENTER>
                                <TH>Date</TH>
                                <TH>Report</TH>
                            </TR>
                            <TR ALIGN = CENTER>
                                <TD><DIV DATAFLD="DATE"
```

```
                                     dataformatas="HTML">
                                     </DIV></TD>
                                     <TD><DIV
                                     DATAFLD="REPORT"
                                     dataformatas="HTML">
                                     </DIV></TD>
                                 </TR>
                             </TABLE>
                         </TD>
                     </TR>
                 </TABLE>
             </TD>
         </TR>
     </TABLE>


     </CENTER>


     </BODY>
     </HTML>
```

And that's it; the result of this page, `hierarch.htm`, appears in Figure 11.7. As you can see in that figure, the XML data source control has deciphered the data in `employee2.xml` and displayed it neatly in tables within tables. This example is a success.

Another powerful aspect of using DSOs in Web pages is that you can work with the recordset objects in DSOs directly, and I'll take a look at that now.

Using Recordsets in Web Page Code

You can use the `Recordset` object in a DSO just as you would any other ADO `Recordset` object. As an example, I'll create a new page here, `rs.htm`, which appears in the HTML folder on the CD, and which will display the names of the employees in the `employees.htm` page in an HTML text area. To create this page, I'll use JScript, the Internet Explorer's version of JavaScript. I start by using an MSHTML data source:

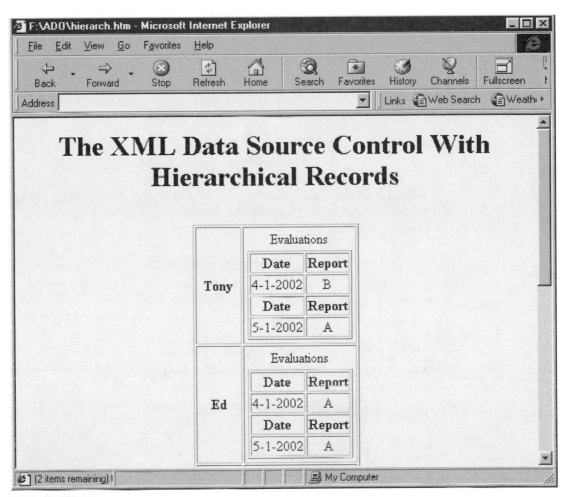

FIGURE 11.7   Using the XML data source control with hierarchical records.

```
<HTML>
<HEAD>
<TITLE>Handling Recordsets in HTML</TITLE>
</HEAD>


<BODY>


<CENTER>
```

```
<H1>Handling Recordsets in HTML</H1>

<OBJECT ID="dsoEmployees" DATA="employee.htm"
HEIGHT=0 WIDTH=0>
</OBJECT>
```

.
.
.

Next, I'll add the text area I'll use. Note also that I'm adding a bound <HIDDEN> tag, which has the effect of keeping the recordset synchronized with the data source:

```
<INPUT TYPE="HIDDEN" DATASRC="#dsoEmployees"
DATAFLD="Name">

<P>
<TEXTAREA NAME="textarea"
ROWS=10 COLS=60></TEXTAREA>

<SCRIPT LANGUAGE="JScript">
```

.
.
.

I'm ready to add code to the OnDatasetComplete event of the MSHTML control to get the names of the employees from the MSHTML control and place them into the text area. Here's what that code looks like—note that I'm free to use Recordset object properties like EOF and methods like MoveNext:

```
function dsoEmployees.ondatasetcomplete() {

    objtext = document.all("textarea");

    rs = document.dsoEmployees.recordset;

    objtext.value = "Here are the employees:\r\n";
```

```
    while (!rs.EOF) {

        objtext.value += rs("Name") + " \r\n";

        rs.MoveNext();


    }
}
```

```
</SCRIPT>
</CENTER>
</BODY>
</HTML>
```

And that's all it takes—the results of this code appear in Figure 11.8; as you can see in that figure, I'm retrieving the names of the employees in the `employee.htm` database and displaying them in the text area.

ADO and Dynamic HTML

You can display data directly in a Web page, without using an HTML control at all. In this next example, I'll take a look at using dynamic HTML in the Internet Explorer to write data directly from a DSO to the page itself.

Using Dynamic HTML

This new Web page, `dynam.htm`, will write the names of the employees in the `employees.htm` database directly to a Web page. To write that page, I start by using an MSHTML control, and bind a `<HIDDEN>` field to that control to keep it synchronized with the code in the page:

```
<HTML>
<HEAD>
<TITLE>Handling Recordsets and DHTML in HTML</TITLE>
</HEAD>


<BODY>
```

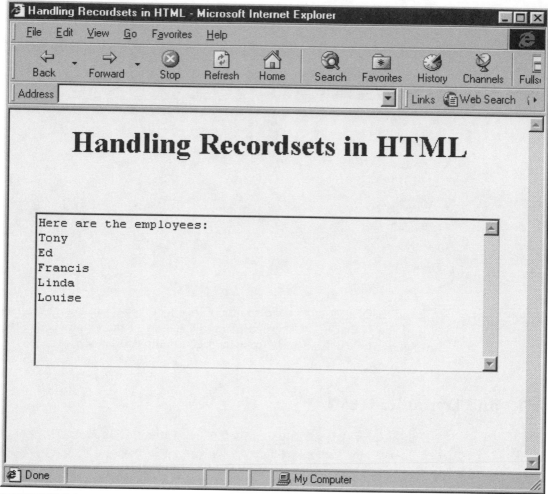

FIGURE 11.8 Using recordsets in HTML code.

```
<CENTER>

<H1>Handling Recordsets and DHTML in HTML</H1>

</CENTER>

<OBJECT ID="dsoEmployees" DATA="employee.htm"
HEIGHT=0 WIDTH=0>
```

```
</OBJECT>
```

```
<INPUT TYPE="HIDDEN" DATASRC="#dsoEmployees"
DATAFLD="Name">
```

.
.
.

Next, I add a <DIV> that originally displays no text. I'll write the names of the employees to this <DIV>, Div1, in code:

```
<DIV ID="Div1"></DIV>
```

.
.
.

Here's the code that writes the names of the employees to Div1—note that to change the text inside the <DIV> tag, I use the dynamic HTML property innerHTML:

```
<SCRIPT LANGUAGE="JScript">

function dsoEmployees.ondatasetcomplete()
{
    var string = "Here are the employees:<BR>";

    rs = document.dsoEmployees.recordset;

    while (!rs.EOF) {
        string += rs("Name") + "<BR>";
        rs.MoveNext();
    }

    document.all("Div1").innerHTML = string;
}
```

```
</SCRIPT>
</BODY>
</HTML>
```

That's all it takes; the result appears in Figure 11.9. As you can see, you can write data from a recordset directly to a Web page without using HTML controls at all.

I'll take one more look at using dynamic HTML and ADO—creating tables and filling them on-the-fly.

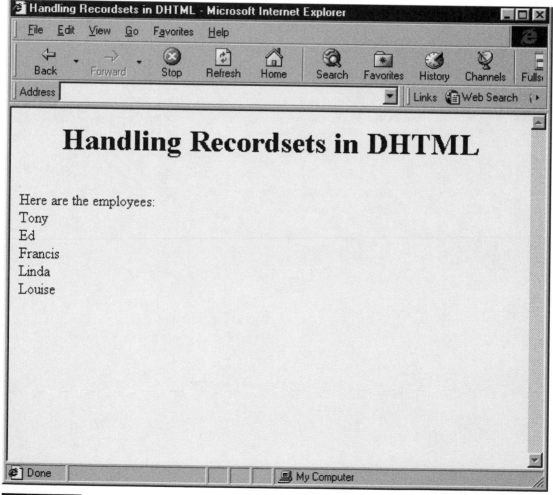

FIGURE 11.9 Using recordsets in DHTML code.

Overwriting Elements and Using GetString

In the last example, I added text to a <DIV> tag on-the-fly. In this example, dtable.htm, which appears in the HTML folder on the CD, I'll show how to create an HTML table on-the-fly, even if you didn't have a table in the Web page before. The previous examples in this chapter have been written in JScript, but you can use any scripting language with DSOs; for example, I'll write this last page using VBScript, not JScript.

I start by adding an MSHTML control and connecting it to the employee.htm database, as well as binding that control to a <HIDDEN> tag:

```
<HTML>
<HEAD>
<TITLE>Handling Recordsets in DHTML</TITLE>
</HEAD>


<BODY>


<CENTER>


<H1>Handling Recordsets in DHTML With GetString</H1>


<OBJECT ID="dsoEmployees" DATA="employee.htm"
HEIGHT=0 WIDTH=0>
</OBJECT>


<INPUT TYPE="HIDDEN" DATASRC="#dsoEmployees"
DATAFLD="Name">
    .
    .
    .
```

As in the previous example, I'll add a <DIV> tag to this page—in this case, however, I'll actually rewrite this tag in code, changing it to a table:

```
<DIV ID="Div1"></DIV>
    .
    .
    .
```

In this case, I'll use the handy `Recordset` object `GetString` method to create the HTML table. This method returns a `Recordset` object as a string. Here's how you use this method in general:

```
recordset.GetString([StringFormat [, NumRows
[, ColumnDelimiter [, RowDelimiter [, NullExpr]]]]])
```

Here are the parameters you pass to `GetString`:

- **StringFormat**—Specifies that the recordset should be converted to a particular format. The only possible value currently is `adClipString` (which equals 2), in which rows are delimited by `RowDelimiter`, columns by `ColumnDelimiter`, and null values by `NullExpr` (note that these parameters are valid only with `adClipString`).
- **NumRows**—The number of rows in the recordset to convert. If `NumRows` is not specified, or if it is greater than the total number of rows in the recordset, then all the rows in the recordset are converted.
- **ColumnDelimiter**—Delimiter used between columns if specified, otherwise the tab character.
- **RowDelimiter**—Delimiter used between rows if specified, otherwise the carriage return character.
- **NullExpr**—Expression used in place of a null value if specified, otherwise the empty string.

Here's how I put `GetString` to work creating the new table—note the use of the dynamic HTML property `outerHTML` here to rewrite the entire HTML of the `<DIV>` tag into a `<TABLE>` tag:

```
<SCRIPT LANGUAGE="VBScript">

Sub dsoEmployees_ondatasetcomplete()

    Dim str

    str = "Here are the employees:<BR>"

    Set rs = document.dsoEmployees.recordset

    str = "<TABLE BORDER = 1>"
```

```
str = str + "<TABLE BORDER = 1>"

str = str +
"<TR><TH>Name</TH><TH>ID</TH><TH>" +
"Hire Date</TH><TH>"

str = str +
"Department</TH><TH>Title</TH></TR><TD>"
```

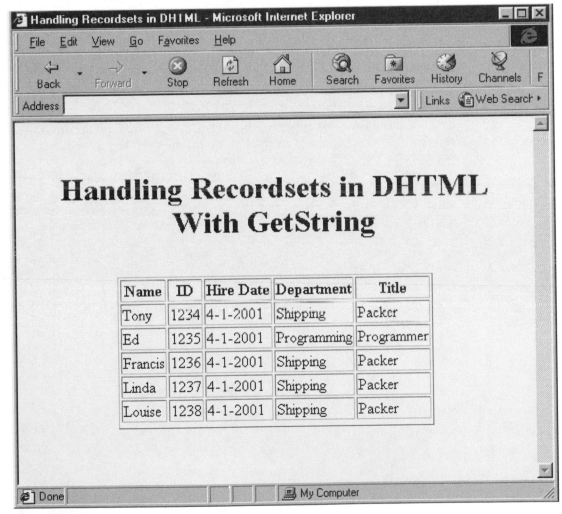

FIGURE 11.10 Using recordsets in DHTML code with GetString.

```
        str = str + rs.GetString(2, -1,"</TD><TD>",
        "</TD></TR><TR><TD>", chr(32))


        str = str + "</TD></TR></TABLE>"


        document.all("Div1").outerHTML = str
End Sub


</SCRIPT>


</CENTER>


</BODY>
</HTML>
```

The results of this page, dtable.htm, appear in Figure 11.10. As you can see, this page generates an HTML table on-the-fly, filling it with data from employees.htm. This example is a success.

That completes our look at using the MSHTML, TDC, XML data source control, and JDBC data source applet. In the next chapter, I'll continue examining ADO and the Internet—but from the server side instead of the client side, as we dig into Active Server Pages and the Remote Data Services.

Remote Data Service and Active Server Pages

This chapter is on ADO and the Web from the server side of things. Here, I'll take a look at Web-based applications that use ADO with the Remote Data Services (RDS) and Active Server Pages (ASP). Microsoft has integrated RDS into ADO as a whole, so it's an appropriate topic to take a look at here. As an ADO programmer, you may be asked to work with data in many different formats, including data on Web servers, and this chapter will show you what's going on. Here, I'll show how to use database systems like SQL Server over the Internet and an intranet using RDS. Besides RDS, you can also use Active Server Pages on the server to work with database systems, and I'll take a look at that here.

Note that this chapter deals with programming on the server, as opposed to the previous chapter, which was all about programming on the client. For that reason, the Internet or intranet server you use has to have some added capabilities.

Web Server Requirements

To use the examples in this chapter, and to use RDS and ASP in general, you'll need a Web server that supports these technologies. The usual choice here is the Microsoft Internet Information Server (IIS). The IIS supports both RDS and ASP, and if your server is running IIS, you're all set.

If your server is not running IIS, and you don't have the privileges to install and run it, you're not necessarily out of luck. Microsoft also provides its personal Web server (PWS) at `microsoft.com/ntserver/nts/down-loads/recommended/NT4OptPk/default.asp` for free download (note that this URL moves around a lot, as do many URLs on the Microsoft site, so you might have to search for the personal Web server by name). You can download and run the PWS as a true Web server; if you want to access Web pages using a browser on the same machine, you can refer to the PWS as `http://default` in your browser. You can also use the PWS on intranets. Although written for Windows NT, the PWS also works on Windows 95. I'll use the PWS in the examples in this chapter; if you're using the IIS, you'll have to change the `http://default` URL to the correct one for your server.

I'll start digging into the Remote Data Services now with an overview.

The Remote Data Services (RDS)

RDS is designed to work with three-tiered architectures. The client tier uses a Web browser or compiled application to view Web pages, the middle tier is the server, which typically runs IIS, and the third tier—called the data source tier—is the database system that handles the actual data, typically SQL Server.

The three tiers don't necessarily have to be in different locations on a network. In fact, it's more usual to use two machines, one for the client tier and the other for the server and database system. You can even use one machine if you're running the PWS and SQL Server on the same machine as your Web browser.

In the previous chapter, we saw four DSOs that ship with the Internet Explorer. RDS is supported by a more sophisticated DSO than the ones we saw in that chapter—the RDS data control. Using this control, you can connect to databases through database systems like SQL Server and work with recordsets over the Web. In fact, there are three components to RDS:

- The RDS `DataControl` is the DSO that you can bind tags to in a Web page.
- The RDS `DataFactory` object is the object on the server that processes and sends data back to the client.
- The RDS `DataSpace` object is the client-side interface to the `DataFactory` object on the server.

Note that you can use the RDS DataControl without explicitly using DataFactory and DataSpace objects, because that control will create such objects automatically. You can also work with DataFactory and Data-Space objects directly, as I'll do in this chapter. In fact, you don't have to use DataFactory objects on the server; you can use custom business objects to handle the way recordsets are returned, and I'll take a look at that here too. This means there are three ways to pass a Recordset object from the server to the client with RDS:

- Use the DataControl methods and properties that automatically call the DataFactory object.
- Manually call the DataFactory object.
- Create a custom business object—an ActiveX DLL component—that supports the data access functions.

The RDS DataFactory object is just a default server-side business object that sends commands on to a data source and passes the results back across the Internet or an intranet for you. If you create a custom business object, that is, a custom ActiveX DLL, such an object can contain methods that aren't provided by the RDS DataFactory, which could implement various business rules.

The easiest way to use RDS is with the RDS DataControl, and I'll take a look at that first.

The RDS DataControl

You can use the RDS DataControl to connect to a Web-based server, and then you bind tags in the Web page to that DataControl's internal recordset (an ADOR object). Here's how you use the RDS DataControl in a Web page:

```
<OBJECT
CLASSID="clsid:BD96C556-65A3-11D0-983A-00C04FC29E33"
ID="dsoRDSControl"
<PARAM NAME="Connect"
VALUE="connection string">
<PARAM NAME="Server" VALUE="http://server">
<PARAM NAME="SQL" VALUE="SQL text">
</OBJECT>
```

To use the RDS `DataControl`, you need to set only the `SQL`, `Connect`, and `Server` properties, which will automatically call the default business object, the `DataFactory` object, to create a disconnected client-side recordset.

Usually, you will bind HTML tags to an RDS `DataControl`, and then add, edit, and delete records in the client-side recordset. After you update the client-side data, you can save the new data to the database by using the control's `SubmitChanges` method.

I'll take a look at the RDS `DataControl`'s properties here.

The RDS DataControl Properties

You use the properties of the RDS `DataControl` to configure that control, and I'll work through those properties here, starting with the `Connect` property.

Connect

This property holds the ADO connection string that you'd use to connect to the database if your application were running on the server. Here's an example:

```
<OBJECT
CLASSID="clsid:BD96C556-65A3-11D0-983A-00C04FC29E33"
    ID="dsoEmployees" HEIGHT=0 WIDTH=0>
    <PARAM NAME="Server" VALUE="http://default">
    <PARAM NAME="Connect"
    VALUE="Provider=SQLOLEDB.1;Persist Security
    Info=False;User ID=sa;Initial
    Catalog=Northwind">
    <PARAM NAME="SQL"
    VALUE="SELECT * FROM Employees">
</OBJECT>
```

ExecuteOptions

This property indicates whether or not asynchronous execution is enabled. You can set this property to one of these values:

- **adcExecSync**—1. Executes the next refresh of the recordset synchronously.
- **adcExecAsync**—2 (default). Executes the next refresh of the recordset asynchronously.

If you set `ExecuteOptions` to `adcExecAsync`, then the next refresh of the `DataControl` object's recordset is executed asynchronously.

FetchOptions

This property indicates the type of asynchronous data fetches to use, and can be one of these values:

- **`adcFetchUpFront`**—1. The complete recordset is fetched before the application is allowed to do anything with it.
- **`adcFetchBackground`**—2. The first batch of data is fetched at once, then additional batches are fetched when required.
- **`adcFetchAsync`**—3 (default). Data is fetched in the background, while the client is also executing.

In a Web application, it's a good idea to use `adcFetchAsync` (the default), because it provides better performance. However, in a compiled client application, a better choice is `adcFetchBackground`.

FilterColumn

This property specifies the column on which to evaluate the filter criteria. You set this property to a string holding the name of the column on which to filter; you set the actual filtering criterion with the `FilterCriterion` property. To perform the filtering operation, you call the `Reset` method.

FilterCriterion

The `FilterCriterion` property specifies the operator to use for a filter; it can be <, <=, >, >=, =, or <>. You use this property together with the `FilterValue` property. To perform the filtering operation, you call the `Reset` method.

FilterValue

This property sets the data value with which to filter records. You use this property with the `FilterColumn` and `FilterCriterion` properties. To perform the filtering operation, you call the `Reset` method.

InternetTimeout

This property holds the the number of milliseconds to wait before a request times out. Note that this property applies only to requests sent with the HTTP or HTTPS protocols.

In general, requests in a three-tier architecture can take a long time to execute; you can use this property to specify additional time for really long operations.

ReadyState

The `ReadyState` property of the RDS `DataControl` holds the progress of the control as it fetches data into its `Recordset` object. Here are the possible values this property can take:

- **adcReadyStateLoaded**—2. The current query is still executing and no rows have been fetched, which means the recordset is not available for use.

- **adcReadyStateInteractive**—3. The first set of rows retrieved by the current query have been stored in the `Recordset` object and are available for use. The rest of the rows are still being fetched.

- **adcReadyStateComplete**—4. All rows retrieved by the current query have been stored in the `DataControl` object's recordset. That data is now available for use.

You use the `onReadyStateChange` event method to monitor changes in the `ReadyStateChange` property during an asynchronous query operation. If an error occurs during an asynchronous operation, the `ReadyState` property is set to `adcReadyStateComplete`, and the `State` property changes from `adStateExecuting` to `adStateClosed`.

Recordset and SourceRecordset

The `Recordset` property holds the RDS `DataControl`'s internal ADOR `Recordset` object that it has fetched from the Web, and you can set the `SourceRecordset` property to specify the recordset the control will use. The `Recordset` property is read-only and the `SourceRecordset` property is write-only.

Using the `Recordset` property, you have direct access to the recordset the RDS `DataControl` is using. You can set the `SourceRecordset` property to a recordset returned from a custom business object, or a recordset you create yourself. I'll use both of these properties later in this chapter.

Server

You use this property to set the name of the server you want to use with the RDS `DataControl`. This is one of the properties you must set before using the control. Here are some of the ways you can set this property using HTTP, HTTPS (secure HTTP), and DCOM:

- HTTP: `<PARAM NAME="Server" VALUE="http://servername">`.
- HTTP: `<PARAM NAME="Server" VALUE="http://servername:port">`.
- HTTPS: `<PARAM NAME="Server" VALUE="https://servername">`.
- HTTPS: `<PARAM NAME="Server".`
  `VALUE="https://servername: port">`.

- DCOM: <PARAM NAME="Server".
  VALUE="machinename">.

Here's an example where I'm using the PWS and setting the Server property to http://default:

```
<OBJECT
CLASSID="clsid:BD96C556-65A3-11D0-983A-00C04FC29E33"
    ID="dsoEmployees" HEIGHT=0 WIDTH=0>
    <PARAM NAME="Server" VALUE="http://default">
    <PARAM NAME="Connect"
    VALUE="Provider=SQLOLEDB.1;Persist Security
    Info=False;User ID=sa;Initial
    Catalog=Northwind">
    <PARAM NAME="SQL"
    VALUE="SELECT * FROM Employees">
</OBJECT>
```

SortColumn

You set this property to the name of the column you want to use for sorting a recordset. To sort a recordset, you should first save any pending changes using the RDS DataControl's SubmitChanges method. Use the SortDirection property to specify the direction of the sort. To actually perform the sort, you call the Reset method.

SortDirection

This property determines if sorts are made in ascending or descending order. Here are the settings for this property:

- **True**—Sort in ascending order.
- **False**—Sort in descending order.

To perform the sort, you call the Reset method.

SQL

This property sets the SQL query string used to retrieve the Recordset object. This is the actual SQL that the database system on the server will execute. You can set the SQL property at design-time in the DataControl object's OBJECT tags, or at run-time in scripting code. You usually set this property unless you're using a custom server-side business object.

Here's an example in which I'm reading the Employees table from the Nwind.mdb database:

```
<OBJECT
CLASSID="clsid:BD96C556-65A3-11D0-983A-00C04FC29E33"
    ID="dsoEmployees" HEIGHT=0 WIDTH=0>
    <PARAM NAME="Server" VALUE="http://default">
    <PARAM NAME="Connect"
    VALUE="Provider=SQLOLEDB.1;Persist Security
    Info=False;User ID=sa;Initial
    Catalog=Northwind">
    <PARAM NAME="SQL"
    VALUE="SELECT * FROM Employees">
</OBJECT>
```

That completes the properties of the RDS DataControl; it's time to take a look at its methods.

The RDS DataControl Methods

The RDS DataControl has quite a few methods, and I'll take a look at them all here.

Cancel

This method cancels the current asynchronous execution or fetch operation, and you use it without any parameters, like this: RDSDataControl.Cancel.

You can use this method to let the user cancel long-running, asynchronous operations. Note that when you call Cancel, the ReadyState property is automatically set to adcReadyStateLoaded, and the Recordset object in the control will be empty.

CancelUpdate

When you call this method, the RDS DataControl discards all the pending changes in its Recordset object, which means it restores the values since the last Refresh method call. This method takes no parameters.

OLE DB keeps both a copy of the original values and a cache of changes for the RDS DataControl, so when you call CancelUpdate, the cache of changes is reset, and any bound tags are refreshed with the original data.

CreateRecordset

You can use this method to create a new, empty, disconnected `Recordset` object in the RDS `DataControl`. Here's how you use this method:

```
RDSDataControl.CreateRecordset(ColumnInfos)
```

The `ColumnsInfos` parameter is a variant array of arrays defining each column in the `Recordset` object you want to create. Each column definition contains an array of four required attributes:

- **Name**—Name of the column header.
- **Type**—Integer of data type.
- **Size**—Integer of width in characters, regardless of data type.
- **Nullability**—Boolean value.

The set of column arrays is then grouped into an array, which defines the `Recordset` object to create. I'll write an example showing how to use `CreateRecordset` later in this chapter.

Table 12.1 holds the data types supported by the `CreateRecordset` method. The Number column is the reference value used to define fields. For some of the variable data types, RDS may coerce the type to the type noted in the Substitution column. You won't see the substitutions until after the recordset is created and filled. Then you can check for the actual data type, if necessary.

Note that each of the data types in Table 12.1 is either fixed-length or variable-length. Fixed-length types should be defined with a size of –1, because the size is already determined. Variable-length data types can have a size from 1 to 32767.

MoveFirst, MoveLast, MoveNext, and MovePrevious Methods

These methods move to the first, last, next, and previous record in the current recordset, and they take no parameters. You use these methods to navigate through a recordset. For example, this script code moves to the next record in the current recordset:

```
<BUTTON
ONCLICK="if (!dsoEmployees.recordset.EOF)
dsoEmployees.MoveNext()" >
&gt;
</BUTTON>
```

| TABLE 12.1 | *CreateRecordset Data Types* |

Length	Constant	Number	Substitution
Fixed	adTinyInt	16	
Fixed	adSmallInt	2	
Fixed	adInteger	3	
Fixed	adBigInt	20	
Fixed	adUnsignedTinyInt	17	
Fixed	adUnsignedSmallInt	18	
Fixed	adUnsignedInt	19	
Fixed	adUnsignedBigInt	21	
Fixed	adSingle	4	
Fixed	adDouble	5	
Fixed	adCurrency	6	
Fixed	adDecimal	14	
Fixed	adNumeric	131	
Fixed	adBoolean	11	
Fixed	adError	10	
Fixed	adGuid	72	
Fixed	adDate	7	
Fixed	adDBDate	133	
Fixed	adDBTime	134	
Fixed	adDBTimestamp	135	7
Variable	adBSTR	8	130
Variable	adChar	129	200
Variable	adVarChar	200	
Variable	adLongVarChar	201	200
Variable	adWChar	130	
Variable	adVarWChar	202	130
Variable	adLongVarWChar	203	130
Variable	adBinary	128	
Variable	adVarBinary	204	
Variable	adLongVarBinary	205	204

Refresh

This method requeries the data source given by the Connect property and updates the Recordset object in the RDS DataControl. This method takes no parameters.

Note that you must set the Connect, Server, and SQL properties before you use the Refresh method. Any data-bound controls on the form connected to the RDS DataControl will be updated to reflect the new set of

note It's a good idea to call the **Refresh** method every now and then when you work with data. If you retrieve data and then work it on your client machine for some time, it's possible it can become out-of-date, because someone might have changed the record and submitted changes.

records, and any unsaved changes will be discarded. Using the Refresh method automatically makes the first record the current record.

Reset

This method executes the sort or filter on a client-side recordset based on the specified sort and filter properties. Here's how you use this method:

```
RDSDataControl.Reset [value]
```

The value parameter is a Boolean that is True (the default) if you want to filter on the current "filtered" recordset; False means that you want to filter on the original rowset, removing any previous filter settings.

SubmitChanges

You use the SubmitChanges method to submit any pending changes of the locally cached, updatable Recordset object to the data source specified in the Connect property. This method takes no parameters.

Note that you must set the Connect, Server, and SQL properties before you can use the SubmitChanges method. Only the changed records are sent for modification, and either all of the changes succeed or all of them fail together. Note also that you can use SubmitChanges only with the default DataFactory object; custom business objects can't use this method.

That completes the RDS DataControl's methods; I'll take a look at this control's events next.

The RDS DataControl Events

The RDS DataControl has a number of events, and I'll cover them here.

onDataAvailable

This event fires each time a batch of data is downloaded. Note that this event does not indicate that the entire data set is downloaded; for that, use the on-DatasetComplete event.

onDatasetChanged

This event fires when the data set is changed.

onDatasetComplete

This event fires when the data is downloaded and ready for use. This event, onDatasetComplete, is usually the event you use to determine when to work with the data you're downloading; if you don't mind working with only partial data, take a look at the onDataAvailable event.

onError

The onError event fires when an error occurs during some operation. This event's handler code is passed four parameters:

- **SCode**—An integer that contains the status code of the error.
- **Description**—A string that contains a description of the error.
- **Source**—A string that contains the query or command that caused the error.
- **CancelDisplay**—A Boolean that, if set to True, prevents the error from being displayed in a dialog box.

You add code to this event's handler to report errors to the user; in any application you release, you should add code to handle errors here.

onReadyStateChange

This event fires when the value of the ReadyState property changes. You can add code to this event handler when you want to watch the progress of asynchronous operations. No parameters are passed to this event's handler.

You can check the ReadyState property in this event to determine the state of the control. In any finished applications, it's a good idea to add code to this event to monitor what's happening and reset counters that you can use to watch if an operation takes too long.

onRowEnter

This event fires when a new record becomes the current one. You can use this event to execute code as the user navigates through a recordset.

onRowExit

This event fires just before exiting the current record. You can use this event to perform data validation, checking the fields in the current record and applying business rules.

That finishes the properties, methods, and events of the RDS DataControl. I'll start putting all this to work now in an example using the RDS DataControl.

Navigating with the RDS DataControl

I'll write an example now, buttons.htm, which you'll find in the RDS folder on the CD. This example will bind two HTML text fields to an RDS Data-Control, and will also support a set of buttons that will let the user navigate through the recordset.

I start by including an RDS DataControl in a Web page, connecting it to the Nwind database on the Web server, and using it to return the Employees table:

```
<HTML>

<HEAD>
<TITLE>RDS Example</TITLE>
</HEAD>

<BODY>

<CENTER>

<H1>Using RDS With Navigation Buttons</H1>

<OBJECT
CLASSID="clsid:BD96C556-65A3-11D0-983A-00C04FC29E33"
    ID="dsoEmployees" HEIGHT=0 WIDTH=0>
    <PARAM NAME="Server" VALUE="http://default">
    <PARAM NAME="Connect"
    VALUE="Provider=SQLOLEDB.1;Persist Security
    Info=False;User ID=sa;Initial
    Catalog=Northwind">
    <PARAM NAME="SQL"
    VALUE="SELECT * FROM Employees">
</OBJECT>
        .

        .

        .
```

Now I can bind two text fields to that new DSO: one displaying the employee's first name, and the other displaying the last name:

```
First Name: <INPUT TYPE="TEXT"
    DATASRC="#dsoEmployees" DATAFLD="FirstName"
    SIZE=20><P>
Last Name: <INPUT TYPE="TEXT"
    DATASRC="#dsoEmployees" DATAFLD="LastName"
    SIZE=20><P>
        .
        .
        .
```

All that's left is to add the navigation buttons as we did in the previous chapter:

```
<BUTTON
ONCLICK="dsoEmployees.recordset.MoveFirst()">
&lt;&lt;
</BUTTON>
<BUTTON
ONCLICK="if (!dsoEmployees.recordset.BOF)
dsoEmployees.recordset.MovePrevious()">
&lt;
</BUTTON>

<BUTTON
ONCLICK="if (!dsoEmployees.recordset.EOF)
dsoEmployees.recordset.MoveNext()" >
&gt;
</BUTTON>

<BUTTON
ONCLICK="dsoEmployees.recordset.MoveLast()">
&gt;&gt;
</BUTTON>
```

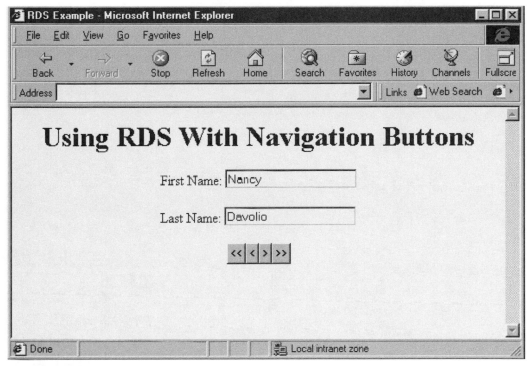

Using the RDS DataControl with buttons.

```
<CENTER>

</BODY>
</HTML>
```

That's all it takes; the result of this code appears in Figure 12.1. As you can see in the figure, we've been able to open a table from a recordset on a Web server.

Just as with the DSOs in the previous chapter, you can also bind the RDS DataControl to tables, and I'll do that next.

Creating Tables with the RDS DataControl

This next example, tables.htm in the RDS folder on the CD, uses the RDS DataControl to populate an HTML table with the first name and last name fields from the Employees table of the Nwind database on the Web server. I start by adding an RDS DataControl to tables.htm:

```
<HTML>

<HEAD>
<TITLE>RDS Example</TITLE>
</HEAD>

<BODY>

<CENTER>

<H1>Using RDS With Tables</H1>

<OBJECT
CLASSID="clsid:BD96C556-65A3-11D0-983A-00C04FC29E33"
    ID="dsoEmployees" HEIGHT=0 WIDTH=0>
    <PARAM NAME="Server" VALUE="http://default">
    <PARAM NAME="Connect"
    VALUE="Provider=SQLOLEDB.1;Persist Security
    Info=False;User ID=sa;Initial
    Catalog=Northwind">
    <PARAM NAME="SQL"
    VALUE="SELECT * FROM Employees">
</OBJECT>
        .
        .
        .
```

Next, I bind this new DSO to a table, as we did in the previous chapter with other DSOs:

```
<TABLE DATASRC="#dsoEmployees" BORDER = 1>
    <THEAD>
        <TR>
            <TH>First Name</TH>
```

```
                <TH>Last Name</TH>
            </TR>
            </THEAD>
            <TBODY>
            <TR>
                <TD><SPAN
                DATAFLD="FirstName">
                </SPAN></TD>
                <TD><SPAN
                DATAFLD="LastName">
                </SPAN></TD>
            </TR>
        </TBODY>
    </TABLE>


</BODY>
</HTML>
```

The results of this Web page appear in Figure 12.2. As you can see in the figure, the RDS DataControl has connected to the DataFactory object on the server and filled the table with data.

The RDS DataControl connects to the DataFactory object on the server by default, but you can also use the DataFactory object's methods yourself. I'll take a look at the DataFactory object next.

The DataFactory Object

The RDS DataFactory object is the default server-side business object. It implements methods that provide read/write data access to specified data sources for client-side applications. This object just passes on the requests from the client to the database system; it doesn't include any business logic or rules itself (if you want to implement such rules, you create a custom business object).

The DataFactory object has only methods (no properties), and I'll take a look at those methods now.

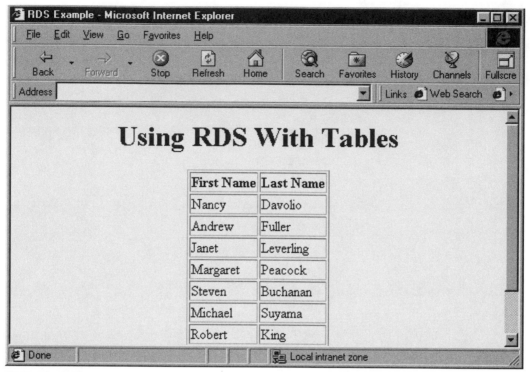

FIGURE 12.2 Creating tables with the RDS `DataControl` with buttons.

The DataFactory Object Methods

The `DataFactory` object's methods are `ConvertToString`, `CreateRecordset`, `Query`, and `SubmitChanges`.

ConvertToString

The `ConvertToString` method converts a recordset to a MIME- (Multipurpose Internet Mail Extension) encoded string that holds the recordset data. Here's how you use this method:

`DataFactory.ConvertToString Recordset`

You can use `ConvertToString` to embed a recordset in an HTML page generated on the server to transport it to a client computer. On the client, RDS can convert the MIME string back into a `Recordset` object. This technique works well as long as you're handling fewer than 400 rows of data with no more than 1024 bytes width per row. In other words, you shouldn't use it for streaming BLOB data and large resultsets over HTTP.

note If you're using versions of VBScript earlier than version 2.0, VBScript caps string size at 32K; to get around that, you can download the latest version of VBScript from **www.microsoft.com/vbscript.**

CreateRecordset

You use the `CreateRecordset` method to create an empty, disconnected recordset. Here's how you use this method:

```
DataFactory.CreateRecordset [ColumnInfos]
```

The `ColumnsInfos` parameter is a variant array of arrays defining each column in the `Recordset` object you want to create. Each column definition contains an array of four required attributes:

- **Name**—Name of the column header.
- **Type**—Integer of data type.
- **Size**—Integer of width in characters, regardless of data type.
- **Nullability**—Boolean value.

The set of column arrays is then grouped into an array, which defines the `Recordset` object to create. I'll write an example showing how to use `CreateRecordset` later in this chapter. Table 12.1 holds the data types supported by the `CreateRecordset` method; see the `CreateRecordset` method of the RDS `DataControl` earlier in the chapter for more information.

Query

This method uses an SQL query string to return a `Recordset` object. Here's how you use this method:

```
Set Recordset = DataFactory.Query Connection, Query
```

Here are the parameters you pass to this method:

- **Connection**—A string containing the server connection information. This is similar to the `Connect` property.
- **Query**—A string containing the SQL query.

This is the method I'll use to create a recordset later in this chapter.

SubmitChanges

This method submits all pending changes of the locally cached `Recordset` object to the data source specified in the `Connect` property. Here's how you use this method:

```
DataFactory.SubmitChanges Connection, Recordset
```

Here are the parameters you pass to this method:

- **Connection**—A string value that represents the connection created with the RDS.DataControl object's Connect property.
- **Recordset**—An object variable that represents a Recordset object.

Note that you can use SubmitChanges only with the default RDSServer.DataFactory object. Custom business objects can't use this method.

That's it for the methods of the DataFactory object. You use DataFactory objects on the server side; on the client side, you use Data-Space objects to work with DataFactory objects. I'll take a look at the DataSpace object next.

The DataSpace Object

The DataFactory object actually sends data to the RDS DataSpace object in the client. The DataSpace object implements a proxy and stub DCOM connection to the server, and marshals data across the connection. The RDS DataControl reads its data from the DataSpace object.

Here's what embedding a DataSpace object in a Web page looks like:

```
<OBJECT ID="rdsDataSpace"
    WIDTH=0
    HEIGHT=0
    CLASSID=
    "CLSID:BD96C556-65A3-11D0-983A-00C04FC29E36">
</OBJECT>
```

The DataSpace object has one property and one method, and I'll take a look at them here.

The DataSpace Object Property

The DataSpace object has only one property: InternetTimeout.

InternetTimeout

This property just indicates the number of milliseconds to wait before a request times out. If your connections are timing out, this is the setting to increase.

The DataSpace Object Method

The `DataSpace` object has only one method: `CreateObject`.

CreateObject

This method creates the actual proxy for the business object and returns a pointer to it. The proxy packages and marshals data to the server-side stub for communications with the business object to send requests and data over the Internet.

Here's how you use this method with various protocols:

- HTTP: `Set` *object* `=` *DataSpace*`.CreateObject("`*ProgId*`",` `"http://`*servername*`")`.
- HTTPS: `Set` *object* `=` *DataSpace*`.CreateObject("`*ProgId*`",` `"https://`*servername*`")`.
- DCOM: `Set` *object* `=` *DataSpace*`.CreateObject("`*ProgId*`",` `"`*machinename*`")`.
- In-process applications: `Set` *object* `=` *DataSpace*`.CreateObject("`*ProgId*`", "")`.

Here are the parameters you pass to this method:

- **ProgID**—String that identifies a server-side business object that implements your application's business rules.
- **servername** or **machinename**—String that represents a URL identifying the server where the server business object is created.

That completes the properties and methods of the `DataFactory` and `DataSpace` objects. I'll put these objects to work in an example now.

Using the DataFactory and DataSpace Objects

In this example, I'll use the methods of the RDS `DataFactory` and `DataSpace` objects to create and update a recordset. This example is in the file `rds.htm` in the RDS folder on the CD.

I start by creating two buttons: one to create a new recordset and one to update the database on the server with any changes the user makes:

```
<HTML>


<HEAD>
<TITLE>RDS Objects Example</TITLE>
```

```
</HEAD>

<BODY>

<CENTER>

<H1>RDS Objects Example</H1>

<INPUT TYPE="BUTTON" VALUE="Get recordset"
ONCLICK="getRecordset()">

<INPUT TYPE="BUTTON" VALUE="Update recordset"
ONCLICK="updateRecordset()">

<P>
    .

    .

    .
```

Next, I add the RDS `DataSpace` and RDS `DataControl` using:

```
<OBJECT ID="rdsDataSpace"
    WIDTH=0
    HEIGHT=0
    CLASSID=
    "CLSID:BD96C556-65A3-11D0-983A-00C04FC29E36">
</OBJECT>

<OBJECT ID="dsoDataControl"
    WIDTH=0
    HEIGHT=0
    CLASSID="clsid:BD96C556-65A3-11D0-983A-
00C04FC29E33">
</OBJECT>

<BR>
```

Now I bind the RDS `DataControl` to a table to display the first and last names of the employees in the `Nwind` database's `Employees` table:

```
<TABLE DATASRC="#dsoDataControl" BORDER=1>
    <THEAD>
        <TR>
            <TH>First Name</TH>
            <TH>Last Name</TH>
        </TR>
    <THEAD>
    <TBODY>
        <TR>
            <TD><SPAN
            DATAFLD="FirstName"></SPAN>
            </TD>
            <TD><SPAN
            DATAFLD="LastName"></SPAN>
            </TD>
        </TR>
    </TBODY>
</TABLE>


</CENTER>
```

At this point, we're ready to add the script that will handle the buttons. When the user clicks the `Get recordset` button, I can create an RDS `DataFactory` object on the server:

```
<SCRIPT LANGUAGE="JScript">


var rdsDataFactory;


function getRecordset()
{


    rdsDataFactory =
rdsDataSpace.CreateObject("RDSServer.DataFactory",
```

```
"http://default");
                .
                .
                .
```

Next, I use the `DataFactory` object's `Query` method to create a recordset from the `Employees` table in the `Nwind` database and then I connect that recordset to the RDS `DataControl` this way:

```
    adoRecordset =
rdsDataFactory.Query("Provider=SQLOLEDB.1;Persist
Security Info=False;User ID=sa;Initial
Catalog=Northwind", "Select * From Employees");


    dsoDataControl.SourceRecordset = adoRecordset;


}
```

In this case, the data is displayed in a table, so the user can't update it; but, if the data is bound to controls, the user can edit and change that data. To update the database on the server, use the `SubmitChanges` method like this:

```
function updateRecordset()
{


    rdsDataFactory.SubmitChanges(
"Provider=SQLOLEDB.1;Persist Security
Info=False;User ID=sa;Initial Catalog=Northwind",
dsoDataControl.recordset);


}


</SCRIPT>


</BODY>


</HTML>
```

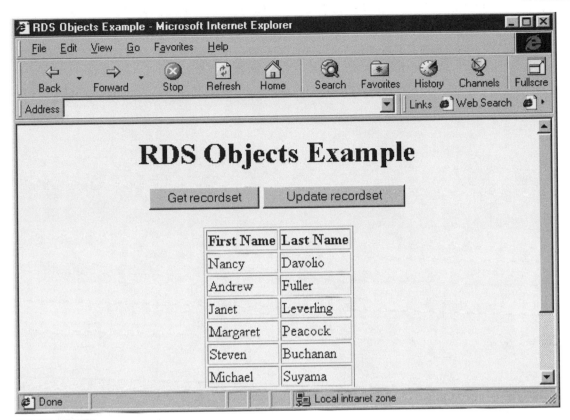

FIGURE 12.3   Using RDS objects.

And that's it; now when the user clicks the Get recordset button you see in Figure 12.3, this example uses DataFactory and DataSpace methods to get a recordset from the server and connect it to the RDS Data-Control, which in turn displays the data in the table you see in the figure.

You don't have to use the RDS DataFactory object in the Web server, however—you can also create and use custom business objects.

Custom Business Objects

You can use data objects of the type we developed in Chapter 10 to create recordsets on the server and return them to the client. These data objects are called custom business objects, and the advantage of using such business objects instead of the RDS DataFactory object is that you can customize business objects to implement business rules—for example, you may want only to list merchandise in a table if it is in stock, and a custom business object can check for such information.

Your custom business object must be instantiable, as any data object is, and it must have a method to return an ADO `Recordset` object. Note that in the recordset you create, you must set the `CursorLocation` to `adUse-Client`, because RDS uses client-side cursors. You also leave the cursor type, lock type, and other options unspecified to create an ADOR recordset. For example, the `Get` function that returns a `Recordset` object in a business object might look like this:

```
Public Function Get()
    Dim adoRecordset As ADODB.Recordset
    .

    .

    .

    adoRecordset.CursorLocation = adUseClient
    adoRecordset.Open adoCommand, adoConnection,
    adOpenUnspecified, adLockUnspecified,
    adCmdUnspecified

    Set Get = adoRecordset
End Function
```

Now in the client, you can use the RDS `DataSpace` object's `CreateObject` method to create a new business object, then use the `Get` method of that object to create a `Recordset` object and connect that recordset to an RDS `DataControl`:

```
Object = DataSpace.CreateObject("Object.Class",
"http://servername")


RDSDataControl.SourceRecordset = Object.Get
```

I'll take a look at one more RDS topic in this chapter: creating a local `Recordset` object.

Creating Recordsets

You can create `Recordset` objects on-the-fly using RDS methods, and I'll write an example now, `newrs.htm`, which appears in the RDS folder on the CD, showing how this works. This example will create a new recordset from scratch and connect it to an RDS `DataControl`; the data in the recordset will be displayed in two bound text fields. In this case, I'm going to create the same recordset that I created in Chapter 8, with `Name` and `Address` fields.

I start by adding the two text fields that will display the names and addresses from the recordset:

```
<HTML>
<HEAD>
<TITLE>RDS Example</TITLE>
</HEAD>
<BODY>

<CENTER>

<H1>RDS: Creating a recordset</H1>

Name: <INPUT TYPE-"TEXT"
DATASRC="#dsoRecords" DATAFLD="Name" SIZE=20><P>
Address: <INPUT TYPE="TEXT" DATASRC-"#dsoRecords"
DATAFLD="Address" SIZE=20><P>
          .
          .
          .
```

Next, I add the button the user can click to create a new recordset, giving that button the caption `Create New Recordset`. I create some buttons for navigating through the new recordset as well:

```
<INPUT TYPE="BUTTON" VALUE="Create New Recordset"
ONCLICK="createRecordset()">

<P>
<BUTTON
ONCLICK="dsoRecords.recordset.MoveFirst()" >
&lt;&lt;
</BUTTON>
```

```
<BUTTON
ONCLICK="if (!dsoRecords.recordset.BOF)
dsoRecords.recordset.MovePrevious()">
&lt;
</BUTTON>

<BUTTON
ONCLICK="if (!dsoRecords.recordset.EOF)
dsoRecords.recordset.MoveNext()">
&gt;
</BUTTON>

<BUTTON
ONCLICK="dsoRecords.recordset.MoveLast()">
&gt;&gt;
</BUTTON>
```

Next, I add the RDS `DataControl` itself:

```
<OBJECT ID="dsoRecords" WIDTH=0 HEIGHT=0
    CLASSID="clsid:BD96C556-65A3-11D0-983A-
    00C04FC29E33">
</OBJECT>
    .

    .

    .
```

At this point, I'm ready to add the code that will create the new record-set when the user clicks the `Create New Recordset` button. I start by defining the types of the two fields, making them character fields (by setting the field type to 129), 40 characters long, and making sure they can't contain null values, like this:

```
<SCRIPT LANGUAGE="VBScript">
Sub createRecordset()
```

```
Dim FieldShape1(3)
Dim FieldShape2(3)
Dim FieldShape3(3)

FieldShape1(0) = "Name"
FieldShape1(1) = CInt(129)
FieldShape1(2) = CInt(40)
FieldShape1(3) = False

FieldShape2(0) = "Address"
FieldShape2(1) = CInt(129)
FieldShape2(2) = CInt(40)
FieldShape2(3) = False
    .
    .
    .
```

Now I construct an array of arrays to structure an individual record:

```
Dim Records(1)
Records(0) = FieldShape1
Records(1) = FieldShape2
```

Having set up the form of a record, I can use the RDS DataControl to create the new recordset, which I call rs:

```
Set rs = dsoRecords.CreateRecordset(Records)
    .
    .
    .
```

All that's left is to use the AddNew method of the recordset to add new records, populate the fields of the new records, and update the recordset, which looks like this for all the records in the database:

```
rs.AddNew
rs.Fields("Name") = "Ted"
```

```
rs.Fields("Address") = "121 Mars Place"
rs.Update

rs.AddNew
rs.Fields("Name") = "Tina"
rs.Fields("Address") = "133 Jupiter Street"
rs.Update

rs.AddNew
rs.Fields("Name") = "Nancy"
rs.Fields("Address") = "16 Earth Square"
rs.Update
```

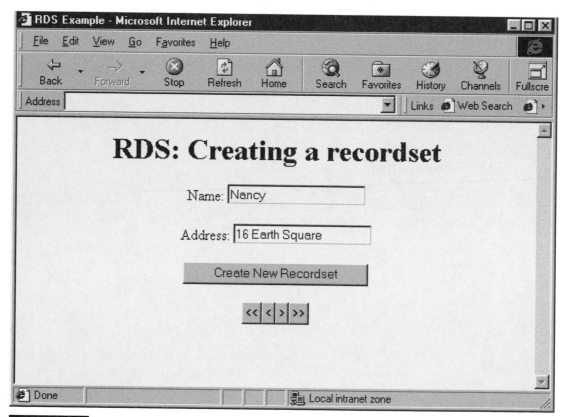

FIGURE 12.4   Creating recordsets in RDS.

.

.

.

The final step is to connect the new recordset to the RDS DataControl:

```
dsoRecords.SourceRecordset = rs
```

```
End Sub
</SCRIPT>
```

```
</BODY>
</HTML>
```

And that's it; the result appears in Figure 12.4. When the user clicks Create New Recordset, the code in this example creates a new local recordset and connects it to the RDS DataControl, and to the bound text fields that you see in Figure 12.4. This example works as anticipated—now we're creating recordsets on-the-fly with the RDS DataControl.

That's it for the coverage of RDS in this chapter; I'll take a look at using ADO and Active Server Pages (ASP) next.

ADO and Active Server Pages

Another way of using ADO on a Web server is with Active Server Pages (ASP). I'll write an example here showing how they works, but won't work through the details of how ASP works here. You can find Active Server Pages documentation on-line for free at: msdn.microsoft.com/isapi/ msdnlib. idc?theURL=/library/tools/aspdoc/iiwawelc.htm, in the MSDN on-line library. Click the Tools and Technologies entry, then the Active Server Pages entry to open the ASP documentation.

This example, db.asp, which appears in the ASP folder on the CD, will open the Customers table in the Nwind database on the server and list the ContactName field for each customer in a Web page.

I start this Active Server Page by creating a Connection object and connecting to the Nwind database like this—note that the <% and %> tags surround commands to the server:

```
<HTML>
```

```
<BODY>

<%

DIM adoConnect
DIM adoRecordset

Set adoConnect =
Server.CreateObject("ADODB.Connection")

adoConnect.open "Provider=Microsoft.Jet." & _
OLEDB.4.0;Data Source=C:\ado\Nwind.mdb"
        .

        .

        .
```

Now I can create a recordset with the Execute method of the Connection object:

```
Set adoRecordset = adoConnect.Execute( _
"SELECT * FROM Customers")
        .

        .

        .
```

Next, I write the text "Here are the customers..." to the Web
page using the Response.Write method:

```
Response.Write "Here are the customers..."

%><BR><%
        .

        .

        .
```

To print out each name in the Customers table, I use a loop like this:

```
Do While Not adoRecordset.EOF
    Response.Write adoRecordset("ContactName")
    %><BR><%
    adoRecordset.MoveNext
Loop
    .
    .
    .
```

All that's left is to clean up and quit:

```
adoRecordset.Close


%>


</BODY>


</HTML>
```

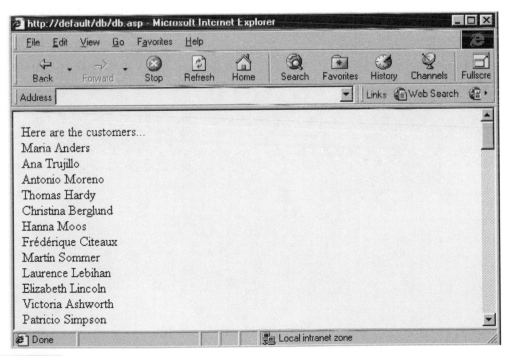

FIGURE 12.5 Using ADO and ASP.

And that's it; the example is complete, and you can see it running in Figure 12.5. As you can see, we've been able to access the database on the server using ASP.

That's it for RDS, ASP, and Web-based applications. In the next chapter, we'll take a look at two advanced ADO topics: data shaping and ADO extensions.

Data Shaping
and ADOX

This chapter is all about data shaping and the Microsoft ActiveX Data Objects Extensions for Data Definition Language and Security (ADOX). Data shaping involves creating records that can themselves contain recordsets in their fields. In other words, you can create hierarchical recordsets using data shaping (properly speaking, you create hierarchical *recordsets* with data shaping, not hierarchical *databases*, which some DMBSs support and which refers to the way data is actually stored). The fields of a hierarchical recordset can be of standard types, such as strings and integers—and they can also hold entire recordsets, which you can access using the field's `Value` property. I'll show how to create hierarchical recordsets in this chapter using the ADO Shape command language. We'll also see how to use the MS Hierarchical FlexGrid control in this chapter when we display hierarchical recordsets.

Microsoft ADOX is an extension to ADO and the programming model. ADOX supports objects for schema creation and modification, as well as security handling. Because it is an object-based approach, you can write code that will work with all kinds of data sources—regardless of the differences in their inherent syntax. ADOX is an advanced database creation and manipulation topic, and I'll survey it in this chapter.

Data Shaping

You use data shaping to create hierarchical recordsets in which fields can themselves contain recordsets, establishing a parent-child relationship between recordsets. Child recordsets are called *chapters* in hierarchical recordsets. In fact, child recordsets can also contain recordsets, making them grandchildren of the parent recordset, and a recordset can contain multiple children, as many as you like.

So what's the idea behind embedding recordsets in recordsets? Why not just use an SQL join to merge two tables? An example will make this clear. Say that you have a recordset with a `Publishers` table and a `Titles` table, which you wish to join so that you can see what titles have been published by what publishers. If both tables have a Publisher ID field, say `PubID`, you can write an SQL join like this to merge the `Publishers` and `Titles` tables:

```
SELECT * FROM Publishers, Titles WHERE
Publishers.PubID = Titles.PubID
```

The result of this join looks something like the recordset you see in Table 13.1.

As you can see, there's a lot of repeated data in Table 13.1. For each new title, the Publisher, Address, and Type fields are all duplicated, and if

TABLE 13.1	A Joined Table		
Publisher	**Address**	**Type**	**Titles**
Publisher1	Address1	Technical	Title1
Publisher1	Address1	Technical	Title2
Publisher1	Address1	Technical	Title3
Publisher1	Address1	Technical	Title4
Publisher1	Address1	Technical	Title5
Publisher1	Address1	Technical	Title6
Publisher1	Address1	Technical	Title7
Publisher1	Address1	Technical	Title8
Publisher2	Address2	Technical	Title1
Publisher2	Address2	Technical	Title2
Publisher2	Address2	Technical	Title3
Publisher2	Address2	Technical	Title4
Publisher2	Address2	Technical	Title5
Publisher2	Address2	Technical	Title6
Publisher2	Address2	Technical	Title7
Publisher2	Address2	Technical	Title8

there are a great many titles, you can see that there'll be a lot of wasted network traffic downloading all the duplicated data. On the other hand, when you work with child recordsets, you get the result in Table 13.2.

As you can see in Table 13.2, there's no duplication of data in the Publisher, Address, and Type fields, because the Titles field holds a child recordset that has the titles listed in its various records. Besides avoiding the needless duplication of SQL joins, child recordsets in hierarchical recordsets are often much easier to work with in code—in the joined table, you'd have to refer to each title for each publisher by working through all the records in the joined table, but in a hierarchical recordset, you can access the titles for a publisher in the child recordset in the Titles field, which means you can use Recordset object methods on it.

Structuring your recordsets in a hierarchical way is the way of the future for data handling, much like how working with hierarchical data on the Web is now supported with XML. In fact, one can envision that in the future, you'll be able to export hierarchical recordsets to XML format.

The columns of a shaped recordset may hold data from a data provider such as SQL Server, references to another recordset, values derived from a calculation on a single row of a recordset, values derived from an operation over a column of an entire recordset, or they may be a newly fabricated, empty column. Here's a brief history of data shaping:

TABLE 13.2   A Hierarchical Recordset

Publisher	Address	Type	Titles
Publisher1	Address1	Technical	Title1
			Title2
			Title3
			Title4
			Title5
			Title6
			Title7
			Title8
Publisher2	Address2	Technical	Title1
			Title2
			Title3
			Title4
			Title5
			Title6
			Title7
			Title8

- ADO 2.0 introduced the data shaping feature, hierarchical recordsets, and the Shape command syntax.
- ADO 2.1 introduced data reshaping, grandchild aggregates, and parameterized commands with intervening `COMPUTE` commands.

The most important event in this history was in ADO 2.0, which introduced the Shape command syntax. Much of this chapter is an exploration of that syntax. I'll start working with data shaping now—the first topic to cover is the data shaping OLE DB provider.

The OLE DB Provider for Data Shaping

You actually use two OLE DB providers when working with data shaping. The Data Shaping Service for OLE DB provider, MSDataShape, supports the actual data shaping, and a standard data provider, like the OLE DB Provider for SQL Server, supplies the data for the shaped recordset.

You can specify the name of the shaping provider as the value of the `Connection` object's `Provider` property, or with the connection string keyword `"Provider="`.

You can specify the name of the data provider as the value of the `"Data Provider"` dynamic property (which is added to the `Connection` object's `Properties` collection by the Data Shaping Service for OLE DB), or the connection string keyword `"Data Provider="`. (No OLE DB data provider is required if the recordset is not populated, as when creating a new recordset; in that case, specify `"Data Provider=none"`.)

Here's an example showing how to open a connection using the data shaping provider with data returned by the SQL Server:

```
Dim adoConnect As New ADODB.Connection

    adoConnect.Provider = "MSDataShape"

    adoConnect.Open "Data Provider=SQLOLEDB.1;" & _
    "Persist Security Info=False;User " & _
    "ID=sa;Password=;Initial Catalog=Northwind"
```

We'll see this connection process later in this chapter's examples. After you've connected to a data source, you use the Shape language to shape the data the way you want.

The Shape Language

The Shape command syntax enables you to make hierarchical `Record-set` objects by appending a child recordset to a parent recordset. As when you create an SQL join, the parent and child must have at least one column in common: The value of the column in a row of the parent is the same as the value of the column in all rows of the child.

Here's an example showing how to create a hierarchical recordset using the `Connection` object configured in the previous topic. In this case, I'm using the `Customers` table in the `Nwind` database as the parent recordset, and the `Orders` table as the child recordset. I relate the two tables using the `CustomerID` field, so that each customer's record in the parent recordset will have a child recordset containing the orders that customer has made. I start by using the Shape syntax to create the parent table:

```
adoRecordset.Open "SHAPE {SELECT * FROM " & _
"Customers} " & _
     .

     .

     .
```

Then I create a new child recordset from the `Orders` table, using the `APPEND` command:

```
adoRecordset.Open "SHAPE {SELECT * FROM " & _
"Customers} " & _
"APPEND ({SELECT * FROM Orders} " & _
     .

     .

     .
```

When you create a child recordset, you must give the relationship between child and parent. Here, the relationship is that the `CustomerID` fields in each table must match, which I specify with the `RELATE` command:

```
adoRecordset.Open "SHAPE {SELECT * FROM " & _
"Customers} " & _
"APPEND ({SELECT * FROM Orders} " & _
"RELATE CustomerID TO CustomerID)" & _
```

.

.

.

Finally, I can name the field that holds this new child recordset (called a chapter) so I can refer to that field by name. To name the child recordset's field, you use an SQL AS clause, as you might expect; here, I'll name the new field ChapterOrders:

```
adoRecordset.Open "SHAPE {SELECT * FROM " & _
"Customers} " & _
"APPEND ({SELECT * FROM Orders} " & _
"RELATE CustomerID TO CustomerID)" & _
"As ChapterOrders", adoConnect
```

Shape commands can be more involved; for example, you can nest hierarchical Recordset objects to any depth (that is, create child Recordset objects of child Recordset objects, and so on). I'll take a look at that later in this chapter. In addition, when you use the AS clause, you're giving the child recordset an alias, and in ADO 2.1, the alias of a shaped recordset can be referenced in an entirely different command. That is, you may issue a new Shape command to change, or *reshape*, a previously shaped recordset.

You use data shaping to define the fields of a shaped recordset, the relationships between the fields, and the way in which the recordset is populated with data. Here are the types of fields you can place in a shaped recordset:

- **Data**—This is made up of fields from a recordset returned by a query command to a data provider, table, or a previously shaped recordset.

- **Chapter**—This is a reference to another recordset. Chapter columns make it possible to define a parent-child relationship where the parent is the recordset containing the chapter column and the child is the recordset referred to by the chapter.

- **Aggregate**—This is the value of the column created by executing an aggregate function (which I'll cover in a few pages) on a child recordset.

- **Calculated expression**—The values in these columns are derived by calculating an expression on columns in the same row of the recordset using the CALC function.

- **New**—This is made up of empty, new fields, which may be populated with data at a later time. You define this column with the NEW keyword.

I'll look at the various parts of the Shape grammar that let you create these types of fields, starting with the most important Shape command of all—the APPEND command, which creates child recordsets in the first place.

The Shape APPEND Command

The Shape APPEND command assigns a child recordset to the Value property of Field objects in a parent recordset. Here's how you use this command:

```
SHAPE {parent-command} [[AS] parent-alias]
APPEND ({child-command} [AS] child-alias
RELATE parent-column TO child-column...) [[AS]
chapter-alias] ...
```

Here are the parts of this command:

- **parent-command**, **child-command**—These commands are queries inside curly braces ("{}") which return a Recordset object, the name of a shaped Recordset object that you want to reshape, another Shape command, or the TABLE keyword followed by the name of a table.
- **parent-column**—A column in the recordset, as returned by parent-command.
- **child-column**—A column in the recordset as returned by child-command.
- **parent-column TO child-column...**—This clause is a list where each relation is separated by a comma.
- **chapter-alias**—This is an alias that refers to the column appended to the parent.
- **parent-alias**—This is an alias that refers to the parent recordset.
- **child-alias**—An alias that refers to the child recordset.
- **...**—The final ... clause after the APPEND keyword is actually a list, where each clause is separated by a comma and defines another column to be appended to the parent recordset.

You can use a *parameterized* APPEND command, which retrieves the entire parent recordset at once, but retrieves the chapter recordset only when the chapter column is accessed (which will improve performance). Here's an example showing how that works:

```
"SHAPE {SELECT * FROM Customers}
APPEND ({SELECT * FROM Orders WHERE CustomerID = ?}
RELATE CustomerID TO PARAMETER 0)"
```

The parent and child tables have a column in common, `CustomerID`. The `child-command` has a placeholder ("?"), which the `RELATE` clause calls `PARAMETER 0`. What happens here is that the data in the chapter column is not retrieved until it is accessed, which can save you quite a bit of time. Here's what happens step by step:

1. The `parent-command` returns a parent recordset from the `Customers` table.

2. The chapter column is appended to the parent recordset.

3. The user can work with the parent recordset as usual.

4. When the chapter column of a parent row is accessed, the value of the `Customers.CustomerID` column replaces the placeholder for `Orders.CustomerID`.

5. The `child-command` is executed.

6. Every record is retrieved from the `Orders` table in which the value of the `CustomerID` column (i.e., `Orders.CustomerID`) matches the value of the `CustomerID` column in the `Customers` table.

7. The child recordset is placed in the chapter column of the current row of the parent recordset.

As of ADO 2.1, you can now embed parameterized commands like this one in an arbitrarily nested number of Shape `COMPUTE` commands. To see what that means, I'll take a look at the Shape aggregate functions, followed by the `COMPUTE` command.

Aggregate Functions, the CALC Function, and the NEW Keyword

Data shaping supports the following aggregate functions:

- `SUM(`*chapter-alias.column-name*`)`—This function calculates the sum of all values in the specified column.

- `AVG(`*chapter-alias.column-name*`)`—This function calculates the average of all values in the specified column.

- `MAX(`*chapter-alias.column-name*`)`—This function calculates the maximum value in the specified column.

- `MIN(`*chapter-alias.column-name*`)`—This function calculates the minimum value in the specified column.

- `COUNT(`*chapter-alias[.column-name]*`)`—This function counts the number of rows in the specified alias or column.

- `STDEV(`*chapter-alias.column-name*`)`—This function calculates the standard deviation in the specified column.

- `ANY(`*chapter-alias.column-name*`)`—This function returns the value of a column (where the value of the column is the same for all rows).

You can also create calculated expressions with the CALC function like this:

```
CALC(expression)
```

The CALC function calculates an arbitrary expression, but only on the row of the recordset containing the CALC function. Any Visual Basic for Applications (VBA) function or expression is allowed.

In addition, you can use the NEW keyword to create a new, empty column like this:

```
NEW (field-type [(width | scale [,precision])])
```

This keyword adds an empty column of the specified type to the recordset.

So, how do you actually use aggregate commands? I'll do that with the COMPUTE command next.

The Shape COMPUTE Command

The Shape COMPUTE command generates a parent recordset whose columns are made up of the child recordset, as well as optional columns whose contents come from aggregate functions, and any columns from the child recordset are listed in the optional BY clause:

```
SHAPE {child-command} [AS] child-alias
COMPUTE child-alias [, aggregate-command-field-list]
[BY group-field-list]
```

Here are the parts of this command:

- **child-command**—This command is a query inside curly braces ("{ }") which returns a Recordset object, the name of a shaped Recordset object that you want to reshape, another Shape command, or the TABLE keyword followed by the name of a table.

- **child-alias**—This alias refers to the recordset returned by the child-command. The child-alias is required in the list of columns in the COMPUTE clause and defines the relation between the parent and child Recordset objects.

- **aggregate-command-field-list**—This list defines a column in the generated parent and results from executing an aggregate function on the child recordset.

- **group-field-list**—This list of columns (from both the parent and child recordsets) specifies how rows should be grouped in the child.

TABLE 13.3	The Customers Table	
State	**Customer**	**Orders**
MA	Johnson	600
NY	Smith	300
NY	Ericson	500
CA	Paulson	900
CA	Clark	400
MA	Hayes	600
NY	Brown	300

If there is a BY clause, then the columns that clause defines are also appended to the parent recordset, and the BY clause specifies how the rows of the child recordset are grouped. If the COMPUTE clause contains an aggregate function but no BY clause, then there will be a single parent row with an aggregate value for the entire child recordset. If there is a BY clause, there can be multiple parent rows, each with a child and an aggregate value for the child.

To make all this clearer, I'll take a look at an example. Say you have a table named Customers that has State, Customer, and Orders (in dollars) fields, as appear in Table 13.3.

Now say you want to sum all the orders in this table and organize the result by state. You could execute this Shape command, including a BY clause to group the results by state, to do so:

```
rs.Open "SHAPE  {SELECT * FROM Customers} " & _
"AS Details COMPUTE SUM(Details.Orders), " & _
"Details BY State", ADOConnection
```

This command creates a shaped recordset with two levels. The parent will be a recordset with an aggregate column (created from SUM(Details. Orders)), a column holding the child recordset (Details), and a column for grouping the child recordset (State). Note that the child recordset detail rows will be grouped by state, but otherwise in no specific order. The resulting parent recordset appears in Table 13.4, and the three children appear in Tables 13.5 to 13.7. You can see how the COMPUTE command has shaped this recordset and created the summation field by taking a look at those tables.

That's it; we've seen how hierarchical recordsets work in overview—now it's time to put them to work in some full examples.

TABLE 13.4	The Parent Table	
SUM	**Details**	**State**
1,300	Reference to Child1	CA
1,200	Reference to Child2	MA
1,100	Reference to Child3	NY

TABLE 13.5	The Child1 Table	
State	**Customer**	**Orders**
CA	Paulson	900
CA	Clark	400

TABLE 13.6	The Child2 Table	
State	**Customer**	**Orders**
MA	Johnson	600
MA	Hayes	600

TABLE 13.7	The Child3 Table	
State	**Customer**	**Orders**
NY	Smith	300
NY	Ericson	500
NY	Brown	300

Using Hierarchical Recordsets

I'll construct some examples showing how to use data shaping now. The first example, named adoshape and found in the folder of that name on the CD, will display a hierarchical recordset in the Visual Basic control designed to work with hierarchical recordsets—the Microsoft Hierarchical FlexGrid control.

Displaying Hierarchical Recordsets

This first example, adoshape, uses SQL Server to connect to the Nwind database and display the Customers table, adding a chapter to display the orders for each customer. I start by creating a connection to the Nwind database using the data shaping and SQL Server OLE DB providers:

```
Private Sub Form_Load()

    Dim adoConnect As New ADODB.Connection
    Dim adoRecordset As New ADODB.Recordset

    adoConnect.Provider = "MSDataShape"

    adoConnect.Open "Data " & _
    "Provider=SQLOLEDB.1;Persist Security " & _
    "Info=False;User ID=sa;Password=;" & _
    "Initial Catalog=Northwind"
    .
    .
    .
```

Next, I create the hierarchical recordset where the parent recordset is the Customers table and the child recordset is from the Orders table where the CustomerID matches the CustomerID field in the parent:

```
    adoRecordset.Open "SHAPE {SELECT * FROM " & _
    "Customers} " _
    & "APPEND ({SELECT * FROM Orders} " _
    & "RELATE CustomerID TO CustomerID)", adoConnect
    .
    .
    .
```

Now that I've created the new hierarchical recordset, I can display it in the Hierarchical FlexGrid control. To do that, you simply assign the hierarchical recordset to a FlexGrid control's DataSource property:

```
    Set MSHFlexGrid1.DataSource = adoRecordset
```

```
End Sub
```

The result appears in Figure 13.1, where we see the created hierarchical recordset in a Hierarchical FlexGrid control. As you can see in that figure, the

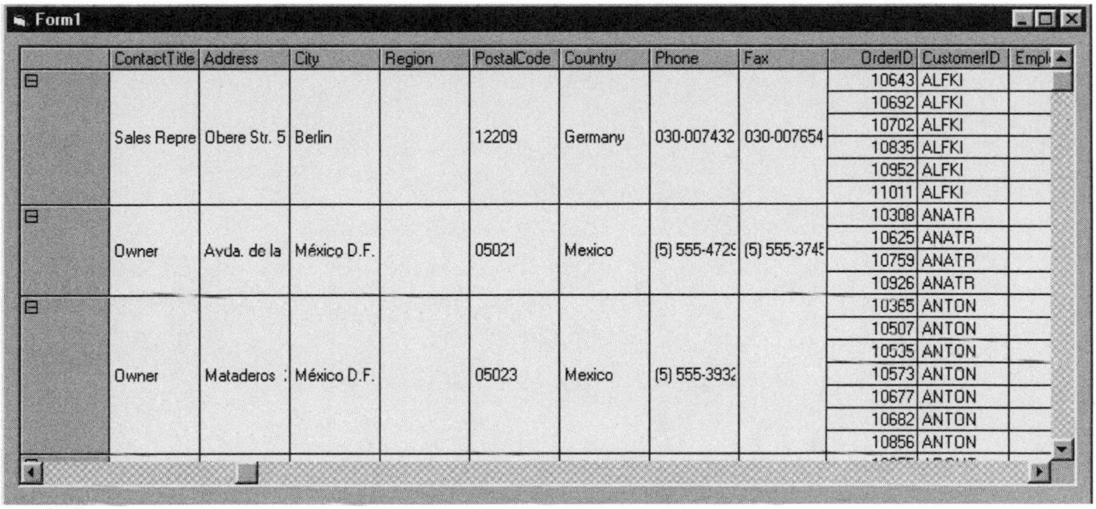

		ContactTitle	Address	City	Region	PostalCode	Country	Phone	Fax		OrderID	CustomerID	Empl
□											10643	ALFKI	
											10692	ALFKI	
											10702	ALFKI	
		Sales Repre	Obere Str. 5	Berlin		12209	Germany	030-007432	030-007654		10835	ALFKI	
											10952	ALFKI	
											11011	ALFKI	
□											10308	ANATR	
											10625	ANATR	
		Owner	Avda. de la	México D.F.		05021	Mexico	(5) 555-472S	(5) 555-374E		10759	ANATR	
											10926	ANATR	
□											10365	ANTON	
											10507	ANTON	
											10535	ANTON	
		Owner	Mataderos ;	México D.F.		05023	Mexico	(5) 555-393;			10573	ANTON	
											10677	ANTON	
											10682	ANTON	
											10856	ANTON	

FIGURE 13.1   Creating and displaying a hierarchical recordset.

records from the Orders table for each customer have been added as a chapter for each parent record.

This example is fine if you just want to view the entire hierarchical recordset at once, but what if you want to work with the records in a child recordset individually? I'll take a look at that next.

Accessing Records in Hierarchical Recordsets

In this next example, adoshaperecords, which appears in the folder of that name on the CD, I'll work with the records of a child recordset individually. In this case, I'll create a recordset of the customers in the Customers table of the Nwind database, adding a child recordset for each customer, holding the orders of that customer. I'll also loop over all the orders in the child recordset for each customer, listing the orderIDs in a text box.

I start by opening a connection to the Nwind database:

```
Private Sub Form_Load()


    Dim adoConnect As New ADODB.Connection
    Set adoRecordset = New ADODB.Recordset


    adoConnect.Provider = "MSDataShape"


    adoConnect.Open "Data " & _
    Provider=SQLOLEDB.1;Persist Security " & _
```

```
"Info=False;User ID=sa;Password=;" & _
"Initial Catalog=Northwind"
    .
    .
    .
```

Next, I create the parent and child recordsets, naming the child record-set, which holds the orders for each customer, `ChapterOrders`:

```
adoRecordset.Open _
"SHAPE {SELECT * FROM Customers} " _
& "APPEND ({SELECT * FROM Orders} " _
& "RELATE CustomerID TO CustomerID) " _
& "As ChapterOrders", adoConnect
    .
    .
    .
```

To let the user move through the new hierarchical recordset, I'll connect the recordset to an ADO data control:

```
Set Adodc1.Recordset = adoRecordset

End Sub
```

In addition, I'll bind a text box, `Text1`, to the `ContactName` field of the parent recordset so the user can see the name of the customer as they navigate through the recordset.

Now it's time to work with the `ChapterOrders` child recordset in the current record. I'll do that in the ADO data control's `MoveComplete` event handler, which fires when the ADO data control moves to a new record. I start by copying the child recordset into the `Recordset` object named `adoRecordset2`, accessing it with the `Value` property of the `ChapterOrders` field:

```
Private Sub Adodc1_MoveComplete(ByVal adReason As _
ADODB.EventReasonEnum, ByVal pError As _
ADODB.Error, adStatus As ADODB.EventStatusEnum, _
ByVal pRecordset As ADODB.Recordset)
```

```
Set adoRecordset2 = _
Adodc1.Recordset("ChapterOrders").Value
    .
    .
    .


Text2.Text = ""
```

Next, if the child recordset contains any records, I'll loop over all the OrderID fields, placing them in a new text box, Text2:

```
If adoRecordset2.RecordCount <> 0 Then
    While Not adoRecordset2.EOF
        Text2.Text = Text2.Text & _
        adoRecordset2("OrderID") & vbCrLf
        adoRecordset2.MoveNext
    Wend
End If
End Sub
```

The result appears in Figure 13.2. As you can see in that figure, the user can click the navigation buttons in the ADO data control, moving through the hierarchical recordset and seeing the order IDs for each customer.

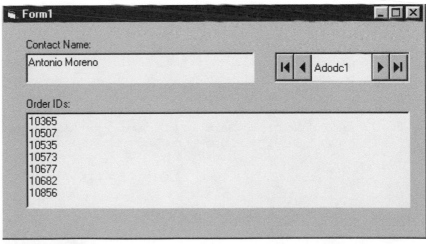

FIGURE 13.2 Accessing records in a hierarchical recordset.

To update any data that you've edited in a bound control using a hierarchical recordset, you just use the normal update commands.

So far, our hierarchical recordsets have only had one child recordset each, but you can have multiple children in a recordset, and the children can themselves have chilren.

Multiple Children and Grandchildren

You can give a hierarchical recordset multiple children; for example, I'll use the Orders table in the Nwind database as the parent recordset, giving it two children. One child will hold the CustomerID and ContactName fields from the Customers table, where the CustomerID field matches the CustomerID field in the parent. The other child will hold all the records from the Order Details table, where the OrderID field matches the same field in the parent. Here's what the Shape command looks like—note that I'm just passing two arguments to APPEND, although the whole thing looks a little complex:

```
adoRecordset.Open _
"SHAPE {SELECT * FROM Orders} " & _
"APPEND ({SELECT CustomerID, " & _
"ContactName FROM Customers} " & _
"RELATE CustomerID TO CustomerID)" & _
"As ChapterCustomers, " & _
"({SELECT * FROM [Order Details]} " & _
"RELATE OrderID TO OrderID) " & _
"As ChapterOrders", adoConnect
```

The resulting recordset appears in Figure 13.3 in a Hierarchical Flex-Grid, and you can see the two children for each record there.

Besides multiple children, you can also support grandchildren. Here's an example; in this case, I'll use the Customers table as the parent table, the OrderID and CustomerID fields from the Orders table as the child recordset, and the Order Details table as the grandchild. Here's what that looks like—note that I'm just nesting two APPEND commands:

```
adoRecordset.Open "SHAPE {SELECT * FROM " & _
"Customers} APPEND ((SHAPE {SELECT " & _
"OrderID, CustomerID FROM " & _
"Orders} As Orders APPEND ({SELECT * FROM " & _
```

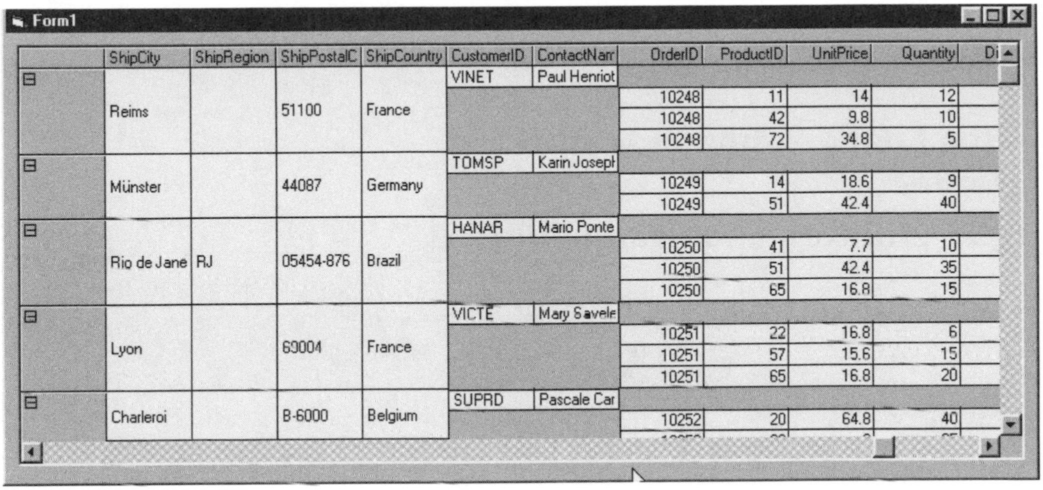

FIGURE 13.3 Multiple children in a Hierarchical FlexGrid.

```
"[Order Details]} As Details " & _
"RELATE OrderID TO OrderID) As Details) " & _
"AS Orders RELATE CustomerID TO CustomerID)", _
adoConnect
```

The result appears in Figure 13.4, where you can see the child and grandchild recordsets. In fact, you can nest children to arbitrary depth using data shaping.

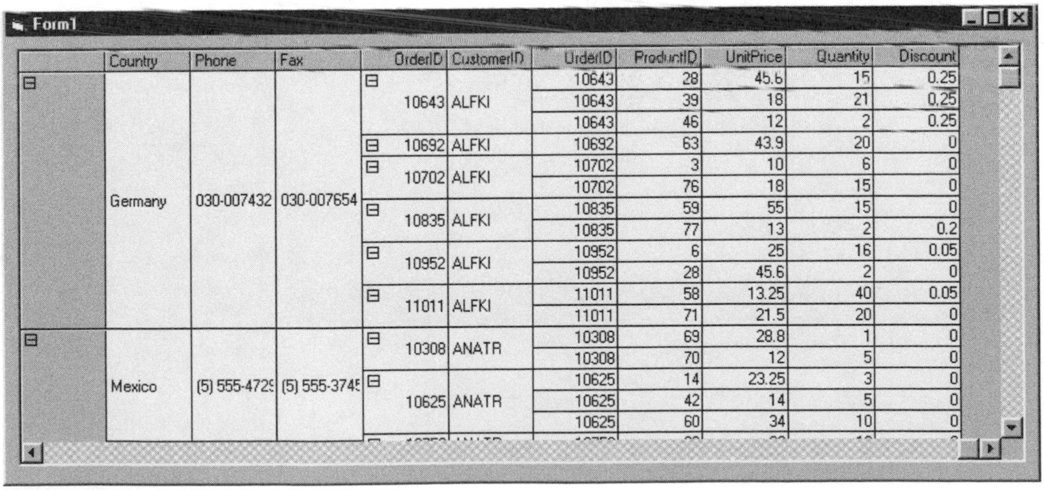

FIGURE 13.4 Grandchildren in a Hierarchical FlexGrid.

Having seen how to create Shape commands the hard way, I'll take a look at the easy way--using Data Environments.

Creating Shape Commands with Data Environments

Visual Basic makes it easy to create shaped recordsets and use Shape commands with Data Environments. As an example, I'll create the hierarchical recordset we first created in this chapter—using the `Customers` table as the parent recordset and the `Orders` table as the child recordset. I start by connecting the default `Connection` object in a Data Environment to the `Nwind` database using SQL Server, then I add a command, `Command1`, to the `Connection` object, and connect that `Command` object to the `Customers` table, as shown in Figure 13.5.

Next, I right-click the new command and select `Add Child Command` from the menu that appears, creating a new child `Command` object, `Command2`. I right-click the new `Command` object and select the `Properties`

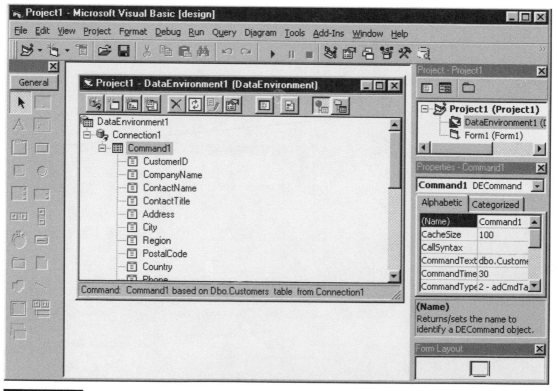

FIGURE 13.5 Command corresponding to the `Customers` table.

item to open the command's Properties Pages, as shown in Figure 13.6. I connect the new command to the Orders table, as also shown in that figure.

In addition, you have to set the relation of child to parent in the Relation tab of Child2's properties, as you see in Figure 13.7, where I'm relating the CustomerID field in the parent to the CustomerID field in the child. I click OK to close the Command2 object's Property Pages.

This creates the new child command in the Data Environment, as you can see in Figure 13.8.

You can now access the hierarchical recordset in the Data Environment as rsCommand1. You can see the actual Shape command that generates the hierarchical recordset by selecting the Hierarchy Info menu item in Command1's menu. Selecting that menu item displays the dialog you see in Figure 13.9.

You can see the Shape command in that dialog:

```
SHAPE {SELECT * FROM "dbo"."Customers"}  AS Command1
APPEND ({SELECT * FROM "dbo"."Orders"}  AS Command2
RELATE 'CustomerID' TO 'CustomerID') AS Command2
```

As you can see, using Data Environments provides an easy way to create Shape commands. You can also add grandchild commands to child com-

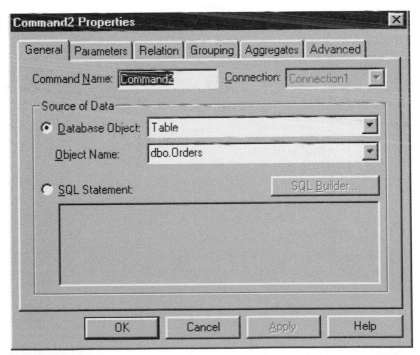

FIGURE 13.6 Connecting the child command to the Orders table.

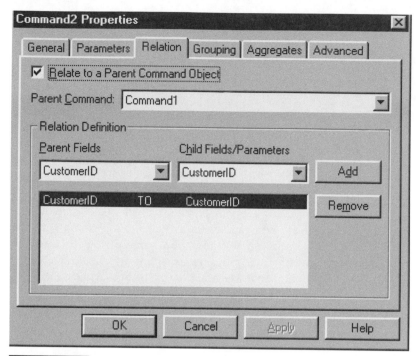

FIGURE 13.7 Setting the relation of child to parent.

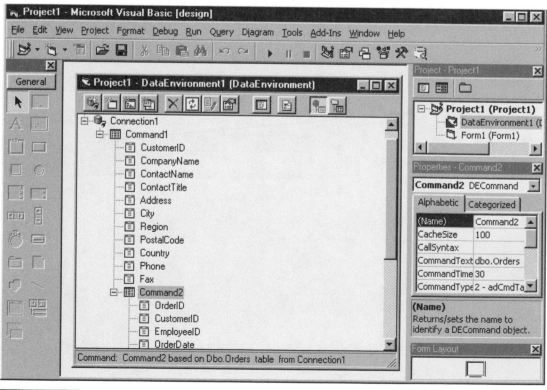

FIGURE 13.8 The new child command in the Data Environment.

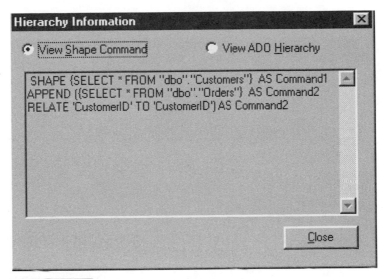

FIGURE 13.9 Viewing the new Shape command.

mands or give commands multiple children in a Data Environment—just use the Add Child Command item as appropriate.

That finishes this chapter's coverage of data shaping. It's time to turn to ADOX.

ADO Extensions: ADOX

What is ADOX? The Microsoft ActiveX Data Objects Extensions for Data Definition Language and Security (ADOX) is an extension to ADO and the programming model. ADOX includes several objects that allow you to create and modify schema, as well as support security by granting or revoking permissions.

To use ADOX, you add a reference to the ADOX library to your Visual Basic project; the description of the ADOX library is "Microsoft ADO Ext. for DDL and Security" in the Components dialog opened by the Project menu's Components item. (The ADOX library file name is Msadox.dll.)

Note that as usual with ADO and its extensions, some features of ADOX may not be supported depending on the data provider you're using. The Microsoft OLE DB Provider for the Microsoft Jet Database Engine supports ADOX fully.

I'll take a look at ADOX in overview here so you can get an idea of what's involved.

The ADOX Objects

ADOX is based on a set of the following objects—note that in applications like Microsoft Access and SQL Server, a catalog is a database:

- **Catalog**—This object contains collections that describe the schema catalog of a data source.
- **Column**—This object contains a column from a table, index, or key.
- **Group**—This object contains a group account.
- **Index**—This object contains an index from a database table.
- **Key**—This object contains a primary, foreign, or unique key field from a database table.
- **Procedure**—This object contains a stored procedure.
- **Table**—This object contains a database table, including columns, indexes, and keys.
- **User**—This object contains a user account.
- **View**—This object contains a filtered set of records or a virtual table.

Note that each object can be contained in a corresponding collection—for example, an Index object can be contained in an Indexes collection. I'll take a look at the ADOX collections next.

The ADOX Collections

Here are the ADOX collections:

- **Columns**—This collection contains all Column objects of a table, index, or key.
- **Groups**—This collection contains all Group objects of a catalog or user.
- **Indexes**—This collection contains all Index objects of a table.
- **Keys**—This collection contains all Key objects of a table.
- **Procedures**—This collection contains all Procedure objects of a catalog.
- **Tables**—This collection contains all Table objects of a catalog.
- **Users**—This collection contains all User objects of a catalog or group.
- **Views**—This collection contains all View objects of a catalog.

The ADOX Properties

As you might expect, the ADOX objects support quite a number of properties. Here's a list of the available properties and what they do:

- **ActiveConnection**—This property specifies the ADO Connection object of which the catalog is an object.
- **Attributes**—This property specifies column attributes.

- **Clustered**—This property specifies whether an index is clustered.
- **Command**—This property specifies an ADO Command object that can be used to create or execute a command.
- **Count**—This property specifies the number of objects in a collection.
- **DateCreated**—This property specifies the date an object was created.
- **DateModified**—This property specifies the date an object was last modified.
- **DefinedSize**—This property specifies the maximum size of a column.
- **DeleteRule**—This property specifies the action that should be performed when a primary key is deleted.
- **IndexNulls**—This property specifies whether or not records whose index fields have null values have index entries.
- **Name**—This property specifies the name of an object.
- **NumericScale**—This property specifies the scale of numeric values in a column.
- **ParentCatalog**—This property specifies the parent catalog of a table or column.
- **Precision**—This property specifies the maximum precision of data in a column.
- **PrimaryKey**—This property specifies whether or not an index represents the primary key on the table.
- **RelatedColumn**—This property specifies the name of the related key column in the related table.
- **RelatedTable**—This property specifies the name of the related table.
- **SortOrder**—This property specifies the sort sequence for index columns.
- **Type**—This property specifies the data type of a column, key, or table.
- **Unique**—This property specifies whether or not index keys have to be unique.
- **UpdateRule**—This property specifies the action that should be performed when a primary key is updated.

The ADOX Methods

Here's a summary of the ADOX methods:

- **Append**—Adds a new Column object to the Columns collection, new Group object to the Groups collection, new Index object to the Indexes collection, new Key object to the Keys collection, new Procedure object to the Procedures collection, new Table object to the Tables collection, new User object to the Users collection, or new View object to the Views collection.
- **ChangePassword**—Changes the password used in a user account.

- **Create**—Creates a new catalog.
- **Delete**—Deletes an object from a collection.
- **GetObjectOwner**—Gets the owner of a particular object in a catalog.
- **GetPermissions**—Gets the permissions for an object.
- **Item**—Gets a specific member of a collection by name or number.
- **Refresh**—Updates the objects in a collection.
- **SetObjectOwner**—Specifies the owner of a `Catalog` object.
- **SetPermissions**—Sets the permissions for the group or user of a particular object.

That completes this chapter's overview of the ADOX objects and collections. I'll take a look at a few ADOX examples next.

Putting ADOX to Work

Creating a new database is easy using ADOX; here's how I create a new MS Jet database, `newdata.mdb`:

```
Dim ADOXcatalog As New ADOX.Catalog

ADOXcatalog.Create _
"Provider=Microsoft.Jet.OLEDB.4.0;" & _
"Data Source=c:\ado\newdata.mdb"
```

I can open this new database and add a table, `EmployeesTable`, to it, using ADOX objects like this:

```
Dim ADOXcatalog As New ADOX.Catalog
Dim ADOXtable As New Table
Dim ADOXindex As New ADOX.Index

ADOXcatalog.ActiveConnection = _
"Provider=Microsoft.Jet.OLEDB.4.0;" & _
"Data Source=c:\ado\newdata.mdb;"

ADOXtable.Name = "EmployeesTable"
```

```
ADOXtable.Columns.Append "LastName", _
adVarWChar, 40
ADOXtable.Columns.Append "ID", adInteger
ADOXtable.Columns.Append "Department", _
adVarWChar, 20

ADOXcatalog.Tables.Append ADOXtable
    .

    .

    .
```

I can also create an internal index on two fields like this:

```
ADOXindex.Name = "TwoColumnIndex"
ADOXindex.Columns.Append "LastName"
ADOXindex.Columns.Append "ID"
    .

    .

    .
```

And I append the new index to the table like this:

```
ADOXtable.Indexes.Append ADOXindex
    .

    .

    .
```

Having created a catalog with a table, EmployeesTable, I can give the user Edward full rights to that table this way:

```
ADOXcatalog.Users("Edward").SetPermissions _
"EmployeesTable, adPermObjTable, _
adAccessGrant, adRightAll
    .

    .

    .
```

That's just a glimpse of what's possible with ADOX—see the ADOX documentation for all the details.

That's it for our coverage of ADOX, and that's also it for our coverage of ADO. We've seen a lot of ADO programming power in this book: from the basics to RDS, from using the ADO `DataControl` to working with shaped data, from creating disconnected recordsets to sorting and searching data, from ADO objects to ADOX objects. The only thing that's left is to put this huge database arsenal to work for yourself—happy programming!

INDEX

LICENSE AGREEMENT AND LIMITED WARRANTY

READ THE FOLLOWING TERMS AND CONDITIONS CAREFULLY BEFORE OPENING THIS CD PACKAGE. THIS LEGAL DOCUMENT IS AN AGREEMENT BETWEEN YOU AND PRENTICE-HALL, INC. (THE "COMPANY"). BY OPENING THIS SEALED CD PACKAGE, YOU ARE AGREEING TO BE BOUND BY THESE TERMS AND CONDITIONS. IF YOU DO NOT AGREE WITH THESE TERMS AND CONDITIONS, DO NOT OPEN THE CD PACKAGE. PROMPTLY RETURN THE UNOPENED CD PACKAGE AND ALL ACCOMPANYING ITEMS TO THE PLACE YOU OBTAINED THEM FOR A FULL REFUND OF ANY SUMS YOU HAVE PAID.

1. **GRANT OF LICENSE:** In consideration of your purchase of this book, and your agreement to abide by the terms and conditions of this Agreement, the Company grants to you a nonexclusive right to use and display the copy of the enclosed software program (hereinafter the "SOFTWARE") on a single computer (i.e., with a single CPU) at a single location so long as you comply with the terms of this Agreement. The Company reserves all rights not expressly granted to you under this Agreement.

2. **OWNERSHIP OF SOFTWARE:** You own only the magnetic or physical media (the enclosed CD) on which the SOFTWARE is recorded or fixed, but the Company and the software developers retain all the rights, title, and ownership to the SOFTWARE recorded on the original CD copy(ies) and all subsequent copies of the SOFTWARE, regardless of the form or media on which the original or other copies may exist. This license is not a sale of the original SOFTWARE or any copy to you.

3. **COPY RESTRICTIONS:** This SOFTWARE and the accompanying printed materials and user manual (the "Documentation") are the subject of copyright. The individual programs on the CD are copyrighted by the authors of each program. Some of the programs on the CD include separate licensing agreements. If you intend to use one of these programs, you must read and follow its accompanying license agreement. You may <u>not</u> copy the Documentation or the SOFTWARE, except that you may make a single copy of the SOFTWARE for backup or archival purposes only. You may be held legally responsible for any copying or copyright infringement which is caused or encouraged by your failure to abide by the terms of this restriction.

4. **USE RESTRICTIONS:** You may <u>not</u> network the SOFTWARE or otherwise use it on more than one computer or computer terminal at the same time. You may physically transfer the SOFTWARE from one computer to another provided that the SOFTWARE is used on only one computer at a time. You may <u>not</u> distribute copies of the SOFTWARE or Documentation to others. You may <u>not</u> reverse engineer, disassemble, decompile, modify, adapt, translate, or create derivative works based on the SOFTWARE or the Documentation without the prior written consent of the Company.

5. **TRANSFER RESTRICTIONS:** The enclosed SOFTWARE is licensed only to you and may <u>not</u> be transferred to any one else without the prior written consent of the Company. Any unauthorized transfer of the SOFTWARE shall result in the immediate termination of this Agreement.

6. **TERMINATION:** This license is effective until terminated. This license will terminate automatically without notice from the Company and become null and void if you fail to comply with any provisions or limitations of this license. Upon termination, you shall destroy the Documentation and all copies of the SOFTWARE. All provisions of this Agreement as to warranties, limitation of liability, remedies or damages, and our ownership rights shall survive termination.

7. **MISCELLANEOUS:** This Agreement shall be construed in accordance with the laws of the United States of America and the State of New York and shall benefit the Company, its affiliates, and assignees.

8. **LIMITED WARRANTY AND DISCLAIMER OF WARRANTY:** The Company warrants that the SOFTWARE, when properly used in accordance with the Documentation, will operate in substantial conformity with the description of the SOFTWARE set forth in the Documentation. The Company does not warrant that the SOFTWARE will meet your requirements or that the operation

of the SOFTWARE will be uninterrupted or error-free. The Company warrants that the media on which the SOFTWARE is delivered shall be free from defects in materials and workmanship under normal use for a period of thirty (30) days from the date of your purchase. Your only remedy and the Company's only obligation under these limited warranties is, at the Company's option, return of the warranted item for a refund of any amounts paid by you or replacement of the item. Any replacement of SOFTWARE or media under the warranties shall not extend the original warranty period. The limited warranty set forth above shall not apply to any SOFTWARE which the Company determines in good faith has been subject to misuse, neglect, improper installation, repair, alteration, or damage by you. EXCEPT FOR THE EXPRESSED WARRANTIES SET FORTH ABOVE, THE COMPANY DISCLAIMS ALL WARRANTIES, EXPRESS OR IMPLIED, INCLUDING WITHOUT LIMITATION, THE IMPLIED WARRANTIES OF MERCHANTABILITY AND FITNESS FOR A PARTICULAR PURPOSE. EXCEPT FOR THE EXPRESS WARRANTY SET FORTH ABOVE, THE COMPANY DOES NOT WARRANT, GUARANTEE, OR MAKE ANY REPRESENTATION REGARDING THE USE OR THE RESULTS OF THE USE OF THE SOFTWARE IN TERMS OF ITS CORRECTNESS, ACCURACY, RELIABILITY, CURRENTNESS, OR OTHERWISE.

IN NO EVENT, SHALL THE COMPANY OR ITS EMPLOYEES, AGENTS, SUPPLIERS, OR CONTRACTORS BE LIABLE FOR ANY INCIDENTAL, INDIRECT, SPECIAL, OR CONSEQUENTIAL DAMAGES ARISING OUT OF OR IN CONNECTION WITH THE LICENSE GRANTED UNDER THIS AGREEMENT, OR FOR LOSS OF USE, LOSS OF DATA, LOSS OF INCOME OR PROFIT, OR OTHER LOSSES, SUSTAINED AS A RESULT OF INJURY TO ANY PERSON, OR LOSS OF OR DAMAGE TO PROPERTY, OR CLAIMS OF THIRD PARTIES, EVEN IF THE COMPANY OR AN AUTHORIZED REPRESENTATIVE OF THE COMPANY HAS BEEN ADVISED OF THE POSSIBILITY OF SUCH DAMAGES. IN NO EVENT SHALL LIABILITY OF THE COMPANY FOR DAMAGES WITH RESPECT TO THE SOFTWARE EXCEED THE AMOUNTS ACTUALLY PAID BY YOU, IF ANY, FOR THE SOFTWARE.

SOME JURISDICTIONS DO NOT ALLOW THE LIMITATION OF IMPLIED WARRANTIES OR LIABILITY FOR INCIDENTAL, INDIRECT, SPECIAL, OR CONSEQUENTIAL DAMAGES, SO THE ABOVE LIMITATIONS MAY NOT ALWAYS APPLY. THE WARRANTIES IN THIS AGREEMENT GIVE YOU SPECIFIC LEGAL RIGHTS AND YOU MAY ALSO HAVE OTHER RIGHTS WHICH VARY IN ACCORDANCE WITH LOCAL LAW.

ACKNOWLEDGMENT

YOU ACKNOWLEDGE THAT YOU HAVE READ THIS AGREEMENT, UNDERSTAND IT, AND AGREE TO BE BOUND BY ITS TERMS AND CONDITIONS. YOU ALSO AGREE THAT THIS AGREEMENT IS THE COMPLETE AND EXCLUSIVE STATEMENT OF THE AGREEMENT BETWEEN YOU AND THE COMPANY AND SUPERSEDES ALL PROPOSALS OR PRIOR AGREEMENTS, ORAL, OR WRITTEN, AND ANY OTHER COMMUNICATIONS BETWEEN YOU AND THE COMPANY OR ANY REPRESENTATIVE OF THE COMPANY RELATING TO THE SUBJECT MATTER OF THIS AGREEMENT.

Should you have any questions concerning this Agreement or if you wish to contact the Company for any reason, please contact in writing at the address below.

> Robin Short
>
> Prentice Hall PTR
>
> One Lake Street
>
> Upper Saddle River, New Jersey 07458

About the CD-ROM

Contents

The CD-ROM contains all the source code from *ADO Programming in Visual Basic 6*.

Installation

For information about installation, read the README.TXT file included on the CD. The supported platforms are Windows 95, 98, and NT.

Technical Support

For issues regarding bad media or replacement software, please contact Prentice Hall at `disc_exchange@prenhall.com`.